PHANTOM LEADER

To

Sir Michael — one of our
greatest Captains & Leaders.

Michael J. Foust

PHANTOM LEADER

THE LIFE AND TIMES OF A FLYING SAILOR

MICHAEL J. DOUST

With a Foreword by
Admiral of the Fleet Sir Michael Pollock GCB LVO DSC

Published in 2005 by
Ad Hoc Publications
Cedars, Wattisham Road, Ringshall, Suffolk IP14 2HX,
England
www.adhocpublications.com

ISBN 0 946958 42 4

Typeset, edited and designed by Roger Chesneau

Printed in Great Britain by
William Clowes Ltd, Beccles, Suffolk

To my family, my wife May and our two daughters
Naomi and Dominique, and to all my friends both in the
Naval Service and in civilian life.

Think of every day,
every challenge,
every triumph and indeed...
every defeat as
feathers on your wings

Then one day, the sum
of all your wisdom
will let you fly...

Where only Eagles dare!

—Mario Fernandez
Feathers on My Wings

Contents

List of illustrations   9

Foreword *by Admiral of the Fleet Sir Michael Pollock* GCB LVO DSC   11

Preface   13

Part I: The Early Days   **15**
1   Arrival   17
2   War   22

Part II: Life on the Lower Deck   **31**
3   In the Navy Now   33
4   To Sea in a Big Ship   36
5   Aircrew Selection and Officer Sea Training   43

Part III: Aviator   **55**
6   Gosport   57
7   Syerston   61
8   Jets   68
9   Flying the Navy Way   77
10 Fighter Pool   82
11 Wyvern   89

Part IV: The Ladder of Responsibility   **117**
12 Failure   119
13 To be a QFI   123
14 Instructor   131
15 Supersonic Instructor   145
16 Big Jet Flying Days   157

Part V: Buccaneer   **165**
17 Return to the Front Line   167

18   Premier Air Squadron   170
19   Buccaneer Squadron   186
20   Buccaneer Operational Flying School   211

Part VI: An American Adventure   **221**
21   AIRTEVRON FOUR   223
22   Visitors and Personalities   242
23   Homecoming   259

Part VII: Command   **267**
24   Landing Safety Officer   269
25   Commanding Officer   287
26   Terra Firma   307
27   Lieutenant Commander (Flying)   326

Part VIII: Back to the Desk   **343**
28   Helicopters and Martels   345

Part IX: Wings of Hermes   **361**
29   The Air Boss   363
30   Refit   379
31   Caribbean Cruise   387

Part X: Goodbye to the Andrew   **401**
32   Back to the MoD   403
33   Finale   408

     Epilogue   417

     Appendix: Aircraft Types and Models Flown by the Author   421

     Abbreviations & Glossary   423

     Index   431

List of Illustrations

(between pages 160 and 161 and pages 320 and 321)

The author aged nine months
The author with his brother Brian, 1938
John Doust, the author's father, in 1955
The author's sisters and mother
The author in 1951
HMS *Collingwood*, the RN Electrical School, in 1950
The author's New Entry Course, March 1951
The Mediterranean Fleet at Malta in 1953
HMS *Theseus* turning into the wind, 1952
USS *Midway*'s SAR helicopter visits *Theseus*, 1952
King Paul of the Hellenes visits *Theseus* off Athens
Commissioned pilot Alfie Wigg makes a hard landing aboard *Theseus*
Sea Furies and Fireflies prepare for take-off from *Theseus*
HMS *Implacable* glimpsed in the Irish Sea, spring 1953
Upperyardmen pose in front of a Provost Mk 1
The remains of Reg Hunt's Provost 'Mike Juliet'
RAF Syerston: Provost trainers and a lone Harvard trainer, 1954
Lieutenant John Beard lounges by a 738 NAS Sea Hawk
The 738 NAS hangar at Lossiemouth in 1955
No 40 OFS starts engines for its flypast, Lossiemouth, 1955
No 40 OFS graduation line-up
831 NAS officers on commissioning
831 Naval Air Squadron in deep maintenance, 1957
The outcome of an argument between a tractor and a Wyvern
The author and Pete Wheatley put the finishing touches to 'Flook'
RNAS Ford's SAR Dragonfly helicopter, 1955
The author starts up his Wyvern, Lossiemouth, 1956
The author manning his 831 NAS Wyvern, winter 1956
A Westland Wyvern S Mk 4 with a full load of 3-inch rockets
Stan Farquhar leading 831 NAS out for the flypast over Ford, 1956
831 Squadron starts up for the Ford flypast, 1956
The author lands a Wyvern S.4 at RNAS Ford

The author's wife's course with HM Queen Elizabeth the Queen Mother

No 16 Air Warfare Instructors' Course, HMS *Excellent*, December 1957

The OFS instructors, 736 and 738 Squadrons, RNAS Lossiemouth

Captain Michael Pollock with 'Jenny's Side Party', Hong Kong, 1963

The world's first supersonic beer, Kenya, 1963

Part of the USS *Essex*'s air group aboard HMS *Ark Royal*, 1963

US Navy Sea Kings approaching *Ark Royal*

A US Navy E-1B Tracer is launched from *Ark Royal*'s port catapult, 1963

Part of *Essex*'s air group parked in *Ark Royal*'s Fly 1

One of *Essex*'s A-4 Skyhawks operating from *Ark Royal*

HMS *Jaguar* detaches from *Ark Royal* and her tanker, 1963

HMS *Ark Royal* refuelling from her tanker

The author fires a Bullpup missile from his Scimitar fighter, 1963

Three Scimitars from 800 NAS work up for the Aden Air Display, 1963

Lieutenant Les Ingham mans his Scimitar fighter

A street scene in Wanchai, Hong Kong, 1963

A Wanchai greengrocer, Hong Kong, 1963

The author's wife May and eldest daughter Naomi, November 1966

HMS *Eagle* in May 1964

Another view of HMS *Eagle*, with Sea Vixens and Buccaneers evident

736 NAS Buccaneer S Mk 1s practise formation aerobatics, August 1966

An 809 NAS Buccaneer S.1 having performed a wheels-up landing

Lossiemouth squadrons practise for the 'Freedom of the Town' flypast, 1967

The author firing 2-inch rockets over the Tain Range

Colonel Paul Sandison presents the Sandison Trophy to the author, 1966

The VX-4 badge

Welcome to Point Mugu: a view of the display park

VX-4's US-2A communications aircraft *Son of Beulah*

The author and his daughter Naomi outside their California home, 1968

The author and his wife May at the US Naval Officers' Ball, 1968

The author as Squadron Commander, 767 NAS, RNAS Yeovilton, 1971

Lieutenant Commander Peter Sheppard is briefed for a Sea Fury flight

The author mans his F-4K Phantom for a training flight

HMS *Ark Royal*, now equipped with a fully angled, 11-degree deck, 1975

HMS *Hermes* heads down-Channel, 1980

Hermes returns to her berth at the Northwest Wall Jetty, February 1981

800 NAS tries out *Hermes*' 'ski-ramp' for the first time, 1981

The Sea Harrier trials team on board *Hermes*.

The author engaged in conversation with the late Senator Childs

Hermes is manoeuvred into her Mayport berth, 1981

The author as Commander (Air) flying an 826 NAS Sea King in 1981

Hermes almost vanishing from sight as she 'takes it green', 1981

The flight deck of *Hermes* after taking a 'heavy one' aboard

Foreword

Admiral of the Fleet Sir Michael Pollock GCB LVO DSC

OWING to the disruption of his education by the War and a period of child-hood illness, Michael Doust failed the cadet entry into the Navy. With typical determination, however, he joined as a rating, taking the risk that he would not be selected as an officer by the 'Upper Yardman' scheme and would have to serve his engagement on the lower deck. In the event, and by constant pressure from him, he was quickly selected for a short-service commission in the Air Branch Supplementary List.

The first part of these interesting memoirs covers the author's childhood and progress towards becoming a qualified pilot, his initial ambition. The next section covers his service as a squadron pilot, during which he became a brilliant airman and which, I suspect, was the happiest time of his life with a single task of flying aircraft safely and to the limit of their performance. He flew Scimitars from *Ark Royal* when I was in command of her in the early 1960s and quickly made his mark as an aerobatics pilot. He flew the heavy jets with sympathy and as if they were an extension of himself, and many times I watched with Commander (Air) as he carried out spectacular manoeuvres around the ship—yet always within sensible safety limits.

The Squadron re-equipped with Buccaneers, and it was after qualifying as an AWI that he found time to write an operations handbook for that aircraft's complicated weapons system—no mean achievement, and one which, as he says himself, cost him a lot of 'midnight oil'.

His exchange service with the US Navy was a revelation to him as he found out that, in spite of its superb equipment, neither its administration nor its operations were as seamlessly perfect as Hollywood films would have us believe.

After a further flying spell as the Commander of the Phantom Training Squadron, he faced the inevitable stint in the MoD, in his case with DNAW. Here, for the first time, he met the inter-services rivalry for funds and, in the case of the civilian providers of aeronautical equipment, anxiety for the preservation of jobs. He was, however, very good at supporting his own case with facts, figures and common sense and was careful to ensure that any controversial issues were backed by a watertight case.

Finally, as 'Wings' of *Hermes*, he achieved his highest peak, the job usually being given to a General List Officer due for promotion to Captain. As he was only on the 'permanent Supplementary List' he then had to retire and the RN lost a very experienced and valuable officer. It is of interest that, in the intervening years, the separate Lists have been scrapped, to be replaced by a single List with various promotion points giving selection to continuing service.

All in all, *Phantom Leader* tells an interesting tale of a most able and determined officer. I am sure the book will be read by all with pleasure, not least of course by his old shipmates and squadron officers.

Preface

THESE memoirs are of my life and my times as a sailor and naval aviator in Her Majesty's Royal Navy, the finest naval service in the world. They are also an attempt to relate the struggle that I experienced to 'climb the ladder' in order to be awarded a commission in the Navy and to rise to positions of responsibility within the Service. My surroundings (the sea), and the aerial combat of World War II that went on about me during those formative years when one should be sitting at a school desk absorbing education, shaped my life. Nowadays, children in England spend their lives in peace, not subjected to the violence that my generation had to suffer because of man's greed and ambition for power.

On leaving home to go out into the world, I chose the sea instead of a comfortable life as a civil engineer. Both careers would have provided excitement and good prospects, but service in the Royal Navy would be much more demanding, offering more opportunities for living life to the full. Eventually, the call of flying proved to be compelling, and I would enter what is probably the most demanding of all careers—that of a naval aviator.

The demands of a naval pilot are many. He has no comfortable, long runway on which to land after a protracted and wearisome sortie, but rather a short length of pitching and rolling steel deck in an ocean or sea, miles from anywhere. It calls for experience, and for a cool and steady nerve, to make a successful flight of this kind—even more so at night when all that lies ahead of one are a few specks of light in the vastness of the waters indicating the flight deck and home. Moreover, quite apart from flying, a naval officer has to take care of his division of men (and now of course women), numbering in some instances as many as thirty. (I hate to use the term 'boys', because to my mind 'boys' of seventeen or a little more are young men doing a man's job.) He is responsible for their welfare, for their advancement within the naval service and for sorting out their domestic problems—of which there are many, often very different from and more difficult than those dealt with by the average social worker in civilian life. It is this aspect of a naval officer's life that makes him stand head and shoulders above his contemporaries in the Army and Royal Air Force.

I received little or no training for what lay ahead of me, apart from a short spell in the Air Training Corps while at grammar school, and neither did I inhabit a home where parents owned and ran a large estate or company within which I could be groomed for future leadership. I had to learn the necessary attributes the hard way, and by experience, watching how others coped under similar circumstances and by following my intuition or 'gut feeling'. Sometimes I had to cope with crusty old captains or heads of departments who thought that, because of their length of service, they had more experience than I although unfortunately they were not close enough to, or sufficiently intimate with, a particular welfare problem. In these instances, one has to stand one's ground. However, in general, senior officers gravitate toward junior officers who have zeal and gumption and are prepared to 'do something' rather than hold back, even though a chosen solution may not be perfect. On one occasion my 'Boss' said to me, 'You have only been here a short time, but you remain cool and calm under the most trying of circumstances, especially during an emergency, when everything about you seems to be going wrong!' Hearing these words, I felt that, at last, I had really learnt and understood what leadership was all about.

A career in the Royal Navy is, then, a demanding one, placing a very great strain both on one's family and on one's daily life. When we were first married, my wife and I agreed that the Navy came first and that neither of us would place our own personal feelings and requirements before those of the Service or the country. This attitude may seem old-fashioned to many people—especially those of the younger generation of today—but one does not join up in order to look proud and smart in a naval officer's or sailor's uniform, catching the eyes of all the pretty girls. The guiding principle is 'What can I give to the Service and to the country?' rather than 'What can they do for me?' I suppose this is what some will call 'commitment'.

Michael John Doust
Newport News, Virginia

I

THE EARLY DAYS

— 1 —

Arrival

I T WAS about 10 o'clock on a Monday morning during August 1933 when I arrived with a push and pull into this world at the Fernbank Maternity Hospital, Hastings. As is commonly the case, I gave notice of my violent arrival from the warm and comfortable surroundings of my mother's womb by letting out an almighty yell of disapproval. With hindsight, nothing much has changed over the years because I am still very good at letting folk know about my innermost feelings and thoughts when the occasion arises.

In continental Europe at about the same time, Adolf Hitler was making himself known throughout the length and breadth of Germany and neighbouring countries. Before I reached the tender age of seven he would have plunged the world into a military conflict the likes of which it had never seen nor has seen since. As a result, thousands upon thousands of young men and women from both sides perished, among them teenagers not much older than me who would never reach the age of maturity, leaving only memories of what they might have achieved had they been allowed to grow up in peace.

On leaving Fernbank I was taken home to a small house at the bottom of Strand Hill, Winchelsea, almost opposite Strand House, the home of Naomi Elizabeth, my late great-grandmother (whose name would, many years later, pass on down to my eldest daughter). My father had by this time taken over as the Harbour Master at Rye, 'old Mr Coote' having passed on. A short while later the family moved to No 1 Coast Guard Cottages in Rye Harbour, where it would remain for a year or two before moving into No 1 Inkerman Cottages in the same village. The new family home was next door to the Inkerman Arms. Mother, somewhat straightlaced, was not too happy about the idea of living next to a public house, but we nevertheless remained there until the summer of 1939—during which time the family was to receive a further three members, Brian, Anthea and Jacqueline, all of whom were born at the Cottages. This was a home of which I have, even to this day, the fondest of memories. In 2001 it was standing forlorn and boarded up.

In August 1939 the family moved once more, this time across the River Rother into a purpose-built harbour master's house and office. I can recall quite clearly the delight and happiness with which my mother and father moved us across the river: not many people had the good fortune to live in a brand new detached house. To this day, as I look across the river from the village of Rye Harbour to that old home—even though it has grown to include of two further terraced houses covered in typical Sussex black clapboard— many happy memories come flooding back to me. I can still see Mother sitting on the huge timbers supporting Dad's old tarred shed which served as an office and storage facility next to the light tower. She often rested there, watching events on the river while Dad strode seawards along the eastern river wall with his fuel can to replenish the harbour entrance lights, still not electrified at that time. Following him at a discreet distance would be our brood of cats, which would sit and preen themselves whenever he hailed an incoming or departing boat. When he started walking again, off they would go, maintaining their distance. Although others live there now, this was my home for nearly thirty years. It was rather isolated, but there was always a constant stream of friends—associates of my parents and my siblings—throughout those years. It would be from this home that I would join 'the Andrew', as the Royal Navy is affectionately called by members of the Service.

* * *

The memories of my first few years on this beautiful spaceship called Planet Earth are somewhat limited. However, I know that a sense of mischief, adventure and daredevil were in me from a very early age. Most sailors are wanderers, and not only through making sea and ocean voyages: they also have the venturesome spirit of roving far and wide when ashore or on leave between jobs. HMS *Orion* could be alongside in Singapore, and one could see her tallies proudly displayed on a sailor's cap at a railway station in Bangkok. Wandering was to be my trait, too.

I can clearly recollect, at the tender age of two and a half, climbing out of the back window of the local barber's shop and walking along the dangerously narrow roof ledge. This was in preference to facing the proprietor's gleaming eyes and grimacing face as he approached with his comb and scissors, poised to despatch my fair locks to the waste bin. It was also the time of King George V's Silver Jubilee, and there was parked on Rye town green a visiting circus. When at the circus with family members, I lost little time in slipping from Mother's grasp, sneaked out of the Big Top by crawling underneath the raised seats and the ground sheet and, dodging the animals, started walking home. Somehow my navigational prowess proved inadequate and I soon became lost. However, even at that age I seemed to have some horse sense, deciding to sit down, stay put and await the arrival of the relations, albeit admittedly not really understanding whether they knew where I had gone. Soon the family did appear, with shouts of joy at having found the errant son—although as soon as I was back in their company I received a resounding slap across the rear end for causing so much distress and alarm.

Although I cannot recall it, my family often used to mention my duck pond exploits. Apparently, I went boating on the village pond in an old tin bathtub borrowed from somewhere and on one occasion ran aground in the middle of it. The pond was a favourite place for dumping unwanted domestic property such as prams, broken bicycles and the like, all waiting to snag and maroon any budding Columbus. In my excitement and panic I did actually fall into the water when Father waded out to rescue me, although prior to going aground and Father's rescue efforts my voyage of discovery was, I believe, proceeding very much according to plan.

On another occasion, at the age of three and a half, I decided to climb out of the living-room window into the village's main street. The problem with this venture was that it took place in the dead of winter. It was a very cold and snowy morning when, with bare feet and a bare bottom and wearing only a vest, I went in search of Father. He had risen early for a morning tide, and it was 5.30 when I waddled around to the Point just past old Mr Blatt-man's tarred lifeboat house, totally oblivious to the conditions. As I approached the Point a shout went up from the local fishermen talking to Dad: 'What have we here? More live bait for our lines?' This was followed by raucous laughter. One can imagine my father's face when he recognised his own son braving the elements with neither fear nor decency.

Sometime during the early spring of 1937—the year before I started school for the first time—I was again walking along the main street and, as I passed the Inkerman Arms, my attention was drawn by the noise of an aircraft engine coming from the west. A huge airship was crossing the coast in a southerly direction between Winchelsea and Fairlight. I had never seen one before but had heard Mum and Dad speak of them. It seemed so graceful and majestic with the bright morning sun reflecting off its skin. Looking back over that moment in time, and remembering the the position in relation to the surrounding hills and downs, the ship must have been flying at between 1,000 and 1,500 feet and cruising at some 60 to 80 knots. Its engines were making a quiet but unfamiliar noise, which was probably due to the airflow from the propellers striking the airframe fabric, causing a sort of 'flapping'. This noise was quite different from that of a fixed-wing aircraft. The airframe was, I recollect, quite long and narrow, with a length-to-width ratio of about 8 to 1, thus placing it in a class of its own. It was quite probably the German *Hindenburg* or *Graf Zeppelin* en route from London to Paris and Berlin.

Many years later I learnt that the *Hindenburg* had been lost in a dreadful accident in the United States. This beautiful ship of the skies, while coming into dock at the US Naval Air Station Lakehurst, New Jersey, on 6 May 1937, exploded into a huge fireball and crashed to the ground, killing many of its crew, its passengers and its US Navy docking personnel. It was never really established what caused the explosion, which seemed to originate at the stern of the craft. The general consensus of opinion at the time was that it had built up a static electrical charge in its airframe while flying through wet and thundery conditions around New Jersey awaiting clearance to dock. The airframe was filled with volatile hydrogen gas, and a leak coupled with a spark would have ignited it with disastrous consequences. This terrible accident swiftly brought to an end the era of airship transportation. The multi-engine airliners quickly superseded the airships, although the US Navy would continue to use the latter throughout World War II for coastal reconnaissance, convoy protection and anti-submarine duties. The Americans have always used helium gas—far safer than hydrogen as a lifting agent.

One aircraft that flew around Rye and Rye Harbour a great deal both before and after the war was an autogyro. This craft had been invented by the Spaniard Cierva, but I was never to know who owned this particular machine. It disappeared during the war but reappeared soon afterwards still sporting its duck-egg blue finish. Light aircraft became quite popular around the district in the immediate postwar years, especially the old de Havilland Tiger Moth, the basic trainer for the Royal Air Force and the Royal Navy.

In 1937 or thereabouts my father was presented with a small tender from the motor yacht *La Toquette*, a converted Thames sailing barge. She was a beautiful craft, owned by one Mr MacGregor, a wealthy Scottish gentleman. MacGregor had decided to give Dad first refusal of the tender, which was due for replacement, in lieu of a payment for his services. She was in fact a small 13/14-foot oar and sailing dinghy, but as soon as Dad took possession of her he quickly removed the centreboard and trunking, extending the stern so that she ended up looking very much like a Hastings beach boat. The sails were replaced by a small Austin Seven motor car engine and gearbox, long levers being fitted to the clutch and gear change pedal. He did all the conversion work himself and then he named the boat *Anthea* after his eldest daughter, my sister.

By the time the family had moved across the river into its new home Dad had increased the topsides of the *Anthea* by about eighteen inches and added a small cuddy in the bows. He had also modified the engine to enable it to run with either petrol or paraffin: he would operate the engine initially on petrol until it had reached a suitable temperature and then slowly introduce the paraffin once it was running smoothly. This modification would be a boon during the war years when boat owners found their petrol supplies severely rationed. A fishing registration number, RX-133, was obtained ('RX' representing the port of Rye and used by all fishing boats operating between Rye and Bexhill, including Hastings), entitling him to fish beyond the three-mile offshore limit.

Dad made his own fishing nets, and initially he used a beam trawl. The beam took up a great deal of room in the small boat and he eventually manufactured some otterboards, thus increasing the available space within the craft. Throughout the war he made numerous fishing trips at night out into Rye Bay, taking both my brother Brian and me with him. These trips helped to supplement his wages and also the food supply for the family. When he did not go to sea the local fishermen would drop off boxes of fish outside his office shed as a 'thank you' for all the hard work he put in for them. This generosity would continue until he retired from his office and left the harbour.

After the war my father acquired an old 18-foot ship's lifeboat. He quickly set about increasing her topsides, built in a bow cuddy and this time installed twin Austin Seven engines. The boat was christened *Margaret* after my mother and was registered as a fishing boat with the number RX-221. When the *Margaret* was completed, Dad gave me the old *Anthea*.

* * *

The village of Rye Harbour was a thriving community, always full of life. The whole of the Doust family worshipped at the church, the roof of which resembles an upturned boat resting on four walls. Dad, Uncle Jim and Uncle Wilfred all sang in the church choir as young boys and teenagers, and, as members of the armed of forces during World War I, Jim's and Wilfred's names are recorded in gold letters over the church's gateway arch. Jim served in the army and was taken prisoner at the age of sixteen, but he managed to escape and make his way back to his regiment. Wilfred served in the Royal Navy and fought at the Battle of Jutland as a Yeoman.

Below and two hundred yards from the church, the school nestled alongside the village green, where soccer and cricket matches were held. Unless one's family had money, one entered the school at the age of five and left to start work at fourteen. Those families able to afford to do so sent their children either to the Rye Grammar School or to the Collegiate School (for girls only). There are still two public houses in the village, The Inkerman and The Conqueror, and two general stores, one of which hosts a Post Office. Alongside the Post Office there was and still is the Church Hall, which was used for Church functions and Christmas festivities. Opposite the Post Office was a garage, owned jointly by Uncle Jim and Bert Hedgeler, who owned and ran the Post Office; Jim eventually bought the garage outright from the Hedgeler family when Bert passed away. Further along the street, just past the garage, was a Seaman's Mission Hall, also used for various village functions. By the river was the Point, where fishing boats were either beached or moored, the old lifeboat house, then owned privately by Mr Blattman, and Mrs Tonbridge's tearooms. Alongside the tearooms was The Conqueror, and on the other side stood the railway terminal, where fish and blue boulders—used in th pottery industry—were loaded up for transportation to towns and cities around the country.

The main jobs in the village were associated with fishing, farming and the concrete factory, where tubes and slabs of all sizes were manufactured, to be transported away in railway wagons. Half a mile north of the village was the chemical plant, which manufactured tar, pitch and other products from coal and oil. There was also a huge beach works next to the church which processed deposits mined to the west of the church for concrete and for use as crushed aggregate for road construction and general building. The jobs provided by these businesses kept the village men in work. There was no television, radio was in its infancy and films were of the silent kind until the mid-1930s, so the villagers made their own entertainment and the two village halls and school were well used for this purpose. As a result, the atmosphere was much livelier than it is today.

— 2 —

War

W HILE I was still attending the Church School in Rye Harbour in 1939, the whole family was issued with food ration books and gas masks, the Government taking no chances in the event of war breaking out. Neville Chamberlain, the Prime Minister, was conducting serious talks with the German Government, and there was little doubt that *Herr* Hitler and his henchmen were dangling him on a piece of string. The Germans were doing the same with the French Government, and despite the strong ties between Britain and France at the time, the German Nazi Party were quietly poking two fingers at us behind our backs.

In the morning of 3 September 1939, a Sunday, while I was visiting Uncle Jim's garage with Dad, cousin Joy arrived to say that the Prime Minister would be speaking to the nation over the wireless at 11 o'clock. Jim switched on the radio and a few minutes later Chamberlain was heard, telling us that he had not had a response from the German Government as he had requested and that, as a consequence of Hitler's invasion of the sovereign state of Poland, Britain and France were now at war with Germany. Several friends of Dad and Uncle Jim were standing around in the garage at the time, and the silence following the PM's announcement was deafening. Suddenly everybody woke up as Joy burst into tears: they all wished each other goodbye and hurried off home to consider the seriousness of the news and how it was going to affect them all.

* * *

Having moved across the river, I was placed in another church school in Rye, just below St Mary's Church, and within a few weeks would move into a new junior school located in Ferry Road opposite Rye Town railway station. In the spring of the New Year all children attending the schools within the Rye borough would be evacuated to the city of Bedford, north of London. The Germans had invaded the Low Countries and France and were now just twenty miles away opposite Dover and seventy from Rye. Aerial bombardment by the Luftwaffe of the south-east of England was becoming a daily occurrence. We had just suffered the ignominy of having our British Expeditionary Force defeated and of having to rescue it and members of the French and Belgian Armies from Dunkirk by means of a huge fleet of naval ships, cross-channel steamers, small boats and yachts—but a third of a million officers and men were recovered to Britain to fight another day.

One Saturday afternoon a German Dornier 17 'Flying Pencil' medium bomber flew along the shoreline to the south of us, turned towards Winchelsea and reversed course to fly across Rye Harbour village. It had very distinctive, large, round-tipped wings and a long slender fuselage with twin fins and rudders. As the aircraft passed overhead I heard a whistling noise from an object dropped by it. A few seconds later there was a huge explosion at the Camber Sands tram station, which was blown to smithereens. Fortunately nobody was hurt or killed as the station had closed for the autumn and winter months. Why on earth the bomber's crew had selected a tarred building was beyond us all, but they had demonstrated how accurate they were with their bombing. War had suddenly arrived with a whistle and a big bang.

Together with my brother Brian, I was evacuated to Ravensden some six miles north-east of Bedford, where we were placed with Mr and Mrs George Harper, a childless couple at that time, who ran a small, hundred-acre mixed farm. They were to be our foster parents for the next six to eight months. However, they were expecting also to receive a couple of foster girls, and when Brian wet the bed one night that was enough: our parents were summoned to come and collect us forthwith!

The night before Mother arrived to take us home she stayed with her parents in Teddington, Middlesex. Unfortunately, this was to be the night of the biggest blitz on London and the Home Counties. Mother spent much of the night under the kitchen table with Grandma Lee, while Grandad Lee was out fire-fighting and young Uncle Horie was on Air Raid Patrol. The Luftwaffe attacked Bedford, Luton and RAF Cardington, just down the road from Ravensden, too. One German bomber was shot down and crashed the other side of the road from our farm cottage. Ever inquisitive, Brian and I were across the road the following morning to view the wreckage, but there was nothing to be seen other than powdered, burnt aluminum and the odd flying boot and helmet—plus the awful smell of burnt human flesh. This sensation was to remain with me for the rest of my life: it was something I wished never to experience again, but I would do so in the not too distant future.

Before we left the Harpers for good they took us over to Thurleigh, where George Harper's brother had a farm. Unfortunately his farm was requisitioned by the Government for building a new RAF bomber base which would eventually house the US Eighth Army Air Force and its B-17 Flying Fortresses. Little did I know that, many years later, I would be teaching Fleet Air Arm pilots from the very same airfield.

Mother duly arrived and we took the train south to London and Teddington, having been diverted via Waterloo station owing to the bomb damage at Euston from the previous night's blitz. We spent a night at Grandma Lee's home and the next day trained further south to Ashford, Kent, and then on to Rye. There Dad met us with one of Uncle Jim's taxis. A day after our arrival back home I was to witness what was probably the last aerial dogfight over the Sussex and Kent borders. It lasted about half an hour, but to me it was like a gladiatorial battle in the sky high above our heads, with machine guns rattling, aircraft falling and on fire and pilots descending on parachutes—and then it was all over, with quietness and peace reigning once more. What I did not realise at the time was that many of the British pilots taking part in the aerial battle were from the Fleet Air Arm—sailors, Petty Officers, Midshipmen and Sub-Lieutenants. They were barely twenty years old, many much younger, on loan to the RAF because of a shortage of pilots. They were fighting for us, to preserve our way of life from the scourge of the Nazi machine that was trampling everything and everybody under its jackboot across Europe.

Brother Brian and I had to receive schooling so over the next couple of years we were either living with Grandma and Grandad Lee or nearer to home with Father's parents in Winchelsea, Sussex. Our two sisters, Anthea and Jacqueline, were still far too young to be evacuated, so they stayed at Camber. Mother was with us at Grandma Lee's because she had to have a goiter operation on her throat at the Teddington Hospital; poor Mother was slowly being poisoned by this terrible growth that had developed in her neck. While I was staying with Grandma Harman, Dad's mother at Winchelsea, various Army units were billeted in and about the town, many from the Canadian Army. One day, suddenly, they were gone, to take part in the ill-planned and ill-conceived raid on Dieppe: nothing was achieved except the loss of many brave Canadian and British, and some American, lives. At about this time the Luftwaffe was starting its daily 'hit-and-run' raids across the south-east and south of England.

During the period of these terror raids—and terror raids they were—Rye Junior School reopened and brother Brian and I moved back home. My two sisters were now of school age, and daily a covered truck from Pankhurst's Removals would collect us and other children from Camber and the surrounding Romney Marsh area and transport us to Rye and school. However, before the Pankhursts were hired we had travelled for a short time in East Kent buses back and forth from Rye Harbour to Rye. On one return trip two of our buses were shot up by a Focke-Wulf 190 fighter, though fortunately the pilot missed us. The aircraft later crashed near Winchelsea Beach, the pilot having been decapitated while attempting to fly beneath some power cables.

The Admiralty was at this time building a new jetty at Rye Harbour in order to berth hundreds of landing craft. In addition, dozens of huge tanks were buried in Rye Golf Course in readiness for the 'Pluto' fuel system for the forthcoming invasion of Europe by the Allies. The man responsible for all these works was Admiral Sir Algernon Willis. He and Father were great friends, and I can recall them standing near Dad's office, the wooden tarred shack by the tide light tower, discussing various matters. Dad was about to be given an RN Reserve commission and appointed King's Harbour Master in Lagos, Nigeria. However, Sir Algernon stepped in and would not allow him to leave: his presence at Rye Harbour was too important, and so, instead, he took on the task of checking and testing all the 65-foot motor fishing vessels then being built by Nichol's boatyard at Rye for the Navy. Many of these craft are still in service around the world today.

With its new construction taking place, Rye Harbour became a prime target for the German fighter-bomber squadrons based on the opposite side of the Channel at Abbeville in northern France. As a result, numerous anti-aircraft batteries—3.7-inch, 40mm and 20mm guns, together with the new American gunlaying radar system—were moved into the region. The batteries were operated by girls from the Women's Royal Army Corps, many of them little more than eighteen years of age. With minefields to seaward, AA batteries almost in our back yard and landing craft jetties and fuel tanks all around, we felt like an armed camp. The Luftwaffe arrived daily to create terror and mayhem, and it was during one of these many raids that my father's deputy lost his home and wife when an FW 190 released a 500-kilogram bomb over the village and hit the Smith's house. In another raid, the MFV *Mizpah*, leaving harbour for a day's fishing, was attacked and strafed by a Messer-schmitt 109. The skipper, old Mr Crampton, was hit in the backside and seriously injured by cannon fire, leaving him a cripple for the remainder of his life. The vessel sank in the entrance of the harbour, where a gateway had been erected to prevent German E-boats from entering and attacking. Dad spent many days attempting to salvage the old *Mizpah*, but she was beyond repair and was consequently laid up on the old gridiron next to the Ferry Steps, to be broken up a year or so later.

By this time the extreme eastern part of Sussex and the western part of Kent had become known as 'Buzz Bomb Alley'. Hitler and his cohorts had devised the first ever cruise missile, the V-1, and during the night of 13 June 1944 they unleashed the weapon from launching sites in the Pas de Calais. That first night about 400 missiles were fired over Britain, and we watched them from our bedroom window as they streaked across the sky at about 2,000 feet and 400 knots. Our AA girls were on the mark, however, and began to knock them out of the sky. The long fire issuing from the V-1's ramjet would be seen first, then the AA shells would start to burst about it, and then a shell would find its mark and there would be a tremendous explosion as the 1,600-kilogram warhead disintegrated in a huge ball of fire. The following day Mr Barnden, the headmaster at my school, had the senior pupils standing Air Raid Patrol at the bomb shelters next to the playgrounds. They blew a police whistle as soon as they heard the distinctive sound of the ramjet—not unlike that of a motorcycle engine—and everybody then ran for shelter from their classrooms.

One weekend I happened to be in the back yard when I saw a 'Buzz Bomb' spinning into the sea south of my home. Then it suddenly levelled off and came straight towards the house. I shouted to Mother and, together with my siblings, we dived into the Morrison shelter that had been erected in the lounge. We heard the ramjet getting closer and closer, and louder and louder, and then it stopped right over the house. We clutched each other in fright. Seconds later there was a huge explosion, doors slammed shut, crockery bounced around on shelves and windows rattled—though no panes were broken as the windows were all open on account of the hot weather. The bomb had struck an embankment just below the Rye Golf Club House, creating a huge crater. Most of the blast had gone up and over the Club House, but its roof and west-facing walls were badly damaged. We all scrambled out of our shelter to see what had happened, and the Fire Brigade, which was billeted next door and had taken shelter under its two bus crew rooms, also arrived to view the crater and the damage. Firemen dashed over to the Club House, but fortunately the Club Steward and his family were out shopping that afternoon, although on their return they had to move into the vacant house next to the Professional's house and shop, below and by the main road. There they would stay until after the war when the Club House was repaired.

It was while I was doing my stint as the ARP warden that I noticed an RAF Beaufighter flying from the south-east towards Rye. As it reached the south-western side of the town an AA battery opened up on it and within a few seconds every battery around the town was firing at the aircraft. I began to jump up and down shouting 'Stop! Stop! It's one of ours!' Then fire erupted from one of its engines and down it went, crashing near Winchelsea railway station. A few days later I saw an RAF 'Queen Mary' low loader parked in the railway station yard and piled high with the Beaufighter wreckage. Amongst it were the flying helmets and radio masks of its crewmen, plus that horrible smell of burnt human flesh. To say that I was very upset would be an understatement. Many years later I would learn that, of the Allies' air crew losses during the war, a staggering percentage were due to misidentification. The US Navy lost one of its most famous fighter aces over the Pacific during the war for the same reason.

Suddenly, on 8 May 1945, the European War came to an end, although the Pacific War would continue until September 1945, brought to a close by the dropping of atomic bombs over Hiroshima and Nagasaki. Uncle Horie, who had served all his time out in the Far East aboard HMS *London* as a Royal Marine gunner, was hospitalised in a Melbourne, Australia, sanatorium. He had contracted tuberculosis in his right lung, brought about by the terrible humid conditions he and his shipmates had had to endure in the cruiser's gun turrets: air conditioning had not at that stage entered Royal Navy service.

Life had by now more or less returned to normal, and at school I, together with all my other class friends, sat the 'Eleven Plus' entrance examination for the grammar school. I flunked the exam, of course: I really had no idea what I was being asked in the question papers. Following an altercation with Mr Barnden, the latter stated publicly in the school hall when the results were being announced that I was good for nothing more than being a labourer—which really upset me! When I arrived home that day I told Dad and he stormed over to the school and set about my headmaster. What made matters worse was the fact that he had announced, again publicly, that his own son had won a seat at the Royal Naval College Dartmouth as an officer cadet, a success I wanted so desperately. However, my guardian angel must have been looking after me at the time for within the year, after I had moved over to Rye Modern School, the Labour Government issued a statement to the effect that all students who had failed the previous 'Eleven Plus' examination could sit a further test and oral exam. I passed for entrance into Rye Grammar School, the oldest such school in the country, founded by Thomas Peacock in the early 1600s. Although I did not know it at the time, the school had the same name as my future wife's father—an extraordinary coincidence!

I eventually joined the school's ATC Flight, commanded by the arts and woodwork master, Tommy Thompson. He had served in the RAF throughout the war and was the obvious choice for the post. However, after a short period of time he relinquished his command to Percy Mitchell, the school's physical training instructor. Percy had been a Chief Petty Officer (PTI) in the Royal Navy and now he donned the uniform of a Flight Lieutenant RAFVR. 'Our Percy', as we used to call him, still wore his old naval PTI garb when teaching us physical training (or PE, as it is known today). He was a good sportsman and was adored by the schoolgirls and schoolboys alike. When the ATC flight was camping at RAF Tangmere near Portsmouth, I met him one night, after I had joined the Navy, at the Trafalgar Club in Portsmouth. I was just checking in when he was going out for the evening, and I queried why he was staying there. 'Well, it's the cheapest place in town Michael, so I used my old naval "official number" and booked in for the night!'. I called him an old skinflint and he laughed.

Just before Percy took command, Tommy Thompson organised some flying practice for the Flight in both the Tiger Moth biplane and an old twin-engine Anson reconnaissance aircraft flown from RAF West Malling, near Maidstone. We flew the Tiger Moths from a grass meadow near Filsham Hill in St Leonards, about a mile from my future home in Bexhill-on-Sea. It was (and is) a wonderful little aircraft, and I would fly it again not long after I joined the Navy. The Mk 1 Anson was very much a 'cloth and wooden bomber', with most of the fuselage covered in fabric and with windows made of celluloid just like the MG sports car. Getting airborne in the machine was rather like launching a small boat from the beach. It bounced up and down as it accelerated across the grass airfield, and then, with a final lurch, it lumbered into the air and away. The pilot had one of us lift the undercarriage, which was done by cranking a lever attached to a drum of wire—all very primitive! Our pilot flew us over and around Rye, and of course across the grammar school, where we saw students on the playground during the morning break. An hour later we were back at West Malling, taxying past Mosquito fighters and Vampire jets which were now entering service with the RAF, I little realising that within five years I would be flying the Vampire as a training jet from RAF Valley in Anglesey. After this experience I was hooked on flying, and by the age of twenty I would start learning to be a naval aviator—which would be my career for next thirty years after joining the naval service until my retirement.

Father had become very friendly with a Cambridge University undergraduate, Harry Leney. He was the son of the Leney brewer based at Ashford, Kent. He had served as a navigator in the Blue Funnel Line throughout the war, and at the war's end he had gone to Cambridge to read mathematics, physics and biology. He bought an old Cornish lugger and my father helped him to convert it into a ketch, as a result of which Harry, together with a group of students from Cambridge, embarked on an ornithological expedition to the Faeroe Islands. After graduating with a Master's degree from Cambridge, he took up a position as House Master at Gordonstoun School in Morayshire, Scotland. He took his old ketch, the *Ellen Louise*, to Scotland and she was frequently used on sailing expeditions about the area.

Dad was very fond of Harry, who offered to give him the money for a cadetship for me in the Blue Funnel Line, although, out of principle, my father could not accept this. However, Harry had a 14-foot Southampton One racing dinghy which he allowed me to refurbish and race in the local Rye Harbour Sailing Club events on the Rother. Over the next couple of years, together with either Brian or a schoolfriend, Don Diaper, I took part in the Anstruther Cup races, even managing to lift the 'pot' with a half-point advantage. At the same time Dad had given me his old fishing boat, the *Anthea*, which I slowly converted into a 17/18-foot cabin sloop, giving her a deep keel and fitting her out with two bunks. Although the old boat leaked like a sieve, I had some wonderful experiences sailing her. So began my long association with dinghy sailing and yachting.

Over the school holiday periods, and when not dinghy sailing, I used to go caddying on the local golf course at Rye. I thoroughly enjoyed myself in the company of such personalities as 'Gubby' Allen, Chairman of the Marylebone Cricket Club, Gerald Micklem, the captain of the British Ryder Cup Team, and Leonard Crawley, the *Daily Telegraph*'s Golf Correspondent. I earned good money each day—as much as one pound, especially during competition tournaments. With this money I managed to pay for my school uniform, books and dinners, as well as to purchase timber, paint and fittings for the *Anthea* as I converted her. Most of these wonderful gentlemen have now passed on, but it was a great pleasure to be in their company listening to their golfing tales and jokes. They were all very good friends.

I was not a brilliant scholar, but by dint of hard work I managed to climb the academic ladder and passed my Oxford University School Certificate. On the other hand, I failed the entrance examination for Dartmouth Naval College. Owing to my late entrance into the school, I had less than a year in which to reach the required standards of knowledge for the Joint Civil Service Entrance Examination. This examination was used for all three Armed Forces Officer Colleges and the Civil Service. Every day I worked until 1 o'clock in the morning but I just did not have the ability to cram all the required facts and figures into my brain, and the result was a foregone conclusion. I therefore decided that I would take the 'lower deck route' to commissioned rank.

So it was that, on or about 19 February 1951, I bade farewell to all my friends at the Kent River Board District Office and went home knowing that the following Monday, the 27th, I would be going to London to enlist in the Royal Navy. I had received my call-up papers, which told me that I would be joining the Electrical Branch as there were at that time no vacancies in the

Seaman Branch—which was, of course, complete nonsense. However, I was keen to go no matter which branch I had been nominated to join because I was quite confident that I would be able to change things when I arrived at Charing Cross Recruiting Station in London. I had been sent a railway warrant and instructions on how to find the recruiting station and at what time to present myself.

It was a dull and overcast morning when I left home to enlist. Mum was already downstairs preparing breakfast for me and I went into Dad's bedroom to say goodbye. He had been on tide duty most of the night and was having a lie-in. He obviously did not want me to leave, but his parting words were 'Have a good time, son. At least I am pleased that you will have an easier career and life than mine has been.' We hugged each other and I went downstairs and ate Mum's hearty breakfast. I kissed her goodbye and with tears in her eyes she replied, 'Take care, son. Don't forget to write.' I set out full of trepidation on a brisk walk across the golf course with my small attaché case to catch the 8.30 bus to Rye, the 9.15 train to Ashford and the connection to Waterloo. Once I had cashed my railway warrant all fear left me, and I knew that I was about to embark upon the greatest adventure of my life.

* * *

This business of being inducted into the Electrical Branch left me wondering what was going on at the recruiting centre. I was of course quite naive about the way the Navy handled its recruitment, and did not realise that vacancies were filled in whichever way was possible, based upon the current requirement. While I was having my medical I again pushed for the Seaman Branch but was told quite firmly that I was not up to standard medically because I was partially colour blind. I was quite convinced that this was merely a ruse to put me off, and I complained bitterly to the contrary. I was given the test again and once more I said that the so-called white light was yellow because of the small aperture. The other two lights were green and red, which together with the white light represented the navigation lights of a ship. Very few white navigation lights are pure white and indeed vary in shades of yellow to orange, but the medical staff were having none of it and told me quite firmly that I was colour blind and that if I did not like the results the door was over there! Having thus been put firmly in my place, I joined the Electrical Branch, took the 'King's Shilling' and was in. Brother Brian had had the same problem when he tried to join the Seaman Branch: he also was told he was colour blind, which is decidedly not the case; indeed, when he joined the RAF for his National Service he entered the RAF Marine Branch and served in air–sea rescue launches at Plymouth, standing night watches on the bridge.

It was almost midday when a Chief Petty Officer gathered us all together and bussed us over to Waterloo station. There we caught a train for Fareham, where another Navy bus picked us up and transported us to HMS *Collingwood*, the Royal Naval Electrical School, a mile outside the town. On arrival we were ushered into two mess decks, where we left our cases. We were then marched over to the bedding department to be issued with sheets, pillow slips, a counterpane with the blue Admiralty anchor woven into it and a blanket—the bare essentials for our first night in the Navy. Once we had returned to our mess decks, Lieutenant Commander Hollis, our Naval Training Officer, gave a short talk and we were then introduced to our Training Instructor, Chief Petty Officer (GI) Springfield. ('GI' in the Royal Navy stands for 'Gunnery Instructor', and not the American term of General Infantryman which was introduced long after the British substantive rate.) He was one of those senior non-commissioned ratings who were ideally suited for training new-entry ratings. He treated his charges like a family and acted as a father figure, which he was: most of us were little older than seventeen years, and juniors as far as the Navy was concerned. The Chief GI's task was to whip us into shape as sailors first, before we became electricians. When he had finished, one felt proud of being in the greatest naval service in the world.

Our first meal in the Navy consisted of toast, butter, jam and a cake and of course copious quantities of tea in huge mugs and lashings of sugar to sweeten it. Back at the mess deck, the Chief GI described where everything was located aboard *Collingwood*, and what the programme would be for the next day. Then it was time for supper, which was always at 1830. After supper my course paid the NAAFI bar a visit *en masse*, although, as I was 'under age'—that is, not yet eighteen years old—I was allowed only a pint of 'scrumpy', a powerful cider which was, however, more alcoholic than beer! At 2200 we had to be back at our mess deck. Shortly thereafter, a bosun's pipe call was made over the ship's broadcast system, followed by 'Pipe down! Pipes and lights out!' This was the executive order to switch off all mess-deck lights except for the emergency 'blue police light', kill smoking pipes and cigarettes, stop talking and get to sleep.

Suddenly things really hit home, I was now in the Navy and subject to strict discipline. My career had begun.

II

LIFE ON THE LOWER DECK

— 3 —

In the Navy Now

ROYAL NAVY recruits go through a two-part training system before they join the Fleet. 'Part 1 Training' consists essentially of 'kitting out' a raw recruit, training him how to march properly and carry out rifle drill, and instructing him in various aspects of seamanship so that he will not be completely at a loss when ne arrives on board one of His or Her Majesty's ships. 'Part 2 Training' consists of academic and professional tuition. Generally speaking, the time allowed for each of these phases of training is six weeks. On graduating from 'Part 2 Training' one is either drafted immediately to a ship or placed in a holding division until a draft becomes available. With luck, one may even know one's draft long before completing 'Part 2 Training' and be off to sea there and then.

On arrival at HMS *Collingwood*, the Naval Electrical School, I was treated with 'kid gloves'—quite the opposite approach to that adopted by the Army in terms of the way new recruits were handled. The thinking in the Navy was that if a new recruit were treated badly at the beginning, either his spirit would be broken or an individual would be created who loathed authority and discipline and would spend his time merely waiting for his discharge date.

Much of the remainder of that first afternoon and evening was spent getting to know the others. We had all come from very different families and backgrounds, and had varying regional accents and religions. Therefore, we all had a great deal to learn and understand. After breakfast, our first day in the Navy began with everybody mustered on the roadway between the two rows of mess decks and instructional rooms. We were then marched across to the Pay Office to 'sign on' officially and receive our pay books and ID cards—a combined item for enlisted men. Our personal details were checked to ensure that there had been no mistakes. Even at this late stage I tried to change to the Seaman Branch, but I was put firmly in my place by a matronly blonde First Officer WRNS overseeing the new entries who bellowed at me, 'You are colour blind and that is the end of it, Doust!' I decided to let the matter rest for the time being and await a more appropriate time, which, I felt, was bound to occur.

The next stop was the Slop Room, where we all received a gratis issue of uniform and kit. We were presented with two blue uniforms, one for everyday wear and the other for parade use. Two pairs of boots and plimsolls were issued also, together with socks, underwear, pyjamas, white fronts, blue jerseys, blue jean collars, blue and white caps and two cap tallies. In addition, we received two sets of No 8 working uniforms, an overcoat, a raincoat, kit bags, an attaché case, a name block and a 'housewife' kit. Burdened with this vast amount of impedimenta, we all staggered back to our mess deck. None of our blue uniforms fitted us very well, and a base naval tailor made the necessary alterations at no cost to us. Tool boxes, together with the appropriate tools for our profession, would not be issued until we had begun 'Part 2'. A second trip was made to the Slop Room to collect our hammocks (two each), mattress and covers, plus hammock slings.

After lunch the Chief GI set about teaching us how to lay out our kit on our beds for inspection. Our first task was to mark all clothing with our name using the printing block issued to us. Everything I owned was thus marked in half-inch black letters. Over the next week, daily, we laid out our kit for inspection, and if there were any body stains on one's underwear then that would be cause for a further inspection. The Chief would stand quietly alongside and ask, 'Does your mother wash your underwear that way? Go and rewash for another inspection this evening!'

Our next task was to sew on our basic trade badges using our 'housewife' kit. Neat stitching was required, 'homeward bounders' (that is, large stitching) being rejected and a cause for re-sewing. Cap tallies were placed on our caps with a neat bow over the left ear, the wartime fashion of having the bow over the forehead being forbidden. 'Bell-bottom' trousers were pressed so that there were seven horizontal creases in each leg, these creases supposedly representing the seven seas sailed by the Royal Navy. There was another reason for the creases: they reduced the size of the trousers and made them easier to fit into a kit bag. Slowly the Chief GI created a group of sailors of which any Sovereign would be proud!

Once our uniforms were in good shape and we were presentable as sailors, the course attended its first divisional parade. *Collingwood* had the largest parade ground in southern England and it was filled to capacity when all the courses of officers and men mustered for roll call, inspection and march past the Executive Officer. This took place daily except Thursdays, which was always 'Captain's Divisions' day. Normally, all of us except the officers wore long, khaki-green gaiters, but on Captain's Divisions these gaiters were left off and we marched around the parade ground swinging our 'bell-bottoms'. A finer group of sailors there never was! During the weekdays after divisions, the course would retire to the drill sheds for further marching and rifle drill. After Captain's Divisions, the course would return to its mess decks to change out of No 1 and into No 2 blue uniform or No 8 working dress. This working dress was much more comfortable than the blue uniform and easier to keep clean.

During one particular session of rifle drill the course was being coached about more intricate weapon handling, such as 'presenting arms'. The Chief

GI had demonstrated how the rifle was taken from the shoulder to a position vertically in front of the body in a 'general salute'. He called the course to attention, gave the order 'Shoulder arms' and then went on to give the order 'General salute: present arms!', for which manoeuvre one had to stick one's index finger into the trigger guard during the movement of the rifle. I missed the trigger guard and my weapon fell with a resounding clatter on the drill shed's concrete floor. The Chief GI, without saying a word, marched over and snapped to attention in front of me. Then, as in the song of Sam Browne and his rifle, he said in a very firm voice, 'Pick up your rifle, Doust. If there had been hairs around it you would have found it!' I of course responded, 'Yes, sir!' My course members fell about splitting their sides with laughter although, being rather naive, I had not a clue as to what he was talking about. When we all took a short break a friend whispered in my ear what the Chief was trying to tell me, and I immediately went scarlet from the neck upwards!

Although all of us had given our preference as to whether we wanted to be an Electrician's Mate (EM) or a Radio Electrician's Mate (REM), the course was given an examination to decide finally which sub-specialisation training we would receive. I was rated JREM, the 'J' meaning Junior as I was still under eighteen years of age.

At about this time I requested, in accordance with an Admiralty Fleet order, a transfer to the Fleet Air Arm as a pilot. Although my request went forward, I would be at sea before any action was taken on it. However, while at *Collingwood* I learnt to fly a Tiger Moth at Portsmouth Airport. After going solo I clocked up about fifteen hours of flying time, and this was to stand me in good stead when I eventually went before the Admiralty Interview Board.

— 4 —

To Sea in a Big Ship

AFTER many weeks kicking my heels around *Collingwood* performing various menial tasks as a newly qualified REM, I was finally on my way to join one of His Majesty's ships. My first seagoing draft was to the light fleet carrier HMS *Theseus*, operating out of Malta with the Mediterranean Fleet. Needless to say, I was overjoyed: this was really why I had joined the Navy—to go to sea. The majority of my contemporaries were already at sea, having received their draft orders almost immediately upon graduating from the REM or EM courses. More importantly to me, I would be seeing the Fleet Air Arm operating at close quarters.

My first task was to visit 'Slops' to collect my issue of tropical uniforms and kit. This included No 6 white suits, white shorts, blue No 8 shorts and sandals. Next I had to pack a 'steaming kit bag' with the bare essentials of kit, my attaché case and a pusser's green suitcase—all that I was allowed to take with me on my flight to Malta. The remainder of my kit, including my tool box, were bundled up and despatched to *Theseus* via a Royal Fleet Auxiliary that made a run to Malta every six weeks, delivering stores and equipment to the Mediterranean Fleet. One had to live in hope that the kit would arrive complete and dry.

Until my final departure I continued to work in the Electrical Officers' Training School (known as 'Whitehall'). Many of the National Service ratings who had been with me in New Entry training as Upperyardmen (L) had now been commissioned as Acting Sub Lieutenants (L) RNR. They were in this section of *Collingwood*, receiving their advanced training before going off to sea to complete their two years in the Navy. Consequently we all knew each other, and during my short time there I learnt a great deal about how officers behaved and conducted themselves. Many of these young National Service officers would eventually transfer to the General List on a permanent commission. One afternoon I received a telephone call to report to the Draftees' Office for my orders, rail warrant and flight ticket. Everybody at 'Whitehall' wished me luck with my draft and success at the AIB.

My departure from the United Kingdom was by means of a British European Airways twin-engine Viking airliner, on charter to the Ministry of Defence, from RAF Bovingdon. The MoD had a contract with British European Airways to fly military personnel and their families around Europe and the Mediterranean, the RAF not having suitable aircraft for the task at that time. The Vickers Viking was the standard aircraft used by most commercial airline companies. It was safe and reliable, powered by two Bristol Centaurus radial engines similar to those used in the Navy's Hawker Sea Fury fighters, and so one felt perfectly at ease when aloft in it.

As I mustered with other draftees to board the airliner, the Chief Petty Officer in charge nominated me to look after an officer's young wife and family who were also on their way to Malta to join husband and father. I was rather miffed at being assigned this task but, as it happened, they were a very nice family and the mother made it a very enjoyable flight. Our first stop en route to Malta was Nice in southern France, where the airliner would be refuelled and serviced for the last leg of the flight. I visited the airport restaurant bar and bought myself a small beer which cost the earth and tasted of onions! After a couple of hours we all re-embarked and proceeded to Malta, landing at RAF Luqa at 1600.

On disembarking, all naval and other military personnel had to wait until the civilians had left the airliner. My young family's husband and father was waiting at the bottom of the steps. He was a newly promoted Commander and I was introduced to him; he thanked me for looking after his wife and children. Together with several other draftees, I was then driven over to Valletta steps, where a ship's launch was waiting to ferry us out to *Theseus*, which was moored off Binghy Point. As the launch approached the forward gangway I could see an Electrical Petty Officer waiting to meet me. He introduced himself and immediately led me below to my mess deck, introducing me in turn to the leading hand of the mess, LREM Robb. As soon as I had stowed my kit temporarily I was taken off to the Electrical Regulating Office, where I met my Divisional Officer. I explained to my new DO that I was expecting to return to Britain soon to attend an AIB, but he did not seem to know anything about this, although he would 'look into it' for me. When all my visits had been completed I returned to the mess for supper— my first meal aboard the carrier—and to sort out where I would be slinging my hammock when it finally arrived from *Collingwood*. In the meantime I would be sleeping on a fold-away camp bed, borrowing sheets and blankets from Slops.

Ship's mess decks in those days consisted of a large flat, perhaps two or three scuttles for fresh air, three large folding tables, side benches for sitting on and a folding chair for whoever sat at the head of the table. Each mess had a couple of sailors who were nominated mess cooks, and they were responsible for preparing the meals and taking them to the ship's galley for cooking. This duty was rotated every week, so we all took a turn at being mess cook. One's reputation stood according to how good a cook one was, and many sailors were very accomplished at preparing and producing a meal; indeed, many requested a transfer to the Cookery Branch, where they did extremely well for themselves. The routine called for each mess cook to go to the victualling store to collect the daily rations. The cooks would then prepare the meal in the mess and return it to the galley, where the ship's chefs would cook it and make it ready for collection about half-an-hour before meal time. Tea and coffee rations, together with sugar and tinned milk, would be issued in a similar way, at the beginning of the day. However, in my mess nobody ever managed to make good tea. It was thick, almost like tar, and a spoon could almost stand up in it. It was always prepared in a large 'fanny' and allowed to stew, which ruined it completely.

In those days there were no fold-away or fixed bunks of the type enjoyed by sailors in today's warships: the Navy was still in the era of Nelson and men slept in hammocks as did cadets and midshipmen. Each mess deck had hammock bars placed across the deckhead and each sleeping berth was allocated according to rank and position in the mess—and woe betide anyone who took another man's berth. In the morning the Duty Petty Officer would burst into the mess at 0630 shouting 'Wakey, wakey! Rise and shine!' He may have added the odd obscenity if, for example, the scuttles had been closed, causing the air to be putrified with odorous body smells, especially after a good run ashore the previous night. We leapt out of our hammocks, cursing the fellow in the next one as we bumped into each other, and stowed them in the metal cage set aside for the purpose outside the mess. Then we dashed off to the ablutions to fight for a wash basin or WC. Those men who had been on watch during the night were allowed to sleep for a further half-hour, although this was difficult with people bumping into one's hammock and with a great deal of talking and cursing going on nearby. Those who were lucky enough to acquire a camp bed usually slept out on the weather decks or in a flat area away from the mess. Eventually I would take my camp bed, sleeping either in the starboard after paravane bay or up on one of the Bofors gun sponsons off the starboard side of the flight deck. What a difference from the smelly old mess deck—clean, beautiful fresh air, and much healthier!

Breakfast was my second meal aboard *Theseus*. It consisted of eggs, sausages, fried bread, beans, toast and marmalade, plus copious quantities of tea. I was ravenous, and went 'around the buoy again'. Eating habits had to be watched, or weight could quickly be put on and uniforms outgrown. At this stage in my naval career I weighed just 7 stone 8 pounds, and I certainly did not have any extra cash to pay for new uniforms. So I quickly settled down to eating just what my body needed.

Following another visit to the Electrical Regulating Office, I met my head of department, Commander (L). He did not impress me as a friendly officer, contenting himself with sitting in a chair with his cap on, looking corpulent, offering neither smile nor handshake and merely grunting with a 'Mind yourself—we want no slackers in this department!' I made a mental note to keep out of the way of this man.

My working station was on the port side amidships, just below the flight deck. LREM Robb, my mess-deck leading hand, who operated out of the same workshop, collected me and showed me the way. Six of us worked out of the same station, dealing in the main with radios and radars located in the island—the carrier's bridge and operations room superstructure. My first job was to assist CREA Gray, who was trying to repair the ship's Type 981Q radar, which had one of the old 'bedstead' aerials. The CREA had been working on it for days without success, and now he was asking me for ideas as to what might be wrong with it. I must admit that I was rather bewildered. As I stood in the radar office I wondered what on earth I was supposed to do: if a highly qualified CREA could not solve the problem, how could I? A short while later LREM Robb joined me and we talked over some ideas as to what might be causing the failure. After replacing a couple of parts we fired up the radar and we managed to transmit and receive. The fault had lain in the klystron, which produces the transmission signal. I must admit that there were moments when I thought we might be fried alive. I suppose the episode is what one might call 'being thrown in at the deep end'.

Theseus was a very clean ship, due entirely to the fact that she had an excellent Captain and Executive Officer. The officers and men liked them both, and if somebody did well during the day, whether in harbour or at sea, they would receive a 'chuck up' in the next day's daily orders. This was the way to run a ship, with everybody on board feeling and knowing that he was appreciated from the very top of the chain of command.

A week after I joined, *Theseus* put to sea and re-embarked her air group from RNAS Halfar in Malta. Over the next ten days the air group practised launches, both from the hydraulic catapults and the axial deck proper, and arrested landings, the angled deck and steam catapult being in those days merely ideas on the drawing board. There were eight to ten arrester wires strung across the flight deck, and if an aircraft missed them on landing, or even caught only the last couple of wires, it was brought to a halt by a heavy wire barrier. A second barrier was erected in case the first was penetrated or 'jumped', to ensure that the aircraft was stopped before reaching the park at the forward end of the flight deck. One pilot, who shall remain anonymous, jumped both barriers and tried to go around again, but he had insufficient speed and promptly landed forward amongst the parked aircraft, writing off a large part of the air group's complement and injuring several flight-deck personnel as well as himself. If an angled deck had been installed in the ship, this type of accident would never have occurred because he would have had a clear way ahead to go around again.

In fact, this particular period of flying practice was to have its share of accidents. One Saturday I, together with a friend, had decided to sleep the afternoon away on the starboard after Bofors sponson. Unfortunately, or perhaps fortunately, Commander (Flying), as he was known in those days, had spotted us from Flyco. Commander Black looked for all the world like a reincarnation of Blackbeard the pirate. He came striding along the flight deck looking like thunder and, bawling at the top of his voice, let forth with 'What the bloody hell do you two think you are playing at? Get below the flight deck before you are killed!' The two of us scampered below decks wondering who this officer was, never having seen nor heard of him before. Within a minute or so we heard the roar of a Centaurus engine, followed by a loud bang, the screeching of metal and a dull thud, and then flecks of cellulose paint came fluttering down into the flat where we had been standing. The next thing we heard was a broadcast over the ship's tannoy: 'Crash on flight deck. No smoking throughout the ship until further notice!' Despite the strong smell of aviation gasoline we plucked up enough courage to peer over the edge of the flight deck to see what on earth had happened.

The aircraft that had come to grief was a Sea Fury fighter, and it was lying in a mangled heap on the forward lift. The pilot, who had survived the crash with only a few minor cuts and bruises, had 'gunned' his engine at the last moment before touch-down and the powerful Centaurus engine had caused the airframe to rotate around the propeller in what is commonly known as a 'torque stall'. The pilot had lost control of his fighter, which veered off to the right. The right wing had slid along the top of the jib of the ship's crane, jamming between the jib and buffers, where it was torn away from the fuselage. The aircraft had spun round, slammed into the after side of the island, jumped both barriers and finally landed on the forward lift, spilling fuel everywhere. To this day nobody understands why there was no fire as a result of the hot engine and the sparks flying everywhere. The pilot had exited his plane very quickly before the crash crews had had time to react and reach him, the fire crew quickly covering the spilt fuel with foam and washing it overboard. My friend turned to me.

'Do you still want to be an FAA pilot after all this?' he asked.

'Yes,' I replied quickly, nodding my head.

It must have been a week later when I was working in the island and another crash occurred on the flight deck. This time it was a Fairey Firefly, which had made a 'full toss' landing into the first barrier. It lay on the flight deck on its belly at an angle pointing toward the island, its undercarriage ripped off, its propeller bent and twisted and with various tears in its wings and fuselage metal. It was the 'mail and money plane' returning from Halfar. At the time I had no idea who the pilot was, but many years later I discovered that he was an old Rye Grammar School friend of mine, Alfie Wigg. He had run away to sea twice: he was caught on the first occasion and returned to school but on the second attempt he made it into the 'Andrew' as a rating pilot. In those days, some 60–70 per cent of the FAA aircrews were either ratings or commissioned pilots, that is, warrant officers. Many of these gentlemen were to climb the ladder to the highest rank in the Navy as either Admirals or Admirals of the Fleet. Admirals Fell, Lygo and Empson, for example, all served as rating pilots, flying Hurricane fighters in the Western Desert of North Africa against Rommel's Afrika Korps.

The main purpose of our flying training was to prepare the air group for a forthcoming NATO exercise in the eastern Mediterranean. Over the next ten days *Theseus*, together with her task group, would be carrying out dummy attacks against a US Navy task group acting as the opposition. On completion of the exercise the two task groups would join up, steam into Piraeus Bay as a combined fleet and drop anchor together—a spectacular event.

My watch had been given shore leave for the first evening in harbour when, at the last minute, just as I was going down the gangway, leave for my part of the watch was cancelled. It was too late: I was in the liberty boat and away ashore. Commander (L) wanted the duty watch plus a part of the off-duty watch to rig floodlighting around the ship. This was really a job for EMs, and a dozen men could have easily completed the task, but no—our gallant head of department decided that it required at least 75 per cent of the Electrical Department! He caused more unhappiness than can be imagined, and very nearly set in train a mutiny.

Later that day, when my part of watch had returned on board, the Duty Electrical Petty Officer was waiting for us. 'You, you and you—report to the Electrical Reg Office now! You are all for the high jump!' At that point in time none of us had any clue as to what we had done, but it was soon made clear when we arrived at the Reg Office. Commander (L) was waiting for us looking very threatening and crimson with rage. We informed him that we were on our way ashore before the order had really been issued changing leave arrangements. Therefore, there was little that he could do except blast us to Kingdom Come and give us a stern warning. However, he singled me out from the others, although to this day I do not know why.

'I've got my eye on you Doust!' he said. 'I believe you to be a trouble-maker!'

'Who, me, sir?'

'Yes, you, Doust! So watch your step!'

I had been in the Navy only a very short time and had not been in any trouble at all, and his accusation knocked me sideways. Immediately I had an interview with my Divisional Officer and Petty Officer, to whom I complained bitterly about the Commander's remarks and accusations. They advised me to forget about it and stay out of the officer's way. This gave me little or no confidence in those responsible for me. Personally, I found this senior officer quite offensive, totally lacking in ability to handle either officers or men. He never visited our workplaces, and I certainly never saw him around the ship. Someone said that he was a direct-entry officer from the dockyard and had spent very little time with the Navy. I was never able to confirm the truth of this, but perhaps he found shipboard life difficult to cope with and took it out on his staff.

I went ashore again in both Athens and Piraeus. Both cities were still in the throes of recovering from World War II. There was still much damage to buildings that had not yet been repaired, and the Greek citizens were 'ripping us off' for as much as they could. I did see a couple of films, one in Athens and the other in Piraeus. They were both foreign films with Greek subtitles, so one could only watch the pictures and try to make out the storyline. The Piraeus cinema was like something from Ancient Greece, fitted out with stone benches similar to those in the old Colosseum. The British Ambassador laid on various visits for us and I took full advantage of them. One was to the Parthenon on the Acropolis and another was to the site of the great sea battle of Salamis. After a week the anchor was weighed and *Theseus* steamed off to Naples, our next port of call.

As in so many naval commands, the time of year dictates which uniform should be worn. It was spring in Europe but the Mediterranean, being that much further south, was a good deal warmer, which warranted our being in tropical uniform or whites. Everybody shifted into whites for entering harbour, and for the sailors this meant wearing white tops and shorts, blue stockings and black shoes. It was late March, and as the carrier swung into Naples harbour, a blinding snowstorm swept down from the mountains around the volcano, Vesuvius, and across the ship. The sudden arrival of this storm and the accompanying low temperature took everybody by surprise, and sailors' legs and arms turned the same colour as their stockings. As soon as the ship docked, a broadcast was made— 'All hands change into blue uniform'—and a cheer went up from the flight deck. The ship's company stayed in blues until *Theseus* arrived back in Malta, where it definitely *was* very much warmer and we changed back into tropical uniform.

Theseus remained in Grand Harbour, Malta, and she was still there when I left her some seven weeks later. My draft orders had finally come through for my return to Britain, to attend the AIB. I was to report to HMS *Collingwood* on my return, whereupon I would be given further instructions. Initially I was transferred to the Kalafrani Barracks, Valletta, to await my flight. After spending a week there I was transferred across the harbour to a unit near Binghy consisting of tents and caves where those on draft were held until their flight home. I had by now been hanging about for at least two weeks ashore in Malta, and once again I felt as if I were being pushed around and getting absolutely nowhere. Finally I plucked up enough courage to visit the Draft Section in order to voice my opinion: I had to be back in Britain by a certain date to attend my AIB. It soon became obvious that my complaining and 'jumping around' began to produce results, and before I knew it I was on another Viking airliner. My aircraft landed at Bovingdon, and after checking in at *Collingwood*, and a long weekend, I moved into RAF Horn-church, Essex, for a two-day psychological and aptitude test. On completion of these tests I was informed that I had passed that particular phase and would be told when to report to the AIB at Lee-on-Solent. In the meantime I would remain at *Collingwood*.

I felt now as if I might be going places!

— 5 —

Aircrew Selection and Officer Sea Training

ALTHOUGH I was at RAF Hornchurch for two days, the aircrew aptitude tests lasted only one, which surprised me. The tests seemed formidable at the time, but, in retrospect, they were in many ways to my mind pointless. Perhaps the RAF psychologist obtained something useful from the results, but what that might have been is beyond me. I suppose that he was trying to gauge and assess the speed and adaptability of a candidate's mind—which is essential when controlling a high-performance aircraft.

On my return to *Collingwood* I was placed once again in Howard Division and I decided, rather foolishly, to take my LREM's oral examination. A friend had just taken his and passed it with no effort whatsoever, telling me that it was easy. I failed miserably and was angry with myself, especially at a time when I was about to go before an officers' selection board. The next event shocked me even more. I was given an overnight draft to HMS *Vanguard*, the Navy's one and only battleship still in commission. Now I was convinced that something, or somebody, was trying to stop me from attending the AIB. I rushed over to Draftees' Office, and the staff there swore that they knew of no selection board for me.

'Why do you think I returned from the Med? For the good of my health?' I shouted.

'Don't take that attitude with us here. Go to *Vanguard* and sort it out aboard her!'

So off I went with my tail between my legs and feeling very disgruntled.

Fortunately *Vanguard* was berthed alongside in Portsmouth, so I did not have far to go. I arrived in mid-afternoon, checked in with the Electrical Reg Office and was allocated a berth in the aftermost gun turret. My Divisional Officer was a friendly young man, and I explained my situation to him, not understanding why I had been sent to this great ship when I was supposed to be attending an AIB. He replied, 'Well don't worry. I'll sort it out for you. Off you go with your Section Petty Officer.' My Section PO was a kind and cheerful person, who showed me around and to my battle quarters, which would be the Operations Room, deep in the bowels of the battleship. There was only one way in and one way out—via a nine square foot, six inch thick armoured hatch. Once inside, one's fate was sealed: if the ship developed a list to port there was no way in which anyone could move that hatch because of its weight. This was, to say the least, all very impressive—and alarming! I suspect that the PO was pulling my leg and that there was another escape route via a hatch in the deckhead, although he never showed it to me.

My new Divisional Officer was as good as his word. Before tea time he had sorted out my draft (which could easily have been done at *Collingwood*): I would return to *Collingwood* and wait there until called forward by the AIB. In the meantime I was cleared to go on a long weekend and leave the ship first thing on Monday morning before she sailed for Gibraltar. I returned on Sunday evening to spend my one and only night aboard *Vanguard*. Next morning I gathered my kit together quickly and was the last person to go ashore before the gangway was removed as the ship started to slip her moorings. I stood there and watched her depart for The Rock, wondering what my experiences aboard her might have been.

A week later I was drafted to Lee-on-Solent for three days to attend the AIB. The first day was taken up with practice parachute jumps from a mock-up of a Firefly cockpit and crossing a canyon by using a couple of planks, an oil drum and a few feet of rope. Then I spent a couple of hours writing an essay on any subject I liked, my choice being a motor yacht fitted with Gardner diesel engines.

The first evening, while I was relaxing in my mess, Dick Godden, an old chum from Rye Grammar School, appeared from nowhere. He also was sitting the AIB for his second attempt, but he had not been successful. He seemed very unsure whether he really wanted to take up flying, and indeed with hindsight it is probably just as well that he did not. He became a Direction PO and as far as I know he went on to complete his time in the Service: our paths never crossed again.

The following day my group was taken one by one before the selection board, which consisted of a headmaster from Bedfordshire, a Captain, a Commander and a Lieutenant Commander. My essay was picked to shreds and I was asked about my Tiger Moth flying. One officer asked me what I would do on a motorcycle when going around a corner. I answered honestly that I had never ridden a motorcycle and did not really know but hazarded a guess by saying that I would lean into the turn, which satisfied him. Then I was dismissed, feeling like a schoolboy. Later that afternoon I was informed that I had been selected to join an Upperyardman (Air) Course some time in February 1953 aboard the carrier HMS *Indefatigable* at Portland.

The term 'Upperyardman' hails from the days of sailing, when only the best were allowed aloft to the topmost yards on the masts to tend the sails. The Royal Navy subsequently applied the term to the 'cream' of the lower deck—those considered to have officer potential. The usual uniform was worn, but a white band was displayed underneath the ship's cap ribbon or cap badge band if wearing fore-and-aft rig, plus white shoulder flashes on the sleeves. On Upperyardman courses there were Able, Petty Officer and Chief Petty Officer ranks, but all were treated the same and were considered to be officer cadets. Ages ranged from eighteen to twenty-six, and on passing the course one was commissioned either Midshipman or Acting Sub Lieutenant, depending upon age. At nineteen, I was the youngest on my course.

* * *

I had not been feeling well for the past few weeks. My stomach was playing me up and was very painful, especially on my lower right side. Before leaving for *Indefatigable* I went home on long weekend leave and during the Saturday evening I kept vomiting. By the next day my stomach had settled down and I returned to *Collingwood*, but by Monday morning I was just as bad again and I finally plucked up enough courage to visit the Sickbay. I spoke to the Sickbay Chief and told him I was feeling awful and needed to see the doctor right away but was told to take my turn in the queue. After I had rushed to the 'heads' a couple of times to vomit he realised that something was very wrong and immediately sent me to the doctor. Before I could sit down I went straight to his office wash basin and promptly vomited again. He called in the Chief and, after asking a couple of questions and poking me about in my stomach, which made me yelp with pain, he ordered the Chief to make ready the ambulance to take me to the RN hospital at Haslar, near Gosport. The next thing I can recall was waking up in a hospital bed and being violently sick once more. On my arrival at the hospital I was 'prepped' and taken straight into the emergency operating theatre for treatment to a ruptured appendix. All that morning and for most of the afternoon I vomited periodically and felt very sore and drowsy. After a couple of days I managed to sit up and take some nourishment in the form of light soups, though trying to 'pee' and 'george' was excruciating. Over the next few days I slowly recovered, but I had had a very close brush with St Peter: fortunately, they had caught me just in time.

One afternoon I awoke from a post-lunch snooze to discover that another sailor had been admitted to the ward. He was at the far end near the main entrance, lying on a special bed with his bed linen suspended above his body. Apparently he was a cook from the Portsmouth Naval Barracks and had fallen into a vat of boiling soup. He was burned severely over about 75 per cent of his body and was suffering from severe pain. The next day his bed was empty. When I inquired of his whereabouts the nurses were very reticent and I could only assume that he had passed away during the night. As I lay back on my sickbed I thought just how lucky I had been at having been given a second chance.

* * *

My Upperyardman (Air)'s course aboard *Indefatigable* had started: I would be weeks behind following my time in hospital and sick leave and it was worrying me. I was assured, nevertheless, that I would join the ship and course and that, somehow, arrangements would be made for me to catch up. After ten days in hospital I was sent home on two weeks' sick leave and then ordered back to *Collingwood*. When I arrived back I was immediately drafted to RN Barracks Portsmouth to await further instructions for *Indefatigable*. It seemed, now, that I was reaping the whirlwind I had sown by being such a pain in the butt to everybody. I spent about a couple of weeks kicking my heels, helping out in the PO's mess and doing odd menial jobs. I was then told to collect my kit together and was driven to the city railway station and placed on a train. A naval bus was waiting for me at Weymouth railway station and I was driven off, to be deposited with my kit and baggage on a jetty in Portland harbour where a ship's boat, manned by Upperyardmen, had been laid on.

Indefatigable was one of two wartime aircraft carriers that formed the Royal Navy's sea-going Training Squadron. She had no aircraft embarked except for a static Firefly parked on the flight deck astern of the after lift, and all the hangars had been converted into huge mess decks and officers' quarters, both officers and men being embarked for seamanship training and ship handling. The two vessels were ideal for the task because the training could be concentrated instead of spread out over a squadron of several smaller ships—which could also be restricted by bad weather. Both ships were moored close to one another, not far from the harbour eastern entrance, and looked massive when compared to *Theseus*.

My sea-going course had been up and running for six weeks or more and the Upperyardmen were well into the course syllabus, and consequently there was little chance of my being able to catch up at this stage. Another course was just about to start aboard *Implacable*, the sister-ship. My course chums were about to commence street-lining practice for our new Queen's Coronation in London, and I was given the opportunity to move across and join the new course, changing back when I had reached the point where my original course had stopped for the new duties. The move worked very well indeed and I was soon amongst old friends again. I missed the *Implacable* Upperyardmen, but they were not quite like my old group, which was a happier and more carefree corps of young future officers.

It was during my time aboard *Implacable* that I was, much to my annoyance, given the nickname 'Punchy'. Both ships of the Squadron visited Bournemouth for the Coronation weekend. I had been landed as part of the Shore Patrol and was supervising the return of some Upperyardmen in one of the liberty boats. One particular individual, 'Tug' Wilson, was a little the worse for drink and being rather obstreperous.

'Wilson, get down in the boat, sit down and shut up!' I said in a loud, commanding voice.

'Oh,' he said, 'Doust is being very punchy tonight!'

The term stuck for the remainder of my naval career.

My voyage to Bournemouth did not actually take place aboard the carrier because I sailed around from Portland in one of the ship's whalers, it being considered that this would present an ideal opportunity for the Upperyardmen to gain some practical sailing experience in an open boat. Each carrier therefore launched a minor armada of half a dozen whalers and cutters to be sailed from Portland harbour to Bournemouth. It was a dull and drizzly day but fortunately the wind and tide were with us all the way to our destination. The boats arrived within a short time of the carriers' anchoring, and by then the sun had come out, giving a fine sail across Studland Bay. Many of the crew were seasick, however, and never wanted to sail in a small boat again! Personally, I found the experience great fun and very instructive, but then I had knowledge of small boats and yacht sailing.

After the Bournemouth visit I was returned to my own ship and course. The Captain held Sunday Divisions on the flight deck, and standing in front of me was UY S——, a former seaman Petty Officer. S—— had had quite a run ashore the previous night, spending a few hours with a certain lady of the city beneath the Palace Pier. Once back on board he had had little time to tidy his No 1 uniform and he failed to notice that he had a piece of female apparel hanging from his right jacket pocket. As he stood in line within his division, small piles of sand began to appear. Lieutenant John Parfitt, our Naval Training Officer, stood behind S—— and complained in a loud voice that he was being buried alive by sand. He pulled out the red panties from S——'s pocket, demanding to know why 'Irish bunting' was hanging from his uniform. Before S—— could say anything, the whole course collapsed with laughter while Parfitt heaped upon him one tirade after another. His leave was stopped for a week and the course was warned in no uncertain terms that, as we were future naval officers, a very high standard in morals and personal behaviour was expected from us.

A Coronation Fleet Review had been scheduled for the early summer, and it had been decided that the Sea Training Squadron, after leaving Bournemouth, would make a quick circumnavigation of the United Kingdom. Its first visit was to the Scilly Isles, those far-flung islands south-west of Land's End that are still at war with the Netherlands from the 1700s. The two ships anchored in St Mary's Roads and virtually the entire companies of both ships managed a run ashore. Late on Sunday the weather deteriorated rapidly and all shore leave was cancelled, those ashore being recalled aboard. The wind soon rose to gale force and the Admiral signalled for the two ships to weigh anchor and proceed north to the Irish Channel. By the time the ships had cleared the islands the gale had increased to storm Force 10 with very heavy seas. The two carriers, about half a mile apart, steamed slowly past Lundy Island and soon afterwards the conditions deteriorated further, to almost hurricane force. Both Captains hove-to in order to ride out the storm. I had seen wartime film footage of carriers riding out severe Atlantic storms with the forward ends of their flight decks plunging into and under the heavy waves, and I managed to take some pictures of *Implacable* with 150 feet of her forefoot clear of the sea and then as she plunged down again, her rudder and propellers showing.

Most of *Indefatigable*'s crewmen were terribly seasick, and with such violent ship motion who could blame them? There was a tremendous thud each time the ship plunged into yet another huge wave. After what seemed a long time, with her hull shuddering, she slowly began to lift her head with the sea cascading down the flight deck. As the water cleared it became apparent that serious damage had been sustained by the forward aircraft lift: it had

47

been knocked down into the lift well and was hanging at a precarious angle. The lift well was flooded, as was the hangar deck to several inches of water. With such a large quantity of free surface liquid slopping about at so high a level, the safety of the ship was in jeopardy since, if a hefty volume of water on the hangar deck was allowed to move to one side of the hangar with the ship rolling or turning, the carrier could capsize and sink. Captain Fisher nursed his ship to reduce any rolling moment and the Executive Officer, together with the Shipwright, Engineering Officer and the Emergency Party, set about shoring up the lift with huge timbers and pumping the floodwater overboard.

While *Indefatigable* was fighting her battle with the sea and elements, away to starboard her sister-ship was having her own problems. One of her men was swept overboard. Captain Campbell manoeuvred his ship and swung out the starboard boat boom so that the end dipped in the sea as the huge carrier rolled. The ship's First Lieutenant, with a safety line about him, shinned out on the boom and threw a line to the man overboard, pulling him back to and up on to the boom. Captain Campbell and his First Lieutenant were awarded the CBE and MBE, respectively, for their gallantry in rescuing this man in such appalling conditions, and the Executive Officer and his team aboard *Indefatigable* received similar awards.

While the Squadron was hove-to in St George's Channel, a fifty-square-metre yacht with just a storm jib set passed down our port side, heading south for Plymouth. It was crewed by officers and men from RN Engineering College Manadon. Many years later, when I was a flying instructor in 738 Naval Air Squadron, I found out that Lieutenant Reg Hillsdon, our Air Engineer Officer (AEO), was one of the crewmen aboard this yacht, and, both being keen yachtsmen, we became great friends.

Slowly the storm moderated, but then a 'mayday' distress signal was received from the Tenby Lightvessel, which had broken adrift from her moorings off the south coast of Wales. Lightvessels do not have engines and are therefore at the mercy of the sea and wind. She was some distance to the north of us and the Milford Haven lifeboat reached her first and stood by until a tug arrived, passed a line and towed her into Milford Haven, where she was later refitted with new anchors and towed back out to her station. Our help was not required and so we steamed on north, into the Irish Sea. Once the storm had abated, the Squadron continued to the Isle of Arran in the approaches to the Firth of Clyde. It had been decided to hold the Squadron Regatta off Arran the following Saturday afternoon.

The two ships steamed slowly into the loch between Arran and Holy Island, a small piece of land just to the east of Lamlash, the main port of Arran. I was very intrigued when Captain Fisher threw a bundle of small sticks into the water to judge his ship's speed. When the ship stopped, the anchor was slipped and we went slowly astern, laying out our cable and to ensure that the anchor made a good grip in the seabed. Engines were stopped and those members of the crew who were off watch prepared to go ashore or make preparations for the next day's regatta. The following day, Saturday, turned out to be fine and sunny with a gentle breeze—ideal conditions for a regatta.

The two ship's companies competed against each other in rowing and sailing events, *Implacable* just beating *Indefatigable* by a couple of points. However, the latter gained some revenge when a team quietly rowed over and commandeered *Implacable*'s motor fishing vessel, bringing it back alongside our MFV tied up on the starboard side of the ship. This was considered fair, our ship having lost out in the tussle to be 'Cock of the Fleet'. All hell broke loose, of course, once *Implacable*'s crew realised that their liberty boat had gone missing. Captain Fisher and the Executive Officer smiled quietly, and after an hour the 'borrowed' MFV was towed back to its rightful owner, the recovery team from *Implacable* being repelled by water hosed on them, accompanied by a half-hearted apology.

On Sunday I went ashore for a walk. I must have covered almost thirty miles, and I also climbed Goat Fell, the highest point on Arran. Once back at Lamlash, I called in at a hotel for a pint of beer and was promptly refused, the reason being that my home—that is, my ship—was less than three and a half miles away, the minimum legal distance one had to travel in Scotland on a Sunday during those years to be served an alcoholic drink! The hotel staff suggested that I walk down the road half a mile to the next hostelry to obtain my beer. One can well imagine how I felt, letting forth in no uncertain terms my thoughts on the Scottish regulations. Fortunately, a very kind local bought me a beer, and the pair of us sat back and chatted away for an hour or two.

On Monday the Squadron weighed anchor for the upper reaches of the Clyde, where it spent a couple of days. UY Phil Cardew and I went racing in an RNSA 14-foot dinghy. The day started very well indeed with a fine, light to moderate breeze ideal for racing, but it soon dropped away and by the afternoon it was calm, with a blazing sun beating down from a clear sky. The race was finally abandoned because of the absence of wind, although late in the afternoon a light breeze sprang up from the south-west and we had a good sail back to *Indefatigable*, arriving in time for supper.

Our next port of call in the Clyde area was Troon. As a port, Troon has little to offer the visitor except its golf course, and I suspect that this was the reason behind the decision to call there. Our visit to this quiet, west Scottish fishing port was to rebound on us a few weeks later when the ship's padre received a letter from a very upset mother. One of our Upperyardmen had met a local girl and had made her pregnant, but he had called himself 'Peter Fox'. Peter was sent for by the Padre, who wanted to know what he intended to do about it. As it happened, Peter had not gone ashore at Troon and he told the Padre this: the girl's condition had absolutely nothing to do with him. Moreover, he was betrothed to a girl in Stroud and so would not even consider such a heinous deed. It did not take us long to narrow down the culprit, who, when confronted by the other Upperyardmen, denied having been with any girl ashore in Troon. He had been seen by one of us and he was told to his face that he was a blatant liar, but he still denied that he was the man responsible. I do not know whether this miserable specimen paid the Padre a visit, but he was thereafter well and truly ostracised by all of us. To this day I do not know how the man was ever granted a commission. He never changed his spots for as long as I knew him, and I felt extremely sorry for his wife, who was a wonderful lady.

The next visit by the Squadron was to Scapa Flow in the Orkney Islands. The two ships' MFVs were sent on ahead with a group of Upperyardmen aboard each of them for navigational training. The voyage north for all vessels was made in excellent sea and weather conditions, and the MFVs berthed alongside the jetty near the old Fleet NAAFI canteen, which was still up and running for visiting warships. The two carriers anchored out in Scapa Flow and the two MFVs stayed moored alongside the jetty, making daily runs for liberty throughout the visit.

While at Scapa the Upperyardmen carried out various small-boat exercises, such as navigation and sounding the water depth. The latter was found by heaving a lead and line ahead of the boat. The marked depth line was allowed to run out until the lead reached the sea bed. The slack line was then gathered in and the coloured depth marking placed in the line noted by calling out 'By the mark six fathoms' or whatever the depth happened to be. The lead was hollow and charged with tallow, and one could ascertain the nature of the sea bed—that is, sandy, muddy or stony—according to what adhered to the tallow. However, for some reason I could never achieve a proper throw and my efforts always ended with the lead falling vertically back into the boat with a tremendous thud. How on earth I never killed anybody or had the lead go through the bottom of the boat I will never know.

Our next major training sortie was an Escape and Evasion Exercise, which was carried out on Hoy, the southernmost island of the Orkney group. This was the first of a number of such exercises with which I was to be involved over the next twenty or so years, ordered in light of the experiences encountered by United Nations prisoners of war held by the North Korean communist forces. Instead of being treated in accordance with the Geneva Convention, our PoWs were subjected to brutal, degrading, sadistic and inhumane treatment to persuade them to divulge intelligence information. In many instances the communists deliberately executed prisoners in front of their friends and comrades so as to break the will of the others. Many of the PoWs treated in this way returned home at the end of the Korean War shattered in both body and mind, and the MoD decided that all aircrew should be trained to withstand this form of abuse.

The training involved our being dropped at specified locations with the minimum of rations, kitted out in flying clothing and armed with a map of the local area. In most instances, three days were allowed for the trainee to return to base HQ, evading the Army and the local police on the lookout. If one was caught, then an extremely tough interrogation would follow to extract any information about one's military background, knowledge and job. Actual physical abuse was prohibited, but there were occasions when the authorities came very close to breaking the rules and on one occasion they did overstep the mark with a young Midshipman, which resulted in questions being raised in the Houses of Parliament. Following this incident, a special training centre was set up at Ashford in Kent to teach military personnel how to withstand the treatment communists meted out to their opponents. We were organised into teams of three and bussed to a remote area of Hoy, dropped off at intervals, wished the best of luck and told to be back at base camp within three days.

In my team there was a former Petty Officer and a Leading Seaman, both of whom were to perish in future aircraft accidents. We were dropped on the western side of Hoy, and in order to avoid the coast road we had to cross the centre of the island. After an hour we came across a cwm, and the obvious way forward was around its lip rather than by descending down one side and having to climb back up the other. However, there was a gull colony on the south side and the birds were very agitated by something or someone. which caused us to be cautious. I decided to go and reconnoitre and left instructions that if I was not back within an hour they were to proceed without me. I discovered that the gulls were merely being noisy and squabbling amongst themselves—it was obvious that there was no other intruder in the area—so I quickly made my way back to my team members. I had hardly been away for three-quarters of an hour, but when I arrived back they had gone without even leaving a message, and there was no sign of them anywhere. I climbed down the cwm, arrived at the coast road and walked to a bus pick-up point, where I found my team members already aboard the vehicle. When I enquired as to why they had left early they had no real reason, and when I heard that they had not reported me separated from them I became angry and told them forcefully that they had been irresponsible.

'Well you got back okay, and we could see no reason why you went off to investigate,' was the retort.

'That's not the point,' I shouted back. 'You didn't abide by the rules, and, what's more important, you didn't even report what had happened to me. I could still be back there injured! What a bunch of friends you turned out to be!'

The officer in charge of the exercise vented his fury upon them.

The day after the Escape and Evasion Exercise the Squadron weighed anchor and proceeded to Lossiemouth, where it was intended to hold the Squadron's annual sports competitions. En route we joined up with several cruisers, destroyers and frigates to conduct ship manoeuvres and escort duties. As the task group steamed south-east another storm blew in from nowhere, producing tremendous seas, greater than those experienced in St George's Channel: the waves were some forty to sixty feet high and the largest I had ever seen. While *Indefatigable* was pitching into a trough, a destroyer ahead of us was literally climbing a wave: the whole of the vessel's upper decks and superstructure could be seen, virtually in plan view. As the destroyer pitched over the crest into the next trough, her stern rose out of the sea to expose her red bottom, rudder and screws, and then she was gone from sight except for the top of her mast.

As the task group moved south-east the storm passed through very quickly and the seas decreased to slight and moderate. When *Indefatigable* arrived off Lossiemouth to anchor, a cruiser had proceeded us and was moored ahead and closer inshore. RNAS Lossiemouth was at this time having its

51

runways rebuilt to NATO standards. The Royal Canadian Air Force was also transiting through with its Sabre jet fighters to a base in Europe, as part of the NATO standing air force. The station had excellent sports facilities and the Squadron intended to make use of them during the visit and competition. The inter-ship and departmental sports events were held over the Saturday and, as usual, the engineering department walked away with nearly all the trophies: most of their many artificers were still in excellent shape from their days as apprentices.

The next day, Sunday, the weather turned foul yet again, all shore leave was cancelled and those ashore were brought off by MFV. The cruiser inshore of us was really straining at her anchor; her cable was out bar-taut and about thirty degrees down from the horizontal. Her Captain had her steaming slow ahead to reduce the weight on the anchor cable and to prevent dragging, and our Captain was doing likewise. The storm passed through quickly, however, and then the anchor was weighed and we were on our way south to Spithead and the Coronation Fleet Review.

As the Squadron steamed along the east coast, the Admiral decided to give the up-and-coming seaman executive officers training in ship manoeuvres. With the two carriers steaming in line abreast, the order was given to 'Corpen 90'. However, although *Indefatigable* turned the right way her sister-ship *Implacable* turned the wrong way. Both ships passed within a cable of each other going in opposite directions—narrowly avoiding another *Victoria* and *Camperdown* incident!* The Admiral logged the young officer aboard *Implacable* responsible for the wrong turn.

When the Squadron reached the English Channel the Admiral decided that it was time for us to try our hand at further ship manoeuvres before entering Spithead. I was with several other Upperyardmen in the Operations Room maintaining a radar watch when we noticed our two ships' echoes merging. Suddenly, the Operations Room began to shake violently as the propellers were put full astern and a broadcast was made for all watertight doors to be closed. We all rushed outside to see the forward end of our flight deck about ten yards from *Implacable*'s stern, so close, in fact, that we could have jumped from one ship to the other! *Implacable* had, yet again, turned the wrong way—and it was the same young officer who had made the mistake. He was subsequently transferred to the Engineering Branch.

The Fleet had moved *en masse* to Spithead, south of Portsmouth, for the Review following the Coronation of HM Queen Elizabeth II. Many of the ships to be reviewed were already at their berths, and they made a grand sight as our Squadron steamed in. The Royal Navy still had many aircraft carriers and battleships in commission on this auspicious occasion. When the Queen arrived to review the Fleet, the FAA flew past in parade with just about every aircraft it had listed on its books. We felt immense pride watching our future fly above us: every Upperyardman was champing at the bit to get his hands on one of these aircraft—and that occasion was not far away.

---

* These two battleships collided during manoeuvres in the eastern Mediterranean on 22 June 1893, *Victoria* sinking with very heavy loss of life.

The Soviets had also been invited to the Review, and they sent their latest cruiser, *Sverdlov*, about which we had little or no information. Admiral of the Fleet Lord Louis Mountbatten considered this new warship a serious threat to the Royal Navy and to NATO and he set in motion a Staff Requirement for a new, fast, low-flying nuclear bomber for the Royal Navy. This aircraft, to be built by Blackburn, was designated the NA.39 and would eventually enter service as the Buccaneer—an aircraft with which I was to have a close association in the future.

Following the Fleet Review, the Squadron returned to Portland. My course time was quickly coming to an end, and the final examinations were sat with great trepidation. We need not have worried: we all passed with flying colours.

III

AVIATOR

— 6 —

Gosport

AFTER graduating from *Indefatigable*, and following ten days' leave, my course joined HMS *Siskin* at Gosport, just across the harbour from Portsmouth. This was one of the Royal Navy's oldest airfields; indeed, it was one of the original Royal Naval Air Service air stations from the 1914 era. It was no longer an operational front-line airfield but it did host the Air Torpedo and Trials Development Unit. The ATTDU was a joint RN and RAF trials unit from which the two services perfected their aerial torpedoes and attack tactics. The unit would eventually move to RNAS Culdrose, Cornwall, owing to the lack of adequate runways at *Siskin*. Most of the accommodation at the base was now empty and very few officers lived in the wardroom, most being married and living ashore locally. A ratings' barrack area was set aside for the Upperyardmen (Air) together with their own dining room. It was here at *Siskin* that our commissioned officers joined the course— a development that we viewed with some concern, though we need not have worried—and it became officially known as No 40 RN Flying Course.

Although the Upperyardmen were technically officer cadets, they were kept apart from the General, Special Duties and Supplementary List Officers, who enjoyed wardroom status. They were not invited into the wardroom except on special occasions, a policy which stuck in many a UY craw. In the classroom, and eventually in the flying training squadrons, the officers and UYs mixed together as brother officers and there were no sides to anyone. Eventually, at RAF Valley, we all lived and dined together, although the UYs still had their own mess quarters for relaxation as they were not allowed in the Officers' Mess for this purpose until they had been given their commissions. It would not be many years into the future that the UY (Air) scheme would fall by the wayside and men selected from the lower deck for flying duties would be granted a temporary commission of either Midshipman or Sub Lieutenant, depending upon age. If they failed their flying courses they would be given the option of either returning to their original naval branch in their previous rank or being discharged from the naval service. This was a much better scheme and made life a good deal easier for the aspiring young 'lower decker' who wished to become a naval officer and airman.

The days at *Siskin* were devoted entirely to Pre-Flight Training. The tuition consisted of aero-medicine, which was given by Surgeon-Commander Ian Mackie. Ian was a veteran FAA pilot who had taken part in the wartime dive-bombing attack upon the Japanese-held oil refineries at Palembang, Sumatra, flying his American-built TBM Avenger, although, like so many veterans of that war, he never spoke about his experiences. He became a good friend and was involved in my flying career for most of my time in the Navy. Other tuition consisted of high-altitude testing, aero-engineering, meteorology and, above all, making sure that we could swim.

The high-altitude testing, although not really required at this early stage of our flying, was undertaken to ensure that there was none amongst us who could not proceed beyond the basic flying phase of the course. One entered a decompression chamber and was taken to a simulated altitude of 30,000 feet and held there breathing oxygen for about twenty minutes. The test was to establish whether the trainee suffered from the 'bends', similar to the condition a diver might suffer if he ascends too quickly. Nitrogen comes out of solution in the body as one climbs. It will find its way into limb joints, causing severe pain, and in the worst of cases it can congregate in the lungs, causing extreme agony, choking and perhaps death. Those who did not experience any effects were determined to be 'Cat A' and were cleared to fly to 36,000 feet in an unpressurised cockpit; those deemed 'Cat B' had to fly in a pressurised cockpit. Those unfortunate enough to be categorised as 'Cat C' were limited to 20,000 feet, and such pilots and observers would be employed only in anti-submarine aircraft or helicopters. I was initially categorised as 'Cat B' because I happened to have scratched my elbow and the doctor in charge considered that reason enough to downgrade me. At a much later date I would go through the test again and emerge 'Cat A'.

The swimming tests were carried out at HMS *Vincent*, the old 'boy seaman' training establishment at Gosport. This site had long since been relegated to other training duties, which was very sad because, like HMS *Ganges* in Essex, it had had a reputation for producing some of the finest sailors in the Navy. *Vincent* had an excellent pool, and it was here that we had to pass our swimming test by completing two lengths whilst wearing a sailor's 'duck suit'—a particularly awful piece of apparel that felt like canvas and was extremely heavy when wet. UY Dennis McCarthy was a non-swimmer, and so the PTI in charge took him down to the shallow end and with the aid of bamboo pole and safety harness coaxed him into swimming two widths in water barely two feet deep. Dennis was absolutely terrified of water and how on earth he ever reached Petty Officer rank without being trained to swim was beyond me—although there are indeed many in the naval service who cannot swim. After being awarded his 'wings', he eventually joined a Wyvern strike squadron. During the Suez Crisis his engine developed serious problems, obliging him to bail out of his aircraft over the Mediterranean. He had learnt enough from his swimming and safety equipment training to be able to board his survival dinghy and was found safe and sound by the rescue helicopter, munching away on his emergency rations and none the worse for his experience.

While at *Siskin* I had my first flight in a naval aircraft—a Bristol Brigand twin-engine light bomber, as used in limited numbers by the Royal Air Force in Malaya against the communist insurgents and also in Iraq. When the RAF laid the aircraft off from front-line duties, the Navy acquired several of them for torpedo trials, to which the type was ideally suited. Every Wednesday afternoon at Gosport, as at all service establishments, was devoted to sports, and at *Siskin* one was given the choice of playing sports or going flying. I elected to do the latter.

I wandered over to the ATTDU one Wednesday afternoon and enquired if there were any flights available, to be told that, if I hurried, I could have a flight in a Brigand. I received a quick briefing from a young RN Lieutenant pilot who was wearing a white shirt and tie and lifejacket but no flying 'cover-alls' (as they are called today). The aircraft was going up on a torpedo-dropping trial over Alvestoke Torpedo Range and I would be sitting behind the pilot on the wing main spar. There was no thought of any safety harness, and if the aircraft had for any reason crashed I would presumably have been projected through the cockpit canopy in the manner of a sixteen-inch shell. The take-off went smoothly and the aircraft had an impressive rate of climb. Before I knew it we were circling over the firing range at 10,000 feet awaiting clearance for our 'drop'. As the pilot circled, he passed over the fairway leading into Portsmouth harbour, and it was then that I noticed several strings or tapes fluttering behind the trailing edge of the port wing. After a further orbit the pilot entered a steep dive of about 45 degrees, levelling off at 250 feet above the sea for a live firing run. After squeezing the trigger, the pilot was informed by range control that no torpedo had been seen to leave the aircraft and there did not appear to be a weapon on his wing. The pilot returned to Gosport—and, sure enough, the weapon was missing.

That evening, while listening to the local radio news, I heard that an aerial torpedo had inadvertently been dropped into the Portsmouth fairway and was being recovered by a Navy diving team. Fortunately, no ships moving along the fairway at the time of the incident, and the weapon had no live warhead although its motor was armed for use. It was soon recovered and returned to the ordnance depot for examination, and the aircraft was also examined to establish why a release signal had been sent to the weapon pylon. I was intrigued as to why the pilot had not noticed any changes in his lateral trim once the weapon had left his aircraft. It was a hot and sunny day and there was some air instability, so perhaps the 'lumpy' air had masked them. When I flew that Wednesday afternoon I was suffering from a slight cold and sore ear. After the steep dive my ear was giving more pain than before and it has given me trouble even to this day. I often wonder whether I damaged it during that flight. I was quite naive about the effects of flying when suffering from a cold, however slight.

A few days later the ATTDU witnessed another incident, this time involving a Wyvern torpedo fighter. An RAF Sergeant pilot was running the aircraft's engine when it suddenly left the fuselage in a ball of fire, finishing up about fifty yards down the runway. In those days the Armstrong Siddeley Python turboprop engine had only one turbine disc and on this occasion it broke loose and carved through the fuselage like a gigantic circular saw. Following the fright suffered by the pilot and the write-off of the engine and its propellers, the aircraft was soon fitted with a more up-to-date engine and new propellers and was airborne again within three weeks.

A week or so later the Pre-Flight Training course was completed and I and my colleagues proceeded on Christmas leave, scheduled to join RAF Syerston, near Newark in Nottinghamshire, for basic flying training in early January 1954.

— 7 —

Syerston

NUMBER 40 RN Flying Course was due to commence basic flying training at RAF Syerston a couple of days after New Year's Day 1954. We had agreed that the majority of us—those who did not have their own cars—would meet up at King's Cross station for the short journey to Grantham station, where an RAF bus would collect us and drive us the ten miles or so to Syerston.

It was a cold and overcast afternoon when we arrived at Grantham and the bus journey added little enthusiasm to our general feelings. Syerston is about five miles north of Newark, just west of the A1 Great North Road to Scotland. The air station was not very impressive. It sat atop an escarpment running north-to-south along the River Trent, by the side of which was located a huge power station generating electricity for the region. The air station was split by the Fosse Way, an old Roman road which ran from the south-west to the city of Nottingham. The Upperyardmen and National Service officers were quartered in an old prefabricated building next to the RAF officers' married quarters. Our commissioned course officers lived on the opposite side of the road in the RAF Officers' Mess.

The Upperyardmen's accommodation had been converted quite tastefully into an anteroom, bar and dormitories. There was a large ablution area plus rooms used by the RAF batmen who looked after our uniforms and footwear. I shared a dormitory with six other UYs, and our Naval Training Officer, Lieutenant Commander John David, had his own suite of rooms at the end of the building nearest the married quarters. Meals were taken in the Officers' Mess, which meant that we had to trudge about two or three hundred yards across the Fosse Way in all sorts of weather and light conditions. There was nothing worse than arriving almost soaked through for a meal while one's fellow commissioned officers were as dry as a bone. It upset me that we had to endure this old British class system of 'them and us', but I bit my tongue and stood the insult along with my fellow Upperyardmen for the next twelve months until we hoped to receive our 'wings' and commissions.

Back at home I had considerable trouble trying to make friends understand that although I was taking up flying duties I was still a sailor and not in the

Royal Air Force; to them, anyone who flew in the Armed Forces had to be in the RAF. I had to point out the fact that until 1 April 1918 there had never been an RAF: up to that date the Royal Navy had been responsible for the air defence of the United Kingdom, while the Army had been responsible for strategic air defence, but then the Royal Naval Air Service and the Royal Flying Corps had merged to form the Royal Air Force, with Major Hugh Trenchard RFC promoted to be its leader. Lord Inskip, who was responsible for the reorganisation of the air forces of Great Britain, had, apart from recommending one armed flying service, laid down various requirements, one of which was that the new RAF would be responsible for the Fleet Air Arm and its pilots' flying training to 'wings' standard—hence the reason for my being at RAF Syerston. Just before the outbreak of World War II, control of the FAA, which was until then considered part of the RAF, was handed back to the Royal Navy, although pilot training remained with the RAF. The training of observers would still be the responsibility of the RN.

Once we had all settled into our new accommodation, the course mustered in the Ground School main hall, where the customary welcomes and introductions to leaders and instructors took place. The air station was owned and commanded by the RAF and under the control of Flying Training Command. The course was divided into two watches with an equal number of General List officers in each. A National Service officer, Midshipman Michael Lawrence, did join us after having been 'back-classed' owing to illness, and later on in the course a Supplementary List Midshipman was similarly backclassed. The Upperyardmen were equally divided into CPOs, POs, Leading Hands and Able Rates, so that each watch was balanced in all respects. It was then arranged that Watch 'A' would be flying in the morning while Watch 'B' went to Ground School. They would change around in the afternoon, and they would then rotate until Ground School was completed and final examinations sat, when everybody would take to the air each day until the flying syllabus had been concluded and final handling examinations taken. It was a sensible way of running the course programme, giving continuity in tuition. On average each trainee flew two flights each day.

My flying course was the first ever to go through the new RAF Provost/ Vampire jet training programme. The Royal Navy had the privilege of having its pilots under training fly the Percival Provost, a single-engine, two seat trainer with a fixed undercarriage, for the first time in service. It was fitted with a Leonides radial engine, which provided good performance, and the aircraft responded well to its controls. In fact, it was a joy to fly. No 39 RN Course, a National Service course, was the last to go through at Syerston on the Percival Prentice/Harvard programme, its members receiving their 'wings' from Admiral of the Fleet Sir Caspar John, a veteran naval aviator and at that time the First Sea Lord.

Sir Caspar was a gangling man well over six feet tall. His father was the famous artist Augustus John, who led a riotous and carefree life as a painter. Sir Caspar was still living in yesteryear, his uniform like something from the turn of the nineteenth century. He wore a small officer's cap, a wing collar with a straight tie and a jacket which buttoned up the front. He was a kindly looking, grey-haired individual with a rather gaunt and sallow face who seemed to be somewhat distant when making a speech. The RAF was at a loss as to how to deal with this venerable old gentleman and veteran flyer. Sir Caspar was one of the pilots who had taken part in the Taranto raid, which had resulted in the Italian battle fleet being knocked out of the war. He was like so many of his time, having very little to say about the war and wishing to forget about an era during which man committed unspeakable acts of barbarism against his fellow man.

There was always, at the back of our minds, the fear of being involved in an air accident. Air fatalities, especially during flying training, were bound to happen no matter what precautions were taken. Many were caused by the overexuberance and confidence of the young flyer, and by his lack of experience. No 38 RN Course was to lose one of its Upperyardmen in a Harvard accident not long after my course had joined Syerston. Various members of the course had been discussing pull-out heights flying a Harvard from an inverted loop. One UY, a former CPO, who along with his other course members was scheduled to receive his 'wings' the following week, maintained that he could achieve a pull-out in 800 feet or less. He had just returned from getting married to the widow of a RAF officer who had been killed in an air accident. The following day, after the bar discussion, he took off in his Harvard for a local flight and became overdue. A couple of hours later a telephone call was received from the Lincolnshire police saying that a Harvard had crashed alongside the London to Scotland railway north-east of Newark. The aircraft had been seen carrying out aerobatics and then went into an inverted loop which it failed to complete. It dived vertically into the ground, its port wing smashing the track fencing. There was little that one could say. The stupidity of it was all so obvious and now his new wife was a widow for the second time in her life.

The next fatal accident occurred when my new flight instructor, Flight Sergeant Mottram, took Upperyardman Haines from No 38 Course for a 'jolly' in a Provost. They went low-level flying across the Nottinghamshire and Lincolnshire countryside. After a couple of hours they became overdue, and once again a message came via the local police informing us that an aircraft had crashed in a field, killing both crew members on board. This accident was yet another case of utter stupidity. The pair were flying far too low and their aircraft hit a tree, pitched forward into the far bank of a dyke, turned upside down and exploded in a ball of fire. Sergeant Mottram was an instructor who, I thought, took demonstrations to the extreme, as he did with me when carrying out tight turns at low level. I could have sworn that our wing tip went through the leafless branches of a tree on one occasion.

What amazed me more than anything following this tragedy was that no effort was made to gather the course together to offer sympathy and explain that such accidents were caused by breaking the rules of flight safety. I suppose the general feeling was that, without people behaving like this, and taking risks, flying would be a dull occupation. For myself, I had a strong sense of self-preservation: I wanted to reach my goal of becoming a naval aviator with a dedicated task and future ahead of me.

The next accident, which shook us all, happened at night. A RAF Varsity twin-engine training aircraft from RAF Swinderby was attempting a single-engine approach into Syerston during heavy rain and a thunderstorm. The pilot had experienced an engine failure, and because of the appalling weather on the final approach he undershot, landing in the very rough threshold area between Syerston village and the runway. The aircraft broke up on impact and exploded, instantly killing all six people on board. I suspect that some of them were trainee RAF navigators from the Navigational School at Swinderby. Phil Cardew and I visited the crash site out of morbid curiosity and left very chastened, wondering whether it was worth all our efforts to reach 'wings' standard. There is little doubt that one became hardened after a while, believing that such a fate could never befall one personally. On the other hand, we were all being trained to be military pilots, and our lot in life was to fight the enemy and defend the realm: death could come on the first combat mission. If this could not be understood, then there was little point in carrying on.

My course was not to be spared: it came very close to losing Upperyardman Reg Hunt. Reg and his instructor were lining up on the grass runway at Syerston when a Midshipman from 41 RN Course landed on top of them. Both aircraft were written off but all three aircrew survived the ordeal, although Reg was severely injured. Reg and his instructor escaped because of their crash pylon, which was built behind the two side-by-side seats: the other aircraft's propeller embedded itself in this pylon. The instructor, Flight Lieutenant Taylor, was up and about in a few days and back flying within the week, whilst Reg spent about four weeks in Newark Hospital recovering from severe concussion and a back injury. The Midshipman just stepped out of his aircraft uninjured except for severe shock and fright; he also was back flying within the week. Reg's father, during a visit, tried hard to have his son removed from flying duties but Reg—and indeed the Navy—would have none of it and, once fit, he was back on the training schedule flying extra sorties in order to catch up.

About two-thirds of the way through my course at Syerston a young Midshipman was back-classed from No 39 RN course. He was checked out in the Provost and sent solo in the aircraft, commencing his flying from the point my course had reached in the syllabus. One day he went up on a solo flight to practise aerobatics. He had been airborne for barely fifteen minutes when he called the tower to say that something was banging about in his rear fuselage. He was instructed to return and land, and as he taxied into the aircraft dispersal his instructor was waiting for him. The aircraft's rear fuselage looked like a pepper-pot. The instructor opened up the rear fuselage hatch and found that the radio set, attached to its electrical loom, had become detached from its mounting and was lying on its side. It was easy to see what had happened: when the young man had rolled his aircraft the radio had swung around on its loom, its sharp corners punching holes in the aluminium skin. The longerons were also damaged, and the aircraft required a complete change of rear fuselage. This youngster had not checked the security of his radio before taxying out to fly, and as a result both the pilot and the radio mechanic paid a visit to Wing Commander (Flying) and had their futures read to them in no uncertain terms.

This errant young Midshipman was to demonstrate that he was capable of further acts of stupidity. I suppose that if certain people are given sufficient rope they will eventually hang themselves. For some unknown reason he was allowed to go solo again in a Harvard trainer, and on his return to the airfield he was to carry out circuits and landings. Unfortunately, he thought that he was in a Provost with a fixed undercarriage and tried landing the Harvard without its gear down, making a perfect approach and flattening out on his belly right in front of the air traffic tower. On top of the tower the reviewing officer of No 39 RN Course's Wings Parade—who happened to be the Air Officer Commanding Flying Training Command—was pontificating to the graduates' guests about what a great job the RAF was doing in training all these budding naval pilots. Then one of the new shoots crashed right in front of him. He was a very senior Air Force officer, full of fire and brimstone, and, scarlet with rage, he ordered the man removed from pilot flying training forthwith. So exited our young Midshipman for pastures new as an observer.

The failure rate during pilot training was quite high, as I know from personal experience: I almost became one of the statistics. My flying instructor was a very young RAF Flight Lieutenant straight out of RAF College at Cranwell. He was above average on his cadet course and had outstanding flying ability, and he was therefore selected to go straight to RAF Little Rissington to attend the Instructors' Flying Course. However, one fact that had escaped the RAF posting officers was that he was unable to handle people with tact and discretion. He was very sharp and dictatorial in his bearing and tuition skills; consequently, as a student I was always very nervous when flying with him and on many an occasion confused. During one particular session of circuits and landings he kept shouting at me, and finally I retaliated and asked him to back off. My next circuit and landing was perfect—except that I had flown the wrong way round; in other words I had flown a right-hand instead of a left-hand circuit! If one was 'up for the chop', events happened very fast indeed. My next flight was with a very elderly Flight Lieutenant, 'Scrubber' Dillingham: following a flight with him, one was generally packing one's bags and on one's way to the Observer Course or back to General Service duty. He had gained his nickname from being the instructor who removed students from flying training because of their inability to fly properly.

'Scrubber' was a short, stocky individual with black curly hair and a fatherly smile. He had been a Battle of Britain Spitfire fighter pilot and had, like all the others, little to say about his exploits during that great conflict, any information about which had to be dragged out of him. As we walked out to the aircraft he asked me what my problems had been. I explained them.

'Um, um, I understand, son. Well, show me around the plane and let's taxy out and take off for Newton airfield just down the road.'

We taxied out, took off and headed for Newton.

'Nothing wrong with that,' he said casually. 'Now I'll take over.'

I had never been to Newton before, and he showed me the procedures and the grass landing strip. He asked me to leave the circuit, re-join and carry out one circuit and landing, returning to the take-off point on completion. The flight went as planned and I taxied back as instructed.

'I'm getting out. Take off and do one circuit, land and taxy back here, where I will be waiting for you. Okay?'

"Yes, sir.' I felt as if a whole weight had been lifted off my shoulders, After all, I did have fifteen hours of Tiger Moth flying under my belt and if I could not fly the Provost something was seriously wrong.

'Scrubber' removed his parachute, fastened the instructor's harness securely, grabbed my right shoulder, gave it a squeeze and shake, followed by a thumbs up and he was gone. I was on my own. I carried out my take-off checks, called for take-off clearance, lined myself up on the grass runway strip, opened up the throttle and was on my way. Going solo in a new aircraft, no matter what experience, is always a thrill and hard to describe: I was the master of my own destiny, in control, and only my knowledge and ability were going to help me. Once those wings lifted me into the air I was free from Mother Earth, free to do as I wished—within the bounds and rules laid down by higher authority. It was a wonderful experience.

When I taxied back to where 'Scrubber' was sitting on the grass, he climbed back aboard.

'Fine, son. Take me back to Syerston.'

On the way back we fell in with another Provost, flown by Flight Lieutenant Taylor and Reg Hunt. Although I did not know it then, Taylor was to be my new instructor. 'Scrubber' took control and immediately he and Taylor were locked in aerial combat. It was the Battle of Britain all over again, and I must admit that, although it was great fun, I had some white knuckles as we passed within a few feet of each other. 'Scrubber' then took charge and the two aircraft returned to Syerston in formation, making a typical fighter low join, breaking upwards into the circuit downwind position. As we walked back to the crew room after landing I plucked up enough courage to ask if everything was all right.

'I don't understand what all the fuss was about,' was the reply. 'You are okay, and I'll brief you for a solo flight, so off you go and enjoy yourself.'

To say that I was filled with excitement would be an understatement. I felt as if the shackles had been released from me. However, I had been taught a salutary lesson: never take anything for granted. Over the next couple of weeks or so I had 'Scrubber' as my flight instructor, and under his tutelage and watchful eye I grew into a steady and competent young pilot.

When 'Scrubber' was totally satisfied I was handed over to Flight Lieutenant Taylor, who became my instructor for a while until a new instructor, Flight Sergeant Mottram, joined the Training Flight and I became his first student. Mottram was a very pleasant man but a very aggressive aviator. On one occasion he was teaching me the use of speed, power and flaps during turns at low altitude. His interpretation of 'low altitude' was the top of a tree around which we turned at the old Ossington airfield: the aircraft was so close to the tree on occasion that I could have sworn its wing brushed foliage. To say that I was frightened would be an understatement: how on earth anyone could place himself, his student and his aircraft in such danger was quite beyond my comprehension. Three weeks later Mottram was to die with Upperyardman Haines in a Provost flying below the briefed height on a low-flying navigation exercise. There was little doubt in my mind as to what had really happened. It was in all probability a preventable accident, and one that had cost the lives of two pilots and a valuable aircraft. For a long time I felt very chastened, realising that it could easily have been me instead of Haines.

Flying continued throughout the summer of 1954, and once we had sat our final Ground School examinations we were all flying two or three sorties a day. By the end of July we had taken our final flight handling tests and were ready to move on to Advanced Flying Training at RAF Valley, Anglesey. Lieutenant Nigel Anderton, the course's General List officer, was awarded both the Ground School and flying trophies. There was little doubt in any of our minds that Nigel was above average in all respects. We had all accumulated 160 hours of flying time by the time we graduated from Syerston. Before joining Valley, however, the Course had to pay a further visit to *Siskin* to make another run through the decompression chamber. This time I came out with a 'Cat A', which entitled me to fly up to 36,000 feet in a non-pressurised cockpit using normal oxygen supplies. This meant that I could become a fighter pilot—the élite of the FAA.

There were many funny moments at Syerston, two such I recall causing particular hilarity. The first concerned the late Lieutenant Michael Bristow. At this time an Upperyardman, he was on his final solo navigation exercise in a Percival Prentice prior to being awarded his 'wings' when he was taken short and felt compelled to relieve himself. This particular aircraft was not fitted with a 'pee-tube', so after a moment's thought he trimmed the aircraft straight and level, slid back the canopy, removed his safety and parachute harness, stood up and discharged over the side of the cockpit. Then he completed his exercise and landed back at Syerston. As he climbed out of his aircraft the 'plane captain' asked him if he had been in a rain shower. Mike replied that he had. 'Funny colour this rain,' remarked the captain. 'It's yellow.'

The other incident concerned an Upperyardman who was on the same course as Mike Bristow. Like Mike, he was on his final solo navigation exercise but was flying a Harvard. Half way through his exercise he became hopelessly lost and, seeing an active airfield below, he carried out a non-radio join, landed and taxied up to the tower and parked his aircraft. Then he quietly sauntered into the tower to see from the notice boards on what airfield he had landed. Unfortunately for him, Wing Commander (Flying) was watching him closely, and he walked up to the Upperyardman and inquired whether he was the pilot of the filthy Harvard parked outside his tower. He was then promptly provided with a bucket, detergent and other materials and ordered to clean and polish his aircraft before returning to Syerston. The tone of the telephone conversation that ensued between two air station Wing Commander (Flying)s can be imagined.

— 8 —

Jets

MY NEW appointment instructed me first to report to HMS *Siskin* and then to join RAF Valley for Advanced Flying Training in Vampire jet aircraft. I was given permission to travel both ways in my old BSA Scout car, and two weeks' leave was granted before I took up these new duties. I felt that I was going to enjoy my time at Valley.

The first day was spent meeting instructors and being taken around the place. RAF Valley was a typical wartime airfield, its hangars the only permanent structures. The accommodation for aircrew and maintenance personnel and the Officers' Mess were temporary buildings consisting of Nissen huts and prefabricated structures. However, a new dormitory and mess hall had been built for the RAF airmen and similar buildings were due to be constructed for the officers. All Royal Navy officers and Upperyardmen messed in the RAF Officers' Mess; however, the officers had their own quarters and the Upperyardmen were provided with their own anteroom, games room and bar and could use the RAF Officers' Mess facilities during the evenings and weekends—as long as they were wearing civilian suits! Owing to the fact that both the Ground School and Training Squadrons were far away, buses were provided to transport the students around the base.

On our second day the Course split into two watches and followed the same routine as that practised at Syerston. Once the final Ground School examination had been taken and passed, we reverted to a daily flying routine. After being taken over the Vampire T.11's systems in Ground School, we all quickly flew ten dual sorties and were then sent solo for twenty minutes, followed by a further dual sortie and then an hour solo in the Vampire FB.5 or FB.9 single-seat fighter. My flight instructor was a young naval Lieutenant, Tommy Thompson. He was a small, dark, curly-haired man with whom it was easy to get along both professionally and socially. Under his tutelage and care my flying improved by leaps and bounds: I was the first in my course to pass the Instrument Rating Test and to be awarded a 'White' instrument card. It was essential to have this card because there were many days when one needed an instrument rating in order to fly solo, especially on 'land-away' solo navigation exercises.

Towards the end of the course, on my final solo navigation exercise, I flew a long, two-and-half-hour sortie to land-away at RAF Oakington in Cambridgeshire. This exercise was carried out in a Vampire FB.5 fitted with overload fuel tanks, which made it quite heavy at take-off. This little jet fighter was just like a racing car, fitting the pilot like a glove. There was no ejection seat, and if it became necessary to bail out one either climbed over the side of the cockpit or inverted the aircraft and applied negative 'g' in order to get thrown free. I was, as usual, wearing my sailor's uniform and 'milk churn' hat. When I climbed out of my aircraft at Oakington the RAF mechanics were quite taken aback at seeing a sailor climb out of a jet fighter.

There was some difficulty entering the pilots' crew room too. As I walked in somebody cried out, 'This room is for officers only!'

Quick off the mark, I replied, 'What do you think these white bands mean? Your trainee pilots shared our crew room over at Valley when you were deployed there during your runway refurbishment.'

'Oh, okay. I suppose it's all right for this time only.'

I grabbed a quick cup of coffee and moved outside into the fresh air . . .

Looking back over the events and happenings at Valley, there were many which were quite frightening at the time but which with hindsight are comical. Upperyardman Pete Atkins, an ex artificer, was on his first solo flight in the FB.5 when he literally blew out his jet engine. He had just taken off and was climbing though 2,000 feet near South Stack lighthouse when he moved his throttle too quickly to the fully open position. This resulted in the engine being overfuelled and the flames in the combustion chamber being drenched, and extinguished, with neat kerosene. In those days the FB.5's Goblin engine lacked any metering device to regulate the fuel flow into the combustion chambers: one had either fuel, and lots of it, or none at all! The Vampire T.11's Goblin was modified, allowing the pilot to slam the throttle open or closed with the fuel flow regulated correctly. There was an emergency re-lighting procedure in the FB.5, but Pete did not have sufficient height at which to try it. He therefore did the next best thing—setting up a glide back to base. He called Valley and the tower cleared him for a straight-in approach downwind on the runway from which he had just taken off. A perfect wheels-down, 'dead stick' landing was made, and after another quick dual check Pete was off again solo in the FB.5 without further incident

Later during his course Pete Atkins was to have two further accidents in a Vampire and one in his car. The next mishap was much more serious. While he was flying with his instructor on a low-level navigation exercise around Anglesey, the canopy of his jet suddenly left the cockpit at a speed of 450 knots. The canopy struck the instructor a glancing blow on the head and knocked him out. In those days very few pilots had 'bone domes', and the instructor was wearing only a leather helmet, although Pete himself had a 'bone dome'. All that Pete can remember was the bang, mist, and high-velocity air. He instinctively pulled up, reducing speed, declared an emergency and carried out a perfect landing back at Valley. He recovered from his tremendous fright and for his professionalism in dealing with the accident was awarded a 'Green Endorsement' —a certificate placed in the pilot's logbook stating what had happened on a particular flight and that the pilot had handled the emergency in a professional manner. However, a short time later he and his instructor had to make an emergency 'wheels-up' landing when their undercarriage failed to lower under either the normal or the emergency procedures. The jet was landed on a foam carpet and received little damage to the fuselage.

After being awarded his 'wings' Pete went on to Culdrose to fly anti-submarine aircraft. He had other aircraft incidents and accidents, including the loss of a Gannet on board HMS *Bulwark* and another at RNAS Eglinton, Northern Ireland. The sea-going accident was a real comedy of errors with a cast of several people, not least Pete himself. He was scheduled to make an axial flight deck take-off—a departure that required the use of the whole of the deck as his runway. The aircraft had been parked aft on the centreline but its nose wheel was cocked to the left. Pete, together with his 'pilot's mate', carried out an external inspection of the aircraft and then climbed aboard his Gannet. Engines were started and all pre-flight checks were completed satisfactorily, except that the nose wheel remained cocked to the left. The pilot then called the FLCO to say that he was ready for take-off and was given a green light. Lieutenant Commander (Flying) had not noticed that the nose wheel was turned to port and now the Flight Deck Officer (FDO) raised his green flag, he also having missed the errant wheel. The pilot raised his hand to indicate that he was ready to go, the FDO checked that he still had a green light at FLCO and lowered his green flag, the pilot released the brakes and the Gannet promptly made a sharp left-hand turn and disappeared over the port side of the flight deck into the sea. Pete abandoned his aircraft, climbed on to his liferaft and was recovered by the rescue helicopter. He was grounded and sent back to RNAS Culdrose for a flying check.

Most people are usually level-headed and prepared to 'give' a little, but the Commanding Officer of 796 Squadron nearly went berserk when he heard that Pete had been sent to him for a flying check. 'He's not going to fly any of my aircraft,' he stormed, 'Neither is he going to be allowed anywhere near them!' He was right, but he was nevertheless ordered to fly him. One day, as Pete ran up his aircraft's engine whilst parked he applied too much power and the aircraft jumped the chocks and pitched forward, damaging the propeller on the concrete hardstanding. Fortunately, nobody was injured as pieces of airscrew flew around. That did it: Pete was grounded permanently and finally went into Air Traffic duties.

* * *

It was during my time at Syerston that I had acquired the old four-wheeler BSA Scout, one of the very first front-wheel-driven cars to be mass-produced for the public. Normally one came across only the three-wheel version, but the four wheel car had improved luggage space, better control and of course greater stability. I had bought it from Upperyardman Richardson's uncle at Farnham, Surrey, for the princely sum of £25— including the road tax, which had still six months to run. With the help of John Milham, an old Rye

Grammar School friend, I had collected the car and between us we had driven it back to Rye. At the time I had only a provisional driving licence—which required me to have a fully qualified and licenced driver with me—and John was my 'safety man'. The next few days were spent carrying out the necessary repairs and repainting, following which, with the help of John Milham and Don Diaper alongside me to keep me legal, I managed to gather valuable driving experience. I obtained my full driving licence while at Syerston.

The car had been in my possession for almost twelve months when I left her at a Worcester garage with a failed gearbox. I managed to find a second-hand gearbox in a motor racing magazine and for £17 10s I had it shipped to the garage for installation. A week later I telephoned the garage and was told that the car was ready whenever I was, and I agreed to collect it the following weekend. The overall repair cost was less than £40, which pleased me because my finances were very low at the time. I caught an early train over to Worcester and took a bus for the last mile or so to the garage, and there she was, looking all spick and span, and as ever she started first time! I thanked the garage owner, he wished me luck and off I went back to Valley.

The Scout was used mainly over the weekends. I always disconnected the battery because of the station's proximity to the sea and salt air. Every time I reconnected the battery and pushed the starter button, the Coventry Climax would leap into life with a healthy roar. Many of the older students who had new, or relatively new, cars would always have trouble starting their engines. Eventually they believed me, disconnected their batteries and dried their sparking-plug leads. It was amazing how the damp salt air quickly discharged batteries if they were left connected.

It was after a Saturday night run ashore in Holyhead that No 40 RN Course came very close to losing almost a third of its complement. The old BSA was loaded up with about five of us, all singing our heads off. As the car approached the bridge crossing the main Holyhead–London railway track, not far from our accommodation, I lost steering. The car veered off the road on to the grass verge, where I managed to stop it a few feet short of the fencing leading up the bridge. Below, about twenty feet or so, was a vertical drop straight on to the railway track. We all clambered out rather shakily and examined the car, discovering that the steering drag link bolt and nut had fallen out, thus disconnecting it from the steering wheel. A search was made back along the road and the bolt was found, but the nut was missing and was probably miles back. The bolt was replaced and was temporarily held in position by wire. The mechanism was now workable, if of course entirely unsafe. The last quarter of mile the car was driven at walking pace, the front wheels being given the occasional kick to ensure that they turned in the right direction. Back at Valley a new nut was found and this time a split pin was inserted to ensure that it remained in place. Afterwards we all laughed about it over a pint of beer, but the potential newspaper headlines can be imagined: 'Five Future Navy Pilots Killed in Freak Car Accident'.

* * *

Advanced flying training was a much more exciting time and the Course had by now blended together as a unit. There were no longer any dividing lines between the officers and Upperyardmen, who had proved themselves just as good as pilots as the GL officers. They did things together and went ashore together and nobody knew any difference. To those off the base we were all a group of future naval pilots training at RAF Valley. When not flying, especially over the weekends—which were free from Friday evening through to Monday mornings—we played golf, messed about with our cars, played other sports or visited Holyhead or other towns or places in Anglesey or North Wales. On Saturday nights we would sometimes visit the Corn Exchange Hops in Holyhead and 'chat up' the local girls. This was how we met the McGee family, of whom more in a moment. At the local dance hops, some of us would join the local band and play their instruments, and I can always remember Upperyardman Richardson strumming away on the double bass. The local girls used to annoy us tremendously by talking about us in Welsh, which none of us could understand—except John Morgan, who was a Welshman.

By the time No 40 RN Course had graduated there were three other naval courses passing through flying training at Valley. There had also been the RAF flying course from Oakington, which had shared facilities during the early autumn of 1954 while their airfield's runways were being resurfaced. General Service and National Service courses ran alternately until the latter were abolished in 1955–56. Young Midshipman Michael Lawrence RNVR had joined us at Syerston and was promoted Acting Sub Lieutenant RNVR. He was very much a gentleman and quietly spoken. He continued with us to Lossiemouth, and then left for university.

It was one of the young RNVR officers from No 41 Course who would provide us with a great deal of excitement one bright and sunny winter's afternoon. Several of us were either on our way out to or returning from our aircraft when somebody shouted and we all looked upwards towards South Stack to see a single seat Vampire jet plummeting earthwards in a vertical dive. The jet disappeared into a bog near South Stack while the pilot descended very fast on the end of his parachute with a rigging line over the top of the canopy. The rigging line caused the 'chute to have two canopy sections, with air spilling out of each very fast, vastly increasing the pilot's rate of descent. Fortunately, our budding aviator landed in the sea; he would have sustained serious injury had he arrived on land. He was eventually rescued by the air station's DUKW crew, which found him lying back in his one-man liferaft gobbling up his emergency rations as fast as he could.

What had caused this accident? It was, quite simply, a question of a young pilot not abiding by the rules. In a Provost one could pull the aircraft vertically to the stall, then turn it 180 degrees by kicking hard on the rudder and holding the rudder 'on' until the aircraft was going in the opposite direction, when the control could be centralised. This manoeuvre was called a 'stall turn' and was forbidden in the Vampire because the aircraft did not have sufficient keel surface. Therefore, if the manoeuvre was attempted in a Vampire there was a high probability that the aircraft would enter a spin—

and this is exactly what had happened to our young National Service officer. Fortunately for him, the aircraft entered an inverted spin, and after jettisoning his cockpit canopy he released his safety harness, the negative 'g' forces catapulting him from his cockpit in the manner of an ejection seat. However, in his panic he had pulled his rip-cord too soon and his parachute had deployed between his legs, resulting in one rigging line crossing the top of the canopy. This young aviator was the only male heir to a family hosiery business, and when the family were informed of his accident they had him withdrawn from flying training; had he been killed, then the family would have gone bankrupt owing death duties. He completed his National Service in a quieter occupation in the Royal Navy.

* * *

The last couple of weeks of the course were devoted to general flying and to building our hours. We all flew sorties that involved high-level aerobatics, and half a dozen de Havilland Vampire T.11s being put through their paces at 35,000 feet was a common enough sight. One would dive to pick up speed, and then pull up into a loop. At the top of the loop a little too much back stick could be applied and the aircraft would flick into a spin, ascending vertically to 40,000 feet, where the controls would be centralised. The aircraft would then fall over into a near-vertical dive until there was enough speed to pull out into level flight. How none of us found ourselves in difficulties is beyond me, but we had great fun building our confidence and abilities.

My course was about to lose two more students, a General List Supply Lieutenant and an Upperyardman. The officer was not very happy about flying and his progress was below standard, so by mutual consent he was withdrawn from flying training. The other student pilot was an ex Ordnance Artificer, Pat Sullivan, who departed for something other than lack of flying ability.

Patrick, who was a very tall, gingerish blond with tight curly hair, had progressed well throughout basic and advanced flying training. He was shy and perhaps a little slow, but he had the makings of a good pilot. While at HMS *Siskin* he had met, become engaged to and married an Engineer Commander's daughter. His wife was a very pleasant and likable young lady, almost as tall as he. They moved into rented accommodation in Holyhead. His problems started during the Christmas leave break. Pat and his wife visited the Officers' Mess, and, as is the custom, went to the Guest Lounge to drink their 'Christmas cheer'. The Station Duty Officer of the Day invited them both into the main bar for drinks, and it was while they were in the bar that the Station Commander paid the mess a visit. For those who do not know, the Station Commander of an RAF base is President of the Officers' Mess, in contrast to practice in the Royal Navy, where the Executive Officer is President. The Station Commander immediately ordered the OOD to 'Remove that woman from the mess!' The balloon went up and Pat had to be restrained from hitting the Group Captain for insulting his wife. Pat left the mess with his wife in tears.

The Navy's SNO was away on leave at the time but was immediately informed of the incident on his return. He was aware that many of the Navy students had their wives with them but had rather turned a Nelsonian eye to the matter. However, something had to be done now, and despite the fact that Pat had, technically, broken the mess rules, he and his wife had been invited into the bar by the OOD. The SNO, when he visited the Group Captain to discuss the matter, politely pointed out that the Sullivans had been invited into the bar by the OOD, that it was Christmas and that he, the Mess President, had reacted in a manner unbecoming a gentleman. There was nothing that the Group Captain could do now—the damage had been done—and he was certainly not going to apologise to the Sullivans. Pat's image of officers had been tarnished to such an extent by this incident that he was all for throwing in his hand there and then.

One can understand the reasoning behind flying students not having their wives with them while under intensive training. It is important that students apply themselves fully to the business of learning to fly, and to becoming professional aviators. Moreover, the authorities did not want the problems attendant on coping with a wife if anything dreadful happened to a husband. This may seem rather callous, but one has to remember that attitudes were rather different in those days and that discipline was stricter. However, whatever the authorities deemed, students did have their wives with them and they were not going to be separated by a group of stern-faced unknown individuals. Thus the question of students having their wives with them while under flying training had to be resolved by Their Lordships. It was decided, eventually, that wives could accompany their husbands while they were on course but that the husband would not be paid any living-out allowances. This was accepted, and the situation which had existed before the Sullivan bar incident remained *status quo*.

However, a further Officers' Mess incident would occur, and this would bring about Pat's departure from the course. It took place during a mess ball, when the Sullivans were accused of having had too much to drink and were instructed to leave. Pat was given no option this time and he was removed from the course for 'un-officer-like qualities'. His removal shocked us all. Pat was quite honest about it, saying that he would rather be with people who were not so false in their attitude to life. Rumour has it that, before leaving, he told the Group Captain to his face what he thought about him as an officer and gentleman. Many years later I met Pat at Portsmouth aboard the aircraft carrier *Hermes*. He was then a Chief Ordnance Artificer, was perfectly happy with his lot and had no regrets about what had happened at Valley. Something stopped me from asking about his wife, and that was the last that I ever saw of him.

At the same ball that ended Pat's flying career, another incident was also taking place. A young Midshipman had taken a fancy to the wife of one of the naval flying instructors. This young blade was taken out into the car park where he received a firm southpaw to his chin, which sent him flying. Of course, the SNO soon heard about the incident and by now he was pulling his hair out with rage and frustration. The young Midshipman was told very firmly that if he did not behave himself he would soon be out of the Navy and looking for a civilian job. Although the SNO sympathised with the instructor, he was told to keep his boxing skills to himself or he would be looking for a job elsewhere in the Navy. The matter was settled and quietly forgotten. The SNO really handled that incident well, because it could so easily have led to a court-martial and the loss of two officers—and the instructor was someone whom the Navy could ill afford to lose.

* * *

The advanced flying training courses came to an end in mid-February 1955. Various naval tailors had visited the Officers' Mess to measure the Upper-yardmen for two suits, a mess kit, overcoat and two caps. Each man was given an initial uniform allowance of £180 to cover the cost of the tailored items, and all other uniform items—shoes, shirts, collars, ties, cap badges, underwear, socks, pyjamas, an officer's sea-going tin trunk and many other items—were issued gratis from Navy 'Slops'. I decided to enlist Bakers of Portsmouth as my tailor because they could keep within the allowance given me. Many others went to Gieves of Old Bond Street, London, paid twice as much and found themselves in debt for some time to come. Perhaps their uniform cloth was of a finer quality, but I was happy with mine and the clothing lasted much longer than my contemporaries'. A naval sword was not required at this stage as it was a very expensive item.

The Wings Parade was held in a hangar because of the windy conditions on that day, and all the wives, girlfriends and sweethearts were invited to the event. After the parade a Course photograph was taken of all together—the first RN course graduation photograph to be hung in the Ground School at RAF Valley. Once this small event was over, we all retired to the Officers' Mess for a party, which lasted for a couple of hours. I did invite a girlfriend, Isabel McGee, to the Wings Parade end-of-course party. Isabel was the daughter of the owner of the Holyhead Hotel. The owner, 'Mother McGee', had four daughters and a son, and most of the daughters were dating future naval officers. The daughters and their mother had been good to us while the course was at Valley, and I struck up a close relationship with Isabel, who was the youngest. She taught English at a primary school near Liverpool and we saw each other quite regularly over weekends, but on my moving to Lossiemouth we drifted apart. I later heard that she had emigrated to South Africa with her eldest sister Angela. That was the last I ever heard of them.

After the party, we said our farewells, changed into 'civvies', collected our bags and departed for a week's leave before joining our various naval Operational Flying Schools. I had sold my old BSA Scout car to Upperyardman Dave Howard, who had taken a fancy to it, and I gathered that he sold it to somebody else when he left Valley. The 'old gal' was fast becoming the officers' jalopy, and I was sad to see her go because she had given me many hours of fun as well as a hobby of mechanical interest. I caught a train from Holyhead for Rye, where Dad, looking very proud that I had achieved my aim in life, drove me home to Camber where Mum was waiting, smiling from ear to ear!

After the Wings Parade and Course party in the Officers' Mess we had all been handed our new appointments as commissioned officers. I was now an Acting Sub Lieutenant (X) (P), Royal Navy, on an eight-year commission in the Supplementary List, to join 738 Naval Air Squadron at RNAS Lossiemouth for Fighter Operational Flying Training in Sea Hawk F.1 jets. The other course members had also been appointed to Lossiemouth, except for four officers who went off to RNAS Culdrose for the Anti-Submarine OFS Course. I arrived back at Rye a newly commissioned officer, having achieved what I had intended when I joined the Navy—to become a naval officer. After my leave break I was on my way again, this time to Scotland to face the future and to tackle whatever lay ahead of me.

— 9 —

Flying the Navy Way

I T WAS ABOUT two weeks later that the fighter element of No 40 RN Course arrived at RNAS Lossiemouth, in the middle of a harsh and very cold Scottish winter. Heavy snow had fallen and blanketed the whole of northern Scotland, and everybody—officers, sailors and Wrens—was out shovelling snow from the runways. In those days the air station did not have dedicated snow blowing machines, merely ploughs fitted to the front ends of fuel tankers and trucks—and hand shovels.

In 1955 there were two squadrons at RNAS Lossiemouth for training newly qualified aviators, 738 Naval Air Squadron, for British-trained and Royal Canadian Navy pilots, and 736 Naval Air Squadron, for US Navy-trained pilots from Pensacola. The latter unit held most of the Vampire T.22 jet trainers—naval versions of the RAF's T.11s—on which were conducted all the dual flying checks and instrument training. A dual flying check was given to each pilot on joining the Operational Flying School before he progressed to the Sea Hawk. Both squadrons were equipped with Sea Hawks, which would be our primary OFS training aircraft, but 738 NAS also had a complement of Sea Fury fighters and trainers, which were used to train the Canadians. No 40 RN Course was to spend all of its OFS time with 738 NAS. The Squadron Commander was Lieutenant Commander Don Morrison, the Senior Pilot Lieutenant Commander Keighley-Peach and the Air Engineer Officer (AEO) Lieutenant Pepper.

A week of general training was carried out both in the Ground School and on the squadrons in order to acclimatise us to the way things were done in the Fleet Air Arm. Another Sub-Lieutenant, a former RAF Meteor pilot, joined the course as he believed that the FAA had more to offer him. As soon as we had completed our dual check—mine was carried out with Lieutenant Rowan Thompson—we were briefed for our first solo flight in the Sea Hawk. It was a beautiful jet and fitted the pilot like a glove, having a cockpit similar in size to that of the Spitfire. Once we had completed six familiarisation flights we plunged into the tactical flying syllabus, which would last until the end of May 1955: it would be Easter by the time all of us had converted properly to the Sea Hawk, and then we all proceeded on two weeks' leave. The Royal

Navy was totally different from the RAF in that it always granted two weeks' leave at Easter, during the late summer and at Christmas to coincide with the school holidays, enabling fathers to be at home with their families. Once a man went off to sea, it could be for eleven months or more before he saw his wife and children again.

Returning from Easter leave, everybody settled down to do some hard flying during the day and at night. It commenced at 0800 and continued until 1730, when the aircraft were wheeled away into the hangar unless there happened to be night exercises. Then flying would continue, perhaps, until midnight. Night flying was usually conducted well before the Scottish summer nights arrived, when there was barely any true darkness at all.

Lossiemouth was originally built for the RAF as a bomber base during World War II. It was taken over by the Navy during the early 1950s as a fighter base and converted to an air station, meeting NATO standards. This part of Scotland is a beautiful area from the point of view of both flying and the extramural activities available. The weather is just about the best in the world except during the winters, which are, however, short-lived; indeed, the weather factor is about 85 per cent, making it suitable for flying for most of the time. Weather systems blow in from the Atlantic, but because the air station is so far north these systems pass within twelve hours, the wind then veering north-westerly to give clear blue skies. One could not wish for better conditions.

One of 738 Squadron's instructors was an RAF Flight Lieutenant, Dickie Wirdnam. His job was to teach us tactical flying and air tactics, turning us into fighter pilots ready for the Fleet. I hated flying with him. After returning to his own service he went on to reach Air Officer's rank as an Air Marshal. Indeed, almost all the Air Force officers who served with the FAA attained Air Rank later in their careers: they must have been very well trained by the Navy.

It is essential that a fighter pilot learn how to handle his aircraft as an aerial fighting machine, and this is the fundamental principle behind aerobatics. Fighter aircraft are fitted with guns, and it is therefore mandatory that the pilot be taught how to fly and align his machine so that the guns are aimed properly at the target in order to achieve a 'kill', that is, the shooting down of the enemy aircraft. At this time, to achieve the objective the pilot was provided with a gyro gun sight, which enabled him to aim and lay off his guns ahead of the target so that his bullets (or shells) and the target arrived in the same piece of sky at the same time. The gun sight was nothing more than a simple gyro, controlled by giving it a variable voltage based upon the wing span of the target aircraft. The gyro rigidity was controlled by this voltage, which was modified by maintaining a circle of diamonds around the target aircraft, the diameter of which was adjusted by twisting the throttle grip: the further away the target the closer together the diamonds and, conversely, the wider apart they were the nearer the target. Thus the gyro rigidity could be increased or decreased depending upon the target range. All the pilot had to do was track the target aircraft with the gyro 'pipper', which was at the centre of the wing span diamonds. In so doing he could then pull the correct 'lead' ahead of his target and give his guns the correct deflection to achieve a 'kill'.

Gyro gun sight tracking was not an easy task, especially at high speed and under high 'g' forces. It required constant training and was an exercise that all fighter pilots practised daily. Film of the pilot's efforts was captured and the frames were analysed by the Wren Range Assessors to determine closing speeds, angle-off and ranging error. If the gyro failed, the fixed ring-and-cross was used to determine the lead angle, and this was a particularly difficult procedure. Those who were good at target tracking and lead angles were those who did a great deal of skeet shooting with a shotgun.

The Sea Hawk was fitted with four 20mm cannon beneath the pilot's cockpit. The day came when we were all let loose with 120 rounds of live ammunition to fire against a banner target towed by a Meteor fighter operating out of Milltown, Lossiemouth's satellite airfield five miles to the east. Our ammunition was marked with various colours so that one pilot's efforts could be distinguished from another's. The banner target was towed at some 3,000 to 4,000 feet over the sea and would hang about 500 feet below the tug. The Sea Hawk pilot positioned himself on the 'perch', 4,000 yards out, 2,000 feet above and forward of the banner, abeam of the tug flying at 250 knots. The tug pilot would then clear the attacking pilot in either 'dummy' or 'live', depending on the range safety conditions. The attacking pilot turned in, dropping his fighter's nose and placing the gyro 'pipper' on the target, and began to track the banner, and at about 800 yards he gave a quick burst of his guns. He then relaxed the 'g' and rolled out to the left of the banner, pulling up and over the tug to return to the 'perch' position, ready for the next attack. When the guns ceased firing, he returned to Lossiemouth to await the results. On most occasions these were telephoned through from Milltown, where the tug pilot dropped the banner, although sometimes the banner would be dropped right in front of 738 Squadron and we would all rush out to see how we had faired. Pilots would return to the crew room either with big smiles or looking glum.

It was during this phase that No 40 RN Course was to suffer its one and only fatality. Nigel Anderton had returned from one of his live-firing sorties to say that he had spun while making a hard turn at low speed on to the target banner during the latter stages of the attack. He was quick to realise what he had done wrong and immediately relaxed on the stick, and the aircraft recovered of its own accord. Phil Cardew was the next to experience the spin, and he also recovered safely. I was on my way out to my aircraft for my third sortie when I was stopped by Dickie Wirdnam and told to swap with Peter Fox, who had as yet flown only one firing sortie. Peter and I passed each other and I wished him luck, little knowing that it would be the last time that I would ever see or speak to him again. He joined the banner firing pattern and was duly cleared in 'live'. During either his first or a subsequent run he flicked into a spin and did not recover, ejecting upside down at about 800 feet straight into the Moray Firth. The Sea Hawk fighter was in those days equipped only with an 800-foot ejection seat, and if a pilot were upside down or below this altitude there was little chance of his surviving.

I cannot recall anyone bothering to gather us together or display any sorrow over what had happened, and the episode was treated with callousness and disregard. Perhaps the Command decided that this was the best way to handle the matter, in order not to cause any further distress. However, the accident did hit home hard. Three weeks later a Buckie trawler netted an ejection seat with the remains of a pilot still strapped in it. Upon investigation the remains proved to be those of Peter, and now a full military funeral had to be prepared for him.

I had no idea at the time why I was selected, but I became the Funeral Officer. Looking back, I suspect that it was because I was the youngest officer on the course. With a dozen sailors, the Chief GI formed us into a Funeral Guard of Honour to march into the cemetery with the coffin, and at the end of the service to present arms and fire three blank shots from each rifle in Peter's memory. As I sat in the station chapel I pondered why this accident had befallen one of our finest newly commissioned officers. As a young man he was totally unpretentious and did not have a bad word for anybody, and yet he died as a result of a simple mistake. We had all made mistakes and had been lucky, but on Peter's day God must have blinked. The accident brought us all down to earth with a resounding thump: we knew now that we were not invincible.

In 1955 the Lossiemouth OFS was, in essence, set up for the sole purpose of converting newly trained pilots to the Sea Hawk F.1. This aircraft was then only capable of carrying out air-to-air missions and strafing. The later marks of the fighter, which would arrive in the Fleet over the next couple of years or so, would be modified to fire rockets and carry bombs. The only rocketing and bombing sorties my course would conduct consisted of making dummy dives against the ORS circles at Dalachy airfield just east of the mouth of the River Spey. Towards the end of the course we all flew live strafing sorties at targets on Tain Range in Ross and Cromarty, thirty to forty miles west of the air station.

About a month before finishing the Sea Hawk OFS I submitted a request to fly the Wyvern strike fighter. I am not quite sure what really happened, but before I knew it I was up before Commander (Air), Dougie Parker and the Captain to be scrubbed from the course. It all happened so quickly that I demanded to know what was going on. Dougie Parker stated that I did not want to fly the Sea Hawk anymore, and I countered by saying that this was not true: I was keen to finish the OFS course but wanted to fly Wyverns on graduation. It was the Navy's number one aircraft, called upon to do all the heavy battle work. The balloon was pricked and I was soon back on the Squadron flying again, with everyone wondering what on earth had happened!

No 40 RN course graduated from OFS on 25 May 1955 with a massive flyby of fifteen Sea Hawks in close formation. We were all appointed to the Divisional Officer's Course at the RN Barracks, Portsmouth, except Nigel Anderton, who went to RNAS Yeovilton, Somerset, to fly Sea Venom night fighters. On completion of the Divisional Officer's Course we were despatched to the Fighter Pilots' Pool in 764 Squadron at RNAS Ford, Sussex. I, along with four other officers, would be selected from my course to fly Wyverns.

While on the OFS course at Lossiemouth I shared a cabin with Sub Lieutenants Phil Cardew and Peter Sausman. Phil and I had always got along together, mainly because he had a mature attitude and was not one for frolicking around as did others. It was because of this, as mentioned earlier, that he was considered rather aloof, although in fact he was not this way at all. He was a very good pilot if perhaps rather too confident of his own abilities. He felt that he was untouchable, thus making himself vulnerable, and this was to come home with a vengeance later in his flying career when on two occasions he nearly killed himself in a flying accident. Phil's second initial was 'P', which stood for 'Peel', but it was a long time before he finally told me why he had been given that name. When we returned from Easter leave in 1955 he had a roll of paper on which was laid out the whole of his family's genealogy, going back to the time of King John. The Cardew family had a long and distinguished history and Sir Robert Peel, who was responsible for introducing the first ever police force, was one of his ancestors.

My other cabinmate, Peter Sausman, was an Anglo-Indian from Delhi and had joined the Navy on a short-service commission. He was very much a gentleman with a pleasant and polite disposition—the quintessential young naval officer. He did have trouble mixing with Englishmen, although the three of us got along together very well indeed. After leaving Lossiemouth he went on to fly Gannet anti-submarine aircraft, but during one of his axial-deck free take-off practices he had an accident. As soon as he had completed his take-off checks Peter raised his hand to the FDO to indicate that he was ready to be launched. The FDO raised his green flag, the signal for the pilot to open up to full power, turned to check that he had a 'green light' from Flyco and then lowered his flag, and Peter released his brakes. The aircraft roared down the flight deck but as it left the deck it quietly settled into the sea ahead of the carrier. No take-off flaps! Peter was quickly rescued but he had no recollection of what had happened to him. He had failed to lower flap during his take-off checks and the error was missed by the FDO and Flyco, but the evidence was on the camera film taken of every carrier launch and recovery and a valuable aircraft had been lost. He was rapped over the knuckles, as were the FDO, Flyco and the briefing officer who was in Flyco.

At the end of his short-service commission Peter returned to India and Delhi University. One day, during a period of rioting, someone murdered him with a machine gun as he ran up the steps to the university. He was a gifted Indian who would have gone a long way in Indian politics and may well have become a great leader in the course of time.

81

— 10 —

Fighter Pool

I T WAS OBVIOUS that the summer of 1955 was going to be very hot and dry. Day in and day out during June, the sun blazed down from a clear blue sky with relentless ferocity. The new Fleet pilots of what had been No 40 RN Course had to attend the Divisional Officer's Course at the RN Barracks at Portsmouth before taking up any other duties. The course lasted less than a week, but it was necessary to show newly commissioned young officers how to look after the sailors in their care, in both the military and the domestic environments. The GL Lieutenants had already been exposed to divisional work and for them the course was thus very much a refresher.

The DO's Course was held in a large classroom with a stage at one end—probably a large briefing room or lecture hall. Various scenes were re-enacted by our instructors, and in my case I had to cope with a 'drunken' sailor returning from a heavy session ashore. The officer playing the part of the sailor was dressed in a seaman's uniform and was brought before me in the role of Officer of the Watch. Our errant sailor had his cap 'flat-a-back' (that is, on the back of his head) and when ordered 'Off cap' by the Master-at-Arms he promptly threw it at me, hitting me in the face. The instructor officer in charge immediately cried, 'Stop right there!' We all turned to look at him.

'Doust, you didn't react fast enough! Our drunken sailor is now in deep trouble for committing the offence of striking an officer—a very serious offence indeed! You must never let or give a sailor the chance of getting into deeper trouble, even if you have to run all the way around the ship to avoid him. Do you understand?'

'Yes, sir,' I replied quietly.

It was an excellent course for all of us, and especially for me: I learnt a great deal.

The DO's Course had finished by Wednesday evening and we all made our way to RNAS Ford. There had been no let-up in the heatwave when we arrived: it was obviously going to be another summer like that of 1940 when the Battle of Britain was raging overhead with clear blue skies over most of the country. On checking in at the wardroom, an old wartime prefabricated building, some of us were accommodated in the few cabins which were built close by but the majority were quartered in semi-detached houses alongside the road to the east and south of the main runway threshold, a couple of hundred yards from the sailors' quarters near the village of Clymping. Each was divided into four officers' cabins with a kitchen unit, a bathroom and a downstairs toilets for us all to share. At the end of the row of houses was the station chapel, and the house next door to the chapel had more or less been converted into dormitories with bunk space for six officers in each room. This house was used by the RNVR officers who came in over the weekends to fly Firefly aircraft of 1832 Channel Air Division, a reserve outfit kept running just in case of an emergency similar to the Korean Crisis. Opposite the wardroom was the FAA Photographic Reconnaissance School, where FAA officers and ratings were trained in the art of PR, an essential part of air warfare. Every day a bus called at the officers' quarters to take the officers to breakfast, lunch or dinner; some used their own cars but I was without transport for the time being so it was the bus for me. The wardroom was less than half a mile away, and if it was not raining or blowing a gale the walk was most refreshing, and a way of increasing the appetite.

During the early days at Ford I was pushed around from cabin to cabin. One day I ended up in a small cabin in the house next to the chapel. I learnt afterwards that an RNVR officer used the same cabin over the weekends. I was not overly concerned because most weekends I went home to Camber, but one Monday morning I discovered that the wretched man had been using my personal clothing. I blew my stack at the Accommodation Officer: borrowing an officer's cabin was one matter, but using his personal effects was beyond the pale. The Accommodation Officer immediately found me another cabin half way along the row of houses, on the ground floor and with a beautiful view facing eastwards towards the South Downs, Worthing and Brighton. I also now had a Wardroom Assistant (WRA), Archie, an ex Seaman Chief Petty Officer who looked after me like an old Dutch uncle. He did my laundry, pressed my uniforms and 'civvies' and polished my boots and shoes so that they had never looked better. I gave him cigarettes and thirty shillings a week—a lot in those days, but he was worth every penny. Over the years as an officer I have never come across another WRA who was so good to me. I asked him once why he treated me in such a fine manner. I could hardly argue with his answer: 'Sir, you are an officer and you must look your best at all times!'

Joining 764 Squadron was a very simple affair: 'What's your name? Okay Doust, there's the crew room but I'm not sure if you will fly today. Here to fly Wyverns I see. Well, you are the only one at the moment and you have a choice of three to fly.' After a dual check I was sent up in a Vampire and then a Sea Hawk, and finally I had a flight in a Gannet AS.4 with Lieutenant Commander Stan Farquhar, who was the Senior Pilot of 700 Squadron, a trials unit located on the western side of the airfield. The purpose of the Gannet flight was to teach me how to handle a turboprop aircraft, engines and propellers. After the Gannet flight I was shown over the Wyvern, given a quiz on the pilot's notes, briefed and then let loose on my first familiarisation flight. I could not believe it: I had achieved what I had requested at Lossie-mouth and was on my way to becoming a strike pilot!

The Wyvern was a big aircraft—getting on for twice the weight of the Sea Hawk—but its general performance was somewhat more sluggish. However, it was a requirement that the aircraft fly steadily in order to deliver a torpedo at the right speed and altitude above sea level. On the other hand, when used for mining missions it had to be able to carry a heavy load, and such missions were, when possible, carried out stealthily at night.

Two squadrons, 813 and 827, were commissioned to embark and serve aboard HMS *Eagle*. The first deployment did not start off auspiciously. *Eagle* lost nine of her eighteen Wyverns in various accidents, the first aircraft during the initial embarkation. Lieutenant Jim Jouitt, one of the Squadron Staff Officers, was making his approach in a very tail-down attitude, indicating that he was either very heavy or slow. As he came over *Eagle*'s round-down the aircraft entered a stall and rolled to the right, crashing into the carrier's funnel. The engine and propellers broke off, remaining embedded in the funnel, while the remainder of the aircraft crashed upside down alongside the port side of the island with Jim trapped underneath. The flight-deck rescue crew and firefighters were quick off the mark, and fortunately there was no fire. However, Jim was trapped with twelve tons of aircraft on top of him. His 'bone dome' took most of the impact and shattered, but he was deeply unconscious and his head and face were dreadful shades of blue and black. The first impressions were that he had not survived, but after the aircraft had been lifted to enable a doctor to attend him he was found to have a pulse. The aircraft was slowly lifted and Jim was cut clear of his harness, pulled out of the cockpit and flown immediately by helicopter to RN Hospital Haslar for emergency surgery. After a great deal of medical treatment and help, he recovered to fly once again eighteen months later. However, he would never be allowed to fly fixed-wing aircraft again, instead becoming a helicopter pilot. A few years later I met up with him at Lossie-mouth, where he was the base SAR helicopter pilot. He was still having problems with headaches and I believe that he passed out on occasions and was eventually grounded. I have not seen nor heard of him since.

Within a month 764 Squadron received more pilots both from the OFS pipeline at Lossiemouth and from Pensacola. The Fighter Pool was by this time so overcrowded with pilots that it became necessary to set up a watch system whereby we flew every other day. When we were not flying we were allowed to do more or less as we pleased, and many played golf, went sailing or went gliding over at RNAS Gosport. On average, pilots managed to fly two sorties every other day but I was lucky and able to fly daily in the three Wyverns available on the Squadron. Eventually Reg Hunt, 'Sam' Spafford, Bobby Sandison, George Humphreys, Mac McCarthy and Bob King received appointments to convert to the Wyvern with a view to joining the two new front-line squadrons which were to be formed in the autumn. With this number of pilots converting to the aircraft, I, like everybody else, was flying every other day, as well as helping out in cockpit briefings and acting as Safety Officer in the tower while pilots were flying their familiarisation flights.

The summer rolled on and the heat did not subside. Then some very nasty thunderstorms drifted in from northern France, during one of which I lost my leader in a formation sortie: the cloud was so thick that one moment he was there and the next he had vanished, even though he was actually only a few feet away. To the west of us, Reg Hunt and Bob King, flying in a Vampire T.22 on a mutual instrument training flight, entered the centre of a thunderstorm. They were thrown around so violently that they spun out of the base of the storm at 2,000 feet, returning to Ford very shaken indeed. After they had made a safe landing and returned to the Squadron line, hardly anybody could believe what they were looking at. The jet trainer apeared to have been through a small-arms barrage: the leading edges of the wings, tailplane and fins had all been flattened and had numerous small holes about the size of rifle bullets, caused by hailstones, while the aluminium clamshell in front of the cockpit had been crumpled down over the batteries and radios. How on earth the pair of them had managed to fly it was beyond understanding, but the fact that the aircraft was not fitted with ejection seats probably saved their lives. Had they ejected, their parachutes would have been shredded in the hailstorm they had gone through and they would have surely died.

On another quiet sunny morning we were all lying out on the grass in front of the Squadron when we were shaken by a huge explosion. A second or so beforehand a Vampire trainer had run up to full power and started its take-off. A pall of smoke looking for all the world like the result of a small atomic detonation was coming from its direction, and from it emerged the jet, careering off the runway and heading towards the Squadron hard-standing. The Vampire finally came to a halt a few yards from the parked aircraft as we were running towards it. The canopy opened and two very startled and shaken pilots leapt out of the cockpit. They were even more shocked when they looked round to discover that their aircraft had no jet engine—just a huge empty bay behind the fire bulkhead and between the inboard edges of the wings. The Goblin engine had exploded as it reached full power, probably as a result of a compressor failure, and bits and pieces of the aircraft and its engine were all over the runway threshold and its immediate vicinity. The instructor and trainee pilot were both extremely lucky. Had the engine exploded after take-off, there is little doubt that they would both have been killed because they had no ejection seats.

The next aircraft accident, although extremely serious, was also very comical. Sub Lieutenant Clive Fleming took off to practise medium-level aerobatics in a Sea Hawk fighter. After having carried out his checks, he commenced a slow roll. To his utter surprise, with the aircraft upside down and under negative 'g', his ejection seat slid down its rails and punched a hole in the canopy and he found himself outside his jet, which was now flying away from him. He fell earthwards and at ten thousand feet his parachute deployed and he floated down to land in a nunnery, his jet meanwhile having dived vertically into a farmer's field and exploded. Clive, to his embarrassment, found himself being gently cared for by the good sisters.

The wreckage of Clive's jet and his ejection seat were recovered and it was soon established that the seat's top locking nut had not been re-fitted following a servicing. The unfortunate Chief Petty Officer responsible was found guilty by court martial and was 'busted' to Naval Airman rank. A new pre-flight procedure was instituted wherein pilots and observers had to check that the locking nut was in place and to ensure that the safety locking pin introduced was also in place.

Another bizarre accident occurred that summer. A division of four Sea Hawks from a Ford-based front-line squadron were in battle formation and returning to the air station from the direction of Farnborough. During a cross-over turn one of the jets experienced a cockpit explosion. There was a load bang followed by rushing air and noise. The port side of the cockpit was suddenly missing, although the throttle and various other controls were still in position and usable. The very frightened pilot informed his leader and made an emergency landing back at Ford, where everyone present examined the aircraft. There were two scratch marks over the port side of the canopy plexiglass but otherwise there was nothing else to give any clue as to what might have happened. It was almost as it the aircraft had been in a mid-air collision, but nobody in the division had seen any other in its vicinity.

Back at Royal Aircraft Establishment Farnborough, a Sea Hawk from the Empire Test Pilots' School had been airborne with its pilot carrying out aerobatics. While conducting his aerobatics, having first checked the area for other aircraft, he pulled up into a loop and felt some juddering on pulling out. Following one or two further manoeuvres he returned to Farnborough, where it was discovered that his aircraft's rudder was damaged and the tail hook missing. There was little doubt that he had hit something, and the remains of grey cellulose suggested that it might have been another aircraft. After telephoning around, Ford was called and the facts emerged about a second mysteriously damaged Sea Hawk. There was little doubt that these two aircraft had experienced a mid-air collision, but why the remaining divisional pilots had not seen the Farnborough jet was baffling. How the Farnborough aircraft's tailplane and wings had missed the other jet was also a riddle.

Throughout the summer of 1955, 764 Squadron took part in every Navy Day and Air Show in the south and south-east of England. The Royal Navy's premier aerobatic pilot, Lieutenant Commander John Kelly, during his last low-level, low-speed loop, had a hydraulic failure and his flap failed to deploy fully down. He managed to roll out but collided with the top of some trees near the wardroom and had to make an emergency landing at RAF Tangmere just down the road. Back in the wardroom that evening he was smoking like a chimney and his hands were shaking. There was little doubt that he was still a very frightened man. He had been very lucky indeed, but his luck was to run out within the next couple of years.

I was not to escape a near-accident. 764 Squadron had a Vampire jet trainer which on two separate flights had developed partially jammed flight controls. The systems had been taken to pieces and thoroughly checked, but nothing could be found which might have caused these defects. The aircraft came up for a test flight, and it fell to me to check out the aircraft in all aspects of the flight envelope. Off I went up into the blue yonder, throwing the aircraft around in high- and low-speed manoeuvres and carrying out aerobatics, and the jet responded beautifully. Then I returned to Ford, requesting to re-join and land. Downwind everything seemed perfect, and then I turned finals to land. As I rolled out at about 500 feet, descending towards the runway, the control stick froze solid. I could not move it in any direction, and had the aircraft been fitted with ejection seats I would have bailed out. I thought quickly: if I pulled the stick backwards and it unfroze I might enter a stall and crash, but if I pushed forward I should be all right. I did so with all my strength, there was an almighty bang and the stick was free if very sloppy. I increased power and gently climbed, at the same time telling the tower of my predicament. I nursed the aircraft around the circuit, landed and taxied back to the Squadron somewhat shaken from my experience. Walking into the Air Maintenance Control Office, I told the AEO firmly that the aircraft was grounded until a positive reason could be found as to why the controls had frozen so many times. I told the Senior Pilot the same thing, and then went off to change and walk back to the wardroom for a well-deserved pint.

A couple of days later I saw the Vampire outside the Squadron hangar with two Chief Petty Officers looking over the cockpit, so I strolled over to ask whether they had found anything. Their answer was no, except for some odd witness marks on the control cables where the latter passed through the throttle quadrant. I climbed up into the cockpit to take a look at the marks. I slid my hand down into the quadrant a felt a foreign object, retrieved it, and found it to be the black-painted head of a No 10 wood screw which had broken away from its threaded portion. One of the Chiefs then felt around and soon found the other half of the screw. The screw threads fitted the witness marks on the control cables perfectly. How the screw came to be in the throttle quadrant was to remain a mystery, but the bang I heard was me pulling the head off the screw as I pushed forward with the control stick. We all smiled and I went back to the crew room feeling very pleased with myself.

Late in 1955 HMS *Eagle* returned from her Mediterranean deployment and the remnants of 813 and 827 Squadrons disembarked to Ford and decommissioned. Early in November of that year 830 and 831 Squadrons were resurrected from wartime days and I was appointed to 831 Squadron.

By the autumn of 1955 many of the 764 Squadron pool pilots were appointed to 897 and 899 (Sea Hawk) Squadrons, to be based at RNAS Brawdy in south-west Wales under the commands of Ray Rawbone and Nobby Clarke, respectively. In one quick move, therefore, the complement of 764 Squadron had been depleted by almost thirty pilots. About the time that 830 and 831 Squadrons were formed, another dozen pilots were appointed to Brawdy to form 898 Squadron under the command of Don Morrison, who had been my Commanding Officer when I went through 738 Squadron on the OFS course. In addition, 764 Squadron was split and another squadron, 767, re-formed under the command of Gil Newby, who had been at Syerston when I went through basic flying training. 767 Squadron had not been around the Fleet since wartime days, when it was known as the 'Clockwork Mouse' squadron and was responsible for the training of Landing Safety Officers and Fleet pilots' deck-landing techniques. The LSO disappeared with the advent of the mirror landing sight but he was to be reintroduced following several heavy jet deck landing accidents. 767 Squadron was soon to go to war; after the war it was decommissioned again, but it would be resurrected yet again in the early 1970s. On this occasion I would be closely associated with the Squadron.

The great exodus to Brawdy was to re-form *Eagle*'s air group. HMS *Ark Royal*'s was yet to be formed: she was still deep in refit at Devonport. It was not yet known which Wyvern squadron would embark in *Eagle*. Their Lordships had decided not to put all their strike eggs into one basket, but which squadron would go to which ship would be left up to Rear Admiral 'Crash' Evans, who was Flag Officer Flying Training. The two Wyvern Commanding Officers visited the Admiral and a coin was tossed. Stan Farquhar lost: 831 Squadron would belong to the *Ark Royal* air group, and so began my long association with that fine ship.

— 11 —

Wyvern

IT HAD BEEN over ten years since 830 and 831 Naval Air Squadrons had last been in commission. They had been based at Kirkwall in the Orkney Islands with Albacores and Barracudas, and at the cessation of hostilities in 1945 both squadrons had been decommissioned and their aircraft placed in reserve. With all the problems suffered by 813 and 827 Squadrons while embarked aboard *Eagle*, Their Lordships had decided to start again with a clean slate. 830 Squadron would be commanded by Lieutenant Commander Vincent, with Lieutenant Commander 'Smokey' Cowling as Senior Pilot, while my own squadron would be commanded by Lieutenant Commander Stan Farquhar, with Lieutenant Commander Jock Tofts as Senior Pilot. 831 Squadron's AEO would be Lieutenant Tony Bastick. From my flying course, only Reg Hunt and I would be appointed to 831, while the others—George Humphreys, Bob King and Mac McCarthy—would go to 830 Squadron. Peter Wheatley, Gus Gray, Bobby Sandison, Treavor Spafford and Gerry McFall would all be appointed, completing 831 Squadron's pool of nine pilots.

Initially each squadron received only a couple of the new Wyvern S Mk 4 aircraft and in the meantime each had to make do with 813 and 827 Squadrons' old aircraft. As a new aircraft arrived so out went one of the old, and it was not long before each squadron had its full complement of nine new machines. There were several changes in the S Mk 4 version. For example, it was fitted with a strengthened canopy, and with finlets on the tail, and the turboprop engine had a number of modifications to improve its performance. To ensure that we understood the Armstrong Siddeley Python turboprop, we all went on a short engine course at the maker's factory in Coventry. Captain Percy Gick RN, the Captain of RNAS Lossiemouth, had already been on the course ahead of us and had left his mark. Percy was a former Navy heavyweight boxer, and when he was wined and dined at the local hotel the first night of his course he was rather offended by a large but young 'skinhead' who was at the bar. It took all of the Armstrong's instructors to restrain him.

Why the Wyvern was fitted with the Python engine is a story in its own right. The original prototype of the aircraft was fitted with a Rolls-Royce

Eagle.* It was scheduled to receive a turboprop from Rolls-Royce but the test programme had fallen behind schedule and Rolls-Royce were not prepared to release an engine for service use until it had been fully tested and proved. Armstrong Siddeley's engine, the Python, had been designed and built originally for the RAF's Avro Lincoln but it had never entered service with the Air Force although one aircraft was fitted experimentally with two of the engines, one on each outboard nacelle, and there was some talk of Royal Australian Air Force Lincolns being so fitted. Armstrong Siddeley were prepared to upstage Rolls-Royce and offered their engine for powering the Wyvern before the completion of its test programme. As a bomber engine it was ideal: one could set the throttle and the engine would purr along happily for hours on end. In the Wyvern, however, the pilot would be frequently changing the throttle position as he manoeuvred his aircraft, and as a result the engine had a tendency to suffer speed control failures, making life somewhat difficult, especially during landing. Generally the Python was a good and powerful engine for its purpose—to drive two 13-foot-diameter contra-rotating propellers, the largest on any turboprop aircraft in the world at that time.

With the commissioning of the two new squadrons, the Westland Aircraft Company took the opportunity to throw a huge Commissioning Ball for them both at the Beach Hotel in Littlehampton. It was a grand and sumptuous affair with delicious food and champagne flowing as if there were no tomorrow. After midnight, when the champagne was becoming short, guests were signing chits for bottles of whisky, and it was a wonder that anybody survived the night.

In late February 1956 my brother Brian came to visit me at Ford. He was a Junior Technician in the RAF and was doing his National Service aboard an air–sea rescue launch at RAF Mountbatten, Plymouth. We took off in a Vampire T.22 and climbed above the overcast, carried out some aerobatics and then decided to recover back to Ford. When we came to call Ford Air Station we received no reply on our radio. To the east of Ford there was a break in the overcast, so I very gingerly let down in a slow spiral and found myself to the north of the Chancterbury Hills. After a few minutes I found a gap, flew through it and came out just to the east of the old Chain Home radar station near Poling. The course home was now straightforward and I made a 'no radio' join, was given a green flare and landed safely. When I look back on this incident, taking Brian up was very stupid and I deserved the roasting that Father gave me when he found out: 'You two are never to fly together again: I do not want all the family eggs in one basket!' Brian thought the experience wonderful, but he never knew about the cold sweat I was having until I found that radar station.

Although all fighter squadrons had an Air Warfare Instructor, neither of the two new Wyvern squadrons had one appointed to it. This was rather odd, especially as they were both strike squadrons. However, Lieutenant Commander Gus Gray became the Squadron Ordnance Officer and he took

---

* This aircraft can still be seen at the Fleet Air Arm Museum at Yeovilton.

on the mantle of AWI. He did a very good job, particularly since he had not received any specialist training. The Squadron flew to Lossiemouth in mid-June 1956 for a ten-day FLAP (Front Line Armament Practice) session, where it could rehearse all forms of weapon attacks on the numerous ranges located in the north of Scotland. The flight north was to be a time of mirth. Peter Wheatley and Tony Bastick, the Squadron AEO, flew on ahead of us in a Vampire T.22, but somewhere over the south of Scotland Tony accidently operated the 'press to transmit' radio button in the jet's right-hand throttle. For at least five minutes the whole world heard them chattering away in good, healthy sailor's language, effing and blinding, until Scottish Air Traffic Control managed to make a broadcast requesting all aircraft check their transmitter switches. The next message we heard was 'Gawd f—! That's us, Tony! You have your f—ing...' Nothing else was heard. When we landed at Lossiemouth, Peter and Tony were ribbed so hard that eventually the Senior Pilot had to step in and put a stop to it.

The Squadron flew hard, day and night, on weapon exercises, using both practice and live ordnance. It also played hard, and went ashore as a squadron to give the lads a 'thank you' for all the hard work they had put in. During this run ashore Peter and some of his friends had decided to walk back to the wardroom from the Lossie Hotel where the party had been held. Gus Gray and a couple of other officers had gone on ahead and decided to empty Peter's cabin on to the lawn outside his window. Every stick of furniture was moved out and set up on the lawn exactly as it was laid out in his cabin. Everybody then hid himself and waited to see what would happen. Peter entered the dormitory block talking very noisily, and then he opened his cabin door. There was an almighty shout. 'Gawd f—! I'll kill them when I get my hands on them!' He promptly changed into his pyjamas, climbed into bed on the lawn and fell fast asleep in the open air. He was awakened a couple of hours later and between us we replaced the furniture back in his cabin and tucked him back in bed!

Throughout our time at 'Lossie' a couple of Arctic terns had fashioned a nest in the grass between our dispersal and the taxiway. They sat on the eggs until they hatched, despite the noise and jet blast from our aircraft. Everybody, without exception, did all they could to protect these two birds, their nest and eventually their young. One afternoon I happened to be walking out to the dispersal and there was a cacophony of avian cries coming from the area of the nest: a gull had found it and was attempting to take the chicks. Despite my efforts and those of the line crew (and the parent terns), the gull took the chicks and had itself a meal. For a few days, the two terns hung around the nest but eventually left, very saddened creatures. Nobody can tell me that birds and animals do not have feelings: this incident proved that they do.

Before the Squadron flew to Lossiemouth there had been an influx of young new officers, including one young Sub Lieutenant who thought that he was God's gift to naval aviation. Late one afternoon at Lossiemouth, while airborne, he called the air traffic tower for permission to make a low pass over our hangar. He approached the hangar from the north-west as fast and as low as he could. The north-western hangar doors were closed and nobody heard him coming. The first indication anybody had of any trouble was an enormous bang that hit us all and seemed to filter in from the open south-eastern end of the hangar. Men working on aircraft ladders fell off them and dropped their tools in fright; everybody rushed out of the Squadron offices wondering what on earth had happened, only to see a Wyvern pulling away to the south-east in a climbing barrel roll. Jock Tofts stood at the hangar entrance looking purple with rage, turned round and told the Duty Officer to instruct 'that idiot' to report to his office when he landed.

The pilot landed safely and walked over to the hangar, cock-a-hoop and with a supercilious grin all over his face. He was told that he was required immediately in the SP's office, and everybody stood around in the hangar close to the office, listening to the tirade that Jock was unleashing on the hapless individual. The miscreant was made Duty Officer for the remainder of the visit to Lossie and his wine bill was stopped in the mess. When he exited the SP's office he muttered that he could not understand what all the fuss was about. However, it was obvious that this young pilot was a very loose cannon and required severe reining-in in order to curb his excessive exuberance, which could have led to disaster.

After three weeks of hard weapons exercises at Lossiemouth, the Squadron returned to Ford to continue its work-up. Apart from a few personnel who stayed behind to carry out essential maintenance, the remainder of the Squadron proceeded on summer leave until the first week of September.

The CO and SP both piled jobs on to me, and at one stage I was the Squadron Safety Equipment Officer, the Navigation Officer and the Photographic Officer. Within a year of Peter Wheatley being promoted to Lieutenant Commander he was reappointed Senior Pilot of another squadron; he was the Squadron Staff Officer, and before I knew it I had been instructed to take over his job. The Staff Officer has much the same job as the Army's Adjutant Officer: he is responsible for the paperwork within the squadron and for issuing daily and squadron orders. A good Staff Officer is worth his weight in gold. Over the next few years I would be the Staff Officer in three squadrons, so perhaps I was good at it—or perhaps I needed more practice!

At Ford both squadrons continued with their work-ups, practising various types of attack using live ammunition when possible. The requirement for torpedo attacks was removed as these were considered suicidal now that warships were being fitted with advanced ship-to-air weapon systems. 830 Squadron carried out its Operational Readiness Inspection (ORI), embarked in *Eagle* and deployed to the Mediterranean.

* * *

The summer airs of 1956 were full of pollen and hay dust, and many at Ford, including myself, were laid low with hay fever. Together with Treavor Spafford, I ended up in Sickbay for three to four days under the care of Surgeon Lieutenant Commander Ian Colley suffering badly from the wheezes. Ever since I was a small boy I had suffered from bronchitis, but over the past few years I had been quite free from the illness. However, it had now returned with vengeance. When I had recovered, Ian Colley bundled me off to RNH Haslar for an allergy and sensitivity test. In those days, testing for allergies was in its infancy and the hospital had only a few test solutions to try on me. These solutions were mainly of grass pollens, and of course I reacted violently to all of them. When they were placed on the inside of my forearm the reaction was incredible—huge, ugly, red blisters. A desensitising solution, which included grass pollens and household dust, was prepared for me and this was injected into my upper arm once a week for nine weeks.

When one receives such treatment, one wonders whether it is going to do any good. In this instance I can honestly say that the treatment did work, and I was relatively healthy for the next couple of years of my life. However, neither the hospital staff nor I appreciated at the time that I was a bronchial asthmatic, and had been all my life. It was a condition I had inherited through my mother from my grandfather. Although Grandad died early, at the age of 65, it was not from asthma but from renal failure. My youngest sister Theresa also suffered from the illness, and far worse than I. She would sometimes be found unconscious on the pavement in Cheltenham, where she lived, and have to be admitted to hospital for treatment. Many years later, in 1992, after moving to North Wales with her husband and family, she suffered a severe asthma attack and died within twenty minutes. It was a great shock to us all, especially to me, because we had been very close. Theresa was just 46 years old when she died, and even now I find it very hard to understand why she has gone and I am still here.

My asthma was to affect me for the remainder of my days in the Royal Navy. I can honestly say that had it not been for Ian Colley's efforts I would have been discharged medically unfit early in my naval aviation career. Of all my close friends in the Royal Navy, I owe him a debt of gratitude more than any other.

* * *

One Monday morning the French Navy arrived at the hangar doors of 831 Squadron with two Magister trainers. These butterfly-tail, twin-jet aircraft were being evaluated for deck landing training. At the time the French Navy did not have a carrier readily available for the task, so the Royal Navy kindly loaned one of its light fleet carriers for the trials. As for the two test pilots, one could smell them from a mile away because of the strong perfume that they were wearing. The reaction from Jack Tar was predictable: 'They're a couple of poofters!'

The future Captain of *Ark Royal*, Captain Frank Hopkins, visited us at Ford. He had just completed an appointment as the Director of Naval Air Warfare, where he had been trying over the previous two years to introduce a new interceptor fighter into the FAA. This new aircraft—the Saunders-Roe SR.177—was a composite-powered fighter with a jet engine for normal flight and a rocket engine for the final interception phase. It was to be armed with two Firestreak infra-red guided missiles. After a great deal of planning by

Frank Hopkins and his staff, the aircraft became the subject of one of the many military cost-cutting exercises beloved of the Government of the era.

The Squadron was also visited by *Ark Royal*'s Commander (Air), Commander Dougie Parker. He had a slight cast in one eye and, somewhat disconcertingly, one never quite knew in which precise direction he was looking. He wanted each squadron to have a distinctive colour so that he could recognise which aircraft belonged to which unit. Ours was to be red, and he gave instructions for our spinners to be painted thus. At this Jock Tofts exploded at the seams. Many of us had already expressed a desire to have a squadron colour and something distinctive on our aircraft, but Jock was not having any of it. He stated quite firmly that Their Lordships, in their wisdom, had decided what the colour scheme should be for FAA aircraft and that we had no authority to change it. To move away from the current scheme would affect the value of the camouflage. Therefore, there would be no change. However, we had now been told by higher authority, the 'Air Boss', to paint our spinners red—the same colour as Jock's face, in fact.

At about this time Treavor Spafford had struck up a friendship with the cartoonist in the *Daily Mail* who drew the comic strip 'Flook'. Treavor thought that it might be a good idea to have 'Flook' painted on the side of our squadron aircraft and he finally managed to get permission from the character's creator to reproduce this little bear on our Wyverns. Treavor and I drew a large cardboard outline of the cartoon and set about painting the CO's aircraft. In view of Jock Toft's opinion about such symbols on naval aircraft—although we knew that Stan Farquhar was happy with the idea—we had to find a time when all was quiet. It was about 1800 one evening when Treavor, Pete Wheatley and I mounted Stan's Wyvern, bear outline, pencil, paintpots and brushes in hand, to carry out the task. I was half way through the painting when suddenly one of the side doors opened and out came Tony Bastick, the AEO, and Jock, deep in conversation. Tony caught sight of us, and within seconds Jock was demanding what on earth we were about. My heart sank, wondering what would happen to us, but Peter spoke up and said that Stan was happy with what we were doing. At that, Jock climbed down a little, but he gave strict orders that no other aircraft was to be touched. Looking back, it was a stupid emblem to put on a military aircraft, the connotations associated with the word 'Flook' giving the impression that the Wyvern was a 'fluke' of an aircraft, which was very far from the truth. However, Jock had his way and only one aircraft was painted with the little bear.

831 Squadron continued with its work-up at a considerable pace. Every day we were up strafing, rocketing or dive-bombing over the Bracklesham Bay Range just to the east of the entrance to Chichester harbour. An old sunken ship there was used as a target, but our weapons circuit came very close to the hospital on the western side of the harbour entrance. Every pilot took great care to stay well away from the the building, but even so I do not believe that a single day went by without the Matron telephoning either Stan or Jock to complain about the noise and the overflying, which, she said, severely affected the peace and well-being of her patients. Nobody actually flew over the hospital, but there must have been considerable noise

from our cannon, rockets and bombs. Eventually the range fell into disuse and other facilities were found for live-firing exercises. The hospital building is still there, but I understand that it is nowadays used for some other purpose.

Another wartime task for the Squadron was the dropping of sea mines. The Wyvern could carry either three 1,000-pound mines, on the centreline and two wing stations, or two 1,000-pound mines on the wing stations and a 2,000-pound mine on the centreline—a very heavy load. Gus Gray had telephoned my father asking for permission to carry out dummy night mining attacks at the entrance of Rye Harbour, using smoke floats. These floats would burn for a couple of minutes on contact with salt water, thereby giving a precise position and evidence of where a real mine would have fallen. The final run-in to the dropping zone had to be made accurately, and we chose the Royal Sovereign Lightvessel as our IP (Initial Point) for the timed run to weapon release. The lightvessel was easy to find but the harbour entrance was not, even though it had a small red and white light on either side, flashing away at regular intervals. However, one had to ignore the lights because these would not be present in wartime. Most of our floats found the harbour entrance, but some of them landed beyond on Camber Sands and did not ignite until the tide came in. Flying low-level at night over the sea was not an easy exercise, even though we had radar altimeters, but it gave us some good practice at a new form of weapon attack that we could have been called upon to perform. It taught us to fly accurately and steadily, on instruments, to a precise weapon-release point—something that I would not do again until many years later in a more advanced aircraft.

Up until September 1956, 831 Squadron had enjoyed a very good safety record. However, this was to change dramatically on our return from summer leave that year. Each pilot was scheduled to make a refamiliarisation flight in order to re-hone his skills in aircraft handling, instrument flying and circuits and landings after the long leave break. September had been a real Indian summer and ideal for getting back into the swing of things. Bobby Sandison took off, heading up country north of Arundel, in his Wyvern. He flew over a motor-racing friend's house with his landing gear and flaps extended and shortly afterwards was seen to pitch up, entering a spin to starboard. Bobby ejected but unfortunately his aircraft was inverted at the time and he hit some trees, and then the ground, before his parachute had time to deploy. He was killed. His Wyvern crashed vertically into a nearby wood, making a huge crater.

I was the last squadron officer to speak with Bobby and to see him alive, wishing him good luck and a safe flight just before he had started up and taxied his aircraft out to the runway. A short while later I was out on the dispersal area, checking to see if my aircraft was ready, when I noticed a huge pall of black smoke rising from behind the hills north of Arundel. At the time I did not connect it with anything in particular but then Jock Tofts came to the aircraft line to tell me that Bobby had crashed. Jock was visibly shaken and very upset, and he said, quite openly, that he had hoped that during his tenure as Senior Pilot the Squadron would be free from incident or accident. Now, in one fell swoop, he had lost both a pilot, who was very well liked by us all, and an aircraft.

The following day Stan Farquhar called Treavor Spafford and me into his office to say that we had been selected to go to Bobby's cabin and muster his effects. Treavor was, like me, very upset at having to carry out this task, the more so because he and Bobby had been close friends, sharing an interest in cars and motor sport. It was a gruesome job: not only did we have to gather up his belongings, we had also to go through all his personal correspondence to ensure that there was nothing at which his relatives could take offence; had there been anything, then it would have to have been handed to the Captain's Secretary for disposal. The dreadful job took all day, and then we locked and sealed the cabin and handed the keys and all personal papers and documents over to the Captain's Secretary, signing various forms to state that we had carried out the task correctly and in accordance with Admiralty Regulations and Instructions. It was a job I did not want ever to do again—and, thank goodness, I was never required to.

The FAA Aircraft Accident Investigation Unit were on site before the evening, having had to travel only from nearby Lee-on-Solent. It did not take them long to establish the cause: the propeller stop was still engaged, preventing the blades from moving into fine pitch. It was essential that the propellers could move into fine pitch in order to allow the Python turboprop engine to continue constant speeding; if they remained in coarse pitch at low speeds they would slow down and cause the engine speed to run down, resulting in high exhaust temperatures and damage to the turbine, which would eventually fail. Normally the propeller stop was withdrawn automatically when the landing gear was lowered, or it could be removed manually by operating a switch in the cockpit. This manual switch was found in the normal 'engaged' position, so the automatic landing gear switch must have failed to withdraw the stop. Therefore, owing to his being so low and slow, Bobby had insufficient altitude in which to dive and increase both propeller and engine speed. As a result, he lost control of the aircraft and entered a spin.

This dreadful accident shook us all out of our complacency. An investigation and Board of Inquiry was held to determine the cause, but the Board could reach only one conclusion—pilot error. Out of flying practice, Bobby had not carried out his flight checks properly and, moreover, he was low-flying unofficially in an area not designated for such operations. A memorial service was held in the Ford Air Station Chapel, which was filled to overflowing with family and friends. Afterwards Colonel Sandison thanked everybody for all the help and kindness shown him, his wife and his family following their sad loss. As a lasting memorial for his son, he decided to present annually a trophy to the pilot in the 'strike world' who had shown the most outstanding qualities as a pilot and an officer. The trophy would be a Wyvern cast in silver, mounted on a plinth. I supplied the scale drawings for a 1/72 scale model of the aircraft and Colonel Sandison took them to Garrards, the silversmiths in Regent Street, London, who produced a beautiful model of the aircraft, perfect in every detail. The first pilot to be awarded the Sandison

Trophy was Lieutenant (AE) (P) Treavor Spafford RN, a fitting recipient who was both an excellent pilot and a superb naval officer. Once the memorial ceremonies were over, the Squadron returned to the task of working up and preparing for war, the prospects of which none of us thought about in earnest. As far as we knew there were no conflicts looming over the horizon. It was, nevertheless, our business to be prepared.

* * *

Ark Royal was now nearing the completion of her refit and Jock Tofts flew Stan Farquhar and half a dozen of us in an old twin-engine Dominie biplane to Manadon airfield at Plymouth to attend the ship's recommissioning ceremony at Devonport Dockyard. The ship was at that time still residing in drydock but within the week would be refloated and moved out for her final refit tasks prior to sailing on her post-refit sea trials. While we were in the wardroom getting to know our new shipmates, somebody turned on the ship's radio for us to listen to some very important news, which was then just beginning to filter through to the nation and the world. The British and French armed forces had just attacked Egypt to regain control of the Suez Canal, which the Egyptians had closed and blocked off. It was 6 November 1956 and 831 Squadron was now placed on twenty-four hours' notice: if need be, *Ark Royal* and her air group would have been deployed within the week and on their way to the Mediterranean. There were already three British carriers on station north of Port Said, but the men at Devonport now worked every hour of the day and night to complete 'Ark's refit. Our sister squadron, 830, aboard *Eagle*, was in the thick of the battle, as were all the other friends who had been with us in 764 Squadron. Gil Newby's squadron, 767, was deployed to join one of the carriers as an extra Sea Hawk fighter-bomber squadron.

After the recommissioning ceremony Jock flew us all back to Ford, but before we took off from Manadon we were given a conducted tour of the Engineering College. All our AEOs went through this college, and quite a number of them went on to become pilots. At the end of a front-line squadron tour they attended the Maintenance Test Pilots' Course and spent between four and eight years at an Aircraft Repair Yard or Air Station as MTPs. Some of the more ambitious MTPs continued on to the Empire Test Pilots' Course, taking up appointments at either RAE Farnborough or RAE Boscombe Down as military test pilots. Jock Tofts was a graduate of the ETPS at Farnborough.

By the time we had arrived back at Ford *Eagle*'s carrier group had made several strikes against Egyptian targets along the Suez Canal. My cousin Kenny Eastwood, who was serving in the Parachute Brigade, had been air-dropped into Kanak and his corps had taken the airfield and secured it from the Egyptians. The RAF attacked Cairo Airport with Canberras flown out of Cyprus, while Don Mills in his Sea Hawk was attacking Russian-built T-54 tanks with rockets and 20mm cannon-fire to the west of the Canal. Unfortunately Don shot himself down by flying into his ricochets off the tanks, but he was rescued by one of the Navy's SAR helicopters patrolling the Canal Zone.

While all this was going on, about 2,000 miles away 831 Squadron was sitting back at Ford nervously twiddling its thumbs and waiting to be deployed.

The Suez conflict was to cause a number of casualties in the Fleet Air Arm. Sub Lieutenant Hall, who had survived a near-crash landing on the top of the Chancterbury Hills while flying wing man to Lieutenant Flowers in a 'pairs GCA' landing (Flowers crashed and was killed), was to be a casualty. He was to be the victim of a fatal deck-landing accident after having successfully carried out a mission over the Canal Zone. 'Mac' McCarthy of 830 Squadron was to bail out of his Wyvern after suffering engine failure but was recovered safely by the ship's SAR helicopter. Then there was a serious hangar accident aboard *Eagle*. A Sea Venom fighter had returned with a jammed 20mm cannon and for some reason the aircraft was taken below into the after upper hangar. The Ordnance Chief in charge of clearing the jammed gun had left a young rating in charge while he went off to seek advice and collect some tools. The rating decided that he had already diagnosed the problem and removed the maxiflux solenoid unit which was causing the jam. As soon as this unit was removed the cannon's breech block was clear to rush forward under the force of its spring, ram a live shell into the breech and fire it. On its return, the breech block picked up another shell, ramming home and firing that one also. Indeed, there was now nothing to stop the gun firing until it had emptied its magazine of 120 live HE and incendiary shells. Unfortunately all the shells were fired into a fully refuelled and armed Wyvern a few yards ahead of the Venom and the Wyvern exploded, causing serious damage to the upper hangar.

Other than on this occasion, I have never heard of armed aircraft being stowed in a carrier's hangar. The weapons are fused and potentially very dangerous, and the slightest mistake or accident can lead to a serious safety problem which can in turn result in the loss of the ship. Although nobody was killed or injured in this Suez accident, the ship was seriously damaged— to such an extent, indeed, that (I understand) it was touch and go as to whether she would be withdrawn permanently from service. Considerable fire damage was caused in the upper hangar, aircraft had to be written off and most of the electrical cabling, which passed up the starboard hangar side to the island superstructure, was destroyed. The ship had to return to Malta dockyard for immediate repairs. The hands there worked day and night, and thanks to their unstinting industry *Eagle* was quickly back on her station off Port Said. Aircraft that had received AA damage were flown back to Britain for repair at the RN Aircraft Repair Yards at Fleetlands, Gosport, or at Sydenham in Northern Ireland and replaced by new machines held in reserve at RNAS Halfar, Malta. The damaged aircraft arrived first at Ford and were parked outside 831 Squadron's hangar, most of them severely mauled and resembling nothing less than pepperpots with canvas patches glued over the holes. Within the month most had been collected by ferry pilots and delivered to the repair yards.

* * *

By the following early spring *Eagle* had returned home and disembarked her air group. 830 Squadron came ashore at Ford and was decommissioned, its officers and men proceeding on leave before being reappointed or drafted to a new job. Bob King went to Sea Venom night fighters while George Humphreys and Dennis McCarthy were appointed to 849 Squadron at RNAS Culdrose to fly AEW Skyraiders. George would eventually marry the widow of the Australian exchange officer who was drowned in a Gannet ditching in The Minches off Glasgow. When he had completed his short-service commission he emigrated to Australia with his new wife and is now running the family wine business. Dennis also left the FAA at the end of his short-service commission but I have no idea what happened to him. Bob King, after his Venom appointment, was granted a permanent SL commission and went on to be a QFI at RAF Linton-on-Ouse, where RN pilots went through basic and advanced flying training to 'wings' standard. On one occasion he and his student pilot had to eject from their Vampire T.11 when it failed to recover from a spin because of a rudder malfunction. Eventually he went on to become the CO of the FAA's Aircraft Accident Investigation Unit at Lee-on-Solent, a task for which he was eminently suited because of his analytical and searching mind. He excelled at the job and was probably the best investigator ever employed in this demanding task. Soon after 830 Squadron's decommission, 813 Squadron was resurrected and recommissioned at Ford under Lieutenant Commander Gus Halliday, thus bringing the Navy back to two Wyvern squadrons.

It was now 831 Squadron's turn to embark in *Ark Royal* and do some sea time. The plan was to embark off Lundy Island. Each pilot would carry out several circuits, touching down on the flight deck without being arrested and overshooting to make a further touch-down. When the command was happy the pilot would lower his tail hook to be trapped. A landing amongst the arrester wires during a 'touch and go' was presumed to have been a 'trap' and would therefore count as a deck landing. However, the sea conditions were considered too rough off Lundy for initial deck landings and so they were postponed until the ship had steamed around to quieter waters off Lyme Regis.

I flew out with Gus Gray's division as his wing man, but dusk was already beginning to set in when we arrived overhead. The wind was from the north so the carrier had to steam straight at the coast and was fast running out of sea room as we made our approaches. There were, moreover, a large number of fishing trawlers in the way, and had the ship continued on her course it would have cost the Royal Navy a great deal of money to replace nets and catches. So the division was waved off, given a new 'Charlie Time' (the time for hook-on) for the next day and diverted to RNAS Culdrose for the night. During the night the weather and seas moderated and the carrier moved back to the Lundy Island area, and on 10 January 1957 I made my first arrested deck landing aboard a carrier in the Bristol Channel. Owing to the weather *Ark Royal* was already a day late, and as soon as Gus's division had landed on board the ship set course for Gibraltar, the Mediterranean and Malta.

99

It was off Malta that I came very close to killing myself. I had been scheduled for an area familiarisation flight followed by a session of deck-landing practice and a final hook-on. Instead of flying the aircraft in a three-point attitude—that is, with all three wheels in the same plane—I came in tail high and slightly too fast and then tried to flare out at the last moment. The aircraft stalled and dropped its left wing. My immediate reaction was to throw the throttle wide open, which exaggerated the aircraft's attitude and the roll to port. I floated down the flight deck almost sideways, somehow recovered the aircraft's attitude to level flight, bolted—i.e., missed all the wires—and was diverted to RNAS Halfar in Malta.

It had been almost ten days since I did any deck landing practice and the CO and Senior Pilot were not impressed with my efforts on this occasion. I was to have a session of dummy deck landings ashore at Halfar under the supervision of Peter Wheatley. This session went very well indeed and Peter could not really see what all the fuss was about. I was, however, very apprehensive when I was launched to make my deck landings because I had done no carrier-based flying since I landed on board off Lundy Island. Peter contacted the ship and I was authorised to fly out to her and carry out a series of touch-and-gos followed by a final hook-on landing. I did some excellent approaches and made a final landing. Jock Tofts then asked me, 'Why on earth did you not do that yesterday?' There were many extenuating circumstances, including the fact that the sun was shining right off the mirror deck-landing sight, but in the end it was bad airmanship and therefore all my fault. However, it was a sobering experience and I learnt more about flying from that incident.

Ark Royal spent a week or so steaming around Malta, the Squadron carrying out some live 1,000-pound bombing against Filfla, a huge rock some five miles off the south-west coast of the island. Filfa was used also for ship-to-shore gunnery exercises, and by the the RAF for live bombing. On completion of this work-up, the air group disembarked to Halfar for ten days while the ship moored in Grand Harbour. It was while we were disembarked that I was to lose a very close friend, Lieutenant Nicholas Chambers.

It was a beautiful day at Halfar and 831 and 898 Squadrons were flying a quiet programme practising low-level flying and dummy weapon attacks. Nicholas took off with 898's Air Warfare Instructor, Lieutenant Robbie Robertson, on a low-level flying exercise around Malta. While at 250 feet above ground level, a few miles north-east of Rabat, two RAF Meteor fighters 'bounced' them. Robbie broke into the attack and, while following him, Nicholas flew into heavy jet wash, flicked into a high-speed spin and hit the ground. His aircraft exploded and he was killed instantly. When the news filtered through to the air group I was absolutely stunned. Like me, Nicholas had come up from the lower deck as an Upperyardman, and while at Ford we often 'went ashore' together. Then he was appointed to join 898 Squadron at Brawdy. I had lost a very good and dear friend, a quiet and kindly gentleman who never had a bad word to say about anybody. A funeral service was held in Valletta and Nicholas was laid to rest in the military cemetery to the south-west of the city. I can still remember Lieutenant Jimmy Moore saluting the grave and then walking away, shaking his head and with a very strained look on his face. He, like many of us, was very close to tears.

A Board of Inquiry was held and the two RAF pilots were found guilty of unauthorised low flying and carrying out unauthorised attacks against other aircraft. I believe that the pair had to face a court martial by their own service. It was a dreadfully sad incident, the more so as we were at peace; had it occurred in wartime and Robbie's flight was on the other side, the Air Force pilots would have been fêted for their success. Now they had to face humiliation and dishonour over their actions, and for evermore have on their consciences the death of a British brother officer.

At the end of our period ashore at Halfar the air group re-embarked and the ship steamed westwards in order to be off Gibraltar for a scheduled visit by HRH the Duke of Edinburgh. It had been intended that a flying display would be laid on in his honour, but unfortunately the ship was shrouded in fog and flying was cancelled for the day. However, he did come aboard, having been brought off by the Flag Officer Gibraltar's barge. The officers entertained him in the wardroom before he had lunch with the Captain and the Executive Officer. I was rather intrigued by the fact that he was not as tall as I had thought. He was barely an inch or so taller than me, and not six-feet plus as I had always believed, and his uniform and gold lace were worse than mine—all rucked up with missing stitching! He was certainly at ease in the wardroom, speaking freely with everybody and with nothing stuffy or pretentious about him.

After this visit *Ark Royal* steamed for the Strait of Gibraltar and her aircraft took part in a flypast over the city and dockyard to celebrate the Queen's official birthday, but I was disappointed at not being selected to participate. After watching the aircraft being launched I retired to the wardroom to read the latest newspapers. It was a quiet moment, but suddenly the crash alarm sounded followed by a broadcast: 'Crash on deck! Wyvern aircraft Fly Four!' I dropped everything and flew up the ladders to the island to see what had happened, and there was my aircraft, '381', with its starboard wing ripped off. Gus Gray, who had been flying it, had landed off-centreline and had pulled out to the right straight into Fly Four, the parking area along the port side of the island. Fortunately Gus was unhurt, but his pride was damaged and he had been frightened, as indicated by his nervous laugh when he referred to the accident. 831 Squadron was now one aircraft short.

As *Ark Royal* entered the Channel her air group disembarked, the Wyverns to Ford, the Sea Hawks to Brawdy, the Sea Venoms to Yeovilton and the Skyraiders and Gannets to Culdrose. After clearance by HM Customs & Excise while at anchor in Plymouth Sound, the ship steamed up to her usual berth at Devonport Dockyard. Wyvern '381' was offloaded and shipped to Westland at Yeovil for a rebuild and a replacement aircraft was flown to Ford to bring the Squadron back to its original complement of nine aircraft.

During the spring of 1957 *Ark Royal* and her air group crossed the Atlantic for a United States Naval Review at Norfolk, Virginia. It was a cold, foggy and dismal day when we arrived and took up our anchorage in the parade of ships from the US and other visiting nations. Most of us went ashore and looked in at the USN Officers' Club at the Norfolk Air Station, which in those days was just a prefabricated structure and had nothing of the grandeur now in existence.

In the United States and its territories, the uniform worn by US Navy personnel is decided by the Flag Officer on whose station one is serving. For the Norfolk and New York areas, the uniform was tropical white, but when *Ark Royal* arrived in the Hudson River the wind was blowing straight out of Canada and was bitterly cold. The Captain and the Executive Officer, Commander Ian McIntosh, decided to go by British rules and the ship's company reverted to blue uniform before everybody went down with pneumonia. The wardroom held a cocktail party in the upper hangar and the uniform for this occasion was, however, tropical white. Bob Edward and Dave Lutter had met some old girlfriends that they knew from Pensacola days, and together we all went ashore in uniform, which we should not have done: certain officers from 898 Squadron were hovering in the background, ready to take the girls off our hands! We hailed a taxi and went to a night club in Central Park then on to a bar in Greenwich Village, where we ran into the Executive Officer. He was in 'civvies' and we were out of the rig of the day by wearing uniform ashore. Ian McIntosh made a play for one of the girls, intending to embarrass us as much as possible. Before escorting the girls back to their hotel and wishing them goodnight, we ended up by having our photograph taken with Ian—which could be used as 'blackmail' to prevent him from dishing out punishment to us for going ashore in uniform! The next day the carrier sailed for Norfolk again, where she would berth opposite the new 'super carrier' USS *Saratoga*.

The purpose of the visit to Norfolk was to transfer some of our aircraft to *Saratoga* and some of hers to *Ark Royal* for cross-deck operations when the new carrier put to sea for trials. Treavor Spafford would be our Wyvern cross-operating pilot, and the aircraft were hoisted aboard by crane while both ships were alongside at Norfolk. Training catapult loading sessions were held aboard each ship in the quietness of harbour routine, so that any problems could be easily sorted out by the experts immediately to hand.

Ark Royal had suffered several engine failures during the past few months and off Cape Hatteras, with both carriers steaming line abreast at about 30 knots, her American companion was to suffer a similar indignity. *Saratoga* looked majestic with a huge stern wave on which her planeguard destroyer was riding with her bow high, just like a fast motor launch. Suddenly the stern wave collapsed, the planeguard swerved off to one side and *Saratoga* dropped astern. Then a signal lamp started flashing from the American carrier, with the message 'Sorry, we seem to have suffered the same problems as you have had—we're down to three engines!' Eventually the American engineers had their fourth engine up and running properly, the cross operations were carried out successfully, all gear was returned and the two carriers parted company. We set course for home, arriving in the Moray Firth at the end of May 1957.

* * *

Her Majesty the Queen had recently made a state visit to Norway, and it was decided to have a Sea Review of the Fleet in home waters on her return to Britain. The review took place in the Moray Firth, and afterwards, with HM Yacht *Britannia* in the lead, the Fleet would steam into Cromarty Firth in style, where all the ships would anchor together on command from the Royal Yacht. As *Britannia* approached the Fleet she was greeted by a massive flypast of *Ark Royal*'s air group and aircraft from RNAS Lossiemouth. When our aircraft had been recovered, the Royal Yacht steamed slowly past the Fleet and we all lined ship and cheered her as she sailed by. It was a grand and moving occasion. The Fleet would remain at Invergordon for weekend leave and inter-ship sports while the Royal Yacht steamed around to the west coast of Scotland for a brief visit prior to the Royal family gathering at Balmoral for the summer holidays.

Invitations were sent out to all the warships from the Royal Yacht for commanding officers to be present on board *Britannia* for cocktails with Her Majesty. Boats were laid on to ensure that all the invited guests arrived on time as commanded, and when I boarded *Britannia* along with other junior officers I was ushered up to the boat deck while senior officers of Commander rank and above went to the quarterdeck. The Queen obviously went to the quarterdeck first to meet her senior officers, but it did not take the Duke of Edinburgh long to persuade Her Majesty that she might prefer to meet the junior officers because their opportunities for meeting the Royals were less frequent than those of the senior officers.

Queen Elizabeth walked over to my small group of officers and must have spent at least half an hour chatting to us about her family. She is a very small and beautiful woman, and very much a 'Mum'. She spoke about Charles and Anne, who were toddlers at that time, just as any normal mother would, with love and affection, and it was obvious that she adored her children. There was no aloofness or pretentiousness: she was a warm, generous person who was obviously doing a splendid job both as a mother and as the Sovereign. Prince Philip was very much 'one of the boys': raucous laughter came from whichever group of officers he happened to be with at the time. He still wore that unkempt uniform and did not seem at all bothered by it. Finally the Royal party left, wishing us all the best for the future, and we disembarked for our own ships. The remainder of the weekend was spent playing sports or visiting the NAAFI, which had been temporarily reopened for the Fleet's visit. The wartime days at Invergordon had long since passed, and it would probably be a long time before another large fleet visited the place again.

After the Fleet Review *Ark Royal* steamed around to the west coast of Scotland for a mining exercise. This was the first time that 831 Squadron had loaded full-size dummy mines while embarked, to drop them in a well-used waterway. Our Wyverns were each loaded up with a 2,000-pound mine on the centreline fuselage station, and these were laid in the entrance to Loch Tarbert. Dave Lutter really put his foot (or rather mine) in it. He made his run up the loch but released his mine a little late, having made an error in his navigation, and the huge weapon landed in the front garden of the local postmistress. The lady was not amused. The weapon buried itself deep

103

into her garden and defied all attempts to dislodge and recover it. Finally, after a couple of days of hard work, the mine was pulled clear and the lady's garden returned as near as possible to its condition before the monster had arrived out of the blue.

There had been one or two incidents during Wyvern deck landings when the aircraft's tail hook had split or nearly cut through an arrester wire. This hook was nothing like that on either the Gannet or the Sea Hawk, both of which were rounded and incapable of cutting into a wire. The Wyvern's, on the other hand, was similar in appearance to a chisel with a very sharp beak. If it hit a wire it did not bounce off but simply cut straight into it. The problem came to a head one day when Gerry McFall, on landing, cut straight through the fourth and last arrester wire. Using his wheel brakes, he managed to stop his aircraft about a couple of feet from the front end of the angled deck, but it was only a question of time before we lost an aircraft and pilot or killed someone on the flight deck with loose wires flying in every direction. It was decided in the meantime, until a solution could be found to this very serious problem, that the Squadron would be disembarked back to Ford.

The ship steamed around to the Firth of Forth and moored off Leith. The entire air group would be disembarked while the ship was at Leith instead of in the English Channel. Weekend leave was given to all off-duty watch personnel, and 831 Squadron challenged the other air group officers to a 'sniff and a snort' golf match on Saturday afternoon at Dunfermline Golf Course. Participants were allowed only two clubs, one of their choice and a putter. An unlimited supply of golf balls was permitted, plus a hip flask of malt whisky. The rules were quite straightforward: the losers were allowed a 'sniff' from the opponent's flask but the winners were allowed a 'snort'. As can be imagined, after a short while the winners were reeling about the course and beginning to lose while the losers were catching up and also beginning to reel; needless to say, by the end of the match every player was inebriated. After the match everybody retired to the club-house bar and by the following morning the wardroom contained very many sore heads.

There was great excitement in the air group on Monday morning as it had been decided to launch all the ship's aircraft by steam catapult while she was moored to her buoy off Leith. This was an unprecedented exercise, and would be a little slower than normal because the rate of steam generation would not quite be the same as if the carrier were under way. The Sea Hawks and Venoms were launched first, followed by the Skyraiders, Gannets and finally the Wyverns. The whole operation went without a hitch and provided a great spectacle for the locals who sat and watched the event from the sea wall. Owing to the slowness of each launch, once they were all airborne the pilots proceeded directly to their respective parent air stations.

Back at Ford, DNAW, Westland and DGNA, together with representatives from RAE Bedford, gathered to discuss the Wyvern's tail-hook problem. The hook was the same as that fitted to 830 Squadron's aircraft, but that unit did not experience the problem while embarked in *Eagle*. The only relevant difference between the two ships was their arrester wires: *Ark Royal*'s had a larger diameter, thus offering a larger surface area to the hook 'beak', enabling the hook to penetrate the wire and break it. A modified tail hook was prepared which included a built-up sole, increased radius to the beak, increased throat and a rounding off of the sides—which had been very sharp indeed and quite capable of cutting a wire with any sideways movement along it. Success-ful tests were carried out at RAE Bedford using arrester wires of the same size as those used in *Ark Royal*, all aircraft were retrofitted with the modified hook and no further wire spearing or cutting was experienced after re-embarkation.

I had just returned from weekend leave when Dave Lutter approached me to say that we had both been selected to go to 813 Squadron aboard *Eagle*. At the time I thought that we were both being reappointed, but Stan Farquhar quickly calmed me down by saying that we were going on loan to the Squadron because it was two pilots short and was entering the NATO autumn exercise 'Strikeback' off the coast of Norway. 813 had embarked in *Eagle* with two engineer pilots, Lieutenants Firth and Hall, both of whom had experienced difficulties deck-landing the Wyvern. One was grounded for his safety and the other quickly followed after he had asked to be removed from embarked flying duties. Dave and I were to replace these two officers for the duration of the exercise. We quickly packed our bags and caught a train north to Scotland to join the ship at Leith in the Firth of Forth. Neither of us was really happy about this temporary arrangement and we both harboured uncertain feelings.

The pair of us were quickly absorbed into the Squadron. Lieutenant Alan Griggs took us in hand and we were assigned to his division. The ship slipped her moorings and proceeded north to the Norwegian Sea, where it was blowing a gale bordering on Force 9, *Eagle* pitching and rolling a good deal out of wind. Dave and I went out on to the flight deck and walked aft to view the ship and the watery scene. Neither of us had experienced this bitterly cold weather, and as we stood there the Squadron CO, Gus Halliday, came down the deck to speak with us. He asked me if I thought it was 'on' for the Wyverns to fly with these sea and weather conditions.

'Well, sir, you're the experts,' I remarked, 'and you know if your pilots are capable of coping, but I think the deck is out of pitch limits for the aircraft.'

'I agree, but you have far more experience in the aircraft than any of us!'

Dave and I looked at each other, grinned and walked back to the briefing room with our new temporary CO.

The next day the sea and weather had moderated considerably and Dave and I were scheduled to fly with Alan Griggs as his No 3 and 4 pilots, respectively. As I left the bow catapult I had no premonition that, within the hour, I was to experience my first aircraft accident. Alan's division had been required to carry out dummy FAC (Forward Air Control) attacks against a simulated enemy in the area east of Ballangen, northern Norway. The attacks were carried out successfully and the division set off back to the ship with Dave and I flying as a pair in trail about half a mile astern of Alan's flight.

It was a beautiful September morning and the visibility was unlimited with an almost flat calm existing in the fjords. Alan took us up Harstadfjord at about 12,000 feet. At that stage none of us had a care in the world, but suddenly my aircraft yawed violently to the right and then straightened itself up again. Then I noticed what to me looked like ice particles flying back from the front of the engine nacelle past the cockpit. My immediate reaction was to check that the de-icing tank had not been switched on, but the switch was in the 'off' position. The flow of ice particles only lasted for a second or two, then the aircraft yawed violently again. My airspeed was falling fast and the aircraft was descending very fast too. I seemed to have lost both elevator and rudder control, and this really worried me. I called Alan about my predicament and I could see that my height was fast vanishing. I told him that I intended bailing out, and at what I thought was 800 feet I jettisoned the cockpit canopy, a flurry of maps and navigation boards hitting me in the face as they were sucked out by the airflow. I needed no encouragement. I pulled the ejection seat handle and suddenly I was outside in a relatively quiet environment. My parachute deployed very quickly, my seat left me, I spun around into the light wind and then I hit the water with a resounding splash.

Dave Lutter had been chasing me closely, taking photographs of the whole event with the F24 cameras that were mounted in his rear fuselage. He told me afterwards that he himself had come very close to disaster: he had been so busy watching me that he had failed to notice that he was closing the mountains quickly, below their crests. He managed to pull up at the last minute to scrape over the top with a few feet to spare.

My Wyvern crashed just a hundred yards from a Norwegian fishing trawler which was proceeding south down the fjord. It did not stop or turn around, and so I imagined that her crew must have been either asleep or too frightened to do anything when this huge aircraft appeared from nowhere out of the sky to crash just astern of them. Perhaps they thought that it was a whale broaching.

I was alone in the middle of an extremely cold Harstadfjord, splashing about, though thankfully in calm conditions. However, my troubles were not yet over: my parachute rigging lines had become entangled about my feet and ankles, and my 'chute was sinking fast into the blackness of the fjord. I had managed to inflate my liferaft and had boarded it, with my legs dangling over the thin end. I could not pull out my survival knife because it was held tight in its pocket, the material having swollen with the wetness. My thoughts were racing now, but finally, after much heaving and pulling, I managed to free the knife and to cut and unravel the rigging lines from around my feet and ankles. I fell backwards into the liferaft somewhat exhausted, and as I did so a small Norwegian rowing boat came alongside. Two fishermen pulled me on board together with my liferaft and survival pack as the parachute disappeared into the depths.

The fishermen made me feel as comfortable as possible in their small boat and a short while later we landed at a fishing village on the western side of the fjord. I was feeling rather cold, due no doubt to delayed shock, as well as somewhat shaken from my experience, so I asked for a cup of tea or coffee. Shortly, somebody appeared with half a bottle of whisky and insisted that I had a 'dram'. I said that I would rather have tea or coffee but they were adamant. By the time we had all had a 'dram' or two there was hardly anything left in the bottle. Then the local headmaster arrived. He could speak broken English and he arranged for photographs to be taken of us all together. Then, out of nowhere, a US Air Force Grumman Albatross search and rescue flying boat flew overhead, landed nearby on the fjord and taxied over to the village. After thanking everybody for their kindness I boarded the Albatross, whereupon an American airman thrust a large beaker of Jack Daniels Kentucky bourbon into my hand. By the time I arrived at the sick quarters at the Norwegian NATO air base at Andoya I could dance the highland fling. The Americans, after a quick medical check-up, gave me lunch and then *Eagle*'s SAR helicopter arrived to fly me back to the ship.

Back on board the carrier, I went straight to Flyco to explain to the Captain, Commander (Air), the ship's AEO and the Squadron Commander what had happened to me out there over Harstadtfjord. Without hesitation, the AEO, Commander Ian McConnackie, explained that I had experienced a translation bearing failure. This bearing was situated between the front and rear propellers and was coupled in with the mechanism which ensured that both propellers were at the same pitch when the throttle was moved. If the translation bearing ever failed, the rear propeller blades automatically moved into fine pitch, producing a very effective disc behind the front propeller that would block any airflow rearwards over the tail control surfaces, rendering them ineffective, lowering air speed dramatically and causing the aircraft to go into a high rate of descent from which it was impossible to recover to controlled flight. These were exactly the effects that I had experienced. The AEO's explanation was accepted and this was entered as the cause of the accident in the A25 Aircraft Accident Report.

Unbeknown to me, Mike Le Fanu, *Eagle*'s Captain, had arranged for a magnum of Long John's whisky to be delivered to the village as a 'thank you' for rescuing and looking after me so well until the US Air Force had arrived on scene. The Norwegian headmaster sent me a letter of thanks together with several photographs, and one with them all holding the bottle of whisky. Although we did not see a great deal of each other, Michael Le Fanu was to remain one of my closest friends in the Navy. He was a person who never forgot. Many years later I was to learn that my old grammar school headmistress had taught him at Bedford throughout World War II during the period that the school was evacuated from Rye to Bedfordshire.

After a couple of days away from flying, I went back to participating in the NATO exercise. Immediately after my first launch of the day I experienced a severe hydraulic failure, had to jettison my drop tanks and landed back on board after the main recovery. On 30 September 1957 I disembarked with 813 Squadron to Ford Air Station to re-join my old squadron, 831.

* * *

A new Senior Pilot, Lieutenant Commander Phil Swithinbank, was appointed to 831 Squadron to relieve Jock Tofts, who had been appointed Senior Pilot of the Navy's new Scimitar fighter Intensive Flying Trails Unit, which was set up at Ford in the old 764 Squadron hangars. 764 had been relocated to Lossiemouth as the new Advanced Air Weapons Training Squadron. Apart from its old Sea Hawk fighters and Vampire trainers, it would start to receive some new Hunter T.8 dual-seaters to give pilots appointed to Scimitar and Sea Vixen squadrons swept-wing training prior to their OFS on those two types of aircraft.

At this time there was a significant change in the Squadron's complement. Pete Wheatley and Gus Gray had both gone and Treavor Spafford was off to do the MTP's course at Sydenham, Northern Ireland. Lieutenants Barry Hartwell, 'Tank' Sherman and Mike Smith, all relatively senior in rank, would join the Squadron as their replacements. Two new Sub Lieutenants, Jerry Smith and John Williams, also joined the Squadron to replace two other pilots who had departed. The Squadron would re-embark once more before its disbandment, but at the end of 1957 both Wyvern squadrons would cease to exist, their task being taken on by either the Scimitar or the Sea Vixen until the arrival of the Navy's new strike aircraft, the NA.39.

Before 831 Squadron disbanded, No 700S Squadron, the Scimitar IFTU, would suffer the blow of losing its CO, Commander Ian Martin, who was killed in a car accident north of Arundel one night while returning to Ford from a visit to the Ministry of Defence in London. He ran off the road at almost the same place as one of our squadron officers. The accident stunned everybody because he was such a careful person: as it was late at night, he must have fallen asleep at the wheel and gone off the road before he knew it. Command of the IFTU shifted to Jock Tofts, who completed the trials and became the CO of 807 Squadron, the first squadron to be equipped with the new Scimitar, at Lossiemouth.

The other loss was that of Lieutenant Mike Smith, who suffered a motoring accident on his return from a Hunt Ball he had been attending up-country. He also, it is presumed, fell asleep at the wheel and drove off the climbing road just north of Arundel. His car rolled over several times, finishing upside down in a field with its headlights still blazing. Fortunately a motorist spotted his wrecked car in the early morning hours. He went to investigate, found Mike, dragged him clear and called an ambulance. Mike had received severe head injuries and was to spend several weeks in Chichester Hospital before he was fit to join the Squadron once more. However, following medical tests and examination he was considered unfit to fly fixed-wing aircraft again and went on to fly helicopters. He would eventually become the Flight Deck Officer on board *Ark Royal*.

While I was with 831 Squadron there occurred a series of incidents which we all ignored at the time but which would culminate in the loss of two Squadron pilots in the same accident. Looking back, I feel that every one of us was guilty in some way or another, for had there been stronger control over these two men the accident might never have happened. It was an instance of an officer who was senior by age needing to exercise influence over a younger pilot who needed stern guidance and control to bring him to maturity as an aviator. However, this did not happen and eventually these two pilots died. I am not blaming any individual because I honestly believe that, whatever orders or instructions might have been given, the two would have ignored them. The real answer would have been to ensure that they never flew together, but this was not always possible.

There were two postgraduate flying courses in the FAA for pilots who had completed their first front-line appointment—the Qualified Flying Instructor and the Air Warfare Instructor courses. The QFI's course was conducted at RAF Little Rissington, Gloucestershire, in those days, while the AWI course started out at HMS *Excellent*, Whale Island, Portsmouth, for the Ground School and then moved to Lossiemouth for the flying phase in 764 Squadron. Over the years the AWIs had always thought themselves the better of the two types of postgraduate pilots but in reality the QFI was generally the better aviator, smoother in his flying and more accurate with his weapon attacks. In a squadron, the AWI would always be the leader of the third division of aircraft. However, the rivalry between them would remain.

After Bobby Sandison's death in 1956, another young pilot, the tall, blond-haired Sub Lieutenant Maurice Maggs, joined to take his place. He was a likable young man but very self-assured and extremely overconfident. He was an ideal naval aviator for war, but needed to be taken in hand by an experienced aviator for guidance and direction. Unfortunately he was to make most of his Wyvern flights as the wing man to Lieutenant Reg Hunt, who I am sure was rather elated by this young aviator's adulation.

One day, on my way to the wardroom for lunch, a 764 Squadron Sea Vampire joined the airfield circuit. The pilot, Maggs, commenced a low-level aerobatic routine. It was a display that required considerable polish and was in some sections quite dangerous. When he returned to the Squadron I asked him who had authorised him to do low-level aerobatics and he told me quite bluntly to mind my own business. I was Duty Officer and he had not been entered into 831 Squadron's flight authorisation book, so he must have sweet-talked somebody in 764 Squadron into letting him fly the Vampire. However, I was never able to establish if he had been authorised to throw his aircraft about the airfield at low level. What worried me more than anything was his attitude, which confirmed what I really believed—that he had not been authorised to carry out the display. It was obvious to me, at least, that this young man was a danger both to himself and to others. He had aleady shown his disregard for safety at Lossiemouth when he had 'buzzed' the Squadron hangar.

The Wyvern was not cleared for aerobatics other than a barrel roll, and positive 'g' had to be maintained throughout even this manoeuvre. One morning I was walking out of the hangar to the aircraft dispersal when I spotted two Wyverns in formation carrying out barrel rolls to the south of the airfield, along the coast. Reg and Maurice were the only two pilots airborne at the time. When they landed, I said to them that I had seen them carrying out the barrel rolls but they blatantly denied it. This devil-may-care attitude was to my mind dangerous and I was quite fearful that sooner or later something dreadful would happen. With hindsight, I should have spoken with the Senior Pilot, but at the time I believed him to be aware of what was going on.

It was a Friday afternoon during the summer of 1957 when Reg and Maurice should have flown together on a quarter attack exercise. I had gone back to the Squadron, which was at this time housed temporarily in the old 764 Squadron hangar. Maurice was in the Squadron, but there was no sign of Reg, who had last been seen playing billiards in the wardroom. This being so, Peter Wheatley changed the flight schedule and wrote me up as Maurice's leader. Peter was at this time a Lieutenant Commander but Maurice was having nothing to do with Peter's change of schedule. Maurice flew into a tantrum on the dispersal: 'I'm not flying with him! Reg is my leader and I only fly with him!' and so on. Peter told him to do as he was ordered and at that Maurice turned his back on him. He was starting to walk back to the hangar when Jock Tofts arrived, having been alerted to the shindig that was in progress at the aircraft line. Jock asked what all the commotion was about and Peter told him. The Senior Pilot then said the sortie would be flown as scheduled: Reg was now back in the Squadron and this would be his last flight with 831 before going off to join the AWI course. Jock's statement was soon to prove all too prophetic.

The fact that Reg was off to do the AWI course was news to me since the appointment had been kept very quiet and was not common knowledge within the Squadron. Maurice left the line with a smirk, his attitude that of a precocious child who thought he had got his way. Jock called me over. 'It's okay, Punchy. I want you to do an engine test flight for me.' So that afternoon Reg and Maurice took off together to practise quarter attacks south of Selsey Bill. Peter and Treavor Spafford also took off to do the same exercise south of Worthing, while I flew out to the west to 20,000 feet for my test flight.

It was early summer and, as is usual at that time of the year, sea fog was rolling in off the Channel over the coastline. On this particular afternoon it was already covering the downwind leg of the airfield circuit. Both Peter and I were advised about the fog by the airfield tower, but the air traffic personnel were unable to contact Reg. I had switched to the same frequency as Peter and Reg. I heard Peter tell Treavor that he was clear in on a dummy attack and a short while later I heard Reg clear in Maurice for a similar attack. Then I heard Peter telling Treavor that they were returning to Ford owing to the fog but I heard nothing more from Reg's flight. The fog was by then very close to the airfield runway, so I made a hasty return and landed a short time after Peter's flight.

After landing, I checked into the AMCO and signed the aircraft's logbook, Form A700, and signed off the test flight as satisfactory. I then strolled back to the Duty Officer's room to sign in the Authorisation Book. I was met by a delegation consisting of the CO, the SP, Peter Wheatley and Treavor Spafford. They all asked me if I had seen or heard anything of either Reg or Maurice as they were now overdue. All I could tell them was that I had heard Reg on the radio about an hour ago when he cleared in Maurice for a dummy attack and, for some reason, I believed them to be due south of Selsey.

What I had dreaded was now becoming a reality. Both aircraft were in 'clean' configuration—in other words they were not carrying overload drop tanks—and thus, on the exercise that these two pilots had been authorised to carry out, they could stay airborne for an hour and a half at the most. It was now two hours since they had taken off and there was growing concern about their safety. RAF Tangmere was contacted, but no Wyverns had landed there that day. The station SAR helicopter was launched and headed to a position south of Selsey Bill, the Selsey lifeboat was also launched and the Duty Naval Safety minesweeper set sail from Portsmouth. The fog continued to thicken, although it did lift a little just before sunset. There was no doubt in anybody's mind that both Reg and Maurice had met with a dreadful accident of some sort.

The Selsey lifeboat, during its search, would find Reg's 'bone dome', part of his lifejacket, his navigation kneeboard and a flying boot, plus a piece of aircraft piping. His 'bone dome' was badly bruised, the lifejacket consisted merely of the back piece with his name on it, and his boot, also with his name inside, had been ripped from top to bottom along the lacing, indicating that it had been torn from his foot in a violent manner. The piece of piping could not be identified as coming from a Wyvern, but everybody was sure that it had because there was no other immediate explanation as to its presence. Whatever had happened to Reg's flight had been extremely violent and catastrophic, resulting in the loss of both aircraft and the deaths of the pilots. The tide runs fast in the area of the ditching, so any fuel slick would have quickly dispersed; aircraft wreckage could have been carried anywhere along the coast and, once on the sea bed, would have been covered by sand or mud quite quickly.

Peter started to make observations about Reg's being awarded a 'Green Instrument Rating' too soon because of his lack of experience and flying hours, but Jock Tofts was not buying that one. However, a little later, when Maurice's flying locker was cleared, an empty 35mm camera case was found. One of the Squadron linemen had seen Maurice with a camera before he boarded his aircraft. It can only be speculation—nobody will know the truth—but Maurice may have placed his camera on the gyro gun sight to take pictures of Reg's aircraft as he closed in during a quarter attack. Reg's aircraft would have looked very small in the camera's viewfinder, and by the time he looked up he would have been too close to avoid a collision. A collision in these circumstances would have been so violent that both aircraft would have exploded, scattering wreckage over a wide area, and the fireball would have consumed most of the fuel—hence the absence of a slick.

The bodies were never recovered. Many years later, when I used to sail over that area, I would sit and reflect in silence about their untimely deaths. After the event my father often asked me if anything more had been discovered because he knew that Reg and I had been friends. Maurice I never really got to know, and when we had spoken the conversation had always been confrontational.

I look back over that dreadful time and wonder if I could have done anything to prevent the accident. One does not 'tittle tattle' about brother officers and one assumes that everybody is aware of what is going on in the Squadron, but, even so, following events such as this there is always doubt in one's mind as to whether more could have been done. Perhaps these two pilots

111

should have been separated and made to fly with others, but of course the accident might have happened anyway. Individuality has to be encouraged, but exactly what is the limit? Every pilot must be allowed to develop his own capabilities to the full within the envelope of flight safety, and when it becomes obvious that he is about to, or is likely to, step out of that envelope then one calls a halt before an accident occurs. Whether this should have been done in this instance I am not really sure, and I believe that most of the others involved feel the same. Nobody saw what exactly happened and nobody will ever know. That said, it was a salutary lesson for us all and we were very much affected by it. Even now, after nearly half a century, I look back and wonder.

* * *

Perhaps one of the most laughable but at the same time very serious moments during the commission of 831 Squadron took place during the Admiral's Inspection of Ford Air Station at the time of my loan to 813 Squadron. There were by now few Wyverns in the Fleet: 830 Squadron had lost at least three, 813 Squadron one and 831 Squadron three. 831 Squadron was about to lose two more on the same night in the most bizarre of accidents.

In the majority of Admirals' Inspections of an air station, most of the flying tasks take place late in the day and at night, in an attempt to raise the workload to something like the level that would be experienced during war and thereby test the capabilities of the station's personnel and their ability to cope in such circumstances. During this particular inspection the personnel were to be tested to the limit by what was about to happen—and it was not on the list of tasks drawn up by the Admiral's Staff.

The Staff had arranged for aircraft to be flown in from Yeovilton, Brawdy and Lee-on-Solent to swamp the air traffic services. Yeovilton and Culdrose air stations had been instructed to be available as night diversion airfields for any aircraft based at Ford. Stan Farquhar was airborne with a division of three Wyverns, with Bob Edward as his No 2 and Jerry Smith as his No 3. When the three had finished their night exercise Stan called for a stream GCA landing in the order of himself first, Jerry Smith next and Bob Edward last. As they entered the recovery pattern Lieutenant Roger Dimmock landed ahead of them in his Sea Hawk fighter, burst a tyre, shattered the runway's 800-yard go-round-again lights and skidded off into an ammunition dump, and glass all over the runway meant that the latter was effectively closed until the mess could be cleaned up. A Gannet anti-submarine aircraft landed on the standby runway and also burst a tyre, effectively blocking that one too. Stan was instructed to overshoot and conserve fuel until a runway could be made available. The second Wyvern behind Stan joined up with him on his left wing and Stan then instructed the pilot to move over to his starboard wing just as the third Wyvern was joining—a movement of which Stan was not aware at the time. Stan felt a lifting of his tail, thought he heard a thump, called the pilot he had instructed to change sides but received no reply. He immediately contacted Ford to say that he thought that his

No 2 had collided with his tail: he was unable to raise him on the radio and intended to make a flyby over the tower to have his tail checked.

There had in fact been a complete misunderstanding about which aircraft were flying alongside Stan's aircraft. Jerry joined Stan on his port wing and was instructed to move across to the starboard wing, but as he moved across he did not see Bob's aircraft and promptly chopped his tail off with his propeller. Bob immediately went into a spin and ejected, and Jerry, with no propellers, also ejected. In the meantime the Squadron Chief Ordnance Petty Officer was out on 831's dispersal, heard the aircraft go overhead and then heard the collision, followed by the bangs of the two ejection-seat guns. He rushed into the hangar and telephoned air traffic control to tell them that he thought two ejection seats had been used just to the south of the airfield. The tower refused to believe him at first but then began to have doubts following Stan's radio call. When they failed to raise either Bob or Jerry on the radio their doubts began to fade.

The Ford Air Operations Branch was now in the middle of the worst situation imaginable. Two runways were blocked, a suspected (and probable) mid-air collision had taken place and an entire squadron of Sea Hawks was overhead wondering what to do next. The Sea Hawks were diverted to Yeovilton and all other aircraft were placed in orbit, conserving their fuel, while the runways were cleared as quickly as possible. Stan eventually landed on the main runway with no damage to his aircraft.

The Commanding Officer of the Sea Hawk squadron, Lieutenant Commander 'Paddy' McKeown, took his aircraft off to Yeovilton. When he was within recovery range he called the station but received no reply. He led his squadron over Yeovilton but it quickly became obvious that it was not open, so he proceeded to Culdrose, which had been listed as the second diversion airfield. When within radio range he called Culdrose, but once again there was no response. It was a clear, moonlit night and the runways could plainly be seen from 20,000 feet, so he descended to see if he could wake up the duty crew in the tower. There was no response so he told his pilots to make an approach and land on the moonlit runway as quickly as possible; they were all by now very low on fuel. Eventually somebody in the tower realised that something was very wrong indeed and had the runway lights switched on, just as the last few jets were making their approaches.

Back at Ford the Admiral's Staff was going berserk. Yeovilton not open, and neither was Culdrose, so what on earth had happened to the Inspection Orders and Instructions? Commander (Air) of Culdrose was dismissed, and I believe Lieutenant Commander Flying also found a new job. I am not really sure what actually happened to the two officers in similar appointments at Yeovilton, but I suspect that they may have received similar treatment. Fortunately, neither aircraft nor pilots were lost—which, in the circumstances was almost unbelievable.

Meanwhile two Wyvern pilots were floating earthwards on silk while one aircraft crashed in the sea and the other into the marshes east of the air station. Bob Edward landed in a nursery to the east of Littlehampton, sustaining several cuts and bruises as he gracefully penetrated a greenhouse.

He walked up to the manager's house and knocked on his door, but when it was opened and Bob tried to explain his predicament it was slammed in his face After banging on the door again he managed to convince the manager that he had just bailed out of a jet and landed in his glasshouse, and he would be grateful if he would telephone Ford and let them know that he was all right. A car eventually arrived from the air station and he was collected and taken back to the tower, and then to the Sickbay for a check-up. The second pilot, Jerry Smith, landed on the outskirts of Littlehampton. He collected his parachute together, slung his dinghy pack over his shoulders and with his 'chute in his arms walked along the High Street to the police station—without anybody asking him what was wrong. When he tried to explain his presence he was asked to wait because the police officers had a serious aircraft accident on their hands. He flung the dinghy and parachute on the Duty Officer's desk. 'What the hell do you think all this is, eh? I am one of the pilots who bailed out! Now can you get me some transport back to Ford, please?'

It was a day or two before Jerry's aircraft was found. Nobody had heard or seen it crash, so at first it was assumed that it had disappeared into the sea as had Bob's aircraft. A couple of days later, however, a local farmer telephoned to ask if we were still missing an aircraft. When he was told yes he revealed that he thought that his Daisy Belle has found it. One of the farmer's dairy cows had discovered the fin of Jerry's aircraft sticking out of the marsh east of Ford and was licking the cellulose.

As a result of this fiasco 831 Squadron had lost a total of five aircraft—nearly two-thirds of its complement. There were now very few Wyverns left in the Royal Navy's armoury, and Their Lordships decided that the time had come to retire all Wyvern squadrons. 831 Squadron was decommissioned in November 1957 and 813 Squadron followed a short time later. 831 would be resurrected a year later as the Navy's ECM squadron with first Avenger and then Gannet aircraft, replacing 751 Squadron and its Avengers, the Gannets being modified to carry electronic countermeasures equipment.

So ended my first front-line squadron experience. I was appointed to HMS *Excellent* to attend the AWI Ground School prior to joining 764 Squadron at Lossiemouth for the flying phase of the course.

* * *

In the summer of 1957 I arrived home at Camber for fourteen days' leave. My father had been away visiting the Kent River Board offices in Rye, but when he came home he said that he had a yacht delivery job for me if I was interested and wanted it. A gentleman he had met required his 21-foot sloop to be brought round from Bosham, near Chichester, to Rye, where he intended keeping it: could he recommend somebody who could deliver it for him? Dad thought that it might be good experience for me, and I grabbed the opportunity of a sail along the south coast.

I gathered together a delivery kit of food, sleeping bag, lantern, navigation charts, equipment and information together with some warm and foul-

114

weather clothing. Dad and I drove over to Bosham in the old Morris E and found the *Dunnolly* tied up alongside a jetty, dried out as it was low tide. She was a centreboard yacht with a sloop rig and fitted with a single-cylinder Stewart Turner petrol engine. The fuel tank was checked and found to be full, and, after a look around the vessel and pumping her dry of water, everything was found to be in order. Dad waited until the tide started flooding and the boat was afloat, and when he was happy he cast off my ropes and I was on my way to Rye.

This was my first experience sailing out of Chichester's tidal basin, and the tide can flow with some very strong currents. The wind was light so I motored until I was clear of the area and out in the Solent, whereupon I hoisted the sails, cut the engine and sat back for a quiet and enjoyable voyage along the coast inshore to Selsey Bill. The *Dunnolly* was a shallow-draught boat and so I decided to stay inshore and clear of the rocks and shoals known as the Owers. With Selsey Bill behind me, I headed straight for Beachy Head, making full use of the east-flowing tidal stream.

The boat was not fitted with any proper navigation lights and it was just as well that I had brought my lantern along; as she was just 21 feet overall, an all-round white light was sufficient to meet the necessary regulations instead of red, green and white navigation lights. Off Shoreham, another sailing yacht flashed me in Morse the letter 'P', meaning 'Your lights are burning badly', but he was some distance away so I ignored him. However, just before dawn, near Beachy Head, I became concerned about a small coaster which suddenly veered toward me. I started the motor in case I had to make a quick evasive manoeuvre, but, to my relief, at about a cable's distance she resumed her original course westwards.

As the day wore on, and with a fierce sun blazing down on me and little or no wind to cool me off, *Dunnolly* drifted slowly across Rye Bay towards Rye Harbour. The two items that I had not brought with me were a broad-brimmed, floppy hat to shield me from the sun and some lipseal to protect my lips from both the sun and the ultra-violet light reflected off the sea. When I finally arrived at Rye Harbour my face looked as though it had been in a roasting oven. It had taken just over a day to sail the 140 miles from Bosham, which was reasonable considering the tides and wind I experienced.

The *Dunnolly* was a leaky old boat and I suspected that much of the water was entering somewhere around the centreboard trunking. She needed to be slipped, thoroughly inspected and re-caulked to make her properly watertight.

Some months later Dad called me and asked if I was prepared to collect the *Dunnolly* again, this time from Ramsgate. I agreed, and a young lad called Richard—a friend of Dad's who wanted to gain some boating experience—joined me as crew. My father drove us over to Ramsgate. The boat was tied up to the eastern harbour arm, the worst possible place for such a small craft: she should have been moored inside the marina for safety and where an eye could be kept on her. When we found her she was sitting on thick mud and once again was half filled with water. We waited until the tide started flooding, when we could pull the craft into the side of the arm and board her. Our first task was to bail her out and make her shipshape before we brought our gear on board. Dad left when he was happy that we had everything in hand and we finally motored out of the harbour in the early afternoon when the tidal stream had reversed to flow westwards.

There was a fresh southerly breeze and we made good time down-Channel and throughout the night. That part of the English Channel is a busy area, so I stayed close inshore to avoid the big ships. Just before sunrise we rounded Dungeness and headed across Rye Bay, but there was a low tide so we had to wait until 10 o'clock, when there would have been sufficient water in the river. I sat down in the stern sheets with the mainsail sheet eased off while Richard was below grabbing a few minutes' 'kip'. It was warm and sunny on that early morning, and although I cannot recall it I fell asleep, to be woken up by the boat sailing ashore on to the beach to the south of Jury's Gut in the middle of the Army's Lydd Firing Range! Fortunately there was little wind and hardly any surf so the old boat did not sustain damage, and luckily the Army were not using the range that morning. For a second or so, however, panic reigned. Richard appeared from below wondering what had happened as I was racing forward to see how shallow the water was and how far up the beach we had gone. I hurried aft, started the motor and told Richard to stay on the helm and do as I said. Then I jumped over the bow and started to push and heave as the boat rose up and down gently on the waves, instructing Richard to go astern on the motor. I prayed hard for strength and guidance and He must have heard me because the boat slowly began to move astern and then she was afloat. I caught hold of the bowsprit and its stay, swinging myself back on board as the boat went slowly into deeper water, and we then turned around and headed for Rye Harbour about a mile and a half away.

I never sailed the old *Dunnolly* again but I believe that the owner sold her on. Some years later I was reading a yachting magazine and spotted an article which reported her as having been wrecked and lost—a very sad end to a lovely old day sailer.

My association with the *Dunnolly* certainly renewed my faith in God. I had not paid much attention to Him for a very long time, but my experience on the beach at Lydd had brought home the fact that He was there, ready to help in times of need. Whenever I flew I always felt that He was there with me, providing a shield against whatever dangers were about to confront me. Flying alone at heights of 40,000 feet, I could never doubt His existence. It is very lonely at night in near-space, with a canopy of stars and planets, but with His presence one never feels alone.

IV

THE LADDER OF RESPONSIBILITY

— 12 —

Failure

O NCE A naval aviator has one front-line tour under his belt he is considered to be of a high enough standard to be appointed to either the
Air Warfare Instructor or the Qualified Flying Instructor course. It is
the QFI's responsibility to ensure that the Fleet receives the best-trained
pilots for front-line service and it is the AWI's responsibility to ensure that
the front-line aviator can deliver the required ordnance on a target. Traditionally, as we have already remarked, the only difference between the two has
been that the AWI leads the No 3 division of aircraft in a squadron; however,
on occasion, if the QFI is senior to the AWI, then the third division may well
be led by him. I had voiced my preferences to Jock Tofts that I was keen to
go on the AWI course, and he told me he would see what he could do.

A couple of months before 831 Squadron decommissioned I received my
appointment to No 16 AWI Course, starting at HMS *Excellent*, where there
would be about eight weeks of Ground School followed by twelve weeks of
flying with 764 Squadron at Lossiemouth. Needless to say, I was overjoyed.
There would be six other officers as my course companions, Lieutenants
Northard, Moorcraft, Mears, Bland, Webster and Josselyn. Colin Moorcraft
had been with me on No 40 RN Flying Course and Bob Northard was with
me aboard *Indefatigable* in No 42. John Webster and Malcolm Bland I had
got to know at Ford after they had returned from Pensacola, having gained
their 'wings' with the US Navy. Lieutenant Josselyn came from 736 Squadron,
where he had been serving as Royal Australian Navy exchange instructor;
he was a former Sea Venom pilot, and he would return to Australia on
completing the course.

The course started in December 1957 but we had hardly begun schooling
when we all proceeded on two weeks' Christmas leave. My course had an
excellent set of instructors—Lieutenant Commanders Eve, Stewart and Miller,
the last the 'Schoolie'. On our return from leave the weather was bitter, and
although the wooden classrooms were, after a fashion, heated, we all had to
wear our greatcoats to stay warm and alert. The instruction was superb,
but for some reason I found it hard going. It should have been easy—the
aerodynamics, for example, were the same as those given in flying training—

but I struggled and only achieved a third class pass in the final examination. This upset me. My results at Whale Island more or less set the tone for the remainder of the course. What grated most was the fact that Malcolm Bland would go ashore partying, returning on board at about 0300 every night and barely staying awake throughout the day, and he then walked away with a first class pass. Perhaps I should have taken a leaf out of his book and done the same.

Looking back over my time at Whale Island, I can remember some very amusing moments. The funniest was during a mess dinner when a 'Long Gunnery' Course was being dined out, having just completed its two years of training. Throughout the dinner the Portsmouth Command Royal Marine Band were seated in the orchestra pit playing various tunes and melodies. Then the band played an oboe concerto and a young marine took the solo part. The 'Royals' have the best of all the military bands in Great Britain or, indeed, anywhere in the world—they are just superb—and this young Royal was absolute perfection, bringing the mess to its feet with cheering and clapping when he had completed his rendition. The poor lad was quite overcome by the adulation; his fellow musicians patted him on the back and then they sat down to complete the concerto.

After the dinner the tables were cleared and, as is the tradition in the Royal Navy, port or Madeira wine was passed for drinking the Sovereign's toast; I always drink Madeira because I find port wine too heavy. In the Royal Navy, it is traditional to toast the Sovereign sitting down—because, in days of yore, the old sailing battleships' deckheads were so low that one could not stand properly to attention. With a band present, when the Mess President announces 'The Queen' the national anthem is played, and on its completion all present raise their wine glasses, say 'The Queen' and take a sip of their wine. Once the 'toasting' is out of the way, the Mess President will make the initial speech. He will go on to say what a jolly good brother officer the mess is losing if he is leaving for another ship or, as in this instance, what a good group of officers it is that has just completed the course and how those officers will be a credit to the Fleet.

Unfortunately, he went on and on with his speech and everybody started to become restless. Suddenly Malcolm Bland blurted out, 'Why don't you shut up and sit down!' The resultant uproar can be imagined: 'I say, I say, I say!'; 'What rudeness!'; 'Who in hell are you?'; 'Sit down, sir!' Malcolm was so inebriated that he had by now slid under the table. He tried to regain his seat but the budding AWIs held him down until the mess had returned to normal. After the dinner and speeches the Executive Officer, who was the Mess President, banned him from the bar. The entire event placed rather a stigma on the aviators and most of us retired early, making our apologies for Malcolm's undignified behaviour.

Following the Ground School element of the course I was scheduled to join 764 Squadron in late January or early February 1958. Colin Moorcraft and Malcolm Bland left for Culdrose in order to complete their flying course in the Gannet anti-submarine aircraft, so at Lossiemouth the course was down to five fighter pilots, including me. At this time I still had my old

Morris Series E, and, loaded up with all my worldly possessions, including my flying kit, I set off for the north of Scotland. The weather was still bitterly cold and the going was slow because of the snow and ice, and consequently I arrived at South Queensferry too late to catch the last ferry, which was just pulling away as I arrived at the top of the loading ramp. I parked close to the sea wall out of the bitterly nor'easter blowing across the firth, wrapped my greatcoat about me and fell asleep across the front two seats. Missing that ferry was going to make me late at Lossiemouth, but Fate was about to take a hand in my future.

It was about 5 o'clock in the morning when I awoke to hear people shouting and a boat approaching from North Queensferry. I quickly bought a ticket and boarded the boat and within half an hour I was on my way again. Stopping at a roadside café for a bite to eat, I heard that during the night a severe blizzard had swept the whole of northern Scotland and that the western route via the A9 to Inverness, which I had intended taking, was virtually blocked with heavy drifts. I had no alternative but to drive to Aberdeen and take the A96 out of that city to Elgin; as it was the main northern route from Aberdeen to Inverness I quite expected it to be reasonably clear and an easy drive. The drive to Aberdeen went well but there was a great deal of snow about and it was late afternoon, with daylight failing, when I drove out of the city heading north-west for Elgin. I had probably gone about ten miles when I ran full tilt into a snowdrift, spun around and ended up on the inbound lane to Aberdeen. Fortunately the car was undamaged, but my nerves were not and so I drove carefully back into the city to find accommodation and somewhere to garage the car while I continued my journey by train. I decided to stay in the Railway Hotel next to the station. I telephoned Lossiemouth and spoke to David Mears so that he could let the Squadron know what had happened and that I would be arriving at Elgin at about 1000 the next day. He put me at ease and told me not to worry since the air station was snowed in and there was no flying because of the bad weather. He would tell the Course Officer what had happened to me.

Lieutenant Commander 'Paddy' McKeown, the CO of 764 Squadron, was a Northern Irishman from Belfast. He was a very likable man but a very aggressive aviator. The squadron was equipped with Sea Hawk F.4 fighters, Vampire T.22s and the new Hunter T.8 jet trainers. The AWI course instructor was Lieutenant Chris Mather, who tried hard to emulate his commanding officer. Following various briefings and lectures, we were all flying by the end of the week when the weather had improved and the runways had been cleared of snow.

Some people thought that I was something of an overcautious aviator, but I have always been a stickler for flight safety. Therefore, in view of the fact that none of us on course had flown for at least two months, I was surprised that we were let loose in the Sea Hawk after only a cockpit briefing and an emergencies check—I personally had not flown the aircraft for two years or more—but, then again, I suppose that we were considered to be above-average aviators who could be trusted to fly safely. Flying is rather like riding a bicycle: once the skills have been mastered they can be summoned up with little or no effort. After three familiarisation flights we all got down to the flying syllabus, the first part of which was target-tracking using the gyro gun sight. Our tracking, angles-off, ranging and closing speeds were all scrutinised by a group of WRNS Range Assessors. Although I had done gyro gun sight tracking in 831 Squadron, it had been very limited and no film had been taken of the gun sight pictures, so I did not have much idea of my ability or progress. My last real tracking exercises had been during OFS flying in 738 Squadron, and my standards were low compared with those of the other pilots on course, who had been flying the Sea Hawk or Sea Venom as a daily routine.

I have always been one of those people who responds to valid criticism. Here, once again, we had a relatively inexperienced instructor/course officer who was rarely constructive with his opinions. Chris Mather was a very capable aviator but extremely rough and gave little thought to those under his charge. For example, he might be leading a stream take-off of four Sea Hawk fighters but once airborne would wrap his aircraft into a hard turn, thus making it almost impossible for the other pilots to join up with him quickly. Consequently, all the other aircraft were strung out well astern of him at full throttle, desperately trying to catch up. He would be miles away before he thought about throttling back to allow his division to join up. As brother officers we all got along well together, but we did not see eye to eye on flying matters. Therefore, my progress on course remained virtually at a standstill and I became more and more unhappy about it. My colleagues tried to help me, telling me not to worry, but it was to no avail. The time came when I appeared before Paddy McKeown to have my progress reviewed, and he told me quite candidly that I was not going to make the required standard. My flying was very good in his opinion, which was nothing more than a reflection of what Chris had told him; however, I was not up to standard as regards tactical flying and weaponry. He then went on to say that he was recommending my removal from the AWI course and sending me south to do the QFI course at RAF Little Rissington, for which he thought I was suited much more as an aviator. When Chris had left his office he told me personally that he understood the real nature of the problem—a clash of personalities between Chris and me. I nodded in agreement and left to carve out a new future for myself.

I came away from Lossiemouth a downhearted and a defeated officer. The AWI course was considered the élite of the postgraduate flying courses and I had been found wanting and, in my eyes, of a lesser standard than my course contemporaries. My greatest ambition was to be a permanent General List officer, and the route to this was via the AWI. It was all a question of being a leader, and being an AWI gave one a much greater opportunity because of the position one held in a squadron. More AWIs were transferred to the General List than from any other sub-specialisation.

— 13 —

To be a QFI

THE NEXT QFI course was scheduled for July 1958. I proceeded on leave for a couple of weeks with instructions to join RNAS Yeovilton for an interview with Lieutenant Commander Ray Rawbone, who was the Fixed-Wing Staff Officer on Flag Officer Flying Training's staff. Ray had been the CO of 897 (Sea Hawk) Squadron during the Suez Crisis of 1956. After the interview, if I was successful, I was to join RNAS Culdrose for piston-engine aircraft refresher flying.

My interview with Ray Rawbone was a success. An outstanding officer who would eventually be elevated to Admiral's rank, he was quick to put me at my ease and make me feel comfortable. He requested that I give him a quick, ten-minute lecture on the hydraulic system of the Sea Hawk fighter. This went very well, and he was pleased with my effort, particularly as I had been given no notice. The QFI can attain four levels of standard or category: Category B2 is awarded on passing the Flying Instructor's Course; B1 is awarded if a rating of 80 per cent is achieved on the course or if three to six months' instructional duties have been carried out; A2 is awarded on completion of 800 hours of instruction, an all-day Ground School and a practical flying examination at Little Rissington; and A1 is awarded also after examination both on the ground and in the air. As an A1 flying instructor one's knowledge of air, space and flying is beyond question. Ray Rawbone was an A1 flying instructor and he had little or no time for AWIs, whom he considered a bunch of opinionated élitists!

Ray considered me good enough to go on the QFI course and I passed the interview. There was a perfectly good reason for the interview: several RN aviators had gone to Little Rissington and had failed the course quite early on. These aviators were totally unsuited to being instructors and had they been interviewed in the first instance and had their weaknesses exposed they would probably have saved the Navy a great deal of embarrassment. As soon as Ray called the Director of Naval Officers' Appointments (Executive) I was cleared to go on to Culdrose.

I was appointed to 849 Squadron Training Flight to fly Sea Balliol aircraft. The Balliol was a twin-seat, high-performance, piston-engine trainer fitted with a Rolls-Royce Merlin engine. The Training Flight was co-located with 797 Squadron on the eastern side of the airfield, although eventually the Flight would be co-located with 849 Squadron HQ Flight near the main entrance. Within a week Lieutenant John Webster—not the same John Webster who had been on my AWI course—had checked me out on the aircraft. John was an excellent instructor and had a feel for teaching people. We had many good flights together and I learnt a great deal about the Balliol, about flying and about instruction. Unfortunately John was to die some months later while I was at Little Rissington when his Gannet crashed on the approaches to the old naval air station at St Merryn, Cornwall, during an Air Day flying practice. I was devastated by the news because not only had I lost a good friend, the Navy had lost an excellent officer, instructor and aviator. A while later I was to learn that the other John Webster—he who had been on my AWI course—also died, in a Sea Venom crash at Yeovilton. It seemed strange that two officers with the same name had passed away within a short time of each other.

While at Culdrose I qualified to fly the Sea Devon twin-engine communications aircraft before the Balliol Flight left 797 Squadron. The Devon was a delightful aircraft and I spent many hours flying around western England on navigation exercises. I gained my 'Green' instrument rating on this aircraft as well as on the Balliol, although this rating was later to be a source of embarrassment to me.

Half way through my time at Culdrose, Lieutenant John de Winton joined as a newly qualified QFI and took over from John Webster. John de Winton and I flew together many times and on one occasion we were faced with a real emergency. We had been practising aerobatics for Culdrose's Air Day when we experienced an engine failure. I had just gone over the top of a loop when John 'chopped' the throttle on me to simulate an engine failure. I set the aircraft up for an engine-out approach to the duty runway at Culdrose. When the throttle was closed we were at 10,000 feet, and the standard practice with a piston engine was to 'gun' the throttle every 1,000 feet to prevent the sparking plugs from oiling up. On the first engine check I did not seem to obtain much response from the Merlin. At first I thought it was just my imagination, but when there was no response to my second attempt it was obvious that something was seriously wrong. I jabbed my colleague in the ribs. 'John, this is not a practice engine failure. This one is for *real!*' He took control and had exactly the same response that I had experienced and I called Culdrose tower to tell them. The tower acknowledged by transmitting 'Call when high downwind.' In retrospect, I am sure that they had not hoisted in that our emergency was for real.

John had been authorised as the Captain of the aircraft and he took control of the flying while I dealt with all the radio calls and the emergency procedures in the cockpit. As we approached downwind it became very obvious that, at our current rate of descent, we were not going to make the end of the runway. I then suggested to John that we turn in on finals half way downwind and land crosswind over the duty runway; otherwise we were going to crash. I informed the tower of our intentions, whereupon they promptly cleared a Sea Prince to land on the runway that we were about to cross! Neither of us could believe what we had just heard. I called the tower and asked them what they were doing just as our old Balliol thumped down inside the boundary fence with the Sea Prince approaching us on a steady bearing at about two o'clock. As I offered up three Hail Marys we streaked across the runway about ten yards in front of the Sea Prince, which was standing on its nose wheel making an emergency stop. The Balliol halted a few yards beyond the runway on the grass and we both exited quickly as the Duty Aircraft Inspections Officer drove up in a Land Rover. It did not take me long to let all concerned know what my feelings were concerning their professional standing. The Inspections Officer drove us back to 849 Squadron. The Balliol was towed away for examination and it was discovered that the fuel carburettor float valve had jammed, preventing any flow to the engine. Our rather heavy landing had dislodged the float, but the witness marks were still present for all to see. The carburettor was replaced and the aircraft continued to fly quite safely thereafter.

On another occasion I flew with Lieutenant David Bridger, who was one of the new Skyraider AEW pilots. David and I had known each other from Syerston days, when we had shared a dormitory cabin. His instrument rating was due for renewal, so I took him up for some simulated instrument flying practice. On the way back he removed his IF goggles and I told him to fly the aircraft around for a while and then carry out the landing back at Culdrose. However, as he made his final approach to the runway it became very obvious that he was undershooting, so I instructed him to apply some power to check his descent. When he realised that he was going to land on the grass threshold, well short of the runway, he suddenly rammed the throttle wide open. The Merlin being a very powerful engine, the aircraft entered a 'torque stall', that is, it started to rotate about the propeller rather than the other way round. The Balliol hit the grass with its right wheel and wing tip and bounced back into the air. I took control, cut the throttle and landed on all three wheels on the runway. 'What on earth were you trying to do David? Kill us both?' He muttered an apology and we taxied back into the aircraft dispersal with a slightly dented wing tip, which was soon beaten back into shape by the 'metal bashers'. This incident taught me one very important aspect about instructional flying: the instructor must never let aircraft control go too far before he himself takes over.

* * *

It was during my time at Culdrose that I was to meet the love of my life, May Peacock. May is a typical 'English rose': she has black hair, is well proportioned and has a petal-like complexion. She was serving in the WRNS as a stewardess in the wardroom. We quickly grew to love each other, and I can recall when I first saw her during my Wyvern diversion from *Ark Royal* that something important would come of our meeting each other. When I joined Culdrose for my refresher flying I had a picture of my girlfriend Joy Baker on my chest-of-drawers, but now, every day when I returned to my cabin, her picture was to be found lying face down. Eventually I discovered that it was May who was turning the photograph, trying to tell me to get get rid of it and that I was hers! I put the picture away in my drawer and our love grew by leaps and bounds.

During the summer of 1958 May was drafted to HMS *Rayleigh*, the new-entry training establishment at Torpoint on the western side of the harbour opposite Plymouth. I had also been reappointed to No 194 QFI Course at Little Rissington, commencing 21 July 1958. I was very reluctant to leave Cornwall since it took me away from May, and to make matters worse it was a glorious summer that year. Until I left we managed to see each other a great deal, but finally I had to pack my Morris Traveller, clean out my cabin and depart for my new military residence in Gloucestershire. On the way to Little Rissington I called in to see May at Torpoint, promising to come down for a weekend as soon as possible. I was saddened to leave Culdrose because I had made many new friends and, above all, I had met my future wife—although at that time no specific plans had been made regarding a wedding.

* * *

RAF Little Rissington was nothing less than the Air Force University of Flying. It was the RAF's task, laid down by an Act of Parliament, to produce flying instructors for all three Armed Forces. Each course consisted of officers from the three services, and from overseas nations as well. My course, No 194, consisted of British officers only, from the Royal Navy, Army and Royal Air Force. I had a naval companion with me, Lieutenant Martin Packhard, who had been back-classed to my course owing to a car accident. There are usually two naval aviators on each course so that they can keep each other company. The same routine was followed as at other RAF training schools: the course was divided into two watches, with Martin in 'A' Watch and me in 'B', the two alternating between flying and Ground School.

Martin had terrible trouble assimilating Ground School. He had been trained at NAS Pensacola, Florida, by men who had spent only two weeks at a training facility; after this extremely short period of tuition, these *ab initio* instructors were then let loose on unsuspecting students! Ground-school examinations in the US Navy consisted of multiple-answer papers, and anybody could achieve a 50 per cent pass with little or no effort. This method of tuition is very much standard throughout the United States and consequently it can, in my opinion, lead to poor understanding. I often used to spend an evening at Martin's home in Reading going through what he had been taught and 'cramming' him for the final ground-school examination—and, would you believe it, he came top of the course and I was almost at the bottom! Examinations always used to worry me deeply; I used to become very nervous about them and rarely did of my best, although as the years passed I managed to overcome this psychological barrier and turn in some first-class results.

The most important aspect of teaching is, probably, the ability to stand up in front of a group of students in order to impart knowledge. There is nothing more soul-destroying than standing on a platform in front of a sea of faces that are looking up at one and expecting something profound. My course had an excellent tutor, a RAFVR Flight Lieutenant who also lectured in aerodynamics at Bristol University. He was hard, and once one had been torn to pieces in front of the course one began to wonder whether one would ever be a qualified instructor, but he taught me and others on the course several important aspects about teaching: be thoroughly prepared, know the subject, speak with authority and purpose and above all remember that one is better informed than those under tuition. From that point on I never felt afraid of standing in front of any group of people to speak or lecture on any subject that I knew.

The QFI course started on 21 July 1958 and finished some sixteen weeks later on 15 November. It was divided into basic and advanced instructional training, plus Ground School, to which one-third of the time was given over. After six weeks' tuition in the Provost trainer, students either stayed for the remainder of the course on this aircraft, learning how to teach basic flying, or were moved across to another squadron or flight to be taught advanced flying on Vampire T.11s; Martin would stay on Provost aircraft while I went on to Vampires. All the officers on course were very experienced aviators and many had come from front-line tours where they had seen action, for example in the Yemen. Not one member of the course failed in any respect, and I would eventually meet many of them later on during my flying career. Our instructors were the best. I was allocated to Flight Sergeant John Webster for basic flying instruction—yet another John Webster although this one would, fortunately, pursue an active life into old age. He was thorough and taught me a great deal about how to handle students and how to teach them. He was of the breed of teachers that I call 'Old Dads': they know instinctively how to encourage, to praise and to extract the best from one's capabilities.

It was during one of my dual instructional rides with John Webster that I noticed that our Provost's engine was gradually losing power, as indicated by the boost gauge, to which he responded, quite casually, 'Oh don't worry. It will get us back on the ground.' It was a final landing, and it was probably one of my best in the aircraft. At the end of the landing I closed the throttle, then turned to clear the runway and 'gunned' the engine to get the aircraft moving again, but the engine stopped dead. John informed the tower, we climbed out and walked back to the training flight and a while later the aircraft was towed into the hangar. The engine was a write-off: one of the piston rods had broken and penetrated the casing, so it had to be returned for rebuild or salvage.

On another occasion, flying a Vampire with Flight Lieutenant Marsh, another student on course, I experienced a very dangerous incident. We were scheduled to do mutual tuition in which we 'pattered' to each other the aspects of 'clean' and 'dirty' stalling. We decided that I would go through the tuition sequence first. I covered the preliminaries of going through the aircraft and flying-area checks, then commenced the 'patter' sequence for a 'clean' stall, that is, a stall with undercarriage and flaps retracted. I brought the throttle back slowly, raising the aircraft's nose as the speed fell off to remain in level flight until the stall was reached. Suddenly, without any warning and at about 160 knots airspeed, the aircraft pitched nose-up and rolled violently to the right and entered a spin. I quickly recovered and climbed back up to 25,000 feet. We both looked at each other and said in unison, 'What happened there?' Marsh then had a go and exactly the same thing happened. Then I went into a 'dirty' stall with undercarriage and flaps fully down, but the effect was the same and the aircraft went into a right-handed spin at 130 knots. There was no doubt now that we had a dangerous machine on our hands. The tower was informed of the problem and we decided to make a fast, flapless approach, closing the throttle immediately the wheels had touched the runway. The landing went as planned and we taxied the aircraft back to the hangar to establish what was wrong with it.

This particular Vampire trainer had recently been in maintenance for major overhaul. Apart from the engine and airframe inspections, both wings had been stripped of all cellulose and fillers and cleaned down to bare metal. However, when the wings were refurbished their original shapes were not restored to the correct aerofoil cross-sections and consequently the right wing had a different shape from that of the left, causing it to stall earlier— i.e., at a much higher speed—than normal. This serious blunder on the part of maintenance could have led to a landing accident in which one or both pilots might have been killed. The evidence would have been lost in any fire and the accident would have been blamed on the pilots as 'pilot error'. The Flight Commander had the aircraft returned to the maintenance hangar to restore the wings to their correct shape. Whether any maintenance personnel were hauled over the coals for this gross negligence I do not know. When I asked the Flight Commander if he had found out anything further, he was very reluctant to speak. Personally, I would have had somebody's head on the chopping block.

* * *

The end of the course hove slowly into sight. While I had been home on weekend leave during October, I had called May and proposed marriage to her over the telephone. She had agreed to marry me and so we made provisional arrangements to wed on 27 December, during the 1958 Christmas leave. May had to make her request to the First Officer WRNS to be discharged from the Service for reasons of marriage. Time being so short and with a great deal to be done, we set about organising our wedding on the next weekend leave.

We both wanted to be married in St Mary's Church, Rye, a beautiful building which stands at the centre of this famous and historic Cinque Port. A meeting was arranged with the vicar, the Reverend Oscar Brooks, to discuss the wedding day and the time of marriage. It was agreed that we could be married at 2.30 p.m. on the 27th, the day after Boxing Day. May no longer had a family home of her own, both her parents having long since passed away, and so she had to change her address to one in Rye, residing officially at the home of Guv and Aunt Esse Diaper, the parents of my best man, Donald. Oscar Brooks gave May and I the usual 'pep talk' about the state of matrimony and we then visited the Flushing Inn Hotel, next to the church, to arrange our wedding breakfast. That done, we left and went to the Mermaid Inn for a beer and then drove home to Camber.

*　*　*

On my graduation from CFS, a combined mess dinner was held both for my course and for the retiring Commandant of the School. It was known that the Commandant was something of a pyromaniac in his early days, so the organisers of the dinner decided to give the retiring officer an evening to remember. They called in an ordnance expert from RAF Valley and he 'mined' both the huge flower bowl in front of the guest of honour and the flower bowl suspended below the orchestra gallery. It was arranged that he would operate a switch and set off a tiny amount of explosive, which would throw the flowers into the air without causing any injuries.

The dinner was a sumptuous affair with the station band playing some wonderful melodies high up in the gallery. Once the Loyal Toast had been made the speeches began and, finally, the retiring Commandant was invited to stand and give his outgoing address. As he rose, everybody in the mess roared 'Up! Up! Up!' until he finally climbed and stood on the table with the bowl of flowers just in front of him. As he started his speech, a nod was given to the ordnance man and the latter pressed the switch. There was a dull thud and the flowers shot up into the air to fall over our gallant Commandant. He almost collapsed with laughter. When he had recovered he went on to make a splendid farewell speech which, when it had finished, brought everybody to their feet with cheering, whistling and clapping. This was an officer and gentleman who was so well liked that he was going to be a great loss to the RAF. Why he was not selected for higher rank I will never know: he was the sort of leader any service could ill afford to lose.

At the time of dining out the retiring Commandant, the new Commandant was also dined into the mess, his name Air Commodore Whitworth. He did not like what he had witnessed and cleared the 'upper deck' of all officers the following day, mustering them in the anteroom of the Officers' Mess. He gave us all hell for what he called outrageous behaviour at the previous night's mess dinner. He was referring to the flower prank, which he considered most inappropriate, and unbecoming of officers. The next day he addressed my course and made no bones about the fact that he could not understand why there were two naval officers on course at CFS. Both Martin Packhard and I were incensed by his observation and almost walked out of the room. None of us could fathom why he had made such a remark and could only assume that, as he had been in the Royal Naval Air Service prior to the formation of the RAF, something must have happened to sour his opinion of the Navy. Our course chums, especially the RAF officers, apologised profusely and asked us to forget about it. Whitworth was not to stay long at CFS for within eighteen months he had been pensioned off.

Martin graduated with a QFI Category B1 and was appointed to basic flying tuition at RAF Linton-on-Ouse. I managed to obtain a B2 and was appointed to 738 Squadron at Lossiemouth. Flight Lieutenant Peter Lewis, who had become a close friend while on the course with me and had been an ADC to an Air Marshal before taking the course, was appointed to RAF Dyce at Aberdeen as the new OC of the Aberdeen University Air Squadron, teaching university students to fly de Havilland Chipmunks as an encouragement for them to join the Air Force as a career. After May and I had married, we would often visit the Lewises at Dyce.

I loaded my new Morris Minor Traveller with my worldly belongings and set forth for my new appointment. As I drove north I wondered what might be in store for me. It was odd that I was going back to the squadron in which I had flown my OFS course some three to four years previously; now I was returning to teach others those aspects of naval aviation that I had been taught years ago. I was also wondering what the Squadron would be like now that it was equipped with Sea Venom, Vampire and Meteor aircraft under the command of an officer I had neither met nor heard of during my time in the Fleet Air Arm.

— 14 —

Instructor

AUTUMN had truly established itself when I arrived in Morayshire. The days were cold, short and bleak, though the weather was good. Storms do blow in off the Atlantic at this time of the year, but they quickly pass through, leaving a bitter nor'wester. Darkness prevails until about 9 or 10 a.m. and night settles in at about 3.30 p.m.

Lieutenant Commander 'Jock' McCandless, a red-headed officer with a red goatee beard, commanded 738 Squadron and his Senior Pilot was Lieutenant Commander Brown, another naval aviator whom I had never met. Jock was the chairman of the Naval Caravan Association at Lossiemouth and lived with his wife in a large caravan home at Milltown airfield, the satellite to Lossiemouth. The Senior Pilot was a tall and rather serious man but his time in the Squadron would soon be up and early in 1959 he would be relieved by Lieutenant Commander Kenny Kemp, an old friend. Kenny would not stay long in the squadron and would eventually move back to Yeovilton as the CO of a Sea Vixen squadron. His relief would be Lieutenant Jimmy Moore. In the New Year of 1959 I became the new Staff Officer, taking over from Lieutenant Ron McClean; it seemed that my reputation had preceded me! There were two Tactical Instructors, Lieutenant Alfie Wigg from my old school at Rye, and Flight Lieutenant Ray Rae. Lieutenant Eddie Cope, who was just about to complete his AWI course in 764 Squadron, would soon join as the Squadron AWI, and another QFI, Lieutenant Peter Sheppard, would join from Linton-on-Ouse. At the end of the Instructors' Crew Room was the Range Assessing Office, which was run by PO WRNS Sally Howells. Sally was to remain a close friend of my family for over forty years until she died from cancer on 1 May 1999.

The Squadron was equipped with twelve Sea Venom FAW Mk 21 night-fighter jets, four Vampire T.22 trainers and a couple Meteor of Mk 7 twin-engine jet trainers. Our sister squadron, 736, was equipped with a similar number of Sea Hawk fighters and Vampire trainers but no Meteors. The newly trained pilots arriving from Linton-on-Ouse were usually split equally into day- and night-fighter OFS courses. The night-fighter pilots would stay with 738 and the day-fighter men would go to 736 Squadron. Within a year

131

736 Squadron would become the Scimitar fighter OFS, while at Yeovilton 766 Squadron would become the Sea Vixen OFS. 738 Squadron would lose its Sea Venoms and become an all-Sea Hawk squadron and be known as OFS Part 1, while 736 and 766 Squadrons would be known as OFS Part 2. Once the newly trained pilots had completed OFS Part 1, they would move over to 764 Squadron to complete a swept-wing conversion course prior to going on to either the Scimitar or the Sea Vixen OFS Part 2.

As soon as I had settled in I called upon the Chief Flying Instructor, Lieutenant Commander Al Fyffe, and Commander (Air), Commander Ian Campbell. Al was also in the throes of moving on to a new appointment, and his relief would be Lieutenant Commander Ivan Brown. As soon as Al spotted in my logbook that I was qualified on twins and also held a current twin 'Green' instrument rating, he nominated me as the air station's communications pilot. This meant that I had to check out in the station's old Dominie as quickly as possible, and my first weekend at Lossiemouth was therefore spent familiarising myself with, and qualifying myself on, the aircraft. 'Dominie' was the Navy's name for the de Havilland Rapide, a twin-engine biplane constructed essentially of wood and canvas. It was a delightful aeroplane to fly, cruising at about 90 knots on its two Gypsy Queen inline engines, with two fixed-pitch propellers. It had a fixed undercarriage faired into the engine nacelles and there was sufficient room in the fuselage cabin for about seven or eight passengers.

After having qualified in the Dominie over the weekend, my first task was to transport some ordnance CPOs from 807 Squadron to the West Freugh Range in Ayrshire. 807 (Scimitar) Squadron was conducting a 2,000-pound bombing trial on the range, and these maintenance specialists were required to carry out some aircraft armament work and modifications. Late on Sunday a cold front had passed through Lossiemouth, leaving us in a fresh and blustery north-westerly air stream. I checked with the Meteorological Office and I was not very happy about the weather prevailing over the west coast of Scotland and south to West Freugh. The eastern half of Scotland had good weather all the way to Edinburgh, so I chose that route, via the Firth of Forth. It was very important that these maintenance men arrived at their destination early.

My entry height into the bad weather south-west of Edinburgh was 6,000 feet, and it did not take long for conditions to become turbulent. Visibility was zero with heavy snow which was beginning to blow in through the sliding cockpit window and pile up over my right knee and the radio control box. While at CFS I had read a book describing how a pilot of yore had had to move his throttle constantly to prevent his carburettor from icing up. The Dominie did not have anti-icing on either of its engine carburettors, so I kept moving the throttles to prevent any ice from forming in the air intakes and the two Gypsy Queens continued to purr along beautifully. I tried calling Scottish Air Traffic Control but had no success.

I had been airborne for about an hour and a half when someone opened the cockpit door to ask how much longer we were going to be airborne before landing. It was obvious that my passengers were becoming very nervous, and when he saw the snow he shut the door very quickly and returned to his seat. Within minutes, however, the old Dominie popped out of the clouds into a clear patch right above West Freugh. I could not believe that my navigation had been so good, and even now I feel that it was more a matter of luck than of judgement. I closed the throttles, quickly descended to circuit height and landed without further ado. I apologised to the passengers for the terrible weather on the last leg of the flight and they responded by saying that they knew they were in good hands. After 807 Squadron personnel had turned the aircraft around and serviced her I went over to the Officers' Mess for lunch.

Lunch was nearly over when I checked into the dining room. In view of the fact that I was wearing my immersion suit, I sat by myself at the far end of a table so as not to annoy anyone. I had hardly started on my soup when an RAF Squadron Leader came up to me.

'You can't dine in here dressed like that old boy,' he advised.

I told him that I was visiting and that at RNAS Lossiemouth we allowed Air Force officers into the mess wearing flying overalls.

'Sorry old boy, not allowed here. I will lend you some clothing if you wish.'

'No thank you,' was my response. 'I will have to forego my lunch and fly back to Lossie on an empty stomach.'

As I was getting up to leave, Lieutenant Commander Paul Millett appeared on the scene and said that it was perfectly all right for me to dine in my flying kit. The Squadron Leader left in rather a huff; Paul, I later found out, was the Mess President.

After my excellent lunch, I filed my flight plan back to Lossiemouth and obtained a weather forecast, which stated that the conditions were essentially fair all the way back to Morayshire though with occasional isolated thunderstorms over the highlands. As I climbed away from West Freugh I could see ahead of me one of those isolated storms. I flew through the eastern edge of it and encountered heavy hail that sounded like machine-gun bullets hitting the aeroplane. I quite expected the canvas covering over the fuselage and wings to be stripped off, but I was through before I realised it and heading north-east towards Aberdeen in beautifully clear skies. It was just as well that I was wearing my immersion suit, because the cockpit was bitterly cold and there was no heating from the engines. The wind was quite strong, which delayed my progress, and by the time I had raised Lossiemouth on the radio darkness was fast closing in for the night. When I arrived I made my one and only night landing in the Dominie.

I did not mind the occasional flight in the Dominie but I could see myself becoming the air station's hack pilot. The next morning, therefore, I discussed things Jock McCandless and Al Fyffe and made it quite clear that my job at Lossiemouth was that of a flying instructor and not a communications pilot. They both received the message, the CO of the Station Flight quickly checked himself out in the Dominie and I was off the hook.

Much of my early work in 738 Squadron involved giving students dual checks and instrument flying in the Vampire T.22. I also gave flight instruction to senior officers who were moving on to other flying appointments. On 11

December 1958 I flew the Sea Venom FAW Mk 21 for the first time. It was a very pleasant aircraft to fly and was really nothing more than a powerful Vampire. Soon I was leading young OFS students on tactical sorties, teaching them air tactics and weapon exercises.

* * *

Christmas was now approaching and I had to arrange accommodation for myself and May on our return to Lossiemouth immediately after leave. I managed to secure rooms on the western side of the town. The house was owned by Captain and Mrs Souter, he a retired Merchant Navy officer and both of them very dour in their approach to life. They had no children and I suppose that this was the main cause for them appearing so stern and unable to understand young people. They did have one young relative who lived at Tobermory on the western side of Scotland, and I suspect that she inherited everything when they passed away. Wedding invitations were distributed around the Squadron and posted on the wardroom notice board. However, I did not expect anybody to drive south and attend.

Rye itself is built high upon a sandstone nodule rising up out of the flood plains of east Sussex and Kent. Right at the very top of this rock stands the church, which can be seen for miles around and from well out to sea in the English Channel. On most days the flag of St George is fluttering from the main tower, telling all that this is England. On the northern side of the tower is a very large clock similar to Big Ben at the Houses of Parliament in London and on either side of the clockface are a pair of golden cherubs with hammers to strike the quarter bells throughout the day and night. Inside the nave, a huge pendulum sweeps majestically cross the church in a fifty-foot arc. One could not have chosen a better House of God for a wedding.

Leave started in the third week of December, and May until then had been staying with either her sister Nancy at Mallerstang, Westmoreland, or her Aunt Mary at Easingwold, Yorkshire. We had agreed that I would pick her up at Darlington railway station during the evening. Although I managed to start off early, the roads were very busy with traffic all the way south to Edinburgh and beyond and I did not arrive at Darlington until 11.00 p.m. Poor May was beside herself with worry, wondering what had happened to me. She was waiting outside the station, which had by then been closed for the night, when suddenly I appeared out of the darkness. We had a good cuddle, threw her luggage into the back of the Traveller and set off south. A short time later we managed to find bed and breakfast accommodation and we fell into our beds and were soon asleep. We were up early, had a sumptuous breakfast and were quickly on our way.

* * *

Christmas was like all family Christmases but May and I were tied up much of the time making final arrangements for our wedding. The night before the wedding I went 'on the town' with my best man and had more jars of beer than were good for me. Don Diaper was ex Merchant Navy, and like me he could put a few pints away, but this evening we drank more than our fill and consequently were not so steady the following day. Somehow Don and I managed to make the church on time by 2.00 p.m. May finally arrived looking radiant and beautiful on the arm of Lieutenant David Cooke, who would be giving her away. After the ceremony we moved to the vestry to sign the Register, and then we all went next door for the reception in the Flushing Inn. After the speeches and toasts May and I quietly slipped away, changed and made a dash with our cases to the Traveller. By the time we had locked ourselves in, Uncle Will and cousins Brian, Malcolm, Roy and Alan had surrounded the car. As soon as I let the clutch in to drive away they lifted the vehicle off the ground, but finally we drove off down the High Street with the usual rattle of tin cans behind us.

Not many leave days remained so we decided to spend a very short, two-day honeymoon at the Two Sawyers country club at Pett, of which I was a member. After a couple of hours' rest we went down for dinner and a drink in the bar, only to discover that all our friends had moved over from the inn to the club in order to continue the party complete with a band. When we entered the bar a great cheer went up; the evening was off to a good start and it became rowdier and rowdier as it progressed. Finally, at about 2.00 in the morning, May and I retired, having reached the limit of our endurance. After our short honeymoon May and I returned to Camber, collected our belongings and set forth for Scotland.

* * *

Christmas leave finished on 2 January 1959 and I was soon back in the thick of giving tuition, my first flight being a dual check for Lieutenant Larry Hallett. The very next day I went down with a severe case of bronchitis and asthma. What a way to start a marriage and a new job! To make matters worse, the weather had turned very nasty, with heavy snow and blizzards sweeping the whole of northern Scotland. My illness became so serious that I had to be turned in at the air station Sickbay for about ten days. Poor May was by herself, in a strange house and not really knowing any friends, but we did manage to see each other daily in the Sickbay and she stayed for several hours on each visit.

Early in the New Year the Senior Pilot, Lieutenant Commander Brown, left the Squadron for another appointment and his position was taken by Kenny Kemp, a large and jovial officer with jet black hair. Because I was temporarily grounded, it was decided that I would take over the Staff Officer's job. Kenny and I shared the same office, sitting opposite one another, with a hatch for direct access to the Squadron CO. Another two QFIs joined the Squadron, Lieutenants Peter Sheppard and David Bridger. Including Roy Noyes, who had joined earlier, there were now four QFIs in the Squadron, although of course for the time being I was *hors de combat*. Kenny had not been with us very long when he was reappointed to Sea Vixens, and Roy Noyes took over temporarily as the Senior Pilot.

At about this time 764 Squadron's task of giving swept-wing conversion courses was really getting under way for OFS pilots who had completed their course in 738 Squadron. It was essential, therefore, that 764 had another QFI, and Dave Bridger was selected to fill the appointment. This made Roy Noyes very upset: David did not have any real jet experience, and his swept-wing flying experience, apart from the odd flight at CFS in a Hunter, was virtually non-existent. Despite Roy's protestations, David went across to 764 Squadron and did an extremely good job as an instructor.

I settled down to my new duties and decided to have a thorough 'huck out' of the Staff Office. The filing cabinet was an utter mess and there were students' reports going back years and including those from Pensacola, Florida. Where possible I forwarded the US Navy reports on to their owners, and after I had reorganised things the Squadron had a well-run Staff Office in which the CO, SP or other instructors could find orders, papers and reports easily and quickly.

Peter Sheppard had been teaching on Vampire T.11s—virtually identical to T.22s—at Linton-on-Ouse and bringing RN students up to 'wings' standard. He was a very likable officer and a gentleman, with an easy-going manner, but above all he was a superb instructor. He was also a first-class aerobatic pilot, indeed the smoothest that I, or anyone else for that matter, have seen. Even May came into the Squadron one day and asked who was carrying out the aerobatics in the Sea Venom. He just slipped from one manoeuvre into the next with the grace and ease of a ballet dancer.

Once I was declared fit to fly again Peter took me up on a dual check and then I was back in the thick of the workload. It was about this time that 738 Squadron received a dozen Indian Navy pilots for conversion to the Sea Hawk fighter. The Indians had bought one of our old light fleet carriers* and were also buying Sea Hawks to equip it and wanted us to train them. It had been agreed that the Royal Navy would give the Indian pilots a dual check before they were let loose in the aircraft, and I was given the task of assessing their AWI. From his logbook it was apparent that he had flown very little during the past year, and what hours he had put in had been in single-seat Vampires. I briefed him and we took off for a climb to 25,000 feet for general handling, stalling and dummy landing circuits. Every time he entered finals on his circuits he promptly entered a spin, and despite my efforts I could not get him to fly the jet safely.

After landing and debrief I went to see both the CO and SP to discuss this particular pilot. I pulled no punches, reporting that he was unsafe to continue flying and in my opinion should be given at least ten more hours' tuition. The CO instructed me to write up my report in his folder, which I did, underlining everything in red. The CFI was informed and he flew with the officer at no cost to the Indian Navy. When he came into my office after the flight he asked for the student's folder and a red pen and wrote almost the same comments as I had. After much haranguing between the RN and IN it

* This was *Vikrant*, formerly HMS *Hercules*. She was not decommissioned from the Indian Navy until 1997 and is now preserved at Bombay as a museum ship. See also Chapter 33.

136

was finally agreed that the young Indian Navy Lieutenant be given an additional ten hours of instruction. When the IN pilots had all converted to the Sea Hawk, together with their squadron and new aircraft they moved to RNAS Brawdy, where they carried out their work-up before returning to India.

The Fleet Air Arm desperately needed pilots for the front-line squadrons but the pilots coming from Linton-on-Ouse were barely of average standard. Two of my students would later die in separate jet crashes. The first, a GL Lieutenant, was sent to Yeovilton to fly Sea Venom night fighters even though I stated quite categorically that his instrument flying was below par for a night-fighter pilot. I was overruled—with disastrous consequences. While going through his night-fighter OFS at Yeovilton he was diverted to RAF Lyneham on account of bad weather. He became disorientated while making an instrument approach into that airfield and crashed, killing both himself and his young midshipman observer. I was extremely upset by these deaths and pushed the point at the next Saturday-morning instructors' meeting that we send only pilots with above-average instrument flying skills to the night-fighter course. The second student, who died within a few weeks of joining his Scimitar front-line squadron in the Far East, should not have been flying the aircraft because he was far too tall. One of his aircraft's engines caught fire, necessitating his ejection. Unfortunately, because of his very long legs, he severely damaged them as he left the cockpit and the resulting traumas brought about his death. We all knew that he was far too tall because he had to fly the Meteor instead of the Vampire when practising instrument flying. How on earth he managed to complete the flying course at Linton-on-Ouse without anybody raising the question of his height is a mystery, but he did. After this accident and a similar one to an MTP at Fleetlands while test-flying a Sea Hawk fighter, the Navy tightened up its requirements concerning height and leg length so that there would be no more accidents of this nature. All of us, including instructors, had to report to the Sickbay to be measured and for a while the FAA experienced a dearth of pilots in the fighter world, but it was quickly overcome by moving people around among Gannets, helicopters and fighters.

Jock McCandless left 738 Squadron in July 1959 for another appointment and Lieutenant Commander Derek Monsell, a night-fighter pilot, became the new Squadron Commanding Officer. Derek was one of the 'Terrible Twins', the other being Lieutenant Commander 'Jock' Mancais, who became the new Commanding Officer of 736 (Scimitar) Squadron. These two officers had been through the same AWI course and had earned reputations for being a couple of tearaways and drinking buddies. They had served more or less together in both ships and sister squadrons, and now they were together again at Lossiemouth.

When Jock McCandless left, the Squadron officers threw a dinner party for him and his wife. May took on the task of preparing the menu, and together with the wardroom Chief Cook (whom she had known for a long time) produced one of the finest dinners that I and my brother officers and their wives have ever been served. There was a delicious light soup, followed by a fish dish, *filet mignon* steaks and a wonderful sweet of fresh fruits, jellies and cream, all rounded off with fruit and coffee. Delightful white and red wines from France completed the meal. It was all of May's planning, and as a result she established herself in the Squadron as a *connaisseuse* of cuisine.

With the arrival of Derek Monsell there was quite a change in the Squadron's character. He was a very lively individual whereas Jock was a dour, quiet Scot. Throughout the whole of Jock's tenure he had led his squadron well and achieved his goal of training pilots for the front line; above all, this had been done safely and free from accident. This was all about to change.

In addition to Derek, the Squadron also received a new Senior Pilot, Lieutenant Jimmy Moore. Within a few weeks of Derek's taking command the Squadron had its first accident for a very long time. Derek was making a 'pairs' take-off from the main runway when his wing man, Lieutenant Hallam, hit the ground with his starboard wing tip, cartwheeled and exploded. Poor young Hallam was killed instantly. We all stood outside the crew room absolutely choked to the core, not believing what had happened as the smoke from the fireball billowed into the sky.

Jimmy Moore rushed across the airfield but there was little that he could do. Nobody really ever knew what had happened, except that the hapless youngster may have turned too quickly on take-off and at too low an altitude to move into battle formation. However, he may have been too close to Derek, entered his slipstream, rocked and over-corrected, causing his wing tip to strike the ground. Derek had no idea what had happened until the tower called him and said his No 2 had crashed just after lift-off. It was an extremely sad day for the Squadron, which had lost a very likable young pilot and officer.

A few weeks later the Squadron lost another Sea Venom just after take-off. The pilot this time was a young Royal Australian Navy man, Sub Lieutenant Franklin. Franklin was the No 4 in a stream take-off and was cutting the corner to catch up with his leader, Flight Lieutenant Rae. As he was staying low and turning left, Rae called a radio frequency change. The radio control box was between the seats in the Sea Venom and would normally be operated by the observer, but when flying solo one had to reach across and look down to make sure that the correct selection was made. As Franklin was doing this, at that instant, his port wing hit a high-tension power cable and was torn off. His aircraft rolled sharply to the left and impacted with a ridge the right way up. The bottom was torn out of the cockpit and Franklin's ejection seat fired, but with a low velocity. His seat, with him still strapped in it, hit various bushes and small trees and ended up in bracken. He was severely injured. The aircraft flew on a short distance and exploded. Some forestry workers nearby rushed over and gave first aid while waiting for an ambulance but the air station helicopter was quickly on the scene and Franklin was airlifted to Dr Gray's Hospital in Elgin.

Flight Lieutenant Rae was beside himself when he landed: he simply could not understand what had happened. Some say he called the radio channel change too soon, but this was nonsense. The student pilot was keen to catch up with his leader and, sitting on the left side of the cockpit, and in a bank looking up at his leader, he would not have seen the power cables until it was too late. In addition, he happened to glance down at a critical moment, just as he was approaching the cables: his fate was sealed. It was an accident arising from inexperience, and one that many pundits would immediately label 'pilot error', but actually there were several factors, and if any one of these factors had been removed the accident might not have happened.

Young Franklin had still been conscious when help arrived, but he was to spend the next eighteen months in hospital recovering from his injuries and unfortunately he was left a cripple. When he was fit enough he returned to Australia, and I sincerely hope that he managed to find a new career in which he excelled and made a good living.

On 13 July 1959 I flew south to RAF Manston to collect the CFI, Lieutenant Commander Ivan Brown. I did not really want to make the flight as I had many other things to do in the Squadron; moreover, I had a gut feeling that something was going to happen. The flight south was uneventful, and after landing I taxied into Station Flight but none of the RAF personnel knew anything about turning a Vampire T.22 around. Thus I had to do my own refuelling and aircraft inspection and sign the maintenance logbook off. Ivan was late and we finally took off for Lossiemouth again. He decided to sit in the right-hand seat and make the take-off while I made all the radio calls and operated the systems. About half way along the runway the engine fire warning light came on. I pointed it out to him, at the same time asking if he wanted me to jettison the drop tanks before he turned back to do a downwind landing with the engine shut down. He said no to the drop tanks being jettisoned, so we turned and I kept the jet running until we were lined up for landing, and then I stopcocked the engine by turning the HP pump off. Ivan touched down at about 160 knots and I yelled at him to watch out for the painters who had walked on to the runway with their backs to us. They did not hear us coming and as we shot past them they dropped their pots in fright. A few seconds later all three tyres burst and we were now proceeding on oleo stubs. I could see the end of the runway coming up fast. Traffic was flowing on the Ramsgate–Deal road and another aircraft/car accident was in prospect; only a couple of weeks beforehand a US Air Force F-84 had careered off the end of the runway, crossed the road and collided with a car, killing the occupants. However, as we left the runway into the overshoot we ran into a potato field and our oleos dug into soft earth, pulling us up as if by a carrier's arrester wire. As I evacuated the jet an RAF fire truck sprayed me with foam and for the remainder of the day I stank to high heaven. Ivan disappeared and travelled back by train, and eventually a Meteor T.7 arrived from Lossiemouth to pick me up. What amazed me most of all was that no RAF officer offered me a change of clothes or even enquired how I was feeling. Extraordinary!

The FAA Aircraft Accident Investigation Unit inspected the jet and it was established that the fire warning had been a spurious indication. I must admit that I suspected as much, because as we turned finals I could see no trail of smoke or sparks. It was an interesting day and I learnt a lesson: one should believe one's gut feelings!

The Squadron was to lose another Sea Venom fighter during night flying. The pilot, Sub Lieutenant Bleakley, took off on a solo exercise and disappeared without trace. As he left the airfield circuit he was observed turning to starboard, but as he called changing radio channels to 'Approach' he disappeared from view in the overcast. He did not check in on the approach channel, and after repeated calls and no trace on radar he was posted as missing. The young Wren working the approach radio channel had to be relieved of duty as she became very distraught, fearing the worst. She and young Bleakley had been seeing each other quite often, and her fears were soon to be realised.

It was about 0300 when a duty civilian driver from the base knocked on my caravan bedroom window requesting that I report for duty in the tower briefing room at 0500. He then informed me that one of our Venoms had gone missing and an air search would commence at dawn. I got out of bed and May cooked me a quick breakfast while I bathed, shaved and climbed into clean clothes. By 0430 I was on my way into Lossiemouth. All the 738 Squadron aircrew mustered in the tower briefing room at 0500 and we were given the details of what had transpired the previous evening. All available aircraft would fly with half a mile between each, in line abreast northwards towards the Orkney Islands. When east of the Orkneys each pilot would turn 180 degrees, moving over half a mile, then fly due south to the Morayshire coastline. Then all aircraft would turn back north again, repeating the search and ensuring that the same piece of sea was covered several times over. After an hour at low level most of the aircraft were running short of fuel and had to return to base. Another search was then made to the west of Lossie and up to the Orkneys, covering that portion of the sea off Ross and Cromarty. Once again a complete blank was drawn: there was no sign of fuel or wreckage. Most of the pilots were by now exhausted and they were stood down.

Early in the afternoon a message was received from two Shackletons out of RAF Kinloss, just to the west of Lossie, that a SARBE emergency beacon transmission had been picked up west of Inverness in the Highlands. HMS *Hermes* was in the Moray Firth at the time, and a flight of her helicopters was disembarked to conduct a search of the area west of Inverness while Lieutenants Dave Howard and Neville Atkinson took off in Sea Hawks to home in on the SARBE transmission at about 10,000 feet. David and Neville crossed each other but could see nothing on the ground. Lossiemouth's SAR helicopter was despatched to the pinpointed location and also found nothing. The SAR pilot, while trying to relocate his helicopter because one wheel had sunk into the soft ground, rolled over and crashed on his side as he attempted to lift off. He was not wearing his 'bone dome' at the time and received severe head injuries, which grounded him for several weeks, and in addition Lossie lost its SAR helicopter. The SARBE transmissions were finally assumed to be false and probably came from a section testing SARBE safety equipment. At the end of the day it was decided to call off the search and Bleakley was posted as missing, presumed dead.

About ten days later aircraft wreckage was washed ashore near Banff on the north-east coast of Scotland. This wreckage came from a Sea Venom, and by plotting back the time and tidal flow the possible location of the crash site was established as being about five miles east of Wick. This correlated with the general direction in which the aircraft was seen to turn after take-off. It was considered that Bleakley had experienced some sort of failure and whilst he was dealing with it, or became disorientated, had flown into the sea. He was a good and promising young officer who could have had a fine future, but it was not to be. We all felt very saddened by his mysterious disappearance and loss.

* * *

The following year, during June 1960, I converted to the Hunter T.8 jet trainer. My instructor was Lieutenant Colin Caspard. Exactly a month later I converted to the Scimitar fighter and carried out my first ever inflight re-fuelling, from a Sea Vixen tanker aircraft. At about this time 738 Squadron changed its aircraft to Sea Hawk fighters and 736 became an all-Scimitar unit. It was after 738 had converted to Sea Hawk fighters that Derek Monsell was to experience his fourth squadron accident. He had briefed two newly trained pilots on formation flying in the Sea Hawk, and on their way back to the airfield these two youngsters collided and hit the silk. In the RAF, the Nos 2 and 3 pilots of a formation of three aircraft fly the opposite way round compared to Royal Navy practice: in the Navy, odd numbers always fly to starboard and even numbers to port, thus No 2 flies on the leader's left side while the No 3 flies on the right. As Derek's flight was returning to Lossie-mouth he instructed his No 2 to transfer to the right-hand side for the run into the break over the duty runway in starboard echelon. The No 2 pilot should have gone outboard of No 3 but instead he attempted to squeeze in between the leader and No 3, with disastrous consequences. Derek did not see exactly what happened because he was in a left-hand turn and banking away from his students. However, he felt what he thought was a bump and drew the conclusion that he had been hit by one of them. When he could not raise them on the radio he was even more convinced that he had collided and requested the tower that he fly by for an inspection. What he actually felt was the turbulence from the aircraft whose pilot was trying to squeeze in between him and No 3. The tower informed him that two aircraft had crashed in the sea north-east of Lossiemouth harbour and that the pilots had ejected safely.

This accident was so bizarre that one found it hard to believe that it had really taken place. Poor Derek walked into the Squadron twittering like a bird, totally unable to comprehend what had happened: 'All I did was instruct my No 2 to change to the starboard side of the formation and into starboard echelon. How on earth could that cause a collision?' When the two rescued pilots returned to the Squadron and related what had taken place we all stood there dumbfounded, not really believing what we were hearing. Both pilots' aircraft had immediately spun after the collision and the two men had waited until the jets were upside down before firing their ejection seats. This allowed for the aircraft's rotation and ensured that they were the right way up as the seats left the cockpits; in view of the low altitude, had they fired their seats right side up they may well had left the cockpit upside down and hit the sea before their parachutes had deployed. They were very lucky.

Before all the Sea Venoms were replaced with Sea Hawk fighters another Sea Venom accident would occur, this time with an instructor at the controls. Lieutenant Charles Manning had joined 738 Squadron as a QFI and would eventually be my relief. While taking off in a 'pairs' formation with Jimmy Moore, the Senior Pilot, with snow piled high on either side of the runway, the formation drifted right. Charles hit the right-hand snow bank, his right undercarriage was ripped off and he spun off the runway in a cloud of white, coming to a halt facing the wrong way round. Charles was, fortunately, unhurt, but he was severely shaken and the aircraft was a write-off.

Derek's final squadron accident involved yet another Sea Venom and an OFS pilot. Lieutenant Arthur Stewart was making a 'pairs' Ground Controlled Approach to the main runway when his student suddenly disappeared from his right wing tip. He broke out of cloud at about 1,200 feet above sea level but there was no sign of his student nor of his aircraft. No radio contact could be made with the student, so Arthur reversed course and flew back along his approach path. He could find neither wreckage nor fuel slick, indeed nothing to indicate what had happened. The SAR helicopter and Lossiemouth lifeboat joined in the search but they also drew a blank. It was a complete mystery, and the only conclusion was that during a radio channel change the young student, who was also an engineer officer, had become disorientated and spun into the sea. What astonished everybody was the fact that no wing-tip fuel tanks were seen floating in the sea, so the aircraft must have entered the water at an extremely steep angle, like a bomb, and not broken up on impact. Arthur was very upset. We put his mind at rest by telling him that it was not his fault; he had done everything according to the book. The student pilot must have looked away at a critical moment, glanced back to see that his leader had vanished into the cloud and become disorientated while trying to sort out his predicament. His lack of experience was, sadly, his undoing and cost him his life.

My time in 738 Squadron was fast coming to an end. I was hoping for an appointment to a front-line Scimitar squadron, and to make sure that I received such an appointment I visited Jock Mancais, the CO of 736 Squadron, who was responsible for training OFS pilots on Scimitars, to see if he would allow me to convert to the aircraft. He agreed to let both me and Lieutenant Commander Murray, who was with 738 Squadron on refresher flying, to familiarise ourselves in the Scimitar before the next OFS course joined his squadron. After going through the Scimitar simulator with Colin Caspard teaching us how to deal with that aircraft's emergencies, we flew seven sorties each and qualified on type. DNOA (X), my appointers, were informed, as was DNAW, although it was not going to matter much which way those directorates thought: my future was planned out for me and they would have their pound of flesh. I would be appointed to 764 Squadron to teach supersonic flying in the Hunter T.8, and then they would review matters after eighteen months. To say that I was disappointed would be a great understatement—but little did I know then what turn my future would take.

Before I left 738 Squadron the instructors were to encounter an OFS course that held strange ideas about the way ahead to the top echelons in the Navy, and also a marked 'them and us' attitude. This particular course consisted mainly of General List officers but there was one SL Midshipman, Brian Jones. When he joined OFS he showed great promise and was a far better aviator than his GL contemporaries. For some reason he started slipping behind and appeared to all of us to be very unhappy. It was brought to our attention that he was being 'got at' by the GL course students, who were ordering him around and using him much as a 'flunky'. In all my life I had never seen anyone move as fast as Jimmy Moore did on this occasion. Jimmy was a GL officer and one of the very best, and he was standing for none of this nonsense. Jones was sent off to do something while Jimmy tore into the 'élitists', who had the idea that the way to the top was via the 'wings' on one's sleeve. He read them the riot act and indicated that if they did not like it he would take great pleasure in removing their 'wings'. After this episode young Jones romped ahead, completing his course as one of the best ever. He went on to fly Sea Vixens and at the end of his short-service career he left for a place in industry, becoming a manager of imports and exports. Despite Jimmy's taking these GL Lieutenants to task, their attitude continued, although fortunately they were never selected for promotion beyond Lieutenant Commander rank. I certainly did not want such officers near me, and neither did the instructors. Since that incident the Navy officer corps has consisted of at least 65 per cent Supplementary Officers, with a significantly high proportion of the GL officers being ex SL. In every unit in which I served the GL and SL officers all mixed together extremely well.

* * *

One of the happiest times during my service with 738 Squadron was the summer of 1959, when both Peter Sheppard and I taught cadets to fly de Havilland Tiger Moth biplanes. Every year the Dartmouth cadets have a summer flying camp, and this particular year it was decided to hold it at Lossiemouth. The officer in charge of the camp was Lieutenant Commander Peter Bailey, a QFI I had met at CFS while going through the QFI course.

As soon as the air station proceeded on leave half a dozen Tiger Moths were flown up from Arbroath and Plymouth. I had not flown a 'Tiggy' since my days as a sailor while serving at *Collingwood*. I was to remain with the camp until September, when Peter Sheppard would take over from me, where-upon I would depart for my fourteen days' summer leave. The cadets were a lively bunch of youngsters, all very keen to fly, and many of them would go on to fly Gannets, Scimitars, Sea Vixens and helicopters. Several of them would eventually pass through my hands again, learning to fly either the Hunter or the Scimitar. It was a wonderful summer with some of the finest weather ever, and we flew every day except Saturday and Sunday.

On 7 August, while flying with Cadet Backus on a navigational exercise, we entered a very strong thermal over Ben Rinnes just south of Elgin, and after circling the mountain several times we had soon climbed to 10,000 feet. The pair of us were so excited that I called Lossiemouth tower on approach and asked if they could see us. They replied that they could just make out a tiny silver speck in the sky and had at first thought it was an airliner!

Following summer leave, the Summer Flying Camp moved to Milltown, where it stayed until the end of September. Timber, a recently acquired Golden Labrador puppy, used to accompany me to the airfield, sitting on my lap as we were transported daily in a Navy utilicon van. He was kept on his nylon leash, tethered to a stake driven into the ground in front of the control tower. He had a great time and on many an occasion the cadets would take him off for a walk around the airfield chasing hares and rabbits. He loved everybody and everybody loved him!

15

Supersonic Instructor

M Y TIME in 738 Squadron came to an end on 29 September 1960. I flew south to the Naval Instrument Flying School at Yeovilton to take the SMAC 7, the Instrument Rating Examiner's course. This was completed in a week and I then returned to join 764 Squadron as a QFI/IRE. While at Yeovilton I flew with Phil Cardew, who was with me on 40 RN Flying Course; he was now one of the Naval Flying Command Instrument Examiners. Once I was back at Lossiemouth my first task was to examine and re-rate Lieutenant Colin Caspard, who had converted me to the Hunter T.8 jet trainer.

Most of my early instructional duties in 764 Squadron were taken up with giving dual tuition to the OFS students from 736 and 738 Squadrons, who were taking the Swept Wing Conversion Course prior to moving on to either the Scimitar or Sea Vixen fighter. However, during my first two weeks I was given mutual flying instruction by Flight Lieutenant 'Toby' Westoby, the resident RAF QFI in the Squadron. At about this time, too, Arthur Stewart moved across from 738 Squadron while Dave Bridger moved south to Yeovilton. With the build-up of the swept-wing conversions, Peter Sheppard joined from 738 Squadron to keep us company.

There was by now a formidable team of QFIs and AWIs in the Squadron, with Lieutenant Commander Dickie Carne as the CO. However, his time in the Squadron was fast coming to an end and his relief would be Lieutenant Commander Chris Mather, who as a Lieutenant, it will be recalled, had been my AWI course instructor some three years earlier. Toby Westoby was about to move on as the Command Flight Safety Officer to No 1 Group RAF based at Bawtry, and Flight Lieutenant Gordon Lewis AFC, who had been instructing at RAF College Cranwell, would be the new RAF instructor to take his place. Chris Mather and I were soon thrown together when I had to give him his instrument rating test. Owing to his lack of recent flying practice, I could at that stage award him only a 'White Card', although he had flown to 'Green Card' standard. However, when he had flown the requisite number of flight hours, and instrument flight hours, I was able to upgrade him.

I had by this time been a B1/QFI for quite a long time, so both Arthur Stewart and I decided that perhaps it was time for us to go south to the CFS and be examined for our A2 Category. Over the next six weeks or so he and I sat down together in his married-quarters dining room, studying the RAF Instructional Manual and indeed everything to do with the Hunter T.8 jet trainer. By the time we arrived at CFS we knew every rivet, nut, bolt and piece of piping. In addition, we had 764 Squadron's handwritten instructional manual for the T.8; there was at that time no RAF Instructional Manual for the aircraft, even though they had the T.7 version. This manual was to stand us in good stead because the CFS examiners could not believe that we had gone to such lengths to produce it. They were so intrigued with it that we left a copy with them, and it would eventually, after some editing, become the standard RAF manual.

We arrived at RAF Kemble, the CFS satellite airfield where the School kept its Hunters and Canberras. Arthur went for his flight test first while I stayed on the ground being thoroughly quizzed on all aspects of aeronautics and meteorology. When Arthur had finished his flight I was briefed, went up and was back on the ground in time for lunch. We both passed the flying examination. The examiners were extremely pleased with our standard of airmanship and handling ability in an aircraft that was not used a great deal for advanced flying training. When lunch was over, they questioned both Arthur and me even further about our academic flying knowledge—until 1800. We thought that the examiners were never going to stop, but suddenly they stood up and said, 'Thank you. Well done both of you! You have passed with flying colours!' We looked at one another, big smiles over our faces, and shook hands with each other and the examiners. We had done it! As it was now so late and the airfield personnel had secured for the day, we stayed overnight at the CFS Officers' Mess and celebrated somewhat. Early the next day we were on our way back to Lossiemouth, where congratulations all round were waiting for us. Paddy McKeown, the CFI, and Ray Rawbone, as Commander (Air), who was an A1 QFI, just could not find enough praise for us. We had done it all by our own efforts: in the RAF we would have had to go to a HQ Flight and spend at least a month being given tuition, and only then been allowed to go forward for examination, if it was considered that we were up to standard. Arthur and I were chuffed to the core!

Shortly after my arrival in 764 Squadron John Kennett took over as the Senior Pilot from Willie Watson, who moved to 809 (Buccaneer) Squadron to be the SP under the command of Lieutenant Commander John de Winton. John Kennett would leave about a year later to take over the task of Senior Pilot of 736 (Scimitar) Squadron, which had by that time moved across into the hangar next to 764 on the western side of the airfield. Eddie Cope, who had been the AWI in 738 Squadron, would move across to 764 and fill the Senior Pilot's shoes. In addition, Andy Copeland, Charles Manning and Richard Wilkinson, all QFIs, would join from 738 Squadron to help in the Swept Wing Conversion Course, which was now our major task in addition to AWI training. By this time the Squadron had received the Navy's first Hunter

GA.11, a naval conversion of the RAF's Hunter Mk 4. These remodelled single-seat jets replaced the ageing Sea Hawk fighters, and with additional Hunter T.8s to replace the odd Vampire T.22 still in the Squadron the latter became an all-Hunter training unit.

Eddie Cope remembered that I had done a good job as Staff Officer in 738 Squadron and I was not completely surprised when I suddenly became 764 Squadron's SO. When I took over the SO position in 764 I found, as I had at all other squadrons in which I had held the job, the office to be in a complete shambles, files being stuffed away at random so that it was always difficult to find papers, orders and reports. Once again I set about tidying up the office and organising the filing cabinet. Finding the task to be extremely time-consuming, I asked for an assistant and Chris Mather arranged for a young Third Officer WRNS to help me. I could continue with my main job in the Squadron as a QFI/IRE as well as being the Staff Officer.

When I returned from my IRE course I began to formulate an Instrument Rating Test brochure for pilots who were due to renew the instrument flying ticket. Over the years I had felt strongly that pilots need not know the 'guts' of their flight instruments, since in reality there was very little that they could do if an instrument failed for one reason or another; in such an eventuality the only ready solution was to cover the offending instrument so that one was not fooled by it. I felt that it was important to know the instrument flight limitations, and the sources of secondary power supply, and also to be able to fly safely on a limited instrument panel—in other words, I was looking for a practical approach to instrument and weather knowledge. When I floated the idea of a brochure, Chris Mather thought it was a splendid idea and a prototype was forwarded to FOFT for his comments before being sent on to DNAW. Lossiemouth's Captain, Commander (Air) and CFI thought it a good idea too, and then Lieutenant Commander Arthur Milne, the CO of the Naval Instrument Flying School at Yeovilton, was asked for his opinions.

Now Arthur Milne was a first-rate QFI and IRE, an excellent instructor who knew his job inside out, but he expected all pilots to know exactly how flight instruments worked internally whereas I contended that this was not necessary. He put forward a strong case for retaining the old standards and methods of teaching instrument flying. FOFT, however, was not against squadrons having such a brochure as mine available for 'brushing up' prior to examination for an instrument test, so I arranged for copies to be made and forwarded to all squadrons. In a way Arthur and I both won the day, but I am sure that, had he not been in the Instrument School, FOFT would have agreed wholeheartedly with my proposal and the brochure would have become standard training material throughout the Command. Nevertheless, my ideas would come to full fruition a few years later.

* * *

It was now time for me to pay my two-yearly visit to the Aero Medical School at Seafield Park near Lee-on-Solent. It was arranged for Lieutenant Bob Ponter, a tactical instructor in the Squadron, to take on my job as Staff

Officer during my absence. Seafield Park is an old country house with a considerable history which includes the ghost of a young lady who, I understand, died in a fire at the house. Her spectre reappears annually round about the time of the anniversary of the fire.

The purpose of these visits was to establish that aircrews were still qualified in their high-altitude pressure category, to bring them up to date with the latest aeromedical information, to refresh their knowledge of first aid and to check their hearts by means of an ECG test. On one occasion the staff famously carried out brainwave tests for the naval hospital at Haslar in connection with a study into epilepsy and other brain disorders, although after the first two or three tests they gave up using aviators because all the results indicated that we were a bunch of lunatics! Perhaps it was the beef dripping we were fed at teatime when the WRAs placed large bowls of it on the tables for spreading on our toast.

It was always a leisurely time at Seafield Park, and one could almost count it as a rest period from all the pressures of flying. The school, which is located at Stubbington just down the road from Lee-on-Solent, was close to Reg Hunt's old home and located in an area for retired and serving officers in the Navy. Evenings were always free and, as at all British military establishments, Wednesdays were given over to soccer in winter or cricket during the summer months. The Solent was clearly visible from the house and enthusiasts could go sailing with the Lee-on-Solent Sailing Club. As soon as Friday lunch was over most of us were on our way back to our respective air bases, and for me of course this meant a long train journey back to Scotland.

* * *

The following Monday, when I returned to the Squadron, I could not believe what I discovered in my Staff Office: it looked for all the world as though a bomb had detonated inside it. The Third Officer WRNS was no longer with us and my tidy filing system was in complete disarray. The filing cabinet, which contained classified documents, was unlocked and insecure and the papers were in a state of complete disorder, making it virtually impossible to find anything quickly. I asked Eddie Cope what on earth had been going on during my absence.

'Well, Bob seemed to be in control and seemed to know what he was doing, so I left him alone,' he explained.

I then asked Bob what he had been up to during my time away.

'Oh, there was no problem, but I didn't like your filing system or methods,' he replied.

'Oh', I said, 'and what happened to the WRNS officer?'

'We didn't need her so I got rid of her.'

At this I exploded.

'For your information, young man, she was brought in to help me because I have three jobs to do in this squadron, and with her help the Staff Office ran efficiently but now it is an utter shambles. Get out of here, and don't ever touch anything in this office again!'

148

Eddie Cope just sat there, but after Bob had gone he said, 'You were a bit rough on him, Punchy.'

'No Eddie. He needed to learn how to go about things correctly and in a tidy manner. His flying is probably just as bad as his office work.'

To say that I was angry would be an understatement.

While serving at Lossiemouth I must have trained or given refresher flying to many young and older aviators who would go on to take up senior appointments within the naval service. One young officer I remember very well indeed was Lieutenant Richard Burns, an engineer pilot. He was a very quiet and studious person with bright red hair and a fair complexion. He was a sound aviator, although he had some original ideas about how an aircraft should be flown. He would eventually be promoted to the rank of Admiral and run an aircraft directorate in the MoD Procurement Executive. However, Ray Rawbone had decided that he and the CFI would give all Hunter graduates their final handling test before they passed on to the Scimitar or Sea Vixen OFS courses. Ray flew with Richard Burns, and when he landed he took me to one side and asked how I taught landings.

'Stick and throttle, sir.'

'I thought so—and that is the way I do it. However, young Burns has a different idea—setting the throttle and then using just the stick to make the end of the runway. In my opinion, he is a candidate for a wooden overcoat! Perhaps, I am getting too old for this lark!'

Richard completed his Sea Vixen OFS course at Yeovilton and was appointed to a front-line Sea Vixen squadron aboard HMS *Victorious*, the rebuilt wartime fleet carrier. Later, while he was night flying off the Philippine Islands, his carrier director vectored him and his observer on to a low-flying target. It was a bright, moonlit night but they could see nothing either visually or by radar. When the director informed them that they were on top of the target they suddenly felt a severe vibration followed by a Zone A fire warning. This very serious alarm meant that they had to eject immediately from their aircraft because it was in imminent danger of exploding. They left safely and were quickly rescued by the ship's SAR helicopter. The aircraft crashed into the sea off the Scarborough Shoals and nothing was recovered from it.

A few months later *Victorious* was visiting Subic Bay, the US Navy base in the Philippines. Richard was having a drink in the Officers' Club when he struck up a conversation with a couple of USN aviators. They had been flying an S2F Tracker anti-submarine aircraft in the same location as Richard during the night of his accident. The Tracker was being flown low level when suddenly there had been a loud bang followed by severe airframe vibration. They had declared an emergency and landed at Cubi Point, the US Navy air station, to find that the top portion of their fin and rudder was missing. It took no stretch of the imagination to realise that Richard had collided with the Tracker. Both aircraft crews were very lucky indeed: had it been a full mid-air crash then they would have not been around to tell the tale.

After Richard had completed his front-line tour he went on to take the test pilot's course and he was appointed on exchange to the US Navy course at Patuxent River, Maryland. He did so well on the course that he walked away with all the trophies and was asked to stay for another two years testing USN aircraft, to which DNOA (E) unhesitatingly agreed. On his return to Britain he was appointed to 'C' Squadron, the RN Test Squadron or Flight at AAEE Boscombe Down, Wiltshire. It was while he was with 'C' Squadron that our paths would cross once again, when I was the LSO of Ark Royal.

Another young pilot I remember was to cause me some embarrassment while serving in 764 Squadron. I had brought this young aviator up to solo standard just before I went off for my Seafield Park course. I handed him over to Flight Lieutenant Gordon Lewis, who briefed him for his first solo flight. This flight went without a hitch, but on his second flight things went decidedly awry. He was instructed to go up to 10,000 feet and carry out some simulated manual control circuits, Gordon carefully briefing him on the checks that needed to be carried out. The aircraft was to be flying at 250 knots straight and level. He was to ensure the that aileron spring load trim control on the control column was in the neutral position and that all aileron and rudder electric trimmers were set to zero and the locking bars removed before he selected manual control. First he was to select the elevator control switch 'off', secondly trim out the aerodynamic loads, and then, when he was happy, select the aileron switch to manual control and trim out the loads. He was then to fly the aircraft around gently for about five to ten minutes before carrying out a simulated circuit. This was a simple exercise, and one which he had conducted with me without any problems.

The youngster took off and headed out to the Banff/Keith area and proceeded with his solo flight. A short time later the tower received a radio call from him that he was having control problems and was requesting an emergency landing. Gordon dashed to the tower but could not get any sense out of him except that he could only hold the aircraft level down to 180 knots, so he carefully briefed him for a straight-in approach and landing on the main runway, which fortunately had the wind down it at the time. He made a steady approach, touching down safely at 180 knots and coming to a stop at the very end of the runway. Gordon raced round the taxy track and when he reached the jet he found the spring trim control hard over one way and the electric aileron trimmer hard the other way. There was absolutely nothing wrong with the aircraft but the pilot had got himself into such a pickle that he did not know what he was doing. After further dual instruction the young pilot was sent on to the Scimitar OFS course and was eventually appointed to 803 (Scimitar) Squadron.

Within the year the young man was back in Britain visiting the Aero Medical School. His squadron had disembarked to RAF North Front, Gibraltar. It was one of those terrible 'fish bowl' days when one is unsure where the land ends and the sky begins and reliance on instruments is mandatory. He was flying with his CO and he called him to say that he was utterly disorientated and that he intended ejecting. The CO calmed him down and joined him in close formation and they flew around for a while, but our aviator was still not happy and said he was going to bail out. After further talking, the pair flew back to North Front and landed safely. The Senior Pilot took the reluctant pilot aside to find out what was troubling him, and to his astonishment he broke down and sobbed his heart out. He did not want to be a fighter pilot: all he ever wanted to do was fly Navy communications aircraft. He was grounded and sent back home for counselling, and to await a decision about his future. Eventually he was appointed to 781 Squadron, the Navy's communications squadron, where I believe he finished his time flying Devons and Herons.

This case worried me. Where had I gone wrong? Why had I not been aware of the young man's problems? Why had he managed to go through the whole of flying training, including his 736/738 OFS and 764 Squadron training, without anybody becoming aware of his fear of fighter piloting? To this day I do not know the answer. Perhaps I should have been more talkative with him, giving him the opportunity to 'open up' to me. Who knows?

* * *

One day I was quietly minding my own business when a parcel was dropped on my desk. It contained a rudder pedal, a leather strap and a length of cotton cord. 764 Squadron was expecting Commander Stan Leonard, a QFI and Korean War veteran, for a Senior Officer's Conversion Course. Stan had been appointed to HMS *Hermes* as Commander (Air), relieving Paddy McKeown. On his departure from Lossiemouth, Paddy had been appointed as Commander (Air) to that carrier but had had to leave early because his wife was seriously ill and was not expected to live.

I had never met Stan but had heard a great deal about him. He was a QFI in 736 Squadron when I went through OFS, and I can remember seeing him limping out to his Vampire jet trainer with his parachute slung over his shoulder. He had been shot down during the Korean War and had parachuted to safety into some sand dunes near the shore. When the SAR helicopter had come to pick him up he had broken cover and run towards the 'chopper', unaware that there was a communist machine gun nest a short distance away. He was badly hit in the right leg and it had to be amputated. Nothing was going to stop Stan, however, and he soon had an artificial leg and foot fitted. He quickly mastered the new limb and before long was flying again. Whenever Stan flew, especially in an aircraft equipped with an ejection seat, the left rudder pedal was removed and a special substitute installed to allow him to strap his good foot to the rudder bar. If he had had to eject, then he would have pulled a quick-release cord which freed the special pedal, his right 'tin leg' and foot being left behind, trapped under the foot strap. Fortunately, he never had to put the system to the test.

Stan was an excellent aviator and a very accurate instrument flyer, but after landing a Hunter jet trainer he had terrible trouble taxying because of its high speed. It was very obvious that he would eventually have a taxying accident involving either running off the taxy track or running into another jet on the hardstanding. After four or five trips he should have gone solo but he was just not making the grade on the ground. I was honest with him, and he understood my assessment of the situation, but to ensure that I was not being overcautious I had the CFI fly with him. He agreed with me. Stan continued to fly dual sorties, however, and thoroughly enjoyed his time with the Squadron.

Some weeks or months later I bumped into Stan once again, this time at a cocktail party at Whale Island when I happened to wander into the wrong room. He grabbed me, pulled me over and introduced me to his friends saying, 'Meet the chap who had the guts to say, "You are not good enough, Stan, to go solo." He was right!' He gave me a big hug and invited me to stay for a drink or two. Stan was one of those wonderful naval officers whom it was ever my pleasure to know. He completed his appointment aboard *Hermes*, where he was thoroughly liked, and was promoted Captain. In time he would be appointed as the Captain of RNAS Culdrose.

I had just returned from lunch in the wardroom one day and had gone into the 764 Squadron briefing room with Eddie Cope to prepare for a briefing to be given by one of the AWI students when there was a colossal bang in the hangar. An ejection seat! We ran out into the hangar towards a Hunter T.8 jet which had smoke rising from the cockpit. Engineers were running from the Air Maintenance Control Office towards the same jet. Eddie and I were the first on scene and we climbed the ladder on to the steel platform alongside the cockpit. The sight that greeted us was one that I never want to witness again: an young ordnance rating had a drogue gun cord threaded through the right side of his head.

Before lunch that day, the engineering watch had prepared the jet's ejection seats for removal from the aircraft during the afternoon by the next watch. However, for some unknown reason the drogue gun sear rod of the right-hand seat had not been disconnected from the aircraft's rear cockpit bulkhead, which meant that the seat was unsafe. The afternoon watch had arrived and had begun to lift the seat without first checking that its firing mechanisms had been disconnected. One of the young ordnance boys was leaning over the drogue gun bolt as the seat was lifted, the gun sear was pulled out and the bolt was fired through the right side of his skull, just in front of the temple and out from the back of the head, via a 'silent' part of the brain. He was deeply unconscious when we gently lifted him out of the cockpit on to the steel table. Eddie had the presence of mind to cut the drogue cord a foot either side of the head and leave it threaded through the poor boy. A doctor appeared very quickly on the scene and administered medication. Everybody was thoroughly shocked by the event but it brought home the necessity of doing a job properly. The seat should have been rendered totally safe before the morning engineering watch went to lunch. If the ordnance warning instructions had been followed correctly, or if a notice of sorts had been placed on the ejection seat, then the accident would not have happened. Every ordnance accident in the Navy that I can recall originated from a failure to follow instructions and guidelines in manuals.

The young rating was flown in a Navy helicopter to the neurosurgical unit at Aberdeen, where he underwent surgery to recover from the accident. However, as a result of the accident he was discharged from the Navy as medically unfit for further service, though he was awarded a pension. Almost three years later Chris Mather met his mother who informed him sadly that her son had passed away after suffering a brain haemorrhage, two years to the day after the accident. This was a very sorrowful end to the life of a young man who had had so much to look forward to and was liked by all who knew him.

Neither Eddie nor I flew again that day. We were utterly shocked by the accident and by what we had seen and had had to deal with. We were both required to produce a report on what had happened while the facts were still fresh and clear in our minds. The CO and AEO both spoke to the Squadron's lower deck about the necessity to follow the instructions and guidelines for engineering practices. We were not at war and therefore care had to be taken with both our manpower and our equipment in order to prevent such accidents from recurring. In spite of these words, however, Chris and I were to experience something similar in the not-too-distant future.

There had always been great rivalry in 764 Squadron between the QFIs and AWIs as to who were the better aviators and weaponeers. One night we all went night flying, carrying out night dive-bombing on the Tain Range over in Ross and Cromarty. The AWIs had been flying first and their fall-of-shot results were awful, not one bomb falling within fifty yards of the target. Then Peter Sheppard and I flew the last two sorties on the range and had a heyday. We placed all bar two of our eight bombs right on the target, with the other two falling within twenty yards of it. The AWIs thought that we had each got hold of a plotting form and filled them in as a prank, until the Range Officer telephoned in to say that the final two sorties produced the best night dive-bombing results he had ever seen. Peter and I could hardly contain ourselves: we had finally convinced everyone that the QFIs were the best aviators and weaponeers in the Squadron!

At about this time another QFI, Lieutenant Andy Copeland, joined the Squadron. Not only was he a very good flying instructor, he was also an excellent weaponeer. He was, moreover, a very good dinghy sailor and yachtsman—far better than me—and he and his wife had won a number of trophies for the Lossiemouth Sailing Club. The two things that I remember most about Andy are his old Rolls-Royce, which he had found in a very decrepit state and had renovated so well it looked as if it had just come out of the factory, and his dog Fergus, a miniature Irish wolfhound. Fergus loved beer, and if one was standing in conversation with a beer mug down by one's thigh, as likely or not the next time the mug was lifted it would be empty. On one occasion the dog's legs failed to support him and he collapsed in the corner of the room, chuntering and moaning. I can remember Fergus being 'hung over' the morning after this rather lively Copeland party. The girls from the Plotting Room took the poor creature away and fed him milk and coffee, and by lunch he was his old perky self again!

* * *

Apart from my task as a QFI, I had become very much involved with teaching the student AWIs various aspects of weaponeering. My time in the Squadron was almost over, however, and so I requested that I be given the opportunity to go through the AWI course again. Chris Mather agreed, and I joined No 29 AWI Course, which consisted of Lieutenants Bill Billett and Jack Smith, at Whale Island in April 1962.

Because just the three of us were on the course we could cover subjects quite quickly, and I had the advantage of having gone through the Ground School once before. However, there were now various new weapons in the naval air arsenal, adding a new dimension to the proceedings. These were the Firestreak IR-homing missile carried by the Sea Vixen all-weather fighter and the 2,000-pound 'special weapons' bomb* carried by both the Scimitar and the Sea Vixen. All three of us passed the written examinations with flying colours, achieving first-class grades.

Bill's home was in Southampton, and he often went home for the evenings or weekends whereas Jack and I stayed in the wardroom until the course had been completed. However, there were times when all three of us used to 'go ashore' for the evening and spend a few hours at the United Services Club in Portsmouth to enjoy some pints of beer together. I can vividly remember one of these occasions. We were all sitting at the upstairs bar watching some RAF officers from Thorney Island playing the fruit machine 'bandit'. Jack had been keeping an eye on them, and when they stopped playing, having temporarily run out of sixpences, he leaned across to us and said, 'Give me all your sixpences. I'm going to get us our beer money for the evening.' He quietly sauntered over to the machine and started playing, and then suddenly he hit the jackpot and coins started pouring forth. The RAF officers were looking quite angry at having been 'pipped at the post', but Jack returned to the bar, cashed in his winnings and graciously bought the Air Force officers a pint each. When they were out of earshot we asked how he had managed it. He replied, 'I had been watching them play for some time and I instinctively knew that it was about to trip any moment—and I was right!'

* * *

We returned to Lossiemouth in mid-June 1962 for the practical phase of the course. Jack had come from 803 (Scimitar) Squadron with the reputation of bombing Arab tents in the Sahara with 25-pound practice rounds and knocking out the windows of the RAF Kai Tak buildings in Hong Kong during a supersonic flyby. In the first incident he had been carrying out low-level bombing on the El Adem range in Libya when he inadvertently released a small practice bomb early, hitting an Arab's tent and knocking it flat. As luck would have it, nobody was hurt. In the Hong Kong incident he was flying wing to Lieutenant Maurice Hynett, who had decided to make a high-speed run over the RAF buildings. However, the high-speed run that Maurice made became supersonic as a result of his dive and the shock wave knocked out most of the building's windows. A very irate Wing Commander (Flying) and the Squadron Commanding Officer were waiting for the pair when they

---

* The euphemistic official title for a nuclear weapon.

landed! Maurice tried to talk himself out of the incident. Jack said that he had no idea that they had gone supersonic as he was flying wing and was following his leader. However, neither Wing Commander (Flying) nor the CO were buying their excuses, and the two miscreants were grounded for a week, had their wine bills stopped in the mess and were made to apologise to all concerned. Eventually Maurice let it slip that he had done it deliberately, and fortunately no injuries were caused by the flying glass other than a few cases of fright.

The flying phase of the course got off to a good start with air-to-air sorties and then with ground-attack exercises at the Tain Range using cannon, 2-inch rockets and 25-pound practice bombs, Jack's favourite weapon. During the low-level bombing phase we flew a circuit which took us right past the verandah and front porch of James Robertson Justice, the film actor. He was a favourite friend of Captain and Mrs Michael Fell, the Captain being the Commanding Officer of the Lossiemouth Naval Air Station, and by the time we had returned to Lossie he had been on the telephone complaining about us. Consequently we moved our circuit further away and higher, to the south of his home, which calmed him down. I can well understand his indignation because he had a beautiful property overlooking the Dornoch Firth and Tarbat Ness to the east, with the Moray Firth visible and with all the Highlands to the north and south of him. He often visited the wardroom at Lossiemouth on Air Days, dressed in his highland garb and with a falcon on his left arm. He was very much a naturalist, a supporter of wild animals and a champion of the environment. One evening he was in the wardroom when a young RAF Aberdeen University Air Cadet was bragging about his afternoon's shooting of seals along the Aberdeenshire coast. James went for him in quite a violent manner, and when Michael Fell attempted to calm him down he too received some verbal abuse. As a result of that incident James was never invited back to Lossiemouth. A year or so later we heard that he had died from a sudden heart attack. In spite of his eccentric personality he was a fine actor and he loved his native Scotland, and I for one will always watch his films with the fondest of memories.

No 29 AWI Course would not be completed without some drama. The first incident occurred to Bill Billett. 800 Squadron had moved in and were sharing our hangar, and one of their Scimitars was parked right outside the door of the aircrew changing room. This particular jet had its wings spread for maintenance, and Bill, rushing out of the changing room, ran straight into the sharp trailing edge of the right aileron. He fell back into the room holding his head and with blood streaming everywhere. He had been almost scalped, the skin and hair being cut back a couple of inches. He was rushed over to the Sickbay, where Surgeon Commander Ian Mackie, our Senior Medical Officer, stitched him up. It would be another week before Bill was flying again.

The next incident involved me. The course had by this time reached the 'Strike' phase, in which students planned and executed a strike on a particular target somewhere in the local low-flying area. After several dummy practices these exercises moved on to live-weapon strikes on Garvie Island just to the east of Cape Wrath. During a dummy strike over Aberdeenshire which was being led by Jack Smith, I was flying fighter cover when two Hunter 'bandits' bounced us. A 'break' to the right was called and we all turned towards the 'bandits' to countermand their attack. The rules were quite specific in that a 'bouncing' fighter had to disengage by turning in the same direction as the strike. Suddenly, while under high 'g', a Hunter crossed my path little more than ten or fifteen feet in front of me, its tailplane so close that I could have reached out and touched it. I pulled as hard as I could to miss this aircraft but there was a bang, my aircraft shuddered and I blacked out momentarily. When I regained consciousness I was tingling all over and the aircraft's accelerometer was registering over ten 'g' and off the clock. The 'bang' had been caused by the high-speed stall I had induced by pulling so hard. I called Jack, telling him what had happened and that I was returning to base. Back at Lossie I found that I had wrinkled the main fuselage, and the aircraft had to be flown, with its landing gear locked down, to Sydenham, near Belfast, for a rebuild.

Following the exercise a debriefing was held and the CO jumped all over me for what had happened. I could not believe what I was hearing and sat absolutely dumbfounded. Eventually I retorted, calmly, 'Bouncing aircraft always turn in the same direction as the strike breaks, disengaging in the same turning direction!' Eddie Cope came up afterwards and told me that it was the CO's fault—he had broken in the wrong direction—and that he was going to have a word with him. Eddie wanted me to drop the matter but I was very angry. Eddie managed to quieten me down and I retired to the Plotting Room, where Petty Officer WRNS Sally Howells gave me a strong cup of coffee and made me sit down and relax.

Once our course had completed its live-strike exercises we were all assessed as suitable to be AWIs. Jack was appointed to carry out the Buccaneer Conversion Course prior to joining 801 (Buccaneer) Squadron in HMS *Victorious* while Bill was reappointed back to Sea Vixens at Yeovilton. I had already been nominated to take the Sea Vixen night and all-weather fighter course, and Lieutenant John Eagle, who was serving in 738 Squadron, was nominated to join 736 Squadron to fly Scimitars. However, behind my back John managed to have this changed and took my appointment. I had a word with Chris Mather and I went to 736 Squadron as its AWI, which suited me as I did not have to move my family and caravan south to Somerset. I had now had appointments to all the training squadrons at Lossiemouth except the new Buccaneer unit, and I would eventually join that too. Above all, I had graduated; indeed, I was the sole serving, triple-qualified QFI/AWI/IRE naval aviator in the Fleet Air Arm!

16

Big Jet Flying Days

W HEN I joined 736 Squadron I was to be with a band of old friends. Lieutenant Commander Peter Newman was the Squadron CO and John Kennett was the Senior Pilot, while Lieutenants Peter de Souza and Don Richardson were both serving as QFIs. The AWI was Dave Howard, although he had already received his new appointment to 800 (Scimitar) Squadron and I was to be his relief in 736. Dave did not know when he departed that he would soon be the Senior Pilot of 800 Squadron. Peter Newman was also due to leave within a few weeks of my joining, to become the new CO of 800 Squadron. Lieutenant Curly Wood would join the Squadron as my Assistant AWI on completion of his course in 764 Squadron. Maurice Hynett was a tactical instructor in the Squadron, though he also was due to leave and join the next Empire Test Pilots' Course at RAE Farnborough. Lieutenant Commander Dai Vaughan, who lived near John Kennett and me on the Milltown caravan site, was the Squadron AEO. There was, moreover, a marvellous ground crew, and all in all we were an extremely happy band of naval warriors.

I was soon refamiliarising myself in the Scimitar and within a week of joining I was accompanying OFS students on their various flying exercises. Many of our Scimitars were the early models, from the first batch of forty built by Supermarine for the Navy. The Scimitar was a very robust aircraft and could withstand any amount of misuse and punishment at the hands of inexperienced pilots. However, the Squadron did have one aircraft that suffered from airspeed and electrical problems. It finally came to light that this Scimitar had ditched in the Persian Gulf, been recovered by the Navy and been refurbished at Fleetlands. It was obvious from the crackling and odd noises that emanated from the fuselage and wings that it had not been cleaned of all the salt that had crept into it during its immersion. After much discussion with the CO and AEO I managed to persuade them to have it exchanged for a new aircraft out of NASU. Now we had an aircraft which spent more time in the air than in the hangar.

When I arrived in the Squadron, Lieutenant Commander Don Mills was going through his Scimitar conversion prior to joining 800 Squadron as the new Senior Pilot, relieving Lieutenant Commander John Ford, who would come to 736 as the new CO. A new RAF tactical instructor also joined to replace Flight Lieutenant Mike Farmer, who had unfortunately died in a Scimitar accident in Banffshire. Mike had been on a Forward Air Controlling exercise and for some reason had ejected from his aircraft. His parachute failed to deploy or he had hit something at low level and was killed, but his aircraft made a perfect belly landing in a ploughed field. Mike was a much-liked RAF officer at Lossiemouth and we got along very well together, the more so since the pair of us were asthmatics. He was laid to rest in the Royal Air Force cemetery at Kinloss and I attended as the representative from 736 and 764 Squadrons. His replacement was Flight Lieutenant Neil Davidson from RAF Chivenor in Devon. I believe Neil went on in his career to become an Air Marshal.

Neil had come from an environment in which the hangar doors were closed once the requisite flying hours had been achieved. He simply could not believe that the Royal Navy flew and flew to get ahead of the task—just in case something untoward happened, for example bad weather or the grounding of an aircraft for some technical reason. We were scheduled to fly together, I teaching him the Navy's approach to air tactics, while at the same time the Fifth Sea Lord, Rear Admiral Michael Le Fanu, was due to visit the air station and the Squadron. John Ford, the CO, was very emphatic about not wanting officers wandering around in smelly flying overalls during the Admiral's visit. John was very much a prim and proper as well as a rather pompous naval officer, and the rest of us thought it strange that we were not to be seen in our working dress by the head of the Fleet Air Arm, who certainly preferred to see his officers and men that way. However, it was of course John's prerogative as CO to decide how we would all conduct ourselves.

Neil and I had landed and taxied back to the Squadron hardstanding to park our aircraft. After we had signed the Form A700 aircraft logbooks we walked slowly back to the hangar. There was a small rise in front of us, obscuring the lower half of the hangar and preventing us from seeing any cars parked outside the hangar doors. We had been told at the line office that the Admiral had not yet arrived, so we carried on towards the hangar, but as we approached over the brow there was the Admiral and his entourage. We did a rapid about-turn and started back towards the line office but had hardly gone a couple of yards when there was a shout.

'Punchy, where are you going? Come here!' The Admiral bounded over to me, shook my hand and put his arm around my shoulders. I introduced Neil and we started back to the hangar. 'Where the hell have you been since I last saw you?'

'Well, sir, I've been ashore, much to my disgust, for the past six years!'

'How the hell did you manage that?'

'Not my doing, sir. Those damned appointers wanting their pound of flesh from me!'

He laughed and talked as we walked towards the hangar, his arm still around my shoulders. The Captain, XO, Commander (Air) and Flag Lieutenant all had big grins on their faces but John had turned almost purple. The

Admiral and I parted company and he carried on with his 'walkabout'. After he had left there was a loud call from the CO's office.

'Doust! To my office! Immediately!'

I had changed out of my flying kit and was looking presentable and more like a naval officer as I entered the CO's office.

'Come in and shut the door,' he said severely. 'What were my instructions?'

I answered him and said that we had asked at the line office if the Admiral was at the hangar and had been told no. We had not seen any staff cars when we taxied in, so we walked up to the hangar and did an about-turn as soon as we saw the entourage.

'And what, may I ask, was all this close friendship with the Admiral?'

'Quite simple, sir. He is an old Captain and friend of mine, and that is how he is with all his friends.'

'Get out of here, and in future pay more attention to my orders!'

'Yes, sir.'

I returned to the crew room, where everybody was waiting to hear what had transpired. When I told them they all laughed.

Until I suffered my Wyvern accident in northern Norway, I had not known Michael Le Fanu. After returning to HMS *Eagle*, his ship, he showed great concern over my welfare and what the Norwegians had done to ease my plight. Out of his own pocket he had, as we have seen, arranged for a magnum of Long John's whisky to be shipped to the fishing village to replace the tiny bottle of spirit the inhabitants had given me. He treated his officers, his men and indeed all other people with great friendship and civility. Richard Baker, the BBC commentator and former newsreader, served under him as an RNR officer and absolutely adored him, later writing a biography of Michael le Fanu entitled *Ginger*. That was the colour of his hair, and he was full of spice and goodness.

Michael Le Fanu would be promoted to become the head of the Navy as Chief of the Naval Staff and then he was selected to be the Chief of the Defence Staff. However, he had been unwell for a time and he was finally diagnosed as suffering from leukemia, so he had to forego the CDS appointment. Everybody thought so much of him that the Chief of the Army Staff arranged for an honour guard of Scots Guards to be present at his farewell from the Ministry of Defence. Wearing a 'dogtooth' suit and bowler hat with an umbrella over his arm, he pushed his invalid wife of many years in her wheelchair through the lines of guardsmen. As he and his wife left in a staff car, the Guards band played 'Auld Lang Syne'—a fitting tribute to a great officer and a gentleman who was very well liked by one and all. Three months later, Michael passed away into God's hands.

It was many years after this that I learnt just how close Admiral Le Fanu had been associated with me through my old grammar school. It will be recalled that, during the war, all the Rye schools had been evacuated, mainly to the Bedford area, my school joining up with the Bedford Grammar School. Teaching space was at a premium and my headmistress, Miss Matilda Turner, used to hold her English and English Literature classes in one of the Bedford public houses. One of her students was Michael Le Fanu, the son of a local farmer. I shall never forget him: he was simply one of the best Royal Navy officers of the twentieth century.

* * *

It was a wonderful autumn during 1962, with the air growing colder each day. The autumnal gales were not quite as fierce as they had been in the past few years, and we had long, golden evenings. Christmas arrived and so, across the whole of the north of Scotland, did the snows. The Scimitar operated well off the hard-packed snow runways. The air station still did not have an effective snow clearing machine, although it would not be long before the engineers invented one by mounting a de Havilland Goblin jet engine on the back of a low loader towed by a fuel tanker.

Early in 1963 the Squadron lost a Scimitar flown by the Senior Pilot, John Kennett. His aircraft caught fire off RAF Leuchars, near Dundee. John ejected from his stricken jet and injured his back, which hospitalised him for a few weeks in Dundee Royal Infirmary. During his time in the hospital I took over as the temporary Senior Pilot. Although John came back to the Squadron, it would be some time before he was fit to fly again.

The Squadron had a young OFS student going through his course who was a law unto himself, and also totally fearless—a bad trait in any aviator. On one occasion I had flown as his chase aircraft during an FAC exercise over Banffshire and at one point had to order him to fly higher. As he approached his target he was so low that his jet wash was parting the grass on the hills. When we returned to the Squadron he did not understand what the fuss was about, not appreciating the danger in which he had placed both himself and his aircraft. He was appointed to 800 Squadron, but before he left 736 I briefed him for his final Mirror and Dummy Deck Landing sortie. It was a dull and drizzly morning with the cloud base between 600 and 1,000 feet, and I watched him take off and head for Milltown airfield a couple of miles away. I must have been sitting down for five minutes only when the airfield crash alarm sounded followed by the announcement, 'Scimitar aircraft crash off the airfield on the approaches of Milltown!' Then the ATC telephone rang: 'Duty controller here, sir. B—— crashed turning finals at Milltown. We are not sure what has happened to the pilot.' I sat down heavily, wondering what on earth had happened because it had only been minutes since he had taken off.

The pilot had ejected just as he had turned finals for his first MADDL approach. Apparently he had roared into the circuit at over 600 knots in a great ball of fog, with low visibility and a low cloud base, broken hard downwind, selected his undercarriage 'down' as the speed fell through 250 knots, followed quickly by all his flap—but he had forgotten to put the 'Blow' switch 'On'. The Scimitar with its flaps down at 170 knots and with no blow would pitch nose-up and stall. Blow, incidentally, is air at high pressure taken from the engine compressors and fanned over the leading- and trailing-edge flaps to maintain the airflow at low airspeeds. It also permits one to land at a much slower airspeed, which is essential in carrier flying when the

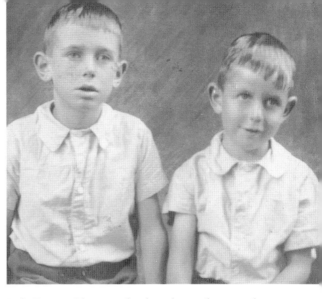

Left: Future Phantom leader: the author, aged nine months, with his father, in 1934.
Above: 'Gormless' and 'Happy': the author (at left) with his brother Brian, in 1938.
Below: John ('Jack') Doust, the author's father, as Rye Harbour Master, in 1955.

(Unless otherwise indicated, all photographs in this book are from the author's collection.)

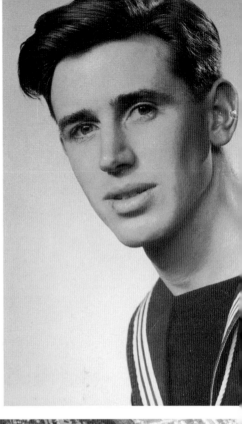

Opposite, upper left: The author's sisters Jacqueline and Theresa, Mother and dog Joey in front of the signal mast at Rye Harbour—apparently in sombre mood.

Opposite, upper right: The author in 1951—and in the Navy now.

Opposite, lower: HMS *Collingwood*, the Royal Navy's Electrical School, in 1950.

Above: The author's New Entry Course undergoing inspection by the Captain of HMS *Collingwood* in March 1951.

Below: The Mediterranean Fleet in Grand Harbour, Malta, in 1953. In mid-channel are (left to right) the cruiser *Liverpool*, carrier *Indomitable* and cruisers *Glasgow* and *Superb*; in the background are the carrier *Theseus* and the cruiser *Cleopatra*. Just visible behind *Theseus*, in dry dock, is the carrier *Ocean*.

Opposite, top: *Theseus* turns into the wind for a land-on, 1952.
Opposite, centre: USS *Midway*'s SAR helicopter visits *Theseus*, 1952. The American carrier can be discerned on the horizon.
Opposite, bottom: King Paul of the Hellenes visiting *Theseus* off Athens.
Above: Commissioned pilot Alfie Wigg makes a hard landing while delivering the mail and pay to *Theseus*. Alfie was an old Rye Grammar School chum of the author's.
Below: Sea Furies and Fireflies prepare for take-off from *Theseus*.

Left, top: HMS *Implacable* glimpsed through the murk with 150 feet of her forefoot above the waves, storm Force 10 in the Irish Sea, spring 1953.

Left, centre: Upper-yardmen (Air) Bob King, George Humphreys, Michael Doust and Phil Cardew pose in front of a Provost Mk 1.

Left, bottom: The remains of Reg Hunt's Provost 'Mike Juliet' after it was landed upon by another Provost.

Opposite, top: RAF Syerston: Provost trainers lined up, and a lone Harvard trainer making a final salute, 1954.

Opposite, centre: Lieutenant John Beard lounges by a 738 NAS Sea Hawk; and (right) the 738 NAS hangar at Lossiemouth in 1955.

Opposite, bottom: No 40 OFS starts engines for its flypast, Lossiemouth, 1955.

Above: No 40 OFS graduation line-up. Back row (left to right): John Beard, Phil Cardew, Reg Hunt, John Weyman, Bill Williams, Michael Lawrence. Front row: the author, Nigel Anderton, Bob King, George Humphreys, Denis McCarthy.
Below: 831 NAS officers on commissioning. Back row (left to right): the author, unknown, Bobby Sandison, Reg Hunt, Mike Smith, Treavor Spafford, Gerry McFall. Front row: George Wilcox (ALO), Pete Wheatley, Jock Tofts (SP), Stan Farquhar (CO), Gus Gray, Tony Bastick (AEO).

Above: 831 Naval Air Squadron in deep maintenance after disembarkation, 1957.
Below: The outcome of an argument between a tractor and Stan Farquhar's Wyvern.

Above: The author and Pete Wheatley put the finishing touches to 'Flook' on Stan Farquhar's Wyvern.
Below: RNAS Ford's SAR Dragonfly helicopter, 1955.

Above: The author starts up his Wyvern at Lossiemouth prior to making a live bombing run on Garvie Island, 1956.
Below: The author manning his 831 NAS Wyvern, winter 1956. The aircraft in this instance is WN330/'381'.

Opposite, upper: A Westland Wyvern S Mk 4 with a full load of 60-pound SAP 3-inch rockets, 1956. The pilot is Lieutenant Pete Wheatley.
Opposite, lower: Lieutenant Commander Stan Farquhar leading 831 NAS out for the flypast over Ford Air Station, 1956.
Above: 831 Squadron starts up for the Ford flypast, 1956.
Below: The author lands a Wyvern S.4 at RNAS Ford.

Above: The author's wife's WRNS course is inspected by HM Queen Elizabeth the Queen Mother at HMS *Dauntless*, the WRNS training establishment near Reading. Below: No 16 Air Warfare Instructors' Course, HMS *Excellent*, December 1957. Back row (left to right): John Webster, the author, Colin Moorcroft, David Mears, Bob Northard. Front row: Ian Josselyn RAN, Lieutenant Commander Eve, Lieutenant Commander Stewart, Lieutenant Commander Miller, Malcolm Bland.

Above: The Operational Flying School instructors, 736 and 738 Squadrons, RNAS Lossiemouth. Back row (left to right): unknown, the author, and Lieutenants Williams, Atkinson, Bristow and Stewart. Front row: unknown, Lieutenant Commander Lee RAN (CO 736 NAS, CFI), unknown, Lieutenant Commander Brown (CO 738 NAS), Lieutenant Commander Monsell, and Lieutenants Moore and Sheppard.

Below: Captain Michael Pollock, the Captain of *Ark Royal*—and future First Sea Lord—with 'Jenny's Side Party' on the carrier's quarterdeck after Jenny and her girls had repainted the exterior of the ship. Hong Kong, 1963.

Above: *Ark Royal* picks up speed after leaving Hong Kong, 1963.
Below: *Ark Royal* passing the Oceanic Hotel as she enters Mombasa harbour, 1963.

working loads both on the aircraft and on the ship's arresting gear need to be minimised. With the pilot still pulling hard as he entered the final approach, his aircraft had pitched nose-up and flicked into a spin from which—at such a low altitude—he could not have recovered. He ejected, and his aircraft entered a near-vertical dive, hit the ground and exploded; his parachute deployed and he and his ejection seat landed on the edge of the crater and fireball. He was very lucky indeed, and apart from shock he received only the usual sore back. Even after the accident he exhibited no fear; indeed, he was convinced that he had not been responsible for the accident, despite the irrefutable evidence found by the AIU team: rummaging through the wreckage, they had found the 'Blow' switch to be in the 'off' position. When he left 736 for 800 Squadron, I was very worried that this young pilot would not live to see another Christmas.

* * *

I had been in 736 for nearly a year and I thought that it was about time that I went back to sea, so I wrote to the Appointing Officer in DNOA (X), Lieutenant Commander Rowan Thompson, after getting no response or reaction from my CO. The next thing I received was a sharp summons to the CO's office.

'What do you mean by writing to the Appointing Officer without my approval?' he shouted at me.

'Quite simple, sir: you have done nothing for me despite repeated requests, and I am tired of being ashore for over six years. If I had wanted to be a shore-based pilot I would have joined the Air Force!'

'Well don't do it again! The appointer is a friend of mine!'

'Yes, sir.'

I had almost said 'So what?' but had held my tongue. A few weeks later my name appeared in the Officers' Appointments List to join 800 Squadron as the AWI *vice* Dave Howard. I was over the moon but there was one snag: it meant leaving May at a critical time in her life. She was now pregnant with our first daughter Naomi. We discussed it and she was happy with so many friends around her, especially Drucie Mills, the wife of the Senior Pilot of 800 Squadron. My parents were also prepared to come north and be with her, so we let the appointment date stand.

When 800 Squadron re-embarked from Lossiemouth its new CO, Peter Newman, did not go because of back problems. Don Mills took over temporarily and Dave Howard moved into the Senior Pilot's shoes. Peter's medical condition did not improve and consequently Don and David remained in their new positions. At one point John Ford thought that he might be rejoining 800 as the CO. Peter's condition had been caused by an ejection from a US Navy Demon fighter while on exchange with VX-4 in California. The day before he was due to embark he had some stiffness with his back and visited an osteopath in Elgin for treatment. The following morning—the morning of the embarkation—he awoke to find that he was virtually paralysed from the neck downwards. So Don embarked the Squadron. Days ran into weeks, and it gradually became obvious that Peter would not be fit for some time to come. Their Lordships decided in their infinite wisdom to leave Don as the CO and Dave as the Senior Pilot, Peter Marshall moving up as the Squadron AWI. My appointment to 800 stood and I would now be relieving Peter.

In 736 a new exercise had been introduced for OFS students—catapulting. This exercise was to be carried out at RAE Bedford, where a large Navy unit had been established for carrying out deck and catapult trials as well as developing other flight-deck equipment. The catapult was underused, so it was considered a good idea to have each Scimitar and Sea Vixen OFS student carry out a number of launches before going to a ship for the first time. The facilities at Bedford also allowed the training of catapult crews, both in the loading of aircraft and in launching them.

I flew south with several OFS students for catapult training, each pilot being allocated two launches. The time came for Sub Lieutenant Ian Frenz to have his catapult shots. Ian was a very short young man, no more than 5 feet 3 inches in his stockinged feet. He manned his Scimitar, was loaded on to the catapult, opened his engines up to full power and gave the salute that he was ready to be launched. The lever was pulled and the jet surged forward along the track. As it left the end of the track the jet reared into an exaggerated nose-up attitude, dropped its left wing and proceeded to execute a left-hand turn around the airfield no more than a hundred feet above the ground. I stared open-mouthed, unable to believe what I was seeing and quite expecting the aircraft to crash at any second. The telephone rang and Commander Pat Chilton, the CO at RAE Bedford, who had witnessed the launch, wanted to know what had happened but at that moment I had no explanation. Ian landed safely and we all ran over to his aircraft to find out.

When Ian had manned his jet he had gone through all the normal checks for catapult launch, including the locking of his rudder pedals and seat straps. However, for some reason his rudder pedals flew away from him and he slumped in his seat as he was launched. Consequently, he could barely see out of the cockpit and had instinctively pulled back on the stick. It was the air cushion between his aircraft and the ground that had kept the Scimitar airborne. He was very lucky indeed, and I do not think anyone realised just how close we had come to losing both man and machine.

I visited Bedford in connection with other trials. The Scimitar was now carrying the American Sidewinder air-to-air, IR-homing missile as part of its armament and it was necessary to establish to what limits the aircraft could land off-centreline on a carrier's deck without causing damage to either the aircraft or the missile's pylon and attachment points. I arrived early on a clear and cold morning, was briefed and made my first run into the arrester wire strung across the runway. Nothing happened, so I was sent back to the starting point but further off-centre, but still nothing meaningful was achieved. After more discussion I was invited to go right back to the beginning of the runway and as far off-centre as I could manage without putting my left wheel in the gutter. I ran up to full power, released the brakes, roared off down the runway and hit the arrester wire at about 180 knots. There was a bang, I nearly went through the windscreen and the missile went hurtling along the runway. The scientists had got what they wanted, and I taxied back to the servicing line. The aircraft was closely inspected and nothing was found to be wrong with it except for the missile attachment bolts, which had sheared due to the heavy side loading. The RAE Naval Unit now had enough data to produce graphs and limitations for deck landings for Scimitars armed with Sidewinder missiles.

I was involved in another trial with the Scimitar, this time firing 2-inch rockets at RAE West Freugh in south-west Scotland. It was necessary to establish the optimum firing range, dive angle and release speed for this weapon when released as a salvo from a rocket pod. The trial went well until I had to go south for my biannual high-altitude test at Seafield Park. My trials Scimitar had been having problems with its fuel booster pumps, which kept on failing. The engines would run under gravity feed even when the pumps had failed and the pilot in these circumstances was limited to non-violent movements of the throttles, otherwise the engines could flame out. Nevertheless, so long as he knew of the defects of the fuel system, and its limitations, then the aircraft was safe to fly and complete the trial. While I was south it was arranged for Curly Wood to complete the trial. I briefed him about the fuel system problem and what he had to do at West Freugh, and he seemed quite happy when I left. When I returned a week later, however, the trial had not been completed and the aircraft was in the hangar, in such a bad state I could not imagine what had happened. This was when I became aware of the fact that Curly was quite a nervous individual where flying was concerned: everything needed to be perfect, and therefore he was unable to cope with anything out of the ordinary. This unfortunate trait would come to a head after his marriage failed and he left the Navy to join the Australian airline Qantas.

Curly, like many other former FAA pilots, joined Qantas and moved out to Australia, where he received his flight training before taking up flying duties. He shared an apartment with several other ex FAA pilots in Sydney. One day he was found dead from self-inflicted gunshot wounds: he had committed suicide. As far as I know, it was never established what had really driven him to carry out this terrible act, but he was obviously very disturbed and distressed about something that must have been so overbearing that he could see no other way out of his problems. He had not confided in any of his apartment friends so they were very much at a loss to explain his decision. When I heard the news I was dreadfully upset: we had been good friends in 736, especially during an Escape and Evasion exercise in Aberdeenshire.

Curly Wood and Chris Wilson were in my escape team. We were dropped at night to the west of the River Deveron. After disturbing a herd of sleeping cows, which we nearly fell over in the darkness, Chris went for a gap in a fence, promptly to run into a strand of barbed wire, which cut his forehead open. After patching him up we continued on our way to a position not far from the town of Keith. It was now very bright, with almost a full moon, as we scrambled down across a turnip field to a stone wall before crossing a road to our next rendezvous point. As we crouched behind the wall, I was certain that I had heard someone, or something, on the other side of the road. Then I heard the noise again: '*Wish noo.*' Somebody was telling someone to be quiet. There was a troop of Cameron Highlanders crouching behind an outcrop of rock and I could just make out their tam-o'-shanters bobbing about above the rocks. Suddenly, they were across the road and we three scattered. Chris vanished completely and Curly dropped to the ground in the muddy farm tracks and pulled his immersion suit hood over his head; he even lit up a cigarette and they missed him completely. They had seen me dive into the turnip field and proceeded to search for me, coming to within two rows when they suddenly gave up. An hour later the soldiers moved away and we made our way independently to the rendezvous. It seemed so odd that a young man who had acted so coolly in this set of circumstances would, at a later date, take his own life.

Before I left 736 Squadron, John Ford would have an aircraft accident. It was not a serious one, but even so it dented his pride. He had been airborne on a solo flight and for reasons unknown had almost run out of fuel. Aircraft were landing on the easterly runway at Lossiemouth, and he called finals with three green lights, indicating that his landing gear was down and locked. When he lowered the nose wheel on landing it collapsed and he skidded along the runway tail-up. John swore that he had had three green lights, but the Station Accident Unit established that the nose wheel had never been locked down. John was so short of fuel that he dare not go round again and was hoping that his nose wheel would lock as the main wheels hit the runway. For quite a long time John was very conciliatory towards us in the Squadron.

At the end of July 1963 I took my leave of 736 Squadron, having packed my bags and flying kit for the long journey out to Singapore to join 800 Squadron aboard HMS *Ark Royal*. Although I had at last obtained my wish to go back to sea, I was quite worried about leaving May behind with a baby due in two months' time. We were still living in our old caravan at Milltown, and although she had many friends about her to help when the time came it was not the same as having a husband nearby at that critical phase in a woman's life. However, we had always said that the Navy came first and that we would never be like certain others, who at the least provocation whined to stay at home because of some domestic matter or other. We drove over to Elgin station chattering away to each other, but May would not stay to see me off and left in tears, which upset me very much. There was still half an hour to go before the train arrived from Inverness and about fifteen minutes later the stationmaster came out and said that my wife was on the telephone. She apologised and we spoke the usual words with nuances of love that one utters in such circumstances. She was now much happier and I promised to telephone her from RAF Lyneham, from where I would be flying out the next morning to Singapore.

V

BUCCANEER

— 17 —

Return to the Front Line

ON ARRIVAL at Aberdeen I transferred my baggage and kit to the overnight sleeper to King's Cross, London, bought a couple of magazines,
had a beer and boarded the train a few minutes before it pulled out
for its long journey south. May had prepared some excellent sandwiches for
me; whatever food she made ready, it was always superb and a joy to eat. I
ordered a pot of tea to go with the sandwiches and laid back on my bunk to
read my magazines in a leisurely fashion. It was not long before I was asleep,
to be woken occasionally, as when the train pulled into Edinburgh and York.
My next recollection was that of being woken by the sleeping-berth attendant
bringing in morning tea half an hour out from King's Cross.

There was plenty of time after I had got off the train so I had a cup of
coffee and then took a taxi to Paddington station for my last journey to
Swindon, from where I would be bussed to RAF Lyneham. It was a beautiful
day in London and I could quite easily have spent a few hours wandering
around the city. I had to be at Lyneham by 1600 at the latest in order to go
through the rigmarole of checking in to ensure that I had received all my
'jabs' and that my papers were in order. Two RAF buses were waiting at
Swindon to transport about four dozen of us—service personnel, wives and
families and a few diplomatic officers. The RAF was very good in taking care
of our baggage, leaving us just with our overnight and small travelling bags.
At Lyneham we were checked through quickly, allocated rooms for the night
and informed that dinner started at 1800 and that breakfast was at 0430
the next morning. Our aircraft was due to take off between 0530 and 0600
so it meant rising at about 0330 in order to make breakfast on time. I quickly
found a telephone and called May to let her know that I had arrived safely
and that there would be a couple of letters in the post for her.

The RAF used the Bristol Britannia aircraft on their flights to Singapore.
I had seen Britannias being built at Filton during my QFI course visit. This
very large, four-engine, turboprop passenger airliner and transport aircraft
was a descendant the colossal but ill-fated Brabazon built by the same
company for future airline travel. The Britannia was an ideal long-haul
transport for the RAF, capable of carrying both heavy cargo and passengers

167

at the same time. Our aircraft would have four huge jet engine crates forward together with seating for fifty passengers in rearward-facing seats—the safest way to fly.

Dawn had broken when our heavily laden aircraft lumbered into the air bound for El Adem in Libya, Jack Smith's favourite bombing range. It touched down at about midday in time for a superb lunch of roast lamb, potatoes and peas, followed by an excellent sweet and bananas. At 1400 the Britannia took off again, heading this time for Aden at the southern end of the Red Sea. Our flight path was across and over the rugged Sahara Desert, then over the dark and bleak mountains near Khartoum. It was by now quite dark so we did not see the Red Sea and our direct path took us straight into RAF Aden. We were served a very good dinner somewhere over Khartoum, though once again the meal included peas and bananas!

We landed in the dark, at 2300—the same time that the resident Hunter squadrons were night flying. Everybody disembarked, some to stay; the remainder of us spent a couple of hours in the NAAFI bar. One of the Hunter squadrons was No 208, which was commanded by Gordon Lewis who had served with me as a QFI in 764 Squadron. I asked around to see if he was available, and before I knew it he suddenly appeared, collected me and drove me out to his married quarters for a 'noggin' or two with him and his wife Di.

One has to visit Aden in order to appreciate the extreme temperatures in that region of the world. I and all the other passengers had been sitting in an air-conditioned cabin, but when we stepped out into the Aden air it was like walking into a furnace even though it was almost midnight. The temperature simply took one's breath away and immediately one was bathed in sweat. It was at that time of night as hot as could be experienced on the hottest summer day in Britain. Aden would later on become a very familiar airfield to me.

At about 0200 our Britannia rose once again into the air, this time heading for RAF Gan in the Maldives, where we would have breakfast. We ate in the NAAFI and were given a hearty meal of bacon and eggs with plenty of toast, marmalade and tea or coffee, plus the RAF's favourite bananas. I was now beginning to believe that the RAF lived on peas and bananas! About 1000 we took off for the final leg to RAF Changi, Singapore, where we were expected to arrive at about 6.30 p.m. local time, which was seven and a half hours ahead of British Summer Time. En route we received our final meal and on the menu were, once more . . . peas and bananas! The RAF catering department had no imagination where cuisine was concerned, but I was not complaining: the food was good and wholesome, and I enjoyed it.

Evening was closing in fast as we made our final approach to Changi. The island of Singapore was a mass of lights, and suddenly our wheels were on *terra firma* in the Far East—the furthest I had travelled from 'Olde Blighty'. Although it was warm when one stepped out of the aircraft, the temperature was pleasant, moderated by sea breezes. However, the air had a pungent odour about it that reminded me of rotting vegetation and sewage. I was picked up by a Navy driver who delivered me to the wardroom at HMS *Terror*, the shore establishment at Singapore. *Ark Royal* was not in harbour as I had been led to believe back home; in fact she was a long way south, en route from a visit to Fremantle in Western Australia. I was just in time for dinner, and after a couple of beers I retired for the night, utterly exhausted by the long journey and two-day flight.

At breakfast the following morning Lieutenant Commander Venables, the First Lieutenant, came up to me to say that I would be embarking in HMNZS *Otago* and would be taken to sea and transferred to *Ark Royal* when she arrived in Malaysian waters. I had a wonderful time aboard the New Zealand frigate, which was crewed by a fine group of officers and men. Eventually *Ark Royal* hove over the horizon and *Otago* took up duties as the carrier's planeguard. Finally, at the end of the afternoon, *Otago* came up alongside 'Ark's starboard side and, with all my baggage and kit, I was transferred by breeches buoy. As I reached the boat deck there were Don Mills, Dave Howard and Peter Marshall all waiting to welcome me aboard. It was as if a group of brothers were meeting again after a long separation. I knew instinctively that I was going to have a happy time both in the Squadron and aboard the ship.

— 18 —

Premier Air Squadron

A S SOON as I arrived on board, my kit and baggage were taken away and delivered to my cabin, which I was sharing with Pete Marshall and Jeremy Nichols. Don Mills whisked me away to meet 'Wings' and the Captain. The Captain was Michael Pollock, a famed destroyer commander and a man who had a tremendous regard for the Fleet Air Arm. Commander (Air) was none other than Ray Rawbone, whom I knew from Ford and Yeovilton and who had also been my boss at Lossiemouth. The ship had an air of happiness about her, and she positively sparkled from stem to stern. It is odd how one always gets a 'feeling' on stepping aboard a warship as to whether she is run well or is unhappy: *Ark Royal* was both very well run and a happy ship.

I checked into the mess office and was given a mess number, and as there was no night flying everybody was down in the wardroom bar. It was like coming home to the family: there were so many old friends, and many of my old students from OFS days at Lossiemouth—some were flying Scimitars and others Sea Vixens—and I also knew many of the anti-submarine helicopter pilots and Gannet AEW crews. It was a happy band of air warriors who respected each other and enjoyed one another's company. As I entered the wardroom bar there were cries of 'Welcome aboard Punchy!', 'Nice to see you again!' and so on. Although there is a standing rule in any wardroom of 'no treating', I soon had drinks thrust in to my hand and in fact I hardly spent a penny that evening. When the bar closed I turned in for a good night's sleep because the next day I was scheduled for an area familiarisation sortie and deck-landing practice.

* * *

The date 31 July 1963 was to have been a happy day for me. I was scheduled to make my first flight from *Ark Royal* in a Scimitar fighter and so I changed into my flying kit and climbed the ladder from the starboard after gun sponson to the flight deck. On the way up the Squadron Line Chief, an old friend from 764 Squadron days, met me.

'Hello Mr Doust! I don't think you'll be flying yet.'

'Why?' I asked.

'Well, Mr Macfie has just gone in!'

He was very sad and upset; aircraft line personnel always take an accident hard because they are the last to see a pilot before he takes off. Off the starboard quarter was a large patch of white frothy water over which the SAR helicopter was hovering, its crew searching for signs of Andy Macfie. I had wondered what had caused the sudden trembling of the ship while I was changing in my cabin. She was going full astern and swinging to starboard to stop; now I was looking at the reason.

Andy had been practising divisional rocket attacks against the splash target, flying as No 2 to his leader. The leader dived a little too steeply for the attack and pulled out lower than normal, and Andy, making sure that his leader was clear, went too low before firing his rockets. He made a hard pull-out, probably 'mushing' as he did, but his tail hit the water and his aircraft exploded, killing him instantly. The only items recovered were his flying helmet and right-hand flying glove. Everybody was shocked by the event. It rocked me because he had been one of my best students in 736 Squadron and was a very steady and likable young naval aviator and officer, and what made it hurt even more was the fact that he had been so pleased to see me in the wardroom the previous evening. Don Mills wanted to postpone my first flight but I refused: 'Let's get it over with. Nothing will change what has happened.' Thus it was in a very sombre atmosphere that I was briefed to carry out my area familiarisation flight and return for deck-landing practice with Don Richardson acting as my chase pilot.

I was catapulted at about midday and climbed to 25,000 feet, heading for RAF Tengah on the western side of Singapore Island. It was a beautifully clear day over the ship and, according to her Meteorological Officer, similar conditions existed over Singapore. However, as I approached the island it became obvious that it was covered in low cloud and fog. I called Singapore Air Traffic Centre for their latest weather report and they gave fog at all the airfields throughout the island, timed 0100Z. I did not hear the 'Zulu' and thought that they were referring to local time. Don chirped in and said, 'He gave GMT, cloth-head!' I felt an utter idiot at having missed it. Arriving back at the ship, I carried out half a dozen roller deck landings followed by a final hook-on. I was back in the carrier saddle again and loving every minute!

There now followed about ten days of intensive flying, including a SEATO sea exercise with ships from Great Britain, Australia, New Zealand, the United States and Singapore. The ships split into two opposing task forces, 'Orange' and 'Blue', making dummy attacks against each other and carrying out various defensive manoeuvres. At the end of the exercise most of the participating vessels anchored for a weekend of recreation off the eastern Malaysian island of Pulau Tioman. Although it was very overcast with high cirrus cloud, there was insufficient cover to prevent the sun's ultra-violet rays from causing us a great deal of sunburn; I spent most of my time ashore swimming but I still ended up looking rather like a beetroot. After this weekend the ship steamed to Singapore Dockyard for repairs to one of her catapults and her engine-room boilers. Before entering Singapore, most of the air group flew off for three weeks, the Scimitars and Sea Vixens to RAF Tengah and the Gannets and helicopters to RAF Seleta.

* * *

800 Squadron was disembarked at Tengah and its officers were billeted in the nearby RAF and Army Officers' Messes while the men stayed in the RAF barracks. As it was the height of summer, a tropical routine was in force and this meant that all squadron flying and non-essential maintenance were suspended after noon for the remainder of the day. Most of the officers retired to the Officers' Mess bar and had a few pints of Tiger beer followed by a curry lunch, which together put one soundly to sleep for the remainder of the afternoon.

The Royal Navy had a NASU based at RAF Tengah. Commander Treavor Spafford, who had served with me in 831 Squadron, was in command of the NASU. Another friend, Chief Petty Officer Roy Mullender, was running the RAF Tengah Yacht Club. The RAF were so pleased with the way he had set about reorganising the Club, increasing its membership and winning races, that they had made him the Commodore. The first Sunday ashore I wandered along to the Club to find out what was available and ran into the Group Captain's wife, who promptly invited me along for a day's sailing with her husband and two small boys in their Chinese junk. It was an excellent sailing boat consisting of a long and narrow hull with an outrigger, a lateen sail and a canopy over the steering position and stern seats. The craft went like the wind and was a joy to sail. The canopy was a great idea because it shielded the occupants from the fierce sun and enabled a cool breeze to flow through underneath. The two sons, who were about six and seven years old, were their second family; the first family of two girls, having grown up, were now nurses. They were very proud of Roy Mullender and the way he had put the Station Yacht Club on the map: it was flourishing much more than hitherto and was making a name for itself on the island.

Young Sub Lieutenant B——, from my 736 Squadron days, was about to prove just how dangerous he was when flying. Before disembarking to Tengah, the Squadron had been practising FAC on the Asahan Range north of Kuala Lumpur. Dave Howard, now the Senior Pilot, was scheduled to fly a Scimitar, which had been piloted by B—— on its previous flight. During his walk around the aircraft he found fresh blades of grass protruding from the starboard wing-tip navigation light cover. Dave refused to fly the aircraft until it had been thoroughly checked over and the previous occupant asked how the aircraft had collected this grass. He said that had no idea. I was on the same sortie as Dave and took off by myself for Asahan. When I arrived over the range I asked the Army Major if B—— had been flying too low or had made a very low pull-out, but he could not recall him having done so. For the time being the episode remained something of a a mystery.

While disembarked, the Squadron once again carried out some FAC training, this time over Jahor Bahru, just north of Singapore. B—— was scheduled to fly one of these sorties. During one of his dummy attacks he pulled out so low that he hit a withy bush about ten feet high, shattering the forward half of his port drop tank and damaging the leading-edge flap, the under surface of the port wing and the port wing flap. He then proceeded to request a further attack. Captain Hunter, the FAC officer, was so distraught that he ordered him home, but B—— repeated his request. The Army Captain then made it very clear that he meant what he was saying, ordering him 'Return to base immediately!', and off to Tengah he went.

I was the Squadron Duty Officer that particular day, and when the young man returned to the dispersal I could hardly believe my eyes: it was almost as if the pilot had been to war. The damage was so bad that the aircraft had to be exchanged for a new one from NASU. What amazed me most was his nonchalant attitude. Don Mills informed Commander (Air), who in turn informed Captain Pollock, who jumped in his staff car, came over to Tengah, picked up the young pilot and took him out to the range to show him exactly how close to death he had come—the bush had been chopped off about two feet from the ground—but still B—— was unimpressed. The Captain grounded him for the remainder of his time ashore at Tengah, made him the permanent Duty Officer and stopped his shore leave and mess wine bill. None of it made any difference, and we all worried that it was only a question of time before something truly dreadful happened.

However, he eventually met a Commander's daughter, to whom he became engaged and later married. He left the Navy at the end of his short-service career, and I understand that he joined British West Indian Airlines. Sarcastically, I would always say, 'Let me know if he is the pilot of the airliner I am travelling on—so that I can get off!' Perhaps I was being rather cynical, and perhaps marriage settled him down. I hope so.

* * *

On 29 August 1963 the air group re-embarked in *Ark Royal* and set passage for Hong Kong, carrying out various exercises en route including dummy nuclear attacks. On 5 September Lieutenant Nick Kerr and I were scheduled to fly and deliver a 2,000-pound shape in OTS ('Over-the-Shoulder') attack mode. This meant flying directly over the target into the wind, crossing the target and pulling up into a loop following the bomb direction and release instrument. After completing about 110 degrees of the loop the bomb is automatically released and the aircraft continues pulling hard to the top of the loop, whereupon it rolls out upright and dives away in the opposite direction as fast as possible. In the meantime the bomb continues an upward flight to approximate 17,000 feet above ground or sea level and it then falls over and descends vertically towards the target, exploding in an air burst similar to that of the Hiroshima bomb. The intention is for the delivery aircraft to be at ground level, flying at maximum speed and four or five miles away when the bomb bursts. Nick Kerr carried out his dummy attack during the forenoon, flying a Sea Vixen against a smoke target placed about a mile off the port side of the carrier. His fall of shot—that is, the distance the bomb

173

fell from the target—was about 1,500–2,000 yards, which, to say the least, was not very accurate. My flight was scheduled for the afternoon.

The ship's Gunnery and Meteorological Officers briefed me, and they, along with the Navigation Officer, checked out my flight plan and navigation details. All were happy. I manned my Scimitar in the hangar, playing the exercise for real, and was towed to the forward flight deck lift, where I started my engines. As the lift reached flight-deck level I was directed to the port catapult from where I was launched for my one-and-a-half-hour sortie. My flight entailed climbing up to about 35,000 feet and then heading south towards the South China Sea. After forty-five minutes I descended to low level, turning inbound for my target, which was, again, another smoke float placed on the starboard side of the carrier at about one mile, with HMNZS *Otago* another mile further to the east. During my low-level run-in I passed an RFA heading south for Singapore, but at the end of forty minutes there was no sign of either *Ark Royal* or *Otago*. My fuel was by this time getting quite low, and all I could see, in any direction, was water.

I quickly checked my compass against both my emergency E2B compass and the position of the sun and it tallied fine. Then I quickly went through my navigation. That seemed all right, so I pulled up and called the ship. The Operations Room replied immediately, asked me to turn and then said they had me identified fifty miles south of the ship. I dropped down to low level again and suddenly the two ships appeared on the horizon, at which point my blood-sweat stopped flowing. I headed for the gap between the two warships and accelerated to 650 knots, aiming for the smoke float, which was now clearly visible. As I passed over the float I pulled up into a 4g looping manoeuvre, keeping my cross wires centralised. As I passed through 90 degrees vertically the aircraft began to shudder a little. A short while later I felt the bomb leave the aircraft and I pulled down towards the horizon, rolled upright, closed my throttles, descended and called the ship for a straight-in approach to the flight deck as I was extremely short of fuel. As I looked back over my shoulder I saw my bomb impact about the same distance from the smoke float as Nick Kerr's—but right alongside *Otago*'s forecastle, covering it with spray!

As soon as I had landed I was 'invited' to the bridge to see the Captain, who wanted to know what had gone wrong. First of all, the upper winds must have been much stronger than forecast, pushing me further south than planned. My navigation plan was checked and found to be correct. The fall of shot was no better than expected, and I for one would not have wanted to be within a mile of a Hiroshima-size bomb! Captain Pollock signalled the MoD (Navy), expressing his serious concern about the accuracy of the OTS delivery mode, and he received a reply saying his concern was noted but that the results were within the expected accuracy of the system.

After some further flying, the ship arrived in Hong Kong for a week's visit. Peter Marshall took me ashore to Wangchi village on the southern side of the colony to buy me a 'Clockwork Orange' wristwatch but with firm intentions of 'fixing me up' with a lady of the bars. He was out of luck—I was not interested—but I had to laugh when the 'madam' thought he had a similar business back in Britain. When he showed her a photograph of his wife and ten children 'madam' threw her hands up in horror and marched off, leaving us alone!

A week later anchor was weighed and the ship steamed south for the Malacca Strait and the Indian Ocean, and by 10 October *Ark Royal* was in the Persian Gulf for Exercise 'Billtong', during which we carried out FAC with the Trucial Oman Scouts and British Army units. The air group created a stir within the Army when it was asked to do a flypast, a Sea Vixen being flown so low by Lieutenant Dunbar-Dempsey from 890 Squadron that sand was blown into the Brigadier's soup, resulting in a signal of complaint to the ship! This was also the first time that I had experienced a mirage. I was returning to 'Ark' at low level and the sea conditions were so smooth that there was hardly a ripple, so much so that the radar altimeter refused to function because of the lack of movement on the water. I could see the ship, which was more than fifty miles away, but she was 'floating' at about 2,000 feet! It was a weird and rather supernatural sight, and then she was gone until I saw her for real at about twenty miles.

Following 'Billtong', *Ark Royal* moved south, back into the Indian Ocean, for some night-flying exercises with the Sea Vixens and Gannets and then, on 17 October, about half the air group was disembarked to Nairobi in Kenya. Don Mills had an assignation in Nairobi and nothing was going to stop him. As his Scimitar moved up to the starboard catapult, however, it developed a hydraulic leak, which was quite serious. The Squadron AEO tried to tell him that he was not serviceable to fly but Don was not having any of it: he gave his salute to be launched and we all stood there in disbelief. Even Captain Pollock was extremely concerned and wanted to know what one earth was going on down on the deck. Don was launched with fluid streaming from his aircraft—and of course he could not raise his undercarriage or flaps—and proceeded to fly to Nairobi. He had two fully loaded drop tanks so he had plenty of fuel to fly the four hundred miles, but he could have lost all his hydraulics and his flying controls. The Captain was furious when he was informed of what could happen, and forcefully made his opinion known.

The Squadron by now had a new Senior Pilot, John Kennett, who joined off Singapore. Dave Howard flew home to become the Senior Pilot of 736 Squadron during its period of run-down. However, John would meet with an accident on the flight deck early one morning when he slipped on some oil and put his knee out, damaging a cartilage. This required him to be medevacked to the military hospital in Aden, where his knee was operated on. He returned on board about two weeks later. In the meantime Don Richardson, being the senior Lieutenant in the Squadron, took over temporarily as the Senior Pilot and flew ashore to Nairobi. I remained on board as the officer in charge of the remainder of 800 Squadron. Just over a week later Don Richardson flew back to Mombasa, where the ship was berthed, and relieved me I went up to Nairobi—'up' literally, since Nairobi is 5,000 feet above Mombasa.

Following the air group's partial disembarkation, our planeguard frigate, HMS *Jupiter*, left just after midnight to enter Mombasa well ahead of the

175

carrier. *Ark Royal* was scheduled to enter the harbour at about 1300, which would have more or less coincided with high tide. As the ship approached the harbour entrance, suddenly a frigate appeared from behind a headland to the north of us steaming at full speed and with a bow wave almost as high as her forecastle. Captain Pollock, immediately recognising the ship as *Jupiter*, signalled her, 'Why have you changed your "Charlie Time"?'—that is, the time given a pilot for making his arrested landing aboard ship.

As quick as a flash, back came the reply: 'Because they have moved Mombasa!'

'When you have berthed your ship, report on board with your navigator, in dress whites, swords and medals, together with your charts and navigator's note book!'

Captain Pollock gave *Jupiter* half an hour to complete her berthing, which was a simple matter of mooring to a single buoy near the dockyard. The ship's company mustered on the flight deck and the officers lined the forward end of the flight deck, with me in the middle. The approach into Mombasa harbour is somewhat tortuous for a large, heavily draughted ship, and 'Ark' had to steam at 11 knots for the Captain to be able to manoeuvre properly, which involves heading straight for the Oceanic Hotel and then making a sharp turn to port, travelling about a couple of cables (400 yards) and finally making a hard turn to starboard into the main harbour. A deep-draughted ship stays on the port side of the channel because that is where the deep water lies. As the carrier made her final turn into the harbour there was *Jupiter*, still attempting to make fast to her buoy and lying right across our path.

The distance between the two ships was closing fast, and from the rumble beneath our feet we knew that the Captain had gone astern on the propellers. By this time *Jupiter* was directly in front of us and our Captain had lost sight of her; indeed, she was so close that we could look directly down on to her forecastle. The frigate was also going full astern, keeping the distance between the two ships about the same. All the officers had moved back about five yards, just in case there was a collision: nobody wished to be pitched over the bow into the shark-infested waters of Mombasa harbour. Then there was a piped broadcast on *Jupiter*: 'All hands on the forecastle! Clear the foredeck now!' There was little need for any instructions: everybody had long gone from that part of the ship! 'Ark' stopped opposite her buoys and was pushed by a tug into position to moor ship, while *Jupiter* disappeared from sight around the corner of the harbour. Eventually she re-emerged to pick up her buoy, and her Captain, Commander John Rowbotham, and navigator, Lieutenant Gerry Booth—both aviators—paid their compliments to Captain Pollock to explain their utter incompetence in the field of navigation and ship-handling.

The reason *Jupiter* had gone so far north was because the navigator did not realise that there was an extremely strong northerly current running — of between five and ten knots in fact. The ship was set on a course straight for Mombasa, and at daylight a town appeared dead ahead. Unfortunately this was Malindi, almost fifty miles to the north of where the ship should have been. John Rowbotham now had to drive his frigate at maximum speed to arrive in time ahead of *Ark Royal*. All the previous night, throughout the flying, he had been complaining about the carrier's speed because he had had so much trouble keeping up with her, although his recent bow wave certainly indicated that he could make 25 knots with little effort. During the visit to Mombasa John and his navigator went up to Nairobi, where Lieutenant Keith Day, the new Senior Observer of 890 Squadron, and I fell in with them. We asked what on earth were they doing, and they both laughed and shrugged the incident off as if it were of little consequence.

While in charge of the remainder of 800 Squadron in Mombasa, I had to contend with a couple of little difficulties. The first concerned my own ordnance division. I was sitting in my cabin going through the daily signal file when the Chief Regulating Petty Officer called on me.

'Sir, we had some trouble this morning at both watches.'

'Oh, and what was that, Chief?'

'Well, as you know, we went to tropical routine for the first time this morning, which meant mustering at 0730, and the Ordnance Division did not muster.'

'The whole division, Chief?'

'Yes, sir, the whole division.'

'Okay, Chief. Clear lower deck of the Ordnance Division, including all senior and junior rates, in the upper hangar in thirty minutes.'

Half an hour later I was in the upper hangar with my division muster two deep, the senior rates to the left and the junior rates to the right two paces apart. I let them have it, telling them in no uncertain terms what I thought of them. Looking each man in the eye as I strolled between the lines of men, I told them straight, looking as fierce as I could. 'The next time you let me down, I will personally knock you from one side of the flight deck to the other, even though you might be bigger than me—and no matter who you are. Do I make myself understood?'

To a man and looking straight ahead, they all shouted back, 'Yes, sir.' Some of them were two to three times my size, but they believed what I said.

'Dismiss them, Chief Regulator!'

From that moment onwards they could not do enough for me. I had spoken to them in the language they understood and they worked hard and kept themselves out of trouble for almost a couple of months.

Keith Day and I had decided to travel together on the overnight sleeper from Mombasa to Nairobi. A request had been received from the disembarked air group for more alcohol because they were holding another weekend cocktail party at the Army Officers' Mess, which was almost out of spirits. So Keith and I loaded our flying holdalls with as much of the liquid as could be crammed into them, our flying kit stuffed on top to hide the bottles from the dockyard police and the customs officials. We held our breath as we were stopped at the dockyard gates, and after a cursory inspection we were waved through on to the town station. The train, carriages, dining cars and sleeping cars were as if out of Victorian times and the whole thing ran on a narrow-gauge system, as a result of which it did not move very quickly for fear of leaving the track. Stops were quite frequent but there were no raised station platforms: one clambered up from the track embankment into the carriages, where one bought the ticket. All sleeping cars had metal mesh guards on the outside to prevent thieves from breaking in.

The train eventually stopped, and what I at first took to be a marshalling yard proved to be the Nairobi's main station. Lieutenant Edwards, 800 Squadron's Air Electrical Officer, was there to meet us with a Land Rover, and he drove us over to the Norfolk Hotel, where a double room had been booked in our name. The next day Keith and I lunched in the hotel dining room, and who should come in and sit down at the next table barely five feet away but Jomo Kenyatta, the future President of Kenya, together with his secretary. He carried a fly swat—the mark of a Chief—and seemed a very polite gentleman, if not as tall and or as thick-set as I had imagined him to be from photographs. He smiled, said good afternoon and then ordered a light lunch, and on our departure we bade him a polite farewell.

On Monday morning I was up with the lark, drove early over to the airport and was briefed by Pete Marshall for a low-level Scimitar sortie—an area reconnaissance flight around Kenya. Nairobi's main runway, pointing to the west, is about 14,000 feet long, and as one departs one immediately flies out over the Rift Valley, a huge geological fault caused by an earthquake millions of years ago. It runs for almost 2,000 miles from the Middle East to Ethiopia to Mozambique. The East Africans live in round, wattle-and-thatch houses enclosed by a circular, high, wooden fence to protect them against wild animals and human marauders. They dress mainly in black and wear red scarves, and these I could see quite clearly as I circled their villages. Then I sped off to Mount Kilimanjaro, flying around it at low speed with my flaps down and 'Blow' selected 'on'. People were climbing the mountain and they waved as I went close by. The wreckage of a DC-3 Dakota was lying about a thousand feet below the top of the mountain; there was also quite a large amount of snow around the summit, adding to the mountain's majestic appearance. Then I flew off south-west towards the salt lakes, which were swarming with millions of storks of all sorts and colours; it is to these lakes that storks fly from Europe to winter, returning in about March or April to breed. After one of the most exhilarating flights of my life, I set course for the return to Nairobi.

I liked Kenya. If I ever had my life over again, I am sure that I would like to settle in that beautiful country, especially down on the coast near the Indian Ocean. The climate is perfect and the people are very friendly; it is surely the spot where God created Man.

* * *

The air group re-embarked on 1 November and, once everybody was safely aboard, the ship headed north for the Horn of Africa for a brief work-up. A course was then set east for a position about 400 miles west of Karachi for an exercise with the Pakistani Air Force. During the passage eastwards the ship was very quiet, all those off watch having their heads down, still recovering from the Mombasa/Nairobi visit. A couple of days later we all flew once more to hone our skills in operating from the carrier, and at 0430 the following morning all the Scimitars and Sea Vixens were launched for a dawn 'strike' against the PAF at Karachi. We lost one Scimitar en route when the French naval officer on exchange in the Squadron returned to the ship with hydraulic problems. The remainder of 800 Squadron, consisting off eleven aircraft under the strike direction of 890 Squadron, continued at low level to Karachi. At 0530, just as dawn was breaking, we pounced on Karachi airport and caught the PAF Sabre jets being inspected by their pilots. They were struck dumb as Scimitars and Sea Vixens appeared out of the darkness, streaked at almost supersonic speed down their lines of fighters only a hundred feet or so above them and then vanished into the darkness off to the west. We came in so close that we could see the pilots using their flashlights to inspect their aircraft. The Pakistanis could not have been more surprised: it was all over in a few seconds, and had it been 'for real' very few of their aircraft would have been left intact.

The *Ark Royal* air group returned safely and a visual CAP was maintained by both 800 and 890 Squadrons, expecting retaliation very shortly. However, nothing happened until about 1000, when a black Canberra bomber suddenly dived out of nowhere to carry out a simulated attack against the ship. The carrier had been maintaining radio and radar silence and the PAF had no idea where we were until that moment; what they had in fact done was to fly half a dozen Canberras in line abreast until they spotted us. Then the Sabres started arriving, jumping our Scimitars and Sea Vixens as they left the catapults. In a short while the entire sky was filled with aircraft in a 'dogfight' the like of which had not been seen since the days of the Battle of Britain. How on earth we did not experience any mid-air collisions is beyond me. Everybody who could be spared from below came up on to the flight deck and superstructure to watch the spectacle, the Captain and Commander (Air) viewing it all from the bridge wings. The excitement in the ship was tremendous: it was the best aviation day for a very long time. By mid-afternoon the exercise was over and the ship steamed for Karachi, where she would be anchored for the coming weekend. We learnt later on that many of the pilots flying the Sabre jets were from the Turkish Air Force, on exchange until the PAF had trained its own Sabre pilots. It was comforting to know that we had some good Turkish pilots flying for CENTO.

Once the Karachi weekend was over, the ship headed west for Aden. The RAF were about to have an air show there but unfortunately one of the Hunter display team aircraft crashed and the pilot was killed, so 800 Squadron was asked to fill in. This meant working up an aerobatic team at very short notice. It was not the first time the Squadron had performed display aerobatics. Danny Norman, when he was 800's first CO, had flown the Squadron at the Farnborough Air Show, so now Don Mills found himself filling his shoes. The team consisted of Don Mills, John Kennett, Jeremy Nichols and Pete Marshall, with Don Richardson as the solo aerobatic pilot. It will be recalled, however, that John Kennett had slipped on the flight deck, injuring his knee, so Don Richardson took over his position in the team; as a result,

179

I suddenly found myself doing the solo aerobatic display. Over the next couple of weeks I practised low-level aerobatics and then gave a display for Commander (Air), Ray Rawbone. At first I practised at 1,500 feet above sea level and then carried out a 'Derry Turn', in which a hard turn in one direction is made, followed by a roll, inverted, to pull a hard turn in the opposite direction. It requires a lot of top rudder to hold the nose up on the horizon, and as I rolled to turn the other way the locking mechanism of my rudder pedals gave way, sending the pedals fully forward out of my reach. Consequently I could not get sufficient of a nose-up attitude and I scooped out of the turn, losing about 500 feet. This frightened Ray Rawbone, who said I was cleared to come down to 500 feet but was to remain above 1,000 for the 'Derry Turn'. I promptly called back and said the display practice had been compromised because of the problem with the rudder pedals. Back on board, the locking mechanism was found to be broken.

It was about 0630 when I staggered out of my cabin bunk to have a shower and shave, and the sun was streaming in through the cabin scuttle as the new AEO, who had relieved Malcolm Scadding, came in to change. He was sharing a cabin with me, as were Jeremy Nichols and Pete Marshall. Suddenly he said, 'Someone has shot the American President!' At first I could not quite take the news in, wondering who on earth would want to do such a thing. It was 22 November 1963, and out of respect the ship did not fly that day. Our ensign would remain at half-mast until he had been laid to rest.

Don Mills, together with his team of four and me, continued with aerobatic practice prior to giving a show on Saturday the 29th. It had been planned that, the team having made a downward 'bomb burst', I would fly vertically upwards through the burst making a 'twizzle'—that is, a high-speed rapid roll. The Air Day dawned fine and sunny and off we went to give our display, although was obvious that because we had not practised over the airfield it would not be possible to co-ordinate the formation and solo displays satisfactorily. The main display went well but when it came to the upward 'twizzle' it became apparent that I was not going to be in the right piece of sky, so I turned my finale into a near-supersonic run across the airfield as Don made his downward 'bomb burst'. On his return to the ship Don was asked to put on a display for the ship's company, and the whole show went perfectly with me 'twizzling' upwards through the burst. Everybody, from the Captain to the most junior seaman, was thoroughly delighted with the show and Don had another feather in his cap!

Earlier in November the Squadron had made its first Bullpup firings over the Indian Ocean. We were allocated about four missiles for practice and I was selected as one of the firing pilots. We had a Bullpup Trainer in the Army Training Room and we all spent a great deal of time on it. The best person on the trainer was the Squadron Line Chief, who could operate it like a ping-pong ball machine. A smoke float was dropped as a target and each of the pilots managed to place his missile within thirty yards of it.

The ship's port outboard propeller shaft had been running hot for some time and it was decided to have a look at it off Kor el Fakem on the southern side of the Trucial Oman. The carrier was taken close inshore and anchored and the ship's company had a weekend on the beaches, participating in banyan parties. When the inspection plate was removed from the after bearing propeller gland, sand was found to be mixed with the oil inside it. It was obvious that someone had deliberately introduced the sand into the system, and that 'someone' proved to be the stoker mechanic who was responsible for maintaining the bearing oil level and recording the temperatures. He was arrested, charged with causing malicious damage and placed in cells under close watch pending the ship's return home, which would be about three weeks later. He was apparently harbouring a grudge and saw his actions as the only way of getting his own back, although we never really discovered what had brought about his unhappiness.

The banyan parties were held on a fine, sandy beach where we could light barbeques and swim in relative safety—or so we all thought until the Deputy Supply Officer rushed out of the sea shouting 'Shark! Shark! Shark!' Needless to say, everybody in the water took the hint. Our DSO had been snorkelling near an isolated rock when he had come face to face with the creature, although the latter had fled in horror rather than fear—I doubt whether sharks have a fear of anything—at seeing the apparition of the DSO clad in his wet suit, goggles, mask and tank. However, it was a shark all the same, a not uncommon sight in the seas in this part of the world. None of us was prepared to risk any further encounters with these denizens of the deep.

The one fact of life in the Middle East and Africa that will always remain in my memory is the poverty. While we were all enjoying ourselves and filling our stomachs with good food, local people were passing by, the women dressed in black, sheet-like costumes from head to foot, their faces covered. They were riding donkeys, carrying bundles of sticks for their cooking fires. This part of the world is so barren that I wondered how they could possibly eke out an existence. Crops must have been very meagre, which left only fish to be caught along the shore. There was little doubt that, in comparison, we were rich beyond their wildest dreams. So also were their sheikhs, who came aboard for lunch with the Captain while we were in the Persian Gulf dressed in beautiful, flowing, silk gowns, their belts made of gold and silver and encrusted with jewels, and with jewel-encrusted daggers. The wealth that each displayed on his person was probably more than I earned in a lifetime while serving in the Navy. I have always found it hard to swallow this sort of inequality and although I am sure that the 'playing field' will eventually level out, I am equally certain that this will never happen during my lifetime.

On Monday morning the carrier steamed round to Aden, where the ship's company was given a couple of days' Christmas shopping before proceeding up the Red Sea. John Kennett returned on board fully repaired and able to take back his job as the Senior Pilot. As *Ark Royal* approached Port Suez, somebody back in the Ministry of Defence realised that ship had been scheduled to pass the stadium near the Canal where Gamal Abdel Nasser would be making his anniversary speech covering the former Suez Crisis. It was considered an inappropriate time for the ship to be there and so her passage was delayed for one day and, moreover, an anti-terrorist watch was maintained both above and under the water, a duty watch of men walking the deck edge looking down into the sea for frogmen and the duty frogmen searching the bottom for limpet mines.

'Ark' had been experiencing severe vibration, especially at high speeds, and the cause was soon found. As our divers searched the stern of the ship they discovered that the starboard outer propeller's 'A' bracket was loose and part of one of the blades was missing, so the shaft was locked and the ship would proceed home on three propellers. The dear old girl seemed slowly to be falling apart, and it was obvious that she was sorely in need of the three-year refit that awaited her back at Devonport Dockyard.

The initial passage of the Canal got under way overnight on Christmas Eve 1963. The first part took us up to the Bitter Lakes and Kanak, near the site of the famous Ancient Egyptian temple of Thebes (now Luxor). It was, and still is, the site for an Egyptian Air Force base and we could see Russian-built MiG fighters parked around the various dispersals. A good many ships were still lying around in the Lakes in varying degrees of dilapidation or resting on the bottom—a legacy of the 1956 war and a very sad sight. *Ark Royal* reached Ismalia early on Christmas Day and entered the last section of the Canal leading north to Port Said and the Mediterranean.

Christmas Eve was very relaxed in the wardroom. In the evening there was a good deal of rivalry between the squadrons at the bar and everybody was in a very convivial mood. Those officers not imbibing were quietly playing bridge, reading or simply talking quietly amongst themselves. It was much the same throughout the ship, the sailors enjoying themselves as the carrier quickly steamed north, homeward bound.

I rose quite early on Christmas morning, washed and shaved, and as I began to clean my teeth it dawned on me that there was something wrong with the fresh water. Only a few 'early birds' were in the dining room, and hardly anyone had tasted their tea or coffee. I ordered a cooked breakfast of ham and eggs and a cup of coffee, but when I sipped the coffee it had been made with salt water! I called the Chief Steward over and pointed out the fact. At first he refused to believe me, but when he took a sip from my cup he was persuaded. However, there was no fresh water for any new beverages: the ship's feedwater pumps had failed during the night and she had only about eighty tons of water to steam on up the Canal to the Mediterranean. C-in-C Mediterranean was signalled for a water carrier to rendezvous with us north of Port Said on Christmas afternoon.

The desert regions of North Africa, Egypt and Israel can be very cold at night, and during the winter months one often sees people wrapped in thick overcoats or blankets to keep themselves warm; so it was on Christmas morning as the ship entered the last section of the Canal. Officially our uniform was still tropical white, but it was not enough to keep us snug that morning. Many of the officers needed the cold brisk air to clear their heads from the previous night's partying and were standing around on the flight deck wearing greatcoats and scarves—a strange sight indeed, with white-stockinged legs protruding from beneath naval blue serge! By mid-morning the sun was well up, the temperatures were more or less back to normal and the greatcoats had disappeared for the day. Some 'gully-gully' men came aboard to sell their wares down on the quarterdeck, but they left us as we approached Port Said. The odd MiG fighter 'buzzed' the ship but remained parallel to the ship's heading. The Egyptians had obviously learnt their lesson from the loss of one of their aviators who had attempted a loop in front of a light fleet carrier. The pilot had pulled out too low and his aircraft had hit the top of the Canal embankment and exploded. British sailors, being British sailors, cheered the event, although this was more in retaliation for the closing of the Canal some seven years earlier. The Egyptian pilot was doing nothing more than showing off, and unfortunately he paid with his life.

At 1300 the ship exited the Canal into the Mediterranean, setting course for Malta. The engine feed pumps were still only producing 80 tons of water—just enough to keep us steaming at about ten knots. At 1430 our promised water tanker came alongside but the seas were too rough to permit a line to be passed and a water hose connected. Water supplied by the feed pumps to the boilers has to be very pure—three parts to one million free of salts—and there, just a couple of hundred yards away, was all the pure water we needed but the sea conditions were preventing us from receiving it!

Ark Royal always seemed to suffer from feed-pump problems when proceeding from tropical to temperate climates. The pump seals would leak very badly until they had readjusted to the lower temperatures, when all would return to normal. The Scimitar had a similar problem with its hydraulic seals, causing the aircraft to experience hydraulic failures, but once the seals had readjusted themselves to the new temperatures all would be fine once more. Our tanker returned to Malta; another was scrambled from Gibraltar, but, as we steamed westwards, slowly feed pump after feed pump came good and we left the Strait back in full working order.

Turning north-westwards, past Trafalgar and then northwards off the Portugal coast heading for the Bay of Biscay, the temperature started to plummet and the entire ship's company was now back in blues. On 30 December the fixed-wing air group was launched for Culdrose, Lossiemouth and Yeovilton, the helicopters disembarking as the ship approached Plymouth. We were all clad in our immersion suits, just in case we found ourselves swimming in the cold Atlantic waters. I was certainly pleased to be wearing mine because soon after I had been launched my cockpit heating failed, and at 31,000 feet it is mighty cold. By the time I arrived at Lossiemouth my body was like a block of ice.

The Squadron had been allocated the old 738 Squadron hangar, that unit having now left Lossiemouth to be relocated to RNAS Brawdy in Pembrokeshire. Hunter T.8 and GA.11 aircraft had replaced the Sea Hawk fighters, and 764 Squadron was no longer required to provide a Swept Wing Conversion Course.

Mine was the last Scimitar to taxy into the dispersal. Wives and sweethearts were already gathering at the far end but I could see no sign of May. I quietly climbed out of my aircraft and walked slowly towards the hangar feeling dejected and sad. Suddenly I heard May calling my name, and there she was, at the southern end of the hangar, waving to me. She had remained in the Morris Minor Traveller as it was too cold to bring Naomi out in the fresh air. My first daughter was fast asleep in her carry-cot, a bundle of joy. I signed in quickly, changed into uniform and drove home with May and Naomi to Milltown. It was wonderful to be together once again, and now as a family. May, I do not think, ever realised just how much I had missed her and the baby. Dear old Timber, our Golden Labrador, nearly went crazy when he saw me; who says that animals soon forget?

* * *

Ark Royal was now in deep refit and 800 Squadron was without a ship. Their Lordships had decided to run down the Scimitar squadrons and re-equip them with the Buccaneer S Mk 1 nuclear/conventional bomber. The second squadron to be so re-equipped was 800. However, throughout January and February we would continue to fly the Scimitar, maintaining our proficiency especially in the LABS (nuclear attack) role, but in March 1964 the first Buccaneer aircraft was delivered to the Squadron and one Scimitar was towed away to NASU.

One January morning, when the sky was clear and the temperature very low, I was scheduled for an engine test flight. I climbed to 27,000 feet, carried out the test and discovered that my aircraft was producing some excellent contrails. It crossed my mind that it might be a good jape to write '800' in the sky, which I proceeded to do. After I had landed the AMCO had a good laugh with me, and as I walked into the crew room Don Mills had a wry smile on his face, shook his head and walked back into his office. Perhaps he was wishing that he had thought of the idea?

In the middle of March 1964 John Kennett, Don Richardson and I reported to 809 Squadron for the Buccaneer Conversion Course and on the 16th I made my first flight in the aircraft with Lieutenant Bill Ryce as my instructor. It was a superb machine to fly, although its two Gyron Junior jet engines could be unpredictable at times. By the end of the month I had flown nine hours in the jet and was back in 800 Squadron flying it on a regular daily basis.

During our conversion we witnessed an accident to one of the training squadron's Buccaneers. I had been scheduled to fly with Lieutenant Rod Richens in an all-white aircraft on an engine test flight. It was an off-the-shelf flight in the rear seat, but I told Willie Watson, the Squadron CO, that unless I flew in the front seat he should forget it, so young Lieutenant Keith Somerville-Jones flew instead of me.

We were all standing in the Weapons Plotting/Navigation Room when the ATC crash alarm sounded, followed by an emergency broadcast: 'Buccaneer returning with engine on fire for runway 29!' We rushed to the window to see the jet fly past, to turn downwind, with both its undercarriage and flaps down and its air brakes partially extended. Although at this stage none of us had flown the aircraft, we all said to a man, 'What on earth is he doing in that configuration, on one engine?' As the aircraft turned it started to lose height, and even though the turning circle was quite large it was obvious

184

that the Buccaneer was not going to clear the ridge towards which it was speeding—the same ridge where Sub Lieutenant Franklin, the young Australian pilot, had crashed. Just as we were shouting 'Come on! Get out of it!', the canopy flew off, followed shortly by a pilot. Another 'chute appeared just as the aircraft disappeared behind the ridge. The bomber dived into a pig farm and exploded in a huge fireball, throwing a large column of black smoke several thousands of feet into the air. Rod Richens landed safely without injury but Keith was off flying for several months until his back mended. For a few days roast pork was the order of the day around Elgin.

— 19 —

Buccaneer Squadron

JOHN, DON and I returned to 800 Squadron fully converted on the Buccaneer. Don Mills had been reappointed and Lieutenant Commander Chris Mather joined as the new CO. He quickly carried out his conversion course and by the end of March 1964 800 Naval Air Squadron was fully complemented with fourteen aircraft in grey and white livery. New pilots and observers were arriving every week from the OFS, and within a month the Squadron was up to full strength.

The Buccaneer was essentially the Royal Navy's answer to the Russian *Sverdlov* class heavy cruisers, which had, as we have seen, appeared at the Coronation Review of the Fleet and had taken everybody by surprise. Under the guidance of the then First Sea Lord, the late Earl Mountbatten, the Navy's response had been to build an aircraft capable of a low-level, high-speed attack to deliver a nuclear weapon against these ships. The aircraft was known initially as the NA.39 and was built by Blackburn at Brough in south-east Yorkshire; it would eventually be named the Buccaneer S Mk 1. The twin jet was capable of approaching its target at Mach 0.9 and throwing a 2,000-pound nuclear bomb a distance of four and a half miles. Much of our flying training was concentrated on making this type of attack, although we also carried out attacks using conventional 1,000-pound 'iron' bombs—of which the Buccaneer could carry eight, four under its wings and four in the bomb bay. The radius to which the Buccaneer could carry conventional bombs was in excess of 500 miles, and to this day—in the year 2005—there is no military jet in service capable of tackling this undertaking, at this distance, without the need to be refuelled. However, the accuracy of the weapon system in the early days of its service left much to be desired, and it was Chris Mather's objective to make sure that it was improved during his time as CO.

Chris had been talking with Lieutenant Commander Peter Walwyn, an ex Sea Vixen observer and electrical officer who had been responsible for improving that fighter's weapon system. It was their contention that the vertical accelerometer in the Buccaneer weapon system could be used to produce a signal for the automatic release of a conventional bomb during a dive-bombing attack. All things being equal, a bomb should fall within twenty yards of the target every time, and this could be accomplished by carrying out a standard twenty-degree dive attack with about 7.5 degrees of depression on the weapon sight. As the pilot tracked the target with his bomb sight, the aircraft would perform a bunt. At 2,000 feet altitude, 450 knots airspeed and a twenty-degree dive angle the aircraft would reach the correct slant range for weapon release for a sight depression angle of 7.5 degrees. This release point would correspond to a specific load factor on the aircraft, and hence the vertical accelerometer. Thus, if the accelerometer was set to this load factor, a signal could be sent to the bomb release mechanism. The Weapon Release Tables produced by the Air Weapons Section at Whale Island, Portsmouth, gave all the necessary data, and all one had to do was select the parameters desired for the attack.

Peter modified a weapon systems computer in the Lossiemouth electrical workshops, reinstalled it and, together with Chris, flew to the Tain Range for the first trial flight. All the bombs fell within a tight twenty-yard area but were landing fifty yards short. Peter scratched his head, made a few calculations, then adjusted the computer, and on the next flight the bombs all fell about the target within twenty yards of it. I do not think that I would want a 1,000-pound bomb going off within twenty yards of me! Chris christened this modified dive-bombing method ADSL (Automatic Depressed Sight Line) bombing. We would encounter some problems with the system once the squadron pilots started practising the attack. Many pilots would select the master armament switch just prior to turning into a dive, but in order to bring their aircraft on to the line of attack they would handle them fairly roughly; consequently bombs started to be released before the actual calculated release point. Bombs were scattered all over the range, causing the Range Officer great unhappiness. It then became standard practice in this attack mode to select the armament master switch only when the aircraft was steady in the dive. The next few months were spent 'fine tuning' the system but Chris had his opponents, not least from the new, third Buccaneer outfit, 809 Squadron.

The CO of 809 Squadron, Lieutenant Commander Lynn Middleton, contended that there was nothing wrong with the standard manual dive-bombing procedure for the Buccaneer. His squadron's pilots were turning in excellent results, virtually as good as our ADSL results, although with ADSL one could reproduce identical results time and again. Moreover, Ferranti, the builders of the Buccaneer's weapon system, joined the fray by stating that the vertical accelerometer was not accurate enough: they had tried a similar system during World War II aboard an anti-submarine aircraft and had abandoned it as useless. Peter did not believe them and pointed out that the accelerometer was accurate to two decimal places, which was more than good enough for his purposes. So 800 Squadron continued with its trials.

Chris Mather was gathering around him numerous officers with an experienced weapons background—men like the Senior Pilot John Kennett, Lieutenant Commander Mike Hornblower, who was a (G) (P) qualified officer (that is, an officer qualified both as a gunnery specialist and as a pilot), and

187

Peter Walwyn. As the Squadron AWI, Doust was at the bottom of the list, and kept very much out of the picture! One day matters came to a head.

I had been scheduled for an ADSL flight on the West Freugh range in Wigtownshire—a trial using range instrumentation—but unfortunately, when I arrived over the range, the instrumentation proved to be unserviceable so I returned to Lossiemouth. Chris, annoyed with me for wasting the flight, asked why had I not attempted a radar-ranging mode of attack, but I pointed out that there was no other range available and that, moreover, I could not be sure of the radar-ranging mode. Then he started commenting about my training as an AWI, and that was enough as far as I was concerned. Furious, I told him straight that I was the AWI in the Squadron, not him, not John Kennett, not Mike Hornblower nor Peter Walwyn, and that if he wanted another AWI he should call the Appointing Officer: I would be willing to go somewhere else, where I would be appreciated. I stormed out of his office not really knowing what would happen over the next hour or so. Much to my surprise, however, nothing did happen and from that point on I was treated with more respect.

Weapon system trials continued throughout 1964 until the Squadron re-embarked, this time aboard HMS *Eagle* under the command of Captain Derek Empson, though not before it had carried out its Operational Readiness Inspection. This is a very important occasion for any front-line squadron, when everybody, the aircraft and the squadron's ability to wage war and deliver weapons is thoroughly checked out. It is an all-day event and can sometimes take longer. Our ORI took place in July 1964 and was conducted by Flag Officer Aircraft Carriers, who was responsible for our operational control.

It had been planned that all fourteen aircraft would take part in a massive bombing operation against Garvie Island, about a mile or so off John o'Groats. A bomb dump was set up a hundred yards or so to the west of the aircraft dispersal. Unlike the RAF, the RN did not possess bomb trolleys to transport the 1,000-pound munitions from the main dump, so a preparation and fusing area was established close to where the aircraft were parked, similar in general layout to the arrangements on the flight deck of a carrier.

I gave the main briefing while the Admiral sat, listened and asked the odd question or two. He was very satisfied and pleased with what he heard and then announced that he would fly in one of the aircraft as an observer. Chris suddenly appeared flustered, worrying whether the aircraft were ready and so forth, so I ran across to the dispersal to see how the arming-up was going, only to be met by Lieutenant Commander Roger Pinhey, the Squadron's Electrical and Ordnance Officer, looking quite pale. I stopped and asked what the problem was, to be informed that four live bombs had been jettisoned on to the hardstanding. I turned in disbelief and walked back with him, to be met by Chris. When I told him what had happened, he went quite ashen and returned to his office.

One of the Buccaneers had not, for some reason, been given its jettison checks. This was a test carried out on the weapon pylons and armament circuits before weapons were loaded in order to establish that a firing pulse was present when the cockpit switch was selected to the 'Jettison' position. The Ordnance Chief had in his wisdom decided to bypass the normal procedure, which would have meant offloading the bombs before pressing the jettison switch. The system clearly worked on this aircraft but with four live bombs should not have done because an undercarriage microswitch should have broken the electrical circuits with the landing gear down and the weight of the aircraft on its wheels. Thus the aircraft was unserviceable. If any one of those jettisoned bombs had exploded, Lossiemouth would have had a catastrophic accident on its hands, possibly resulting in a chain reaction with the bomb dump exploding, all the aircraft written off and a significant loss of life, not to mention the damage to the hangar, the offices, the control tower nearby and other buildings. God was surely smiling on us that day.

Chris initiated a quick investigation and by the following morning the Ordnance Chief was off the air station. If Chris had taken it further, the culprit would have received a court martial, been 'busted' to ordinary rank and lost all his gratuities and his pension. Perhaps Chris thought that, owing to the pressure created by the occasion, we were all at fault. He did not discuss it with me so I do not know what was going through his mind, except that he was extremely upset by the incident. However, it is my firm conviction that ordnance men are usually responsible for disasters such as these because of their failure to follow proper procedures. The same sort of thing has happened in the RAF, with appalling consequences: I know of two such terrible accidents that occurred during World War II resulting in a tremendous loss of life and in equipment. I believe there was such an incident at RAF Marham in Norfolk during the 1960s when Canberras were being bombed up: a thousand-pounder had partially fallen off its trolley and the trolley wheel had been rubbing against the bomb casing, which had become so hot that the explosive in the bomb ignited, killing everybody nearby and damaging numerous aircraft.

The Squadron nevertheless continued with its ORI and the Admiral was obviously impressed with what he saw from his aircraft because on landing he cleared upper and lower decks in the Squadron and told us that he was very pleased. He then signalled his staff, MoD (Navy), FO Flying Training, HMS *Eagle* and RNAS Lossiemouth that 800 Squadron was now ready for deployment in all respects. The Squadron cleared away the remaining bombs, put the aircraft to bed in the hangar and the following afternoon took a Make and Mend—half a day off duty.

Over the next couple of months the Squadron continued improving its modes of attack and during late September 1964 all the pilots carried out deck-landing practice aboard *Eagle*, which by now had emerged from her long refit at Devonport. Each pilot made about half a dozen touch-and-gos on the flight deck, followed by an arrested landing. Immediately on being arrested, each aircraft was then directed on to the bow catapult and launched back to Lossiemouth. On completion of this short practice period *Eagle* returned to Devonport for minor rectification and 800 Squadron continued with its work-up and trials ashore. A month later, during October, the carrier put to sea once again with a team of television and newspaper reporters on board and the Squadron carried out a live demonstration with 1,000-pound bombs. Unfortunately one of my bombs hung up, and while I was approaching Yeovilton to have the weapon removed one of my engines failed on finals to the air station. My observer, Lieutenant John Eatwell, was very calm and a successful landing was made. An engine exchange team was flown down from Lossiemouth and Mike Hornblower took me back in a Hunter T.8.

The day finally arrived—2 December 1964—when the Squadron re-embarked with its new aircraft for a year's deployment to the Mediterranean and the Far East. Apart from the odd test flight, virtually no flying was carried out during our Mediterranean passage. The ship waited in Grand Harbour, Malta, for HMS *Centaur*, which was on her way home from the Far East. After her arrival all confidential documents were passed over to *Eagle* together with all foreign currency, and we set sail for the Suez Canal, East Africa and the Far East. It was planned to spend Christmas in Mombasa and to depart the day after Boxing Day but owing to the ship having a defect our visit lasted almost three weeks. *Eagle* had been fitted out with four new generators capable of producing 200V AC electrical power, required for all the new aircraft and equipment installed aboard the ship, but all of them failed! A frigate fitted with a similar generators came alongside in Mombasa and, using special, heavy-duty cables, supplied the carrier with power, while a team was flown out from Devonport laden with spares. Eventually all four generators came back on line, the frigate was detached and we set sail for Singapore.

While we were at Mombasa nearly everybody made use of the Oceanic Hotel's swimming pool, especially over the Christmas period. However, two officers from 800 Squadron were responsible for having the ship's company barred from the hotel. On Christmas afternoon Steve Park and Bob Woodard, who made up one of our Buccaneer crews, decided that it would be a good jape to leap into the swimming pool fully clothed. They were somewhat inebriated and were egged on by the hotel residents, who were shouting encouragement from their hotel rooms, as they dived into the pool. Unfortunately, after the prank they walked through the hotel foyer in a very sodden condition, creating an unseemly mess and considerably upsetting the hotel manager. He telephoned the XO and told him forcefully that people from *Eagle* were henceforth barred from the hotel during the ship's stay at Mombasa. When the hotel residents got word of what had happened they threatened to leave unless the manager withdrew his decree—it was the only bit of fun they had seen around the hotel during the entire holiday—and *Eagle*'s complement were duly readmitted.

On arrival at Singapore the Squadron disembarked to RAF Changi, the site of the notorious Japanese prisoner-of-war camp. The NASU had moved from RAF Tengah to Changi and they helped the Squadron with various engine changes and other modifications. Then we re-embarked preparatory to our first exercise, 'Irongate', designed to test the defences of Singapore. Malcolm Carver, the Squadron's Senior Observer, was flying with me. Prior to the catapult launch I had stupidly jammed my Pilot's Notes between the starboard windscreen and demisting pipe and as the aircraft got under way

190

the booklet flew backwards. I raised my right hand to catch it but missed; Malcolm thought that I was reaching for my ejection seat handle and was about to depart from the cockpit when my Pilot's Notes slapped him hard in the face. Fortunately, he quickly realised that I was still there and that nothing was wrong.

While at Changi, Bob Woodard, skylarking about with his observer in the officers' swimming pool, broke the tail of his spine. Leading Steve Park down the water chute, he shouted 'Eject! Eject!' and he hit his coccyx on the bottom lip of the chute and fractured it. He was grounded for something like three months until it had healed. Chris Mather was furious to say the least, but the 800 Squadron pilots did not mind because it meant more flying for them.

Another strange incident occurred at Changi. An aviator whose name I cannot remember came up to me in the RAF Templar Officers' Mess and said to me, 'I thought you were dead, having been killed in a Sea Vixen accident off *Victorious!*'

'Sorry to disillusion you, old fellow, but I am very much alive and I do not fly Sea Vixens!'

'But you were on the same AWI course as Jack Smith and Bill Billett?'

'Yes I was,' and then the penny dropped. It was Bill Billett who had died. I was struck dumb, hardly believing that Bill had gone—first his father, then his mother, and now him. Bill had apparently been up on a tanker sortie with his new CO, Lieutenant Commander 'Sandy' Sanderson, as observer. Bill had problems transferring fuel and had requested a landing back on board *Victorious*. On his first pass he was too fast and bolted, so he flew round again for a second attempt. Nobody will ever know why, but he made an axial deck touch-down, bolted again and flew through the aircraft forward park, crashing into the sea off the starboard bow. Both he and Sandy went down with the wreckage and were never recovered. Very upset, I had a neat double scotch and went back to my cabin. Bill had been a good friend, and now he had gone.

During the SEATO exercise 'Irongate' we had to fly out to the Anamba Islands and turn inbound, 'attacking' the Singapore Dockyard at low level from the north. It was near these islands during World War II that Britain had lost the battleship HMS *Prince of Wales* and the battlecruiser HMS *Repulse*, and their hulls could (and can still) be seen quite clearly, lying on the sandy bottom in about 250 feet of water. It was at about 1000 when we crossed the coast and I was accelerating to 550 knots. At that time of day the thermals begin to take effect and I hit couple of them, causing the wings to flex so much that I could see the upper surfaces in my rear-view mirror and Malcolm lost most of his navigation kit about his cockpit. I was forced to slow down to about 450 knots and when I landed back on board I had the aircraft checked for possible structural damage although, thankfully, none was found.

Eagle steamed slowly north for Hong Kong and an FAC exercise was carried out on the old Asahan Range over on the west coast of Malaya, when live Bullpup missile firings were made against an isolated rock off the west coast of the Philippines. The Squadron had some good results and the local fisher-men ended up with plenty of scrap metal. They would wait at a respectable distance in their canoes—which were fitted with high-speed outboard motors—and as soon as a missile hit they would race in and quickly gather the remains before another one arrived. This weapons exercise was followed by live 1,000-pound ADSL bombing, our target an old shipwreck on the Scarborough Shoals to the north-west of the Philippines. Unfortunately on this occasion all my bombs hung up in the bomb bay and I had to divert to USNAS Cubi Point at Subic Bay in the Philippines. The US Navy parked us well away from everything and close to the perimeter fence. I left Dick Pearce, my observer, to look after the aircraft while I went to the tower and called the ship. An ordnance team was flown ashore and the weapons were quickly rendered safe, a check was made that they were still attached to their bomb mountings safely and I flew back to the ship to offload. There were far too many Filipinos watching the aircraft from outside the perimeter fence, so it was necessary for Dick to be seen guarding the aircraft. These people almost daily stole bombs from the USN dump in order to sweat out the explosive and then make terrorist bombs. On one occasion a young USMC sentry caught some thieves trying to steal a bomb, challenged them and, as they ran away, fired a shot, killing one of their number. All hell broke loose on the islands over the shooting and the young Marine had to be smuggled back to the US for his own safety.

Eagle continued to steam north to Hong Kong for a three-week visit, anchoring off Junk Island seven miles west of the Crown Colony. A couple of our aircraft, a Gannet and a Scimitar tanker, were disembarked to Kai Tak Aviation for repainting. The people here did an excellent job and at the finish the aircraft looked better than when they were first built. Long periods of inactivity are bad for aircrews, who can quickly fall out of flying practice from a carrier's deck. However, full use was made of all the recreational facilities, and then the anchor was weighed and the ship was off south again with a full complement of serviceable jets and helicopters. Peter Walwyn was still with the Squadron and Chris Mather was not about to let his right-hand man out of his grasp. My time was taken up with maintaining the Squadron weapon plots, of which there were many—more than I had had to keep in the old Scimitar squadron. In addition, I started writing an aircraft weapons manual for the Buccaneer—something available for no other aircraft in either the RN or the RAF. It would be almost two years before I completed the manual and I would see it in its published form some years later after I returned from the United States.

After a short stay in Singapore and some disembarked flying from RAF Changi, the air group re-embarked and the ship steamed westwards for Mombasa and some night flying south of Aden, using Aden as our diversion field. All aircrew carried sidearms while flying around the Aden Protectorate—a Browning.45 automatic pistol holding thirteen rounds or, as we always used to say, twelve for the rebels and the final one for ourselves. If the rebels made a capture, the victim would be brutally treated until finally killed, so it was a better option to take one's own life than to suffer sadistic torture.

During one session of night flying I was diverted to Aden and was instructed to return at first light the following morning immediately after the first launch of the day. The Officers' Mess dining room was closed, so after a small meal in the NAAFI restaurant I retired for the night, leaving instructions that I was to be called at 0330. I placed my.45 pistol in a cocked condition under my pillow; there had been numerous killings of military personnel about Aden over the recent months.

I have always been a light sleeper, wide awake at the slightest sound. In the semi-darkness I sat bolt upright in my bed with my pistol pointing at the door as it was quietly pushed open. There had been no knock, and the door handle had been turned very quietly.

'Yes, who is it?' I said sharply.

'It's your batman, sir. It is 3.30 a.m.' He was a local from Aden, and locals were often forced by rebels to carry out acts of terrorism.

'Well, next time knock before turning the door handle and walking into an officer's bedroom!'

There was no RAF Duty Officer available to whom I could report the matter, but to this day I am convinced that the steward was in the pay of the rebels. I had a quick cup of coffee and some toast and marmalade at the NAAFI and then started my Buccaneer, and by 0630 my observer and I were both back on board, thankfully safe and sound.

Once our night flying—during which we had all participated in flight-deck lighting trials—had been completed, the ship steamed into Aden for a weekend visit prior to returning home. Our passage through the Red Sea went quickly, and *Eagle* had soon left the Suez Canal behind and was back off Malta. There we carried out some live 1,000-pound bombing against the island of Filfla to the west of Malta. Once again I had a live bomb hang up in the bomb bay and on this occasion I had to divert to RNAS Halfar, where an ordnance team defused the weapon and removed it—a much more difficult task because the bomb had fallen off its pylon and was lying on the rotary bomb bay door. Once the fuse had been removed, the bomb was tied down, the door was opened slowly and the weapon was lowered on to a trolley without further ado. The ordnance men who carried out this dangerous task should have been awarded a medal but to them of course it was all in a day's work.

After the visit to Malta *Eagle* steamed westwards, homeward bound for England. Off Algeria the heavy jets were launched for their home bases, 800X (Scimitar Tanker) Squadron accompanying us to the south coast of France and refuelling us at about 25,000 feet. Mine was the last Buccaneer to be launched, and with Dick Pearce as my observer I climbed to 29,000 feet, descended to 25,000 just off France to join up with Roger Dimmock and start taking fuel. At 250 knots, and with my aircraft growing heavier every minute as I refuelled, my port engine started 'banging' and complaining because of the aircraft's attitude. Finally, with both aircraft still joined up, we plunged into some of the thickest cloud I had ever experienced. I thereupon decided that enough was enough and I uncoupled and steered a diverging course away from Roger. Although the Buccaneer was now at its maximum weight, I managed to coax the jet slowly back up to 29,000 feet and headed for home.

Crossing France, I got the distinct impression that French Air Traffic Control were not happy with our presence in their airspace. They tried everything in their power to make us divert to Châteauroux, but I was having nothing of it and continued on my way, making out that I did not understand their instructions. One of our Buccaneers, unsuccessful in its inflight refuelling, did land in France short of fuel but the crew were treated cordially by the French Air Force and were not detained. Dick and I left French airspace north of Le Havre and crossed the Sussex coast over the old Ford air station.

At this stage of the flight we were down to 7,000 pounds of fuel. This was not enough to reach Lossiemouth, 450 miles away, and in the face of a 110-knot headwind we were going to run dry near the Scottish border. Dick was all for diverting to Yeovilton, but I insisted that we carry on until about Newcastle; if the headwind did not decrease then we could turn around and indeed land at Yeovilton. As luck would have it the headwind disappeared completely, so we elected to carry on to Lossiemouth; if the worst came to the worst we could always land at RAF Leuchars near Dundee. With less than fifty miles to go, and being down to 2,000 pounds of remaining fuel, we called Lossiemouth and requested a straight-in approach to downwind and a final landing. We touched down safely and were directed to NASU, where, much to our surprise, no other Buccaneers were on the hardstanding. I taxied in, folded my wings and shut down the engines, and there was May with Mother and Naomi, together with Dick's wife and family, all waiting for us. Captain David Kirk, Commander (Air) and others came over to greet us, the first thing they all asked being, 'Where are the other aircraft?' At the time we had no idea, but as we walked into the hangar, they began slowly to arrive and within a couple of hours the Squadron was home once again.

With our groundcrew still thousands of miles away, the aircraft were stowed away for two weeks, maintained by a small team of mechanics from NASU, while the aircrew proceeded on leave. On our return from leave we all flew refamiliarisation flights and I gave instrument flight rating tests to those whose instrument tickets were running out. The groundcrew had by now all returned to Scotland; half of them proceeded on leave and then rotated with the other half when they returned. We were now back flying and we moved across to the old 736 hangar next to 764 Squadron; the old Scimitar squadron (had disbanded and the squadron number had been reassigned to the Buccaneer training squadron, hitherto designated 809 NAS.

One day, out of the blue, the air station and the Squadron received a signal from MoD (Navy) stating that no further modifications or changes were to be made to the Buccaneer's weapon system. This order had been instigated because the aircraft was essentially a nuclear bomber, and under international agreement no modifications could be made to any nuclear system without international approval, the rationale being the prevention of an inadvertent release of a nuclear weapon. The order caused something of a stir, with Chris Mather going round in ever-decreasing circles. He and Peter Walwyn rushed south to London to visit DNAW/DGNA to discuss the matter, and after some hard talking by them the *impasse* was overcome, the embargo was lifted and we continued improving the conventional weapon release modes. Ferranti, however, like a dog with a good bone, were not going to let the matter rest, but eventually Chris and Peter nailed them down: if the modifications were approved by MoD (Navy), they would get the contract to modify all Buccaneer weapon systems.

On 12 May 1965 the Squadron received an award for its work on the system—the Australia Shield, an trophy presented to the Fleet Air Arm by the good people of that nation and awarded to the squadron that had achieved the highest degree of operational readiness. The citation was as follows:

> The Buccaneer Weapon System has been developed from comparative ineffectiveness into the best Ground Attack system currently in service anywhere in the world. This is due entirely to the work of 800 Squadron, who have done more for the Fleet Air Arm in 1964 than any other Squadron.

H. R. Janvarin, Rear Admiral
Flag Officer Aircraft Carriers
12th May 1965

The Australia Shield had not been awarded for some considerable time, and the fact that it was awarded at all was thanks to the dedication and drive of Chris Mather. He had been determined that the Buccaneer would become the Fleet's best airborne weapon system, and indeed the best in the world. He encountered a great deal of opposition along the way, but in the end he achieved what we all wanted—an aircraft weapon system that was second to none.

A second award was made to me, and it came as a shock. I was totally unaware that the Sandison Trophy would be awarded to anyone during 1965, least of all to me! As the reader will recall, Colonel Sandison had presented this trophy to the FAA in memory of his son, who had been killed while flying with 831 Squadron at Ford. It was awarded to the officer in a strike squadron who had made the greatest progress as a strike pilot and possessed outstanding officer-like qualities. I had no idea that I was even being considered for the award, those 'in the know' having kept the fact very close to their chests. One may imagine my utter surprise when I opened an envelope in my pigeonhole containing a signal from FOFT, Admiral Smeeton, congratulating me on being selected for the award. Everybody was standing around near the bar, staring at me: 'Come on, Punchy! What does it say?' Of course they all knew, and a great cheer went up when I said, 'Thank you all gentlemen! Drinks all round, barman—and on me!'

Although we never lost a single aircrew officer as a result of an accident while I served in the Squadron, we were to lose by other means one of the best-liked officers in the unit and indeed at Lossiemouth. Lieutenant Commander Alan Griggs joined 800 Squadron having been the FAA's Photographic Officer. He had built a fine new Photographic Unit at Lossiemouth to replace the old Photo School at RNAS Ford and Whale Island. When he joined the Squadron he had been suffering from swollen and enlarged lymph glands in his groin. He had spent a short time at Doctor Gray's Hospital, Elgin, and the swellings had disappeared, but by October 1964 they had returned and so he was admitted to RN Hospital Haslar. It was now quite obvious that something was seriously wrong with Alan's health. He remained at Haslar and missed the Squadron's embarkation. The Squadron received regular reports on his progress, thanks entirely to Chris Mather's insistence that both he and the Squadron be kept informed of Alan's condition. It was during March 1965 that a brief telegram arrived on board:

> We regret to inform you that Lieutenant Commander Alan Griggs passed away during his sleep. Funeral arrangements are being made for his burial in the Haslar Naval Cemetery, Gosport. Our deepest condolences and sympathy to all of 800 Squadron.

A wonderful officer had passed on and the Squadron was very saddened, not only for having lost an outstanding officer and pilot but also for his wife Barbara and daughters, who were still residing at Lossiemouth. Barbara moved south back to Salisbury, which was, I believe, her home town, and returned to her old profession of nursing sister in a operating theatre.

Alan's death affected us all, but I felt it probably more than most because I had known him for some considerable time. He had been my division leader when I had bailed out over Norway inside the Arctic Circle. Like me, he had joined the Navy as a sailor, though as a P2 sailor pilot. In those days, most naval pilots and observers were enlisted men, but he went on to receive a commission and finally transferred to the Supplementary List to be promoted to the rank of Lieutenant Commander. He took over the new Photographic Unit at Lossiemouth when the first CO retired from the Navy. Alan was very well liked by all in the FAA, and there really was no one who could easily replace him.

* * *

It is an old saying that every sailor has a wife in every port. I would not necessarily go along with that, but sailors certainly do seek out companionship while away from home, especially on voyages lasting almost a year. One day I received a letter from my wife telling me that somebody in the Squadron was writing home and telling his wife personal details of various officers' friendships with the opposite sex. Quite naturally, this caused tremendous dissension amongst the wives. She did not know exactly who was passing the information home, although I had a fairly good idea. During a brief visit to a shared cabin I let it be known that I thought it despicable of the officer or officers concerned, whoever they might be, to be conveying such information, upsetting wives and families in the process. A little later May told me that no further information had been posted home, so my suspicions as to the identity of the two officers had been absolutely correct. It had been pique on the part of these two because they were never invited to any party organised in our favour.

One can say with conviction that officers should remain loyal while away from home, but on the other hand man is a creature that requires companions about him, be they male or female. There is also little doubt that a man will strut when a person of the opposite sex displays interest in him. Unattached men, especially those far away from home, will always be attractive to females, who will often go out of their way to strike up a friendship or relationship. This does not necessarily mean that a man has forsaken his wife or family: he is merely seeking consolation because of the separation. On the other hand, there are males who are quite happy to remain totally loyal, their minds never straying from the straight and narrow. Most are in this group. Sad to say, however, on the odd occasion a relationship develops into something more and leads eventually to the break-up of a marriage.

Officers are not the only people who experience amorous approaches: sailors and NCOs come up against exactly the same problem. The odd thing about it is that an individual who is the greatest 'player' while abroad will be, once back home, the most attentive husband and father possible. Perhaps God leans heavily on these people; or perhaps their consciences work overtime!

* * *

During July 1964 the Squadron attempted to catch up with its night flying. This meant taking off at late hours owing to the long, light evenings at these latitudes. We flew south to Yeovilton for a GCA touch-and-go landing followed by a return to Lossiemouth, arriving just as dawn was breaking. On one occasion I flew south with Dick Pearce, and as we flew along the coast of Sussex we entered the edge of a thunderstorm, with St Elmo's fire running all over the cockpit canopy and the leading edges of the aircraft and its wings. Poor Dick nearly went crazy in the rear cockpit.

'You're going to kill us both!' he screamed over the intercom.

'Rubbish!' I replied. 'It's only St Elmo's fire and it's harmless!'

It took him some time to calm down, and after a smooth approach to Yeovilton and touch-down we roared off into the night to return home to Lossie.

As I approached Lossie I called for a GCA to overshoot into a 'quickie' GCA and final landing. My request was granted and I started to roll into my overshoot, but as our aircraft passed the GCA caravan a grey mist rose in front of the aircraft followed by what sounded like an intense AA barrage. Suddenly there was a cacophony of alarm bells and a flashing of warning lights around the cockpit signifying the failure of the starboard engine. I called the tower, dropped my arrester hook and took the 'Chag' arrester gear* at the end of the runway. When we opened the cockpit there was blood and guts all over the front of the canopy and windscreen; the starboard engine intake was totally blocked with birds and the port engine was very similar but was somehow still running. I told the tower of our predicament and shut both engines down. A tractor arrived from the airfield emergency team and we were towed back to the Squadron hangar. Back on the runway were about 300 dead seagulls; they had apparently taken up residence opposite the GCA caravan, attracted by heat from the radar transmissions, and nobody in the tower had thought about scaring them off before we

* Chain arrester gear, sited as the beginning of a runway to halt tail hook-equipped aircraft in the event of an emergency.

made our approach. 'Wings' had a few words to say the next morning to SATCO. The episode had resulted in a totally unnecessary slaughter of wild creatures and the writing-off of two valuable jet engines, had placed both our lives in jeopardy and could have caused the loss of a Buccaneer.

The sequel to this incident occurred out in the Far East. The Buccaneer that I had flown, call-sign 107, was parked at the after port side of *Eagle's* upper hangar when somebody complained of the smell of rotten fish. The awful odour seemed to be coming from the fin of the aircraft, and after extensive searching a decomposed seagull was found. The bird had been rammed right into the ventilation intake on the leading edge of the fin and had been missed at Lossiemouth. The remains were pulled out and thrown overboard and some sweet-smelling, non-corrosive disinfectant was sprayed over the intake and radiator. This aircraft had been 'robbed' to such an extent that it could not have been returned to flying status overnight had it been required, and a short time later an instruction was issued from MoD (Navy) to the effect that squadrons must cease such severe plunder. The sad thing was that this aircraft crashed on its first flight after so long in the hangar. Squadron Leader Graham Smart RAF was piloting the aircraft and, as he and his observer turned finals to deck-land, one of the engines stopped and they had to eject. Smart and his observer were recovered safely and apart from the unexpected dunking were both fine, but the aircraft was lost.

* * *

On 25 August 1965 the Squadron re-embarked in *Eagle* and headed straight for the Mediterranean and Malta. Off Malta the air group started an intense work-up, including some night flying, before proceeding through the Suez Canal to East Africa and the Far East. It was the intention that at least five crews from 800 Squadron would work up as the carrier's night-flying strike element; I was one of the pilots and Dick Pearce was my observer. Since our previous night sortie a new flight-deck floodlighting system had been installed, supposedly giving a mottled lighting effect and thereby enhancing depth perception. The system had been tested in American carriers with some success but nearly all the pilots aboard *Eagle* disliked it because of the patchy effect it produced. I certainly did not like it, much preferring the standard arrangement—that is, an unilluminated deck except for the centre-line lighting, the 'donkey's plonk',* the two mirror projector lights and the mast lighting. Taken together, these were entirely adequate to enable me to judge both depth and distance.

While night flying off Malta, Andrew Gleadow was diverted to US Naval Air Station Sigonela in Sicily with an engine problem. When he arrived at the airfield visibility had been greatly reduced by fog, so he elected to make a single-engine approach and landing, lowering his arrester hook because he would be landing fast. The runway suddenly appeared out of the fog, and he threw his aircraft at the runway and caught the 'Chag' gear, which brought

---

* A vertical array of red lights fixed over the stern of a carrier in line with the flight deck's centreline lights. When a pilot is off-centre, the red lights indicate which way he should turn.

him quickly to a halt. After being disentangled from the gear he was towed to a hangar, where it was soon discovered that his engine had a serious oil leak and would need changing. Together with a USN Petty Officer, and a Squadron Petty Officer who had been hurriedly flown ashore by helicopter, the three of them removed the engine and placed it on mattresses because of the unavailability of an engine cradle.

A spare engine was made ready aboard *Eagle* and also placed on a pile of mattresses—again because there was no cradle—so that the Senior Pilot of 815 Squadron, Lieutenant Commander Mike Harvey, could hoist it and fly it ashore by Wessex helicopter, the Captain placing the ship as close in as possible to reduce Mike's time over water during the lifting and transfer flight. The entire operation was carried out during the night in total blackness; there was no moon. Within twenty-four hours Andrew and his two Petty Officers had changed the engine, fired it up and checked it out. He flew back to the ship with the Squadron Petty Officer in the aircraft's rear seat. There was only one hiccough, and this concerned the type of engine oil for use in the replacement engine. The Americans did not carry any of our oil but the ship's AEO selected an oil which was close; it would be used for one flight only, that back to the ship, where it would be changed for the right grade.

Andrew and his two Petty Officers, one of whom knew absolutely nothing about the Buccaneer, had done an outstanding job, and I have always felt that they did not receive due recognition for a job well done. It is not often that one hears of a pilot having to change his own jet engine, test it and then fly his aircraft back for a deck landing. I have always admired this young officer for his skill and professionalism: he was certainly one of the best.

It was while the ship was off Malta that the air group suffered its first aircraft accident, resulting in two fatalities. I had just closed the ship's dive-bombing circuit and *Eagle* had turned into wind to recover the heavy jets. The Buccaneers landed first, followed by the Sea Vixens. The Vixen pilots were flying a very tight circuit of about 30 seconds between aircraft. One was a little too close and started to take a wave-off when he was told to continue by Flyco. The pilot, having gone high on the approach, took a 'high dip', pulled back on his stick and stalled just above the deck. His left wing dropped, the aircraft bolted and, with full power applied by the pilot, the Vixen assumed a very high, nose-up attitude and auto-rotated into a spin to the left, crashing upside down into the sea to port. It all happened so quickly that for a few seconds everybody was speechless. Apart from an aircraft panel and a dinghy pack, there was only a large, frothy patch. The Flight Deck Officer rushed to the ship's side, shaking his head in disbelief at what had happened. Steve Park, who was standing alongside me on the Gun Direction Platform, nearly passed out with shock, and I had to ask somebody to offer him a cigarette to calm him down.

The accident shook us all to the core: we had completed the previous deployment without an incident or accident, and suddenly we had a totally unnecessary mishap resulting in two good officers—a pilot and an observer—being killed instantly. Even now, thirty-five years later, I wonder whether, if

I had been quick enough over the radio to tell the pilot 'Full right rudder, stick forward!', I would have prevented the accident. I honestly do not know— it all happened so quickly—and in truth the aircraft was probably beyond recovery by the time it had reached the middle of the flight deck. Steve Park was so upset that he had to sit down. The young observer was an old course friend of his whose wife had given birth a couple of weeks before the re-embarkation. It difficult to apportion blame, but I feel strongly that, having started a wave-off, the pilot should not have been encouraged to land by Flyco. The LSO had the whole matter taken out of his hands and was in my opinion blameless. There is nothing that can be done now; it happened so long ago. However, it did point up the fact that, once a pilot has made his decision about landing on a carrier deck or has decided to go round again, then nothing should be done to countermand it—unless of course there is a serious safety reason for doing so.

This accident had a sobering affect on us all. Until then we had all had the feeling that nothing could happen to any of us. Death in the air sneaks up suddenly, taking those who are not vigilant or wary of the dangers that lurk around the corner. I have always maintained that if God had intended us to fly He would have given us wings, and as He did not give us natural wings we have to remain fully alert at all times!

* * *

While *Eagle* was in the Mediterranean she was harassed continuously by a Soviet warship. One day Captain Derek Empson decided that he had had just about enough of this interference with our normal operations in inter-national waters and determined that he would give the Soviet Captain, his commissar and his ship's company the scare of their lives. Normally, when turning into wind for a launch or recovery, a carrier turns to starboard. The Soviet had stationed himself off our port bow anticipating this manoeuvre. When flag 'Foxtrot' was hoisted to indicate that we were about to commence flying operations, the Russian started a turn to starboard but Captain Empson gave two blasts on his siren indicating a port turn, and started to come port. Now we had two ships turning towards one another in inter-national waters, one having given the proper 'rule of the road' signal of her intentions and the other having given no signal at all of hers. The Soviet suddenly realised the seriousness of the situation and increased speed and helm. The ship passed down *Eagle*'s port side about twenty yards away, so close that we could have sprayed her with our fire hoses; I was standing on Fly 4 on the port quarter at the time, and there were some very white knuckles gripping the bridge sides as she passed us; the very fact that *Eagle* was heeling to starboard during her port turn might have ensured that both ship did not collide. There was little need, subsequently, of a diplomatic signal: the Soviets learnt their lesson and kept a healthy distance from us in all future operations.

It had been very hot, so the Captain decided to allow 'All hands to Bathing Stations!' The ship stopped, gangways were lowered and all off-duty officers and sailors took a dip. Our Soviet friends came across our stern and hove-to about two cables away on the starboard quarter, utterly confused by this peculiar British behaviour. They even signalled us suggesting the direction of Valletta. Then we recovered all our people and steamed towards Malta for a brief visit, leaving our terrier behind.

While in Malta, Dave Howard had been invited to a water-skiing party with Admiral Sir Andrew and Lady Cunningham. The Admiral was our C-in-C Mediterranean, and he had a tremendous affection for the Fleet Air Arm, having served as Flag Officer Air (Home) at Lee-on-Solent some years earlier. It was Sunday when the Captain's Secretary came banging on my door to see if I could stand in for Dave, who had for some reason declined the invitation at the last moment. I was happy to go and had a thoroughly enjoyable day with the Admiral and his wife. I had never water-skied before so it was going to be quite an interesting time. I changed into my 'swimmies' at the same time as the Admiral, down below in the barge cabin.

He turned round to me and said, 'I bet you never thought you would be changing in the same small compartment with an Admiral and Knight of the Realm?'

'No, sir,' I replied.

Then we got talking, he asking where I had been since we had last met at Lossiemouth, which was many years ago as he remembered. I then asked where he would be going for his next appointment. First Sea Lord, maybe?

'No, I shall be retiring. My face doesn't fit: I'm of the wrong political colour!'

'What on earth does that have to do with it?' I enquired in my naivety.

'Well, Michael, when you reach time for promotion to Flag Rank, then your political persuasion has a great deal to do with whether you are elevated or not.'

I merely shook my head in disbelief, although I supposed that those in charge of the Armed Forces must be seen to be going along with the policies of the Government of the day.

The Cunninghams were a charming couple and one could not have wished for a better host and hostess. Many years later I saw them again at St Martin-in-the-Fields during a memorial service for one of our late Admirals. Lady Cunningham was now in a wheelchair, an invalid—a sad contrast to her condition when I had last seen her, frolicking about on water skis.

* * *

A couple of days later *Eagle* sailed for Port Said and the Suez Canal. The transit south through the Canal went without incident, and after a quick passage of the Red Sea we were once again off the Aden Protectorate to carry out some FAC exercises. Our tame Scottish Border Regiment Major was landed and flown up-country to an area considered more or less free from rebel activity. Mike Hornblower and Dick Pearce were off at first light, heading for the FAC range. However, Mike was making a low-level approach to the IP when Dick noticed that he was flying lower and lower. Dick told him to increase his height but received no reply. The aircraft was by now dangerously low, so Dick took his long navigation ruler and prodded him hard in the shoulder. Mike suddenly stirred and pulled out—so low that he overstressed the aircraft. He had fallen asleep! I had always had my doubts about Mike's flying ability, especially after my experience with him in a Hunter T.8 over Tain Range in Scotland!

During one of my FAC exercises Dick Pearce and I arrived over the range to be informed by our Army Major that he was being shot at by a rebel hiding at the top of a 2,000-foot cliff. Our Buccaneer was fitted out with four pods of practice 2-inch rockets and the Major asked if there was anything that we could do. 'Yes, sir. Give us the co-ordinates of the target and I will fire a few rockets at him!' I flew in straight and level at the target position given to us and fired a burst of about a dozen. Although neither Dick nor I saw any movement, the Major was convinced that we had hit the rebel because our rockets had fallen right on target. After a slow flyby neither of us could see anything, so we had either blown him to pieces or he had taken to his heels before the attack.

By mid-October *Eagle* was back in Mombasa for a visit of ten days. Chris Mather's time in command was up and Chuck Giles had been appointed as his relief. We all wondered what Chuck would be like because he was totally different from Chris—he was not an AWI and, as far as we knew at the time, he had never had command of a squadron. Chuck arrived while the ship was in harbour, and the Squadron threw a big 'goodbye and welcome' dinner for the pair of them in the large dining room aboard the carrier. Our two resident comics, Steve Park and Bob Woodard, staggered into the bar after dinner to find 'Wings' with one or two friends playing dominoes. They set about singing him a song—'Wings, Wings, show us your ring . . .'—while Steve played the wardroom piano. I had had an appointment with Mother Nature while they were trilling away and arrived back in the wardroom just as the XO was ejecting them. I received his fury also and was told to get out, though for what reason I did not know. We all retired to the dining room where the Squadron officers were still enjoying themselves.

Chris was selected for promotion to Commander—a well deserved appointment considering all that he had done to improve the Buccaneer's weapon system. I also was selected for promotion, to Lieutenant Commander on the Supplementary List on the March 1965 Selection List, effective from 1 September 1965. A team saw Chris off at Mombasa. Although we had had many differences in the past, I had grown very fond of him and we had become great friends.

Chuck Giles was a totally different Commanding Officer; I believe that he may have been wondering what he had taken on. Malcolm Carver had also gone and his relief was Rob Helliwell. Dave Howard was the new Senior Pilot. To get Chuck really settled in, the Squadron officers took him ashore for dinner at the Mombasa Club. This famous old colonial establishment had been founded by a family for officers serving in East Africa. It had accommodation so that guests could stay overnight, and some of our officers did spend a weekend at the club. The elderly lady who ran and owned the club was one of those delightful, matronly women of yesteryear whose word was law. She had an excellent staff of East Africans who treated the guests wonderfully well and with great respect and who, consequently, were treated likewise by us.

We ordered our dinner at the upstairs bar and then we all sat down at a large, round table on the ground floor. Most had ordered T-bone steaks, as did I. However, in addition I had decided to try lobster thermidor for starters, believing it to be a small seafood course. As everybody began to receive their steaks, my dish arrived, an enormous offering on an oval platter. I could not believe my eyes and neither could anybody else believe theirs.

'Yes, that is mine,' I observed, 'but I thought I was ordering just a small shellfish for starters! No, don't take it back—I'll have it!'

'Wow, Punchy! Where are you going to put it?'

'Well, let's wait and see!'

I tucked into the lobster, steak, fruit salad, coffee, brandy and a beer. I really thought that I had overdone things, but I could not let that lobster go back to the kitchen. I suppose, with hindsight, I could have shared it around but the others did not seem keen so I was stuck with my order. At the end I was so full that my brother officers almost had to carry me back to the ship! After this little meal I became known as 'Nosher Punchy'. Most people did not realise that I had a pretty big appetite and could put away several large meals a day—although most of the calories were quickly consumed in nervous energy!

Dick Pearce and I experienced one rather funny incident during a diversion to RAF Khormaksar, Aden. We went into the NAAFI for a cup of coffee and doughnut while our aircraft was being serviced by the RAF and met up with a Colour Sergeant Royal Marines. He was a huge man and not a person I would wish to encounter in the dark. He related how, one day, up-country, his platoon had been playing soccer and suddenly rebel mortar rounds began to rain down on them. The CSRM was very upset to think that anybody might have the nerve to interrupt something as important as a soccer match. The platoon finished their game, collected their artillery fieldpieces and, in retaliation for their bad manners, for fifteen minutes proceeded to bombard the village whence the heathens had come.

During Chris Mather's final weeks 800 Squadron lost a Buccaneer in a most bizarre accident, though fortunately the crew managed to parachute to safety. The ship had been carrying out 'throw off' firings of live HE/AA shells against aircraft—achieved by interrupter safety mechanisms which caused the guns to fire 45 degrees off the line of attack so that the shells exploded about half a mile to the side of any approaching aircraft. Together with our two USN exchange officers, Lieutenant Commanders Chase and Markley, Dick Pearce and I manned our Buccaneers for a 2-inch rocketing sortie against the splash target. We started our aircraft, checks were carried out and we were about to taxy to our respective catapults when Flyco told us to hold our positions to have our rocket pods removed. Our exercise had been changed to enable us to act as targets for the AA guns. The Operations and Gunnery Officers briefed us over the radio and then we were launched. It was a beautiful day and there was about half-cover cumulus at some

2,000–3,000ft. Chase was the first to make a target run at high speed and low level.

Dick and I were on the opposite side of the gunnery circuit when we heard Tom Markley make his 'Running in!' call. Seconds later we heard Tom's panic-stricken voice: 'We've been hit!' I could not see Chase's aircraft but I pulled round hard, telling Dick, an ex Sea Vixen observer, to look at his radar and check whether he could see him. Within seconds he said, 'I've got them! Follow your target marker signal!' Soon I had Chase visual and was up alongside. There was no obvious damage to the aircraft, but his speed was down to less than 250 knots and he had experienced a complete hydraulic failure—which also seemed odd because we could not see any leaks from the aircraft. Chase said that both his engines were running at considerably reduced revs and for some reason he could not increase power. Dick and I looked his aircraft over carefully and then noticed that there was a small servicing panel hanging down in the airflow beneath the fuselage, inboard of the starboard engine intake. Also hanging down in the airflow was the hydraulic ground servicing handle.

Prior to its flight this particular Buccaneer had been in the hangar for servicing work on its undercarriage and flying controls. The Gyron Juniors were fitted with hydraulic fuel pumps, and if the engines were not running, then these pumps could be damaged during hydraulic servicing. A cut-off valve had therefore been fitted to isolate them, and this valve was operated by the servicing handle—and if the handle were down in the airflow then the hydraulic fuel pumps were cut off and the engines would receive fuel by gravity feed only. Moreover, in the tropics, gravity-fed fuel would not be enough to sustain maximum engine rpm: if the pumps were suddenly isolated there would be a sudden drop, causing the engines to stall in flight and producing a huge 'bang'—which is what Chase and Markley heard.

There was no possibility of a landing back on board *Eagle*, so the next move was for the aircraft to head for Aden. However, if anything went wrong there was the virtual certainty of a political storm—the United States was not involved in the Aden troubles—and so every effort was made to ensure that neither Chase nor Markley flew over land. Then Chase decided to try to improve matters by lowering cruise flap and droop, and before I could stop him he had made the switch and his airspeed had immediately dropped to 170 knots and continued to reduce. Now the situation was beginning to worsen. He could have made a flapless landing at Aden, lowering his undercarriage during the last stages of the approach, but his chances had now gone. They both decided to bail out. I told them over the radio to apply full right aileron and nose-down trim before ejecting, thus ensuring that the aircraft spiralled. They were at 5,000 feet and about three or four miles off the port side of the ship when the cockpit canopy left the aircraft, followed by Markley in his ejection seat and, a second or so later, Chase. Their parachutes opened perfectly.

I was flying outboard and slightly astern when the aircraft started to roll right, stopped and immediately rolled left towards the ship, entering a steep dive straight for her. Dick let out a yell: 'Oh my God!' I pulled hard round to follow the unmanned Buccaneer, and as I dived towards the ship I could see the flight deck swarming with personnel in whites. Suddenly they all rushed to the sides to find safety below. As Chris scrambled down a ladder a sailor ran over him, putting his boot in his face; everybody had one purpose only—to find shelter. At about 300–400 feet the unmanned jet pulled out of its dive and passed between the masts of the carrier. It now went into a right-hand turn a hundred feet above the sea and I saw to my horror that it was having another go. Our new Captain Roxburgh was jumping up down: 'Why isn't Doust doing something?' I was flying nearby and it did enter my mind to close in and put my right wing tip under its left and then roll left, thus causing the errant Buccaneer to roll right and thence into the sea. The trouble was that our aircraft were fitted with vortex generators near the wing tips, and if they were damaged then I would have had serious problems landing. The pilotless aircraft kept pulling up and stalling, its speed and height gradually decreasing, and then suddenly its right wing tip touched the water and it was no more. The jet flew into a million fragments of metal, the largest piece recovered being a panel from the top fuselage surface. Chase and Markley were both in the Sickbay swigging brandy a long time before their aircraft crashed.

An inquiry was set up and the accident was ascribed to maintenance error, Dick having managed to take several clear photographs of the panel and handle hanging down in the airflow. Now we all had positively to ensure not only that this particular panel was secure but also that the handle was locked in the 'up' position. Goodness knows what would have happened had the jet struck *Eagle*. Dick and I landed back on board, and the ship turned south for Mombasa for a visit of ten days before heading east to Singapore once again. It had been a very sobering day.

* * *

We were beginning now to use the Buccaneer on missions for which it was really suited, one of these being long-range photography. The aircraft had an excellent photographic pack which carried several cameras and a mass of flares for night photography and which fitted on to the bomb bay door. The ship was steaming south of Aden and it was decided that Dick Pearce and I would fly nearly a thousand miles to the island of Socotra at the eastern end of the Gulf of Aden—in fact, in the Indian Ocean. Twenty minutes would be spent photographing every aspect of the island before flying back to the carrier.

Our aircraft was fitted with two large drop tanks because the Squadron had not as yet been issued with the overload bomb-bay fuel tank, which would have given a considerable increase in the bomber's range. A Scimitar tanker aircraft would accompany us half way to the target and then refuel our drop tanks, providing us with enough fuel for the flight there and back. The Squadron's aircraft had all by this time been fitted with automatic pilots which could maintain heading, speed and height control, and in a photographic mission this equipment would be very useful.

The S Mk 1 was a difficult aircraft to fly at 30,000 feet when fully laden with fuel. The best way to fly it was to set the autopilot on 'Mach Hold' so that as the fuel was consumed the aircraft would become lighter and would slowly gain altitude. I set the hold at 0.85 Mach at about 27,000 feet and as we closed Socotra the aircraft was flying comfortably at well over 30,000 feet. At fifty miles Dick and I commenced our descent to 500 feet, flying around the island to take pictures both with the aircraft's cameras and with Dick's hand-held 35mm Canon. Then we departed, heading west again and climbing to 30,000 feet, whereupon the Mach Hold was engaged at 0.85. By the time we reached the vicinity of *Eagle*, our aircraft had climbed to 42,000 feet. The circuit was clear and so we made a straight-in approach to downwind and carried out a perfect landing. Dick and I had made an round trip of 1,900 miles—one of the longest ever made in the Buccaneer to that date— and above all had obtained some excellent photographs of Socotra.

Following our visit to Mombasa *Eagle* departed for Singapore, a distance of nearly 4,000 miles. En route we carried out various missions both in the Indian Ocean and overland to the east of Aden. Our task was to relieve *Ark Royal* on station in the Far East so that she could return home for about nine months in dockyard hands and be ready to relieve us next year. However, as we closed Singapore a rumour began circulating the ship and its air group that we would not be disembarking because *Ark Royal* was not ready for sea. By the time we reached the north-western end of the Malacca Strait the truth was out: 'Ark' was *hors de combat*, having experienced a serious fire in 'A' boiler room which had caused extensive damage to the engine room. Neither RAF Changi nor RAF Tengah could accommodate both air groups, so, on the face of it, our aircraft would not be disembarking. As the ship entered the Malacca Strait word came through that 'Ark's air group would relocate to RAAF Butterworth near Kuala Lumpur. This was very good news because 800 Squadron' machines required some heavy maintenance.

At this particular time Britain and Indonesia were at political loggerheads. Indonesian forces were making nightly incursions into Singapore and Malaya, as well as attacking our warships at sea in the surrounding local waters. Our intelligence reports informed us that Indonesia's Soviet-built motor torpedo boats, armed with 'Styx' missiles, were holed up among the islands off Sumatra and might well attempt an attack on *Eagle* as she transited the Malacca Strait. Together with three other crews, I was despatched to RAF Changi, our four aircraft armed with four 2-inch HE rocket pods—one of which was sufficient to cut an MTB in two—to act as an airborne attack group, and there we sat, waiting for the order to scramble from either the ship or the control tower. As *Eagle* steamed through the strait we talked with the Operations Room on SSB radio and by early afternoon she was clear and approaching the Johore Strait for a clear run to the dockyard. We stayed alert at Changi until a message had been received that the ship was tied up safely in the dockyard.

After disembarking, the Squadron set about standing down for two weeks so that the maintenance could proceed as planned. Engine changes had to be made and numerous modifications undertaken, and as a result time aloft would be limited to test flights. Dave Howard, who was now the Squadron's Senior Pilot, went sick. The RAF doctor thought he had malaria, but when Ian Mackie, the ship's SMO, saw him he had no doubt: it was jaundice, and he had him removed to the ship's Sickbay. Don Richardson took over as the temporary SP.

Our daily routine proceeded quietly for two days and then Commander (Air), Commander Duncan Laing, arrived to tell us that we would be re-embarking within twenty-four hours. The CO had a fit—understandably so as we hardly had a single aircraft that was not in bits and pieces or had its engines out. 'Wings' was virtually asking the impossible, as well as posing a serious flight safety problem since engines that had been removed would require test flights. However, 'Wings' was adamant: twenty-four hours it was, and the test flights could be made en route to the ship. Treavor Spafford's NASU pitched in with its manpower and somehow all the aircraft were made ready to re-embark the next day. The price would be one of them, although fortunately the crew escaped.

I briefed the last but one division returning to the ship. Lieutenants Andrew Gleadow and Peter King were flying one of these bombers, their bomb bay stuffed with golf clubs, another officer's pay and other items. After thirty minutes I took off with my three aircraft and headed towards the ship, which was steaming at full power in light winds off Raffles Lighthouse, the Squadron CO and Senior Pilot having already embarked ahead of us. I saw two Buccaneers carrying out deck-landing practice: one landed on and the second aircraft then made an approach, touched down and either bolted or was making a touch-and-go. Within seconds there was a huge splash ahead of the ship. The Operations Room came up on the radio and instructed us to return to Changi; we would be given a new 'Charlie Time'. Andrew was making his final approach to hook-on but had missed the arrester wires and bolted. His port engine had apparently stalled, and with full flap, full air brake, drooped ailerons and tailplane flap his good engine could not produce enough power to keep him airborne.

Peter King was the first to eject from a near-vertical position, while Andrew left the cockpit at an attitude of almost ninety degrees and therefore hit the sea at over one hundred knots and travelling horizontally. He was knocked unconscious but for some reason his ejection seat's automatic inflation system worked, activating his lifejacket and separating him from the seat. He was found floating face down by the SAR helicopter diver, who lifted him and gave him resuscitation. In the Sickbay his face was swollen and black-and-blue, for all the world as if he had run into a London bus. He was a very lucky officer but of course it would be some months before he was fit to fly again. The NASU at Singapore supplied us with their only reserve aircraft, which, however, was not quite up to the same modification standard as our own.

Although the exact position of the ditching was known, a dan-buoy having been dropped to mark it, a minesweeper spent an entire month fruitlessly searching for it. The water was quite shallow at that spot and there was a sandy bottom, but unfortunately the tidal currents were fairly strong and so it is possible that the aircraft had ended up in an entirely different location. Andrew lost his golf clubs and an officer was parted from his month's pay, although there was a 'whip-round' and our impecunious colleague got his money after all.

We had no idea why we had been required to re-embark so quickly: nobody would tell us and none of the squadron COs was any the wiser. However, as the ship steamed at 25 knots back up the Malacca Strait and westwards out across the Indian Ocean, there could be only one destination—Rhodesia. A BBC World Service news broadcast more or less confirmed where we were heading, though why on earth we could not be told was baffling: there was no way that we could let the 'cat out of the bag' considering that we were in the middle of the Indian Ocean!

Mr Ian Smith, a World War II RAF fighter pilot and now the Prime Minister of Rhodesia, had brought the colony into an open state of rebellion, and because he could not get his way with the British Government had initiated a Unilateral Declaration of Independence. The Buccaneers and Sea Vixens were each armed with four pods of 2-inch HE rockets and parked on the flight deck for immediate manning and launch. FOAC, who had embarked while the ship was at Singapore, closeted himself away with his staff, the ship's navigator and Operations Officer but still the Squadron COs were excluded from any briefings or discussions. However, we were all convinced that we knew where we were going. One evening a young engine room officer put a map of the Indian Ocean and East Africa up on the wardroom notice board with a plotting pin stuck in it bearing the message 'We're here!'; by using the engine revolutions and repeater compass headings, he had us within ten miles of our true position. The Admiral flipped his lid, sent for him, gave him a severe rollicking and logged him for disclosing this supposedly highly secret information. The next morning, in a relatively calm sea with occasional patches of fog, there appeared the sand dunes of the Mozambique coastline and the Beira river. So started the 'Beira Patrol'—which would continue for many months to come.

The objective of the Beira Patrol was to prevent raw materials, oil and food from reaching Rhodesia. However, it made little or no difference since these crucial imports still got through from other directions. Many questions went around the ship. Why were we doing this to a Commonwealth country? It made no sense at all. Rhodesia was staunchly British and we all knew that, sooner or later, she would be given independence like the other African colonies. The result of our actions was that left-wing policies were fomented by Robert Mugabe and his followers, terrorism began to break out across the country and many lives were lost amongst both civilians and Rhodesia's Armed Forces. Friends of mine who had taken up residence in the country had to carry assault weapons in their car in order to assure their personal safety. Owing to the fact that the British Government of the day would not back Ian Smith, he was left with only one alternative—to declare UDI and remove Rhodesia from the Commonwealth. The British Government, however, was not standing for any such rebellion.

Looking back, one can perhaps understand Ian Smith's attitude. To the north of Rhodesia lay Kenya, and since independence this nation had experienced a significant drop in Gross National Product. White-owned farms had been confiscated and shared out amongst black Kenyans, resulting in the loss of productive farming land, which soon reverted to scrub. However, that country has since improved its standards and is now very prosperous. To the east of Rhodesia was Tanzania (recently known as Tanganyika) and this country was amongst the poorest in Africa. Thus Ian Smith, by retaining the old colonial policies, was trying to ensure that the white population would continue to run Rhodesia, and in this he was supported by the South African regime. It would be many years before Rhodesia gained full independence under the new name of Zimbabwe, and with Robert Mugabe as its president, but until this independence was granted the Beira Patrol remained in force, maintaining sanctions against the white regime.

Eagle moved off to the north, towards Aden, after a couple of weeks off Beira. The British Government had decided to move RAF Javelin squadrons into countries adjacent to Rhodesia to show its resolve and determination, but eventually the Royal Navy would maintain the Beira Patrol as the most effective method available to the Government of carrying out its policy. 800 Squadron practised day and night shipping strikes, and during this period I received my new appointment to 736 (Buccaneer Training) Squadron as the AWI; in addition, I would be Peter Walwyn's Buccaneer Trials Assistant.

One day, following a very hectic day of flying, I was packing my bags in my cabin ready for departure the next day at 1000 by COD (Carrier Onboard Delivery) Gannet. I was also scheduled to night-fly, as I was one of the only four remaining flyers in the Squadron qualified to do so, and I was, moreover, extremely busy completing my latest set of squadron weapon plots. It was almost 2100 when Dave Howard came into my cabin and told me that I had been scrubbed from the flying programme. Commander (Air) had spotted my name on the schedule and had blown his stack, wanting to know what on earth the Squadron was thinking when I was due to leave early the next day. He gave Dave specific instructions that I was to clean up, go down to the wardroom bar and have a good stiff drink on him, and to relax for the rest of the evening. I needed no encouragement, and the next day I thanked him from the bottom of my heart for his wise decision. Commander Pridum Price would be promoted from his position as 'Wings' to Captain, and he would eventually become my Director when I served as a Staff Officer at the Directorate of Naval Air Warfare.

* * *

On 15 December 1965 I boarded the COD Gannet and was flown ashore to RAF Khormaksar. A naval driver collected me and drove me over to a safe hotel in Crater City, Aden, where I would spend the remainder of the day and night prior to flying out in a Britannia airliner of Britannia Airways to Luton via Benghazi. I spent a couple of hours wandering around Crater City buying last-minute presents, always keeping a watchful eye for any rebel

209

who might be lurking about to take a pot shot at an Armed Forces man in 'civilians'. I had a good dinner that evening in the hotel restaurant and retired early to bed, exhausted.

I checked into the flight the following morning and eventually we thundered off down the runway and into the Aden skies, turning north-west for 'Olde Blighty' and home. I have always had good meals on most airline flights, and I must say that Britannia Airways did us proud on both legs of the flight home. We crossed the English coast at Dungeness at about 25,000 feet and soon afterwards entered the edge of a thunderstorm. The old Britannia really bounced around until we popped out of the storm north of London. The descent into Luton went without incident, and we had a smooth landing. My train to Edinburgh turned out to be a slow one, stopping at every station en route. I arrived just in time to catch another slow train to Aberdeen. I finally boarded *The Inverness Flyer* for Elgin, where May and Naomi were waiting for me. It was bitterly cold and I needed my overcoat; indeed, I quickly went down with a good dose of bronchitis and asthma and spent most of Christmas in bed. What a way to come home!

Buccaneer Operational Flying School

FOLLOWING the death of Willy Watson, the CO of 809 Squadron, in a Buccaneer flying accident on a Caithness mountain, the Squadron was renumbered 736. John Kennett was reappointed from 800 Squadron as the new CO and eventually, in 1967, Dave Howard would relieve him. John had been the CO for almost a year when I joined as the Squadron AWI. My health was far from good, asthma having dragged me down again and consigned me to Dr Gray's Hospital, where I spent some considerable time in an oxygen tent. After ten days I had recovered and was released into the care of the Sickbay at Lossiemouth, though was not declared fit to fly again until March 1966. However, I would put my sick time to good use by working hard with Peter Walwyn and writing my Buccaneer Weapon System Manual.

The new Buccaneer S Mk 2 had arrived at Lossiemouth and 700B Squadron, the IFTU, was formed under Commander Freddie Nelson. It was housed in the old 738 Squadron hangar, next door to 736 Squadron and the Buccaneer OFS. The S Mk 2 was fitted with two Rolls-Royce Speys, the new powerplant essentially an RR Avon fitted with a bypass compressor section, imparting increased power and, more importantly, offering reduced fuel consumption. Fitted with these engines, the Buccaneer was now the long-range strike bomber that it was originally intended to be. Nevertheless, it did have one serious problem. Extra range had been obtained also by removing the vortex generators from the upper wing surfaces, but this made the aircraft unstable at deck-landing speeds and so the generators were replaced and the reduction in range was accepted in the interests of flight safety.

The new aircraft had various other modifications, for example longer and broader underwing overload fuel tanks and a bomb-door fuel tank. The new underwing tanks were to cause the loss of two aircraft off the catapult. This very serious problem was resolved by fitting an enlarged stabilator and by ensuring that the new drop tanks were either completely full or completely empty for any catapult launch. Fortunately, no crewmen were lost in either of these accidents, but they did highlight the fact that, perhaps, the manufacturers had not done their calculations correctly. I am doubtful whether the catapult trials were carried out properly, if indeed at all.

801 Squadron would be the first unit to be equipped with the new mark of Buccaneer, and 736 Squadron would form the new unit known as 736B Flight with four aircraft, which would carry out further trials on the weapon system. Peter Walwyn would be the Trials Officer and I would be his assistant. The Flight would remain in the old 738 hangar together with the South African Air Force Buccaneer squadron. The SAAF had bought fourteen S Mk 2s,* and once they had completed their conversions and training their personnel would fly them home via the Canaries and Cape Verde Islands using the long-range drop tanks and bomb-bay overload fuel tank. They were to lose one aircraft during this flight home owing to a serious mechanical defect.

It was Peter's task fully to evaluate the modified weapon system in the new aircraft and recommend improvements where necessary, and the Flight was airborne incessantly, day and night, to this end. Monthly reports were written to DNAW in MoD (Navy) until it was decided that the optimum solutions had been met and then the Flight was disbanded and absorbed into 736 Squadron proper. The Squadron would be equipped with a 50/50 mix of Mk 1 and Mk 2 Buccaneers, and then the early mark would slowly be phased out until 736 had only the Mk 2.

Peter was a first-class project officer, and an excellent mathematician and scientist, but he could not write a report to save his life—an extraordinary state of affairs for an MA graduate from Cambridge University. As a graduate from a grammar school who had not attended university, I had to take his reports and put his words into sentences, paragraphs, chapters and sections, whereupon I gave them to John Kennett, who edited them further until they were suitable for transmission to DNAW.

It had been decided by FONAC that I should receive the Sandison Trophy during March 1966 while I was at Lossiemouth and thus it was arranged for Colonel Sandison, the father of Bobby Sandison, to visit the Station and stay overnight with Captain and Mrs Dougie Parker at their residence on the premises. Captain's Divisions would be held on the Friday, when I would be ceremonially presented with the silver trophy, a model of a Wyvern strike fighter mounted on a plinth. We, with our wives, had lunch at the Captain's residence before Divisions. It was a marvellous occasion, and it was a delight to see Colonel Sandison, a grand old gentleman farmer, once again after so many years. This event had a funny side. The local newspaper, the *Northern Scotsman*, made a hash of its report in saying that I was leaving the Navy and was not sure what I would be doing next, whereas in fact I had just been transferred to a Permanent Supplementary List Commission and I would be serving until the age of 50; moreover, the newspaper published a photograph of me standing next to Mrs Parker, who was identified as my wife!

I was still busy with my Weapon System Manual for the Buccaneer, the object of which was to enable the aircrews who flew the aircraft to know and understand their weapon system properly. It would give a squadron AWI a ready reference with all the weapon release tables in the form of graphs so

---

* The SAAF Buccaneers were known officially as S Mk 50s.

that he could pick off points instead of having to calculate them by interpolation. This manual virtually became my life in the Squadron until I delivered it in person to DNAW for publication prior to my joining the US Navy on exchange.

I had to take the draft manual to the MoD's Publishing Department at Chessington to discuss the rationale behind the book. This was to prove a difficult task. The civil servant with whom I spoke tried hard to belittle the concept of such a manual and have me say that there really was no need for it. I told him in no uncertain terms that it was required: it was a vital book for both the aircrews and ground crews of the Fleet Air Arm, and I would not have spent two years writing it had I not believed in it. With hindsight, I am sure that he must have been ex RAF because he raised so many objections to having it printed, although in the end he seemed to accept my arguments. I left a copy with both him and DNAW, who thought it a splendid work. I also apprised DNAW of the problems I had encountered at Chessington, he promised to ensure that the manual was printed and saw the light of day and I left London and returned to Lossiemouth feeling much happier.

The manual did appear, in somewhat modified form, during my absence from the Royal Navy. Very similar to that produced for the Avro Vulcan nuclear bomber, it had all the methods of working out dive-bombing sight settings and of course the 'g' settings for ADSL dive-bombing. Other than my wife, people were unaware of the long night hours that went into the publication. I was pleased with the final book, even though it did not have everything that I had included in my original draft edition—but that is ever the author's lot!

The job in 736 Squadron was very rewarding. The Squadron personnel not only taught naval aircrew to fly the Buccaneer, but whole courses of newly trained RAF navigators were coming through from RAF Swinderby to make up for the shortage of trained RN observers. Many of these RAF navigators would never see service in the Royal Air Force except for their initial 'wings' training and would complete their time in the Navy; others would transfer to the RN, having become fully indoctrinated in the requirements of naval aviation.

Don Richardson joined us from 800 Squadron and became the Senior Pilot, with Dave Venables as the Senior Observer. Both Don and Dave would leave the naval service, Don to fly with Britannia Airways out of Luton and Dave to take up a posting with a company dealing in weapons information and data for the RN and RAF. When Don retired from the Navy I took over his position as Senior Pilot, Peter Matthews becoming the Senior Observer. At about this time 800 Squadron's two RAF exchange officers—the two Grahams, Smart and Pitchfork—joined 736 Squadron as instructors. John Kennett left early in 1967 and Dave Howard became the new CO. Before John Kennett left the Squadron he received a well-deserved 'chuck up' from FONAC for all the hard work carried out by the 736B Flight, the Buccaneer Weapons Trials Unit. It was a fitting tribute to him and to all who had participated in what had been the most intensive trial to improve a naval air weapon system and make it the most potent in the world.

While serving in 736 Squadron during this period I had more aircraft incidents and near-accidents than I can remember throughout the whole of my naval aviation career. All of them raised a few hairs on the back of my neck. The first involved an engine test flight in a Buccaneer Mk 1. One of the engines had been changed, and the new engine required a full test flight, which involved taking the aircraft to altitude, taking readings all the way up and then descending to 25,000 feet, shutting it down and restarting it. Everything was fine until I attempted to restart the engine. It refused to relight, so I closed the fuel HP lever, waited a while for the engine to be drained of excess fuel and then attempted a second restart. Once again I was unsuccessful and had to go through the shutdown procedure, wait a while and attempt a third relight. On this occasion there was a dull thud, which shook the airframe, the aircraft shot forward like a rocket and the engine tailpipe temperature rose rapidly. I quickly secured the engine and informed Lossiemouth tower of what had happened and that I would be returning to make a single-engine landing. This went without incident, and after the engineers had reset the engine relight sequence the next flight was trouble-free.

The next incident occurred over the Tain Range in Ross and Cromarty. I was flying with Dick Pearce on a weapons trial flight in a Mk 2 at the time, carrying out LABS manoeuvres with practice bombs. The cloud base was about 1,500 feet, and after we had released our bomb the aircraft entered cloud and I commenced the roll-out recovery to the right. The aircraft was almost upside down when we heard a loud grinding noise from the starboard engine. The engine rpm had started to run down, and I quickly rolled the aircraft the right way up and descended below cloud to establish exactly what was happening. The rpm was by now quite low and the temperatures high, so I shut the engine down, declared an emergency and carried out yet another single-engine landing without further incident—though with a very frightened observer in the rear cockpit. The cause of the problem was a compressor shroud that had come loose and was touching the bypass compressor blades. This was the second such occurrence of this engine problem, and as a result Rolls-Royce came up with a modification to prevent it from happening again.

The next mishap occurred during the 1966 Lossiemouth Air Show. The Squadron, together with 764, had just carried out a dummy attack on the airfield and both were forming up into a huge 'Balbo' formation for a flypast finale. The Buccaneer that Dick Pearce and I were flying was the last aircraft to carry out a simulated OTS nuclear attack. The Station's Gunnery Officer exploded a huge dummy weapon in the middle of the airfield, producing what looked like a nuclear mushroom of smoke and fire, as I dived away to join the flypast formation—a good distance since I was on the formation leader's right wing. My Buccaneer was travelling very fast as I swung round on the right side of the formation, and as I came up to the leader I put my air brakes out and all hell broke out in the cockpit, alarms buzzing in my ears and flashing across the instrument panel. Another pilot called us and said we were on fire. I selected the audio alarm 'off' and looked at the instrument panels but no fire was indicated anywhere. However, my starboard engine had gone out, together with all its associated systems. The 'smoke' that everybody had seen streaming from our aircraft was in fact fuel vapour, which disappeared as I secured the engine while pulling out of formation. Poor Dick was beside himself with worry, but I quickly put his mind at rest by saying that we were not on fire: our starboard engine had failed for some reason. Then I set the starboard engine up for relight, which was successful, and I quickly re-joined the flypast formation and made a simulated single-engine landing on completion.

The engineers examined the starboard engine but could find nothing wrong with it. The flame-out must have been caused by the sudden reduction in hydraulic pressure when I had selected my air brakes 'out'. This reduction would have caused a reduction in fuel pressure—because the fuel pumps are hydraulically driven—and induced an engine stall and flame-out. Why the port engine did not also flame out was never really understood. Various hydraulic components were changed in the aircraft, which was later test-flown without a problem. A few weeks later, however, when a student was returning from Roseharty Range near Fraserburgh, flying very fast, selected his air brake 'out', the starboard engine flamed out in exactly the same manner as I had experienced. He quickly re-lit his engine and carried out a precautionary single-engine landing. Once again, nothing wrong could be found with the aircraft systems, but after the air brake hydraulics and selector switch had been changed the problem seemed to disappear.

* * *

While serving in 736 Squadron I decided to sit the Squadron Command Examination at Yeovilton. This examination is very similar to that for ship command but excludes such subjects as navigation, 'rules of the road' and ship safety. The air station's Sea Prince twin-engine communications aircraft was made available to take me and four examiners south with Les Wilkinson at the controls and me as his co-pilot. The take-off was scheduled for about 0730 and there was fog hanging around the airfield, but Les held a 'Master Green' instrument rating on type and the Duty Lieutenant Commander (Flying) was happy to let us depart. The take-off went smoothly and no sooner had we left the runway than our aircraft was enveloped in thick mist and cloud. As the aircraft climbed to 2,000 feet I noticed that the starboard engine boost gauge was slowly falling back to zero and drew Les's attention to the fact. He was by this time also experiencing right yaw and I remarked gently that we had an incipient engine failure on our hands. I called the tower about our predicament and suggested to Les that he return to base and let down over the sea; I would work all the services while he flew the aircraft.

God was taking care of us that day because as we rolled out on the recip-rocal northerly heading I saw Covesea Lighthouse pass underneath and to the right of us. I told Les to reduce height to a couple of hundred feet and then make a 'rate one' turn on to the runway heading. We were passing through broken cloud and fog and suddenly there was the golf course and

215

the runway ahead. I selected undercarriage 'down' and full flap and Les made a perfect landing, rolling out in less than 500 yards. As we touched down the starboard engine stopped of its own accord. With the emergency services were all around us, our very frightened passengers quickly exited the aircraft, telling us that thick smoke and flames had been issuing from the bad engine as we had made our approach to the runway—although we had not seen anything nor had received any alerts in the cockpit,. A Petty Officer friend of mine was having breakfast in the Stotfield Hotel when suddenly an aircraft appeared out of the cloud and fog right in front of him, banking hard to the right and with thick black smoke pouring from its starboard engine; he then lost sight of it as it disappeared in the fog towards the airfield. Apparently the smoke had been caused by a heavy oil leak flowing against the exhaust stack, where it caught fire, and eventually the lack of oil had caused the engine to seize on touch-down.

Later that day I flew a Hunter T.8 jet trainer south to Yeovilton with the Deputy Supply Officer—one of the examiners—as my passenger, quite calm and apparently unafraid in spite of his earlier ordeal. I sat and passed my Squadron Command Examination. It is strange that in such circumstances I have always managed to remain calm—albeit admittedly concerned—and have tackled whatever I have had to do whereas all about me people were behaving like the proverbial headless chickens. I have been fearful, of course, but I try never to let on, going about my tasks in as logical a manner as possible. When my aircraft were back on *terra firma* I would utter a sigh of relief and a prayer to the good Lord for looking after me and my crews.

* * *

My time in 736 Squadron was coming to an end, though not before we were to experience some excitement . On 28 March 1967 I was in the process of manning my aircraft when I was called to the tower to see 'Wings' to discuss a live attack using the ADSL technique. I was a little apprehensive at first because this attack mode had not been fully cleared for use with live ordnance, but after some pressure I agreed that we could go ahead as an adjunct to our weapon system trials. Bombs were ordered up immediately, and I briefed a couple of crews. We had been ordered to bomb the wreck of the *Torrey Canyon*, a Liberian-registered, 120,000-ton 'super tanker' that had gone aground on the Seven Stones Reef to the north-west of the Bishop's Rock lighthouse and begun to leak huge quantities of crude oil. The objective was to set it on fire and reduce the pollution that was threatening the entire south-western coastline.

I was at this stage the new Senior Pilot of the Squadron, Don Richardson having retired from the naval service to become an airline pilot. Dave Howard was the CO and was airborne at the time, so he had no idea of what was happening until after he had landed. My aircraft was prepared, and while I was back in the Squadron carrying out some final planning I noticed Dave manning it, starting it up and taxying out loaded with eight 1,000-pound bombs. He had landed while I was in the Squadron offices, rushed to the tower to find out what was happening, grabbed the Form A700, the aircraft maintenance and log book, told the tower that the crew had been changed and started up and was on his way. To say that I was livid would have been an understatement—and I told him so when I eventually caught up with him! However, another aircraft had almost been readied and I took off in it about fifteen minutes behind him.

My observer was, again, Dick Pearce, and because of the distance to target—almost 600 miles with external weapons—it was necessary to carry out inflight refuelling. A final briefing had to be made at RNAS Brawdy prior to the attack, then we all flew out to the wreck and bombed it, although with limited success: a fire was started but it did not burn for long. What was really needed was a method of puncturing the hull to allow the oil to flood out so that it could be set on fire with napalm. Eventually delayed-action bombs were dropped against the hull and the RAF joined in with rockets and napalm. A huge fire was created, the black smoke from which could be seen well over a hundred miles away. At the end of the operation the hull was empty of oil but a vast amount of it had nevertheless managed to reach the south-west coastline, causing a terrible problem with pollution and one that lasted some considerable time. The 'Torrey Canyon Flight' returned to Lossiemouth after three days of bombing, everybody satisfied with a job well done.

* * *

The usual 'silly season' arrived with the preparations for Air Day. 736 Squadron had formed an aerobatic team with five Buccaneers, but, although we practised some excellent loops and barrel rolls, Commander Ted Anson, who was 'Wings' at the time, swiftly vetoed the idea: the fin and stabilator of the aircraft were not really designed for the rough treatment they were likely to encounter. Ted had been the original naval test pilot and had carried out the majority of the test-flying on the aircraft, so he knew what he talking about, and we ended up carrying out the usual display of dummy attacks against the airfield. I cannot exactly recall whether it was during this Air Day or during the previous year's event when a brand new Gannet AEW Mk 3 crashed in front of the crowd—and before the eyes of the Flag Officer Flying Training, Admiral David Kirk, and HRH Prince Charles, who was on leave from Gordonstoun Boys' School at the time.

The Gannet pilot was straight out of OFS training at Culdrose and should not have been authorised to take part in such an event. He flew down the runway at 1,000 feet; dumb-belled round back on to the runway heading again, raising his flaps and undercarriage; returned back down the runway, going quite fast; stopped one engine; and dumb-belled to fly back along the runway on one engine. As he turned back on to the runway heading it was obvious that he was in trouble, losing height rapidly as he came round the turn. May was quite alarmed and asked what was happening, and it very quickly became clear that he was going to crash—which he did, to the west of the display runway, where his starboard wing tip dug into the ground.

The aircraft spun around so that it skidded away from the crowd across the airfield on its belly, throwing off panels and pieces of metal until it finally stopped just short of the GCA van. The pilot and observer scrambled out and disappeared over the hill. FOFT was meanwhile leaping up and down purple-faced, calling for the 849 Squadron CO, 'Butch' Barnard. He wanted to know why a newly trained OFS student was flying the aircraft and what training he had been given for the display. 'Butch' somehow talked his way out of the problem but he was merely greasing his slipway: following another incident he was more or less on his way from the Squadron, though since he had almost run his full time as the CO it was something of a non-event.

'Butch' Barnard—six-feet-plus, built like an ox and blessed with a heart of gold—came from the Transvaal and sported an unkempt, red 'Trekker's beard that reached almost to his navel. I have a permanent image in my mind of an occasion during my service in 738 Squadron when he had come north for a weekend, flying up in a Sea Hawk fighter. On the following Monday morning there was a howling gale and I watched 'Butch' walk out to his jet with his pusser's green case under his arm just as if it was a lady's handbag, his red trekker's beard blowing over his right shoulder. He incurred the displeasure of Their Lordships when he was the CO of 849 (HQ) Squadron following his decision to take a weekend off down south in Gibraltar, flying direct from Culdrose across the Bay of Biscay to the famous Rock. En route, over the Bay, he had engine problems and had to make an emergency landing in France, but he and his crew had failed to submit a proper flight plan to clear themselves across French territory. The aircraft was nearly confiscated and the crew interned, but somehow 'Butch' again talked himself out of the mire. I understand that when he retired from the Navy he returned home to manage his family's ranch in the Transvaal. Despite his rather severe exterior, he was a very colourful character who was liked by one and all. He was one of those people who made the FAA what it was—one of the finest Armed Forces in the world!

* * *

On the banks of the River Clyde a new Cunard passenger liner was being built. Her building number was 736 and on the day of her launch she was to be christened *Queen Elizabeth 2* by Her Majesty. As soon as it became known that her building number was the same as our squadron number, what more fitting gesture could be made than to fly the whole of 736 Squadron in a flypast formation over the great ship as she left her slipway for the Clyde? The event was due to take place on 20 September 1967 and everybody prayed for good weather. For a couple of weeks we practised flying sixteen Buccaneers in formation, and then Lossiemouth's FAC Army Major travelled south to install himself in one of the cranes overlooking the ship's slipway so that he could act as our controller.

The take-off from Lossiemouth went without a hitch but it was a very heavy, overcast day although our Major was reporting reasonable conditions over the Clyde. When the Squadron arrived the cloud base was at about

3,500 feet full cover but the launch was behind schedule, so the Squadron went immediately into an endurance holding pattern to the south-east. Time was fast running out, however, and our fuel was becoming marginal, but then, suddenly, the Major came up on the radio with 'Start your run-in now' and all four divisions scrambled to regain the formation. The flypast was a great success and our Major began shouting congratulations over the radio but now we had to return to Lossiemouth before we ran out of fuel: it was going to be a very close call for many. Although the weather had deteriorated somewhat since our take-off I called for a straight-in radar approach to the duty runway and my division all landed safely with less than 1,000 pounds of fuel remaining in each aircraft. The whole experience had me sweating since the Squadron should have remained at altitude for lower fuel consumption until it was certain that we could start our flypast run-in with safety. However, discounting a few shattered nerves it was a great occasion, and whenever I read about or see photographs of the 'QE 2', as she is affectionately known, I always recall that very special day.

* * *

I now had less than three months to tie up my job in the Squadron and hand it over to another pair of hands. My appointment to the US Navy on exchange had been approved in both Britain and the United States, the USN having ensured that they were not getting a Russian spy in Royal Navy clothing! I had to make sure that my house was taken over by the Navy as an officer's naval hiring, and in this respect I had Dave Howard and his new wife Mary lined up to move into it as soon as we departed. The family Morris Minor Traveller was handed over to Ray Fielding, a Fleet Air Arm pilot of World War II days who owned P. S. Nicholson in Forres. He gave me £100 on the understanding that a new car would be bought from him on my return home.

Our pets were another problem. However, Timber was handed over to my good friend Jonathan Todd and his family for safekeeping—Jonathan was my assistant AWI during my last days in the Squadron and had also served with me in 800 (Scimitar) Squadron—and we tried hard to leave our two cats with friends, though without success. Father eventually took Zebbie but it looked as if Sweetie Pie was heading for the pound. She obviously had a sense that her ninth life was in jeopardy for one day Naomi inadvertently left the kitchen door open and she was gone. We searched for days and finally had to ask our neighbours, if they were not prepared to take her in, to arrange for a vet to collect her. She had been with us since she was a tiny kitten and I for one did not want anything to happen to her.

It must have been about six weeks into our American tour when we received a letter from Dave saying that Sweetie Pie had been found—and could he keep her? She had been hiding in the furnace chimney of the kirk opposite our house; the verger knew where she had come from and carried her back to her old home, Eilean Mhor. Dave loved her because she saw his new wife's whippet off at the feeding bowl. Dave was a 'big dog' man and, having once owned a Golden Labrador like Timber, he had a hard time taking to this small dog; Sweetie Pie obviously had guts and character. I could not have been more delighted and we wrote back telling Dave that she was his until the good Lord took her.

Finally the day arrived for us to leave. Our very good neighbours Alex and Jane MacCreadie, together with Peter and Joan Gault, drove us to Elgin station with our baggage on the start of our great adventure. We travelled south to Camber to stay with my parents for the Christmas holidays—our last in Britain for the next two years. For the next ten days we had a wonderful holiday, but it would be just as wonderful to leave behind a bitterly cold, blizzard-filled winter for the sunshine of California!

VI

AN AMERICAN ADVENTURE

— 21 —

AIRTEVRON FOUR

ONE DAY I happened to be speaking to Lieutenant Commander Jack Worth, who had just returned from an exchange appointment to Air Test and Evaluation Squadron Four at USNAS Point Mugu, California. He had been the Project Officer for the US Navy's Bullpup missile programme in AIRTEVRON, more commonly known as VX-4, and I wanted his thoughts about the missile concerning its carriage on the Buccaneer. Once we had sorted out my questions we got around to discussing his job in VX-4, and he suggested that it would be a very good appointment for me. I went home that evening mulling over the idea in my mind: the chances of my becoming the Senior Pilot in a front-line squadron were very remote, since such appointments were usually kept for a General List officer as a stepping-stone to squadron command—although I was in time to be proved very wrong, much to my surprise!

During dinner that evening May asked me what was on my mind and I asked her whether she liked the idea of spending two years in the United States. Her initial reaction was that she was not sure that she really wanted to go there at all, although when I asked her the reason she could not come up with anything definite. I dropped the subject, but a couple of days later, after discussing it with her friends, May changed her mind. I then put in my request to my CO, John Kennett, and a while later he informed me that the appointment was mine and that I would be relieving Peter Marshall, the present Royal Navy incumbent in VX-4.

* * *

Early on 16 January 1968 the SS *United States* steamed slowly up the Hudson River, heading for her New York berth. The forward half of the ship was totally covered in ice and snow from a blizzard encountered during the night. After docking we made our way aft with our baggage, awaiting the arrival of Mr McDonald, the New York Consulate's man who saw to all new arrivals, and following some difficulty—he was, it transpired, not expecting us— we settled into our hotel. It must have been about 9 o'clock on that first evening in New York, when we heard, quite distinctively, the sound of a gunshot; our room was very hot and we had opened the window to let in some fresh air, and the noise was clearly heard by us all. The next morning we discovered that there had been a jewellery heist in a store next to the hotel and that the owner had been shot dead. Welcome to America!

On the third day at the hotel Mr McDonald came up trumps with two Consulate cars, collected us and drove us out to La Guardia Airport for a six-hour flight aboard a TWA Boeing 707 to Los Angeles, and within two hours we were on our last leg to California and sunshine. The flight to LA went very well indeed, although because much of the northern United States was covered in deep snow we had little chance of seeing the countryside from 35,000 feet. About six hours later our 707 was on its final approach into LAX, the skies absolutely clear, bright and sunny.

The disembarkation went quickly, and Pete Marshall, with two US Navy station wagons and drivers, was waiting for us. Our baggage was thrown into one vehicle, and together with Pete we climbed into the other. The journey to Point Mugu took us along Pacific Coast Highway 1, through Santa Monica and Malibu, and after fifty or sixty miles alongside the beautiful, blue Pacific Ocean we passed Mugu Rock and there lay USNAS Point Mugu before us.

Our first task was to check in with Base Security to obtain temporary passes, and then we drove over to a USN married quarters that one of the VX-4 officers had very kindly loaned to us while he and his wife were away for ten days. After we had offloaded our baggage and thanked the two drivers, Pete took us over to his quarters, where his wife, Caroline, and their brood of thirteen (!) children were waiting with a barbecue. We had arrived in the 'Golden State', wondering what our future held.

Pete Marshall had our programme well and truly sorted out but it was now the weekend and we were on our own for a couple of days. On the Saturday we drove south to Woodland Hills to visit Eunice Diaper (now Eunice Rawlings) to stay a night with her and her family. Pete had loaned us his old station wagon for a few days until we managed to find a suitable car, a Dodge Dart sedan in excellent condition, with one previous owner and 80,000 miles on the clock. Within half an hour, having parted with $800, we were driving it out of the other end of the lot. It was worth every cent and it gave us yeoman service throughout the whole of our time in the United States. Hal, the officer who had loaned us his married quarters, was due back in a few days so as a family we moved into the Wagon Wheel motel on the northern side of Oxnard, and there we stayed until we moved out a week later to drive south to San Diego and USNAS Miramar for an instrument flying course.

While Caroline Marshall was fussing around with May and Naomi I was introduced to the CO, officers and men of VX-4. Straightaway I was confronted by the Squadron XO, Commander Foster.

'Where the hell were you on Saturday?' he enquired. 'You should have called upon Captain Pierozzi, the Squadron Commander!'

'I'm sorry, sir, but I wasn't told anything about that, and my joining date is today, the nineteenth of January.' Pete backed me up and said he had not been given any specific instructions, and in any case the Captain was away for the weekend. I thought that only British Army and RAF officers made calls upon their Commanding Officers, but it appeared that the US Navy still followed the tradition of officers leaving their calling cards. It was soon brushed over, however, and the following Saturday afternoon May, Naomi and I paid our respects to the Pierozzis for tea and cucumber sandwiches. Somehow we got around to discussing the game of bowling.

'Oh, you mean the game that Sir Francis Drake was playing on Plymouth Hoe awaiting the Spanish Armada long before America was discovered!' I said, jokingly.

'Out of my house!' the Captain shouted, and then burst into laughter. 'I like you two—you would make good Americans!'

'Yes, sir! Thank you!'

From that time onwards we could not put a foot wrong. What we did not know at the time was that the Doust family had been in North America since the 1700s, and eventually our second, as yet unborn daughter Dominique would marry an American who was a descendant of one of the original *Mayflower* immigrants. In many ways we were as American as our Captain and his officers and men, the majority of whose families had come to the country very much later.

Our accommodation at the Wagon Wheel motel was excellent, but it was a long drive along the PCH to Point Mugu. My first requirement was to pay a visit to the Married Quarters Officer to arrange accommodation for four weeks hence, when I would have completed my course at Miramar. The officer, a Scottish immigrant lady, promised us quarters on our return: a USN officer was moving out of Sparrow Drive in less than three weeks, so they could be repainted and redecorated ready for our return. I mentioned furniture but was told that the USN stopped supplying furniture to MQ's some time ago. The next item on the list was to revisit the Security Officer and obtain proper ID cards for us all, for which we had to be photographed and fingerprinted. We were also issued with commissary ID cards and bumper stickers for the car, blue ones because I was an officer (ratings were issued with red stickers).

After a week at the Wagon Wheel, we packed up and left for San Diego and Miramar. We drove along the PCH rather than the freeways through Los Angeles at this stage of our American driving experience. The PCH was much more pleasant and one could drive at a comfortable speed. Our journey south took us through Long Beach, San Clemente and Oceanside. We pulled off into the Mission Bay area, where we found a relatively cheap motel with adequate accommodation and a small kitchen.

On Monday morning I set off at about 6 o'clock in thick fog to report to VFT-125, the Skyhawk Instrument Training School. This was located next to VF-121 'Fighter Town', the US Navy's West Coast F-4 Phantom training squadron, at which the Royal Navy had four FAA officers teaching USN pilots and Radar Intercept Officers how to fly and fight the aircraft. The first week was taken up with Ground School, going through the TA-4F aircraft systems and the ejection seat—not, in this instance, a Martin-Baker product. Air traffic control and meteorology were covered and then we all took an open-book test, which, naturally, we all passed! The second week was taken up with flying around the local area to practise instrument flight procedures and culminated in a trip to NAS Moffett near San Francisco, landing and taking off at night and then returning to Miramar. At the end of the course I was awarded a 'White Instrument Card'. However, before I left the Squadron I was to have a run-in with the XO.

At first I had difficulty settling down to the US Navy's way of conducting instrument flight practice. One had to file a flight plan for each trip, but in the middle of a sortie, perhaps in the middle of a complex manoeuvre, the instructor would tell the student to call the ATC centre to change the flight plan. In my mind such action was totally unrealistic and fundamentally unsafe—especially in the Skyhawk, which had its instruments scattered around the front of the cockpit. US cockpit designers have never really accepted the advantages of grouping the primary flight instruments—compass, artificial horizon, airspeed indicator, altimeter, turn-and-slip indicator and vertical speed indicator—together in one centralised panel in front of the pilot where he could concentrate his vision, although they finally arrived at the British way of doing things in the F-8 Crusader and F-4 Phantom. Consequently a Briton confronted by an old-style American instrument panel could readily become disorientated. There were, moreover, no aural signals for angle of attack, having only the old 'V's and 'Donut' visual indicators which really did not fall completely within a pilot's instrument scan. Perhaps I had become too totally swept up in the British system, which I thought to be the best in the world. At least we did not suffer from the instrument accidents that the US Navy frequently experienced. The end result was that I had to see the XO as my progress was considered below normal. When he started criticising me, and my attitude, I pointed out that I was a very experienced instructor and instrument examiner and it was my opinion that he did know what I was talking about. I was amazed that US aircraft were so poorly equipped and laid out for instrument flying. I also said that I considered that the way instrument flying was practised to be extremely poor. Perhaps I did not tackle the matter in a very diplomatic manner, but when he started reminding me that 'their boys' were fighting a hard and difficult war in Vietnam I was left wondering what the relevance of this remark was to instrument flying practice. I asked him and he realised that he had gone too far. I was dismissed and I thought no more about it.

After receiving my instrument card I returned to Point Mugu with May and Naomi and was then given the position of Project Officer for the F-8H Crusader Ground Attack Project, although before I was allowed to fly the jet I had to attend the F-8H Ground School at Miramar. On my return Major Don Keast USMC briefed me for my first flight, and with an F-4 chase aircraft in tow I took off to the east, heading for the Grand Canyon. It was a delightful fighter to fly—a fighter pilot's dream, in fact—but it suffered from one major shortcoming: it had a very high landing speed. In addition, the nose rode so high while landing that it was very difficult for the pilot to see where he was going. The manufacturers overcame this problem by the very novel expedient of raising the wing's leading edge by two feet via a hydraulic jack, thereby allowing the nose to be lowered at landing speed and giving the pilot a good forward view. The trailing centre section of the wing was held on by two huge bolts. The aircraft was never really cleared for carrier deck operations although it was to become the US Navy's principal day and night fighter until the F-4 entered service. A modified version known as the F-8K entered service to replace the F-8E/H models. This was the same variant that had been sold to the French Navy, and it was fitted with an all-blown wing: now, by merely moving the throttle, a pilot could land the jet anywhere, and its landing speed was almost thirty knots slower, making it much safer on a carrier deck.

It was while I was at the F-8H Ground School that I met up with Commander Jerry Higgins, who was to be VX-4's new XO. He had just completed the two-year postgraduate course at the US Navy College at Monterey, near San Francisco. He was a very small and likable officer, full of fun, and he walked like a penguin with his feet well splayed. Jerry joined the USN via the AVCAD (Aviation Cadet) programme from having been a clarinet player in a dance band; as a matter of fact he could play at least half a dozen musical instruments very successfully, and it was he who taught my daughter Naomi how to play the piano. He was a very generous and kind-hearted but something of a disciplinarian with his own children. His wife Anne tried her hardest to organise the squadron officers' wives, but May was having none of it. On one memorable occasion she approached me about writing May's half-yearly report and I quickly had to point out that British officers' wives were not reported upon. Jerry left before I completed the course but I was to meet up with him again when I re-joined VX-4.

Once I had flown the F-8, I quickly set about building up flight hours both in that jet and in the T-33 training jet and the old Beechcraft UC-45, a small twin-engine communications aircraft christened *Beulah* by the Squadron. I was then sent back to Miramar to join the F-4 Ground School course, and it was while attending this course that I met up with Commander 'Tooter' Teague, a former F-8 XO who was due to join VX-4 as the future Chief Projects Officer. Tooter came from Louisiana and was full of himself—hence his nickname. However, he was very likable and one day he invited me home for dinner. It was while we were driving there that we heard over the car radio that Dr Martin Luther King had been murdered. At that time I did not know too much about the racial tensions that existed in America between blacks and whites. Perhaps I should have read up on them but I thought, rather naively, that they were very much something of the past. I was soon to be disillusioned in VX-4.

* * *

May was beginning to be known about the base from having joined the Navy League, a civilian organisation which, among other commitments, helps US Navy sailors experiencing financial problems. It was hard to believe that, in such an affluent country, the majority of ordinary sailors at that time were living below the poverty line. In many incidents, their credit loan interest exceeded what the USN was paying them. To May it was a real eye-opener that such a state of affairs should exist. President Nixon actually passed a bill to bring the ordinary sailor, airman and soldier above the poverty line with increased pay, but with inflation it was not long before they were back where they started.

May and I joined the Officers' Bowling Club and once a week we used to go along to bowl for VX-4. I was useless at the game but May was good. She had a keen eye for bowling and knocking pins flying in all directions, whereas my ball often ended up in the adjoining alley! Later on in the year we were both attending the prize-giving ceremony at the Officers' Club down on the beach. VX-4 did quite well and May received an award for the most promising beginner. However, while at the club she experienced one of her severe migraine headaches and I had to take her to the base Sickbay for an injection of propranol in the upper left arm. The base duty doctor who gave the injection had been in the Officers' Club drinking quite heavily and was somewhat the worse for it. When he administered the injection he dug the needle into the bone and she let out an almighty scream of pain; her arm immediately swelled up, turning black and blue with bruising. Apart from injuring May, this incompetent fellow was supposed to be on call for any aircraft accident; the air station was night flying at the time. The next day I spoke with Bill Browning, VX-4's Medical Officer, about the incident, he had a word with the base's Senior Medical Officer and within twenty-four hours the young doctor had been reappointed elsewhere. The SMO apologised to May for the dreadful treatment she had received and took charge of her health problem personally. She recovered from her migraine; indeed, she has not suffered an attack since that time.

I flew many project sorties and also qualified in the F-4. The old Beechcraft was withdrawn from service and the Squadron received in its place a modified S-2F Tracker, a twin-engine former anti-submarine aircraft. Before 1968 was out I was fully qualified on this lovely old machine. Pete Marshall was allowed to stay with VX-4 to complete the current phase of Project OV-63. He would eventually return to Britain to become the CO of 767 Squadron, the RN's Phantom training squadron, responsible for training both Royal Navy and Royal Air Force crews for 892 NAS and No 43 Squadron.

* * *

Time was hanging on our hands after I returned from my course at Miramar, so I contacted my cousin Gertrude Pye, who lived in Oakland across the bay from San Francisco, and arranged to visit her and her husband Archie one weekend. We drove north at the end of February after Archie had returned home from hospital, where he had been recuperating having suffered a mild heart attack. Neither May nor I had ever met Gertrude and her husband although she had visited England and seen Dad and Uncle Jim at Rye Harbour. The only image I had of Gertrude was that of a three-and-a-half-year-old dressed in a sailor's suit and straw hat, sitting with Dad and Uncle

Jim on a pony trap near the Martello tower at Rye Harbour—a couple of years or so before the outbreak of World War I. Gertrude had gone to San Francisco as an eighteen-month-old with her mother (who was also called May Doust) and had acquired a job as a lady-in-waiting to a wealthy Californian woman. With her mother she had arrived in San Francisco in 1906, just before the tremendous earthquake that year which shook the city to the ground. Gertrude remembered little of the 'quake but did recall the fire engines racing around to extinguish the thousands of blazes that had broken out as a result. Six weeks after our visit Gertrude telephoned us at Mugu to tell us that, sadly, Archie had suffered another heart attack and had passed away. We were all very upset at this news.

* * *

We had been in the United States eight months without taking any long leave so it was decided that we would spend a month travelling around the west of the country and into western Canada. We hired various pieces of camping equipment, including tents from the base Special Services Section, topped up the car with everything that we might need and set off before dawn for Yosemite National Park, our first stop going north. Our route then took us towards Eureka on the Pacific coast, then to Portland, Seattle and Canada. At the border post the Americans gave us a cursory search but the Canadians were much more thorough—they were searching for guns and ammunition. We called Clive Tanner, an old friend from grammar school days, and he was overwhelmed and delighted to know that we were in Vancouver. He instructed us where to find his home, and after a few wrong turns we finally found him, his wife and family. We stayed with Clive and his family for three days.

Our next call was planned to be Banff National Park, but Clive advised against it. The first snows had already fallen and the grizzly bears were on the prowl prior to hibernating for the winter. Apparently, two young girl campers had been killed by a grizzly in their tent about the same time the previous year, so we decided to give Banff a miss, head off south-east towards Spokane and then into Montana. One fascinating aspect of North America is the countryside. North of San Francisco there is an amazing transformation from desert, semi-desert and arid country into verdant pastures and woodland that continues all the way to Canada. The one contrast is the high mountain region around Spokane, where it is very bleak and bereft of vegetation of any sort. However, to the south-east, in Montana, there is green as far as the eye can see, with cattle roaming and cereals being grown just about everywhere. In Wyoming there is mixed farming, with plenty of pasture and trees in evidence—genuine rural America, and very similar to Europe in many ways.

After leaving Helena we headed south-east and then south into Yellowstone National Park. It was now autumn, and with Labor Weekend behind us the roads were not quite so congested. We stopped for a while at Old Faithful, the largest hot geyser in North America, and witnessed it 'blowing' twice.

From Yellowstone we continued south, heading for Salt Lake City. Our hotel here, which was Mormon-owned, was very clean and comfortable, but our room contained just the barest of essentials. The hotel proprietor also owned the restaurant opposite and we enjoyed a very good evening meal, but, as Clive Tanner had warned us, we had to pay to use the rest rooms. The hotel/restaurant owner meticulously counted every dollar bill, placed them in numerical sequence and entered them one by one into a ledger. We could not believe what we were seeing, but to pay ten cents to 'water the lawn' took the candy for the day!

We called in at Las Vegas and then set off for Barstow and finally Point Mugu, having travelled exactly 4,000 miles throughout the western United States and Canada in four weeks. We planned to tour the eastern half of the US the following year but a very happy event would prevent our doing so.

* * *

While I had been away from VX-4, Major 'Shad' Devorak USAF had been flying the remaining sorties for the Crusader Project and it was now time to write up the report for COMOPTEVFOR, our Admiral, who had his head-quarters in Norfolk, Virginia. Each and every project conducted by VX-4 had a Project Officer on the Admiral's Staff. Everything we wrote went through this officer and upwards to the Admiral, then on to the Pentagon, finally to be placed in Congress's archives, from where any Congressman with a bee in his bonnet could call up a report to substantiate any topic he might wish to raise. The reports had to be written in a special format laid out in COMOPTEVFOR's Instructions and Orders—a simple, quite excellent format so arranged that anybody could readily locate the information sought in order to back up whatever argument it was intended to make. It was a format that I would continue to use throughout my naval career.

It was now time for the annual USN and USMC Officers' Balls. These were held towards the end of October, that for the Navy preceding the Marines' Ball. Every year the Chief of Naval Operations would signal the Fleet, announcing the theme for all the balls for that particular year. For our first year in VX-4 the theme was 'The Old and the New Navy' and May and I were given the task of decorating the Officers' Club guestroom. We decided to turn it into the Admiral's dining room aboard an old 'wooden walls' battleship, similar to that aboard HMS *Victory* berthed at Portsmouth Dockyard. Over-head we fitted black-painted hardboard with 'P' lamps* inserted to represent star constellations. The whole guestroom was re-panelled with light varnished plywood and imitation ship's windows and a dining table was placed in the middle, set for the Admiral and his staff officers. The bar was decorated throughout with ensigns and pennants. With the lighting and a subdued setting, the room looked very realistic and everybody was very pleased with the effect. After the ball, the Club was reluctant to remove our handiwork but I insisted because of the fire hazard it presented.

_____

* Tiny lamps used to illuminate cockpit intstrument panels.

Every three months VX-4 visited the mental hospital near Camarillo known as the Southern California State Hospital. It was a fairly large facility which housed patients who had been committed either by their families or by the state, for a period of time or perhaps for life. In the United States it was at this time possible for one to be put away by a member of one's family merely if one was 'considered' to be insane or mentally ill. One old gentleman, 77 years of age, had been there all his life. He was a cobbler and he had been committed by his family for the simple reason that he wished to be a cobbler—a career that was not in keeping with his relatives' social position. It was the only home he knew, and when the truth finally emerged he did not want to go home. This cruel decision on the part of his family almost brought me to tears: how could one human being do this to another, especially to his or her kith and kin? It was as aspect of American life that I found very disturbing. By contrast, however, there was also present a young male nurse who had been admitted for offences relating to drug abuse. He had been in and out of the hospital several times but had decided to train as a nurse within the facility and stay there because he knew that he would fall prey to drugs once again were he to be released. He seemed very happy now that he was doing something useful in his life.

The purpose behind VX-4's quarterly visits to the hospital was to provide entertainment and party fare and to talk to the various inmates who were allowed to mix with us. We saw only those who were considered stable enough to socialise with visitors, and even so they had to be given tranquillisers to keep them calm throughout their time with us. It was wonderful to see the way in which these poor folk looked forward to our visits, the music and the food provided.

With the approach of Christmas, VX-4 regularly organised a roving carol service around the married quarters. A flatbed was decorated and illuminated with lanterns and was driven around the quarters, and, wrapped up in overcoats and mufflers, we went a-carolling at the tops of our voices. The event was very popular and everybody looked forward to it each year. Christmas in the United States is not marked in quite the same way as it is in Britain and Europe; the big holiday in America is Thanksgiving Day, which is celebrated on the last Thursday of every November. The Squadron would secure early on Christmas Eve and Christmas would be an official holiday, but if the following day were a weekday one was back at work: there was no Boxing Day holiday. Then of course there followed the New Year's Day celebration, but, once again, if this fell on a weekday one returned to work the following day. The main problem with this routine was that most people were not fit to work, and certainly not fit to fly, the day following the holiday. Within the first week of January 1969, for example, the US Navy lost 32 aircrewmen in various accidents; it also lost approximately 500 personnel as a result of road accidents over the holiday period—more than two months' worth of recruiting! The CNO was beside himself at this tremendous loss and waste of life. Although the aircrew casualties included twelve airman in a single P-3 Orion accident, the overall impact of losing so many experienced and trained aviators, including the cost to the nation of much hard work and expense, and of valuable equipment, was still unacceptable. The emphasis was now on flight and vehicle safety, and ship safety would be added following a collision involving the USS *Belknap* and the aircraft carrier *John F. Kennedy*, when eleven officers and men lost their lives. The accident occurred during night-time manoeuvres in the Mediterranean, a huge fire engulfing *Belknap* as, scraping down the port side of the carrier under the latter's angled-deck sponson, her aviation fuel lines were ruptured. Much of the missile cruiser's superstructure had been constructed from aluminium, which melted in the intense heat from the fire, blocking escape routes for the ship's crew in the process. Following this terrible accident it was decided that an all-encompassing 'Safety Center' would be set up to cover all aspects of marine safety—an excellent idea that was accepted by all in the US Navy as a sensible solution to a problem that was threatening to grow out of control.

VX-4 won the Flight Safety Trophy for having made 10,000 flights free of mishap, an achievement of which everybody was very proud. It was not beyond the realms of possibility that the Squadron would pick up the next trophy but, alas, it was not to be. I was airborne in an F-4 with Lieutenant Bruce Marshall USN as my RIO, carrying out simulated missile attacks against a frigate. Before leaving the ship we decided to make a slow flypast with everything down and the inflight refuelling probe extended, but unfortunately I extended the probe above its speed limit and the probe door promptly broke off as a result of the excessive wind pressure. The door went end over end and impaled itself in No 2 fuel tank directly behind the cockpits. Fuel was immediately sucked out by the airflow and the level in the tank began to drop very quickly. Bruce began screaming at the top of his voice: 'Mike! Mike! We're losing fuel from No 2 tank and we will not make it back to Mugu!' Sure enough, I could see fuel streaming from the rupture but somehow the level in the tank stabilised at about 1,000 pounds, which was more than enough to enable us to reach Mugu and land safely. I set about calming Bruce, who was by now becoming quite hysterical, and called Mugu, requesting a straight-in approach to the seaward end of the runway because of a serious fuel leak.,

'Are you declaring an emergency?' they asked. I could hardly contain myself. I called back.

'If I say that I have a serious fuel leak, then that statement in itself is enough to indicate that I have an emergency on my hands!'

'Okay, sir, you are cleared for a straight-in approach.'

'Thank you!'

We landed with more than enough fuel to make a further circuit and we turned off the runway to taxy back to the Squadron hardstanding, where the good Colonel, Don Keast, was waiting to meet us for an explanation of what had happened. I told him that I thought I had extended the probe at 250 knots because that was what I had seen on the airspeed indicator. He accepted my statement, but later Bruce and I discussed the incident further and we came to the conclusion that perhaps I had misread the indicator and extended the probe at a speed as much as 100 knots above the limit.

I was very embarrassed about the incident and for the next couple of weeks or so kept a very low profile. I was unhappy that I had let the Squadron down by making a stupid mistake and had prevented it from winning the next trophy.

* * *

It was now almost time for Pete Marshall to take his leave of VX-4. He was scheduled to return home early in March 1969 to become the first CO of the newly re-formed 767 Squadron, the Royal Navy's F-4K Phantom training unit at RNAS Yeovilton. He was thrilled with the idea of going to 767, and this was the reason he was left a year longer in his appointment to VX-4. The next few weeks were taken up with cleaning Pete's married quarters—quite a task given the size of his family, though made easier by placing him, his wife and his children in a transit MQ. Then the rains arrived: March 1969 took the record!

I had arranged for four US Navy station wagons to transport the Marshall family to Oxnard airport together with all their baggage. It was still raining, and there was flooding just about everywhere. After the fond farewells from all the Squadron friends, with me driving the lead wagon we set off for the airport in plenty of time, but when we arrived at Five Points Junction in Oxnard the streets were flooded to a depth of about eighteen inches. I turned slowly on to the road taking us to the airport, not quite knowing whether we were going to make it. However, we arrived with a few minutes to spare—or so I thought. The twin-engine Fokker Friendship was waiting and about to taxy when the Marshall clan arrived and the poor loadmaster had to unload and redistribute the aircraft's cargo in the pouring rain in order to get the family baggage aboard. After half an hour's delay, however, the travellers were on their way back to Britain via LAX and New York, where they would board the RMS *Queen Mary* for her final transatlantic passenger crossing.

* * *

We returned to Mugu but there was no flying on such an appalling day. It continued to rain heavily into the night, the cloud virtually on the ground. The following day I was the Squadron Duty Pilot and Lieutenant Colonel Keast wanted me to go south in the T-33 to collect an officer from NAS Miramar so that he could complete his project report. The weather was no better than the previous day's, with continuous heavy rain and runway flooding at Miramar, and I told the Colonel that I was not flying south in such conditions in an aircraft type that I had not flown for over a month—and one that sported such an awful instrument panel layout—for the sake of a project report. He looked quite shocked when I refused and then ordered Lieutenant Ron McKeown, our young test pilot to do the job. After Ron had, rather unhappily, departed I sat around feeling guilty, and extremely worried about his safety. Three to four hours later, to my relief, he returned. 'You were right, Mike, to refuse. The runway was badly flooded and I went sideways down the runway for nearly 500 yards and almost filled my pants!' I suggested that he tell the Colonel what had happened, which he did. Don Keast came through to both of us and apologised, saying that I had been correct to refuse the flight. Ron was a very experienced pilot and had been very lucky not to have lost his undercarriage and crashed—possibly to his death. I was seething with indignation that my knowledge and experience had been called into question and that Ron had been ordered to carry out the flight. The Colonel and I remained at arm's length for a week or so until the air had cleared!

During July 1968, while carrying out my familiarisation flights in the US-2F Tracker aircraft with Jerry Higgins, we flew south to Miramar and pick up a new officer for the Squadron, Lieutenant Commander Sandy Button USN. A Bostonian, he was an ex F-8 pilot with over 3,000 hours in that fighter, and on the way back to Mugu he sat in the right-hand pilot's seat while Jerry took a nap in one of the rear passenger seats. At first I thought Sandy was an Englishman as he spoke exactly like one. He was a very quiet and polite officer who neither smoked nor drank alcoholic beverages, and he had two wonderful small sons who were the apples of his and his wife's eyes. He took over as the Assistant Projects Officer and within the year had been selected for promotion to Commander's rank; he was also selected to take command of VCR-35 in Hawaii mid-1970. He ran the base Boy Scouts troop and softball league, and while in VX-4 he also, for two years, organised the Mugu Air Show, for which the Squadron was responsible. Both shows were a huge success, thanks entirely to Sandy's professionalism and attention to detail.

At the time of Sandy's arrival there was quite a changeover of officers. Commander Jack Tallman, who had been on exchange with the Royal Navy at RNAS Yeovilton flying Sea Vixen fighters, departed to become the XO of VMF-92 while Commander Bobby Morton, who had been the Squadron Maintenance Officer, moved off to become the XO of VMF-96. Both of these squadrons were scheduled to be embarked in the USS *Enterprise* operating out of Honolulu. Commander Gunn, who commanded GMU-41, the unit responsible for preparing all the guided missiles for our project, retired from the Navy and his relief was Lieutenant Tom Treanor USN. By the end of 1968 more than half the Squadron's officers had been reappointed and fresh blood had moved in. Captain Pierozzi was appointed to a sea command as the captain of a US Navy oiler and Captain Jim Foster USN became our new Commanding Officer.

With Peter Marshall and his family on their way back to Britain, I took over the F-4J/AWG-10 Project OV-63 for the remainder of my time with VX-4. Much of the work was, quite understandably, focused on the continuing conflict in Vietnam. All our officers had flown in the war and experienced combat conditions. One young RIO, Lieutenant Wright, had been awarded four Navy Flying Crosses for his gallantry, the first of which was for his maiden flight in the Vietnam war zone. En route to a target in a divisional bombing mission, the lead aircraft, together with its flight leader and RIO, had been shot down and, as a 'rookie' RIO with the rank of Ensign—equivalent to Sub Lieutenant in the Royal Navy), Wright had taken over the lead and steered the division to its target for a successful bombing run. At the end of his short service career he entered law school and graduated to become a successful lawyer.

* * *

One September day during 1968 the US Navy fired a total of nineteen Sparrow and Sidewinder air-to-air missiles over North Vietnam and all either missed their targets or failed in some other way. It was a very bad day for the Navy and the CNO wanted to know why. A US Navy Commander from the Naval Missile Center at Point Mugu was despatched post-haste to Vietnam to interview all the aircrews involved in these failed firings. His comments on his return were: 'They didn't have their fingers up their bums: they had the whole of their arms up them!' The aircrews did not know the missile firing parameters and certainly did not understand the PLM (Pilot Launch Mode) modification that had been installed in some aircraft. They had no idea that, in a dogfight, the missile launching envelopes and parameters have to be dramatically reduced for a hit to be achieved; some of them even thought that they could fire a missile in a tail-chase from the same range as when they were approaching head-on! When we had listened to this dismal story, we in VX-4 sat heavily in our chairs in disbelief and wondered where we had gone wrong.

VF-121, the USN Operational Flying School at Miramar, was teaching everything that we were putting out and the RN exchange officers in the Squadron were nearly all AWIs and therefore the best. They were certainly teaching the pilots and RIOs going through the Squadron the correct information, tactics and capabilities of the F-4B/G and J weapon systems. After some agonising days Naval Air Systems Command (NAVAIR) at the Pentagon called for a conference to be held at Point Mugu. It was organised in the cinema and no quarter was given, the one aim being to find the cause of the missile failures. It was then decided that the conference would break up into syndicates to investigate various aspects of US Navy fighter flying and tactics and that the groups would report back that afternoon. 'Tooter' Teague took off with several officers to investigate flying training.

At 1400 everybody mustered once more in the cinema and each syndicate was asked if it had any answer to the problem. All said no except for 'Tooter', who boldly stood up and said that the problem lay in operational flying training. He was asked to expand on his statement, and he came up with the following points:

1. The pilots were given very little instruction in aerial combat and aircraft manoeuvring under high 'g' forces.
2. The aircrews had little idea of the missile envelopes despite the training they were given.
3. The aircrews had almost no idea that high 'g' forces dramatically altered a missile's envelope.

4. Those aircrews posted to F-4J squadrons had only flown the aircraft about four times, the remainder of their experience having been built up on the F-4B/Gs, which had a totally different weapons and radar system. (When the Admiral asked why, it transpired that VF-121 had only about six F-4J aircraft compared with 76 F-4B/Gs, the latter having pulse radar inferior to the F-4J's pulse-doppler equipment.)

The cat was out of the bag. The Admiral concluded the conference, instructing 'Tooter's syndicate to stay behind together with the higher echelons of VX-4 and VF-121 to discuss the matter further and make some initial recommendations for the way ahead.

The afternoon dragged on but eventually VX-4's team returned from the Conference Hall and we all sat down in the Briefing Room to hear what had taken place after the 'workers' had left. It had been decided that fighter aircrews required more tactical training in air combat and that this could be achieved only on a dedicated tactical range. Moreover, every effort would be made to increase the complement of F-4Js in VF-121 so that aircrews destined for F-4J squadrons would receive sufficient, if not most, of their training in that type of fighter. This would give VX-4 a great deal of work over the next few months, especially in putting together a suitable combat training range. The F-4J question was something which had to be resolved at NAVAIR level because at that time all J aircraft coming off the production line were destined for Vietnam—a fact of which I was aware because I was having great difficulty obtaining spares for Project OV-63.

It was decided that the dedicated Combat Tactical Range would be set up in the desert near NAS El Centro. Beacons similar to TACAN beacons, coupled with telemetry as used at the Point Mugu range, would be installed on the El Centro range and in the training aircraft, enabling a three-dimensional read-out to be obtained during a simulated combat exercise whenever the pilot squeezed his firing trigger to simulate a gun or a missile firing. On the ground there would be an immediate three-dimensional read-out establishing the actual parameters at the time of firing—whether the pilot was within the firing envelopes for the 'g' being pulled, the speed being flown, the range and the angle-off from the target. Within a few days of the range's being set up it had proved itself to be an ideal training facility and a wonderful tool for the fighter school at Miramar. In addition, it enabled the training to be accomplished with fewer aircraft—which meant that there would a great saving not only in aircraft and but also in manpower. When pilots landed they were immediately confronted with a read-out at the time of firing and the ground instructor would have an immediate opinion as to their success or otherwise.

The other major point raised at the conference was the lack of a dedicated air warfare instructor in any of the US Navy's squadrons: the USN had no officer who had been trained as an AWI and aerial combat suffered accordingly. The Americans, in their inimitable way, therefore created the Naval Air Warfare Training School, which became more commonly known as the 'Top Gun' School. An officer passing through this school would be appointed to a squadron as its dedicated Air Warfare Officer, responsible for training and maintaining weapon standards. Two of the first officers to pass through this facility were Lieutenants Randy Cunningham and Willie Driscoll, having returned from Vietnam as 'aces' after shooting down three MiGs in one sortie and two more later on over North Vietnam. The 'Top Gun' School was to prove its worth: in short time the Navy would have dedicated air weaponeers in its squadrons, men who knew their stuff, could pass on their knowledge to other squadron members and would turn their outfits into true fighting machines. We Royal Navy AWIs could not suppress a quiet chuckle: the US Navy had got there, albeit in its own good time. There was of course never an admission that the 'Top Gun' School had sprung from seeds sown by exchange Royal Navy aviators and by USN exchange officers in the RN!

My work as the Project OV-63 officer continued. I sat down and pored over the project instructions, objectives and results and was not particularly impressed with what I read. The first aspect of the project which jumped out at me was the fact that no missile firings had been scheduled or programmed into the project to date. I sat down with the Operational Evaluation Group representative, Al Rosen, and pointed out the serious gaps that were evident in the project, and between us we came up with a missile programme that included high-, medium- and low-altitude firings over both the sea and the land from every possible aspect, from head-on through beam to tail shots, including dogfight and 'look-down' firings. Our programme called for the firing of three dozen Sparrow and Sidewinder missiles. The CPO, Don Keast, threw up his hands in horror, wondering where on earth we were expected to obtain 36 missiles! It was really his fault that there were no missile firings in the original project plan, for which he had been mainly responsible. Al Rosen promised to re-evaluate the programme to see if it was possible to combine some of the firings, and eventually the list was reduced to 26 missiles. Although the CPO was still not very happy, we had won the day.

I had to visit the Naval Air Weapons Center at China Lake out in the Mojave Desert to discuss the project's overland firings, especially the look-down firings against BQM targets. Bruce Marshall, my Assistant Project Officer, and I flew over to the NAWC in the T-33. On landing, we went immediately to the Security Officer to obtain our clearances and badges. Somebody drove us over to the section we had come to visit, having already cleared our visit over the telephone from Mugu. I met the civil service officer who was responsible for organising my missile firings and Bruce departed to do something else. The officer showed me what he could arrange, we came to an understanding and I promised to mail him all the necessary data. Bruce and I then returned our security passes and badges and flew back to Mugu.

The flight back was uneventful but I had hardly been back in the Squadron a few minutes when Don Keast called for my presence.

'What the hell have you been up to, Michael?'

'What do you mean, Col?'

He said that I was not allowed access to the section that I had entered at China Lake.

'What on earth are you talking about, Col?' I queried.

'The section you entered was classified as "No Foreign"!'

'Well, I cleared my visit with you, Col, and the Security Section at China Lake took all my details and checked my security clearances and they issued passes and badges accordingly, so I do not see what all the fuss is about!'

'You entered a very sensitive area which was not cleared for foreigners.'

'Well, I didn't make the mistake, Col. It was your security people, who don't seem to know their elbows from their a——s!'

The Colonel then telephoned China Lake and sorted the matter out, and it was quickly all forgotten.

About the same time I ran into another security problem, but this time in the Squadron. The Israeli destroyer *Eilat* had just been sunk by a Soviet-made 'Styx' missile fired from an Egyptian motor torpedo boat. All hell was let loose in the US Navy Department as the CNO demanded to know if we had any defence against such an attack. The Soviet missile's performance and characteristics, together with the types of vessels on which it was carried, were listed in a publication used by all the NATO forces; indeed, I had used this book on many an occasion back in Britain when devising various attacks by Buccaneer aircraft. However, the VX-4 publication was stamped—would you believe it?—'No Foreign'! When the Colonel saw me reading it he went ballistic and demanded to know what I was about because of the book's classification, even though the CNO had designated Project OV-63 the vehicle for devising counter-attacks against this potential threat to US Navy warships.

'Col,' I said, 'this is a NATO publication, and if you go to pages so and so you will find this and that.'

'How do you know this?'

'I've already told you, Col. The book is a NATO publication, and I have been using it for years in developing various types of attacks for the RN's Buccaneer aircraft.'

'Well, I will brief the crews who are to go out and fire the missiles.'

'No, Col. I will do that because I know exactly what is required and how the interceptions should be done.'

Finally he gave in and I won the day, but my goodness! One would have thought that I was out to steal the gold from Fort Knox!

I arranged for Commander Jack Tallman, a former exchange officer with the RN and one who had flown Sea Vixens at Yeovilton, to fire my first missile against a simulated 'Styx', an unaugmented BQM drone set up on a low-level profile over the Mugu sea range. Jack took off with two AIM-7E Sparrows under his F-4 and flew the profiles I had briefed with great success. After some difficulty because of sea clutter the target was acquired and locked up and a Sparrow was launched in a 'look-down' aspect. The target was 'killed' on the first firing and crashed into the sea. An 'Immediate' signal was sent to CNO telling him about the success, and that the 'Styx' presented no threat to the US Navy with the F-4J's pulse-doppler radar weapon system and Sparrow missile. CNO sent us a congratulatory signal and retired to bed that night very much relaxed, knowing that his Fleets in the Mediterranean, the Far East and Asia could cope with the threat.

* * *

It had been arranged for Admiral Luis Le Baylis, the Chief of the British Naval Staff, to visit California and meet all his exchange personnel—of whom there were many, especially in southern California. He first visited those who were in and about San Diego, and Mugu would be his last call. Lieutenant Commander 'Mac' Melhuish RN, our immediate contact at CBNS Washington, DC, was organising things. He telephoned me first before making the final arrangements, and once the visit had been cleared with Admiral White USN, the CO of the Pacific Missile Range, his Flag Lieutenant and I got down to finalising the details. A room was set aside for CBNS to change from his flying overalls into his dress uniform, and a programme was laid out for a briefing by Admiral White and his staff, followed by luncheon at the Officers' Club and then a visit to VX-4 before a trip south to Los Angeles for CBNS to pay his respects to the British Consul General. CBNS was flying up from NAS North Island in a E-2C Hawkeye flown by a group of British exchange officers. They had filed their Flight Plan the evening before but when they called to taxy the next morning their Flight Plan was missing. The Hawkeye crew had to return to the flight line and file another Flight Plan, delaying them for almost ninety minutes. It transpired that there had been a near mid-air collision the previous evening involving two F-8 Crusaders and an airliner over San Diego. During the subsequent investigation all flight plans had been confiscated and in the confusion CBNS's plan had gone astray.

The Flag Lieutenant and I called on Admiral White to explain what had happened and that there would be a delay, and we returned to the room set aside for CBNS only to find that it had been taken over by the air base's Flight Safety Officer. This USN Commander informed us that he had no intention of giving up his room for a British Admiral. When 'Flags' told Admiral White what had happened, the Commander had his rights read to him, but Admiral Le Baylis was charm itself when he arrived. There were only the rest rooms in which to change but with an 'Oh don't bother yourselves: I have changed in worse places in my naval career!' he simply got on with things. The briefing and luncheon went very well indeed and Admiral White was impressed with CBNS's depth of knowledge about the activities at the Pacific Missile Center. After luncheon we retired to VX-4, where I showed the Admiral round, and then he went to the CO's office, where he was briefed on what VX-4 was doing. He took his jacket off and lounged around in the office in red braces, much to the delight of all present, and then I took him in my car to my married quarters for a quick cup of tea. We arrived at my front door to be greeted by May in her dressing gown and curlers, getting ready to go out. The Admiral barged in and introduced himself with a 'Hello, May! Do you have a good cup of tea for an old codger like me?' Poor May did not know where to put herself but the Admiral soon set her at ease and told her not to worry. After this refreshment Mac Melhuish rushed him off in a staff car to be at the Consul General's office by 1530. He had vanished as quickly as he had arrived, and we saw no more of him in the US.

A sequel to this visit occurred on our return to Britain. I was visiting Yeovilton, and who should be there but Mac Melhuish, who had also returned back home for good. I happened to mention to him the fact that my USN Captain had overmarked me on my officer's report, awarding nothing but a 'nine' in each category—the highest possible mark in all respects. I asked Mac if my report had been amended to 'sevens' or 'eights', and he said, 'Hell no, Punchy. They stayed at nines because the Admiral did not like your Captain, and he said that if anyone could stand him he was worth nines!' I had to laugh: such marking has little effect on one's overall standing when being considered for promotion—and I was now entering the zone for promotion to Commander.

* * *

The F-4 Phantom's weapon system was very much dependent upon the RIO, and if he was rendered *hors de combat* for any reason there was no way in which the pilot could control the radar and fire a missile. There was a very resourceful electronics Chief Petty Officer in VX-4 who worked out a method whereby the pilot could take control of the aircraft's radar in the event of the RIO becoming incapacitated. If the equipment in the rear cockpit were modified by inserting a small electronic board in the radar set control handle, the pilot could, by depressing his nosewheel steering button on the starboard engine throttle, gain control of the radar. It was a simple device, easy to manufacture, and it allowed the pilot to 'bore-sight' the radar to the aircraft's centreline, and thus, by pointing the nose and gun sight at the target, ranging data could be fed to a missile in order to achieve a successful launch and interception. Several live missile firings were made against BQM targets over the Pacific Missile Range, but when Westinghouse heard about the modification they were extremely unhappy.

As in Britain, there is a law in the United States that forbids the modification of weapon systems which have a nuclear capability. Westinghouse could see big dollars on the horizon and promptly decreed that if this modification were to be inserted unofficially into their weapon system its warranty would be invalidated. The company's attitude was extraordinary. The *ad hoc* modification cost less than $200 whereas Westinghouse's modification would cost in excess of $40,000. When it was finally agreed that Westinghouse would install it, the cost rose to $140,000, although, to be fair, one or two other modifications were swept up with it.

At about the same time I made matters worse by publishing an Advanced Evaluation Note in which I stated that the F-4J weapon system failed, on average, once every 45 minutes. Westinghouse vehemently denied this and sent an inquiry team to VX-4. The company wanted to know how I had arrived at such an outrageous figure so I told them to read the AEN—it was all written down. Being a person of straightforward thinking, I had obtained a list of all the spare parts that had been ordered by the F-4J squadrons both in the US and in South-East Asia together with a record of all the flying hours and had divided one into the other. Then, before I published the AEN, I telephoned the Pacific Missile Center at Mugu, which was conducting missile firing trials with the aircraft, and asked for the MTBF (Mean Time Between

Failures) on the system. Without any prompting they came up with exactly the same figure, and so I told Westinghouse. I also pointed out that there were many F-4J aircraft in South-East Asia that had 'hard down' AWG-10 weapon systems and could only carry out 'iron' bombing and strafing missions. Were they aware of this fact? There was utter silence in the Captain's office. I was not giving up because the British had a stake in the F-4J with the F-4K and M models. I asked what their field representatives were doing with all this information—which was readily available to them. Should they not all be aware of the system's shortcomings? There was no answer. Game set and match: I had them—and Captain Foster was delighted that VX-4 had come out on top.

Eventually Westinghouse were tasked by the US Navy to improve the reliability of the AWG-10 system in the F-4J and to make the PLM modification available to all systems, and with other modifications to improve the overall effectiveness of the weapon system this new system was redesignated AWG-14. The British F-4s would benefit from some of these modifications though since many of them were 'No Foreign' we had to come up with similar modifications through Ferranti, who were responsible for the system in the F-4K and M models.

— 22 —

Visitors and Personalities

URING the VX-4 exchange there were many visitors to the Doust household other than from CBNS. Our first visitors were Lieutenant Commander Peter Walwyn and his wife Maureen, who stayed at our married quarters for almost a week. Peter was the Royal Navy's Project Officer for the F-4K, then entering service at RNAS Yeovilton. He was very interested in the F-4J's weapon and navigation systems. The F-4J and K had essentially the same systems but there were many modifications to the AWG-10 radar that could not be released to Britain because of their security classification—although in the course of time these modifications did become available. The VX-4 team were very impressed with Peter, his knowledge and his expertise and quite openly stated that it was a great pity that they did not have officers of the same calibre. Over the weekend we took them to the Port Hueneme base PX (Post Exchange—the equivalent of the NAAFI) so that they could buy some presents to take home. Although Peter was allowed entry, the naval sentry at the PX door would not let Maureen in because she had no military ID. I tried every trick under the sun but, despite my protestations, the sentry would not budge, so Maureen and I sat in the car while May took Peter around the exchange. The following week they left for Miramar to visit VF-121, where the Royal Navy had half a dozen exchange aviators.

Our next visitors were from Canada—Don and Drucie Mills with their family. Don was the Naval Attaché in Ottawa. Drucie was Naomi's godmother. They arrived during the early summer and stayed with us for a couple of days, their children camping out in the trailer in our driveway. It would be another two years before we all met up again in Somerset. After the Millses came the Vaughan family. Lieutenant Commander Dai and Barbara Vaughan had been friends back in our Lossiemouth days, when he was the AEO of 736 Squadron. He had an exchange appointment in the United States. The next visitor was Lieutenant Commander George Wilcox, who had been the ALO in both 831 and 736 Squadrons, in which we had served together. He was also involved in the F-4K project and was in the country seeing how the US Navy went about their F-4 maintenance and servicing. I was visiting Miramar when I literally bumped into George. He was keen to see what we

242

were doing in VX-4 and, in company with his USN Liaison Officer, we flew back to Mugu in a twin-engine Convair C-131 used by NMC for various transport and communication tasks.

An hour or so after George's departure Don Keast, the Chief Projects Officer, called me in and wanted to know who had given George security clearance to visit VX-4. I told him that he was one of the British F-4K Project Officers, like Peter Walwyn, and that CBNS and the US Navy had organised his visit to the United States. Apart from anything concerning EW,* he had blanket coverage to go anywhere he liked as organised by his USN Liaison Officer. As ever, Don was trying to create a storm in a teacup. He rather seemed to have it in for me, although I had no idea why; perhaps it was all to do with my rearranging the objectives of Project OV-63. He was worried about making any mistakes, which could affect his possible promotion to full Colonel, and this may have coloured his attitude towards me. I think he may have felt that I was a loose cannon in VX-4. I caught him going through my Embassy and CBNS briefing papers on one occasion, and I became convinced that he thought that I was passing information to the British establishment in Washington. This of course could not have been further from the truth. Many years previously a well-known RN exchange officer in VX-3 (the forerunner of VX-4) based in Rhode Island, passed information regularly to CBNS. He was eventually caught, and his activities caused a serious rift between the two nations that almost stopped the exchange programme. I had no intention of doing anything as stupid. Sooner or later the Americans briefed us on what was happening: if there were money to be had without compromising security, they would release the equipment and brief us on its use. I would certainly verbally brief any visiting British officer but I would never pass on documentation, and USN exchange officers would take the same attitude in Britain. Eventually I plucked up the courage to say to our gallant Colonel, 'You know, Colonel, we are all on the same side. It is not "you and us", and I hope you appreciate it.'

* * *

Every year in October or November the companies involved in the manufacture of US Navy aircraft and equipment would stage a weekend gathering at Las Vegas for those naval aviators who had landed aboard an aircraft carrier using a tail hook, and event that became known as the Tailhook Convention. I gave the 1968 Convention a miss because I was not in a position to afford the trip. The new XO, Jerry Higgins kindly offered to 'stake' me but I refused. He appeared offended until I pointed out that, in the Royal Navy, brother officers did not lend money to each other as this put the recipients in a position of indebtedness, which was frowned upon by the authorities. I also pointed out that if anything happened to me then there was nobody to reimburse him. He finally saw my point of view. However, the following year I did attend.

---

* Electronic Warfare.

It cost each of us $180 to attend the '69 Convention, this sum covering our hotel board and entertainment. Point Mugu arranged for a C-121 to fly 129 of us, including the Admiral, to Las Vegas airport. This number included just about all the qualified pilots from Mugu and I wondered as we climbed out for Vegas what would happen if there were an accident: to have all the air station's aircrews aboard the same aircraft seemed to me the height of folly. However, despite my fears we all arrived safely and we dispersed to the International Hotel, which, I was led to understand, was British-owned; it probably was not, but it made me feel good. Many others had already arrived from various parts of the US and from overseas. The first meeting was scheduled for 2000, at which the organisers would make a speech, pass champagne and distribute small 'eats' so that we could make the acquaintance of the manufacturers' representatives and of other US Navy personnel. We were free to do as we wished for the next couple of days, but we were requested to attend a show at the Tropicana Hotel on Saturday evening. Lieutenant Tom Treanor USN, the new CO of GMU-41, and I shared a room for $16 a piece, which was very cheap indeed.

The Tropicana Hotel show was something else. At the start of the show gilded cages were lowered from the ceiling, each containing a girl scantily dressed in beautiful blue and white feathers. All were British lasses; in fact, they were the finest English roses I had ever seen (apart from my darling wife!). There were well over 2,000 naval aviators in the auditorium, all of whom had been given glossy brochures. These were quickly folded into paper darts and launched to drift down on to the stage or into the gilded cages. Then the aviators settled down to watch the show. An hour later there was an interval, and then the second phase of the show began. During the interval the stage had been re-rigged to represent a spider's den with a huge web strung across the backdrop curtain. The second part of the show was a dance act by a relatively elderly couple representing a spider and a fly. During the act the lady was carried out on to the apron, held high in an arched position above her partner. Someone still had a brochure and this was fashioned into another dart and sent noiselessly on its way high into the auditorium, entering a steep dive as the female dancer was lifted. The whole of the audience went silent—so silent, in fact, that one could have heard a pin drop: everybody was watching the paper dart as it accelerated towards the couple on the stage, finding its mark in the artiste's crotch between her lower stomach and her leotard. As one, the entire auditorium erupted into a deafening cheer and the poor woman rushed off the stage in tears. If anyone had tried to do anything like this deliberately, it would never have succeeded!

The flight back to Mugu took about an hour and a half and because of a failed engine we were cleared for a straight-in approach to the duty runway. At about three miles out from touch-down, the second engine on the starboard wing was feathered and shut down. No doubt many prayers were uttered throughout those last few thousand yards but our 'Connie' Captain knew his stuff and made a perfect landing. I expect that questions were asked as to why there were so many naval aviators on board a single passenger aircraft but I was not privy to them.

Some twenty-five years later the Tailhook Convention was to bring about the downfall of many senior and junior officers. At one particular gathering many female naval aviators were present, all of them 'Tailhookers'. However, they were subjected to a great deal of sexual harassment which culminated in their having to run the gauntlet along a hotel corridor during which they were groped by male officers. A few months later one of the female officers 'blew the whistle' on what had happened—with, as can be imagined, serious consequences. The Naval Department conducted an investigation, court-martials were convened resulting in severe disciplinary action being taken against defendants and many senior officers were forced to resign early from the Navy. It was a very sad occasion for the USN's Aviation Branch and resulted in very bad relations between the male and female aviators. The annual convention was temporarily suspended, and although it has now been reconvened it is, I understand, no longer held in Las Vegas. I find it difficult to believe that the incident ever occurred, especially when there are so many prostitutes available at such events. I must admit that some American males, when they have had too much to drink, become difficult and are often very aggressive. Eddie Cope and I encountered this phenomenon while visiting the USS *Saratoga* off Cannes. We had walked into a small beach promenade café for a drink when we ran into two Americans who were trying to latch on to two French girls. The Americans immediately turned on us and told us to get out, and because of their formidable stature neither Eddie nor I were inclined to argue.

* * *

While serving in VX-4 I had two Captains, the first being Nello Pierozzi and the second Jim Foster. Both men had engaging personalities, but in other respects they were as different as chalk from cheese. Nello was a suave and dashing officer of small stature. He was a former Blue Angels pilot and therefore one of the US Navy's élite. I was not quite sure what his appointment had been prior to taking command of VX-4. Nobody ever mentioned it, but I suspect that he had been the CO of an F-8 Squadron or had served on an Admiral's staff. He was a very keen golfer and spent many hours at the Camarillo Golf Club. Nello was a very dapper man and we became great friends. His wife Marcia tended to be rather aloof, although I suspect that this was due to shyness.

The days of the AVCAD had long since gone and most US Navy officers now went through Annapolis and gained a degree. The possession of an academic degree was considered by the USN to be essential if one aspired to Flag rank or even to a sea-going command. Although he did have command of a naval supply tanker, Nello unfortunately did not achieve a degree in time to be selected for carrier command. Ex aviators always command US Navy aircraft carriers, whereas in the Royal Navy the Captain can be of any specialisation other than engineering. After his tanker command, Nello retired from the USN and took up an executive position with the Teledyne Ryan company in San Diego.

245

Jim Foster was quite the antithesis. He was a rugged, 'go-getting' individual impossible to keep on the ground. Within hours of his arrival in the Squadron he was off night flying in an F-4. When I took over as the Duty Officer and Pilot, I nearly threw a blue fit because Jim was not current on type and had certainly not flown it at night for some time. When I voiced my opinion I was told that since he was the Boss and the Captain he could do as he pleased. I was put in my place, but I was of the school where flight safety is well and truly drummed in: there were standards to be met no matter what one's rank might be. I shrugged my shoulders. Jim was a fair person and would help people in any way possible. After leaving VX-4 he moved to NAVAIR's staff in Washington, DC, where he became the F-18 Hornet Project Officer.

* * *

During the last year of my time with VX-4 there was quite a change-round in the senior officer appointments. One newcomer I remember especially, because he had a Jaguar Mk VII with British number plates in addition to his Californian registration plates. He was very fair-haired, and with the name Fred Ferranzano he quickly gained the sobriquet 'The Italian Blond'. We got on well together and he often took over as the Squadron XO or as the CPO. When he first joined the Squadron I had to give him his Instrument Rating test. Although he was quite good on instruments, he could not fly the instrument approaches very well. On one occasion we had flown north towards San Francisco and I had instructed him to make a TACAN approach into Salinas airport; at 2,000 feet Salinas would take over and give a talkdown to the runway threshold. The approach went well except that he was 90 degrees out on every heading, and as we turned inbound at 5,000 feet I instructed him to level off and look outside the cockpit. He was heading straight for a mountain, and if he had continued on alone he would have impacted half way up. We levelled off, turned and climbed back up to altitude, heading back to Mugu, where I had him make several instrument approaches and also one into Oxnard Air Force Base, an F-102 quick-reaction airfield just down the road from Mugu. When we finally landed and taxied into VX-4's dispersal I was happy enough to issue Fred with a 'White Instrument Rating', which would allow him to fly in most weather around Mugu except in the very worst of conditions.

Some months later Fred went to Nellis AFB, Las Vegas, to pick up an F-8 pilot who had blown one of his aircraft tyres while attempting a take-off in a severe crosswind—way outside the jet's operating envelope. The weather had been very cold for that autumn and we had heard that snow had fallen in the Las Vegas region. When Fred returned I had been instructed to take the S-2F back with another pilot and a few maintenance men to fix the F-8. I asked Fred if everything was all right with the Tracker, and he said that it was except for the wing de-icing, which was not working. I needed that de-icing system in view of the forecast weather conditions but Fred would not place the aircraft unserviceable because in his opinion the cold front had gone through and there was now clear weather astern of the front. I took the aircraft but warned everybody that if the weather showed any sign of deterioration I would turn around and return to Mugu. So off I flew to Nellis. We had a good flight but the crosswind was still very strong when we arrived and the aircraft was 'crabbing' badly until touch-down when I kicked it straight. The fact that the F-8 pilot had attempted to take off in such conditions was incomprehensible. I had Commander 'Tooter' Teague with me and he, as the Acting CPO, decided that we would stay overnight because it would be a few hours before the F-8 would be ready. The following morning dawned wet and blustery but the wind was much closer to the runway heading. The F-8 had been repaired, and so we waited until it was safely airborne and on its way back to Mugu and then we taxied and took off for our return flight. The flight went without incident but the weather back at Mugu was far from good, with low cloud base, poor visibility and heavy rain. 'Tooter' flew the aircraft while I worked the overhead throttles, and finally we landed on a very wet runway without incident.

* * *

Standards of flying ability vary from pilot to pilot in the US Navy. I found them to be either very good or below average in general, there being very few steady, middle-of-the-road aviators. Many flew 'by the seat of their pants' and were excellent fighter pilots, but when called to undertake precision flying, as required when on instruments, they tended to be very rough indeed. Many pilots who made it through the 'pipeline' training system either wrecked their aircraft eventually or killed themselves. However, with the advent of the F-14 Tomcat this would all change because the USN could not afford to lose these $15 million aircraft. Those aviators who did not come up to standard were either ruthlessly 'scrubbed' from training or were transferred to helicopters or Long Range Maritime Patrol aircraft.

The US Navy had a training procedure wherein a pilot flying a new type of aircraft for the first time would have a chase aircraft following him, flown either by an instructor or by a very experienced pilot. This happened to me on my maiden flights in the F-8 and F-4. I must admit that it was comforting to have someone close by to rely upon, provided, of course, there was no radio failure. At Miramar, however, before carrying out my instrument flying course I had one flight in the TA-4F Skyhawk. One flight is not enough to get used to a cockpit instrument layout and the handling peculiarities of an unfamiliar aircraft. Until the F-8 and F-4 came along, instrument layouts in most American aircraft were quite the worst in the world, as I have already remarked.

Maintenance in the Squadron was something else to be believed. On many an occasion I would place an aircraft unserviceable only to find that it had been given 'up' status without any work having been carried out on it or any restriction placed or recorded in the USN equivalent of Form A700. This really worried me, and taking into account the terrible tool control that existed within the Squadron I was more than concerned about aircrew and aircraft safety. A box of tools was not issued with each aircraft but instead there would be a large tool panel in the hangar from which maintenance personnel could take whatever equipment they required without being required to sign for it or its replacement. Tools could, therefore, be left inside an aircraft and nobody would be aware of the fact until a pilot encountered control problems. In the Fleet Air Arm, if a tool was missing from a toolbox the aircraft being worked on was grounded until that tool was found or until the AEO was convinced that it was not present in the aircraft. On one occasion I happened to be walking through the hangar and found several tools lying in the tailpipe of an F-8 fighter!

A sequel to the F-8 incident occurred as I was waiting for the delivery of a new F-4J fitted with the latest DAWG-14 digital weapon system for Project OV-63. The aircraft did not make it out of McDonnell Douglas's facility at St Louis. The Captain called me into his office to say that I would not be receiving the new Phantom as it no longer existed. On the final test flight prior to being delivered to VX-4, the pilot of this particular aircraft was at the point of rotating for take-off when he found, as the aircraft left the runway, that he could not check the nose attitude: the stick was immobile in the fully aft position. The F-4 went into a near-vertical climb, the pilot and observer ejected and the jet then fell back on to its tail and exploded. When the wreckage was sifted a set of pliers was found in the stabilator system and a $2.5 million fighter had been lost because of a $2 tool. This crash was captured by cine camera and was subsequently included in all FAA and USN Flight Safety films.

On another occasion one of the F-4Js was in the hangar and scheduled for heavy maintenance. There was a requirement to replace the 'O' ring seals on the fuselage where the wing blow ducts were located. These ducts took air from the engine compressor and directed it over the trailing edge flaps to reduce speed and improve the low-speed characteristics of the aircraft. The replacement 'O' rings provided looked exactly the same as the old ones and fitted easily into the ducts—too easily as it happened, because they were a millimetre out. The Maintenance Officer, Bobby Morton, took the aircraft up on a test flight and just after becoming airborne the 'Blow Duct' fire warning light illuminated. He called an emergency and requested an immediate landing. When the aircraft was towed back to the hangar there was found to be a large hole in the side of the fuselage where the incorrect ring had been fitted. With fuel tanks situated so close by, Bobby was fortunate that his jet had not gone up in flames.

VX-4 had only four F-4J fighters with which to prosecute Project OV-63 and only one was fitted with an AWG-10 radar weapon system. Although we had asked for a further system, the Squadron was at the bottom of the list owing to the fact that the front-line squadrons in Vietnam had priority. One morning Chief Petty Officer Workentin, my Weapon System Chief, came into my office to say that the klystron in our only radar had blown. I instructed him to apply for an immediate replacement because without it the project would be stalled, and within twenty-four hours we had a replacement part and it had been fitted. A short while later Chief Workentin entered my office to say the new item had also blown. I asked him if everything on the radar had been thoroughly checked and he assured me that it had, so I told him to go ahead and order another replacement. However, these things cost $25,000 each, and after thinking about the failures I called the Chief in and told him that the radar was not to be switched on until a thorough and complete search of the system had been made to establish the reason for the previous failures. Now I was acting as the Squadron Maintenance Officer, which was not my job. We did not have an Electrical/Ordnance Officer in the Squadron and it was really up to either the Chief or me as to what should be done next. I asked what they had been doing to the radar and it transpired that the maintenance men had dismantled the waveguide to the antenna in order to replace something. What they did not tell me was that they were missing a screw that was used in joining the sections of the waveguide. Eventually the screw was found—inside the waveguide. It had caused the energy passing along this guide to be concentrated on the klystron, overloading it to the point of failure. Thus a 2BA screw costing no more than a few cents had cost us $50,000 in damaged equipment. The Squadron could ill afford such stupid incidents: this was $50,000 out of its quarterly budget for stores and spare parts.

In the Fleet Air Arm, maintenance is done very much 'by the book' except in wartime, when it is essential to turn aircraft around quickly in order to make the next mission. Consequently, many procedures tend to be carried out from memory, and this can lead to nasty accidents, especially where ordnance is concerned. Although US Navy squadrons each carried a 'Mustang Officer'—that is, an officer who had risen from the lower deck, similar to the FAA's SD (Special Duties) officer—they did not carry dedicated professional engineering and electrical officers. A Line Officer, i.e. a pilot of the Executive Branch, was appointed to a squadron as its Maintenance Officer, which was a very unsatisfactory system of manning. Many of these officers were totally dedicated to their task, but they had not received proper professional training in either mechanical or electrical engineering and consequently the squadrons had to rely upon their 'Mustang Officer' and the engineering Chiefs for their knowledge and expertise. In my opinion, although there were some shortcomings, the FAA system was quite the best system of maintenance in the world, in a different league from that of either the USN or the RAF. No doubt my friends in both services will consider my opinion nonsense, but I believe sincerely that I am right. The FAA system certainly improved flight safety, and, ultimately, this is what counts more than anything else.

* * *

Every Monday morning the Squadron held Divisions on the hardstanding in front of the hangar, when the opportunity was taken to read out citations to officers and men for awards received while serving in the Vietnam war zone. Men were rated up to higher rank or told that they had passed various examinations to that end. Good-conduct badges were awarded, and if there were anything special that we should all have known the Captain or XO would brief us on the facts. After a quick march past, the men returned to their maintenance tasks and the officers retired to the main Briefing Room for the weekly Monday-morning 'All Officers Meeting', or AOM as it was more commonly known. There we were briefed on facts not for the sailors' ears, and the Squadron Safety Officer would go through various aircraft emergency procedures. Project Officers would give a quick rundown on the progress of their projects, and if there was anything 'No Foreign' I was asked to leave. These AOMs could last for a couple of hours—or longer if the weather was inclement. I enjoyed these meetings because I learnt a great deal about what was going on within both the Squadron and the USN Air Branch, but above all I saw just how good the officers were both in their standards of knowledge and in their ability to impart that knowledge, as well as how they behaved towards one another.

The Ventura County Police Narcotics Branch was introduced to us all during one of these AOMs. The Squadron had experienced several cases of drug abuse amongst the sailors and the Captain had decided that we should see some special films on the subject and receive a lecture from the Narcotics Branch police sergeant. The films were both revealing and frightening. The squadron wives also asked to see the films but they found them so disturbing that their show was stopped.

The Squadron held a court-martial for three sailors and a Petty Officer who was a 'pusher'. All three were found guilty of dealing in drugs and were dismissed from the naval service. To a Royal Navy officer, this appeared most unusual; in the US Navy, however, a Naval Air Squadron is considered to be on a par with a cruiser and is authorised to conduct courts-martial. Every effort was made to keep the event quiet but I inadvertently barged in upon the proceedings, which were being held in the Staff Office. No notice had been published and sent around the officers, so I had no idea that a court-martial was in progress. It was then decided to move to another venue where there was no likelihood of anybody intruding upon the proceedings. The verdicts were signalled to the Flag Officer, who then gave his approval after discussing the matter with the Judge Advocate's Branch. The defendants were then stripped of all their badges of rank, insignia and naval buttons and quite literally thrown out of the main gate. Their lives were wrecked: never again would they be able to enter the Armed Forces, and never would they be allowed hold a federal job, join a police force or even take up a teaching post.

On the whole, though, the VX-4 team were a fine group of officers and men. There was hardly any rancour within the Squadron and everybody got along with each other. This was probably because the Squadron did things as a unit: it was inclusive—officers, men, wives, families. However, when May and I first joined, the Chief Projects Officer, a Navy Commander from the deep South, had an intense dislike of African-Americans and did not mince his words. Both May and I were appalled when he vented his feelings at an evening party that he and his wife were throwing in their married quarters; at one point we came close to walking out. I felt even more incensed over this officer's attitude because there was in the Projects typing pool an African-American Petty Officer with whom I had struck up a close friendship.

This young man was one of the gentlest, most courteous human beings that one could ever wish to meet: he was, in other words, a gentleman who outshone his boss. Perhaps this was the CPO's problem.

* * *

One day OV-63 ground to a halt through lack of spares. I had four F-4Js and only one serviceable weapon system between them, so I compiled an urgent signal, consisting of four pages, to NAVAIR, copied to CNO, requesting spares so that I could continue my project. Before I sent it I had the Acting Chief Projects Officer, Lieutenant Commander Heisner, check it over, and he released it. Early the following morning there was a shout from the Captain's office: 'Doust! My office! At the double!' Everybody sniggered as I rushed to the Captain's office, all of them expecting me to be flung out of the Squadron because they had seen the signal and could not believe that anyone, especially an alien, had such nerve. My final statement in my signal was: 'It is vital that these stores be made available soonest in order to reach a meaningful conclusion to Project OV-63, so that our airmen in South-East Asia will be able to fight the F-4J Phantom to its full potential.' As I entered Captain Foster's office he asked firmly whether I had written and sent the signal.

'Yes, sir!' was my response.

'Well done! The CNO has responded personally, "Let the Brit have all he wants!" You must have some pull there somewhere! Oh, and by the way, I have had a phone call that you will further receive a more up-to-date F-4J plus an additional DAWG-14 radar system.' Captain Foster had a big smile on his face. 'Well, you know how to get things done, Michael. It's a pity we don't have more like you around here!'

I left his office grinning and chuckling to myself.

* * *

COMAIRMAT, from Miramar, was scheduled to inspect VX-4. He was a very senior US Navy Captain, holding the rank of Commodore although he wore only four gold stripes instead of the broad single stripe. Following his material inspection of the Squadron, Divisions were held for his inspection of all the officers and men. The unattached officers stood in two lines to the left of the daïs with the Honour Guard, consisting of the XO, Jerry Higgins, the Colonel and me, out front, swords drawn. The remainder of the Squadron, with the Divisional Officers and Chiefs, was lined up behind the Honour Guard.

As in any navy, all personnel on parade wear dress uniform, swords and medals. However, there was an Air Force officer in VX-4, Major Ron Markey, who had medal ribbons but, as is the custom in the United States Air Force, did not wear the actual medals on parade and moreover did not wear or carry a dress sword. We took Ron aside and told him quite firmly that he could not go on parade without a sword: it simply was not done. In the Officers' Club there happened to be a huge Scottish claymore hanging on the wall behind the bar, so we asked the Club President if we could borrow it for our parade and we presented Ron with the weapon, which he inserted between his tunic belt and tunic. A few cardboard 'medals' were cobbled together and painted for him to wear and his shoes were dusted over with French chalk. He was then squeezed into the middle of the officers' ranks, ready for inspection.

It was a very sunny Californian autumn day and Divisions were obviously going to be an enjoyable event. Wives, families, fiancées and girlfriends were all given seating from which to watch the parade. With Jerry Higgins in the Honour Guard, Fred Ferranzano took over as the Acting XO and called the parade to attention as the Commodore appeared with the Captain. The Commodore was invited to inspect the officers and the divisions, and he started along the line of unattached officers first. When he reached Ron Markey, he let out a roar.

'Gawd! Who the f—— is this?'

Captain Foster quickly replied. 'Oh, he is our resident Air Force exchange officer, sir.'

'Well, tell him to get his boots polished!' He then fell about laughing, saying that it was the best joke he had come across in a very long time.

The Commodore moved across to the Honour Guard and then spent the next half an hour inspecting the sailors. After a quarter of an hour with the wives and families he returned to the podium and the Squadron retired for the march past. The Air Station Band struck up a lively tune and off we went with the Honour Guard leading and with the National and Squadron Colours preceding the Guard. Just after the Guard passed the podium, I told Jerry Higgins, quietly, that his trousers were slowly falling down.

'I know,' he replied. 'I forgot my belt and the top button has given way. Can you shield me while I make an adjustment?'

'Not to worry, Jerry. We are about to turn right and pass out of sight behind the hangar.' As soon as we were out of sight, we all fell about bursting our sides with laughter and I asked him why he did not have a belt.

'I forgot to bring one with me, you bloody Limey!'

A belt was found and we all retired to the Officers' Club with our loved ones for cocktails.

* * *

In the summer of 1969 Robert Kennedy visited Oxnard on his Presidential campaign. The next evening he was shot dead in a Los Angeles convention hall. The entire nation was shocked beyond belief that such a fate had now befallen two brothers from the eminent political family. The following morning I had a range operation, and my Range Officer was an ex US Army man. When I entered the Range Control building, he asked me what I thought of Americans. I replied, quickly, that I thought that they were all mad.

'Well, how do you cope in Britain?'

'Quiet simple. The average person interested in shooting does not have anything more than a shotgun for rabbit hunting, and the police keep an up-to-date list of all firearms owners.'

'Can't have that here, because when the communists invade America they will go straight to the police stations, find the list of firearms owners, round them up and shoot them!'

I could not believe what I was hearing.

'When do you expect the communists to invade this country?' I enquired.

It was impossible to discuss the matter with anybody of that sort of mentality so I dropped the subject.

The very next day a policeman on foot patrol was called to a small shop in Los Angeles that had just been robbed by a teenage boy. As the thief ran away from the shop the policeman ordered him to stop but because he did not do so the officer pulled his gun and shot the lad in the back, killing him. The people of Los Angeles were horrified, and hardly a single radio station had a good word to say about the police. There was little doubt about the case: it was the cold-blooded murder of a petty crook.

That same week a citizen called into a police station, complaining about being shot at on Sunset Boulevard. A day later, while a police patrol car was cruising along the Boulevard, another call came in for the same reason. The two officers in the car had spotted a man walking along the sidewalk and had stopped to question him. As is the custom, one officer had stood back while the other approached the man to establish his identity. The young man had reached for his hip pocket to pull out his identity wallet and had immediately been shot dead by the second officer because he thought that the man was going for a gun. It transpired that this poor fellow was a deaf mute. This incident, occurring so swiftly after the killing of the boy thief, brought Los Angeles almost to the point of riot: it was proof of what everybody had been saying all along—that the nation's police forces were too trigger-happy. Something had to be done about the number of small arms in circulation. The whole of my life has been concerned with weapons and firearms, but I have never had a reason for owning one. To me, firearms are for two purposes only—to defend the realm and for use in war. The killing of animals and birds by firearms is also abhorrent to me, and will continue to be so for as long as I breathe.

* * *

Four officers in VX-4 and GMU-41 were to become close friends of May and me, especially during the latter half of my exchange appointment—Lieutenant Tom Treanor, Lieutenant Phil Anselmo, Commander Jerry Higgins and Captain Jim Foster. Tom and Joy Treanor joined with their family in mid-1968. Tom was a quiet Virginian and for some obscure reason had trouble initially being accepted within the Squadron. I suppose it was because he was a 'bomber pilot': he had come from flying A-3 Skywarriors. However, May and I, together with Naomi, hit it off with him and his family from the very beginning and have remained close friends ever since. Tom had been aboard the USS *John F. Kennedy* when the carrier experienced a dreadful flight-deck accident resulting in 130 officers and sailors losing their lives. He had just landed back on board when an aircraft fired its load of rockets into another fully armed aircraft. This set off a chain reaction of rocket and bomb explosions across the entire after flight deck, causing ruptures that allowed burning fuel to pour below into the accommodation quarters immediately beneath. Personnel were caught by the inferno and many pilots escaped by the simple expedient of ejecting from their cockpits and parachuting into the sea astern of the carrier; there was no other escape route. Tom and his crew jumped into the catwalk alongside the forward flight deck to obtain shelter from shrapnel and weapon blasts, occasionally taking dramatic pictures with his 35mm camera. The carrier was so badly damaged that it was thought at the time that she would have to be scrapped, but after an extensive survey she returned to Norfolk, where she entered drydock for a rebuild of her stern section from the waterline upwards.

The Treanors had a family of two boys who were just of school age when they arrived in California. They were a couple of bright lads and were the delight of their parents. Tom was very much into building and flying model aircraft, which was wonderful for the boys, who used to help him. Naomi made friends with them, and when the Treanor family moved into a Navy married quarters their new home became a frequent destination for her.

A few months after Tom had joined VX-4, Commander Max Gunn, the OC of GMU-41, reached retirement age and another officer was required to relieve him. It was decided that Tom would take over his appointment even though he was at the time only a Lieutenant, albeit nearing promotion to Lieutenant Commander. Although GMU-41 was very much part of VX-4 because it shared the same hangar and facilities, the unit was responsible for preparing missiles for air trials, and for organising visiting squadrons: the Naval Missile Center conducted the majority of these trials and were active every week, and visiting fighter squadrons required missiles for their annual training sessions. Tom therefore had a very responsible job, and he did it very well indeed—so well in fact that there was, it has to be said, some envy within the Squadron.. After running GMU-41 Tom was reappointed to USNAS Oceana, Virginia, and I would meet up with him and Joy later in my naval career.

One of VX-4's RIOs was Lieutenant Phil Anselmo, an officer of Italian descent from New York. He was related to Joe Campanella, the film actor. Phil was very much a devout catholic, non-smoking and not for frolicking around with women. I can remember one day when he turned up as the Duty Officer and found a copy of *Playboy* open at the centrespread on his desk. He immediately picked it up and in disgust threw it into the trash bin where he felt it belonged!

While in VX-4 Phil became engaged to a beautiful girl named Ailene, an air hostess with American Airlines. They were very much suited to each other, and would be married in the base church. However, before the marriage the Squadron boys threw a stag party for him in the Officers' BOQ, inviting both the Station Commander and the XO. They also invited a stripper to provide a little excitement and to manoeuvre Phil into a compromising situation that could be photographed. Although Phil did not drink very much, someone managed to slip him a potent cocktail. Bill Browning, the Squadron Medical Officer, then plastered his left leg and sprayed his genitalia with magenta-coloured dye. Phil passed out and was put to bed with somebody watching over him. The following morning the CO received a very irate phone call from the Base Commander wanting to know who had given permission for a woman to be in the BOQ. The CO somehow managed to talk the Squadron out of any serious problems.

On Saturday, the next morning, Phil arrived in the Squadron in an awful state, the plaster still on his left leg. He looked around us all. 'What am I going to do? What am I going to tell my future wife?' At that moment Bill Browning stepped up, told him to drop his trousers and promptly set about cutting off the plaster cast. Bill then asked him if he could move his leg, and Phil replied that he could, only to be told that there was nothing wrong with it in the first place. He looked at us all and slowly the penny dropped. We needed no bidding and fled in all directions, hotly pursued by Phil to shrieks of 'You bastards!' The magenta dye could not be removed but it disappeared after several baths.

Phil and Ailene had a wonderful wedding in the Station Church and they subsequently moved to San Diego, Phil joining a front-line F-4 squadron at Miramar. Phil went on to become the first RIO in command of an F-4 unit— the first Lieutenant Commander, I believe, ever to have been appointed to the command of such a squadron. When May and I saw Phil and Ailene again it was at a reunion party in Del Mar just north of San Diego in the 1980s, when he was just about to give up command of the 'super carrier' USS *Constellation*. I asked him how on earth he had become Captain of such a large vessel because while serving in VX-4 he did not really know one end of a ship from the other! By hook or by crook he had managed to talk his way into various executive appointments, climbing the chain of command until he was appointed Captain of 'The Connie'. He was later promoted to Rear Admiral and given charge of the US Navy's Airborne Early Warning Division in the Navy Department.

I first met the Squadron XO, Jerry Higgins, on the F-8 Crusader Ground School Course at Miramar. He was a short Irishman, full of himself and great fun to be with. He had just completed the two-year postgraduate course at the Naval College at Monterey, south-west of San Francisco. On completion of the F-8 course he was scheduled to join VX-4 as the new XO. Jerry joined the Navy as an AVCAD, having been a clarinet player in a night-club band in New York. He then transferred, becoming a permanent line officer, the equivalent of a General List officer in the Royal Navy. Jerry, it will be recalled, was a proficient musician and also taught Naomi pianoforte; as a direct result of his influence, she has grown into an excellent pianist with a touch that has impressed all piano aficionados.

Towards the end of his appointment Jerry flew around the country attending this and that university and gaining credits for a political science degree, and eventually he qualified for his PhD. He chances of squadron command were virtually zero at this stage of his career. The US Navy has an odd scheme whereby if one is selected for promotion to the rank of Commander, one's name goes into a hat for command selection and appointment. He was unlucky when he was promoted to Commander, but he would eventually have two squadron commands. After VX-4 he was appointed to Washington as the USN representative at the Federal Aviation Administration—in the rank of Commander even though his predecessor in the job had been a Captain. Jerry and his family left before Christmas 1969 and we more or less dropped out of each other's orbit until 1975, when I met up with him again at Norfolk, Virginia.

Jim Foster, my Captain, I will always remember as a person of kindness and friendship. His life was blighted with sadness at home, and even more sorrow after we left to return home to Britain. Before we departed he loaned us his old Cadillac and beach hut for a few days until our departure. He did not want us to leave, and he told me quite candidly that he wanted me to transfer to the US Navy in the same rank and seniority, but I declined the offer: the Royal Navy had been good both to me and to my family, and I did not think it right and proper to change horses in mid-stream. Jim went on to command USNAS Dallas following his stint at the Pentagon overseeing the F-18 Hornet project. He then retired, but he was subsequently recalled to run the Naval Transport Division at New Orleans.

* * *

The reader will recall that I have always been a keen yachtsman, but somehow I had never been able to find anyone really interested in sailing within the Squadron. Then, out of the blue, Commander Chuck Kluse mentioned that he had a small 21-foot sailboat moored over in Ventura—and would I like to help him bring it around to the Channel Islands Harbour? Quite naturally, I jumped at the offer and so May drove us over to the harbour together with his wife and the Labrador dog. In those days the whole of Ventura harbour was just a series of muddy creeks with small, scattered wooden jetties; now it has been dredged out and is a properly built-up facility for yachts, pleasure craft and fishing boats. The tide was up and the boat was afloat, so we quickly backed her out and set sail for Oxnard and the Channel Islands Harbour to berth her not far from the Whale's Tail restaurant, which in those days was a small wooden shack. This harbour was very similar to that at Ventura but had a better entrance and a deep-water area where fishing boats could moor. Like Ventura, over the next couple of decades, Channel Islands Harbour would be expanded and developed to accommodate several marinas for yachts, pleasure craft and waterfront properties. The fishing port would be extended also, and a large charter fishing fleet would take root on the southern side of the harbour.

Santa Barbara Channel off Ventura, Oxnard and Port Hueneme is a pleasant sea area for sailing, fishing and motorboating. Ten to fifteen miles to the west lie the Channel islands of Anacapa, Santa Cruz, Santa Rosa and San Miguel, which are favourite places for yachtsmen throughout the summer. Most of these islands were privately owned but they now belong to the National Parks Trust and one cannot land without a permit or a guide. There are few places to visit on the Pacific west coast except in the far north and in Baja California, in contrast to the east coast from the Caribbean to the New England waters which offer hundreds of excellent harbours and bays. Catalina Island off Long Beach is also a favourite haunt for summer and weekend sailors. However, if one feels brave enough there is the 2,000-mile voyage to Hawaii or further to the various archipelagoes scattered across the Pacific Ocean.

The weather is generally quite good throughout the year in this region, except north of San Francisco during the winter, when severe storms blow in from the North Pacific accompanied by winds often approaching hurricane force. Thanks to the rocks and the poor entrances to rivers and harbours, the coastal regions are therefore treacherous. To the south of Baja California, hurricanes are the order of the day from July through to December, although their frequency varies from year to year. The water temperature is as low as 50°F throughout the year because of the Californian Current which sweeps down from Alaska; for anyone falling overboard, unless wearing proper protective clothing or hauled back on board within ten minutes, the chances of survival are extremely slim. Because of the cold waters and the warm, moist air blowing in from the Pacific, the region suffers more sea fog than any other spot on the planet except the Arctic and Antarctic. These fogs are dense and have been the cause of many marine accidents and losses over the years. I have flown in worse weather in California than any experienced in Britain.

Although, in general, the weather is excellent for all-year-round sailing, Californians seem to follow an annual routine of launching their boats at Easter and hauling them back out of the water immediately after the Labor Weekend at the beginning of September. Once the air temperature drops to 70°F it is considered too cold here for further sailing, whereas New England sailors, if presented with these conditions, would be sailing all year round!

* * *

With the introduction of the F-4J Phantom into the US Navy it became obvious that, because of the complexity of its weapon system, a new form of teaching tool to instruct aircrews was required. The method selected was the slide/tape presentation, in which an instructor projected pictures on to a screen and gave a verbal briefing on what was being shown. It was a very good idea at the time, video cassettes having as yet not been invented, so the method was implemented across the board in the US Navy.

A team of experts arrived in the Squadron from Orlando, Florida, the location of the company that manufactured these teaching aids. We sat down to discuss what was wanted and it soon became clear that the visiting team knew very little about teaching methods and techniques. They wanted to make presentations of upwards of an hour or more, but I firmly squashed that idea, explaining that people soon begin to lose interest and fall asleep after twenty minutes. After much discussion I got my way and we had more presentations that could be shown at any time, and quickly.

Of course, since that time much has happened and teaching tools and systems have advanced considerably. Now we have video cassettes and DVDs with continuous commentary while a film is being shown. Even so, the durations of these presentations have to be kept to about twenty minutes in order to retain the recipients' interest. Many people will observe that television videos last longer than twenty minutes and indeed they do, but there are usually several generous intermissions for advertisements throughout a hourly showing, allowing the viewer to refocus his or her mind.

Following the introduction of the 'Top Gun' School, the US Air Force latched on to the idea and built a similar ground-attack range near Nellis Air Force Base in Nevada. This range became known as the 'Red Flag' Range, and British squadrons used regularly to deploy to Nellis for training. The range was very realistic because captured Soviet weapon systems were scattered throughout and video cameras were fitted to them to assess whether any 'hits' had been scored on attacking aircraft.

In my first full report on Project OV-63, 'The Evaluation of the F-4J Weapon System in a Tactical Environment', I raised the question of flying training. The US Navy was in effect two Fleets, the Atlantic and the Pacific, and for all practical purposes these were two independent navies. The F-4 training programme for the Atlantic Fleet was conducted from VF-101 at NAS Oceana, Virginia, while that for the Pacific Fleet originated from VF-121 at NAS Miramar. Although the flight training was common to both in many respects, there were great differences in the type of sorties flown. VF-121 had by far the greater number of aircraft—almost 80 F-4Bs together with half a dozen F-4Js. VF-121 was training a hundred pilots and RIOs every month, nearly all of them going to Vietnam. Crewmen going to F-4J squadrons received six flights in the aircraft, a totally inadequate number given that the men were being trained to understand and operate a complicated system effectively in a tactical environment. My recommendation was that both squadrons be equipped immediately with F-4J fighters to the level of fifty per cent of establishment. In addition I proposed that every effort be made to rationalise the flight training so that it became standard in both squadrons, and that an instructor be established in each squadron similar to the Royal Navy's AWI to assure high standards and thorough tactical training. Finally, I recommended that more training be devoted to tactical air-to-air warfare so that pilots would be capable of fighting enemy aircraft and of knowing the limitations of both their aircraft and their weapons. I was glad to see that most of these recommendations were put into effect within a year of my departure. The Americans do not like being upstaged (I suppose that goes for us all): they might agree with a recommendation but will let it settle for a while and then introduce it later as if it were their own idea. The reader may think that I am being churlish here, but it is the way that they are and I do not think that they will ever change. At least I feel happy that I had left seeds to germinate, which eventually they did. As a result, a far better training system was enjoyed than when I first arrived in VX-4.

— 23 —

Homecoming

I T WAS about Easter 1969 that May learnt that she was pregnant again. She was attended by a former US Army Major, Dr Smith, who had his practice in Camarillo. He looked after her as if she were his own daughter. It was determined that she would, once again, have to have a Cæsarean section when the time came for the birth: she was not to go into labour.

It had been our intention to tour the eastern half of the United States during the autumn of 1969. We had put a great deal of planning into the holiday but Dr Smith put his foot down when he heard of our intentions. Thus we decided on a few days' camping at Inverness, just north of San Francisco, and when September came we took two weeks off with the idea of taking the other two weeks when the new baby arrived, which would be some time after Christmas. We spent our time at Morro Bay, Inverness and Tahoe and arrived back at Mugu happy and exhausted after a thoroughly enjoyable break.

* * *

The next day I was back at work finding out what had happened during my absence. A new 'add-on' had arrived for Project OV-63—a helmet-mounted sight for the pilot. US Army helicopter pilots had been using such equipment in Vietnam, and someone at Miramar had suggested that perhaps it might be a good idea for fighter pilots to have something similar. Our inventive Chief Petty Officer, the electronics wizard (who had now been promoted to Warrant Officer status for his previous efforts in modifying the F-4's weapon system), went ahead and developed a 'breadboard' helmet-mounted sight for the fighter pilot. The idea was that cockpit-mounted signal generators would be placed around the coaming, projecting signals on to sensors fitted on the pilot's helmet. The electrical signals picked up by these sensors would vary according to the position of the pilot's head, and the reflected signal would be conducted from the helmet by means of a loom to the weapon system and then on to the radar scanner, which would be slewed to the direction in which the pilot was looking. In addition, a small ring-and-bead sight was mounted on the pilot's visor in front of his right eye, and therefore wherever the sight was aimed so also was the radar, and hence the aircraft's missiles, which were slaved to the radar scanner. Consequently a pilot could pick up infra-red signals for his Sidewinders and reflected radar signals for the Sparrows, giving him the full dogfighting capability hitherto denied.

A series of test flights was conducted with a modified F-4J and the results were extremely gratifying. Finally, Sidewinder missiles were fired against targets turning at high 'g'—with similar results. However, the system was in need of considerable refinement. A shortcoming that I encountered concerned the helmet, which, because of the increased weight from the electronics and the 'pigtail' behind it, had a tendency to be 'left behind' whenever a pilot moved his head quickly. This was quite a serious defect and one that needed to be addressed immediately. The underlying cause was the very poor design of the 'bonedome', so the US Navy went shopping globally and purchased samples of every friendly nation's equivalents. The RCAF helmet proved to be the best, and with this the system worked perfectly. It was eventually introduced into service as the VTAS (Fighter Tactical Air Sight) modification. The F-4 was the first aircraft to be fitted with the modification and it also featured in the future VFX fighter as standard equipment. I was very surprised on my return to Britain to discover that the RAF was reluctant to accept this modification as a necessary item of equipment; a lack of money, unfortunately, determined the decision. The US Navy, however, never regretted installing it.

* * *

It had been anticipated that the US Navy would eventually receive the F-111 (TFX) as its primary long-range interceptor, but experience in Vietnam was demonstrating that the service still needed a dogfighting aircraft.* The F-111 had the size and weight of a bomber and could carry six of the new AIM-54 Phoenix ultra-long-range missiles, enabling the aircraft to destroy any threat to the Fleet at a range of well over 100 miles. The aircraft used to fly out of Mugu quite regularly on test flights under the control of the Naval Missile Center. However, following two serious accidents the US Navy rethought its policy concerning this new aircraft, and from its deliberations arose the VFX conferences and meetings, which were held at North Island, San Diego, and at Miramar. These meetings were classified 'No Foreign', which meant that neither I nor any other British naval officer could attend—or indeed have any involvement in the project. Nevertheless, a former adversary, Adolf Galland, of World War II Luftwaffe fame, was permitted attend and to speak, which made me rather cross.

The CNO gave the VFX conference one constraint: the new fighter jet was to have the same weapon system and jet engines as the F-111; there would be no new money available for redevelopment. Meetings were held between

---

* The Navy version of the TFX, as the project was officially termed, was designated F-111B. Seven examples were built before cancellation. The Air Force version was proceeded with and entered service in some numbers.

VX-4 and a number of aircraft companies at which the latter put forward their ideas and proposals. One of the best was from North American Rockwell, who came up with an aircraft design based upon the Concorde wing. The designer of this jet was British: he had moved to NAR from Avro Canada when that company had folded following the scrapping of the Arrow, the RCAF's new supersonic interceptor. It had one major flaw—under high 'g' loading the wing tips tended to break off (!)—although the designer maintained that this could readily be corrected. This particular design, when run through the US Navy's simulators, outflew all known and future fighter aircraft from both the Western and Eastern Hemispheres, but it was not to be: the USN had for political reasons decided which company would provide its new fighter, and that company would be Grumman. Like the F-111, the new aircraft was based upon Barnes Wallis's 'swing-wing' invention, which he had sold off to the Americans.* The new USN fighter would arrive in VX-4 some time in 1970 as the F-14 Tomcat and my relief, Lieutenant Commander Tim Notley, would be one of the first VX-4 pilots to fly it.

A sequel to the VFX/NAR episode came about when two new Russian fighters, MiG-29s, flew into the RAE Farnborough Air Display. These aircraft were virtually identical to the model of the NAR proposal that had been shown to us in VX-4—fuselage shape, wings, intake design, twin fin configuration and undercarriage. The performance of the two Russian jets was also very similar to that of NAR's proposal, and I am convinced that either it was somehow stolen or else access had been surreptitiously gained to the design information with a view to passing it to the Russians. It was just too much of a coincidence.

* * *

Throughout 1969 the British Labour Government was still in the throes of reducing the strength of the country's Armed Forces, the particular victims being the Royal Navy and its carrier force. The new 50,000-ton aircraft carrier, CVA-01, had already been cancelled, the task envisaged for her air group to be undertaken by F-111 bombers which, Defence Minister Dennis Healey had been assured by the RAF, could do the job just as well from air bases located around the Indian Ocean. Healey swallowed the argument, over-looking the fact that it would require numerous inflight refuellings, and consequently a huge aerial tanker fleet, for the F-111 to reach its targets. The British Government also naively assumed that it would always be able to rely upon the co-operation of the foreign governments which owned the bases around the Indian Ocean.

It was eventually decided to replace the ageing British carrier force with three new 'through-deck cruisers' capable of operating V/STOL Sea Harriers

---

* The British Government could not, in it short-sighted wisdom, see any reason for employing such a revolutionary concept. How wrong they were! Eventually, British Aerospace, as part of the Panavia consortium, would develop the swing-wing Tornado and this would enter service with the RAF, but by that time Barnes Wallis had long gone to meet his maker.

and Sea King helicopters. The ships were designed at Bath, and Victor Doust (no relation, as far as I can ascertain), a ship designer in the Naval Construction Department, had considerable responsibility for them—as indeed he had had for CVA-01 and would have for the new Royal Fleet Auxiliaries which came into service in the early 1980s. The original design called for the bridge and operations room superstructure to be placed on the starboard side, similar to the arrangement for an aircraft carrier, in order to offer the maximum amount of deck area for air operations. However, the First Sea Lord, Admiral of the Fleet Sir Varyl Cargill Begg, would have none of it. Very much a 'Labour man', he ordered the design to be changed so that the bridge superstructure was placed on the ship's centreline in the conventional manner. Everybody knew that his time in office was limited, however, and a set of the original design plans was retained so that, when he left office, they could be implemented as originally intended. The ships would eventually arrive in the Fleet as the *Invincible* class carriers, the name ship joining in 1980. *Illustrious* followed her into service, and then the new *Ark Royal*.

The FAA fixed-wing element would be run down and its aircrews transferred to general service, to helicopter duties or to the Royal Air Force. The RAF was prepared to take a limited number or Navy personnel, but one had the option of resigning from the Navy altogether. I received a letter from my Appointer stating that I had six months in which to make up my mind: if I hurried, the RAF were willing to accept me. I could not believe what was going on, and I mentioned the dilemma to my CO in VX-4, Captain Jim Foster. He was quite prepared to arrange for me to transfer to the US Navy in my rank and seniority. I thanked him but declined. I often wonder what would have happened had I accepted.

The next letter that I received from the Appointer informed me that the Government had decided to retain the old *Ark Royal* and that she would operate an air group of F-4K Phantoms, Buccaneers, Gannet AEW aircraft and Sea King helicopters. I would be required to join the ship as the Landing Safety Officer some time early in 1970 and I would stay with VX-4 until that time. This was of course good news, though I was a little uncertain about the LSO appointment.

* * *

Time was now running short for me. With only a few months left before returning to the United Kingdom, I would have to start writing the first full report on Project OV-63. Bruce Marshall, my USN assistant, Al Rosen, the OEG man, and I began to collate the results and form conclusions and recommendations for the CNO and the Fleet. A set format for the report had been provided by COMOPTEVFOR, so it was quite easy to prepare and lay out the first few sections covering the aims of the project, the equipment used and the personnel employed throughout its schedule, and the results; the difficult part was drawing the conclusions and formulating the recommendations—how the aircraft and its weapon system should be used and deployed within the Fleet. Draft after draft was compiled, amended and rewritten until a finalised document had been produced for editing by a group of officers within VX-4. This process was know colloquially as 'murder boarding', the report being metaphorically torn to pieces and then rewritten yet again until it was considered that it represented what was called for in the Project. The Captain read the final draft and gave his blessing and then it was forwarded to the Staff Project Officer on COMOPTEVFOR at Norfolk, Virginia. If he gave the nod, the report was then printed and bound and copies were forwarded to CNO, NAVAIR, at the Pentagon. It would finally end up in the archives of Congress. This report was now to occupy me for most of my time until my departure from the United States.

* * *

Thanksgiving 1969 came and went and was swiftly followed by Christmas: time was fast flying by. Dr Smith had been insistent that May was not to go into labour in any circumstances, but when I arrived home on 1 January she was experiencing contractions every five minutes. I rushed Naomi over to the Markeys, gathered up May's overnight bag and drove her to St John's Hospital just in time to catch the anaesthetist before he went on holiday. He was in a grumpy mood, muttering about being told so late, especially when he was going on vacation. I pointed out to him the obvious fact that the birthtime of a child cannot be predicted; moreover, we had telephoned the hospital some time earlier and he therefore should have been warned. Our second daughter, Dominique Sarah Victoria Anne, was born at 4.20 a.m. on 2 January 1970. Everybody in the Squadron thought we had produced quadruplets and my parents thought that we had had a son because, in the telegram we sent them, 'Dominique' had become corrupted to 'Dominic'! We had a beautiful American baby daughter, and we were both very proud of her. Guv and Eunice Diaper came over from Callabasas with Kimberlie, who was only a few months old, to visit May and the new arrival. A week later mother and daughter were released and I took them home to Sparrow Drive.

* * *

The dreadful loss of life amongst USN personnel over the 1968/69 Christmas and New Year holiday periods had galvanised the CNO into issuing a Fleet Order instructing all those serving in the Navy and Marines to attend a car safety programme, and as a result all the Mugu base personnel crowded into the cinema to watch half a dozen films compiled and issued by police forces across the United States. They were in full colour and very graphic. The police representatives gave a brief description of what had led up to the accidents featured and the injuries and fatalities that had arisen, and then each accident was re-enacted with close-ups of the final scenes. Many officers and men, veterans of Vietnam, left the cinema unable to stomach what they were looking at. Although I found the scenes extremely gruesome, I had become somewhat hardened by the RN's practice drills for first aid and battle, full of simulated gaping wounds, severed limbs and spurting blood. I can recall an old and bold Lieutenant Commander from wartime days coming upon a simulated battle scene at Seafield Park, being stopped in his tracks and going into a faint. We all had a good laugh, but of course had it been for real it would have been very much a different matter. CNO's film session did the trick and holiday accidents for 1969/70 were virtually nil.

* * *

My new appointment as *Ark Royal*'s LSO arrived. I was to report to the ship in late March after I had completed various aircraft refresher flying courses and safety lectures as well as the short LSO's course. I had agreed to take the leave due to me in half-days across the next couple of months, tying it in with the completion of the first draft for the Project OV-63 report. I flew the odd sortie to keep my hand in and started to prepare for the family's departure. The base shipping department made me some excellent crates, which were delivered to our married quarters. However, our leavetaking was to be gravely marred by the death of Sandy Button in an F-8 Crusader accident.

Sandy, in company with a couple of F-4s, had taken off to carry out some tactical exercises over the Santa Barbara Channel. At 17,000 feet he pulled up into a stall turn, a manoeuvre which he had flown a hundred times or more, when suddenly his aircraft flicked into a spin. His Crusader entered a steep, spinning dive and there was little time to recover. He should have ejected at 10,000 feet but for some reason he rode the aircraft straight into the sea like a dart. Nobody will ever know what really happened, but the Squadron was numbed by the accident. He was one of the US Navy's best officers—someone it could ill afford to lose. Even now I can still hear Phil Anselmo, who was the Duty Officer, saying, 'Sandy has just gone in!' Sandy would, I am sure, have made Admiral's rank. The entire base turned out for his memorial service at the Station Church. As we left the service a traditional flyby of three aircraft in formation was made, the lead aircraft pulling up into the sun and disappearing from sight. There was hardly a dry eye in the congregation on that very, very sad afternoon.

* * *

We sold our red Dodge Dart to a Squadron Petty Officer who was keen to have it despite the fact that it had been driven over 100,000 miles. Captain Foster loaned us his old Cadillac, which guzzled fuel so fast that it needed an oil well in tow. Our reliefs arrived—Lieutenant Commander and Mrs Tim Notley. I had arranged a married quarters for them, not far from where the Marshalls used to live. We sold them all our old appliances for a few dollars, and a couple of days later we moved out to live for a few days in Jim Foster's beach hut near the Officers' Club. A huge removals van arrived to take all our crates across to New York for shipment back to Scotland and home. We had left Britain with little or nothing but were returning with a lot of goodies— and also, of course, a new addition to the family. On 7 March Major Ron Markey drove us to LAX while the Squadron wives and menfolk followed with our hand baggage, which was considerable, and gathered round at the airport to wish us farewell and *bon voyage*. There were many tears: we knew that we were leaving good and true friends. Before we knew it we were aboard our TWA 707 heading for New York.

After we had landed at La Guardia airport Mr McDonald took us to the British-owned Royal Manhattan Hotel for one night. Our return flight would be made in an RAF VC-10 jet transport, departing at 11.00 p.m. the following evening. We had dinner in a pleasant restaurant and, exhausted from our travels, quickly returned to the comfort of our hotel for a good night's sleep. The next day was spent wandering around New York, and then we had dinner, ordered a taxi and drove out to the airport, boarding our VC-10 at about 10.30 p.m.

The RAF VC-10 was the same aircraft as that operated by BOAC but the Air Force used it mainly for transporting cargo and limited numbers of passengers back and forth across the Atlantic. The RAF personnel were extremely efficient and very kind, taking charge of all our baggage and presenting us with our boarding passes far more competently than any airline. Unlike civilian carriers, the RAF arranged their seats facing aft, a much safer way of carrying passengers, as had been proved when a RAF Varsity aircraft had crashed with the Service's rugby team on board. Everybody in the team survived, although some had received serious injuries. Had they been facing forward, however, there was little doubt that most would have been killed. Airline companies have considered rearward-facing seats but have rejected the idea on the grounds that their passengers would be ill at ease with the arrangement.

By 11.00 the next morning we were approaching Brize Norton, and then suddenly we were touching down with the beautiful English countryside all about us. A homecoming always stirs great emotions within me: there is simply no any other place on earth like England. It took about an hour and a half to check through Customs & Immigration, and then an RAF bus took us to Swindon, where we caught a train for London. A taxi took us across the city to Charing Cross station, where we caught a train for Ashford and Rye. Dad was waiting for us at Rye, as pleased as Punch to see us again.

The following day broke very damp and bitterly cold and with the wind still in the north-east. There was a cold drizzle falling which gave way to snow by mid-morning. Dad had decided to drive over to Camber and our old home. I must explain at this juncture that my father had by this time more or less retired and was in the throes of handing over his office as Rye Harbour Master to a much younger man. My parents had very recently moved out of our old home to a small end-of-terrace house in Peasmarsh, north of Rye. The following day the whole of south-east England was under a good foot or more of snow, with many roads blocked by snowdrifts, including the one to Camber—to which Dad needed to return in order to collect a few things.

After three days, however the weather had improved, and as most of the roads were now open we decided to head off back to Lossiemouth and our own home. However, before we left we drove over to Rye Harbour to visit Uncle Jim and his family in their new home. Jim spoke of a lady called

Kathy Mann, and instinctively I knew whom he was talking about: a few days earlier, at the Royal Manhattan in New York, we had spotted a copy of *Country Life* and there, on the front cover, was a very matronly lady in furs with her husband, showing off a racehorse. We did not know it at the time, but this lady was related to me: she was my cousin; in fact she was Kathy Mann. Unfortunately, Mr Mann had passed away since the magazine had been published, but we would eventually meet her in a St Leonards hospital visiting Uncle Jim when he was ill. We would also visit her on many an occasion during our travels south and north on the A1, which went almost past her front door in Wetherby.

Seats and sleepers were booked on the overnight *Aberdonian* from King's Cross station, London. We arrived at Elgin at about 11.00 in the morning and there waiting for us were Jane MacCreadie and Joan Gault with their two cars to pick us up. Half an hour later we were back at Eilean Mhor: home at last!

VII

COMMAND

Landing Safety Officer

WITH the advent of the mirror landing sight, the requirement for the LSO was considered unnecessary. However, following a series of Sea Vixen day and night deck-landing accidents, Their Lordships decided that an LSO was indeed called for on board a carrier if the Fleet Air Arm were to reduce what had become an unacceptable casualty rate. The F-4K Phantom was about to be introduced into service as the replacement for the Sea Vixen fighter, and with so few fixed-wing aircraft now in the Fleet it was essential that every carrier landing be accomplished safely. Having regard to my background experience, it had been decided by both DNAW and DNOA (X) that I was the officer for the job aboard *Ark Royal*—the only carrier which would, in the event, embark these new fighters. I was upset by this decision, because prior to my departure to North America I had been promised command of a second-line training unit, probably 736 (Buccaneer) Squadron. Everybody did a great deal of fast talking to convince me that I was the man who was wanted: they could not, they told me, trust anyone else! I found this all very hard to swallow, but eventually I agreed to take up the appointment provided that I was given a training squadron as my next duty. This was accepted.

I had just one week's leave remaining before I started on my LSO's course. While I was visiting Ray Fielding at P. S. Nicholson's in Forres to arrange the purchase of a new car, Ray received a call from David Dobson, the Senior Appointing Officer in DNOA (X) for aviators. Goodness knows how he managed to track me down. He wanted me to start a Gannet conversion course in two days' time. I was thrilled that I would be flying again; furthermore, I had only to travel a mile down the road from my home to 849 Squadron HQ Flight, which was now based at Lossiemouth in the old NASU hangars. It was very good news; so I agreed.

As we have already noted, it had been decided by the Government of the day in its 1966 Defence White Paper that, owing to reduced commitments overseas in the Dominions and Commonwealth, Britain's Armed Forces would be cut back. The most important effect of this was to do away with the Royal Navy's fleet aircraft carriers and the fixed-wing element of the FAA. The

Royal Navy lost its new 'super carrier', CVA-01; the RAF lost its new super-sonic nuclear bomber, TSR.2. With the demise of the fixed-wing element in the Fleet Air Arm, the naval air station at Lossiemouth reverted to RAF custody. As far as I was concerned, this was a terrible decision by DNAW. Lossie had the finest weather factor in the country; it had the finest weapon range facilities on its doorstep; the airspace in the north of Scotland was free from civilian air traffic; there were excellent low-flying facilities throughout the whole of northern Scotland and nearby Norway; and, above all, the local people enjoyed having the Navy in their midst. However, in spite of the fact that it had been decided, for both political and military reasons, to retain one fleet carrier and her fixed-wing air group, DNAW decided to split up the fixed-wing element. The F-4Ks would be based at Yeovilton (and within three years at RAF Leuchars in Fifeshire), the AEW Gannets at Lossiemouth and the Buccaneers at RAF Honington in Suffolk. This was, in my opinion, a bad decision for another reason: the RAF only accepted the Gannets and Bucc-aneers under sufferance, knowing full well that it would not be long before these units were disbanded.

When I returned to Lossiemouth I found that many of the old naval Ward-room Assistants were still employed by the RAF in the Officers' Mess. They were not happy. The brand new wardroom, built only a few years beforehand, was, according to the RAF, below the standard required for officers. In fact there was absolutely nothing wrong with the building, but I suppose that the Air Force had different aspirations and more money to spend on such facilities; ships were far more expensive than aircraft. The RAF have never understood the reasons for the existence of the Fleet Air Arm, nor the nature of its operations: they have always believed that they can 'do the job' far better than the Navy. They also tend to forget that the RAF was created out of the Royal Naval Air Service and the Royal Flying Corps, and that both RNAS and RFC had shouldered the brunt of the air warfare over the Western Front during World War I.

The reader might imagine that I am prejudiced, but that would be very far from the truth. I have great respect for the Royal Air Force and have many good friends in that service. Over the years, RAF personnel have fought and flown valiantly in the face of the enemy, especially in the period 1939–45 when many officers and men were lost. Their accomplishments during the Battle of Britain are renowned, and deservedly so, and the missions over Germany during the war were some of the finest feats of heroism imaginable. In all, almost 80,000 Bomber Command officers and men took off never see the green grass of England again.

However, there were during my time people on both sides of the Navy/Air Force argument who went out of their way to cause inter-service rivalry and antagonism. Our two tasks, although complementary on occasions, were totally different. The Fleet Air Arm was required to defend Royal Navy ships in times of war, support land invasion forces, take on tasks which were out of the sphere and reach of the RAF and counteract the submarine threat. Ironically, during the two to three decades following the Labour Government's decision to kill off the FAA, the Navy was involved in several wars and skirmishes about the world in which naval air power was a precondition of their being fought—the Falklands War of 1982 being the obvious example. When I returned home to Britain, the new military environment was *fait accompli*, however, and there was nothing I could do but voice my opinion, accept what had happened and, of course, do my very best under the new arrangements

* * *

I spent a week with 849 Squadron and went solo in the Gannet T.5, but I did not fly the AEW Mk 3 because there was none to spare from the OFS programme. However, I was happy at having flown the Mk 5 as this gave me the chance to understand the problems associated with making single-engine landings, especially aboard an aircraft carrier. I left at the end of the week, heading south for Yeovilton and the LSO's course. This was run by Lieutenant Commander 'Dusty' Milner, a former Sea Vixen pilot attached to the naval element in the Airwork Services detachment at the air station. The course consisted of talking pilots down to the dummy carrier deck at the beginning of Runway 23 at Yeovilton. A flight-deck layout had been painted on the runway alongside the deck-landing sight so that practising pilots could make realistic approaches and touch-downs. As a prospective LSO, I also sat on the landing sight seat with helmet and radio, looking through an approach sight to judge and check an approaching aircraft's glide path, attitude, airspeed, landing gear, flaps and arrester hook. I found that I had a natural ability to talk to a pilot with a reassuring commentary—an essential element in any pilot's approach to a flight deck that is pitching and rolling in heavy seas, especially at night.

My next course was the F-4K Ground School run by 767 Squadron at Yeovilton. Commander Lynn Middleton, who was to be FOFT's next Staff Officer responsible for fixed-wing flying training in the FAA, joined me on the course. It had been intended to give me a couple of flights in the aircraft, but Lynn stepped in and quashed that plan: I had had more than enough F-4 flying experience, in his opinion. This peeved me somewhat, because in this way he ensured that he got his own familiarisation flights—the crafty old so-and-so! Then I went to RAF Honington for refresher flying in the old Buccaneer, returning home to Lossiemouth on the completion of my course.

I spent a few days at home before travelling south once again, this time to join the old *Ark Royal*, which was moored at Spithead off Portsmouth. My asthma had reared its ugly head again. I wondered whether perhaps the cool British climate was responsible, but the truth was that I had developed a slight case of bronchitis, triggering the asthma. I flew south to Lee-on-Solent in one of 781 Squadron's Herons, and the ship's SAR helicopter was waiting to pick me up and fly me the last couple of miles out to the carrier. As I stepped out of the 'chopper', there were Pete Marshall and Derek Monsell waiting to greet me and show me to my cabin. Pete was Lieutenant Commander (Flying) and Derek was Commander (Air), the 'Air Boss' and head of the Air Department. My 'cabino,' as I used to call it, was quite the smallest

271

accommodation imaginable. Situated just abaft the port paravane bay, inboard of the passageway leading to the quarterdeck, it was a poky little hole in which one had to jam one foot against the bulkhead to steady oneself while shaving. Inboard of my cabin was a seamen's mess deck, and there was a wire mesh grille at the top of the bulkhead separating us. Lying in the bunk, I could hear all sorts of conversations going on in the mess deck. Opposite my cabin and outboard of the passageway was the Deputy Supply Officer's cabin, which was a palatial affair compared with the hovel that was to be my home for the next eighteen months. Somehow, though, I became quite attached to it.

As soon as I could I visited the Senior Medical Officer, rather concerned about my asthma. He arranged for me to pay a visit to Royal Naval Hospital Haslar, less than a mile away. The chest specialists gave me a thorough going-over and, as on the last occasion when I had suffered with this problem, carried out a desensitising test. About three dozen allergies were placed on each of my forearms and within minutes the test solutions had created large blisters. The Petty Officer Sick Berth Attendant carrying out the test could hardly believe his eyes, and neither could the surgeon attending me: I had reacted to just about every solution available. They ordered a desensitising solution, which was to be injected into my bloodstream once a week over a nine-week period. This would, it was hoped, allow my body to build up an immunity to these allergies. Whatever was concocted in the medical laboratory ashore seemed to work, because I remained relatively free from asthma for the next couple of years.

* * *

After a week anchored at Spithead, *Ark Royal* slipped her buoy and put to sea, embarking a flight from each of her air group squadrons. The idea was to work up the flight-deck handling crews and squadron personnel while testing all the systems such as the catapults, arrester wires, deck landing sight and Carrier Controlled Approach. Everything appeared to be going fine and I was settling into my job as the LSO when the arrester wire jigger ropes suddenly started to fail. The jigger ropes are sheaths of wire cables under the flight deck that provide the resetting mechanism for the arrester wires and tension them to the correct setting for the next aircraft to be recovered. When an aircraft picked up an arrester wire, the jigger sheath was pulled at such a rate that the individual roved wires in the ropes would break; as the jigger began to function, the broken wires caused the system to jam and the arrester wire did not reset itself. It took the flight deck engineers a considerable time working high up in the hangar deck head to unravel the mess and replace the ropes. One incident raised the eyebrows, but then the ropes started breaking frequently and now the ship had a problem. DNAW, DNAE, RAE Bedford and British Ropes were all called in to review the matter when 'Ark' had returned to Devonport Dockyard. British Ropes produced a modified cable, but when this had been installed and the carrier had put to sea once again the new rope also broke. By this time everybody was seriously puzzled as to what might be causing the failures. The problem was associated only with the Phantom; it did not occur when a Buccaneer or a Gannet landed-on. After frantic discussions British Ropes manufactured a further improved cable and after more trials it appeared that the problem had been resolved.

Our next task was to clear the F-4K for night flight-deck operations, and a couple of aircraft were embarked from 'C' Squadron, the Naval Flight at A&AEE Boscombe Down. Three crews came aboard, Commander Freddie Hefford, the OC of the Squadron, and Lieutenant Commanders Richard Burns and Michael Tristram, together with their civilian test observers. I briefed them all to follow my instructions implicitly: if I considered their approach unsafe, I would wave them off for a further approach or divert them to RNAS Yeovilton, which would remain open for the duration of our night-flying exercise. Freddie and Michael followed my instructions to the letter but Richard was going to do it his way. During one pass at the deck he came out of the low cloud base a mile astern of the ship but a quarter of a mile off to starboard. I gave him strict instructions as to what to do but he would not follow them and overshot into a missed approach pattern. His second approach was exactly the same as his first—there was no response to my instructions—so I waved him off and told him to divert to Yeovilton. The Captain, Ray Lygo, Commander (Air) and Lieutenant Commander (Flying) all agreed with my decision. The latter two, Freddie and I sat down and discussed the sortie. I was quite emphatic about Richard's ability to deck-land, which in my opinion was below par. I was not going to allow him to place his aircraft, himself and his observer in a situation which could result in their loss whilst I was the LSO. I could not care less if he were a test pilot: my responsibility was quite clear: it was my job to ensure that a pilot made a safe landing, be it in daylight or at night.

The discussion with Freddie Hefford went on for quite a while but I was not going to shift my stance. Freddie stated that Richard was a far better test pilot than Michael, and in this matter I did not disagree with him. 'However,' I said, 'he is not a very good deck-landing pilot and was not so when he flew Sea Vixen fighters. If you insist on his continuing in the night test programme then you could well end up with a serious accident on your hands—and it will not look good at the Board of Inquiry when it is established that you all disregarded the LSO's advice!' That clinched the matter, and it was decided that sufficient sorties had been flown to clear the F-4K for night flight-deck operations from *Ark Royal.*

The next day Freddie frightened us all. Whilst in the air, he had decided at the last moment, without briefing anyone in Flyco or the LSO, to make an auto-throttle approach. In this type of manoeuvre the pilot pre-sets one throttle to about 90 per cent power and the second throttle is automatically moved by an electrical input from the angle of attack indicator. Depending upon the aircraft's angle of attack, the throttle is either opened or closed to maintain height and speed. *Ark Royal,* however, was not fitted with the fully automatic glidepath facility available in the big American carriers. As the aircraft approached, I thought that there was something wrong with the port engine, which was emitting large puffs of smoke, and as it touched down the nose fell forward heavily, power was reduced and the aircraft bolted. As the jet left the forward end of the flight deck and sank out of sight towards the sea, there was a tremendous roar from its engines and clouds of spray rose from the water. For a moment I lost sight of the aircraft, but then it reappeared, slowly clawing its way into the sky. 'What happened there?' I asked Flyco on the intercom. They had no idea, and at that stage neither had I. Goodness knows what Freddie was about, but he apologised on landing back aboard ship. The funniest part about the incident was that his test observer had had his head down writing notes and had failed to notice what was going on about him.

With the F-4K trials completed, the test aircraft were launched for their return flight back to Boscombe Down and the ship returned to Plymouth Sound and anchored for the night. The next day the carrier weighed anchor, recovered the whole of her air group and proceeded up-Channel for her first work-up. It was early summer and, as is normal for the time of year, there was plenty of sea fog and the waters were calm. The Buccaneers, F-4Ks and Gannets were launched on various exercises, to return for a session of touch-and-go deck landings followed by a final arrested landing. A couple of Sea Kings were also launched for anti-submarine exercises. Everything went well until the last Phantom was due to return. He never appeared. After five or ten minutes I called Flyco, asking where he was, but they had no answer. Slowly it came to light that the aircraft had disappeared off the radar scope during an interception while descending from altitude to low level. In view of the fog and sea conditions, I was beginning to have very uneasy feelings in my stomach.

The ship headed towards the last known position reported by the Direction Room, and both SAR helicopters and the Sea Kings then airborne were scrambled towards the same position. The area was searched extensively but nothing was found, either of wreckage or of an oil slick. One could only assume that the aircraft had dived straight into the sea, either because the pilot and observer had misread the altimeter or because one or both had become disorientated. After a fruitless day of searching, the operation was abandoned, the aircraft presumed lost at sea with its crew. A few days later a small European coaster steaming down-Channel made a radio call stating that the crew had spotted what appeared to be an aircraft wing tip with a British roundel on it floating in the sea. The SAR helicopter was quickly sent to the position given by the coaster's crew but after an hour of searching found nothing. It was a great pity that the wing tip could not be recovered, because it might have given us a clue as to what had happened to the jet and its crew. This was the first F-4K to be lost by the Fleet Air Arm; regrettably, I would be intimately involved with two more in the not too distant future.

* * *

Ark Royal was due to steam north, towards the Norwegian Sea, where she would be involved in the regular autumn NATO exercise. However, before this exercise took place the ship embarked a flight of V/STOL Harriers from No 1 Squadron RAF under the command of Wing Commander Ken Hayr. The Harrier maintenance personnel and ground equipment were embarked off Leith and the aircraft taken on board shortly after the carrier left the Firth of Forth. The Squadron CO had been one of the first RAF officers to go through the Navy's AWI Course—a course that the RAF neither had nor thought necessary, although in time they would implement a similar course under a different name.

The Harrier was fitted with an inertial navigation system, which required that an up-to-date position be fed into the aircraft before it took off. Ashore at an airfield this was easy, but aboard a moving platform such as an aircraft carrier there were problems. These were initially overcome by the use of a device known as the 'Ice Cream Trolley'. The ship's satellite navigation position was fed into this trolley via a data cable from the carrier's catwalk. The trolley, which had its own power supply, would then know exactly where it was positioned and, by means of a short cable, its position could be fed into the Harrier to update the aircraft's INS. It was a simple if rather cumbersome system which, in time, would be replaced by a system of 'wandering' cables running from various flight deck outlets to the aircraft parking spots.

The RN Liaison Officer for the Harrier project was Commander Jimmy Moore, formerly the CO of 800 (Buccaneer) Squadron. After one rather frightening take-off by a Harrier, we had to establish what had gone wrong. The CO was attempting a vertical take-off just outboard of Flyco but had hardly become airborne when the aircraft rolled to the right, the pilot cut the throttle and his machine fell back on to the deck. He tried again, but with the same experience. He was then repositioned slightly forward and further outboard, and on this occasion he lifted off with no difficulty. Jimmy and I then took a bucket of water and a smoke flare and went to a position at the end of the angled flight-deck sponson and plunged the flare into the bucket. The smoke was carried aloft by the wind in an arc, descending again exactly where the Harrier's right wing had been; thus a pilot trying to lift off from that position would have had vertical wind pressure on his right wing, forcing it downwards and inducing a roll to the right. By altering the ship's head to port slightly, the angled deck sponson could be placed in a wind 'shadow', thereby eliminating the downdraft. This was a very important piece of information, and it was passed on to the National Physical Laboratory at Teddington, where carrier windflow trials were conducted, and to the Naval Unit at RAE Bedford.

The opportunity was taken to test the Harrier as to its suitability as a fleet air defence fighter, and we scrambled them on several occasions when Buccaneers were making dummy strikes against the ship. It was an odd sight to see a Buccaneer pulling up into a loft-bombing manoeuvre with a Harrier 'viffing' on its tail.* No night flying trials were carried out, although I would eventually become involved in such trials in my next ship on the opposite side of the Atlantic. The RAF maintenance personnel had a hard time

---

* 'Viffing'—vectoring in forward flight—is manoeuvring by means of the aircraft's vectored thrust, and often therefore at zero airspeed.

understanding carrier operations. I can recall one occasion when a Flight Sergeant appeared alongside me on the flight deck while a Harrier was landing on. A Flight Deck Director was standing near the landing spot, holding his hand aloft to indicate that it was safe to continue the landing; I suppose he was about fifteen yards from the spot and perfectly safe, but the Flight Sergeant did not think so.

'What's he doing there, sir?' he enquired nervously. 'It's highly dangerous, and it wouldn't be allowed in the RAF for anyone to be so close to a Harrier landing.'

'Well, Flight, where do you suggest he stand? This is not the RAF, Flight, and it is perfectly safe when you know what you are doing and are protected with goggles, ear defenders and the right clothing.'

Then he spotted an F-4 being loaded on to the catapult and the ordnance men crawling around underneath checking that the weapons were properly plugged in and the armament safety breaker was closed. This he found totally unacceptable and said so, whereupon he quickly disappeared below to the safety of the upper hangar, believing that we were out to kill every airman in the ship. He did not give me time to tell him that in the FAA one has to have one's wits about one while working on the flight deck—which can be the most hazardous place in the world.

The Harrier trial was completed successfully and No 1 Squadron disembarked and returned to RAF Wittering, its home base. Five days had been spent operating Harriers from the 'Ark', and these revolutionary machines really proved themselves to be sailors' aeroplanes, ideal for close-in air defence against attacking enemy aircraft.

* * *

Ark Royal now steamed off north to take part in the NATO exercise. The actual exercise area was to the north-east of the Shetland Islands. We had not been flying very long before the F-4K started breaking the jigger wires again. This time we disembarked 892 Squadron to RAF Lossiemouth and continued with just the Buccaneers and Gannets. At this stage of events the ship was down to one arrester wire, and we had to ensure that aircraft were returning with enough fuel to cover any eventualities. The weather had deteriorated and the wind was up to Force 9 or 10 with heavy seas.

A task came in for 809 Squadron to fly as many Buccaneers as possible into northern Europe on simulated strike sorties and photo-reconnaissance missions. The Squadron had fourteen bombers and every one was launched in the most appalling conditions. The weather was quite fair but the ship was pitching so badly that the forward end of the flight deck was almost disappearing under the water. Bill Credland, the FDO, waited until the deck pitched downwards, then lowered his green flag for the catapult to be fired. The aircraft broke out as the deck pitched down and left the catapult as it was level and in the upswing, as if being fired ballistically off the flight deck. The American observers on board could not believe that we operating in such conditions, and were quite candid about it: their carriers would not.

We pointed out that in wartime one sometimes has to operate this way, so it might as well be practised. With all the Buccaneers away and half the Gannets and Sea Kings airborne, the ship was very quiet indeed; the fun would begin when all the fixed-wing aircraft returned to catch only one wire.

Almost an hour and a half had gone by before the first Buccaneer called to join the circuit. The aircraft had been in contact via SSB MF radio, and it appeared that every sortie had been successful. Each Buccaneer had been allocated a different mission, so they arrived back individually—which was a relief in view of the heavily pitching deck and the single wire. Each pilot made a steady approach and each caught the wire; not one bolted or was sent around again. A great cheer went up as the last aircraft landed on board. Our American friends stood there dumbstruck at the efficient and professional way we operated our ship.

The exercise debrief took place at Dunfermline at the Headquarters of FOSNI. The ship anchored in the Firth of Forth for the debriefing, plus a well-earned weekend break. On the Monday morning we weighed anchor to return to Devonport to resolve our jigger wire problem. The air group was disembarked while we steamed south along the east coast of England, and we tied up in our normal berth in the dockyard.

* * *

While 'Ark' had been away, HMS *Eagle*, fresh from a refit, had been to sea on a post-refit sea trial. Prior to sailing, both her Captain and Navigator had been aboard *Ark Royal* to oversee a departure and entrance to Plymouth Devonport. However, despite this training they were to experience a serious accident that delayed their ship's planned schedule by six months.

I was standing on the flight deck when Captain Lygo rushed to me.

'LSO,' he ordered, 'get those letter cards out and have the handlers line up on the flight deck and display the following: "I'm only jiggered not buggered!" In addition, we'll have the Marine Band play a lively tune!'

'Aye, aye, sir!'

We all dashed into action as *Eagle* approached us, and as she came abeam she blew her whistle and saluted—no smiles, just grim faces—as we carried out our little stunt.

'What the hell's wrong with them?' exclaimed Captain Lygo.

'I don't know, sir, but *Eagle* appears to be trailing a slick of oil.'

What none of us knew was that the carrier had damaged herself severely on a submerged rock off Plymouth Hoe.

The approach into Plymouth Devonport is via a narrow channel, with a 90-degree bend off Plymouth Hoe. At the corner of this bend is a submerged rock, which is marked by a buoy. Entering Plymouth, large ships always move well over to the port side of the channel so that, as they turn to port, the bows cling to the left-hand side, allowing the stern to swing clear of the rock. On this occasion, *Eagle* had been brought up the channel too near the centre, and as she was turned to port her stern had swung out and ridden up and over the rock, tearing a 40-foot gash in the hull plating and damaging the starboard outer propeller and rudder. The gash had allowed fuel to start flowing out of the ship's bottom tanks. Everybody aboard knew exactly what had happened, and a deep silence had descended upon the company as the carrier steamed further up the channel to Devonport Dockyard.

Eagle had to re-enter drydock in order to be repaired, and her Captain, her Navigator and the Plymouth pilot all faced courts martial. There were, to be sure, extenuating circumstances: the buoy marking the rock had been moved off-station following a severe storm. However, despite this evidence, all three were found guilty of hazarding their ship and navigating without due caution, although the sentences handed down by the court martial board were quashed by the Naval Legal Branch at the MoD. The Captain went on to be promoted Admiral in due course—quite inappropriately, in my opinion—but his Navigator's career was ruined and he retired from the Naval Service, while the Harbour Pilot found another job. It was a sad and sorry affair, initiated by two officers who had been told exactly how to enter the harbour safely and who had had a pilot to help them who failed in his advisory capacity when he saw that things were going wrong. Ray Lygo, not knowing at the time what had happened to *Eagle*, was very upset at the way his joke misfired and quickly called upon *Eagle*'s Captain and apologised. Fortunately, nobody was injured or hurt, although there were serious dents in professional pride. However, but for the grace of God, how many of us have been so close and been lucky?

* * *

Ark Royal was in for a long stay this time because the jigger rope problem would not be resolved quickly. The damaged ropes were inspected by RAE Bedford, the naval engineers from Bath, DNAW, DNAE and British Ropes. They were now failing regularly and no obvious reason could be found. After some considerable time new ropes were laid up, of different material and in a different way. They were fitted and the old ship went off to sea once again to try them out. This time no failures occurred, and it appeared as if the problem had been finally resolved.

While in Devonport, Commander John Neilson and his team from DNAE visited the ship to look at her flight-deck night lighting. They wanted to see how it appeared from astern and ahead, and to discuss a deck landing sight for the Sea Harrier when it was brought into service. The options for the 'through deck cruiser' were very limited and money was a problem. A moratorium had been placed on the her such that no further finance would be forthcoming: her cost had almost doubled over the past couple of years due mainly to the extra equipment that had been deemed necessary and now the Admiralty had called a halt. This new ship, the first of class, was due to be launched in less than two years' time.

Now that *Ark Royal* was fully operational once more, she re-embarked her air group north-west of Land's End and everybody buckled down to the first work-up in which everything functioned properly. Our first objective was that every fixed-wing pilot be day-qualified in deck-landing. It was not too much of a task with the Buccaneer pilots, many of whom were old hands, but the majority of the F-4K pilots were new to deck-landing a Phantom fighter, although many were experienced Sea Vixen deck-landers. The task was less difficult with the Gannet and Sea King pilots: the Gannet pilots were also all very experienced, and landing a helicopter is, in my opinion, relatively easy (except at night). The ship now steamed off again into the North Atlantic and the Norwegian Sea to participate in another NATO exercise.

The Soviets were obviously very interested in 'Ark' and her new all-weather interceptors and followed her wherever she went. On the way north through the Irish Sea our sonar team, carrying out some practice listening on their equipment, located a submarine out on the starboard bow at about half a mile, travelling with the ship and at about the same speed. There were certainly no British or American nuclear submarines in the area and it could therefore only have been a Soviet vessel. Two Sea King helicopters from 824 Squadron were scrambled to locate and identify it. However, they were unable to find it and after a couple of hours the two crews landed back on board, frustrated and disappointed that they had been unsuccessful. It definitely was not a whale!

A couple of days later, north-west of the Orkney Islands, someone on the flight deck spotted a submarine's periscope passing down the starboard side of the ship, moving from forward to aft. The bridge was immediately called and a Sea King helicopter was scrambled, but once again no submarine was located. At the same time, however, a Soviet Il-38 'May' LRMP/ASW turboprop aircraft flew down the starboard side of the ship, in the same direction as the elusive submarine. I rushed up to the bridge to ask whether anybody had seen it but nobody seemed to have any idea what I was talking about. Even the Operations Officer did not appear to understand what I was reporting.

'Get the identification books out and I'll show you what's flying around us!' I said, exasperated.

The intruder made another pass at the ship, and suddenly everybody was aghast.

'Now do you believe me?'

An 'Immediate' signal was sent to the MoD, who tried to play the incident down. We were mistaken; it was not flying in our area; they knew of its existence. Ray Lygo, our Captain, refused to stand for this nonsense and sent a further signal telling the MoD to sort out its intelligence section: this aircraft was flying over North Atlantic waters and the Norwegian Sea, had taken an interest in his ship and had been working in conjunction with one of its own submarines as well. A very short reply came back, thanking him and asking for further information and photographs. Of course, the darned aircraft flew off!

What surprised the Soviets more than anything was our knowledge of their 'Bears' and 'Badgers' rounding North Cape, heading for our fleet. They came round northern Norway in droves and 892 Squadron regularly waited for them and pounced. As the pilots brought their fighters close alongside the Soviet bombers, the tail gunners in the latter would wave to them and 'offer' a cup of coffee. Personally, I have always found the Russians a friendly people. One of the most personable Russians I ever knew was John Ford's mother. She was a White Russian lady, very matronly and with a very strident voice. She came into the Lossiemouth wardroom one Sunday just after church. It was a very cold and blustery day, and the bar was open and with both coal fires roaring away. John was standing by one of the fires as his mother sailed into the anteroom like a battleship under full sail, booming at the top of her voice, 'John! Where is my son John?' John cringed out of sight but she soon caught a glimpse of him and went storming over, haranguing him for leaving her alone at the hall porter's desk. Poor John wilted under the onslaught. What a woman! John went as red as anyone could in such embarrassing circumstances.

On completion of the NATO exercise nearly all the participating ships steamed into Oslo harbour and anchored for the weekend. The visit was very pleasant, although it would have been better to have stayed ten days and seen more of the capital and the surrounding countryside! After the visit the anchor was weighed and the ship proceeded back to Devonport. A fierce storm was blowing through the North Sea with winds of Force 9 to 10 and heavy seas. As we made our way south towards the Channel, the carrier rolled and pitched so dramatically that some of her after-quarter 25-man liferafts were plunged under the sea, activating the automatic inflation devices and ripping the rafts away from their stowage. We must have lost at least a dozen, and even though we were unable to sink them by machine-gun fire a Soviet guided missile ship, which was trailing us, managed to recover many of them. The weather and sea conditions moderated sufficiently for the aircraft to be launched to their parent air stations and then we entered the Channel.

Our passage through the Channel was governed by the Traffic Separation Scheme, whereby those vessels proceeding south-west stay to the north side and those sailing north-east keep to the south. It was dull and misty as we steamed south-east and there was a great deal of heavy shipping about. Suddenly, to the east, a huge warship, travelling some five to ten knots faster than us, loomed into view. It was an American *Iowa* class battleship returning home to Norfolk, Virginia, and looking very sleek and menacing. I do not think that I have seen so many ships in close proximity as I did on that occasion, and navigation must have been a nightmare. Goodness knows what it would have been like in seriously foggy conditions.

The Sea Kings were the last aircraft to disembark, and did so as we approached Plymouth Sound, where the ship was anchored and HM Customs & Excise came aboard to clear us before we proceeded up-harbour to Devonport. The attitude of British Customs & Excise officers has always irritated me. They always believe that British seamen are determined to smuggle as much contraband as they can. The allowances given to British sailors are a fraction of what US Navy personnel are permitted to bring in when returning home, and as a consequence American sailors do not smuggle. If Jack Tar attempts to bring a shilling's worth more than he is entitled to he is detained! The Customs officials were out to squeeze every last penny out of us and consequently were hated by everybody.

Once the air group had disembarked I set about analysing the landing films and preparing my results and report for RAE Bedford, which would enable the Naval Unit there either to expand or to restrict the landing envelopes of the fixed-wing aircraft. I then arranged to spend time at the various air stations where our air group squadrons were disembarked, for the purposes of refresher flying. 809 and 849 Squadrons were at Lossiemouth and 764 Squadron was still operating and completing the final AWI courses before it disbanded. May and our two girls were still living at Eilean Mhor, so quite naturally I spent most of my time at Lossiemouth. Bob Edward was the last CO of 764 Squadron, and, before it disbanded, his AWI course arranged for the final lecture to be on the production of malt whisky. All the old AWIs—those still serving and those able to attend from retirement— were invited to the shindig and were presented with their old course reports. The lecture lasted from 1400 until 1630 and after sampling the various stages of whisky production very few of us had steady legs. Then we retired to the wardroom for a sumptuous dinner and a good deal of frivolity.

Before leaving 'Ark' on this occasion I had discussed my future with Derek Monsell, Commander (Air). DNOA (X) had promised me a second-line training squadron after I had returned from the United States. I had expected 736 (Buccaneer) Squadron, but during my absence Graham Hoddinott had been given that job so I was rather out on a limb as to where I would go next. I was far more qualified than most officers who were being appointed to training squadrons at that time. While at Lossiemouth and visiting the bar before lunch I met Dave Eagles, who had been the Senior Pilot of 800 (Buccaneer) Squadron. He seemed to think that I was in line to take command of the new Phantom training squadron at Yeovilton. I thanked him for being so optimistic on my behalf but my feeling was that one of the many ex Vixen pilots would be taking that job. However, at the same time Commander John de Winton from DNOA (X) was also visiting Lossiemouth so I 'nobbled' him and asked if he had any idea what my future would be and where he might be sending me after I had finished my stint in *Ark Royal*. He smiled and told me to watch out for the next Officers' Appointments List. I grinned, offered him a beer and afterwards I went home feeling rather pleased with myself.

* * *

The Christmas of 1970 came and went and I re-joined the 'Ark' at Devonport. The ship had gone through quite a great deal of re-work by the Dockyard, which included the spray painting of the sailors' mess decks. My cabin adjoined a mess deck, and, when I unlocked it on my return, because of the grille opening between the two just about everything was covered in a coating of white—my bunk, my bedding, my personal clothes hanging on their pegs and the wash basin area. I grabbed the wardroom cabin officer and the First Lieutenant and demanded that they arrange for the mess to be cleaned up, provide me with new bedding and arrange for compensation for my damaged clothing.

'We don't see what it has to do with us,' they said in unison. 'We tried to enter your cabin but it was locked.'

'You mean to tell me that the wardroom does not have a duplicate set of keys to officers' cabins? Why didn't you call for the Dockyard locksmith and have him open the cabin, and why wasn't the grille to the mess deck covered up?'

I did not believe a word they told me: no effort had been made by anyone to ensure that my cabin and personal things were not damaged. I told them in no uncertain terms that they were both incompetent. The First Lieutenant became most indignant, and I responded by asking him what *he* would have done had he found *his* cabin in such a state. There was nothing more to say, but I moved temporarily to another cabin while mine was restored and re-painted and all my damaged effects were replaced.

* * *

In the New Year *Ark Royal* steamed to a position west of Land's End and re-embarked her air group. A few days were spent re-qualifying everybody in deck landing and then the Captain set course across the Bay of Biscay, heading for Gibraltar. The weather and sea conditions were fine all the way. A weekend was spent anchored in Algeciras Bay and everybody went ashore, wandering around the colony and buying presents. On the following Monday the anchor was weighed and the old ship steamed into the Mediterranean, pausing to lay a wreath over the position where the previous *Ark Royal* had been sunk by a U-boat in November 1941. Our next destination was Malta, and on the way we began a work-up using RAF North Front as a diversion airfield.

The ship now steamed eastwards towards Cyprus and participated in a small NATO exercise. A Soviet DLG was harassing us continually and on one occasion *Ark Royal* hove-to and all hands were piped to Bathing Stations, officers and men diving off the side of the ship into cooler waters and enjoying a good swim. The Soviet ship also hove-to a couple of cables off our starboard quarter: her crew could not understand what was going on. In a repeat of the incident when I was aboard *Eagle*, they signalled 'Ark' saying, 'Valet [Valletta] that way—to the west!' An hour later all hands were recovered and the ship got under way again, the Soviet remaining on our starboard quarter.

That evening we went to Flying Stations and the first night launch would be made by the 892 Squadron Phantoms. It was now quite dark, but the moon was slowly climbing the heavens from the east. I had gone aft to my cabin to collect something as the carrier started her turn to starboard into wind—the standard manoeuvre—when I heard an F-4 running up to full power on the bow catapult. Suddenly the roar ceased and the ship began to shake hard as the engines were put into full astern. My immediate reaction was to turn about to go back to the flight deck, thinking that the F-4 had had a 'cold shot' and gone into the sea. There was a great deal of shouting and then a set of ship's lights appeared from under the port overhang of the angled flight deck. I then thought that perhaps we had made contact with

HMS *Yarmouth*, which had joined us as our planeguard. There was still a great deal of shouting as the shadow of a ship moved away to port, and then there was a broadcast: 'Scramble the Sea King SAR! Away lifeboat!' I reached the flight deck in record time and was informed that we had collided with the Soviet DLG.

Ark Royal had struck the Soviet warship just abaft the latter's port propeller guard and the force of the impact had ejected several Russian seamen into the dark night waters. Although the collision had been quite severe, the hull of the DLG had not been breached but the force of the impact had apparently caused severe damage in the ship's engine room and she began blowing thick, black, oily smoke from her funnel stack. 'Ark's lifeboat and SAR helicopter searched the waters and recovered eight young Russian seamen, none much more then eighteen years old and all of them conscripts. They were adamant that there were no other Russians in the water and were brought back to the carrier's Sickbay, where they stripped and were given a hot shower. Fresh, dry seaman's clothing was issued to them and they were given a snack, a large brandy and cigarettes. Our Captain's Assistant Secretary, who spoke Russian, had a word with them and then accompanied them back to their ship. He climbed the destroyer's side ladder first and was promptly met by a Russian brandishing a machine gun. He was barred from boarding and forced back into the lifeboat. To our astonishment, on reaching the deck each Russian was made to strip naked and all the clothing and cigarettes were thrown back into the lifeboat. Eight naked young men were then marched off at gunpoint—presumably to be interrogated by the Soviet commissar concerning what they might have seen while aboard the carrier.

The stem of the 'Ark' had been severely damaged in the collision. A six-foot vertical section was missing and the bows of the ship were open to the sea. The ship's engineer and shipwright trimmed the carrier down by the stern so that the hole in the stem was now well above the waterline and the compartment immediately behind the hole was filled with quick-drying cement. While the repair was taking place the Soviet cruiser *Sverdlov* arrived on the scene and conducted a further search, signalling that a further two Russian seamen were missing. It was an obvious political ploy, placing the blame on *Ark Royal*, holding us responsible for the accident and no doubt accusing us of manslaughter too. However, the Russian seamen we had rescued had been quite sure that all who had gone overboard had been accounted for. The following afternoon *Sverdlov* and the DLG left the scene of the collision and disappeared over the horizon. The latter was no longer making black smoke so we presumed that the engine room damage had been repaired—if, indeed, there had been any damage in the first place. The Russians were bent on making as much capital out of this incident as possible, delivering a strong letter of protest to No 10 Downing Street to complain about the cavalier fashion in which the 'British Navy' conducted itself on the high seas, repeatedly placing their ships in harm's way. A tit-for-tat reply was despatched to the Soviet Embassy in London and to the Soviet Foreign Office in Moscow listing the number of occasions on which their warships had continually harassed both British and NATO ships with little regard for

283

the 'rules of the road'. Our reply quickly shut them up and nothing further was heard.

'Ark' steamed slowly back to Grand Harbour, Malta, for more permanent repairs to her stem and en route a distress signal was received for HMS *Hampshire*, which had a serious engine-room fire, compelling her company to go to Emergency Stations. In the wardroom the officers were getting ready to celebrate Trafalgar Night at a mess dinner when a broadcast was made from the Operations Room: '824 Squadron muster in No 1 Briefing Room at the rush! Range all serviceable Sea King helicopters on the flight deck!' Those of us who were in the wardroom having our first drink at the bar crowded around the broadcast speaker wondering what on earth was happening. Immediately following the broadcast, the XO made a further announcement:

> This is the Commander. You have heard the broadcast for 824 Squadron to be made ready for flying and are wondering what might be going on. To the west of us, about thirty miles away, the *Hampshire* is in distress with a very serious engine-room fire and we are going to her aid. I will keep you informed of further developments as they happen. The wardroom Trafalgar Night dinner is cancelled.

The wardroom emptied fast as everybody rushed topsides to see what was happening. As soon as the Sea Kings had been ranged they were loaded with drums of foam for fighting oil fires and they took off heading for *Hampshire*, which was now clearly visible and had black smoke pouring from her.

Within a couple of hours 'Ark' was abeam of *Hampshire*. Her engine-room fire had been extremely fierce, as evident from the scorch marks amidships; in fact, the fire had been of such an intensity that the deck temperature at the Sea Slug missile magazine, which was above the engine room, had reached 175°C—too hot for anyone to stand there. Consequently the crew had had to stop moving the missiles out of the magazine either to fire them or dump them overboard. It was at this stage that the destroyer's Captain had decided to go to Abandon Ship Stations, fearful that the magazine would explode. I am quite sure that had *Ark Royal* not arrived in time, *Hampshire*'s crew would have had to abandon ship and the ship herself would have blown up and gone to the bottom.

The fire was eventually brought under control, stocks of foam aboard *Ark Royal* having been completely exhausted: every single available drum had been sent across. Technically, therefore, the carrier was now not in a position to conduct flying operations owing to the lack of proper firefighting equipment. However, we continued to fly our Sea Kings, rendering all possible assistance to the destroyer.

How had the fire started? *Hampshire* was equipped with gas turbines in addition to steam plant. Apparently, one of these gas turbine engines had been overfuelled and the excess fuel had been bled off into an overflow tank. The overflow tank was situated high in the engine room above the engines, and the overflow outlet from this tank was not being led away either overboard or back into the main tanks, instead flowing straight on to the gas turbines and immediately bursting into flames. The fire being continuously fed by diesel fuel, a major conflagration quickly developed. The ship managed to make her own way slowly back to Grand Harbour with us in company. A

Board of Inquiry was convened, Lieutenant Commander Dave Mears, the CO of 809 Squadron being a member. During its investigations it was discovered that four out of the five similar ships in service with the Royal Navy had the same technical defect. How on earth this serious design fault had been missed remained a mystery, but within a week all the ships had been modified and *Hampshire* had steamed to Gibraltar, where she was taken into dry dock for overhaul.

Back in Malta, the naval dockyard team set about repairing 'Ark's stem and within the week we were at sea and conducting flying operations. However, whilst we were in Malta, Captain Lygo had given his account of the accident to the *Malta Times*, and as soon as it had been published the Ministry of Defence blew a fuse: MoD (Navy) had not as yet received its full written report of the accident but it had certainly read the *Malta Times*. Poor Ray Lygo was called to account for talking to the newspaper, his next appointment—as Director of Public Relations (RN)—went flying out of the door for the time being and his promotion to Rear Admiral, also in the offing, was delayed. However, the whole affair was in reality a storm in a teacup and he was soon reinstated and back on the 'fast track'. He was eventually promoted to Admiral and soon found himself as Vice Chief of the Naval Staff; very swiftly he would rise even further. The Chief of the Defence Staff, a tri-service appointment that rotated through the three services every three to four years, was at this time held by Marshal of the RAF Sir Michael Humphries, new in the appointment, but during a visit to RAF Germany he contracted pneumonia and died. At the time the RAF did not have another officer of equivalent rank and experience to fill the post, so as it was the RN's 'turn' Admiral of the Fleet Lord Lewin was promoted to CDS. This left the Navy without a Chief of the Naval Staff and so Ray Lygo was promoted full Admiral and appointed as CNS. On retirement he joined the board of British Aerospace and was responsible for air-to-air missiles and this was to cause the RAF a great deal of bother because they did not relish the idea of a retired Admiral naval aviator being involved in their missile requirements.

* * *

My new appointment arrived in the ship: I had been chosen to be the next CO of 767 (Phantom Training) Squadron at Yeovilton, relieving Doug Borrowman, who had been selected for promotion to Commander and as the next Fixed-Wing Desk officer at DNAW. To say that I was over the moon is an understatement. May and the girls were also thrilled, while to be going south to slightly warmer climes had my wife grinning from ear to ear.

Following her deployment to the Mediterranean, *Ark Royal* berthed at Portsmouth. The wardroom held a cocktail party in the upper hangar and the ship's Royal Marines Band and Detachment carried out the traditional Sunset Ceremony. One of our guests was the commander of HMS *Juno*, Captain Ted Anson, Captain F1 and in charge of six frigates. Ted had been nominated to be 'Ark's next Captain after Ray Lygo—which was something of a coincidence because Ray had also gone to *Ark Royal* via *Juno*, in which he had also been Captain F1. May and I both went aboard *Juno* to visit Ted and for further 'eats' and drinks. Ted and his wife Rosemary still had our Sweetie Pie, our tortoiseshell cat taken in by David and Mary Howard when we had gone to the United States; when David and Mary departed overseas, the cat had been passed on to the Ansons.

* * *

My time as LSO in *Ark Royal* had come to an end and Lieutenant Commander Jack Frost came from Yeovilton as my relief. I proceeded on leave to my home in Scotland to finalise the sale of Eilean Mhor. May had been very busy during my absence and had more or less found a buyer, an officer from 849 Squadron who would be staying at Lossiemouth as an exchange observer with No 8 Squadron, which, flying Shackletons, would be taking on the AEW role for both the Air Force and the Navy. The sale was finalised and I drove south to Yeovilton to organise a married quarters—our first in the RN. May called in the house movers and then took the train south with the two children. We stayed at the Ilchester Hotel while our furniture was driven south and the married quarters was made ready. One problem arose out of the fact that the Married Quarters Officer would not move the naval furnishings from our new home, so we had to find storage for them in the loft and at the back of the garage, which was, thankfully, very large. It was a very good quarters with generous garden space, a vegetable patch, a back-garden lock-up and a huge tank for heating oil. Best of all, however, was the fact that we had many old friends from *Ark Royal* about us; moreover, we were now only six hours from my parents in East Sussex. It was obvious to us both that we were going to have a good time at Yeovilton.

— 25 —

Commanding Officer

T AKING command of a naval air squadron is not an easy business. All sorts of thoughts rush through one's mind, the uppermost being whether one is up to the task: Their Lordships had gone to great lengths in singling me out as having the potential and necessary capabilities. Having command of an air squadron is like having command of a frigate, but there is much more constraint over what one can and cannot do because of the authority of the air station Captain and Commander (Air). It did concern me that I was not of the night-fighter world, but then neither was Peter Marshall when he had commissioned 767 Squadron as its first CO. This point was to be raised one day when I went into the wardroom and overheard Commander Simon Idiens, who was about to relieve John Ford as Commander (Air) at Yeovilton, ask the latter what I knew about nightfighters. I quickly spoke up: 'Quite a great deal,' I said, 'as I was responsible for the F-4J Project in the USN, their equivalent to the F-4K.' This knocked any further discussion of the topic on the head. I laughed quietly to myself because John Ford was not a night-fighter man and neither, originally, was Simon; John, moreover, had held his appointment as Commander (Air) at Yeovilton for eighteen months and I never heard anyone complaining about *his* background. The crux of the matter was that I was a Supplementary List Officer relieving a General List Officer, and this stuck in the craw of a good many people. It has never been in my nature to blow my own trumpet, but in this instance I was a senior naval aviator with all the appropriate qualifications and was therefore the right candidate for the job.

Doug Borrowman, the outgoing CO of 767 Squadron, was delighted that I was taking over command from him. What we did not know at the time was that our lives would be linked together over the next few years. He had done a thoroughly good job as Squadron Commander, and as a consequence he had been promoted to Commander's rank. Doug took me on a tour of the air station, introducing me to all the people I needed to know, including the Staff of Flag Officer Naval Air Command, whose headquarters were at Yeovilton. FONAC had taken over the old task of Flag Officer Flying Training and was now the Flag Officer responsible for all shore-based aviation; he was also the fifth member of the Board of Admiralty when it wanted advice on naval aviation matters.

My command consisted of nine F-4K Phantom aircraft and 180 officers and men, housed in two hangars. The Squadron also had the use of a couple of Hunter GA.11 fighters for practising tactical flying. The F-4Ks in 767 were not of the same modification standard as those of 892 Squadron, the one and only front-line Phantom squadron in the RN. My task was to train aircrews and groundcrews for both 892 Naval Air Squadron and No 43 Squadron RAF. The RAF squadron was based at Leuchars in Scotland, and, also equipped with F-4K fighters, was responsible for the air defence of the North Atlantic and Norwegian Sea to a range of almost a thousand miles, covering the Arctic Circle and beyond.* Until my Squadron disbanded in August 1972, it would be a very busy time for me and my flight and engineer instructors, training pilots, observers/navigators and groundcrews to the standards required for front-line service.

The command of 767 Squadron passed to me on 6 March 1971. I had a very good team of officers and men. My Senior Pilot was Neville Featherstone, my Senior Observer Gerry Kinch and my AEO Paddy Carr. My Staff Officer was Sammy Manchett, a retired World War II observer. Ed Beadsmore ran the Phantom simulator and he did an excellent job, ensuring that all staff and students knew their checks and emergency procedures correctly. There were only two simulators in the country, one at Yeovilton and the other at RAF Coningsby for the F-4M ground attack aircraft. In addition, there were in the Squadron half a dozen pilots and observers who were very experienced former Sea Vixen aircrew. A typical day would start off with the Senior Met Officer giving the Squadron a run-down on the local and national weather forecast. This was followed by various briefings on the daily flying programme and anything else of importance. Then flying commenced.

The students consisted of both Royal Navy and Royal Air Force officers. The RN students were obviously destined for 892 NAS as replacements or reliefs, while the RAF students were destined for No 43 Squadron at RAF Leuchars. Visitors or senior officers appointed to staff or carrier posts would pass through the Squadron occasionally for familiarisation flying. There were four RAF students going through the Squadron when I took command— Wing Commander Jerry Cohu, who was to become the next OC No 43 Squadron, a Squadron Leader who was to become his new NavRad Leader, and two Flying Officers.

After three familiarisation flights and some general flying, my first instructional flight was with the Squadron Leader Navigator. He had been on exchange with either the USAF or USMC flying F-4s in the United States and had supposedly written their night intercepts manual. Our flight was a high-altitude navigation exercise with a radar/GCA approach into RAF Valley followed by a return flight to Yeovilton. It was a straightforward and simple

* Had CVA-01 had been built, together with a couple of follow-on carriers, the FAA would have had about 250 of the aircraft. The Armed Forces cut-backs extinguished that plan and only 48 were built (designated Phantom FG Mk 1), of which twenty went to the RAF. The Air Force received 116 F-4M fighter/ground-attack/reconnaissance aircraft (FGR Mk 2).

exercise. I had drawn the route out on my kneepad chart, listing all the necessary frequencies required en route. During the briefing I had instructed him that he was in charge of the navigation and to tell me what to do, when to turn and so forth. Our course took us initially to Land's End, then we were to turn starboard on to a north-easterly heading for RAF Lyneham in Wiltshire, then north-west to RAF Valley in Anglesey. He missed the first turn, and a few minutes later I asked him what he wanted me to do—turn or continue towards New York? After a few seconds of deliberation and hesitation he instructed me to turn right for Lyneham. All the time we were under the control of Southern Radar. The same thing happened at Lyneham, and after further prodding he had me turn north-west. As we proceeded towards Valley we started to have intermittent communications with Southern Radar and I casually asked him if it might be prudent to switch to an alternative frequency as we would soon be crossing airway Green One. I knew the frequency and had it written down on my chart, but he had to look it up in the Air Traffic Manual. In the nick of time he switched us to an alternative frequency for Southern Radar to control us through Green One. We were now approaching Valley and it was time to contact its approach control, but there was silence from the rear cockpit. I was now very concerned about this aviator's proficiency and promptly took charge of the situation, made the approach into Valley and then overshot to return to Yeovilton.

At my debrief of the flight I told the young Squadron Leader that I was not very impressed with his navigational prowess. He had been through the RAF navigational refresher course at Donnington, so this simple exercise should have been second nature to him. He had obviously not prepared his charts properly nor listed the necessary frequencies required en route. An *ab initio* navigation student would have coped better than he had. I wrote him up in his flight report docket and underlined everything in red, informing him that he was below par and under review. He seemed rather knocked sideways when I had finished, and personally I felt for him. Then I went round to the Staff Officer, Sammy Manchett, and asked for the student's previous reports, and a while later half a dozen one-inch-thick folders containing every single report dropped on to my desk. I spent the remainder of the morning reading through them. This RAF officer had performed in much the same way throughout his career, and I saw reason after reason why he should have been removed from flying duties. I then called in Wing Commander Jerry Cohu and apprised him of his future NavRad Leader's flying abilities; he was rather shocked, but he had heard rumours. I then took an unprecedented step: I told him that his future NavRad Leader would fly with him and that I would appreciate his opinion. After the flight Jerry Cohu came into my office and confirmed my opinions. I had now a major problem on my hands.

After Jerry's flight, I recalled the Squadron Leader to my office along with Gerry Kinch, my Senior Observer, and warned the student that he was under official review for possible suspension from the course. I then sent Gerry out of the office and had the student sit down while I talked to him like an old father. Personally, I was sure that there was more to this officer than he was admitting. Following some gentle persuasion, he confessed that he was having domestic problems and was travelling north to Edinburgh to see his wife and daughter every weekend. His marriage was rather rocky and the daughter was suffering from a illness the severity of which would probably turn her into an invalid. In addition, he was also studying for the MNIB Diploma, which the RAF considered equivalent to their Staff Course—a necessary requirement for promotion to Wing Commander rank. I asked him how on earth he expected to concentrate on his intensive flying course. I told him straight that he had to sort out his priorities and seriously to consider taking a week's leave to resolve his problems. Then I called in Jerry Cohu and told him what I had found out and asked him to have a private word with the Squadron Leader: he could have a week's leave, put his MNIB correspondence course aside for the time being and concentrate on finishing his Phantom course to a satisfactory standard.

Every week, as the Squadron Commander, I wrote up each student and forwarded the reports to Commander (Air), who then forwarded them to the Captain for comment. The Squadron Leader's report was underlined in red. First 'Wings' telephoned me and suggested that I was being rather too severe, then the Captain, Ray Rawbone, telephoned asking me to visit him as soon as possible. Ray Rawbone was left with no doubts about my opinion of this officer's ability—and that it was not my opinion alone. My position was that I was not prepared to lower the Royal Navy's standards to accommodate *anybody*. I returned to the Squadron via 'Wings' office to brief him on my conversation with the Captain. An hour later the telephone rang and Ray Rawbone spoke. He had had a lengthy conversation with the RAF appointers. They had said that the Squadron Leader was one of their best, etc., etc. and that we must have it all wrong. No, we were not wrong. Further, we were not questioning the student's ability as an officer—he was one of the best, in fact—but only his flying capabilities. The FAA was not prepared to lower its standards and would expect the RAF to behave in the same manner had the problem concerned an RN officer under their authority. The RAF finally accepted what the Captain was trying to tell them and arranged for the student to be removed from the course. When I broke the news to him, he, somewhat to my amazement, took it very calmly and said it was for the best. Jerry Cohu was also informed and declared himself in complete agreement with the action we had taken. So ended my first squadron command hurdle.

* * *

The RAF decided to hold a Phantom Symposium at RAF Coningsby, to which the Navy were invited to attend. Doug Borrowman telephoned me from DNAW and asked me to go with him: we would be the two RN representatives. It sounded as though it were going to be a very interesting gathering, and so it proved to be. The symposium lasted for two days and covered both air defence and ground attack. One of RAF Germany's F-4M squadron commanders, Wing Commander Bryant, spoke quite candidly concerning what he felt about the role expected of his squadron. His squadron, in the event of war, would be required to carry out low-level attacks against Warsaw Pact airfields, and he had asked what studies had been conducted to establish survivability rates. 'Well, I will tell you,' he said, 'because none has been done—less than 50 per cent of my squadron will return from such an attack! Do you think that that is right?' There was a great deal of seat-shuffling and coughing amongst the RAF Staff Officers from both the MoD and the Air Commands. Doug and I nodded our heads in approval, in agreement with Bryant's statement. He went on to say, 'We will do our duty, but don't expect many of us to return home!' It was the first time that I had ever heard an RAF officer stand up and say what was on his mind without fear of being booted out of his job, and it was a very refreshing occasion. He went on to be promoted to Air Rank: the RAF needed officers of his calibre.

While attending the evening cocktail party I fell in with Air Marshal Allison, an old friend whom I had first met when he was Wing Commander (Flying) at RAF Luqa in Malta in the 1950s. Whilst we were talking, the Chairman of the Armed Forces Pay Review Board, an Admiral, joined us and asked the Air Marshal what he thought about the proposed pay scales. The Air Marshal gave him an 'earful'.

'Why do people like me need to be paid so much?' was his response. 'I have a house, my kids have all left home to find their way in the world, and I have a reasonable pension to look forward to on my retirement from the RAF. So why do I need more?'

The poor Admiral was rather taken aback.

'Well,' he said, 'we thought you would all wish to be on a par with industry.'

'Not really, Admiral. They are overpaid for what they do.'

There the conversation ended and I drifted away to talk with other old Air Force friends.

Returning to Yeovilton, I sat down and set about preparing a report from the copious notes that had been taken at the symposium. It must have taken about six to eight weeks of writing, typing and correcting and then binding for distribution. Doug telephoned me from DNAW and said that they were very impressed with it. Then one morning, during Station Divisions, Admiral Sir John Treacher inspected the officers on parade. After passing me, he paused and came back.

'I liked your report, Mike. It was excellent.'

'Thank you, sir.'

When he had moved on I was prodded from both sides. What report?

'Oh, just a few pieces of paper that I had cobbled together and posted around the bazaars.'

'It must have been important for him to come back and praise you!'

'Oh, it was nothing really . . .'

* * *

Every summer the Fleet Air Arm displays itself by staging Air Days at all its air stations and facilities throughout the United Kingdom. Yeovilton, being the home and headquarters of the FAA, holds the largest event, and aircraft visit from Europe, NATO and France. Although it was an honour to display our aircraft in public and to let them know where their taxes were going, I was always fearful that something dreadful might happen. Memories kept flooding back of that day at Lossiemouth when my starboard engine failed following a dummy nuclear attack on the airfield; I had been lucky that the engine had failed when it did and not during the attack. The F-4 solo aerobatics were always carried out by Neville Featherstone, who was also in demand around the country throughout the summer weekends. The Squadron had to keep in store a series of small underwing panels, which were always popping off when he made negative 'g' manoeuvres. 767 Squadron's participation in the 1971 display included a dummy attack against the airfield culminating in the usual 'Balbo' formation flypast and stream landing. On this particular occasion the day was marred by the death of the RAF Harrier pilot. He had completed his display and had landed beside the tower. As he climbed out of the cockpit his ejection seat fired, throwing him on to the concrete of the hardstanding, where he received fatal injuries. Until that dreadful moment, it had been a wonderful event.

* * *

The next event was the annual inspection of RNAS Yeovilton by FONAC. The Admiral's staff would make a thorough inspection of all departments of the air station, checking paperwork and allocating tasks that were to be completed within a certain period of time, in order to establish whether the base was ready for war. Command inspections made by Admirals were preceded by Full Dress Divisions. All departmental Divisions would be mustered for inspection by the Admiral and his staff, and it was after Divisions that the fun and games would start.

I was standing out in front of my squadron when a runner appeared from Air Traffic Control with a message from Commander Middleton requiring my immediate presence in my Squadron Office. I handed over to Neville and doubled off to the Squadron, just a hundred yards away, to find out what the problem was. The previous day the Squadron had received its usual buff-coloured envelope in which resided the Squadron's inspection task: six F-4 aircraft were to be loaded with thirteen dummy 500-pound bombs apiece and then they would be flown on a strike mission against a splash target towed by HMS *Leander* south of Land's End.

The evolution had obviously been dreamt up by Lynn Middleton and George Oxley, the two Air Commanders on FONAC's staff. Lynn probably thought that, as I was a former Buccaneer AWI, the project would be second nature to me. In that respect he was right, but what he did not appreciate was that 767 Squadron was not equipped to the same standards as 892 Squadron. Being a training squadron, it had been equipped only to carry practice bombs or 2-inch rockets; it did not have the inventory for carrying 500- or 1,000-pound bombs or for loading the weapons or the test equipment. However, we were not to be beaten. We managed to scrounge from the ordnance section enough heavy bomb racks, and by modifying AVO meters the Squadron

292

ALO was able to produce a 'make-do' test meter for checking the aircraft's armament circuits. The racks and bombs were loaded the evening before the inspection, the flight crews were briefed and all that was needed was an up-to-date weather and air traffic brief before take-off. As far as I was concerned, my squadron was ready to go.

As I walked into my office, Lynn was waiting and he immediately tore into me, asking where I had been and accusing me of having got all my priorities wrong. It was obvious where I had been, standing as I was before him in dress uniform, sword and medals. When he had finished I quietly pointed out that it was Admiral's Divisions and that it was my duty to be with my squadron when the Admiral inspected it. The aircraft were standing by and the aircrews were briefed and ready to go when the signal to do so was given. I then pointed out that 767 Squadron was not equipped to carry either 500-pound or 1,000-pound bombs and that its maintenance ratings were not trained for loading these weapons nor did they have equipment to carry out the proper armament tests. If anything goes wrong, I told him, I would hold FONAC's staff responsible.

'You should have this equipment,' he retorted.

'No, sir. It is only held by 892 Squadron because only a limited amount was purchased by the RN—and you should know this.'

'How come you have loaded the weapons?'

'We scrounged everything and made do because I have an excellent group of officers and men that I can rely upon.'

My squadron had just returned from Divisions when the telephone rang. It was the Operations Room. 'Scramble the Phantoms against the prearranged target!' I shouted down the hall. 'Scramble the Phantoms!' Aircrew and men ran in all directions. Lynn and George left my office for the line while I remained in my office by the telephone, still breathing fire and brimstone.

The weather for the day was far from perfect, with low overcast and drizzle. None of my Phantoms was fitted with drop tanks and the aircraft's range was thus very limited—a problem aggravated of course by the high-drag load beneath the wings and fuselage. No tankers were available, and so the aircrews were instructed to land at RNAS Culdrose after the attack if they needed to refuel. The whole sortie should not have taken longer than an hour, and I waited with bated breath as the hands of the clock slowly turned.

Suddenly, out of the gloom, an aircraft came into view and landed, and eventually, after what seemed like a lifetime, the sixth aircraft touched down from a GCA. However, every aircraft had landed with hung-up ordnance. I called in on Sammy Manchett and had him prepare six A25 Aircraft Accident Forms and I sent off six aircraft accident/incident signals to all concerned, including MoD (PE) and the RAF. The air station AEO, ALO and Aircraft Inspection Officer all visited the Squadron to ascertain what might have gone wrong, and all the initial indications seem to point to the bomb distributor unit in the observer's cockpit. The problem would evolve into a major defect—and one that had to be put right quickly.

The Admiral's inspection finished on a jovial note. The Air Engineering Department had been required, as an exercise, to produce ornithopters of the type constructed at the turn of the century. There was general hilarity as these contraptions appeared and, like all their predecessors, collapsed in heaps of wire, fabric and wood. However, in the time allotted to them the AED had done a superb job: to be sure, some original thinking had gone into the designs and their manufacture!

I had hardly reached my office when the telephone rang again. Doug Borrowman was asking exactly what had happened and I gave him the facts. He was extremely angry that Lynn Middleton had placed the Squadron in such a position, but it had brought to light a serious defect in the Phantoms; the RAF had apparently experienced similar incidents both in Strike Command and in RAF Germany but they had been hushed up. Now the truth was out: the F-4Ks and Ms were suffering from a fundamental problem which downgraded their operational capability. The problem was given to A&AEE at Boscombe Down, who quickly established what we had diagnosed at Yeovilton—a defective bomb distributor in the rear cockpit. 767 Squadron had provided the evidence. The correction would not be in the form of a modified distributor but a completely new piece of equipment. It was, thankfully, manufactured in quick time and fitted to all British Phantoms, which were soon fully operational again.

* * *

As the autumn progressed the Squadron fell into a steady routine. However, before summer had faded for good I had Jerry Cohu organise a land-away navigation exercise 'anywhere in NATO Europe except Italy'. He asked me if it would be acceptable to fly to RDAF Vaerlose near Copenhagen and I told him that it was, and that he could use the facilities of 781 Squadron at Lee-on-Solent to transport gear and personnel. Italy was a non-starter: the Squadron had had an F-4 stranded at Naples—a NATO airfield—for about a month because a difficulty concerning customs and excise duty on a replacement generator could not be sorted out, an argument that, unbelievably, almost became a government-to-government issue.

Jerry planned the exercise very well. The 781 Squadron Sea Heron arrived and into it were loaded tool packs, minor spares, a dozen maintenance men and the most important item of all—the bonded whisky. The Heron took off ahead of the four F-4s and had arrived by the time the fighters flew in at about 1530. All the aircraft were parked at the far end of the airfield in a secure area out in the open so that they could be observed from the control tower throughout the weekend. The RDAF arranged transport to take us all to the hotel which Commander Jeff Maltby, the RN Attaché Officer, had booked for us. Following a reception at the British Embassy, again organised by Jeff, we all moved out into the city of Copenhagen to view the delights. On Saturday we were up with the lark, raring to see the sights in daylight. On the Sunday we all visited the Tivoli Gardens, had dinner and a few beers and then retired early so that we could be back at the airfield first thing in the morning. Monday dawned dull and overcast, and one felt as if something might go wrong. It did.

Jerry Cohu's starboard engine would not start, no matter what was tried. The odd part was exchanged but still it refused to fire. I instructed the other two crews to leave and then telephoned Yeovilton to advise them of the problem, whereupon the AEO organised a new starter and control unit and had it flown up by 781 Squadron. I briefed Jerry on what to do, arranged accommodation for those still left behind, started up my Phantom and departed.

The following day I had a call from Air Traffic Control. Jerry Cohu had been diverted into the Royal Netherlands Air Force base at Leeuwarden with an engine failure. He had been controlled by Clutch Radar* and had handed over to the approach control at Leeuwarden; although the base was closed for the day its approach radar and GCA were operating in case there was a NATO emergency. Leeuwarden was thick with fog, but the Dutch Air Force had given him an excellent talk-down on to the duty runway. As he had turned off the runway a tractor tug had been waiting for him, had clipped a towing arm on to his nosewheel and within minutes had whisked him away to an empty hangar, whereupon Dutch mechanics had begun to swarm all over the fighter. The engine bay was covered in oil and the shut-down engine had seized. Within a couple of hours the Dutchmen had lifted the engine out of the aircraft, ready for a new one.

RAF Germany did not have a spare engine—an admission that I found rather odd—so we had to send for a Spey from Yeovilton. DNAW, DNAE and FONAC all did their best to arrange air freight via the RAF out to Leeuwarden, but for some reason no C-130 was available: RAF Lyneham, the training base for Hercules crews, could not, apparently, be enticed into making a training flight to the Netherlands. All in all the RAF treated us in a very off-handed manner, and Jerry Cohu found it strange that he could not even obtain an aircraft through his Air Force contacts. The RAF was for unfathomable reasons being bloody-minded yet again: the Royal Navy would always bend over backwards to assist *them*; furthermore, we were training their F-4K crews!

Paddy Carr, the Squadron AEO, managed to find a 'Queen Mary', the spare engine was loaded on to it and over the following weekend, accompanied by a group of maintenance Chiefs and Petty Officers, it set off for Leeuwarden via Harwich and the Hook of Holland. The entourage arrived on Monday morning and with the help of the Dutch had the engine installed and running by late afternoon. Jerry called me and said that the Phantom was ready for its test flight, and I told the senior Chief to clear the aircraft en route back to Yeovilton. The Chief was instructed to take his time returning home but not to go wild. He and his team therefore spent a couple of days at Leeuwarden, during which the Royal Netherlands Air Force entertained them handsomely. Jerry arrived back at Yeovilton with a perfectly functioning engine after an hour and a half's flight.

* * *

---

* North-West European NATO air defence radar.

Another course of RN and RAF officers arrived after summer leave in 1971 and they were put through an intensive day- and night-flying experience. In mid-December I went down with a bad bout of asthma and was confined to the Sickbay for a few days, not being cleared for flying until the second week of January 1972. It had been a very cold and damp Christmas, but it was good to be in one's own home for the holidays. On Christmas morning we had visited the Mills family, who were now living at South Petherton, Somerset. While we were there the entire Marshall family turned up—now with fifteen children in all—and so with our two and the Mills' children there were twenty or so around the house.

At around this time Simon Idiens, Commander (Air) Yeovilton, had also gone down with a severe case of bronchitis and asthma, and he came good to fly on the same day as I did. There were three Phantoms on the line, one for my refamiliarisation flight and two spare aircraft. I telephoned Simon and asked him if he would like to fly and he accepted. He was briefed by the Senior Pilot, and we were both to fly the same area near Lundy Island, carrying out supersonic head-on interceptions against each other. We were briefed for some general handling, including slow flying, and then for recovery to Yeovilton on a GCA with some circuits and a landing—a straightforward sortie for both of us and one requiring no special aircraft handling skills. Simon's was the first aircraft away, but when I approached the runway take-off point for my pre-flight run-up checks Simon was having problems. I instructed him to go back for the spare aircraft while I proceeded out west to the training area.

Having carried out my general handling, I headed for Lundy Island and contacted the GCI Station at St David's in Pembrokeshire. Steve Park, my observer, tried contacting Simon but without success, so we entered into dummy attacks—that is, entering a dive to go supersonic—and then, after reaching 35,000 feet, pulling up to 45,000 feet flying at about 1.5 Mach. We had carried out two or three of these when Simon came on to the range. I told him we would have to return home because of a fuel shortage, and instructed him to carry out the part of the exercise as we had done. Steve then steered us home for a radar pick-up by Yeovilton and a feed into a GCA. I was about to enter the descent pattern when Yeovilton instructed me to hold my height, querying my remaining airborne time. I asked what the problem was and was immediately told that 'Wings' had ditched. Steve and I made an immediate about-turn, heading for south of Lundy, 'Wings' last known position, and climbing to our best height for our remaining fuel. Rod O'Connor was the instructor observer with 'Wings' and I was at a loss to understand what might have happened with such experience on board. The only information available was through St David's, who told us that both crew members had ejected and that therefore no further messages had been received from the aircraft. As Steve and I approached the search area we could hear one SARBE chirping away loud and clear so we homed in on it. An SAR Sea King had been scrambled from RNAS Culdrose and would be on scene within the hour; its crew were also picking up the SARBE. Our fuel was now becoming critical, so I decided to leave the search area and return to Yeovilton, where I would be of more use in the Operations Room. The Newtown Quay lifeboat had been launched and was on its way and a Nimrod had been scrambled from RAF St Mawgan.

When I taxied in and parked my F-4 Neville Featherstone and Gerry Kinch were there waiting for me. They had no more information other than that Rod O'Connor had been found by the Sea King's crew and had been recovered safely; 'Wings' was still, unfortunately, missing. Neither of them had any idea what might have happened. The wind was Force 9 and the sea was running heavily in the Lundy area. There was an added complication: darkness was fast falling, and 'Wings' had to be found soon or he would not survive, even in a dinghy and wearing an immersion suit. I was now very fearful that this accident was going to turn into a very unhappy event.

Flag Officer Plymouth despatched a frigate to Rod's recovery spot, which had now become the Search Datum Position. There was a ray of hope when a lady who lived near the cliffs opposite Lundy telephoned into to say that she had spotted what she thought was a body wearing a white helmet floating near the base of the cliffs. The Coastguard raced to the site but an extensive tideline search yielded nothing and they gave up and returned to their station.

Although there was a good moon that night, it was still blowing very hard around Lundy and the chances of finding Simon were diminishing by the minute. Rod O'Connor arrived back at Yeovilton at 2000, and we quizzed him about what had happened and why they had both bailed out. He said that the flight had gone according to plan except for the delay caused by the previous aircraft going unserviceable. They had started their high-speed descent, building up speed to go supersonic, but as they had pushed over into the initial descent both engines had flamed out. They had initiated a turn towards the coast, gliding at 250 knots, and had extended the RAT (ram air turbine) to provide electrical power for re-lighting the engines and to provide emergency hydraulic power. Several attempts had been made to re-light the engines but they had all failed. The tail drag 'chute had been deployed to lower the nose so that a better airflow could be made though the engine intakes, but this had done nothing to help them. They had then decided that if neither of the engines re-lit they would commence ejection at 16,000 feet. Rod had indeed ejected at that altitude and was positive that he saw Simon eject, his parachute deploying as the aircraft entered cloud at 10,000 feet. There was little more that he could add to his statement. He was sent to the Sickbay for a check-up, changed and was taken home to a very happy and thankful wife.

Simon had practised dinghy and parachute drill with us in the Yeovilton swimming pool on several occasions and it had been noticed that he had had difficulties disconnecting his parachute harness's Koch fasteners—the dual-pronged clips at the top of the harness that connected pilot to parachute. In order to release these fasteners one had to lift a spring-loaded flap and pull down on another flap to allow the prongs to slip out. Wearing chamois flying gloves, which become slippery in the water, it could be difficult to release the fasteners, and Simon had found this even more so: some years earlier he had received serious injuries to both his hands and fingers in a toboggan crash at St Moritz during an inter-services competition. If he had been dragged through the sea by his parachute in those Force 9 winds he may have had extreme difficulty releasing himself and it was quite conceivable that he had drowned.

There was another possibility, however: he may have never ejected from his cockpit in the first place. Although Rod thought he had seen Simon's parachute, he may have seen only the aircraft's tail 'chute through his legs as the aircraft disappeared into cloud. It was known that if the observer in a Phantom ejected first at high speed, the suction caused by the loss of the rear cockpit canopy could be sufficient to prevent the pilot's canopy leaving the front cockpit, thus making it impossible for the pilot to eject.

A Board of Inquiry was held at Yeovilton under the presidency of Commander 'Rip' Kirby, who had been 'Wings' at Lossiemouth. The Board found that the aircraft had been in good working order when it took off on its fatal flight, that the crew had done everything possible to re-light the engines, and that both the pilot and observer were fit to fly. The briefing had been carried out correctly in accordance with Standing Orders, and both crewmen were up to date in their emergency practices and simulator drills. Why the engines had flamed out was a matter of conjecture. Simon may have caused the flame-out by throttling back too fast at high altitudes while under negative 'g' loading. However, Rod had been adamant that Simon had throttled back slowly when the engines 'popped' and flamed out almost simultaneously. Just a short time beforehand I had carried out the same manoeuvre, though without experiencing problems with my engines. Perhaps Simon's engines had been set up too sensitively and any change in ambient air pressure or temperature or the shock waves across the engine intakes could have caused both to flame out. We will never know, because the wreck was never located, the airframe probably having smashed on impact with the sea and scattered over a wide area.

A couple of recommendations did come out of the inquiry. The first was that an urgent investigation be made into the Koch fasteners with a view to ensuring that they would be easier to release. Secondly, training flights— that is, those made by OFS students—should not be conducted over the sea in winds greater than Force 7. The second recommendation was easy to implement but the first required a meeting of air station representatives, DNAW, DNAE, MoD (PE) and the RAF. I represented 767 Squadron. The people from the Ministry were totally unaware of the problems that the US Navy had experienced with these fasteners and of the fact that lives had been lost because they had not operated properly. All sorts of modifications were proposed and discussed—even the introduction of small explosive charges to separate the pins. During my remaining time in 767 Squadron and my next job at MoD (Navy), however, I was unaware of any further investigation into the fastener problems and, as far as I can recall, none was ever made.

A couple of weeks after the accident a memorial service was held for Simon at Trent in Dorset. The retired Archbishop of Canterbury, Donald Coggan, an old friend of Simon's, officiated. The tiny church was filled to overflowing and there were very few dry eyes that afternoon. I have always found such services most disturbing and upsetting. I try to recall the good times I have shared with the deceased, and wonder how the relatives are going to fare once the reality of it all has sunk in. Both Simon and Debbie thoroughly enjoyed having dinner at our home, as we did at theirs just after Doug Borrowman had handed over to me.

When Simon had first been reported missing, the Air Station Padre and Surgeon Captain Mackie had driven over to Trent to call upon Debbie. As she opened the door she had known instinctively what was wrong and said, 'Oh God! Not again!' Debbie had been married once before to a naval aviator (also called Simon) and he had been killed in a Sea Vixen night-flying accident. She had now once again been deprived of a husband.

* * *

Yeovilton's next 'Wings' was to be Bob Northard, who had been an Upper-yardman (Air) with me in HMS *Indefatigable* all those years ago. Bob and I had been on the AWI course together and had attended the same interview for transfer to the General List; he had made it and I had not. Looking back, I believe, however, that I had, thus far, pursued a more interesting career than he. After much persuasion I managed to have him fly the F-4K, but I always had the feeling that he was not very happy flying and would rather have been a Seaman Officer driving ships. He did have command of a frigate, HMS *Tartar*, for a couple of years, mainly on the West Indies Station, where he thoroughly enjoyed himself. Bob had been lucky, and as far as I know had never had an air accident; I suppose that he considered himself fortunate and did not wish to tempt fate any further. Our lives would be interwoven again later in our careers.

* * *

Every year Yeovilton entertained the Senior Officers' War Course from the War College. A small air display was always put on for them and this included naval aircraft from other air stations. In one of these displays a Gannet from 849 Squadron, flown by a young Lieutenant pilot, with Lieutenant Commander 'Lofty' Nash, the Flight Commander, as the observer, gave a spirited display which ended in an accident. The pilot had made a couple of flybys, one with both engines running and the second with one engine shut down; then, with both engines again, he made a dummy carrier approach to the display runway. I was outside the Squadron hangar watching the display and the pilot's final turn on to the runway with undercarriage, flaps and hook down. However, as he turned through the last few degrees I was not happy about his landing configuration: the flaps did not appear to be all the way down. The aircraft struck some tree-tops short of the runway, crashed and started burning. The crash site was only a short distance from the airfield Fire Station. One of the very heavy fire and rescue vehicles thundered through the padlocked gate near the main road and was on the scene at about the same time as the SAR helicopter arrived with the huge powder extinguisher. 'Lofty' was out of the aircraft as soon as it came to a stop but the pilot was trapped in his cockpit and was released by firemen. He was badly injured and burned. The SAR helicopter crew together with the duty doctor and sickberth attendant rushed him to Yeovil General Hospital but he died en route. The pilot was a very likable young officer and I am sure that with time he would have gone a long way in the naval service. Apart from the odd bruise and scratch 'Lofty' was fine, but shaken considering the circumstances. He had been selected for promotion to Commander that very day. The Senior Officers' Course were very upset that a fellow officer had been killed demonstrating the capabilities of his aircraft to them, and so were all of the station personnel.

Lieutenant Commander Bob King was soon up from Lee-on-Solent with his Aircraft Accident Investigation team. I met him in the wardroom bar that evening and he asked me if I had been watching the display up to the moment of the crash. He then went on to ask me what I thought, and I told him that I was certain the aircraft only had take-off flap selected down. He confirmed that full flap had been selected in the cockpit, but that the switch was corroded and only take-off flap had been lowered, agreeing with my external observation. 'Lofty' had also realised that full flap had not been selected and had called to the pilot for full flap and more power. The aircraft had entered a high sink rate from which it did not have sufficient height in which to recover. Had the trees not been in the way, the aircraft might have bounced off the grass field, over the fence and on to the runway.

'Lofty' returned to Lossiemouth, was promoted Commander and took up an appointment in DNAW. As far as I can recall, he never flew again, and a few years later he retired from the Navy.

* * *

The time had arrived for the next European land-away navigation exercise. Four F-4s would visit Leeuwarden in the Netherlands. The usual planning was done by the senior student on course, and a Heron from 781 Squadron was once again organised to transport tool kits, spares and about ten or so maintenance personnel. The flight took off early one Friday afternoon and had landed at Leeuwarden by 1530. The aircraft were quickly stowed away in a spare hangar. By the time we had showered and eaten dinner, a call came through from 303 Squadron, who flew American F-104 Starfighters, inviting us to a party being held in their crew room. Jokes were cracked and presents were given to those who were leaving for other duties elsewhere and at about 2200 we decided to leave, have a good night's sleep and be prepared for a run into Amsterdam on Saturday morning. On Sunday, following a late breakfast, we strolled around the local area. We were amazed that 90 per cent of the population spoke good English.

On Monday morning we were all up with the lark and down at the hangar by 0800. Our four fighters were neatly lined up and ready for us. However, there was a panic on when we arrived: 303 Squadron had just lost an F-104—

although, thankfully, the pilot was safe, having ejected from his aircraft. He had been carrying out cannon-firing against a towed banner target and had collided with it, and the towing cable had ripped off part of his starboard wing. The local SAR helicopter had recovered the pilot, rather wet and with his pride dented.

After a meteorological and flight briefing, I led my aircraft back to Yeovilton, taking off to the north-east and with a left-hand turn on to a westerly heading, climbing to 31,000 feet. No sooner had I rolled out on the climb heading than I heard a 'Mayday' emergency call. Believing it to have come from my No 4 aircraft, I initiated a tell-off but finally No 3 called in to say that he was alongside safe and well. The distress call had come from another NATO aircraft, which was by then being controlled by Clutch Radar. The return flight back to Yeovilton, apart from the initial hiatus, was uneventful and we landed safely. Within the hour all four aircraft were airborne once more on OFS course sorties.

A new OFS course joined after Easter 1972, as did two future COs for 892 Squadron, Chris Hunneyball and Bill Pepe. They had both gone through 738 Squadron at about the time I was serving in the Lossiemouth Fighter School, and at a later date Bill had completed the AWI's course. It had been decided that Chris Hunneyball would be the first to take command of 892 Squadron, relieving the current CO Nick Kerr. Chris had been elevated from Senior Pilot to CO when Lieutenant Commander Brian Davis had tendered his resignation; this was at the time I relinquished my LSO appointment to *Ark Royal*. The Senior Observer of 892 Squadron, Peter Goddard, had been selected ahead of his Squadron CO for promotion to Commander's rank. Quite naturally, Brian was put out by this resounding slap in the face, while Peter was so embarrassed that he really did not know what to do with himself. Both the Captain and Commander (Air) were up in arms over the decision and told the Admiralty that they had made a very serious blunder in their promotion selections, but there was no backing down. This OFS course was to be the last for 767 Squadron before it disbanded at the end of July 1972.

* * *

The squadron lost two F-4Ks during its commission. The second accident involved FONAC's new Staff Captain, Bill Hawley. Bill was scheduled for five flights in the aircraft but in the event he flew only one. With Lieutenant John Love as observer, he proceeded to the ORP to go through his pre-take-off checks, one of which was to ensure that the pneumatic pressure gauge showed 800psi and building; the RAT required more than 800psi to blow it out into the airstream over the top of the fuselage and a minute or two soon established whether the pressure was at the correct level. However, Bill did not positively establish that the pressure gauge was building and his instructor observer did not double-check either before Bill roared off down the runway.

While carrying out low-speed handling at about 25,000 feet south of Lundy Island, Bill had both of his engines flame out. He deployed the RAT, but although the compartment doors opened the generator did not flick out into the airflow. He therefore had no electrical power to relight his engines and at 10,000 feet both crewmen ejected. John was soon located and picked up by an SAR helicopter, but it was an hour or so later before Bill was found. John was wearing an immersion suit but Bill was just wearing coveralls, which did little to protect him from the very cold water; he said afterwards that had the helicopter not arrived when it did he would have thrown in the towel because of the cold. After this accident it was ordered that all aircrew were to wear immersion suits when flying over the sea until the end of June, or if the surface wind was likely to be in excess of Force 5.

Bill was the second senior officer to have been involved in an aircraft accident over a period of two years. The third was Commander David Dunbar-Dempsey, who was killed in a mid-air collision. 'D-D', as he was known, was the SNO at RAF Linton-on-Ouse. He had decided to go flying in his Sea Prince, a twin-engine communications aircraft, around the local area. Out of the blue a Jet Provost trainer with an instructor and student on board collided with his aircraft. 'D-D' had managed to pull on his parachute and was at the rear door when his aircraft hit the ground; the Jet Provost crashed and both occupants were killed also. It was decided after much consultation between DNAW and FONAC that senior officers of Commander's rank and above should not be allowed to fly solo unless they put in at least ten hours a month plus simulator flights. It was a sensible decision.

* * *

Although I had not been informed of my next appointment in writing, I had been told privately that I would be going to DNAW as one of the Fixed-Wing Staff Officers in Doug Borrowman's section. I had not hitherto held a Staff Officer's appointment and neither had I attended the Staff Course. The DNOA (X) Appointing Officer asked me if I needed to do the Staff Course, and I quickly said no; he told me that this was the opinion of DNOA (X) also. A stint in a headquarters staff appointment was considered far more important than the average Admiral's Staff Officer's chair. I would be working in London, and May and I began to look for a new home.

Early in 1972 May noticed that the former Somerset Police Chief's residence in Yeovil was being auctioned. It was on the outskirts of the city and alongside the road to Yeovilton, and therefore ideally situated for commuting either to Yeovilton or to London, and for Naomi's school; Dominique, at this stage in her life, was still a crawler. We obtained the keys from the estate agent and spent an hour going over it with a fine-tooth comb. The guide price was £9,500: we agreed that I would pull out at £11,500 and I was outbid. A little later I drove the family over to East Sussex to see Mum and Dad at Camber. Passing through Bexhill-on-Sea, we noticed a large house for sale. We called in at the estate agents, were loaned the keys and before we knew it had another property.

I quickly visited the Married Quarters' Officer and informed him that we would be vacating our Ilchester quarters within the month. There was a tremendous amount of work to be done at our new home, but when I arrived back at Bexhill for Easter leave everybody was well and truly settled in and all the services had been connected: all that was required was a plumber (Uncle Will) to sort out the bathroom and boilers for the hot water and radiators. Our intention was to turn the place into a small bed and breakfast guest house. We had three spare bedrooms, and during the summer, while we were renovating the place, we had our first guests. Most of them would come either from the Netherlands or from Germany, and May quickly gained a reputation for providing a good service with excellent meals.

I was personally very pleased that we had bought St Norbert's, as were May and the girls. It offered us a home in which we could entertain our own family and enjoy ourselves over the winter months when we were not busy with guests. It was a far better house than that we had originally viewed at Yeovil. We would keep it for nearly twenty-five years.

* * *

It was almost the end for 767 Squadron, and arrangements were put in hand to disband it by the end of July 1972. I had received no instructions or orders from anybody as to what I was supposed to do with the aircraft, equipment, officers and men. Nothing was received from the Air Station, from FONAC, from DNAW, from DNAE, from DNOA (X) or from the Draft Office at HMS *Centurion* at Gosport. All I knew was that four of my aircraft had to go to RAF Leuchars to form the RN's F-4K Training Flight. I initiated a Disbandment Movement Order and issued it as a 'preliminary' to alert everybody that 767 Squadron would be disbanded in late July 1972. Suddenly the whole world woke up and wanted to know what was going on; had I not done anything, I am sure that 767 Squadron would still be resident at Yeovilton to this day! Everybody was probably so involved in relocating 892, 849, 809 and 707 Squadrons that 767 was totally forgotten about, even though the RN Training Flight was in the process of being formed at Leuchars. 892 Squadron would also be relocated at Leuchars when disembarked from *Ark Royal*.

The first SNO at RAF Leuchars was to be Commander (AE) (P) Alan Tarver, who had been awarded the George Cross for trying to save his observer's life in a crashing Sea Vixen fighter. He was a very affable young officer who had been promoted early, but he would retire from the Navy after this appointment and enter the world of finance. On the disbandment of 767 Squadron, 707 Commando HQ flight from RNAS Culdrose would move into our old accommodation and offices. My office was scheduled for use by HRH Prince Charles, who had been appointed to the Commando helicopter OFS course.

Flying training continued at quite a pace in 767 Squadron right up to the end. The Squadron even took part in 'Capricorn', an Air Defence of Great Britain exercise. We were required to have three F-4Ks and a spare available, armed with live Sparrow and Sidewinder missiles and carrying three drop tanks. Once again nobody appreciated the fact that the Squadron did not have the necessary modifications to carry Sparrows, but we 'frigged' the system yet again and took off with four dummy missiles. The Squadron was split into two watches and I took the midnight-to-0600 duty with the Senior Observer, Gerry Kinch. We were all dozing in our armchairs when the Operations Room Officer issued a 'Scramble' order at 0330. Three aircraft were airborne within five minutes, climbing into the first light of the day. None of us had flown with three fully laden drop tanks, and even with the full power of their Spey engines the aircraft required the entire length of the runway to become airborne and climbing speeds were lower. We flew over London under Southern Radar, heading for our three independent CAP stations over the North Sea.

Gerry and I had a CAP station not far from Heligoland, where we sauntered at 20,000 feet in a large left-hand orbit. Suddenly we were given three 'bogeys' heading south out of Norway, descending to low level. Gerry was quick off the mark and locked up the lead target, and I rapidly made a simulated head-on 'look-down' Sparrow missile firing, assessing it as a 'kill'. Gerry then swung me around on the next two targets and we shot them down. By this time we were fairly low on fuel and the GCI station near Torness vectored us on to a waiting Victor tanker aircraft. As we approached, two RAF Lightning fighters pulled away from the tanker having just been refuelled, and we slotted into the starboard wing station, took a full load of fuel and then returned to our CAP station. Further north, 767's two other fighters were also having success, although one had to divert into Leuchars with an emergency. After nearly three and a half hours on patrol we were diverted to RAF Binbrook for refuelling and re-arming.

We taxied up to the visiting aircraft dispersal and were met by a group of RAF maintenance men who had no idea how to refuel or re-arm an F-4, so I had the other crew turn our aircraft around while Gerry and I visited the Operation Rooms to discover what exactly was going on. The Group Captain in command in the Operations Room did not know what was required of us and suggested that we all go to the Officers' Mess for breakfast. At that stage of the exercise we needed no persuading—and the RAF certainly know how to serve up bacon and eggs! We then received a call from the Ops Room to say that the exercise had been completed and that we were free to return to Yeovilton. It was now 1230 and within half an hour we were airborne for Yeovilton, in a very tired state. Back at base I fell on to my cabin bunk and was soon fast asleep, not waking wake until about 2000. We had all been on watch far too long, and should probably have stayed over at Binbrook. Nevertheless, the exercise taught us a great deal about air defence and flight safety.

* * *

The summer of 1972 was hot and seemed to drag on and on. The Squadron took part in its last air show displays at Yeovilton and Culdrose and flew on its final European Navex, this time at RAF Bruggen in West Germany. The navigation exercise was notable for two incidents; first, we were unable to obtain clearance from Customs & Excise to take our usual allowance of duty-free drink from Yeovilton; and secondly 781 Squadron lost a Heron in the Irish Sea.

Our flight to Bruggen went smoothly enough. The RAF Officers' Mess put on a small party for us, and we met up with Group Captain George Black, who had been on exchange with the FAA at Lossiemouth flying Sea Hawks in 801 Squadron; George had requested a transfer to the RN, but the RAF were having none of it. He was eventually promoted to Air rank, and would probably have reached Flag rank had he transferred to the Navy. On the Monday morning we were delayed by thick fog at Yeovilton and along the south coast of England, and while we were sitting out on the Officers' Mess patio drinking coffee and waiting to fly back to Yeovilton an RAF officer mentioned that the Navy had lost an aircraft in the Irish Sea. He had heard that the aircraft had ditched between Liverpool and the Isle of Man, but that all the crew and passengers had been rescued. It could have only been the Monday 'clipper' making its rounds. I did not know it at the time, but this accident was to be a thorn in my side when I joined DNAW.

At 1300 I gave Yeovilton a call and spoke to the Duty Lieutenant Commander (Flying) to find out if the fog had lifted and whether it was safe for us to return. He said that the fog was slowly dispersing, and that if we took off right away it should be gone by the time of our return. We were airborne within the hour and soon back at our own dispersal, which was now basking in bright sunshine. Our Heron arrived about three hours later.

The last course was virtually complete and ready to ship out to 892 Squadron or the holding unit at RAF Leuchars: all that was required now was to wind down 767 Squadron for the last time. Equipment, aircraft and personnel were readied for their transfer to Leuchars, to the air station or to the RN Repair Yard at Sydenham. Four aircraft—the latest machines, with the highest modification state—would go to the new RN Flight at Leuchars and the remaining aircraft would be flown to Sydenham for extensive rework and upgrading. A disbandment parade was held at which FONAC gave the farewell speech, and there followed a hangar party for all the Squadron personnel and their wives, sweethearts, girlfriends and families.

* * *

This was a very sad time for me. I hoped that I had left a lasting impression of having done a good job. I had had my ups and downs during my tenure of command, but I believe that there were far more of the former than of the latter. May, Naomi and I had made many good friends at Yeovilton, and we were going to miss them all; Dominique, of course, was still too young to appreciate anything. No doubt I had made some enemies at Yeovilton; to think otherwise would have been foolish and unrealistic. I had thoroughly enjoyed doing the job I liked most—teaching others to go about flying a fighter aggressively but in a safe manner. Had we gone to war again I felt sure that those who had been brought through 767 Squadron would have acquitted themselves well in combat. Some of my instructors I would see again in other appointments, some would leave the naval service and one would die in an unnecessary F-4K accident at Leuchars. They were all my friends and brother officers, and I would like to think that a close bond exists amongst us to this day.

The last air show in which 767 participated was at Yeovilton. The weather was far from good for the airborne display and most of the big jets did not fly. The usual post-event cocktail party was held on the tennis courts in a huge marquee. Partying went on all evening, moving to the wardroom about 2000 where a buffet dinner was available for all officers and their guests. I had invited May along and had booked us in at a hotel in Yeovil. By 2.00 a.m. the pair of us were back in our room and fast asleep.

* * *

Before leaving Yeovilton finally for the MoD (Navy) I flew to Lossiemouth for the disbandment of 764 Squadron, then under the command of Bob Edward. The last AWI course was just completing—thereby bringing to an end an era of advanced weaponry—and Bob had decided that it might be a good idea to throw a party for all past and present AWIs and distribute old course reports. The 764 Squadron wardroom dinner was a great occasion, with the dining room filled to capacity. The feeling was that, with the disbandment, the Navy was having one of its arms chopped off; the heady days at Lossiemouth were certainly coming to an end. Speeches were made, a few tears ran down cheeks, and with the demise of 764 another chapter in the story of the Fleet Air Arm came to a close.

Once 767's aircraft had been flown away to either Leuchars or Sydenham, it was just a question of moving the ground equipment, some to Leuchars and the remainder elsewhere within the air station, and giving the Squadron premises a thorough clean. The CO of 707 Squadron arrived, took charge of the keys and moved in with his team of officers and men. My old office was quickly redecorated for Prince Charles, his medical officer and detective. Sam Manchett and his Staff Office team remained in place and became the new Staff Officer for 707 Squadron. Then it was time for me to leave. With my mess bill paid, I quickly made my rounds of the air station and FONAC, bade them all farewell and drove off east for Bexhill and home, wondering what awaited me at the Ministry. At least I had three to four weeks' leave to look forward to—and there were plenty of jobs waiting for me at home!

— 26 —

Terra Firma

A LL MY LIFE I have been one of those people who like to be back at work a week after starting leave. Although there was much to do about St Norbert's, I knew that there would be many an occasion when I could work on the place in my spare time. By September 1972 I was more than ready to start my new job at DNAW. A week beforehand, May and I had visited various 'bed-sits' in and about Central London but could not settle on any one in particular. In the meantime Malcolm Carver offered me the use of a spare room in his London flat and I gladly accepted.

I joined DNAW on a Monday morning with great trepidation, wondering what was expected of me. Doug Borrowman would be my immediate boss, as the Commander in charge of the Fixed-Wing Section in DNAW. Lieutenant Commander Mike Darlington was FW2, the second officer on Doug's team responsible for fixed-wing projects and the day-to-day running of fixed-wing aircraft, and for future policy. It was Mike whom I would be relieving, and with less than a week before the handover there was barely enough time in which to meet all the military and civilian personnel in the MoD and outlying areas with whom I would be working. He and I went to BAC at Warton to see the Canberra T.22 project for the FAA, to RAE Bedford, to RAE Farnborough, to MoD (PE), to DNAE and to numerous other places and establishments throughout the country. We spent evenings going through the various documents, which he locked away in his filing cabinet. Then he introduced me to MoD Security. I had the riot act read to me, watched all the while through half-closed eyes, and left feeling like a criminal. After some tidying up I had a nice clear desk and filing cabinet, and Mike departed for his leave and next appointment, the command of a minesweeper.

My first three months were very much a time of learning. I took to wandering around the Ministry to meet people, especially the civil servants and my opposite numbers in the RAF departments on the same floor as DNAW. The first task in which I became involved was the Canberra project. A cockpit layout meeting was scheduled at BAC Warton. The first instrument panel had been manufactured and installed in the first 'production' aircraft, a former RAF photo-reconnaissance aircraft. The Navy had purchased several

307

of these PR Mk 7s to replace the ageing Sea Vixens flown by Airwork Services at Yeovilton for Direction Officer training and to act as missile trainers and radar targets for the Fleet. The aircraft had to be modified to meet the RN's requirements, which consisted of altering the nose to take the Buccaneer's radar system and installing electronic equipment for EW training in the bomb bay, formerly used to accommodate cameras and flare packs.

I had not flown either of the Canberras at Little Rissington on my QFI's course because one was in deep maintenance and the other had been wrecked during a landing accident with a Luftwaffe Colonel at the controls; now I was expected to sit in the pilot's seat and offer my opinion, and approval, of the new instrument panel. As I sat down I imagined myself flying this aircraft at low level, perhaps into a setting sun. I did not feel at all happy. The Sea Vixen's radar altimeter had been selected for giving indications of height above the sea, and it was hidden away in the bottom left-hand corner of the panel. To make matters worse, it was obscured by the left 'spectacle' of the control column, and therefore by the pilot's left fist. Moreover, there were no height-limiting lights indicating whether one was flying at the correct altitude above the sea, as fitted in the Buccaneer bomber. Such a modification allowed the pilot to fly 'heads up', knowing that he would be safe and could see exactly where he was going. I had a vision of someone flying himself, his crew and his aircraft into the sea and I said quite candidly that the system was unsafe. There was an immediate reaction from BAC and MoD (PE).

'You can't say that!' was the anguished retort. 'We've had people from Boscombe Down checking the aircraft, and they are perfectly happy.'

'Sorry,' I said. 'I will not put my signature to this.'

'But it has taken months to draw out this panel and manufacture it, and we will now have to go through the whole process again, placing the project back several months.'

'Well, keep the panel and put the instrument together with its limiting lights on top of the cockpit coaming—but I will not accept the modification as it is, and that is final. And, by the way, replace the altimeter with that used in the Buccaneer: the Sea Vixen instrument is not good enough for the task envisaged for this aircraft.'

On my way back to London I was quite worried that I had delayed the project by several months. Perhaps I was wrong; no, I was right. Flight safety came first, and I was not going to be held responsible for allowing a stupid thing like this to slip though the net. When I arrived in London I told Doug Borrowman what I had done and he wholeheartedly agreed with me. However, this was not to be the end of the Canberra's problems.

One day I was idly reading through some RAF signals concerning the Canberra when I came across one dealing with the failure of its rear-fuselage longerons; in fact, the RAF repair centre at St Athan in South Wales had found that nearly all the Canberras going through rework had several broken. I telephoned MoD (PE) and they in turn contacted Warton: all our new aircraft had the same problem. This meant that the rear fuselage would have to be de-skinned and have stronger longerons inserted, adding to the time before the first aircraft could come off the line. A few weeks later I intercepted another RAF signal, this time concerning a failure in the Canberra's crew cabin. The Air Force had experienced several incidents of explosive decompression following a rupture of the metal skinning: apparently, after so many thousands of pressure inflations and deflations, it had fatigued and cracked. BAC had a Canberra cabin structure on a test rig at Warton and were putting it through high-speed inflations and deflations under simulated flight conditions. It failed, but they could recommend a modification to eliminate any future failures. Hence there was a further delay to the T.22 entry into service.

A final meeting was held by MoD (PE) on the Canberra T.22 prior to its first test flight in early 1973. I asked if the instrument panel had been modified as requested in 1972 and there was a deadly hush in the room. Both MoD (PE) and BAC asked what this proposed modification might be. I could not believe my ears. The company denied all knowledge of this modification, at which I rose and voiced my anger.

'The BAC representative at the top of the table knows all about the modification,' I fumed, 'and it was recorded in the minutes of the meeting held at Warton last year!'

'Oh,' came the response, 'Boscombe Down decided that they were happy with the arrangements—it was to stay as it was.'

At this I exploded. 'The Naval Department will not accept this aircraft unless the modification is installed. It's a question of flight safety. Boscombe Down does not have to fly the aircraft operationally. The Navy does, and it will not accept something which, under certain flight conditions, is considered a serious flight safety hazard!'

The meeting was now in uproar and the Chairman called for a recess so that each department could regroup. DNAE was perfectly happy with my stand and eventually MoD (PE) accepted it. A compromise was reached in which the aircraft would be height-limited until the new instrument panel was made available together with a repositioning of the radar altimeter indicator and limit lights. However, I made it very clear that this modification was to be on the fourth and subsequent aircraft off the production line and that the first three were to be modified within six months. This was accepted and the meeting closed, and by the end of 1973 the Canberra T.22 began to arrive at Yeovilton.

* * *

With the coming of the New Year a great many new projects would begin at DNAW. The largest of these would be the Sea Harrier Staff Target. Doug Borrowman would be the Project Officer and Lieutenant Commanders Dusty Milner and Bob Edward from the Future Policy Section would be his two assistants. My workload within DNAW would more than double over the next few months. There was also a change in our offices. Together with Peter Matthews, I moved around the corner into the main corridor next to Nigel Greer-Rees, who was responsible for air armaments.

One morning I arrived at work very early at 7.30 and, much to my surprise, found Nigel in his office, smartly dressed as if he were going for an interview.

He appeared very unhappy and depressed, however, and I asked him if there was anything that I could do. He thanked me, said he was going away on vacation for about two weeks and asked whether I could look after his department during his absence. I quite naturally agreed and he showed me his files and gave me the key to the filing cabinet, remarking that there was nothing of importance that needed immediate attention. He finished his coffee and cigarette quickly and then left. However, I did notice that his hand was shaking quite badly.

Peter Matthews was surprised at Nigel's behaviour, as was the Assistant DNAW, Captain Dave Stanley. In fact, Nigel had taken two weeks' leave without requesting it, and nobody knew exactly where he had gone. Later on in the day, when I had an hour to spare, I started going through the filing cabinet, and what I found appalled me. File after file marked 'Urgent', some going back several months, had received no attention. Dave Stanley ordered me to drop everything else to do with fixed-wing projects and concentrate on clearing Nigel's backlog. The whole of my desk was quickly cluttered with weapons and armament files, but by about 7 o'clock that evening I had managed to clear a good many of them for onward transmission to the next addressee. What really worried me was the fact nobody had raised any queries about the progress of these files. DNAW himself telephoned DNOA (X) for a temporary replacement for Nigel until his return, and Joe Billingham, who was on leave, was temporarily appointed to Nigel's vacant chair.

The two weeks passed and there was no sign of Nigel. Then one morning Peter Matthews and I boarded a train at Waterloo station for Farnborough to attend a navigation equipment conference. I had bought a copy of the *Daily Telegraph* and Nigel's name caught my eye. It was in the obituary columns. It appeared that he had died following an accident in Dartmouth, where he had lived with his wife. It was not until several months later, while May, the girls and I were staying with the Todds, who lived near Dartmouth, that I would learn the truth.

Nigel had had serious domestic problems, which had disturbed him greatly, and he had been admitted to the psychiatric section of the Naval Hospital in Plymouth. Somehow he had managed to leave the hospital and make his way on foot to a field not far from the Todds' Devon home, where Jonathan and his two boys found him entangled in briars. He was badly cut and in an awful state both mentally and physically. Jonathan took him home and called an ambulance. Nigel was eventually discharged fit from the hospital, and he returned to his home in Dartmouth. One morning he decided to trim the branches of a tree outside his home, which were overhanging the road. He elected for some unknown reason to sit on the wrong side of the branch he was cutting off, it broke and he fell to the hard pavement, where he sustained serious injuries. He was then run over by a car and killed.

The death hit us all badly. Nigel had been a fine officer and, as a Midshipman, one of the pages to Prince Philip at the Coronation of Queen Elizabeth II. He had survived a terrible night injured in both leg and arm in the snowy Cairngorm Mountains after ejecting from his Scimitar jet fighter in a supersonic dive. He had been promoted early to Commander and was obviously a rising star, destined to be a Captain at least, and would have gone on from DNAW to command a frigate. However, his marriage had run into difficulties, and instead of seeking help and advice he had allowed his marital problems to fester in his mind, bringing about a mental breakdown. Had Nigel confided in me, or in anyone else for that matter, an appalling tragedy might possibly have been averted.

* * *

Commander Dave Howard was eventually appointed to take over Nigel's job and Joe Billingham decided to retire from the Navy. When Dave Howard arrived the Sea Harrier project was well under way. I was glad that the Directorate now had an officer to run the air armaments section, but with the Sea Harrier project gaining momentum I was soon inundated with further work. First of all I took on Doug Borrowman's FW1 job temporarily, and then found myself doing both Dusty Milner's and Bob Edward's jobs in addition to my own as FW2. One day Dave Stanley came into my office, saw the huge piles of files and documents on my desk and was flabbergasted. Fortunately, many of these papers required merely a quick comment or even nothing at all before being passed on out of the Directorate, and I was therefore able to keep abreast of most things. However, my days were long. I usually started at 7.30 in the morning and did not finish until about 9 in the evening. It all began to tell, and so I had a quiet word with Doug. He managed to twist DNOA (X)'s arm, and Lieutenant Commander Peter Burgess was appointed to help out in the Fixed-Wing Department. I moved into Malcolm Carver's office where Milner and Edward used to work, and soon found myself running Malcolm's desk when he was off sick. The workload in DNAW was at that time extraordinarily heavy, and there were simply insufficient officers available to tackle it properly.

The first project that I became acquainted with in the Future Policy Section was that of writing a joint RN, RAF and Army Staff Target for a night vision device to be fitted to helicopters. I had never written a Staff Target before and had little idea where to start. Malcolm gave me a copy of the MoD Manual for preparing and writing both Staff Target and Staff Operational Requirements papers. After studying this huge tome for a couple of days, I sat down and sketched out a vague draft of what was wanted by the three Armed Forces. Malcolm gave me some leads on whom to visit for information so that I could spell out the requirements and capabilities of the equipment.

My first visit was to Shell Mex House in the Strand in London. The RAF had a directorate located in this vast building which dealt in night vision and low-light devices. It transpired, however, that they were interested only in laser-marking for their Jaguar strike fighters. I then moved on to MoD (PE) and did no better there, but they arranged for me to visit RAE Farnborough, where there was a department devoted to these devices; it had already made flights in a Hunter T.7 jet trainer fitted with an LLTV sensor. However, they had hit a problem: the sensor could not identify electricity-grid cables slung between pylons. At low level and at high speed, these of course presented a very serious hazard, and there was, as a result, a great deal of development work ahead.

While at Farnborough I was informed of research work being carried out at RRE Christchurch, not far from Bournemouth, so I arranged to visit this establishment and found a very helpful team who were prepared to loan me image intensifiers for trials at sea. They were developing these systems and also night-vision goggles for use in various fighting vehicles and helicopters as well as for the soldier in the field to use with his rifle. These devices did require a degree of light in order to function effectively: on a totally overcast night with no moon, for example, they would not work at all. They put on displays for me in specially darkened test huts and I was amazed at the capability even of the simplest of the image intensifiers. The staff at Christchurch gave me a great deal of information for inclusion in my Staff Target, and I left feeling that at last I was getting somewhere.

My next stop was RRE Malvern in Worcestershire, the establishment responsible for the development of all radar and anti-submarine defence systems. At that time the scientists there were involved in the research and development of FLIR devices for detecting ships, aircraft and vehicles in overcast and other bad-weather conditions. They had developed a ground-mounted device which could be used to investigate ships at long distances, and here was something right up my street. The RN had an Air Electrical Engineer Officer, Commander Don Ross, based at Malvern and directly associated with this particular project. The prototype equipment had reached the stage of being tested, and a trial was to be conducted at Portland. Our man at Malvern kept me informed of progress and a few weeks later I was advised of the date and cordially invited to attend.

While at Malvern, I was shown some very good FLIR film taken during an earlier test at Lulworth Cove, just to the east of Portland, and using inshore minesweepers and the cruiser HMS *Blake*. It was night time and the cruiser was blacked out and showing no navigation lights but suddenly there was a brilliant flare on the bridge starboard wing. Challenged about their darkened ship, the cruiser replied that it was complete. The test officer told the ship to check the starboard wing area, and standing there was a sailor having a quiet smoke. When he drew on his cigarette it looked, to a FLIR device, like a shining beacon: the increased glow could be seen from eleven miles away.

The second test at which I was an observer was also most impressive, the performance of the 'breadboard' test equipment passing all expectations. Oil tankers steaming up-Channel could be seen from 'The Bill' over eleven miles away. Moreover, the oil bunkers, engine room and other areas where steam was being used could readily be identified. Warships could be recognised easily by type and class, just by means of the 'hot spots' around the vessels. Helicopters flying around the ranges could also be recognised and identified by type.

Back at the Directorate I briefed DNAW himself and Malcolm about my visits, and I felt that we were well of the way to having something available within the next couple of years. However, I was very concerned by one thing: there were four major establishments working independently for the Navy,

Army and Air Force on very similar equipment, the effort being quadrupled and involving an obvious waste of money. I mentioned this to the naval scientist working with me and he was appalled. All these research and development establishments could be relocated under one directorate, leading to a co-ordinated effort and programme: one sensor head could quite easily be used for all the aircraft, and developed for use in ships and fighting vehicles. My naval scientist could see the logic of the argument and arranged for me to see the Director of Guided Weapons and Electronics, a civil servant of equivalent four-star rank. I spent two and a half hours with this gentleman arguing my case in a logical and straightforward way, but I could see that I was not getting anywhere. He smiled, deliberated and finally advised me that a review was in progress to 'rationalise' the present arrangements, but that it would be at least nine months before any recommendations could be made. When I left his office I felt as if I had been given the brush off—and indeed I had, because when I returned to DNAW four years later the only change had been the amalgamation of RRE Christchurch with RRE Malvern. It was obvious that the then DGWE had no intention of reducing his empire while he was in office. At one stage there was even talk of moving RRE Malvern to RAE Bedford, which would have made a lot of sense. The only serious side-effect of any changes would fall upon those local people who would have to uproot themselves or be out of a job.

My Staff Target had by now grown from a few scrap pages to a document which was, in draft form, nearly three quarters of an inch thick. After many revisions and corrections, I finally produced the first draft for circulation to all directorates, departments and establishments. It had taken me about three months to reach this stage, which was, in the circumstances, not too bad for a 'slow coach', especially as it was my first project of this nature. Now I had to wait for the comments to arrive, although in the meantime I was scribbling my own amendments and additions.

By this stage it had been decided that a further office shuffle would take place. I moved back into my old corridor office with Peter Matthews, and what had been the 'Odds and Sods' office became Malcolm's and Wally Hall's. We had a connecting door so that we could stay in close contact with each other. The Sea Harrier project team moved *en bloc* into Malcolm's and Wally's old office.

Another project gathering speed was the Sea King replacement ASW helicopter, eventually known as the Merlin. Ben Bathurst was hard behind this project, an international collaborative effort involving Westland and Agusta of Italy.

* * *

One of my other many tasks was the so-called Major Fields of Research. This comprised half a dozen areas of interest to the FAA for the development of improved airborne equipment. One area was devoted to LLTV, FLIR, radar, gyros, navigation systems and anti-submarine equipment. It was a most interesting task, and one calling for a great deal of time and energy. Much of

313

the research was associated with my Staff Target for an LLTV device for helicopters.

I was about to get into hot water again, this time with the civil servants who controlled these Fields of Research. DGWE's civil servants called a meeting to discuss the agenda for a conference to be held at Farnborough for the following year's aims, objectives and expenses. Together with the Army and Air Force representatives I joined the meeting, which was held in Shell Mex House. The agenda was quite straightforward until we reached the subject of allocating £2.5 million for the research and development of an infra-red detection device capable of 25 mils resolution. I quietly enquired of my Army and Air Force friends whether they had asked for anything of this capability and they both said no. I then asked the chairman what exactly the money was being spent on.

'So that we can do research to produce a device of this capability,' came the explanation, 'thereby knowing that we can produce in large quantities a similar device of 10 mils resolution.'

'Excuse me, Mr Chairman, but none of the Armed Forces has asked for this research, and you can buy a FLIR device of 10 mils resolution off the shelf in New York for $10,000. Now if the money were used to improve that piece of equipment, I would not object; otherwise I do not see the purpose of spending such a huge sum of the defence budget.'

For a few seconds there was utter silence. Then all hell broke loose, the chairman glowering at me.

'It has nothing whatsoever to do with you,' he exploded, and if I didn't mind what I said, I would be asked to leave. That was enough.

'Mr Chairman, it is the defence budget which is being spent here. The three Armed Forces have not asked for a piece of equipment with this capability. If you persist with your attitude then I shall take the matter to my Director and then to the Chief of the Naval Staff.'

I was absolutely livid that an attempt was being made to obtain monies for keeping civil servants in work of their choosing, and my Army and Air force colleagues supported me to the hilt. The chairman quietly backed down and agreed to put it aside for further discussion. He in fact did not, because it appeared on the agenda of the conference I attended at Farnborough. From that moment onwards, I never really trusted a civil servant again. My eyes had been opened fully.

The next meeting concerned LLTV devices and radars. On the agenda was a subject concerning high-definition radar. I had asked around the naval representatives whether anyone had put forward a request for research into such equipment and none had been made. Once again I asked the Army and the Royal Air Force representatives whether they had a requirement for this equipment and once again their reply was in the negative. When I raised the subject with the chairman of the meeting neither he nor any other members of the Board had any idea as to what it might refer, although one person had a vague notion that it might have had something to do with the Meteorological Office. The subject was set aside for the afternoon session and we all went to lunch.

On our return the Head of the Meteorological Office was available and he confirmed that the matter concerned research into weather radars, adding quickly, 'Of course, there will be a throw-off into improved airborne radar systems.' He was more or less saying that if we agreed to the research work, the Armed Forces would get something for nothing. The Meteorological Office were developing weather radars that would enable them to give up-to-date forecasts, with less than two hours' warning of impending bad weather, to the nation's farmers!

When I returned to DNAW, Peter Matthews informed me that the Director wanted to see me again. The word had been quickly passed along that I was rocking the boat at these meetings and that the civil servants did not like it. The Director asked me what had happened and I told him that our defence budget was being spent on projects that none of the Armed Forces had requested; I did not think it right and had challenged it.

'Well done!' he exclaimed. 'It's about time those fellows were brought up with a round turn! However, don't rock the boat too much, because they can be useful to us sometimes.'

'Yes, sir, I appreciate that,' I replied, 'but I'm just letting them know that these meetings are not called to rubber-stamp their requirements—and I believe the message has finally got across to them!'

* * *

Even though by this time I was officially working for Malcolm, I was still Doug's 'fixed-wing man', and one project which crossed both sections was the Multi Role Combat Aircraft, or MRCA. This was a new, multi-national, strike aircraft being developed and built by Panavia for the British, German and Italian air forces. The aircraft would eventually be named Tornado. It had been conceived back in 1969 and would be manufactured by three European companies, BAC, Messerschmitt-Bölkow-Blohm of West Germany and Società per Azioni Fiat of Italy. The work carried out by each country was based upon a fixed rate of exchange decided in 1969. However, by 1973–74, when I appeared on the scene, the rate of exchange had altered considerably but no account had taken of it. The reason for the fixed rate was to ensure that each participating country received an equable percentage of the work involved in the project as a whole, including the production of the aircraft: if the rates fluctuated then these percentages would change dramatically, shifting the percentages more to the advantage of one or other of the three countries.

Malcolm, Wally and I were still in the old office overlooking Whitehall when the MRCA file dropped on my desk. After ploughing through this huge tome I discovered that the Staff Requirement had overrun its financial limits by £12 million; the 'capping' limit set by the Staff Target/Requirements Manual was £10 million, which meant that the project had to go back to ACDS (OR) for fresh approval before it could be proceeded with. The Air Force had not resubmitted its costings and was therefore, technically, in violation of the procedure.

At about this time Chris Mather had joined the staff of ACDS (OR), and he happened to visit my office together with my old naval scientist as I was going through the MRCA Project file. I pointed out the overspend; they were, at that time, unaware of it. Within a few days another paper had dropped on to my desk stating that the MRCA project was being put forward for further approval because of the cost overrun. Then I received a call from the Secretary to ACNS (OR) directing me to prepare a brief for the Admiral so that he could study it over the following weekend, before the next tri-service meeting chaired by ACDS (OR). This meant that I had to work extremely quickly and come up with all the salient facts covering research, projected in-service and armament costs for the next ten years. The task seemed daunting, especially as I knew little or nothing about the MRCA—and I could be certain that the RAF would not give me any help. I now worked from 7.30 a.m. through to 10 o'clock each night. I sketched out the bare bones of the draft covering all aspects of the project right through from conception to in service. As I completed each section I passed it to Malcolm for comment and embellishment where necessary, and when it was complete it was passed to the Director for comment.

I had learnt that an old friend of mine who had been the AEO of 830 Squadron back in the 1950s was now the MoD (PE) Project Officer for the MRCA in the Civil Service rank equivalent to four stars. I telephoned him to ask a few pertinent questions. From all the information I had managed to cobble together the research and development costs of the airframe and weapons, but I had been unable to find out much about the engines. I asked what had been spent to date and how much each production engine unit would cost once Rolls-Royce had started to manufacture them. He could give me no information, and I asked whether this was for security reasons. His response was that he honestly could not give me any specific figures. I thanked him and sat back in my chair, speechless. My naval scientist friend was tackled next, but all he could come up with were the expenses to date— though no unit costs. I felt that, somewhere along the line, somebody was covering up the expenses. The only figures, therefore, that I could give my Admiral concerned the engine research and development costs to date. I had a vague idea of the unit cost per engine because I had a figure showing the price at which Britain had intended to sell them to the Indian Government for installation in their MiG-21 fighters.* Airframe, maintenance, personnel, training and armament costs were quite easy to calculate, and they were all listed in separate appendices. The final draft was sent to the Secretary of ACNS (OR) and the Admiral went away to read it and make his comments. I had begun to think that I had done a pretty decent job in the time available, but I was about to be brought back to earth with a resounding thump.

Monday morning happiness was shattered when ACNS (OR)'s secretary telephoned me to say that the Admiral was unhappy with the format of his briefing: he was content with the information itself but he wanted it laid out

---

* I tried in every way possible to halt this sale, fearful that the engine and its technology might fall into the hands of the Russians.

in another way. I could not understand what he wanted and went to the Director, Captain Jock Tofts, advising him of the Admiral's requirements. Jock, a former test pilot, thought I had done a very good job. We sat down together in an empty office and set about redrafting the brief, and by 4 p.m. it was back on ACNS (OR)'s desk in finalised form. It was approved.

The MRCA meeting was scheduled for the following Wednesday and my Admiral asked me to accompany him. Like all the other junior officers, I took a seat behind him, but he instructed me to sit alongside him so that I could brief him on matters that might require amplification. The meeting lasted all day. When I saw who was chairing the meeting—Air Marshal Peter Giddings, who had relieved Admiral Sir Ian McIntosh on the latter's retirement after a long and distinguished career in the Royal Navy—I quite expected the project to sail through without much hindrance. I was about to be proved wrong. The Air Force had not done its homework at all well and were unable to answer many pertinent questions—the cost of an F-4 versus the MRCA and so forth. It was becoming very apparent that the RAF were slowly but surely being backed into a corner from which they would not be able to extricate themselves. ACDS (OR) told the RAF to go away, to revise their presentation and to bring to the next meeting all the facts he had called for.

I could not believe what had happened. This was the RAF's major aircraft project and they had made a howling mess of it. The MRCA was scheduled to replace the Buccaneer, the F-4M and the Canberra, as well as the 'V-Bomber' force; moreover, in its air defence guise, it would replace the Lightning and F-4K fighters. It was a major re-equipment programme on which hundreds of millions of pounds would be spent over the next two to three decades, and it needed to be presented properly. Air Marshal Giddings was making sure that the Air Force did its job properly but his persistence would rebound on him later: although he would receive a knighthood he would go no further in the Air Force, which was a great shame because he was one of the best senior officers the RAF had at that time.

Although the MRCA had some excellent features, such as a swing-wing and a terrain-following radar system that really worked, in the maritime role it was nowhere nearly as good as the Buccaneer. The Buccaneer had a far greater fuel-carrying capability, and it could also carry six or eight 1,000-pound bombs twice as far. Oh, but it will have long-range tanks, the RAF told me; however, even with these the MRCA could not outperform the Buccaneer, which could fly twice the distance with four 1,000-pounders. It would be better to build more Buccaneers and retain them for the maritime attack and strike role, but the logic of my argument escaped them. The real problem was that the Air Force had set its heart on a major re-equipment programme and nothing, and nobody, was going to stop them. As for the air defence variant of the MRCA, this was still a long way into the future, mainly because the radar system had yet to be developed for it. The Tornado Mk 2 did begin to arrive in service a year or so after I left DNAW, but it flew for a long time as a 'lead nosed' aircraft, i.e. with ballast instead of radar.

* * *

One of my first tasks on joining DNAW was to attend a Buccaneer CATWEP (Clearance, Aircraft Trials and Weapons) meeting, a conference called every three months by the MoD (PE) Buccaneer Office to discuss progress and the latest developments, both in RN and RAF service, the latter having taken delivery of this bomber as a replacement for the ageing Canberra following the collapse of the F-111 procurement.*

I had never been to one of these meetings before and neither had my opposite number from DNAE, a newly promoted Commander AEO, Dave Donnolly. We had both decided to sit and listen, to learn what these meetings were all about and to discover what the aims and objectives were of this organisation. A glance at the meeting's agenda suggested that there was little of substance except for an item at the end that called for trials to be carried out at Boscombe Down regarding the vortex generators fitted to the top of the Buccaneer's wings. The RAF believed that they could achieve greater range without these devices. They did not know how right they were! Dave and I both sat patiently until this agenda item came up for discussion. The Chairman was attempting to breeze through it quickly, saying that he could see no reason for not going through the trial but I stopped him in mid-flight.

'Excuse me, Mr Chairman,' I interjected. 'I do not see the reason for wasting money on this trial when it had been done for the Navy some years ago. I can tell you what range increase it gives the Buccaneer with the vortex generators removed—twelve per cent.

The Chairman huffed and fluffed around and the Air Force looked uneasy. Dave and I grinned at each other.

'Mr Chairman,' I continued, 'the facts are available if you care to go back to both Boscombe Down and Brough. The Naval Department will not approve the spending of further monies on tests which have already been completed satisfactorily. If the Air Force Department had walked around the corner in the Main Building and liaised with DNAW they would have been given the facts. We have nothing to lose by helping them!'

That did it. There was a great deal of shuffling in Air Force chairs, and the Chairman promised to look into the matter.

After the meeting, the Chairman came over and thanked Dave and me, explaining that he was unaware of the earlier trials with vortex generators. Even the RAF representatives came over and thanked us, and said that they would visit DNAW more often to seek advice. Following this meeting there was far more contact between the RAF and the RN, not only concerning the Buccaneer but also with the F-4K and M Phantoms. There was also considerable liaison with regard to helicopters since the Navy, having the largest inventory of helicopters, was responsible for all three services' deep maintenance and spares. It was a time of continuing pain, with reductions and rationalisation taking place in the Armed Forces. There had even been talk of amalgamating all three services into one, but the Canadians had done that and it had not been a great success so the idea died a quick death. The

*See Chapter 23.

Air Force had in the past pulled a few tricks on the Navy—the F-111-versus-CVA-01 débâcle, for example—and in the end this had resulted in both services losing and neither obtaining what they really wanted. I used to take great delight in tweaking the tails of my Air Force friends, explaining that they were our 'sons': had it not been for the Army and Navy, there would be no Air Force!

* * *

Soon after my arrival at DNAW Captain Dave Stanley joined as the new Assistant. I had known him at Yeovilton, and he had been a Commander in DNAW while I was serving at Lossiemouth. I do not know why, but he took an instant dislike to me, not seeming to approve of anything I wrote. Matters came to a head when Peter Goddard took over from Malcolm Carver in the Future Policy Section.

Peter was immediately thrown into the deep end by having to look seriously at cutting costs and projects. The effects that this work had on everybody at the MoD can well be imagined, involving as it did the loss of equipment and swingeing cuts in the payroll. One day Peter came into my office and asked me to write a paper entitled 'The Way Ahead for the FAA'. This was, to put it mildly, a tall order, but I visited the various sections within DNAW soliciting ideas and asking the heads of each section whether they minded writing the way ahead for their particular element of the FAA. When I had gathered together these papers I sat down and began to collate everybody's ideas into a single document. Ben Bathurst wrote the best paper—one dealing with helicopter anti-submarine warfare. After two or three rewrites I gave my draft to Peter, who approved of what I had produced, but when he returned from having seen Dave Stanley he said that the latter wanted to see me. As soon as I entered his office, I was set about in anger.

'What do you call this?' he exploded, slashing through my report with his pen with such violence that he tore the sheets of paper. 'Where did you get this drivel on anti-submarine helicopters?'

I pointed out to him that Ben had written that paper, and that I thought it excellent.

'Oh," he said. He flicked over it and then flung the document at me and dismissed me.

I went straight back to Peter and told him what had happened. I thought he ought to telephone DNOA (X) and ask for someone to replace me: I refused to be treated in such an outrageous manner—by anyone. Wally Hall was appalled at what he heard and shook his head in disbelief. A cloud of despair settled over the Future Policies Section.

It was time for the half-yearly officers' reports. Dave Stanley produced a derisive and derogatory report on me but DNAW, Captain 'Spiv' Leahy, did not even call me in to discuss it. Peter told me what Stanley had written, a cloud of doom settled over my head and when the Secretary of ACNS (O) called for me to visit the Admiral I felt as though I was about to meet a firing squad. When I arrived at the Secretary's office, however, he was all smiles and ushered me into the Admiral's office, where I was offered a chair. Admiral Gerard-Pearse had been my Captain in *Ark Royal* and I had always had great respect for him.

'Just been reading your half-yearly report, Michael,' he said. 'I don't believe a word of it and have said so. I know you from our days in "Ark" and I know that you are not like this. So don't worry over it.'

'Yes sir. Thank you, sir, but that is going to go against me even though you have said otherwise. You are the only person apart from my direct boss who has spoken to me about it. Neither ADNAW nor DNAW have said a word to me.'

'Leave it to me and, believe you me, you will be all right.'

We talked about old times and had a cup of coffee together, and I returned to DNAW feeling on top of the world, knowing that I had some friends in this world. Both Peter and Wally were delighted, and a short while later we saw Stanley hurrying past our door heading upstairs. I was sitting at my desk when he put his head through the door.

'I see you have friends in high places,' he observed sheepishly, and left.

* * *

Late in 1973 Grandma Lee died and I took the train over to Teddington in Middlesex to attend her funeral. It was a very sad occasion for me because I was her first grandchild and there had always been a special bond between us. The whole of mother's family had gathered at Field Lane for the funeral. Great Aunt Rose sat in the old rocking chair in the corner of the living room where we had all held so many family parties. She was very upset because she and Grandma had been very close indeed. When her husband died, she had returned home from New York where she had lived all her married life— since the early part of the century. Grandad Lee was always her favourite brother-in-law and Annie, as Aunt Rose called her, her favourite sister, so it was natural for her to return to them. Grandad had passed away when he was only 65 years old; Grandma followed him nearly twenty years later. Aunt Rose wept, not understanding why she had lost them both; now all she had for company was the three-legged dog which Dad and Mum had given her a few years back. Donald, my cousin and Aunt Winnie's eldest son, came too, and he proved to be the spitting image of Grandad Lee: he had the same dark hair parted in the centre and sported the same black moustache. However, before he reached his fortieth birthday he would have passed away following a heart attack.

The hearse arrived and we all boarded our various cars and headed off for the Teddington cemetery. A small service was held in the chapel, and then Grandma was laid to rest alongside Grandad and mother's two siblings, Horie and Rose. Mother was extremely upset, realising that she and Winnie were now the only remaining children from Grandma's family. Now they are all gone.

* * *

Above: 'Presented with the compliments of Allsopp (East Africa) Limited to commemorate the world's first supersonic beer—a bottle of Allsopp's pilsner lager taken through the sound barrier by *Capitaine de Corvette* Michel Borney from Embakasi Airport, Kenya, on Tuesday, October 29th, 1963.'
Below: Part of the USS *Essex*'s air group aboard HMS *Ark Royal* in the Indian Ocean, 1963.

Above: US Navy Sea Kings approaching *Ark Royal*. One of these three helicopters later crashed at night while approaching their ship, the USS *Essex*, and three officers were lost.

Below: A US Navy E-1B Tracer AEW aircraft is launched from *Ark Royal*'s port catapult in cross-deck operations in the Indian Ocean, 1963.

Opposite, upper: Part of *Essex*'s air group parked in *Ark Royal*'s Fly 1.

Opposite, lower: One of *Essex*'s A-4 Skyhawks operating from *Ark Royal*.

Opposite, upper: HMS *Jaguar* detaches from *Ark Royal* and her tanker following refuelling in the Indian Ocean, 1963.
Opposite, lower: HMS *Ark Royal* refuelling from her tanker.
Right, upper: The author fires a Bullpup missile from his Scimitar fighter over the Indian Ocean, 1963.
Right, lower: Three Scimitars from 800 Naval Air Squadron work up for the Aden Air Display, 1963.
Below: Lieutenant Les Ingham mans his Scimitar fighter at five minutes' notice to scramble.

Opposite: A street scene in
Wanchai, Hong Kong, 1963.
Above: A Wanchai greengrocer,
Hong Kong, 1963.
Right: The author's wife May and
eldest daughter Naomi, November 1966.

Opposite, upper: HMS *Eagle* in May 1964. The carrier was a half-sister of *Ark Royal*, both ships having originally been drawn up to the same basic design. *AH files*

Opposite, lower: Another view of HMS *Eagle*, with Sea Vixens evident aft and forward and Buccaneers amidships. *AH files*

Right, top: 736 NAS Buccaneer S Mk 1s practise formation aerobatics over the Banffshire countryside, August 1966.

Right, centre top: An 809 NAS Buccaneer S.1 having performed a wheels-up landing at Lossiemouth early 1964. The author did fly this particular aircraft— XN928/'224'—but not at the time of this incident! *Courtesy Phil Jarrett*

Right, centre bottom: Lossiemouth squadrons practise for the 'Freedom of the Town' flypast, July 1967—seven Buccaneers with eight Hunter trainers flanking, and with four Sea Venoms and a lone Sea Vampire taking up the rear.

Right, bottom: The author firing 2-inch rockets over the Tain range in northern Scotland. His aircraft for this sortie was a Buccaneer S.2 of 736 Squadron.

Left: Colonel Paul Sandison presents the Sandison Trophy to the author, March 1966. Captain Doug Parker is at left.
Below: The VX-4 badge.
Bottom: Welcome to Point Mugu: a view of the display park, with the author's specially painted, all-black F-4J Phantom on its pedestal. This aircraft was used for visibility trials in the US Navy's Project OV-63, with which the author was intimately associated.

Top: VX-4's US-2A replacement communications aircraft, a former S-2 Tracker christened *Son of Beulah*.
Above: The author and his daughter Naomi outside their California home in 1968.
Right: The author and his wife May at the US Naval Officers' Ball at USNAS Point Mugu, 1968.

Left: The author as Squadron Commander, 767 Naval Air Squadron, at RNAS Yeovilton in the summer of 1971.
Below: Lieutenant Commander Peter Sheppard being briefed by Duncan Simpson prior to his 're-famil' flight in Sea Fury '123', Yeovilton, late 1970.
Opposite: The author mans his F-4K Phantom for a training flight.

PULL
HANDLE
TO JETTISON
CANOPIES

RESCUE

7

PUSH TO OPEN DOOR

CANOPY
JETTISON
HANDLE INSIDE

133

133

AN/APG-60 PWR
SUPPLY 8 VOLTS SW
FUSES & FLM JACK

145

145

5L 5L

PG-60
SUPPLY

6L 6L
EQUIPMENT
REFRIGERATION UNIT

Above: HMS *Ark Royal*, now equipped with a fully angled, 11-degree deck, in 1975, with a visiting US Navy F-4 Phantom and A-7 Corsair at the bow.
Courtesy Richard L. Ward

Left: HMS *Hermes*, with throttles 95 per cent open, heads down-Channel in February 1980.

Opposite, top: *Hermes* returns to her berth at the Northwest Wall Jetty at Portsmouth for her refit to be completed, February 1981.

Opposite, left: 800 Naval Air Squadron tries out *Hermes*' 'ski-ramp' for the first time, spring 1981.

Opposite, far right, upper: The Sea Harrier trials team: Danny Norman, BAe representatives and (foreground) the author, on board *Hermes*.

Opposite, far right, lower: The author engaged in conversation with the late Senator Childs.

Above: *Hermes* is manoeuvred into her Mayport berth, with the USS *John F. Kennedy* astern, 1981.

Left, top: The author as Commander (Air) flying one of 826 Squadron's Sea King helicopters in 1981.

Left, centre: *Hermes* almost vanishing from sight as she 'takes it green' over her 'ski-ramp' south of Iceland in 1981.

Left, bottom: The flight deck of *Hermes* after taking a 'heavy one' aboard.

One day I had a call from Dad asking if I would like a trip helping him deliver the film producer David Mallett's ketch *Malibu of Birdham* from Rye to Burnham-on-Crouch to have its rudder mountings repaired. I asked the Director for a long weekend from Friday to Monday, and he was happy to give me some time off.

Dad had decided to go up-Channel on the highest spring tide and full moon that had occurred for nearly twenty years. We took with us a young man named Richard, and we slipped our moorings at Strand Quay at around 11 p.m. There was still an hour or so to go before high water, and Dad was just turning into Rock Channel, leading out to the Rother, when he shouted that he had no propeller response from the throttle. He steered the yacht into the left bank of the channel, Richard jumped ashore and I passed a line to him. Richard then proceeded to pull us back into Strand Quay while Dad steered as best he could back to our old berth. The engine room floorboards were lifted and we discovered that the locking nut had come adrift on the propeller shaft: the assembly had backed away from the gearbox and had become totally disconnected. With Richard upside down and with Dad and me holding his legs, he fished about with an old wire coat hanger and finally found the locking nut. We reassembled the shaft, locked it and threaded a split pin through the nut, had a quick cup of tea and set off again. The delay was fortuitous.

It was the top of the tide when we left Strand Quay once again—so high, in fact, that it was over the capping wall, flooding the A259 and all places around to a depth of about three feet. We slowly made our way out into the Rother and headed for the open water. There was a brilliant full moon and visibility was perfect. As soon as we were outside the harbour entrance all sails were set and we headed off towards Dungeness. With the motor switched off, it was a wonderful experience sailing along at about eight knots with nothing more than the slap of the waves against the steel hull. Rounding Dungeness, we headed for the North Foreland and by dawn we were almost off Dover harbour. At 6.25 we turned on the radio for the shipping forecast, only to hear a storm warning of Force 10 winds for the Thames and Dover areas, so I suggested we perform an about-turn and head straight into Dover harbour. Dad agreed. However, a cross-Channel ferry had just left Dover and the harbour entrance signals were set against us. I told Dad to head straight for the entrance—to hell with the signals!—and leave the sails as they were until we were inside, out of harm's way.

As we approached the entrance the signals were altered in our favour and we shot into the outer harbour like a scalded cat. We rounded up into wind, dropped all sails, motored to a shallower anchorage and let out all our chain, the motor kept running at half-ahead to take some of the strain. One of us stayed on watch every two hours while the others had some rest—which was almost impossible owing to the yacht's bouncing up and down. A Polish timber ship outboard of us had two anchors out, her chains were almost horizontal and she was listing quite badly. At about 2 o'clock in the afternoon the wind had moderated to about Force 8 and we weighed anchor and headed for the locks and the inner harbour. As soon as we had tied up Dad telephoned

David and told him where we were, and within a couple of hours, he had motored over to take us all back home.

Had it not been for the propeller problem, we would have been off the North Foreland when the storm arrived and could well have ended up a maritime casualty. The ferocity of the storm, and the speed with which it blew up, was quite unbelievable. I returned early to DNAW and everybody asked whether I had had a good sail. 'Oh yes,' I smiled. 'A wonderful sail in beautiful full-moonlit conditions. You would have loved it!'

* * *

The ditching of the Navy's Sea Heron in the Irish Sea in the summer of 1972 was to return and concern me towards the end of my time in DNAW. The aircraft's young pilot had faced a court martial and had been found guilty of failing to carry out the challenge-and-reply checks, of failing to keep a proper check on his aircraft's fuel load and of poor airmanship. He had been dismissed his ship and reappointed to the Staff of FOSNI as an Assistant Operations Officer. FONAC had requested that an Order in Council be made by the Sovereign for his flying brevet—i.e., his 'wings' badge—to be removed. It was for this reason that the huge tome relating to this matter came to me for comment before proceeding to the Naval Legal Branch. The file landed with a thud early one afternoon with an 'Urgent' tag on it for comment that day.

The file was well over an inch thick and there were also the 'Findings of the Court Martial', and I had to read through every page and then make a rational comment for my Director to sign before passing the document on. As I read I found glaring errors and faulty conclusions that would, in normal circumstances, be enough to quash the findings of the Court Martial Board. However, the 'big guns' were out to 'get' this young officer, and this was enough for me to take up my sword in his defence. My first move was to try to establish why the aircraft had ditched where it had, half way between Liverpool and Douglas, Isle of Man.

The aircraft's crew had been made up of the pilot, a Chief Petty Officer crewman under final test for his Aircrewman endorsement and the 781 Squadron Senior Observer, a very experienced Lieutenant Commander aviator on board to monitor the Chief Aircrewman's test. The aircraft had been scheduled to fly to Sydenham via Yeovilton, where several more passengers would embark. After the aircraft had left Yeovilton, its flight path would take it via the Brecon Air Navigation Beacon, on to the Wallasey ANB near Liverpool and then straight on to Sydenham. The aircraft had ditched twelve miles out from the Wallasey beacon. The weather was clear, the sea was calm and the aircraft was piloted to a perfect ditching. All the crew and passengers were either rescued by helicopter or by the RNLI lifeboat from Douglas. The aircraft sank in quite shallow water and was recovered complete within a week by a naval recovery vessel. It was placed aboard a barge and the FAA Aircraft Accident Investigation Unit quickly set about discovering what had happened to cause all four engines to stop within seconds of one another. The AAIU established the following:

1. All the fuel tanks were empty.
2. What fuel had been found remaining on board was tested and found to be uncontaminated.
3. The engine de-icing levers were all in the 'On' position.
4. There were no signs of broken fuel lines or leakages.
5. All the fuel gauges appeared to be functioning correctly.

My first reaction to the AAIU's findings was that the aircraft had been immersed for almost a week and consequently it was impossible to establish what fuel had been on board at the time of ditching; most of it would have leaked away by then, and the under surfaces of the wings and fuselage had been damaged quite extensively during the heavy contact with the water on ditching. The environmental conditions prevailing, although the weather was clear, could have caused carburettor icing to have formed in all four engines, and of course none of the icing would have remained once the carburettors had been immersed in salt water. The question of fuel really worried me, so I asked Peter Matthews for his copy of the Heron's Flight Data Manual and I set about calculating fuel consumptions and miles flown for various fuel loads.

At the court martial it had been established that the aircraft was three-quarters loaded with fuel while at Yeovilton; the Squadron Senior Observer had sworn to this. Using the climb-out figures and the rate of fuel consumption for the altitude flown, and assuming a 50-knot head wind all the way, the aircraft would, in my estimation, have run out of fuel and come down about 100 miles north-west of Northern Ireland. I had Peter Matthews check my figures twice and he came up with the same answer. Had the engines been running on a rich mixture, they would have failed well before reaching the Wallasey beacon. There was, therefore, something very wrong with the court martial's findings.

It was almost 8 o'clock in the evening when Doug Borrowman called in to see how I was getting along. I told him what I had found, and that Peter had confirmed that my calculations were correct. Peter left to go home and Doug and I went along to the Director, Jock Tofts. I told him that I found it totally incomprehensible that three aircrew officers had all failed to notice the fuel remaining on board throughout the Heron's flight; if they had all failed in this respect, then all three were guilty of poor airmanship and all three should have faced a court martial. Personally, I felt that the pilot was being 'railroaded' because he had been involved in two other aircraft accidents at sea in questionable circumstances although, unfortunately, neither of the aircraft concerned had been recovered for AAIU investigation. Jock was having none of it: the pilot had been found guilty by the Court Martial Board of failing to carry out the challenge-and-reply checks and that was enough for DNAW. The following day the file was returned to Naval Law with DNAW's comments and the pilot lost his 'wings'—and the job he had waiting for if and when he left naval service.

To this day I feel strongly that we let this young officer down. He could have won on appeal and had the findings of the court martial quashed.

Officers of much senior rank, for example the Captain and navigator of HMS *Eagle*,* had had their findings quashed after hazarding their ship. This young officer could reasonably have been accused of hazarding a total of eighteen lives, including his own, but to lose his wings as a result of a relatively minor technicality of which just about every pilot in the three Armed Forces was guilty was in my opinion both severe and unjust. He had been treated unfairly by the naval system.

* * *

I had known for some time where I would be going next after DNAW. DNOA (X) had informed me privately, but I was to keep it quiet for the time being. I would be going to *Ark Royal* as the next Lieutenant Commander (Flying), relieving Bob Edward. Bob had been in the job for almost a year and had been passed over for promotion to Commander. I had also learnt that Commander David Cowling from the Directorate of Naval Plans would be joining with me as the new XO, relieving Commander Briggs. However, David had been none too well over the past few months and his appointment did not look firm—or so Peter Goddard informed me. However, in the event he did join the ship at about the same time as I did.

Christmas 1973 came, and in the New Year I received my official appointment to 'Ark', which I would join the following October in Malta. Needless to say I was extremely excited, hardly able to wait to start my various courses. It meant that I would the Number Two of the Air Department, responsible for all flight-deck and circuit operations, as well as being the ship's Flight Safety Officer. I was scheduled to leave DNAW in mid-1974.

There was still plenty of work to do at the Directorate concerning the Sea Harrier. The project had now passed to the Staff Operational Requirement phase and would eventually lead to the purchase of the aircraft for the Royal Navy. There was planning to be done for pilot training, maintenance matters, stores requirements, armaments and numerous other aspects of the project. The new 'through-deck cruiser' project was well under way, the first ship, HMS *Invincible*, having been launched and now engaged in builder's trials off the Clyde. She would soon make her maiden voyage and carry out her shake-down cruise before being handed over to the Navy, an event that was scheduled for later in the year at Portsmouth. Her first Captain would be Jock Slater, who had been in an office on the opposite side of the corridor to me in the MoD Main Building. I was kept quite busy right up until the last moment.

Three other officers were leaving DNAW at about the same time as myself, so we arranged to have a bumper leaving party in the registry office. Under the control of the Head of Registry, Kathy, the girls all produced lots of splendid 'eats' and, being the Directorate Wine Secretary (!), I arranged for the wine and sherry and then handed over the task to Peter Burgess who had officially relieved me at DNAW.

---

* See Chapter 24.

I was going to miss the people in the Directorate. The post had been very rewarding—far more so than I had expected, in fact—and I felt that I had done a reasonable job. Even Dave Stanley came up to me, thanked me for all my hard work and assistance and wished me luck in *Ark Royal*. The world was not such a bad place after all!

Lieutenant Commander (Flying)

ONE OF THE MOST demanding jobs in the Fleet Air Arm is that of Lieutenant Commander (Flying) in a fleet carrier. One is totally responsible for all that goes on about the carrier, on the flight deck and below in the hangars, and for the flight safety of the air group and the ship—the 'right hand' of Commander (Air), the head of the Air Department and, in American parlance, the 'Deputy Air Boss'.

My first task was to take the various courses considered necessary for a budding Lieutenant Commander (Flying) afloat. First I had to return to flying practice on the various types of aircraft that I would be controlling in *Ark Royal*. My first flying course was known more commonly as the 'Helicopter Geriatric Course', designed for old and bold aviators who had never flown helicopters before. I would spend the whole of September 1974 at RNAS Culdrose learning how a helicopter flew and how to control it. Many of my instructors were old friends going back a very long time in the Navy, which made for a really happy time. The experience also brought back many wonderful memories of my courting days with May when she was serving in the WRNS at Culdrose. While there I flew every helicopter the Navy had on its inventory, except for the Wessex Mk 5 and the Lynx, which I would fly at Yeovilton. I was, however, saddened by the fact that people of my seniority were not allowed to go solo on type, although, had I spent another week or two at Culdrose, I am sure that I would have persuaded someone to override the ruling. However, I proved to my instructors that I was quite capable of flying any helicopter the Navy had in service. My day was made when I was up flying the Whirlwind Mk 10 and my instructor turned to me and said, 'You have flown helicopters before, haven't you, sir?' I replied that I had not: all I had done was watch 'Whirlybirds' on TV with my children!

I thoroughly enjoyed my time learning to fly helicopters, and by the time I had finished the course I had flown nine different types. Nevertheless, the message somehow got abroad that I was a 'turncoat', and my Appointer challenged me when he visited Culdrose

'What's this I hear?' he asked me. 'You wish you had been a helicopter pilot?'

'No,' I replied. 'I find them very much a sailor's aircraft, capable of going in any direction he wants, whereas in a fixed-wing aircraft you are very much confined as to what you can do.'

I practised just about every type of mission a helicopter was capable of undertaking and relished the hover over heavy seas, dropping and recovering divers and picking up stretchers and simulated casualties. I never had any qualms about feeling one of the helicopter team: helicopters were just as essential to the Fleet Air Arm as were the fixed-wing jets. Of course, the two types of flying would, in a sense, come together when the Navy took delivery of the Sea Harrier.

After my helicopter course I visited Yeovilton to renew my instrument rating and also to spend a few hours in the Wessex Mk 5 Commando and the Lynx helicopters. Then I moved on to RAF Honington to fly the Buccaneer, and after that to RAF Leuchars to fly the Phantom F-4K again, whereupon I returned to Lossiemouth to fly the Gannet. I managed flights only in the Gannet T Mk 5 owing to the lack of availability of the AEW Mk 3. 849 HQ Squadron was located right opposite No 8 Squadron RAF, which was flying Shackletons with old naval AEW radar systems under the aircraft's noses. Several naval observers were helping the RAF fly these wonderful old four-engine former ASW aircraft; one of them had bought our old house in Lossie-mouth, and, looking back, I often wish that we had never sold it. I had really grown to love dear old Lossiemouth, and May and I had many friends in the town and around the local countryside. It was a great pity that I did not fly the Gannet AEW Mk 3, because, leaving aside the Sea Vixen, I would then have flown every aircraft type in service with the RN up to that time.

When I checked into the Officers' Mess at Lossiemouth I met many of the old naval Wardroom Assistants now employed by the RAF. However, most of them were quite unhappy. The told me that the mess did not have the same atmosphere as it had in the Royal Navy days, and that the Air Force was not liked much in the town. I was sure that they were exaggerating, but they were quite adamant. One of the Navy's great virtues was that it would easily blend in with the local inhabitants and become an integral part of the local community. The residents of Lossiemouth were very appreciative of the Navy, so much so that they had conferred on it the Freedom of the Town. In a wonderful ceremony, a naval guard of honour marched through the town centre with bayonets fixed and with the Air Station Band playing naval and Scottish tunes. The local schoolchildren were given the day off and the whole of the town was decked out in flags and bunting. In addition, a huge 'Balbo' of air station squadron aircraft flew over in formation, to tremendous whoops and cheers. We were part of that marvellous town, and its people were part of us.

I returned to Yeovilton for a Flight Safety course, given by the FAA Flight Safety Centre led by Commander Vic Sirrett. Several of us were on the course, for example newly appointed Commanding Officers, Senior Pilots and the future Flag Officer Aircraft Carriers, Rear Admiral John Jarvis. Our course started with a flight safety film which opened with an F-4J going vertical, both crew members ejecting and the aircraft falling back on to its tail and exploding. I gave a loud chuckle and everybody looked at me. 'Sorry,' I said. 'That was my old—or, rather, new—F-4J on its last flight before delivery to me in VX-4. The cause of the crash—a set of pliers left in the stabilator mechanism, which jammed it fully nose-up!' On completion of this course I had a few days' leave and then proceeded to RAF Lyneham for a flight out to RAF Luqa, to join dear old *Ark Royal* once again.

* * *

The flight out to Malta went very quickly and I arrived at about 1300. There was a mad scramble to process everybody through the Maltese Customs & Immigration. I quite expected to find a helicopter waiting to transport me out to the carrier; instead, however, a Petty Officer took charge of me and I was bundled into a naval 'tilly' van and driven out to Binghy Creek, where 'Ark' was firmly moored to two buoys: thanks to winds in excess of 40 knots, she was stormbound in harbour, with steam up and at two hours' notice to sail. I had arrived just in time to have lunch and meet up with Bob Edward, whom I was relieving. I left my baggage in Bob's harbour cabin, we went topsides to Flyco and I was introduced to the Captain and to 'Wings', who was Jack Worth, another old DNAW chum. Bob launched the SAR helicopter to check on the strength of the wind and the Captain decided that he would leave the creek and put to sea as it had by then moderated sufficiently to be within limits for handling the ship. The Captain deftly took his ship out of the narrow creek and turned her starboard, and we were quickly on our way out of Grand Harbour and heading for the open Mediterranean. It was good to be back at sea once again—a feeling hard to convey to a landbound person. A sailor is never very happy unless he can feel the motion of a ship beneath his feet, and to me the sea has always been my true home.

Ark Royal steamed off to the south of Malta for a couple of hours' flying. Bob Edward took me through the procedure of working out the fixed-wing launching speeds from the bow and waist catapults. These speeds depended upon the aircraft's all-up weight, the wind-over-flight-deck and the available steam pressure at the catapult. As Lieutenant Commander (Flying), I could launch aircraft from 10 knots below the minimum to 10 knots above the minimum launching speeds. The lower end of the scale was used in wartime and for very experienced pilots who were being launched 'heavy' in light wind and high ambient temperatures, the higher end being for those pilots making their first catapult launches or taking off during dusk and at night. The launching speeds for each type of aircraft had been computed by the Naval Section at RAE Bedford. As the aircraft left the catapult, its speed had to be such that it could safely accelerate and climb away; when there was a launch below minimum, then the height of the flight deck above sea level would be more than adequate to assure a safe climb-away.

As soon as the ship secured from Flying Stations, Bob took me down to the Operations Room to meet the Operations Officer, Lieutenant Commander Bob Woolgar, and his team, whose task was to produce the daily flying programme after consultation with the various squadrons' Senior Pilots or

Senior Observers. Then we retired to Bob Edward's harbour cabin—which was about four times as big as my old LSO cabin on the other side of the ship—to go through ship and departmental orders.

While we had been in Flyco just prior to the ship's departure the alarm had sounded: 'Fire! Fire in Lieutenant Commander (Flying)'s harbour cabin. Ship's Emergency Party muster on the quarterdeck.' Bob leapt from his chair in Flyco, and flew aft to his cabin. While in his cabin he had banged out his pipe into the waste bin but some of the tobacco had still been alight. This had caused some paper to catch fire, and the flames had reached his flying overalls and raincoat, both of which were charred. However, nothing important had been damaged, but because of the smoke damage my new cabin was repainted.

Bob Edward spent two days handing over to me and then he was ready to leave and return home to Britain. He had not, unfortunately, been selected for promotion to Commander, and he suspected that FOAC, who was Rear Admiral Cassidi at the time, was responsible. The Admiral tended to stand behind Bob during flying operations with his hands on the top of his chair, twisting his knuckles into Bob's back and asking very awkward questions at critical moments. Eventually Bob rounded on him and asked him not to bother him while he was busy. Admiral Cassidi never spoke to him again. In contrast, 'Wings', Jack Worth and Admiral Cassidi were always together and talking like old buddies. In Jack's case it paid off, and he was promoted to Captain even though he had little time left to serve. The Admiral invited me to dinner one evening on the Admiral's bridge just before night flying. It was a very convivial gathering of four officers, but I had to leave early to ensure that the launch speeds were ready for the Flight Deck Engineer Officer. I always found the Admiral very friendly; I had the impression, however, that he was rather a shy and lonely man—and was probably more so after the death of his wife.

Now that I was on my own, Jack Worth proved to be a great mentor. Between us we built a strong bond which went back to the days when he was Lieutenant Commander (Flying) and I was the LSO. In retrospect, this was probably the reason I had been selected for the appointment—and I could have not been more fortunate in having such a boss. Normally my appointment was given to a General List officer, and although there were quite a few available who could have filled it I suspect that they did not have the qualifications or experience that I had gained over the years. I was certainly going to ensure that I lived up to the hopes that everybody had placed in me.

After returning to Britain for a short while, 'Ark' departed for the Caribbean and the western Atlantic. On the way over we conducted 'non-diversion' flying, wherein we flew our air group with no diversionary airfield available. However, we did have a Buccaneer tanker aircraft flying a holding pattern half way between the ship and USNAS Roosevelt Roads in Puerto Rico, just in case anything untoward happened—and it did! The CO of 809 (Buccaneer) Squadron, Mike Bickley, returned to the circuit with a red light on his undercarriage. He had as his companion the Squadron Senior Pilot, Tony Morton.

I ordered them to divert to Roosevelt Roads and to take on extra fuel from the tanker. They departed, and nothing more was heard until two hours later when 'Wings' had a telephone call from the Ops Officer. Bickley and Morton had crashed. Jack turned round and looked at me with a very white face. I said to him that I had no idea how it could have happened since he had plenty of fuel; the only thing that could explain it would be the collapse of the undercarriage, the red light indicating an unsafe condition. What had actually happened was that the aircraft had swerved off the runway into a monsoon ditch when the port undercarriage leg collapsed. Mike and Tony had decided that if anything happened on touch-down, Mike would eject followed by Tony, but owing to the rough ride Tony did not have a chance to eject before the aircraft came to a grinding halt. However, he was able to return to the ship. Mike landed heavily with both feet on the edge of the taxi track and broke both ankles, grounding him for nine months. He was admitted to the USN hospital at Roosevelt Roads was eventually returned by Sea King helicopter while the ship was visiting Barbados. After the wardroom cocktail party Mike was last seen hobbling ashore under escort by a group of lovely young ladies attending to his every desire. He was clearly their hero, so much so that when he returned to the ship he almost needed to be readmitted to the USN hospital!

The ship spent Easter 1974 at Barbados. The wardroom threw a cocktail party for the local Government members and other people of importance in the running of the colony. It was held on the flight deck under a clear starlit night with a warm breeze blowing. I was speaking to one very tall, white-haired Barbadian gentleman from the Government who said that he had come along to drink the Queen's cocktails and that he was always keen to have something free at her expense.

'Sir, it is the ship's officers who are paying for this cocktail party, and not the Queen.' I told him quietly.

'I don't believe you,' he replied.

'Sorry, sir. Ask the Captain over there and he will tell you the same.'

He then disappeared into the crowd very quickly. I was of the opinion that most of our guests had no idea that it was the ship's officers who paid for their eats and drinks, and not the Queen nor even the British Government. The Governor invited the officers to his house, but he was away on holiday, as were most of the ex patriots, who had gone north to New York or Canada to escape the heat of the summer. After four days we weighed anchor and steamed for Florida and Fort Lauderdale.

At Fort Lauderdale *Ark Royal* created a pollution scare when neat furnace fuel oil was accidentally discharged into the harbour. The clean-up cost the Navy $65,000. The stench was awful, and of course there was a nasty tide mark around the quayside, the ship's side and other nearby vessels. However, after a couple of days everything was back to normal.

On our return voyage Jack Worth called me into the Admiral's bridge quarters, where he was leafing through the Air Department Officers' reports. His face was so severe that I thought for a moment that I was in serious trouble.

'Sit down. Mike,' he said. 'You've been on board only a few months but have settled in well and control the flight deck and circuit with a firm and cool hand, as you did with Mike Bickley's emergency. Well done!'

He smiled and I grinned. 'Do you have anything to say or suggest?' he went on.

'Well, no, sir. I enjoy working with you and the rest of the Air Department and squadrons,' I replied. 'It's a very satisfying job and I thoroughly enjoy it.'

'Good—and thank you.'

I returned to Flyco feeling on top of the world.

* * *

Following a short port call at Devonport for some minor repairs, the ship sailed once again, this time for waters off the north of Scotland. It was August and HM the Queen Mother was celebrating her seventy-fifth birthday at her Scottish retreat, the Castle of May. As Queen Elizabeth, the wife of the late King George VI, she had launched the carrier from Cammell Laird's yard at Birkenhead in 1950. The 'Queen Mum', as she was affectionately called, always visited 'her' ship on her birthday, and she was coming aboard for the day to see the ship's company.

Arrangements had been made to fly the Queen Mother out to the ship in a bright orange Wessex Mk 2 helicopter of the Queen's Flight. Because the flight was over a considerable stretch of water, a signal was sent stating that one of our Sea Kings would escort the Wessex from the coast to the ship. We soon received a stiff reply from the Queen's Flight telling us that this was not necessary. Neither I nor the ship were going to be caught out if there was an emergency, however, so unbeknownst to the Flight I stationed a Sea King midway along the Wessex's flightpath. The RAF, which was responsible for the Queen's Flight, would have pulled the rug out from under us had we not made such a contingency plan.

Nearly all the air group had been disembarked to RAF Lossiemouth for the day, except for two aircraft of each type that remained on board for a static display; the aircraft that went ashore had been armed to give Her Majesty an aerial display on their return to the ship. As the last fixed-wing aircraft left the ship, the 'Queen Mum' arrived overhead in her Wessex and she flew around the ship, leaning out of the side door and waving to us all. Then the Wessex was landed on the forward lift and our illustrious guest stepped on to the flight deck to be met and greeted by the Captain and XO. Wilf Graham then introduced her to the heads of departments and conducted her to the bridge and Flyco, where a large cocktail bar had been laid out for her. She gladly took a large, neat, malt whisky and came and sat next to me for the air display. We chatted away to each other and then the Buccaneers and Phantoms arrived overhead in a splendid 'Balbo' formation and commenced their display. The ship then turned into wind to recover about twenty jets. The recovery went like clockwork, each aircraft landing with an interval of 30 seconds and not one of them missing a wire. The 'Queen Mum' then turned to me and said, 'Thank you Lieutenant Commander. That is quite the best air show I have seen, and it is the first time that all the jets have landed on board without having to go around again!' I stood up and thanked her, she smiled, and then the Captain and XO escorted her below to the wardroom for luncheon with the off-duty officers. It was obvious that she knew something about carrier operations.

An excellent static display had been arranged for Her Majesty in the upper hangar. As she went round each display she spoke with every officer and sailor, chatting to them about theirs lives and families. Then, at about 1530, the XO escorted her to the Chief Petty Officers' Mess, where she was entertained with tea and cakes, after which it was up to the forward upper hangar extension, where the Captain made a speech and presented Her Majesty with a birthday gift of Caithness glass. At about 1600 she boarded her Wessex and took off for the return trip to Castle of May. However, before departing, she flew around the ship a couple of times, waving her light blue chiffon scarf and leaning out of the side door—and with no harness! My heart was in my mouth until I saw the aircraft level off and the door slammed shut. Once again I had a Sea King helicopter follow her at a discreet distance until she had crossed the coast safely.

It had been a wonderful day and everybody thoroughly enjoyed having this most gracious lady aboard their ship—*her* ship. I will never forget her sitting right next to me in Flyco. She was kind and attentive, and chatted away as if she had known me all her life. A truly great lady!

* * *

The ship reverted to normal routine and proceeded north for the autumnal NATO North Atlantic exercise. The weather had deteriorated somewhat, with drizzle, low cloud and heavy seas in attendance as we approached the Norwegian Sea. Our Phantoms were launched on CAP to a position near the North Cape, but as the second pair were launched to relieve the first pair on patrol, intelligence came through that the Soviets had sent off over two dozen 'Badgers' from their base near Archangel. As these Soviet bombers rounded the Cape, our F-4s—now four aircraft, and joined by Phantoms from RAF Leuchars and USN carrier aircraft—pounced on the unsuspecting Soviets aviators. The Russians were surprised that they had been met so soon after take-off, received the message and turned about and went elsewhere.

The recovery of our fighters took some time owing to the heavy seas, which caused the deck to pitch beyond the F-4's landing limits. One or two aircraft were forced to go round again for a second attempt, but there was no anxiety because I had placed a Buccaneer tanker overhead, orbiting at 20,000 feet in case any of the aircraft wanted extra fuel.

FOAC—Rear Admiral Jim Eberle, my old XO from *Eagle* days when I was serving in 800 Squadron—was embarked with his Flag and staff. By the time we had recovered our fixed-wing element the carrier was at least thirty miles away from the main task force. Just as the Navigator was about to reverse course, one of our Sea King helicopters returned to refuel and rearm, but the Navigator insisted that the ship had to be back with the force. The helicopter landed on board facing aft, but because of its all-up-weight—at the maximum permissible—it had to make a running take-off, and this meant that the ship had to be turned back into wind. The Navigator, however, refused to turn the ship. I called the Ops Officer on the 'bullhorn', asking him to tell the Admiral's staff that unless the ship were turned into wind to give us anti-submarine protection we would be a dead duck. What I did not know at the time was that FOAC was sitting alongside the Ops Officer going through the daily signal log. Apparently, he turned quietly to the Ops Officer and said, 'Let "Little F"* have his way', and suddenly the ship started turning into wind. The Navigator walked through to Flyco.

'You have some mighty influence down below!' he remarked

'No—just being sensible and playing the game as if for real,' I grinned.

Ops called me and told me what had happened, and I had a quiet chuckle. The Navigator had learnt a good lesson: never leave your ship without anti-submarine protection, otherwise you will be sunk.

Out of the blue, a request appeared from HMS *Hermes*, which was carrying out her usual early-autumn cold-weather exercise near Bodø in northern Norway. The ship—by now officially designated a CVH—wanted four of her Wessex Mk 5s to conduct deck-landing practice in heavy seas and then be refuelled for the return flight. The request reached 'Ark' just as the aircraft appeared out of the drizzle. We could not refuse because they were all down to minimum fuel so we landed them on board and refuelled them, but deck-landing practice was denied because there was insufficient time, the next fixed-wing launch aircraft having to be re-spotted and prepared for their flight. I believe that this little 'exercise' was something that FOAC's staff had thrown at us as a test: they were probably hoping that it would cause chaos. Needless to say, however, the Air Department coped in its inimitable way and the ship continued to close the main task force without further delay.

By this time various Soviet warships had joined the task force, following us around though keeping a reasonable distance. One of the latest anti-submarine cruisers was about two cables ahead and her 'Hormone' helicopter came alongside the port side of the waist catapult to within about 25 feet. I quickly called the FDO on the loop to wave him aboard, but the Soviet pilot shook his head, waved back and flew off to land aboard his ship just ahead of us. The CO of 824 Squadron was standing alongside me and remarked that it was a pity that we did not have engines like theirs. I asked why and he replied that Soviet helicopter engines were very 'agricultural' and could operate in just about any type of environment, including conditions of severe icing. This was a pretty damning statement, especially when one had been brought up to believe that British equipment was the best in the world!

After the usual post-exercise debrief the ship made her way back to Devonport. It had been arranged for one of our helicopters to pick up Jimmy Saville, the radio and television personality, from Newcastle Airport. It had been a very wet, cold and foggy morning but as we neared our destination the fog was already lifting and blue sky could be seen, so I decided to send

---

* Nickname for Lieutenant Commander (Flying).

the SAR CO in under positive radar control until he could be taken over by Newcastle Approach Control. As he crossed the coastline we lost radio contact with him but after a radio-telephone call to the airport it was established that he had landed safely but that Mr Saville had not yet arrived. A while later Jack Worth appeared in Flyco.

'Well, that little shindig is off,' he said, rubbing his hands.

'Oh no,' I replied. 'Our chopper is ashore at Newcastle waiting for Jimmy, and he should be back within half an hour.'

Jack looked at me. 'You launched him in this?'

'Yes. The fog was patchy when he left and it was well within limits at Newcastle. He was under radar control all the way to the coast, so I was happy for him to go.'

The Ops Room called up to Flyco to say that they had the helicopter on its return flight and that he had gone to the CCA control frequency. I placed a couple of tractors at the end of the flight deck with their headlights on fully facing aft, and a short while later the helicopter was alongside the ship and landing-on safely.

When the FDO brought Jimmy Saville up to Flyco I almost burst out laughing. He was wearing a beard but the right half of his face had been shaven clean. When the Captain saw him his eyes almost popped out of his head in amazement. For the next twenty-four hours, up to the time we docked at Devonport, Jimmy interviewed as many people as he could throughout the ship, the entire programme being transmitted live over BBC Radio 2. He was entertained in the wardroom afterwards, smoking the biggest cigar imaginable and sipping a glass or two of 'the hard stuff'. As soon as the ship had docked he left and went over to RM Barracks at Stonehouse, where, as an honorary 'Green Beret', he had many friends.

* * *

With the air group disembarked the ship settled down to a quiet period in port over Christmas 1975 and the following New Year. Jack Worth departed and his relief was Bob Northard. Jack would be selected for promotion to Captain in the New Year Promotions List, which pleased us all in the Air Department. Reg Hillsdon, the ship's Air Engineer Officer and a friend of long standing, also departed for a job ashore. There was plenty of work to be done around the ship, repainting inside and outside and replacing equipment. The old flight deck intercommunications system, which had survived by kind permission of a 'little brown jug',* would be replaced by a brand new system manufactured in St Leonards-on-Sea, a mile from my home in Bexhill. Another company a couple of hundred yards away on the other side of the road outside my home was producing armament explosive release units for the FAA. One never quite knew who was making equipment for one's aircraft!

May drove over to Devonport to collect me for Christmas leave. Winter had set in hard and there were all the signs of a white Christmas—which

_____

* Used for replenishing the communications cooling system.

duly arrived. I always enjoyed being at home with my family at Christmas time. St Norbert's was a very welcoming home, very warm inside, and we adored the place. The only family absent member was our old dog Timber, missed by all of us since his death a few years earlier. However, we now lived close to a main road, and another dog in these circumstances would have been the stuff of nightmares. We still had Zebbie, Sweetie Pie's son, and just before the celebrations we acquired another cat, still very much a kitten. The new addition was named Tinkerbell, and she promptly went down with cat 'flu. However, with the help of Mike, our friendly vet who lived two doors away, she was given a 'jab', kept wrapped up in warm blankets and placed in a basket in front of the fire in the dining room to which we retired every Christmas holiday. Naomi and Dee Dee fussed over the patient, feeding her warm milk and choice pieces of turkey, and it was not long before she was up and about, romping around the house as if she owned it.

* * *

It snowed heavily throughout Christmas 1975, making it impossible for May to drive me back to the ship. Instead, after the New Year celebrations, I took a train to London and caught *The Cornishman* from Paddington to Plymouth. At Plymouth, Leading Airman Somerville picked me up with the ship's Land Rover, and I was soon back on board a warm and comfortable ship, the gangway staff offering their usual welcome with big grins and handshakes. With just a couple of days to go before slipping our moorings, Bob Northard realised that he had left his Commander's hat at home and had only his beret. A quick call was made to Gieves in Plymouth giving his size and a new hat was delivered on board just as the gangway was being lifted.

A small drama unfolded as I stood in Flyco monitoring the ship's departure. I was told that one of my Flight Deck Leading Hands was AWOL—a very serious offence since he had 'missed his ship on sailing' knowing full well that the carrier was under sailing orders. He had married an Army Major's daughter and the marriage was not working out very well—his wife was having affairs with other men during his absence at sea—so he had decided to extend his leave in order to resolve matters. However, by his action he had merely sunk into deeper waters. He reported to the RN Barracks and I sent a helicopter inshore to pick him up. It was a very sad case, because he was charged both with being AWOL and with the aggravated offence of missing his ship, resulting in his being disrated to Naval Airman 2nd Class although, with the consequent loss of pay, this perhaps did not matter too much. With the help of his Divisional Officer, divorce papers were issued and the marriage came to an end. He was well rid of her

* * *

The Director of Public Relations (Royal Navy) had, without consulting the Captain, arranged for a BBC television crew to come aboard and shoot a documentary about life aboard an aircraft carrier, to be shown on BBC 1 over an eight- to ten-week period. The first we knew about it was the arrival of an 'Urgent' signal at about 1530 the day before our early-morning sailing. The BBC team was on its way and would be aboard early that evening, but they wanted a helicopter to carry a filming team aloft to capture the ship's departure. As the ship's Flight Safety Officer, I said, very firmly, no: I would not authorise a helicopter to fly around the dockyard amongst unlit cranes in semi-darkness. Commander (Air) backed me as did the Captain, and a signal was sent to that effect. However, we were overruled by Their Lordships.

The BBC team had a quick dinner and disappeared off ashore with their cameras and equipment to film the first episode of *Sailor*, entitled 'The Lads' Last Night Ashore'. They picked a sleazy nightclub in Plymouth where the dancing girls discarded just about everything and then fondled the sailors! These scenes would be shown in their entirety, uncensored, enabling the mothers, wives, fiancées and girlfriends to see what their menfolk got up to ashore before a ship sailed, the implication being that this was the sort of activity the men went in for once they had disappeared over the horizon. The show achieved high ratings and the public could hardly wait to see the next episode. However, the ship's complement was in for some difficult times ahead when it returned home six months hence and had to explain away what had been seen on 'the box'.

There are events in one's life that one wishes had never happened, and our Captain, Wilf Graham, was soon to experience one. Hours before a ship sails, all her systems are checked through by the engineers, electricians and operators to determine that everything is functioning properly. Officers and men had been carrying out this work since 0400 aboard *Ark Royal* to ensure that all was ready for our departure at 0730. Everything had been found to be in good working order and the tugs duly arrived to help pull the ship off the quayside and to carry out a 'pinwheel' manoeuvre in which she would be turned around on to a southerly heading and pointing down the harbour. With the ship about two hundred yards off the quay, the tugs started the 'pinwheel'. All was going well until the starboard engine telegraph failed, robbing the Captain of his starboard outer engine and propeller. Using a telephone was too difficult because the Captain would then be moving from one side of the bridge to the other and he needed to give instant orders to the engine room, so we went to sea with only three engines.

Ahead of the ship was the Torpoint–Plymouth ferry, and the normal procedure is for the ferries to wait on either side of the harbour until a departing ship has passed them; this is because they haul themselves across by chain, which is just a few feet below the surface of the water except when they are at the departure points, when it lies on the bottom. As Wilf Graham straightened up his ship, the chain ferries, to his horror, started across the harbour. None of us could believe that the ferry captains could be so stupid. We waited to feel the ship snag the chains, but for some reason they were just below our keel and we slipped over safely.

Our next difficult passage was through the Hamoaze, the tortuous S-shaped channel linking the Dockyard and the outer harbour. First the other starboard engine telegraph failed, leaving the Captain with just two propellers—on the 'wrong side' with a port turn coming up—and as we app-roached Drake's Island to turn port on to an easterly heading the port inner engine telegraph failed, leaving him with only the port outer propeller for a very difficult manoeuvre. The Captain was heard to say, 'S——! I can't believe this!' The BBC television crew was filming the entire departure and caught every word Wilf uttered, and although he was unaware of what he had said it made him the 'man of the day' for the natural manner in which it was delivered. The tug was out at right angles to the carrier's bow with the towing hawser bar taut; had it failed, the tug would have shot off across Plymouth Hoe like a rocket. There was one more turn to make, but fortunately that was to starboard. Now that the Captain was free to move about the bridge as he wished, the other engines were brought up to the same speed as the port outer and we left Plymouth Sound mopping our brows while the electricians and engineers tried to discover why three telegraphs had failed us.

The Captain headed for a position off Land's End, where the whole of the air group was re-embarked, 824 (Sea King) Squadron landing-on as we steamed westwards to be stowed safely below before the heavy jets arrived back on board. The fixed-wing aircraft carried out some limited flying and deck-landing practice, after which the ship turned south, heading for Gib-raltar for a weekend visit prior to departing for Puerto Rico.

After a three-day passage to Gibraltar and a long weekend, 'Ark' left for a few days' flying practice for the air group before steaming west for the Roose-velt Roads flying area off eastern Puerto Rico. When the ship was about 300 miles from the Azores a signal was received from C-in-C Fleet ordering us to divert towards the Azores to airlift a US Navy seaman from an American nuclear submarine. He was suffering from severe appendicitis and needed to be sent ashore to the USAF base hospital at Lajes. At the time of receiving the signal Ark Royal was at the extreme range for launching and recovering a Sea King, so it was decided to send the CO of 824 Squadron with his best rescue team plus a back-up helicopter. Although we tried to keep the oper-ation from the television crew, they soon found out and wanted to go along in the second helicopter. However, because of the weight of their equipment, some of the machine's fuel had to be offloaded, thereby reducing the aircraft's range, so the ship closed another fifty miles before launching the Sea Kings. As the helicopters disappeared over the horizon, Wilf Graham slowly closed the islands but making a westing at the same time. Then an SSB broadcast was received from the CO 824 Squadron saying that they had landed at the US Air Force base at Lajes and were refuelling before proceeding to the submarine.

The medevac of the severely ill American seaman was to be a very dramatic event. When the CO of 824 Squadron arrived over the submarine the latter was being swept from end to end by heavy seas—impossible conditions for carrying out a stretcher lift—so the American Captain took his boat to a quieter cove, the seaman was brought out on to the upper casing and down went the Chief Aircrewman on the end of the wire. Just as he was hooking on the stretcher, however, a huge wave swept the submarine, washing overboard the seaman in his stretcher together with the Chief Aircrewman.

The CO manoeuvred his Sea King back quickly over the pair in the water and by a supreme effort managed to attach the lifting hook and hoist the two inboard. All the while this dramatic event was taking place the BBC team were filming every second, hardly able to contain themselves at 'scooping' such an event. The American seaman was immediately flown to the USAF hospital, where he was operated upon and quickly recovered, and the BBC team arranged for their film to be flown back to Britain for inclusion in the next episode of *Sailor*.

Honours were soon forthcoming in respect of the rescue, the CO receiving the Air Force Cross and the Chief the British Empire Medal for their bravery and the quick and expert manner in which they both handled the extremely difficult circumstances. When the CO returned to the ship he said that they were all very lucky in that neither aircraft had sustained serious damage: both had only just made it to Lajes because of the headwind, and they had landed with barely a gallon of fuel remaining between them. At Lajes the wind had been gusting up to 100 knots and it was impossible to shut down the rotors in such conditions. Refuelling was carried out in the lee of a hangar but it was still extremely rough. However, by the time that they had returned to Lajes with the patient, the winds had moderated considerably and they had been able to refuel once again in relative comfort.

The Captain altered course south-west and increased speed for the Caribbean. It was imperative that we arrive there as quickly as possible, so that our air group could continue practising. The BBC team carried on filming all over the ship. I had dubbed them 'The Jonahs': everywhere they went something seemed to happen over and above what had been planned, and always for the worst of reasons or with the worst of results. I would not have them in Flyco, although they did manage to sneak some footage of me at work there.

One day they came to me requesting permission to set up their cameras in Fly 4, the parking area just below Flyco. I turned down the request, explaining that it was far too dangerous a position for them to be standing during landing operations, but I was overruled and they set up their cameras and started filming the landings. It must have been the second Phantom to land that had the accident. The aircraft's right tyre inflated to 400psi and burst with the force of a 1,000-pound bomb, pieces of rubber and fragments of metal wheel flying everywhere like so many sharp knives—right opposite the television camera crew. Everybody ducked for safety and fortunately nobody suffered any injuries. The head of the team came up to Flyco to apologise for not taking me seriously concerning the hazards on the flight deck and promised to listen to me more carefully in future. I had at last managed to get through to them.

* * *

It had been arranged for 892 Squadron to conduct Sidewinder firings against BQM-37 target drones. The missiles were live in the sense that they had active homing heads and rocket motors, though not live warheads. It was during these missile firings that a US Navy C-130 drone carrier was nearly shot down. The Phantom crew locked up on a target (which they could not see) at some considerable distance; the target was within the firing range and the Range Safety Officer confirmed that the target had been correctly identified and gave clearance to fire. Off went the Sidewinder with a firm lock-up. However, for some reason the C-130—which apart from carrying BQM drones was also on an engine test flight—had entered the danger area. Suddenly the aircraft's crew felt and heard a thud from the starboard outer engine—the engine under test—and a fire warning light illuminated in the cockpit. The fire was quickly extinguished and the crew declared an emergency and headed back to their base at Roosevelt Roads, where they landed safely. When the engine was examined the remains of a Sidewinder were discovered in the exhaust pipe. Had the missile been fitted with a warhead, there is no doubt that the C-130 would have been shot down with the loss of its entire crew.

* * *

Following flying practice in the Puerto Rico area the ship put into Fort Lauderdale for a short visit. It was while we were alongside here that the catapults were found to be defective when inspected by the flight-deck engineers. There had been several reports from flight-deck personnel that they had seen the huge metal blocks being lifted during the catapult runs, especially when Phantoms were launching, and when the engineers inserted the end of a crowbar under the centre section of the blocks it was discovered that they could be moved a couple of inches. Slowly, as the blocks were lifted out one by one, the dreadful truth revealed itself: the bottoms of the blocks, which rested on narrow troughs running from one end of each catapult to the other, were badly corroded, as were the blocks themselves. So much metal had been eaten away, in fact, that the blocks were free to float outwards and upwards. This was a very serious engineering defect and one that was beyond the capability of the ship to repair; moreover, the ship was now non-operational, except in an extreme emergency. Signals flashed back and forth between and among the ship, MoD (Navy), Bath and Devonport Dockyard as to how to the defect might be quickly rectified.

We made our suggestions, and then a signal arrived instructing us to proceed to Norfolk Navy Yard, where heavy engineering facilities would be made available. The ship would launch all her fixed-wing aircraft at half fuel loads to NAS Norfolk and NAS Oceana for the duration of the repair. The catapults were quickly reassembled and we left Fort Lauderdale. Once all the flyable fixed-wing aircraft had been launched, the flight-deck engineers quickly set about lifting all the catapult blocks and stacking them on the starboard side of the flight deck near the aircraft crane—which promptly went unserviceable when its jib electric motor failed to cut out and jib itself collapsed and was severely buckled. It appeared that someone did not like us and was putting every obstacle in our way; Wilf Graham, the Captain, was almost pulling his hair out in despair. However, MoD (Navy) arranged for Norfolk Navy Yard, along with personnel from Devonport, to repair the catapult blocks and rail troughs and the jib.

Admiral Kidd USN, SACLANT (Supreme Allied Commander Atlantic), was not going to have one of his carriers *hors de combat* for long and so as 'Ark' arrived alongside at Norfolk the USN Dockyard staff were waiting with flatbeds and cranes, and before the mooring ropes were made fast the blocks were going over the side, followed by the crane jib. Another team worked on the catapult troughs, grinding and cleaning them back so that they could be built up by welding and then ground down once again to the correct configuration. The efficiency with which the work was carried out was almost incredible, the teams toiling day and night until the job was finished, and within ten days the catapults were fully operational and the crane jib had been repaired and was back in place. The cost to the British Government was $38,000. None of us could believe it.

* * *

As soon as the repairs had been completed *Ark Royal* proceeded to sea, showering thanks and congratulations upon the US Navy for a job well done. The air group was re-embarked and we headed off for the Puerto Rico sea training areas, where we spent ten days flying hard both during daylight and at night. Then we went alongside at Roosevelt Roads for a long weekend, where we were visited by the Second Sea Lord. He gave us a long and interesting briefing on the way ahead, and judging by his looks in my direction I gained the impression that I was in the running for promotion to Commander (SL). Sure enough I was; indeed, *Ark Royal* gained a fair share of promotions on the Supplementary List. I could not believe my luck because I was certain in my own mind that there others more worthy—for example Bob King and Graham Hoddinott, both of whom were senior to me. However, I was very pleased and those of us on the list threw a huge lunch party in the wardroom.

Following our visit to Puerto Rico the ship returned to Norfolk, and one Sunday lunchtime the Captain's Secretary came to me in the bar and asked if the British Phantoms could carry the American AIM-7E Sparrow missile. At the time I was sure that they could not because of the different modification states of the US and British aircraft, and Roger Pinhey, 892 Squadron's Weapon Engineer Officer, and the ship's WLO both confirmed this. I told the Secretary and he passed the message on to the Captain, who then informed Admiral Kidd—who went ballistic! Everybody had been telling him the opposite. We had always known that most NATO weapons could not be crossed-operated within the allies, though whether the Russians ever realised this I do not know.

* * *

My time aboard the ship was nearing its end. It was about this time, while at Norfolk, that Commander Lynn Middleton and his cohort Commander Jeff Hunt from FOAC's Staff decided to visit the ship and conduct an inspection of us and other ships in the task group. I was on duty the day they both decided to visit the Royal Fleet Auxiliary *Olmeda*, which was at anchor in the outer harbour. It had been intended to use the Captain's gig but its motor was poor and was due to be replaced by the engineering department. Lynn jumped up and down, demanding to know why it was not serviceable and ready. As the Duty Lieutenant Commander for the day, I tried to explain and also pointed out that the wind and sea conditions within the harbour were totally unsuitable for a passage in such a small craft. So they decided to go ashore to inspect the disembarked helicopters. What they did not tell me was that they intended to use an SAR helicopter to ferry them out to *Olmeda*; had they done so, I could have informed them that they needed to take lifejackets with them because there were not enough in the helicopters. When they discovered that there were no lifejackets for them, they blew their stacks and had to borrow from 824 Squadron. This was, in my opinion, no big crisis: all they had had to do was ask. They seemed to think that all these details should have been organised for them but their problems were caused in the main by their being so secretive about their visit. When I informed 'Wings' what had happened he told Lynn exactly what he thought and the Captain backed him up to the hilt. So ended a small fracas, and one that had not been helped by the very wet and miserable weather. Back at sea, Jeff Hunt tried to interfere with the way I worked out my aircraft catapult launch calculations. I asked him whether he had ever conducted launches and whether he had ever been Lieutenant Commander (Flying) or Commander (Air), the answer to both questions being no. I asked him then please to leave me alone before he caused an accident. I knew exactly what I was doing, and had been doing it safely for a very long time. Bob Northard jumped in at this moment and told him to leave me alone for the same reasons.

Nobody likes inspections by the Admiral's Staff because they usually interfere with a ship's daily routine. However, if an itinerary is arranged properly so that everybody knows exactly what is happening, the inspection can go off like clockwork and to everybody's satisfaction. These two wanted to take everybody by surprise, to catch people off their guard, and in my book that is not the way to conduct an inspection.

* * *

The ship's XO, David Cowling, was due to leave at the same time as myself. My relief was Lieutenant Commander Charles Manning, who was a very good choice. The ship's Land Rover was still ashore at Norfolk for liaison purposes, and after being flown ashore the four of us who were returning to Britain were driven to Norfolk Airport to be flown up to Dulles Airport in Washington, DC. I was on my way home after eighteen months in the ship— although at one point I wondered whether I was going to make it safely. The Boeing 727 in which we were flying home was taking off in a severe cross wind, and it had travelled barely a hundred yards when the port engine backfired owing to its being the downwind powerplant. The huge bang had me almost leaping out of my seat with fright. The take-off run continued,

341

however, and soon the jet was airborne and turning for Washington. CBNS had placed us all in a very good transit hotel, which we shared with Lynn and Jeff. We all had a few drinks together and there were no hard feelings over their inspection visit. The next day we boarded an RAF VC-10, landing at RAF Brize Norton at 0800 the day after that. As soon as I had cleared Customs I was on a train for London, having been dropped off by Lynn at Swindon station. After arriving at Paddington I took a taxi over to Victoria station and caught the next train for Bexhill, where May and the children awaited me.

* * *

I would not serve again in the old *Ark Royal*. A few years later she was paid off, and she ended her days in a the breaker's yard in Scotland. So ended the life of a wonderful ship—a ship that was loved, revered even, by all who served in her, and one of which, and of whose complement, I will always have very fond memories. Simply stated, there was no other ship like her.

VIII

BACK TO THE DESK

— 28 —

Helicopters and Martels

I WAS DUE for promotion to Commander's rank on 1 September 1975, and the Appointer had to find a job for me until there was a vacancy for a Commander's appointment. At Yeovilton, Commander Nick Bennett had returned from being on CBNS's Staff in Washington. He was conducting an investigation into flight safety from the operational side in parallel with FONAC's air engineering flight safety investigation. He had become rather overloaded and needed somebody with experience to assist him; I was considered to be the man for the job.

The summer of 1975 was one of the hottest on record in the British Isles. For day after day at Yeovilton, the sun blazed down from a cloudless sky. C-in-C Home finally issued an order for all personnel who wore Fore-and-Aft rig—i.e., officers' uniform—to shift into modified Red Sea rig. This meant open-necked, short-sleeved shirts with rank shoulder boards but no cummerbund. The Royal Navy was finally moving into the twentieth century!

Nick Bennett and I went through every FAA aircraft accident and incident report for the past twenty years to try to establish a trend, if indeed there was one. It was an interesting task albeit a gruesome one. However, it did appear that some aircrew had experienced accidents or incidents more often than others, and in many cases they seemed to follow a pattern. When we looked into the background of one helicopter pilot, for example, we discovered that he had come from a university having read psychology. Neither Nick nor I could understand why a young man with this type of background would be suitable for military flying duties. He had suffered a number of accidents, all of the same general nature, and we could not see how he could be suited for flying on a dark and stormy night forty feet above the waves of the North Atlantic searching for submarines. Mentally, he did not have the aptitude for such a situation. There were other similar accident or incident reports, but, on the whole, those we investigated could be ascribed to pilot or aircrew error, command error, mechanical failure or merely sheer bad luck. No particular trend was apparent, and the obvious lesson to be drawn was that everybody needed to be more vigilant during flight operations. Nobody went out of their way to cause an accident. In one instance, the

Command brought about a court martial because of a stupid mistake in the local command flying instructions, a glaring error that should have been spotted during a recent Command Inspection. The Command was holding a helicopter test pilot responsible for an accident in which an anti-submarine sonar ball became entangled with an underwater explosive dumping site. He had to jettison it, at great loss and expense to the Navy. This explosive dumping area should assuredly have been highlighted in the local Flying Orders but in fact it was not.

After six months Nick was ready to finalise his report, which was then forwarded to FONAC and DNAW. His recommendations and proposals were accepted, and he was reappointed to an MoD (Navy) directorate while I 'moved sideways' to join a team looking at Commando helicopter squadrons and carriers. I was duly promoted to Commander (SL) on 1 September, joining an élite group consisting of two other aviators and an electrical officer on the Supplementary List.

* * *

The Commando Helicopter team consisted of Commanders Dave Howard and Martin Johnston and Lieutenant Commander Jeremy Knapp, who had been a former Commando Helicopter Squadron Commanding Officer, plus me. Dave Howard was the initial team leader, although I would take over from him later when he was appointed to an intelligence unit at Wilton near Salisbury. Martin was the engineer and Jeremy was the commando helicopter expert, while I was the fellow with the uncluttered mind, not having existing knowledge of such operations.

With the demise of the helicopter commando carriers, it was my contention that, if we were to reorganise our commando airborne force properly, we had to look at the RAF. They operated their helicopter army air support out of RAF Odiham, not very far from Yeovilton. This was considered a good idea and Dave Howard arranged a visit. The Royal Marine Commando helicopter unit and its base at Stonehouse Barracks, Plymouth, was also visited. Both the RM and the RAF had some very good ideas and ways of doing things, so it was essentially a question of reorganising our helicopter commando force into a more effective unit based at Yeovilton, using the experience and knowledge of these other armed services.

It occurred to me also that the best way forward was to have just one large helicopter squadron under the command of an officer of Commander's rank. This squadron would be subdivided into five smaller flights, four under the command of a Lieutenant Commander and the fifth the HQ and training flight. This would be very similar to the arrangements for 849 (AEW) Squadron, each flight being identified by a letter appended to the squadron number. This principle was accepted, and we could now move on to tackle the support, engineering and supply facilities, and the ships for the task.

Dave Howard's new appointment left me in sole charge of the project, the proposals for which now had to be gathered together into an acceptable report. Fate would play a part in making available a young Sub Lieutenant who had been a civil servant before joining 'the Andrew'. He had been to Oxford and gained a degree in English, which would be of use to us in formulating a readable document for civil servants, politicians, and of course those in the Navy. This young officer had been involved in a traffic accident in which he had lost one leg a couple of inches below the knee; he had been fitted with an artificial limb and foot and was using his time with us to become adapted to them, and to regain his strength prior to, perhaps, taking up helicopter piloting once again. He quickly read through our draft report and suggested changes and corrections that certainly made it a much better document, and, having endorsed his work, I sent it off to all the interested parties for their reading.

Prior to joining the Commando Helicopter Project I had received notification of my next appointment—Royal Naval Liaison Officer in the Central Tactics and Trials Organisation at RAF Strike Command at High Wycombe in Buckinghamshire. Soon afterwards, I received a most pleasing letter from the RAF Air Commodore commanding CTTO, Air Commodore George Park. I wrote a reply gladly accepting the post; it would be my first real appointment as a Commander. I would be relieving Russell Abrahams, who was retiring from the Navy. Many of the RAF officers in CTTO were known to me personally from their days while they were on exchange with the Fleet Air Arm, while another RN officer was at Strike Command serving as an AEW advisor.

* * *

It was just like joining the US Navy all those years before. I was full of apprehension at what was in store as I drove north to High Wycombe in our old white Austin Maxi, but I really had no need to feel that way as I would soon find out. CTTO is co-located with RAF Strike Command at the top of a ridge to the north-west of High Wycombe. Leaving Wycombe, one drives up a valley and then turns right to climb through a heavily wooded area in which much of the subterranean control and command organisation is hidden. The Officers' Mess proved to be exactly like all RAF Officers' Messes in style and pattern. As is the way, I left my 'calling card' in the Mess President's tray at the entrance to the hallway and in due course was invited to his residence for drinks or tea. I was to have a very pleasant surprise: the Mess President was Group Captain Mervyn David, an old schoolfriend from my days at Rye Grammar School. I could not believe my eyes!

Mervyn and I had attended RGS together and had both been in the Air Training Corps School Flight, where he was the Cadet Flight Sergeant. When he left to join the RAF, I took over from him as the Cadet Flight Sergeant. He had won a seat at the RAF College at Cranwell but had been found unsuitable for flying duties so had joined the RAF Regiment, which is responsible for the protection and air defence of all RAF bases. It was as a Flight Lieutenant RAF Regiment that I had last seen him at the RGS, but then our paths had taken totally different directions and it would be nearly thirty years before we met again. At some time during his career he had decided to transfer to the RAF Provost Branch because of the greater opportunity it offered to rise to higher rank than in the Regiment. He was right, because he was eventually promoted to Air Commodore, becoming head of the Provost Branch before retiring from the Air Force.

Mervyn came from Winchelsea, three miles west of Rye, where his father was the railway stationmaster. The actual railway station was about a mile north of the town, sitting in the valley through which the Southern Railway passed on its way to Hastings and Ashford. Before and after World War II it was a busy little station because sheep and cattle were taken there and transported by rail to the Rye or Ashford markets. The stationmaster and his family lived above the station in relatively comfortable quarters, and of course Mervyn had free travel by train to Rye to attend school. However, in the early 1960s Lord Beeching had been retained by the Government to 'rationalise' the British railway system, and Winchelsea station was one of those on his 'chop list'. The dual-track line would be reduced to a single track with passes at each of the main stations; the Davids' home was reduced to rubble and replaced by a boarding and disembarkation platform. The marshalling yards and cattle yards would all disappear except for those at Ashford and Hastings.

When I met Mervyn again at High Wycombe he was totally dedicated to the RAF. This was no surprise. He now had no mother or father, only his immediate wife and family. He had lived most if not all of his life at Winchelsea until joining the RAF, and to return and discover that one's former home no longer existed must have been a heartbreaking experience. In that respect I was very lucky because my old homes in Winchelsea, Rye Harbour and Camber still survived.*

When I arrived at CTTO, Russell Abrahams was still the resident RNLO although he was due to retire shortly and take care of his wife, an invalid in a wheelchair. I had not seen him since my days at RNAS Ford when he was flying Wyverns. He was ready for retirement because he always felt uneasy being away from his wife. It would take a week for him to hand over to me because we had many outlying posts and organisations to visit and many projects to review; many of these latter were of vital interest to the FAA, and it was therefore important that I understood them.

The CTTO threw a splendid leaving party for the Abrahams. It was a grand affair, and there was little doubt that they were very well liked by the RAF. I would have some big shoes to fill. Once Russell had left I settled down to reading and exploring the corridors of power. Russell had organised appointments for me to meet UK (Air), Air Chief Marshal Sir David Evans, who was a Canadian, and the Senior Air Staff Officer to Sir David, Air Marshal Charles Maughan, a former Navy pilot. SASO was dined out of the RAF during my time in CTTO, and it was at this event that I learnt that he had been in the Fleet Air Arm. He had transferred to the RAF some time during 1946 as a Flight Lieutenant and slowly climbed the ladder of responsibility. When he

---

* I would still, if I had the chance, return to Rye Harbour and move into No 1 Inkerman Cottages, renovate the property and spend the remainder of my life there in retirement. No doubt it would require extensive work, but it would be worth every penny—and there is of course the Inkerman Arms next door!

left the RAF he became the Secretary of the Royal British Legion. Both he and Sir David had a healthy respect for the Fleet Air Arm, and said so to my face when I called upon them. I was very pleased to hear this; after all, our one aim in life is the same—the protection of the Realm. I left them feeling that my time at High Wycombe was going to be enjoyable.

Air Commodore George Park was the Officer Commanding CTTO when I joined, but his time in command was coming to an end and his relief would be Group Captain John Pack, the Officer Commanding RAF Kinloss, who would be promoted to Air Commodore prior to taking over CTTO. Although I was directly responsible to CTTO, there were two Group Captains to whom I had to report concerning attack, strike, air defence, anti-submarine, maritime reconnaissance and helicopter matters. They were both very amenable, so it did not matter too much one way or the other.

In the office adjacent to mine was the Strike Command Flight Safety team. It was through them that I learnt that the FAA had lost one of its F-4Ks at RAF Leuchars, piloted by the SNO, Commander Carl Davis, with Lieutenant John Gavin, one of my old 767 Squadron instructors, as his observer. The SNO survived the crash but John was killed, and I sat and worried about that accident for days. The SNO had been practising low-level aerobatics and had lost control coming out of a tight turn on to the runway heading with his flaps and gear down. The aircraft's rate of descent was so high that there was little chance of recovering before hitting the ground. He had ejected sideways and was arrested by a barbed wire fence but John never left his cockpit before the aircraft hit the ground and was killed instantly. The SNO received injuries that left him a paraplegic.

For days I sat in my office turning over the accident in my mind. It should have never happened, but it did and it was due entirely to Command error. FONAC's Staff should never have given permission for Carl to practice low-level aerobatics with so few hours on type—he had only 120—and Carl should never have taken it upon himself to practise such demanding manoeuvres, despite his flying experience. It was a case of overconfidence on Carl's part and sheer stupidity on the part of FONAC's staff. I would have thought, following Simon Idiens' and Bill Hawley's accidents, that everybody would have been more vigilant, but this was evidently not so and John Gavin had had to pay with his life.

I was to spend eighteen months at High Wycombe and would enjoy every moment. Although I lived in the Officers' Mess, like so many others I commuted over the weekends. Perhaps I should have taken a married quarters, and driven the family back home to Bexhill over the weekends and for the holiday periods, but, with money tight and a mortgage to finance, I decided against it.

My quarters in the Officers' Mess were quite excellent. I lived at the south-western end of the Mess, where I had a suite of rooms of my own plus a bathroom, and toilet facilities which I shared with a Group Captain. I was certainly amongst the élite, with Group Captains on either side of me and along most the corridors plus an Air Marshal on the floor below. This was Russell's doing, although, as he had pointed out to the Mess Officer, Royal

Navy Commanders were on a par with RAF Group Captains. My batwoman was a local lady who came in daily to look after her officers. She always ironed my clothes and pressed my suits, and would have done my washing had I not stopped her. In many ways she looked after me as old Albert had at Ford all those years ago. These people are the salt of the earth, and are hard to find these days: they were very proud to look after us and we were very proud to have them doing so.

* * *

My time in CTTO was fully occupied with both Navy and Air Force matters. I had been placed in charge of the RN and RAF Martel TV missile firings at Aberporth in west Wales and of the Martel AR missile firings at Biscarrosse in western France. At Aberporth the Martels were fired against an old RN frigate anchored in the middle of Cardigan Bay. On one occasion, the target was set on fire when the linoleum on the decks in the old operations room and the sailors' mess decks was ignited by missile rocket fuel. Fortunately the range also had one of the Dartmouth training squadron frigates at the time, and we called her over to extinguish the blaze. This they did, though as a result the old target frigate almost capsized due to the amount of free-flow water on the upper decks. During my tenure at CTTO the RN and RAF must have fired between six and ten missiles, with some excellent results.

The anti-radar missile firings were carried out over the Bay of Biscay from the French Air Force base at Cazaux, and were made after I had left CTTO. However, I did the organising and wrote the missile firing orders. In company with a Flight Lieutenant from the armament division at MoD (PE), I visited l'Armée de l'Air at the Ministère de la Défense in Paris to discuss our firings. Unlike the British, the French wear uniform every day at their Ministry; we were all wearing civilian clothing. Then a visit was arranged to Cazaux followed by one to Biscarrosse, the Biscay missile control centre, to discuss our firings and requirements. The meetings in Paris were rather protracted because everything was spoken in French and was then translated for us. Our French Liaison Officer, a Major in l'Armée de l'Air, was very amiable and spoke quite good English. After the meetings we discovered that the other Frenchmen present could speak quite reasonable English but that the President, Général de Gaulle, had decreed that only French was to be spoken at political and diplomatic meetings. At Cazaux our task was made much easier by the presence of a RAF exchange officer who could speak French like a native.

Our first visit to Cazaux went very well indeed. The MoD (PE) RAF Flight Lieutenant—the equivalent of an RN Special Duties Officer—led the team as he knew all the French Air Force personnel involved at Cazaux and Biscarrosse. He organised all our air passage and our transport to and from Bordeaux. After landing at Bordeaux, we picked up a hire car and drove over to Cazaux to check into our quarters. Our cabins, or 'rooms' as the RAF would call them, were very spartan though I had lived in worse. Then our gallant RAF leader took us off to dinner at a restaurant he knew in Arcachon, a small town on the edge of the Bassin d'Arcachon. Although it is basically a fishing port, over the years Arcachon had become much more of a yachting centre, but the season was over and autumn was fast approaching. One of the other reasons for visiting Arcachon was to meet up with the RAF Squadron Leader exchange officer at Cazaux, who lived in the town. I would have thought that, in the circumstances, he might have met us at Bordeaux and ensured that we had better accommodation than we were given, but he did not and now here we were trying to find him!

At about midnight we returned to our quarters at Cazaux. The young corporal manning the hall porter's desk appeared sleepily in his 'long johns' and gave us our keys. During our absence, our FAF Major liaison officer from Paris had arrived and changed our accommodation. I had been moved to a cabin befitting a 'Commandant' and I was overawed: there was a circular bed, with 'his and her' towels in the bathroom, there was a 'booze locker' full of the best of French drinks, and the whole room was decked out in the best of furnishings. What a change from my previous hovel! It was obvious that the French treat their Commanders with more respect than we do in Britain. I called the team in and we all had a good nightcap before retiring.

It was still quite dark the following morning as we made our way to the dining hall for breakfast of croissants, marmalade or jam and coffee—hardly enough to send a soldier to work on! The men dined at one end of the mess hall and the officers at the other end, which was all very republican. Our RAF exchange officer picked us up from the mess hall and drove us out to the Station HQ Flight where our French Air Force Liaison Officer was waiting. The HQ Flight would be responsible for loading the Martel AR missiles on to the Buccaneers and for carrying out all the safety checks. After three hours of discussions we were driven out to Biscarrosse Range Control on the eastern coast of the Bay of Biscay. After being shown around by a very helpful French officer who would be responsible for the control of our missile firings on the range, we returned to Cazaux. The following morning we left early in our hired car for Bordeaux and flew back to Britain, happy that all that could have been done had been done. It was now my task to put everything into a set of orders for use by the RN, the RAF, the MoD, the FAF, the French MoD, FAF Cazaux and the Biscarrosse Range. The orders would have to be in both English and French, and fortunately there was residing at MoD (Air) a civil servant who was fluent in French.

I had left CTTO by the time the RAF and RN fired their Martel AR missiles, and my relief Commander, Tony Morton, became responsible for the project. I understand that there were several hiccoughs but that these were resolved and the firings were successful.

* * *

Another project that took up a great deal of my time while at CTTO concerned the fitting of anti-collision lights to military aircraft, starting with high-speed jets. The RAF had suffered two nasty mid-air collisions, the first involving two Harriers in which the pilot of one aircraft was killed and the second the Station Commander at RAF Coningsby, who lost his life, as did his navigator and the pilot of a civilian crop-spraying aircraft. In this second accident, wreckage had been scattered over a large area of the Lincolnshire countryside, but fortunately nobody had been injured or killed on the ground. As the project was dropped in my lap a near mid-air collision occurred over a Welsh reservoir when a Buccaneer from RAF Honington just missed a Hunter fighter from RAF Brawdy. In this accident the Buccaneer pilot saw the Hunter at the last moment and pulled so much 'g 'on his bomber that he wrenched the tail off his aircraft. Both he and his navigator ejected from their aircraft, but in so doing the navigator collided with the tumbling tail and stabilator, sustaining severe injuries. The main reason for the accident was the fact that both aircraft were camouflaged overall and were very difficult to make out against the rugged Welsh countryside. The RAF requested the assistance of a naval diving unit to recover the wreckage on the edge of the reservoir and the FAA's AAIU conducted the crash investigation.

The Air Force had decided on two models of bluish-white anti-collision lights, one manufactured by Halle of West Germany and the other by a US company. There was little doubt in my mind that the German equipment was far superior to the American, which looked as if it had been thrown together at the last moment for the purposes of the trial. I was given two sets of each light, and it was planned to place one of each type on a couple of Buccaneers and the other two on two Jaguars going through re-work at RAF Andover. The two Jaguars were destined for one of the squadrons based at Bruggen, RAF Germany.

At RAF Honington I found nothing but enthusiasm for fitting the two lights to two aircraft in No 208 Squadron. The pilots and navigators were keen to conduct a trial as soon as possible, and when they started they thought them to be a tremendous advantage, especially during low-level flying and in poor visibility. However, at Bruggen I encountered opposition, the general attitude being, 'What do we want these for? We have no problem seeing each other over here!' I visited Wing Commander (Flying) as well as the Station Commander, and I spoke up saying that I was rather worried about the Jaguar squadrons' general attitude. The RAF had had enough air collisions and this was a positive step in the right direction to reduce their frequency. He agreed, and they both promised that they would do their best to ensure that a proper trial was carried out for CTTO. When I returned to CTTO I informed the Air Commodore of my misgivings where the RAF Germany squadrons were concerned, and he had a quiet word with the Air Station Commander, who promised that he would get us the facts.

Within a couple of months I had enough information for a preliminary report, which was forwarded to UK (Air) SASO, a new Air Marshal who had taken over from Charles Maughan. He was very enthusiastic about the lights and wanted to visit the trials unit at RAF Honington. The squadron had parked a Buccaneer in a hollow some distance from the taxi track, and as we drove past it neither SASO nor I could see it because of its excellent camouflage. Then the ground crew switched on the anti-collision light and SASO spotted it. He was persuaded there and then that we needed to fit it to all aircraft.

352

'Okay, Doust, we'll get them installed in all front-line aircraft right away!' he said on the way back to the Squadron.

'Whoa, sir! MoD (Air) and MoD (PE) have to give their sanction to the purchase and will find the money to install the modification, but it is not quite so easy as you think.'

'Well, leave it to me and I will pull some strings, but in the meantime you get on and complete your report as quickly as possible.'

This was a senior RAF officer I liked. He acted in the traditions of the Navy: 'Do it, and any problems will be sorted out later!'

Our report was to be illustrated by a message that came in via UK (Air)'s Flight Safety Centre office, next door to me at High Wycombe. An RAF Germany Jaguar—one of the aircraft carrying my modified anti-collision light—was on detachment to Lossiemouth for low-flying and armament practice. Also detached to Lossiemouth were Hunters from RAF Brawdy. It was while one of these Hunters was flying south along the western side of Loch Erich that the pilot spotted a brilliant blue/white flashing light moving north along the eastern side of the loch, though he could not see the aircraft to which it was attached. The Hunter pilot altered course to intercept the light and came up alongside the Jaguar. The Jaguar pilot was most surprised to find another aircraft alongside him; he had not detected it because it did not have the light.

The pair flew back together to Lossiemouth, discussed the incident with the Flight Detachment Commanders and reported it to the Station Flight Safety Centre, which passed the details on to Strike Command at High Wycombe. The Hunter and Jaguar pilots were all most impressed with the new light and endorsed its safety aspect with enthusiasm. Little interest had been shown hitherto by the Bruggen squadrons, whose reports back to CTTO had given the impression that it was all too much bother and that the light was not required. My answer to that was: tell that to the families of the aircrew who have been killed in mid-air collisions! This one report from Lossiemouth tipped the scales.

I finalised my report and together with the results and conclusions it was forwarded to Strike Command, to MoD (Air) and to MoD (PE). My recommendation was that it should be installed on all military aircraft, starting with the high-speed jets and aircraft involved in low-level flying duties and then moving on to the transport and bomber aircraft. When MoD (PE) received the report it balked immediately, protesting that it had to go out to tender, official trials on both lights and on any other possible contenders had to be undertaken, and so forth. The Chief of the Air Staff said no: this was a matter of flight safety, and the CTTO report and recommendations had to be implemented immediately before there were any further accidents and loss of life. After a great deal of prevarication MoD (PE) backed down and the equipment began to be purchased and installed, first in the ground attack aircraft and then in the helicopters, transports and bombers, in that order of priority. I had won the day but only with the help of some very senior RAF officers who saw the wisdom of having this essential piece of flight safety equipment installed in all aircraft. As far as I know, there is not one aircraft, military or civilian, in the Western world that is these days not fitted with the bluish-white anti-collision light as standard equipment.

* * *

One of my most enjoyable experiences at CTTO was a visit to RAF Kinloss with one of the Group Captains, culminating in a flight in a Nimrod MR Mk 1 aircraft on a day's 'fish patrol' over waters to the east and north of the Shetland Isles. The Nimrod was (and still is) the RAF's large anti-submarine aircraft, which at the time was based both at Kinloss, near Lossiemouth, and at St Mawgan in Cornwall. The Nimrod was derived from the old de Havilland Comet airliner and was built at Hawarden near Chester. While going through Advanced Flying Training at RAF Valley, I, together with the others on my course, had visited the building facilities at Hawarden. Old Comet airliners were being flown in and stripped down and a new bulbous section was fitted beneath the fuselage of each one to carry torpedoes and sonobuoys. The engine bays and nacelles were enlarged to accommodate Rolls-Royce Speys for increased power and lower fuel consumption compared with the old Avon jets, a new anti-submarine radar was fitted in the nose and an enormous Magnet Anomaly Detector boom was added to the tail section of the aircraft. The passenger cabin was converted to an anti-submarine tactical control bay, kitchen and air electronics cabin. All in all the aircraft represented a huge improvement over the old Shackleton. The Nimrod carried a crew of eleven officers and NCOs, including the two pilots, a navigator and a tactical operations officer. The aircraft I flew in was from No 120 Squadron and was piloted by the Station Commander, Group Captain John Pack—who was about to be become my Commanding Officer at CTTO.

When I boarded the Nimrod there was officially no seat for me, so I sat on the cockpit floor behind the Group Captain, the aircraft's commander. Had there been an accident, my chances of survival would have been nil; and here was I, the great spokesman for flight safety, busting all the rules, flying with no seat or harness! The purpose of the mission was to check and monitor all fishing vessels within northern waters to ascertain that they were British. It was a rough day to the north of Scotland and the Shetlands, with heavy seas and storm force winds. It was hard to believe that small vessels would be out in such conditions catching food for the nation.

As we flew over fishing vessels the Air Electronics Officer took photographs. A radio call was made to the Flag Officer Scotland & Northern Ireland operational centre at Dunfermline giving the fishing registration number, name and port of registration to determine whether the vessel was genuine. Between midday and 1300 the designated cook appeared with a hot lunch, an excellent meal that had been prepared back at Kinloss (and this time containing no peas or bananas!). The patrol was then resumed. On the way back to Kinloss we received a call from Dunfermline that a distress message had been intercepted coming from an oil rig barge north of the Shetlands. The barge was being towed to Norway but its towline had broken, the onboard generator had failed, huge seas were sweeping the vessel and the crew had gone to

Abandon Ship Stations. Would we divert to overfly the barge and establish the situation, and then advise on what could or should be done?

Within half an hour we were overhead. Heavy seas were washing over the barge and we could not see how the crew would be able to launch lifeboats in the atrocious conditions. The men were standing on the upper decks in dayglo lifejackets and they waved as we flew close by. The tug, painted dayglo, was minuscule compared with the barge. The only way of rescuing the crew would be by helicopter, which would mean flying one of the 'Jolly Green Giants'* up from Lakenheath; it would not arrive before nightfall. We stayed with the rig for an hour in some of the worst weather imaginable. Suddenly lights began to appear all over the barge and its crew came on the international distress frequency to say that they had managed to fire up their emergency generator and that they were cancelling the distress call; while we had been flying around, moreover, the tug had managed to re-establish its towline. We wished them luck, informed Dunfermline of what had happened and that we were leaving the scene, and returned to RAF Kinloss.

After we had landed, a couple of hours were spent debriefing and listening to Soviet submarine noises that the Nimrod crew had taped while we were airborne. I had a session in the Nimrod flight simulator, dined in the Officers' Mess and went off to bed for an early night. My CTTO Group Captain had already returned to High Wycombe; I would be catching a BEA Viscount out of Inverness the following morning at 0800 so it would mean an early call and breakfast.

There was a delay at the airport but while there I met Alastair MacFarland, an old friend from Findhorn sailing days. He was seeing his son off to boarding school. I have since learnt that Alastair has passed away. He was a fine Scottish gentleman and May and I always enjoyed his company. The Viscount pilot proved to be Captain Dennis Lucas, who had been on two courses ahead of me at RAF Syerston during basic flying training, and I was soon invited up front to the flight deck for a fifteen-minute chat—something that nowadays would be totally against company regulations. On my return to High Wycombe I briefed the Air Commodore and the Group Captain on my visit to Kinloss and on the flight, and after going through the mail and papers that had piled up I returned to my cabin for a quiet nap before dinner.

* * *

It was early in 1979 when David Dobson, my Appointer, telephoned me from DNOA (X) to ask whether I liked the idea of being the next Commander (Air) of HMS *Hermes*. I sat at my desk speechless until he shouted at me.

'Are you still there, Michael?'

'Yes,', I replied, 'but are you sure that you have the right officer? I am a Commander on the Supplementary List, and that appointment's usually reserved for General List officers like yourself, as a stepping stone for promotion to Captain.'

---

* Sikorsky HH-3 rescue helicopters.

'Yes, I agree, but I have the right officer, because out of four or five possible candidates you are the best qualified.'

'Well, I think that you should go over this very carefully, David, because it is going to make many GL officers unhappy. I am not turning the job down and would be very pleased to have it.'

'Good! I'll call you back in a few days!'

A week later he telephoned me again to confirm the appointment, informing me that I would be relieving Tony Walsh as 'Wings' in late November 1979. It was a job that, even in my wildest dreams, I had never imagined being given and both May and I were overjoyed.

I now had to attend various essential courses. I had never been to a Tactical Course at HMS *Dryad*, the Navigational and Operations School at Fort Southwick, so I arranged to go on the next available, in March 1979, and to live in the wardroom there. The wardroom was an old mansion that had been left to the Navy by a lady in her will. It had been used during World War II as General Eisenhower's headquarters for the planning of Operation 'Overlord', the invasion of mainland Europe. It was a beautiful old house and the 'Overlord' painted maps were still on the walls in the anteroom, reminding everybody of those tremendous days spent battling against the tyrannies of Nazi Germany.

I met up with many old friends on the two-week course. We were divided into six syndicates that would eventually become the executive teams of six warships headed by future warship Captains Designate. There were lectures on intelligence and we acted out dummy scenarios, either in our own classrooms or in the main lecture hall. On Friday at the end of the first week we left the school for weekend leave at about 1530. It was a bitter afternoon, with the wind blowing strongly out of the north-east, when I drove home to Bexhill, about eighty miles away. Commander Bob Woodard had gone over to Lancing College in Sussex to see his two boys who were boarding there; Bob's great-grandfather had built the college when he was a clergyman as a refuge for the orphaned sons of gentlefolk. Then he drove to his home, which was west of Yeovil, Somerset. The Australian Commander on the course left for Weymouth to visit his family.

On Friday night and early Saturday morning the weather turned extremely cold and snow began falling. By dawn a full-blown blizzard was raging. The whole of the south of England, from the North Foreland to Land's End, was covered in deep snow, cutting off communities and blocking roads and railway tracks throughout most of the countryside. The west of England was particularly hard hit. I started my return journey early on Sunday afternoon and arrived at the top of the Portsdown Hills leading down to Southwick village to find a snow plough about to clear the road, so I slipped in behind it and I was shortly turning into *Dryad* in time for late afternoon tea and sandwiches. There were very few officers in the wardroom, and the bar was virtually empty except for the duty officers. At dinner there were no more than half a dozen of us. I had telephoned May to let her know that I was safe and sound and she had said that it was so bitterly cold that the two cats would not even put their noses outside the back door.

It was fairly obvious that something was wrong the next morning when the duty steward failed to bring the morning tea. I quickly had a hot shower, changed into some warm clothing and strolled into the wardroom for breakfast to see the same faces I had seen the previous evening. At 0900 I reported to the school to find only a couple of my syndicate present and the other five syndicates not fairing much better. Telephone calls started to come in as various officers reported being snowbound though making every effort to reach *Dryad*; most of the officers had gone west for the weekend, and of course that was the area hardest hit by the blizzard. By Wednesday, however, the course was all together once again but there were certainly some tales to be told.

The Australian had found himself totally blocked in at Weymouth, and it would be two days before a relief train steamed into the town station. Bob Woodard and his wife had skied across the Somerset and Devon hills to see how their parents were doing. They eventually found the top of their house protruding out of the snow, a wisp of smoke spiralling from the chimney. They entered the house via an attic window and walked downstairs to find their parents sitting on a couple of mattresses in front of the living room fire, reading books, drinking tea and unable to understand what all the fuss was about. They had food, water from melting the snow and logs from the shed, which they had reached by digging a tunnel from the kitchen door. So, after a cup of tea, Bob and his wife departed through the attic window and skied home before the night came on.

The final day of the course was spent carrying out mock battles in the simulator building. We were divided into 'Blue' and 'Orange' forces, the 'Orange' forces being the teaching staff and the operations Wrens. I had command of a destroyer or frigate but was 'sunk' half way through the battle when I was caught by torpedoes coming in from different directions with nowhere to turn for safety. At 1530 the battle was terminated and we retired to the auditorium for afternoon tea and sandwiches followed by a debriefing with the staff on how we had fared and what we should have done. This afternoon had been the best session of the course. I felt that I could have gone to sea as a destroyer or frigate captain and fought my ship with knowledge and understanding. Although the course had been rather compressed owing to the blizzard, we did manage to throw a small party for our instructors, which they much appreciated.

One lunchtime towards the end of the final week I was sitting down opposite a Captain Barnden. For a while nothing was said but then I plucked up the courage to ask if his father had been the headmaster of my junior school in Rye, East Sussex. He said that he had, we chatted about his father and mother and I asked him to remember me to his father. I had been, according to Mr Barnden, one of his worst pupils. A couple of nights later I met the Captain and his wife in the bar. 'Dad remembers you well, Doust,' he said. ' "Made Commander did he? Well it takes all sorts to run a world!" ' We both laughed heartily.

* * *

I arrived back at High Wycombe to write a report on the RN and RAF Martel firings to date and to form some conclusions from the results, although I was rather left on my own because my Operational Evaluations Group officer in Strike Command had suffered a stroke during my absence at *Dryad*. However, I managed to draw up some recommendations for onward transmission to CTTO and Strike Command.

My time in CTTO was almost over, and David Dobson had arranged for me to attend a Senior Officers' course on Air Power at the RAF College at Cranwell. I arrived at Cranwell to find that our man there was Bob Woodard. Somehow he had managed to persuade the RAF and the Navy that, as he was the Senior Naval Officer at Cranwell, he was entitled to have a flagstaff outside his married quarters where he could fly the white ensign daily when he was in residence. It was a nice gesture but it was pure 'bull'; Bob always had a sense of showmanship. When he left Cranwell he took command of HMS *Active*, a frigate that Princess Anne had launched earlier in her career as Rear Admiral of the WRNS. Bob would eventually rise to the rank of Rear Admiral and be the last Captain of HMY *Britannia*. He would be responsible for decommissioning and laying up the Royal Yacht as decreed in a series of Armed Forces 'cuts': 11 December 1997 was a very sad day for the Royal Navy, for the Royal family and of course for the country as a whole.

On my return to CTTO from Cranwell, my relief Commander Tony Morton joined and I began my handover. As Russell had done for me, I took him around all the establishments and the personnel with whom he would be working during his tenure. Most of the RAF people knew him from his days in 809 (Buccaneer) Squadron so in a sense he had his 'feet under the table' already. A leaving dinner was held for May and me. Both of us had enjoyed our time with CTTO and it was a sad day when we left. I personally had made many new friends in the RAF and had worked with them as if one of them, never allowing my rank nor my service to get in the way. My most fulfilling moment had probably been when John Pack called me into his office to tell me that he was recommending me for promotion to Captain. I thanked him from the bottom of my heart, but had to tell him that I had reached the pinnacle of promotion on the RN's Supplementary List and that I could only go further on the General Officers' List. 'Well, whatever you say, Commander,' he had replied, 'but I am going to recommend you all the same!' I left CTTO feeling very proud indeed that John Pack had thought so much of me but saddened that the end had been reached for promotion. After a few days' leave I joined DNAW for a short period before going to *Hermes* because my services were needed for a special project.

* * *

David Dobson had appointed me to DNAW to help out Commander Keith Somerville-Jones, the FAA Armament man in the Directorate. Keith was swamped with both conventional and special armament projects, and I was required to finalise a RN and RAF joint service special weapons Staff Requirement. Once again I had to go through the business of being cleared Top

Secret so that I could talk to all the people involved with the project. The Navy, being the service with the greatest requirement for this weapon, had the lead. The weapon was associated with the Sea Harrier, the new Merlin helicopter and of course the Nimrod Mk 2 that was entering service.

Keith still occupied the same office that David Howard had used before him, and Wally Hall and now Commander James Ingham, who had taken Pete Goddard's old chair, were still in the next-door office. Sharing an office with Keith had one great disadvantage: he smoked like a trooper. He used to go through at least three packets of cigarettes each day, and his ashtray of dog-ends resembled a small pyramid. Being an asthmatic, I could not stand cigarette smoke and used to throw the windows open to clear the air. Keith would accuse me of trying to kill him with cold air, and then Wally would call out from next door that it was Keith's cigarettes that would kill him, not fresh air. This daily fight went on with me accusing him of trying to give me lung cancer and he accusing me of trying to give him pneumonia. In the end, the cigarettes killed Keith because sadly, at the age of 52, a couple of years or so after retiring from the Navy, he suffered a heart attack and died.

One day, on the way back from visiting an RAF Directorate concerning the new special weapon project, Keith took me to the Naval Intelligence Section to find out some facts about the Soviets' VTOL carrier fighter, dubbed 'Forger'. We ventured no further than the entrance hall of this highly classified department, but they did not have what he wanted so we returned to DNAW. I had barely sat down when two civil servants barged into our office demanding to know who I was and what right I had to be in the Naval Intelligence Section. In reality, Keith was the only person allowed from DNAW to enter that section; not even the Director had clearance. They wanted to know what my security clearance was, and who had cleared me to enter the section. They were beginning to make me feel like a criminal, and I rounded on them. 'If you are so worried, why did you not check my credentials when I entered the entrance hall? I did not see anything because there was nothing to see, so what is all the fuss about? It was you who failed, not me. And, by the way, I have a security clearance of Top Secret '——';do you have that? I believe it is higher than your clearance?' This shut them up, but they wanted me to sign a form to the effect that I had not seen anything that could be compromised. I refused. The whole affair rather reminded me of the incident that had occurred at China Lake many years before while I was serving in VX-4. The security people had failed in their duty and then had tried to place the blame elsewhere.

While he was serving in *Ark Royal* as the CO of 809 Squadron, Keith's marriage had begun to fall apart. His wife was having an assignation with a RAF navigator from Honington. She came to the United States whilst the ship was alongside in Mayport, Florida, and created mayhem to such an extent that Keith was not in the proper frame of mind to be safe to fly. Despite attempts by CO 824 Squadron and myself to try and help the marriage, it went downhill, the pair divorced and she married her navigator. Keith was promoted to Commander and he moved to DNAW as the new FAA Armament officer, taking up residence in Wandsworth in south-west London.

359

When I arrived at DNAW Keith seemed to be much his old self. He had taken on a number of extracurricular activities, such as singing tenor in the Westminster Abbey choir. He had also a bevy of young ladies in tow, all of whom thought the world of him. However, remarriage was for him off limits. One morning he paid a visit to the RAF on the other side of the MoD and returned in a very disturbed of state of mind. After I had calmed him down, I managed to drag from him the fact that an RAF Germany Buccaneer from No XV Squadron had crashed, killing both the pilot and navigator. His ex wife's husband flew with that unit, and Keith was somehow convinced that the navigator was her new husband and that he would be saddled with her once again. I told him to stay put, poured him a very large sherry, gave him a cigarette and went round to the RAF Buccaneer directorate to see if I could find out who victim was. At first there was considerable reluctance to tell me—the accident had not as yet been officially announced—but I pointed out the problem and asked them to say, yes or no, whether the navigator was ———. They said no, I thanked them and then I rushed back to Keith and told him that he had nothing to worry about. While I had been away Wally Hall had been talking to him, and once he heard my news he perked up. We took him across to the Sherlock Holmes public house for a stiff noggin and sent him home for the day.

The special weapon project for which I had been seconded to DNAW was now coming to fruition and I started putting together the Staff Requirement for distribution to all the people who needed to know, for their comments and suggestions. With this task completed my time in DNAW came to an end, and together with several other Staff Officers who were leaving I threw a huge party in the Registry. The 'Registry Gals' came up trumps once again, producing lots of wonderful food, and after yet another farewell from my favourite Directorate I was off to join *Hermes*.

IX

WINGS OF HERMES

— 29 —

The Air Boss

THE HIGHLIGHT of any naval aviator's active career is an appointment as Commander (Air), the Head of the Air Department—or 'Wings', as he is more commonly known (and in US parlance the 'Air Boss')—of either an air station or, preferably, an aircraft carrier. For a General List officer the appointment represents a stepping stone for promotion to Captain's rank, although for a Supplementary List officer, as I was, this would never happen. These 'lists'—General, Special Duties and Supplementary—had been a thorn in my side for years, and by the time I was half way through my appointment I would be writing a paper for circulation around the Fleet and along the corridors of power proposing the amalgamation of all officers' lists into one 'Corps of Officers'—of which more later.

After a weekend at home in Bexhill I took a train to Holyhead. An RAF driver picked me up and took me to RAF Valley, where I boarded one of the ship's SAR helicopters for the flight out to *Hermes*, at that time carrying out Sea Harrier trials over the Irish Sea from a position off Anglesey. The carrier was hove-to about five miles off Holyhead in bright sunlight though with gale force winds and heavy seas running. It was wonderful to step aboard and on to a flight deck heaving in the heavy swells. I was met by Tony Walsh, the outgoing 'Wings', and immediately whisked away to the bridge to meet the Captain. He was a friendly enough senior officer who would be promoted Rear Admiral in the New Year, but at the same time he seemed a little aloof and in fact I would never really know him since he left a week after my joining the ship. His relief would be Captain David McKenzie, the last Captain of HMS *Blake*, the helicopter cruiser that had been withdrawn from service to be decommissioned prior to heading for the breaker's yard.

I had known Tony Walsh from Lossiemouth days when he had been flying in Buccaneers as an observer. It had been a very long time since an observer had held the position of 'Wings' aboard a carrier, but although he was a GL officer he would not, unfortunately, be promoted to Captain, which was a pity because he had done a very good job. His deputy was an ex Commando helicopter squadron CO whom I had known at Yeovilton, where he was Lieutenant Commander (Flying). It was apparent that he was unhappy at my being appointed as his 'boss', especially as he was a GL and I was an SL officer, and there was a degree of rancour between us over the remaining months he was aboard prior to his reappointment.

Hermes was scheduled to enter dry dock at Portsmouth early in the New Year for a twelve-month refit. However, there was union trouble in the Dockyard—the men were striking over pay and allowances—which meant that the carrier would be laid up idle, rusting, while the unions sorted out their problems. C-in-C Fleet therefore decided that the ship would sail to the Caribbean for three months on a sea training mission, taking all sailors who were awaiting draft and a limited number of helicopters that had not been assigned to any particular ship. It was even envisaged that a contingent of Wrens would be embarked under the command of a Chief Officer WRNS, but the First Sea Lord decreed that no member of the WRNS would ever go to sea during his tenure in office and the idea faded. However, the Cadet course from Dartmouth was embarked, and amongst its members was HRH Prince Andrew, who was destined to become a Sea King helicopter pilot and would fight in the Falklands War—which, in the event, was less than eighteen months away. We also embarked a contingent of young boys, the sons and nephews of personnel serving in the ship. An Instructor Officer and a Lieutenant Commander seaman officer were placed in charge of them to give schooling and instruction and to look to their general well-being.

It was decided that my air group would consist of a flight of four Sea King anti-submarine helicopters and a flight of four Wessex Mk 5 Commando helicopters commanded by a Flight Lieutenant who was the son of an Air Marshal. The helicopters embarked whilst the ship was still alongside the South Railway Jetty in the dockyard and the cadets from Dartmouth were the last contingent of men to embark. We were now ready for sea.

The departure from Portsmouth was rather tortuous. As the ship left her berth, her starboard engine failed and the Captain, who had never commanded a carrier, struggled to leave the tight harbour entrance with a very strong crosswind from starboard, the side for which he had no propeller. With the help of a powerful tug, however, he cleared the harbour and headed for open waters, and by the time *Hermes* was off the Isle of Wight her engineers had the starboard engine up and running once again.

Departure late in the day is always rather a subdued affair, most people unpacking their belongings and settling in to their cabins and quarters. There is usually a film in the wardroom for the officers and one forward in the main dining hall for the sailors. The Captain stayed on the bridge until the ship had left the confines of the Channel and was clear of all heavy shipping before he altered course for Gibraltar. It had been planned to spend a long weekend at 'The Rock' and then set sail for Port of Spain, our first port of call in the 'Caribee'. On the way over the Sea Kings carried out some practice ASW flying while the Commando helicopter pilots carried out deck-landing practice. The passage across the Atlantic went very quickly and we were soon anchored five miles off Trinidad for a week's visit.

The first task on arriving at Port of Spain was to collect the mail. The Operations Officer went ashore and returned to tell us that it was locked away in a dockside warehouse and would not be distributed until Monday morning. Our XO was soon ashore meeting 'our man in Trinidad' to inform him that it was necessary that the ship's company received its mail forthwith. After a great deal of prevarication the warehouse was unlocked and the mail delivered to the ship. Mail always seemed to present a problem wherever we went; the same difficulty had occurred while I was aboard *Ark Royal*. The people ashore could not comprehend just how important it was for a ship to receive her mail quickly and on time: regular deliveries were very important to the morale of the ship's company and therefore to the running of the ship.

The ship spent about a week anchored off Port of Spain. Together with the other heads of departments, I had luncheon with members of the Trinidadian Government in a beautiful house situated on a hillside east of the city. It was a pleasant gathering, but it was obvious that there existed on the island a great deal of corruption. This small West Indian nation was receiving a handsome income from oil and tarmac but there was little evidence of its being invested in the island to improve the lives and amenities of the general population. The roads, for example, were very poor indeed, and the majority of people appeared to exist in extreme poverty, their homes nothing more than hovels with corrugated tin roofs. It was hard to understand why, with so much 'black gold' flowing, the nation was not more prosperous.

* * *

The Air Department has traditionally been responsible for the Captain's gig, which aboard *Hermes* was a small, high-speed motor launch. One particular afternoon while we were anchored off Trinidad the boat's engine failed and the Captain was stranded ashore. I was waiting for the officers' boat, and invited him to return with us in our launch and he accepted. On the way back to the carrier, standing alongside the coxswain, I noticed that the starboard engine's boost gauge was slowly falling back to zero. I drew the coxswain's attention to the gauge and told him that he had an impending engine failure on his hands and that it would be wise to shut things down before any more damage was done; he could easily return to the ship on one engine at reduced power. He took my suggestion and advice, shut down the starboard engine and continued towards the carrier. The Captain immediately asked what the problem was and I told him, whereupon he ordered full power on the remaining engine. I respectfully suggested to the Captain that such a procedure, apart from thrashing the good engine, would make it extremely difficult to steer the launch. He reluctantly agreed with me and soon we were alongside the ship. Here, however, I had to hold back the junior officers, who were intent on disembarking before the Captain. Somehow this small courtesy had not been drilled into these budding commanders while at Dartmouth.

When the Captain had disembarked, I had a word with the coxswain in order to discover when he had done his Small Boats Course. It transpired that he had not done one at all, and had received all his training while aboard *Hermes*; in other words, he had received training 'on the job'. Over the years I had noticed that ship's boats were driven at high speed wherever they went. It seemed that each ship's small-boat coxswain was intent on outdoing his counterparts, and that this was probably the main cause of so many engine failures over the years. Many years later I would teach civilians to drive high-speed motor yachts, the engines of which ran at speeds very similar to those of aircraft piston engines. At maximum throttle, the engines were screaming at 3,300rpm, the power used for take-off or in an emergency, but one could, if one wished, drive at 2,700rpm ('maximum continuous power') or, better still, at 2,400rpm ('continuous cruising power'), a setting at which an engine could, in theory, continue to drive the boat for ever, at a good cruising speed. Everywhere I went senior officers believed in one power setting only—'Full Throttle'! None of them seemed to understand that boats' engines had to be limited at full power lest they be overstrained, 'overtemped' and worn out within a few hours. It was as if these officers were totally unaware of mechanical limitations.

As soon as I returned on board I set about writing a paper in an attempt to resurrect the old Small Boats Course, which had been scrapped in one of the earlier rounds of 'defence cuts'. My contention was that it was costing the Navy more in engine repairs than it would in running a proper boat-handling course. My paper went forward but nothing more was heard of it during my time in *Hermes*. In many ways it angered me that there existed such short-sighted planning in the Service, but, as so often is the case, it was considered that the problem had been dealt with and that any further discussion would be a waste of time; errors of judgement in this regard were rarely admitted to.

* * *

Our next port of call was Willemstad in Curaçao. The island was a Dutch dependency and Willemstad was an open port, so one could buy jewellery and other *objets d'art* duty-free and at a fraction of the cost elsewhere. The ship stayed there for about five days. The approach to our berth took us beneath a huge bridge spanning the harbour. We all stood on the flight deck looking up in trepidation, wondering whether the navigator had done his sums correctly as our tall mast passed beneath the bridge. There were just a few feet to spare, and then we were in the inner harbour and alongside, astern of a huge container ship. The ship went into Tropical Routine for our visit, the crew rising early, working hard until midday and then spending the afternoon as leave or Make and Mend, as one wished, if one's watch was not on duty. As soon as midday came round, officers and 'Jolly Jack' streamed ashore to taste the delights or to spend their money on presents for mother, wife, fiancée or girlfriend. The town was set up for rich American tourists, who visited in their droves from the cruise liners, spending millions of dollars over the year. Any currency was accepted at a good rate of exchange.

The Air Department was responsible for the ship's two Land Rover pick-ups, which were embarked for various duties as well as giving the Captain some form of transport during a short port visit. However, within a day we were to experience a serious accident with one of them. A group of sailors driving into town somehow managed to overturn one of the vehicles, seriously injuring two of their company. After this accident the use of the Land Rovers was restricted and such journeys forbidden, and only a selected few, of which I was one, were permitted to drive them.

* * *

While we were at Curaçao the sun blazed down out of a clear blue sky. It was an idyllic island with a climate that was neither hot nor uncomfortable, the soft Caribbean winds keeping the temperature at a level which made life very pleasant indeed. I spent a day sailing from the Yacht Club aboard a vessel with a canopy over the stern cockpit, although even with this the ultra-violet light reflected off the sea and my lower lip was burnt; it would be almost a month before it had healed properly. We departed on yet another sunny day, heading for the island of Aruba, where we were to carry out a marine landing with Royal Netherlands Marines, of which we had embarked a small company while at Willemstad. Our Commando helicopters would be used to ferry them ashore in a mock battle, rather along the lines of those practised at HMS *Dryad*, the RN Tactical School. When we had concluded the 'battle' our Dutchmen were left ashore to return to their barracks in Aruba and *Hermes* steamed off for Grand Cayman, an offshore tax haven for both the honest and the criminally inclined.

The Captain anchored the ship a few miles north of Georgetown for a weekend visit and to 'show the flag'. The Governor was invited on board together with his family, friends and political colleagues. He was rather an arrogant man who upset the Captain from the moment he stepped aboard by his demanding attitude. He gave the impression that he was only present out of courtesy, and that he did not want one of Her Majesty's ships around his island.

While we were anchored off Grand Cayman 824 Squadron took the opportunity to conduct some wet safety equipment drills, which have to be practised periodically by aircrew. A Sea King had just landed and was being pushed back on to the after flight-deck lift when an urgent message came from the 'banyan party' ashore. They had a sailor who was in a serious condition, having been dragged from the sea unconscious. The same Sea King was ranged again, and with the duty doctor on board it was scrambled to meet the landing craft bringing the sailor back to the ship. He was by this time semi-conscious, but he had been to all intents and purposes half drowned. The ship's Diving Officer and the Marine Major had found him on the sea bed twenty feet under and lying face down while they were swimming underwater. They had brought him to the surface and dragged him ashore, where he had been given resuscitation. He was one of the Commando helicopter flight engine mechanics and had been partying aboard a luxury motor yacht anchored offshore. He had been fed large rums and 'Coke' with more of the former than the latter and in his inebriated state he had dived over the side of the yacht to swim ashore. Everybody had cheered as he departed but nobody had witnessed him surfacing and had continued with their merriment. The sailor became unconscious as he entered the water and had sunk straight to the bottom. However, in his comatose state his heart rate had so reduced that he was hardly breathing, and he was indeed exhaling more than he was inhaling. It was this that had kept him from drowning. It was estimated that he must have been underwater for at least fifteen minutes before being found by the Major and the Diving Officer.

The duty doctor was lowered into the landing craft, where he gave first aid, and as soon as the vessel was alongside the sailor was rushed to the Sickbay Operating Theatre. His mouth was thoroughly washed out and he was given further oxygen and injections to assist his heart. Slowly the young man came round, a bedside vigil being maintained until it had been established that he was on the mend. Then he was shifted to a bed in the Sickbay, which was where I visited him to ascertain what had happened out there off the beach. Our young sailor appeared in high spirits, and it seemed that he had suffered no ill effects from his clash with death. His mind, and therefore his brain, was fully alert, so he had suffered no permanent damage to them. Owing to his high state of inebriation, his body and brain must have entered a form of hibernation. All of us, especially the doctors, were astounded by what had happened. However, after talking with him, he promised me faithfully that he would in future stay away from the 'demon drink' and I believed him. He could so easily have been left a cripple for life.

* * *

Our next port of call would be New Orleans in Louisiana for the final days of Mardi Gras. This meant a long overnight passage through the tortuous Mississippi Delta leading to the city, where we arrived at about 1100 the next day. *Hermes* was berthed alongside the largest jetty just down from Bourbon Street, at the bend of the river—as far upstream as the carrier could go because of a low bridge ahead. The final approach to our berth was made under overcast skies, and the river itself was thick with mud and debris washed down from up-country, almost all the way from the Canadian border. The whole of the Mississippi delta was strewn with oil rigs and platforms for as far as the eye could see, and in the last stretches of the river leading up to the city itself many old oil tankers had been laid up, awaiting either an upturn in business or the breakers' torch.

Hermes was scheduled to remain at New Orleans until the end of Mardi Gras—Shrove Tuesday—and to depart the following day. Many invitations were sent to the ship for the various Krewe balls, the Captain receiving one for the 'Hermes Krewe Ball' the second night we were in harbour. The ball had nothing whatsoever to do with the ship; it so happened that 'Hermes' was the name of the Krewe. Various balls would be held every night around the city, culminating in the Rex Krewe Ball, the 'king' of all Krewes.

I was sitting in my cabin going through some Air Department papers when the Captain's Secretary put his head through my door curtain to ask me to take the Captain's place at the Hermes Krewe Ball that night. Dress was to be mess kit, and the Captain of RFA *Olmeda* would be accompanying me. I was happy to go and at 1900 *Olmeda*'s Captain called for me and we set off in the US Navy staff car that had been provided for the occasion.

The Hermes Krewe Ball was being held in a large theatre, where we arrived bang on time at 1930 to find a couple of gentlemen dressed in dinner jackets and bow ties sorting out white and red carnations. We introduced ourselves and were immediately told what our duties would be: we would be searching out young ladies whose company was required by the masked men dancing on the floor of the main auditorium. Then they informed us that we would be wearing red carnations, and we quite naturally asked why, to be told that the white carnations represented the landed white gentry and the red denoted the coloured hands of the various families of the region. The Captain and I looked at each other and I shook my head. 'I want nothing to do with this recalling of colour segregation,' I said, and the Captain agreed with me. The Louisiana gentlemen were quite confused by our attitude. We left their company and walked into the auditorium to find hardly a soul present. However, there was noise aplenty coming from the enclosed rooms surrounding the auditorium which, we discovered, had been hired by various members of the Hermes Krewe for pre-ball parties. The pair of us stood around like stuffed dummies wondering what to do. No one offered us a drink, although the other two we had met on our arrival were moving around from party to party. Finally, the ball got under way shortly after 2000.

The New Orleans Krewe balls are really a hangover from days of yore when the landed gentry brought out their marriageable daughters for the local eligible bachelors to inspect. However, they had grown into something more than just that: men dressed in harlequin-type costumes would parade around the auditorium wearing masks and then each would demand a dance with the young woman of their choosing. The fairer sex had no idea with whom they were dancing—boyfriend, lover, brother, father, uncle, or indeed stranger. After an hour of this the Captain and I decided that enough was enough and quietly left. We found a bar where we had a few drinks and then we caught a taxi back to our respective ships. The next morning Captain McKenzie asked me how we had enjoyed ourselves and I told him straight what had happened. He was furious and eventually reached the organisers of the ball and told them in no uncertain terms what he thought. An apology was forwarded to the ship although nobody turned up in person to offer it.

During the visit the wardroom held its customary cocktail party in the hangar for city and military guests. While I was talking to one of these guests a friend drew my attention to my old VX-4 CO, Captain Jim Foster, and his new wife. Jim had left the Navy after his final appointment commanding USNAS Dallas but then out of the blue had been recalled to run the USN Transport Division at USNS New Orleans. He and his wife invited me out to their married quarters on the naval base for a weekend visit. Together we attended a Mardi Gras carnival parade, watching from a hotel balcony. It was bitterly cold and snow had been forecast for the area. The young girls manning the carnival floats were all wearing off-the-shoulder ball gowns and must have been frozen. All the parades had school bands playing music but, in every instance, the black school band was placed at the tail end of the parade. I asked Jim why this was—a silly question as I knew full well what he was going to say. 'Now you see the truth, Michael,' he said. 'Nothing has changed in this part of America. The whites still rule supreme, and nothing will change that attitude.' I told him that I had noticed, and related what had happened at the Hermes Krewe Ball. After the parade, the Fosters took me out to dinner, we telephoned May back in England and there was a long conversation about old times in VX-4 and what they were doing now. Their time in New Orleans was coming to an end, and it was their intention to move back to northern California for retirement.

The final night of Mardi Gras arrived and the city went crazy. Bourbon Street was packed solid, especially outside the House of Joy, a famous brothel. The throng was so great that it was almost impossible to pass through. Everybody was shouting at 'Les Girls' parading about on the verandah, inviting them to 'take it all off', which they gladly did to the waist. All the young women were well endowed, and every time they removed their upper garments a tremendous cheer went up from the crowd. Down on the main street things were little different, although most people had painted themselves in gaudy colours and were sporting broad-brimmed straw hats. As the carnival floats came by the people aboard threw out quantities of plastic 'gold doubloons' and necklaces in various bright colours, which everybody scrambled to retrieve. This was the first parade for two years, the previous year's celebration having been cancelled because of a police strike. However, this final parade was rather different because *Hermes* provided a Guard of Honour, which marched behind 'Rex's float. The British sailors had terrible problems trying to keep at bay the young women, who were intent in taking their honour. The whole city was just one enormous rowdy party, but at the stroke of midnight, *à la* Cinderella, the partying stopped, the streets emptied and the population magically vanished, leaving the city's cleaners with a mountain of rubbish to clear.

Departure day dawned warm and sunny but by lunchtime a cool breeze was beginning to flow in off the Gulf of Mexico. A small tug had been assigned to assist in pulling the ship off the dockside. The plan had been to haul the carrier's bow off to port into the fast-flowing river current and then, by use of the ship's engines and the tug, the Captain intended to turn the vessel slowly around to port and head off out to sea. It was a simple enough plan of action and a straightforward manoeuvre, but things were about to go askew.

I was below in the wardroom drinking coffee when the XO made an urgent broadcast over the ship's tannoy system: 'All personnel clear the starboard side of the ship immediately! Close all watertight doors throughout the ship now!' The officers in the wardroom looked at each other, stopped whatever they were doing, and headed topside to see what the emergency was. What we found was that the carrier was drifting broadside down-river, missing some of the other ships by only a few feet as the current carried her downstream at five knots or more. One ship narrowly missed was one of the US Navy's brand new guided missile destroyers on her acceptance trials. Apparently the tug's tow had parted, the current had taken hold of the ship and all that Captain McKenzie could do was to go astern to give clearance ahead of the ship as she drifted fast to starboard. However, by keeping a clear head he gradually turned the ship to starboard by going ahead on one propeller and astern on the other, then astern on both until he knew that he had sufficient room to turn safely downstream. As the ship straightened up and headed for the sea, a great cheer went through the ship for the 'Old Man's wonderful show of seamanship. It must have been the worst moment that he had ever experienced throughout the whole of his fifteen years at sea as a seaman officer.

Having recovered from that hair-raising incident, however, the ship entered thick fog a mile or so down-channel. I was standing on the Gun Direction Platform above the bridge at the time. I had never seen such thick fog: the only objects visible were the masts and funnels of other vessels projecting out of the blanket. Nevertheless, some twenty or thirty miles further south *Hermes* safely cleared the fog and, as evening came on in a riot of bright oranges, mauves and purples, the ship left the Mississippi Delta and headed for open water.

* * *

Our next port of call was Pensacola, Florida, the old US Navy pilot training base. HRH Prince Andrew would be joining the ship there, together with the rest of his Dartmouth course, to complete his naval cadet training prior to being promoted Midshipman. En route members of the British Press would be embarked from US Navy Sea Knight helicopters. The USN had requested both CCAs and deck-landing training for their helicopter pilots as we made our passage toward Pensacola; the ship did not have CCA equipment and we had to refuse this request but we gladly offered our flight deck for deck-landing practice. At this juncture Lieutenant Commander (Flying) tried to prevent the exercise from going ahead, saying that the wind was out of limits. I gently advised him that it was not, whereupon he rounded on me, informing me that I did not know what I was talking about. In as quiet a voice as I could muster I ordered him to land a Sea Knight on a forward helicopter spot, and to read NATO publication so-and-so which gave the wind limitations for all NATO helicopters landing aboard ships. The Sea Knight had no limitations, and the first USN pilot to land was female. I pointed out that if a woman could make a perfect landing in a very heavy helicopter I could see no reason why a male pilot could not do the same. Our USN female pilot went on to make several more perfect landings and then returned to Pensacola.

Hermes now entered a narrow channel leading to Pensacola harbour and all flying had to cease because local regulations forbade such activity within the passageways outside the harbour. The ship was quickly tied up close to the American training carrier *Lexington* and the Captain went ashore to make his number with the civil and military dignitaries. Mrs McKenzie, the Captain's wife, also came aboard, having flown out for a few weeks' holiday, and the next day Prince Andrew's course joined the ship. The cadets were given a sailors' mess deck, and until they had been promoted to Midshipmen they all dined in the sailors' mess hall forward. There was no favouritism for His Royal Highness, and he expected none. Once they had been promoted the cadets messed in the 'Gunroom' under the flight deck on the starboard quarter. They were allowed entry into the wardroom for the odd drink or two, but otherwise they remained in their own mess.

Now that Prince Andrew had embarked, British newspaper correspondents followed us everywhere. They congregated around the dockside telephone booths, preventing officers and sailors from making private calls, and they dropped their coin wrappers, littering the place. Eventually the Master-at-Arms, in conjunction with the local police, moved them on.

Jon's Bar in Pensacola—an establishment set up essentially for naval aviators ashore for a drink or two from the training air bases nearby—was full of naval aviation memorabilia. Aircraft instrument panels and 'joysticks' from famous fighters were hanging from the ceiling or were fastened to the walls together with hundreds of photographs of squadrons and personalities, including of course the Blue Angels aerobatic team. In one of the Blue Angels team photographs I came across my old VX-4 Captain, Nello Pierozzi, then a Navy Lieutenant. The bar was also famous for its 'go-go' girls, who performed their nightly shows on a stage discreetly tucked away in the far corner of the bar, unseen from the road outside.

On his first night ashore Prince Andrew found himself in Jon's Bar and of course the dutiful British press followed him there. The representatives from the *Sun*, *Daily Mirror* and *Daily Express* newspapers were particularly nauseating, dogging the poor chap wherever he went. On one particular occasion the young Prince visited the gentlemen's lavatory, the ablutions facilities within which had walls open at both top and bottom. The *Mirror* reporter climbed the outside wall and asked him for an interview. When Prince Andrew related the incident to me I was appalled that anyone could behave in such a manner.

'Well, young Windsor,' I said to him, 'I would have had an elevation problem and would have peed in his eye!'

He roared with laughter. 'I'll remember that next time!' he said.

As Prince Andrew left, the photographers were waiting outside. Flashlights went off in his face, making him wide-eyed with surprise. One of the resulting published photographs showed a naked 'go-go' dancer superimposed above his left shoulder as he was coming out of the main exit—a faked montage and a deliberate attempt to besmirch the Prince since, as remarked earlier, it was impossible to see the performers from outside the building. We had quickly discovered that these newspaper men knew no bounds.

The ship had been in port hardly a couple of days when the Captain's Secretary burst into my cabin informing me that the Captain wanted to see me right away. I rushed round to the Captain's cabin and he thrust a copy of an 'Immediate' signal into my hands, asking me whether I had seen it. The signal was from C-in-C Fleet and was explosive. It concerned a photograph that had appeared on the front page of the *Daily Express* showing a youngster scrubbing the flight deck and, according to the signal, accompanied by the headline 'Child Labour Aboard Our Warships!'—or words to that effect. Questions were about to be asked in the Houses of Parliament that afternoon.

As mentioned earlier, we had taken to sea a couple of dozen boys between the ages of 10 and 15, the sons and nephews of personnel serving aboard. They were under the strict control of an Instructor and a seaman officer, and there were parts of the ship from which they were excluded, the flight deck being one of these: they could venture out there under supervision when the carrier was in harbour, but otherwise it was out of bounds. A newspaper photographer had taken a picture of a boy scrubbing out his mess deck and someone connected with the *Daily Express* had superimposed this on a photograph of the flight deck. The faked image had then been published in the newspaper along with a heap of journalistic lies. I told the Captain straight about the earlier photograph, a copy of which had been transmitted to him. I told him also that the boys were banned from the flight deck and that the picture was fraudulent. I called in Lieutenant David Elliott, my Photographic Officer, and asked him what he thought of it. Without any hesitation he replied that it was a montage: from where the picture had purportedly been taken, it was impossible see past the electric winch to the flight deck. We thanked him and drafted an immediate reply to C-in-C Fleet that we were not guilty. Within the hour we had a reply: 'Thank you. I knew that both you and "Wings" were playing the game straight. Leave it to me. There will be no questions in the House over this matter—ever!'

The *Daily Express* had been somewhat biased against the Royal Navy for as long as I could remember. While serving at Lossiemouth, for example, the newspaper had always referred to the air station as a Royal Air Force establishment. I suppose it went back to the days of Lord Beaverbrook—who had owned the *Daily Express* during the wartime days, when he was also the Minister of Aircraft Production—or before, when the Admiralty was still wrestling to gain operational control of its aircraft from the Air Ministry. This was not to be the last encounter with the *Daily Express*'s man on the scene, as we would discover within a couple of weeks.

* * *

While at Pensacola the Captain received a request from the US Navy for two USMC AV-8A Harriers to embark and conduct some night-time deck-landing trials during our passage across the Gulf to Fort Lauderdale. I was more than happy and we duly obtained the necessary clearance from DNAW and FOAC: it would result in further information concerning the Harrier's clearance envelope, and USN Test Center Patuxent River, Maryland, were prepared to forward their results and conclusions to DNAW. The US Marine Corps detachment and the two aircraft embarked while we were alongside at Pensacola, and we went through the intentions and aims of the trial. They would carry out some day flying to familiarise themselves with the ship and its deck arrangements, and the actual trials would commence with dusk

373

flying, moving into full night flying as the evening progressed. The day before we sailed there was liver and onions on the wardroom lunchtime menu. I had always believed that Americans did not like offal, but I was wrong: the Marine Corps officers could not get enough!

Our flight-deck handlers were already practised in organising Harriers from the earlier Sea Harrier trial, so they quickly fell into routine, handling the two jets as if they been doing it all their lives. It had been arranged that the USMC Major in charge of the trial would man Lieutenant Commander (Flying)'s chair in Flyco, with me sitting beside him, in the event of any unforeseen incident. It was quite dark when Lieutenant Commander (Flying) suddenly burst into Flyco demanding to know what was going on. He wanted the flying stopped immediately. He was dressed in his best No 5s and if anyone had put a match to his breath he would have gone to the moon. The Major wanted to know what was wrong with him, and I turned quickly to 'Little F' and ordered him off Flyco and to return to his cabin at once and stay there. The Captain had witnessed the scene from the darkness at the back of Flyco and asked me if he wanted him to deal with the problem. I politely declined and said that I would see to things after flying had been completed. I knew that if the Captain took the matter in hand it would mean a court martial for 'Little F' and that this was something that the Captain did not want, his having just been selected for promotion to Admiral.

The trial was completed successfully and the USMC were very happy with the results. The following day the two jets disembarked, the officers and maintenance personnel leaving when we reached Fort Lauderdale. Then I had 'Little F' call upon me in my cabin, where I read the riot act to him. I told him to his face why he did not have my position in the ship: he drank far too much for his own good, and that was the main reason he had not been promoted further in the Service. He was one of those naval aviators who was qualified fully both as an observer and as a pilot. Personally, I believed that something had happened while he had commanded a helicopter squadron— something that had blighted his chances of promotion. He would not tell me and I could not drag it out of him, so I let the matter rest. He was due for reappointment immediately on our return to Britain.

* * *

The ship was to experience another invasion by the British press corps before her arrival at Fort Lauderdale. They embarked on board by helicopter, fully expecting everything to be laid on for them and demanding this, that and the other. I caught the *Daily Express* reporter and photographer trying to arrange for Prince Andrew to be scrubbing the flight deck; the pair were quickly told where to go. The entire team of reporters and photographers were sent to the aircrew briefing room, where they were given written briefs and told what they could and could not do. Then the *Express* man stood up and demanded that Prince Andrew be ordered to carry out various tasks. He was quickly put in his place by the Instructor Commander in charge of this group. He was told that he could witness the Prince working the ship's anchors and cables on the cable deck while preparing for entering harbour, but nothing else. If he did not like it, then he could stay in the briefing room. I was absolutely in awe of the manner in which the Commander handled the situation: he really put the *Daily Express* man down and, more to the point, the other members of the press corps got the message.

The press were to remain around the ship throughout her Fort Lauderdale visit and would then follow us to Bermuda. It was while the ship was visiting Florida that the Prince was promoted to Midshipman, and to assure his safety while ashore he was given an escort of armed Florida police officers. As is customary, the wardroom threw a cocktail party for the local dignitaries and senior US military personnel, after which Midshipman Windsor went ashore in uniform with his escort to some of the local 'dives'. I happened to be at the starboard after gangway space seeing ashore some guests when I heard a commotion, and there was young Windsor waving his arms about and letting the gangway staff know that he had been seen off. His escort had apparently had a good time ashore, but they had prevented any young women from approaching the Prince and he had not liked it. His language was rather blue, and he had lost his officer's cap and was somewhat inebriated, so I told him to be quiet and go aft immediately to his cabin, in company with another officer so that he arrived safely. He responded with a 'Yes, sir, Commander Wings' and scuttled off. I detailed the OOD to ensure that HRH was visited regularly for his own safety. He was like any other young officer of his age: he had found freedom and he wanted to have fun.

The ship stayed at Fort Lauderdale for five days and then set sail for Bermuda, our last port of call prior to setting passage home. This would be my first visit to an island of which I had heard so much from friends who had served on the West Indies Station. However, the days of glory had long gone and the West Indies Fleet had been reduced to a couple of frigates and a Senior Naval Officer of Captain's or Commodore rank.

Our departure from Fort Lauderdale did not take place without incident. As the ship left the harbour entrance a high-speed motor launch intercepted her from the north and pulled up on the port side fifty or so yards outboard. Two grey-haired men dressed in shorts were driving the craft, and in its well deck were three scantily dressed young women. As soon as they were in steady formation with us, the girls went into a 'go-go' dance act, removing their upper clothing and flaunting their natural assets; one of them even went as far as to mime copulation she bent over backwards. Of course, the whole of the off-duty ship's company appeared on the flight deck as quick as a flash. The ship's 'tom-tom' system worked overtime and before long there were about twelve hundred officers and men crowding the port side; even the Captain was leaning over the bridge wing with his powerful telescope! Then the motor launch roared ahead, crossed our bows and dropped back to the starboard side of the ship. Suddenly its engines quietened—I suspect that it had run out of fuel—and it fell astern, disappearing from sight in the Florida haze.

* * *

The passage to Bermuda took a couple of days in fine weather and gentle seas. *Hermes* entered harbour via the Hamilton Passage and proceeded at ten knots toward Somerset Island. Our anchorage was about a mile from Hamilton and half a mile from the old Royal Naval Dockyard. The passage was thrilling: the water was shallow and extraordinarily clear and rocks overgrown with underwater flora waving in the currents could easily be seen. Here there was no pollution—just beautiful, clean waters of green or blue as far as the eye could see.

Bermuda is an unusual place. The colour of the roofs is the first thing to catch the attention: they are all white, for the perfectly good reason that in this way they reflect the heat of the sun. The roofs are also used to trap water during the rainy season. Although it is very much a British colony, Bermuda is heavily influenced by its proximity to mainland America; indeed, the US dollar is the local currency. The ship spent five days anchored off Hamilton and as soon as we arrived Prince Andrew was taken in hand by the local Governor and his family and so little was seen of him during our visit. Thankfully, the press were kept at bay.

A cocktail party was held for the ship's officers at the Governor's residence, a very pleasant house in beautiful surroundings, following which nearly everybody moved into Hamilton for dinner and jollity for the remainder of the evening. Bermuda was not a place for late-night revelling except at the large hotels, which organised their own entertainment for their guests. I would imagine that Hamilton was quite lively in former days when there was a large naval base for the West Indies Fleet. Now that there was only a token British naval presence in the Caribbean, however, the naval facilities had virtually died away. Even the US Navy's flying boat air station had gone, and these departures had had their effect upon the island, especially the capital.

One of the former Captains of *Hermes*, Captain Sir Michael Tibbets, was resident in Bermuda at this time and he came aboard to look over his former command. The old lady had changed somewhat since his days. The Type 984 radar antenna atop the island, looking like an enormous searchlight, had long since been removed, along with the angled flight deck and the two steam catapults. Otherwise she was much as he remembered her.

After our final run ashore the anchor was weighed and *Hermes* was moving off, bound for Portsmouth. The day after leaving the island the ship ran into a very heavy swell, nearly fifty feet in height, rolling in from the south-west. The carrier was struck on the starboard quarter and corkscrewed badly, heavy seas sweeping her starboard side for many hours and causing considerable damage. All the ship's boats on that side were smashed, including the brand new, semi-rigid Atlantic air–sea rescue inflatable. Fortunately, the two landing craft, at flight deck-level, escaped being hit by the seas, but the 'Alaskan highway'—the catwalk built outboard of and beneath the island—was twisted beyond all recognition. The cause of this tremendous swell remained a mystery: there was certainly no tropical depression or hurricane to the south.

The day after leaving Bermuda it was planned to have a 'dining out' night in the Gunroom for those Supply Officers leaving the ship on our arrival back in Britain. One of these officers was the Captain's Secretary, who had been invited to the Supply Chief's and POs' messes over the lunchtime. Needless to say he had quite a few 'stiff ones' and should have gone to bed early that evening. The dining table in the Gunroom had not, for some reason, been fastened to the deck to prevent its sliding about as the ship rolled and pitched, and it required a good deal of dexterity to hold on and feed as the table moved around the mess—and move it did, though, curiously, no cutlery or china left the table. The ship's motion soon took a toll of the diners, however, including the principal guest, the Captain's Secretary, who turned a ghastly shade of green and then departed, never to return. I always feel sorrow for sufferers of *mal de mer*: it can be an excruciating sickness, but I have been very fortunate in never having been afflicted by it. Before long only a few stalwarts were left in the mess, so we finished off the sherry and the brandy and retired for the night very contented.

The Captain, the ship's engineer and the shipwright were deliberately running *Hermes*' fuel down so that her draught would be less than 27 feet when she reached Portsmouth—a figure that would enable her to enter the dry dock safely. However, as we were steaming to the north of the Azores a signal came in from C-in-C Fleet instructing us to divert south to assist a German timber ship that had put out a distress signal. Her deck cargo had shifted and she was listing heavily and required immediate help. 'Fleet' was informed of our fuel situation and that, if we diverted, there was a strong probability that *Hermes* would run dry by the time she reached the Channel. Fortunately, however, there was another ship much closer than ours, and within a short period of time we heard that our assistance was no longer required and we resumed our original heading.

It was a quiet Sunday afternoon in the wardroom following an excellent lunch of roast beef, Yorkshire pudding, roast potatoes and vegetables when the ship's emergency alarm sounded, followed by the announcement 'Fire! Fire! Fire! Fire in the ship's funnel! Emergency Party muster on the flight deck opposite the island at the double!' The Deputy Engineer Officer—in charge of the Emergency Party aboard a carrier—calmly put down his cup of coffee and then bolted for the Emergency HQ located amidships. A running commentary was maintained on the fire and what was being done to extinguish it. A funnel fire is very dangerous: the actual steel lining of the funnel burns and any use of water is like throwing petrol on to it, the water, owing to the tremendous heat, being converted into its component chemical parts, hydrogen and oxygen. Inside the funnel casing were two uptakes, and one of these had caught fire, probably because of an accumulation of soot, but the huge updraft from the furnaces had caused the metal itself to start burning. There was only one way to stop the fire: shut off the flue below and above it, thereby removing any source of oxygen. Water was then sprayed on the outside of the funnel to reduce the temperature, and after three or four hours the fire was out, although the flue remained closed for the duration of the voyage. *Hermes* now had, in addition to her refit, two major repairs for the dockyard—the 'Alaskan highway' and the funnel, and as a result she would be out of the water for a further three months.

The 'old girl' was riding high when she entered harbour, and with the aid of tugs she was berthed alongside the Northwest Wall Jetty facing Whale Island. Waiting on the dockside were all the wives and families, the girlfriends and the fiancées. The majority of the ship's company would be proceeding on leave and draft, while a team would stay behind to de-store ship and prepare her for going into dry dock a couple of weeks hence. May was there with our two girls, Naomi and Dominique, so after presenting them with their gifts I departed to Bexhill for a very long weekend with them. It was good to be back home with one's loved ones

— 30 —

Refit

MS *HERMES* was scheduled for a twelve-month refit but it actually lasted for fifteen. Although the first 'through-deck cruiser,' HMS *Invincible*, had been commissioned and was operating Sea Harrier V/STOL fighters, the next ship of her class was a long way from being completed and ready for sea. It had therefore been decided by Their Lordships that *Hermes* would be made ready and capable of operating the Sea Harrier. This refit would make her able in all respects to operate in the same capacity as *Invincible*, but with more aircraft—and with Royal Marines, if so required. At that time Their Lordships did not know just how prescient their decision would be (although I believe that they were also hedging their bets in case the third ship of the *Invincible* class did not materialise).

A ship's refit requires a great deal of planning and organisation. A vessel does not simply enter drydock for the work to begin. A tremendous amount of preparation by both the ship's and the dockyard's staff is called for, as well as planning by the Ship Engineering Division at MoD (N) at Bath. Every operation has to be drawn up carefully on a flow diagram; new equipment and materials have to be acquired and pre-positioned well ahead of time, so that the refit progresses smoothly and to schedule. Moreover, it is important that there be sufficient manpower from both the ship and the dockyard to meet the various tasks that need to be completed. In order to ensure that a refit goes smoothly and according to plan, a Naval Construction Corps Officer, equivalent in rank to either a Captain or a Commander, is placed in overall charge. Not only does he visit the ship daily to inspect the work and monitor progress, he also holds weekly meetings to review the work and to resolve any difficulties that may arise. The ship's furnaces and boilers have to be 'killed' and allowed to cool to temperatures with which men can cope. The ship has to be de-stored, de-ammunitioned and de-fuelled, which reduces her to an empty steel hulk, without life. Holes are cut into the decks and the sides of the ship to remove heavy equipment and to provide easy access. It is almost as if the vessel is in the last stages of fitting out, having just been built; it is indeed a time of great activity and hard work for all involved. Of course, the ship has no facilities of her own, so these have to be provided on the dockside. Those officers and sailors who remain behind move into barracks for accommodation and meals, but vital quarters such as the Captain's Office and the Regulating Office remain open and operational in order to address the everyday requirements of the reduced ship's company. One office on board vital to the refit is that of the Ship's Engineering and Shipwrights' Department, which becomes a hive of activity controlling the refit from the shipboard side.

Drydocking *Hermes* was carried out at the height of a spring tide, in calm winds. She was nudged in by carefully positioned tugs and dockside 'mules', the dock gates were closed and, as the tide receded, the dock was gradually emptied while divers ensured that she settled on her pre-positioned keel blocks. The emptying of the dock was stopped once she was on the blocks, to enable huge side beams to be put in place around her to ensure that she remained upright and did not lose shape. Once this shoring up had been completed the remaining water in the dock was emptied at low tide and the refit commenced in earnest. This docking took two days to complete.

A special high crane had been placed alongside the island, and this lifted the prefabricated sections of the Sea Harrier 'ski-ramp' on to the centre of the flight deck. When this had been completed, the funnel was lifted off on to a low loader and taken to the dockyard metal fabrication shop. The 'Alaskan highway' was cut loose and hauled away as scrap. The landing craft and ship's boats had all been offloaded while the carrier was at the Northwest Wall Jetty and taken to the boat shop for overhaul and rework. Scaffolding appeared around the island and steel plate cutters appeared with their torches to remove those sections of bow plating and framing that had been badly dented and distorted by the heavy Atlantic seas. The bow had to be restored to its original condition before the 'ski-ramp' sections could be moved into place for fastening to the forward flight deck. Beneath the forward flight deck, where the ship's bow plates and framing had to be removed, were the Petty Officers' cabins.*

As soon as the bow section had been restored the 'ski-ramp' was lifted into position to be welded to the flight deck. It was a major task, and one which required precise alignment before any welding could take place. I had been informed long before the refit that the ramp would be welded and bolted to the flight deck because of the differences in the ages of the adjacent metals. However, this was not to be, and I expressed my fears that perhaps, with ship movement, the welds might open when placed under severe stress. Higher authority assured me, however, that such would not occur. I was not convinced.

The welding of the ramp was an engineering job, and other than my reservations it required no input from me.† Work started late one Friday and it was

---

*How on earth anyone in his right mind could have placed cabins under the flight deck immediately behind the bow plating was beyond me. This was where the catapults had been originally located, and in addition was an area in the ship where one would experience severe ship motion, noise and thumping!

† This was not quite so, because my attention was drawn to the step of the ramp, where the metal deck plating was about an inch and a half proud of the old flight deck. I told the

intended to complete it over the weekend. However, when I arrived back after weekend leave I found that the welding had not been finished. I asked if there had been a hold-up.

'The weather, sir!' was the response.

'What weather?' I queried. 'It's been bright and sunny all weekend!'

'Well, sir, the ambient temperature was so high that the ship warped and assumed a banana shape, lifting her forefoot a couple of inches off the blocks. Consequently we were unable to weld until the ship had cooled off and resumed her original shape. It will probably be tomorrow—Tuesday—before we can recommence welding again.'

It was hard to believe that the sun could change the shape of ship so much, but it had done so.

The welding was completed the following weekend, but when I returned from leave I found that much of the ramp-deck welding was being removed and replaced with new. It had failed a stringent test and was below Category 1 or 2 welding, the same as that required in the building of the hulls of nuclear submarines. The second welds met the necessary standard.

Once the flight deck refit tasks had been completed, the deck was dressed with a new anti-skid paint, the work being carried out under canvas to ensure that drying took place in a relatively controlled environment. Over the years each 'Captain of the Flight Deck' had acquired gallon upon gallon of flight-deck paint, which was stowed beneath the deck. Most of this paint was out of date and had to be discarded; it was sold to an enterprising individual for a song, and he then resold it off at a ridiculous price, making a fortune in the process. With this paint offloaded, the old ship was considerably much lighter topside.

The ship's hull required a good deal of renovation to make it seaworthy. The hull bottom plates had worn so thin that it was possible to poke a finger through them. The wearing effect is brought about not so much by the water *per se* as by the impurities in it, such as salt and sand. Together these ingredients act like sandpaper and slowly but surely rub the steel plating thin. New plates were welded over the old as the quickest and cheapest method of effecting a repair. At the stern, both propellers had to be removed to improve the ship's anti-submarine acoustics and the two rudders also had to be removed, for overhaul and re-skinning. The removal of a propeller or rudder is an extremely difficult task, and one that requires skilled engineering. Once they had been removed from their respective shafts, it was a relatively easy matter to lift them from the bottom of the dock and tow them to the propeller and rudder maintenance shops.

Flyco was 'gutted', including the flooring. New instrumentation and communication systems were installed, making it a much better place in which to work. I had seen the mock-up in the dockyard sail loft together with the new layout for the Operations Room. Users of these facilities were invited to

---

foreman in charge that it was unacceptable since it could cause aircraft tyres to shred or burst as they hit the edge of the ramp at high speed. A wedge was then manufactured and welded into position, giving a smooth transition from the original flight deck to the new ramp deck.

sit in their new surroundings and comment on the position and location of the equipment. If all was not well, then a new mock-up would be made out of wood and the user asked to make further comment. When everybody was satisfied, the layout was 'frozen' and then the ship was modified accordingly. No steel was used within the island superstructure, aluminium being the major material used for bulkheads, hatches and doors plus other fixtures. Building the spaces within the island superstructure was fairly simple, but the most difficult task was the running of the numerous electrical looms from one area to another. Within the island a special intelligence flat was constructed which was accessible only to the Admiral and his Intelligence Officer when they were embarked; not even the ship's Captain was allowed to enter—a most extraordinary state of affairs!

While at the dockyard sail loft to view the mock-up I enquired what would happen to all the wood and plywood once the project had been completed, to be told that it would be donated free of charge to local schools for their woodworking departments; if they did not want it, then it would be burnt. I thought that the destruction of the wood by burning was totally unnecessary, and said so, because much of it could be used again and again. One begins to understand, perhaps, why the Armed Forces cost so much.

* * *

Prior to taking command of HMS *Blake*, Captain McKenzie had had command of HMS *Hermione* and had placed that frigate into long refit at Chatham Dockyard. Prior to her refit *Hermione* had had to be completely de-stored, and this arduous and difficult task had been delegated to a young Leading Stores Assistant. While his Stores Officer and Chief proceeded on leave, he was left alone to clean the ship out of all stores, prepare the paperwork and load the chacons and forward them to the various stores depots. There was nobody in authority over him, and during the operation he slipped on some ice on the dockside and broke his leg. However, with his leg in plaster, he gamely carried on with the task until it was completed. Quite naturally, because he received no help, some of the stores ended up in the wrong chacon, as did some of the paperwork, but in general he did an outstanding job in the circumstances. He was then drafted to Yeovilton Air Station, where he was deservedly promoted to Stores Petty Officer. Then, out of the blue, and on the recommendation of the officer who had investigated the mix-up, he was summoned to be court-martialled. The venue was to be HMS *Nelson*, the RN Barracks at Portsmouth, and I was nominated as one of the court-martial board officers.

It is the tradition in the Royal Navy that a presiding court-martial officer is 'piped ashore' as he leaves his ship dressed in No 2 uniform, sword and medals. As I left *Hermes* I was given full honours as I proceeded ashore to be driven to the court-martial. The Court-Martial Board convened at 0930 and the charges were read out by the Naval Judge Advocate, the list so long and serious that I began to think that this young man had committed treason. The prosecution described the sorry tale of events, but the more I heard the more I became convinced that this newly promoted Stores Petty Officer was nothing more than a scapegoat, and that the wrong person was on trial. Finally, unable to contain myself any longer, I slipped the President a handwritten note asking why we were court-martialling this young man. We had the wrong person before us. The President looked towards me, nodding his head in agreement.

At 1100 we took a recess and it became obvious that all the members of the board were feeling the same as I did. However, under the rules we had to allow the proceedings to continue to a conclusion. At noon we retired for luncheon in our own dining room, where we could discuss the proceedings at our leisure, and as we left to continue the court-martial it was already clear what our findings would be. By mid-afternoon the court-martial had been concluded and we retired for a couple of minutes, returning to deliver our verdict to the court: 'Stores Petty Officer —— has been found not guilty of any of the charges laid against him. He is free to leave this court and return to his place of duty with no stain upon his character.' The entire courtroom erupted with cheering and clapping. The President went on: 'Petty Officer ——, you have been most grievously accused of charges which should have been laid at other peoples' feet. I shall be sending a letter to higher authority concerning the conduct of your superiors, and recommending that they be investigated. Good luck and God speed to you!' The President was as good as his word. *Hermione*'s Supply Officer was severely censured by Their Lordships and given an 'Admiralty logging' that would remain permanently on his report, and the ship's Stores CPO was severely reprimanded for his shortcomings. The Board walked *en masse* across to congratulate and to shake the hand of the Petty Officer.

The young PO was a likable lad and I sincerely hope that he went on to do well in the Navy. He was badly 'used' in every respect. Unfortunately, there are in this world many people who take advantage of others. In most cases the truth comes to light, but sometimes the innocents pay the penalty and have their lives ruined. Fortunately in this case, the Court-Martial Board was alert and mature enough to recognise the injustice that was being perpetrated. The Judge Advocate was most unhappy at the outcome. He should have seen through all the evidence and dismissed the case before it even reached court-martial stage. In this respect he failed miserably in his duty, but the Board quickly saw what was being done to an innocent party. That evening, I felt that I, together with my fellow board members, had done a good day's work.

* * *

As the summer of 1980 progressed the refit continued apace. However, a further dockyard strike then loomed: the Dockyard unions wanted management staff to be paid at the same rates as naval officers. I happened to be visiting the office of the foreman in charge of erecting the 'ski-ramp' and he showed me a pamphlet which laid out the pay rates that the unions were trying to obtain for their members; for example, a union member who held a position similar to mine would be paid almost double what I was receiving. I pointed out that their figures were grossly inaccurate, and that my pay was just £21,000 per annum, which included flying pay; it was a matter of public record if it were not believed. The figure being quoted by the union was based on that asked by the Armed Forces when an officer was seconded to industry for development and research; the higher figure was required to recover and make up for the loss from the service and for training costs but the officer himself was paid his normal salary. I also pointed out that *Hermes'* second-in-command received less pay than I did because he was not an aviator nor did he have the seniority that I held. The foreman was staggered by what I told him. I went on to advise him that the union was lying to its members. I agreed that his pay should be raised, because at the time it was nothing more than that received by a Leading Rate or Corporal, which was unjust in view of the responsibility he carried. Eventually the Dockyard workers' pay dispute was resolved, and they did receive an equitable and substantial rise, albeit well short of the outrageous demands being made initially.

* * *

Hermes was now afloat, and the next most important step in the refit was to re-install the engine-room pipework and fittings that had been taken away for replacement or overhaul. The hangar deck was littered with tubes of all shapes and sizes, and it was hard to believe that they had all come from the engine room. They were all labelled so that the engineers knew exactly where to place them. There were no official engine diagrams or instructions for the ship, everybody having to rely upon textbooks and drawings that each engineer officer either owned or had had handed down to him on joining the ship. This was an odd state of affairs, if understandable since the Navy was in the throes of changing to an all-gas-turbine fleet.

The boiler rooms had a good deal of asbestos fitted around the boilers and pipes, all of which had to be removed and replaced by new, non-carcinogenic material. Men dressed in green plastic suits and breathing masks, working on twenty-minute shifts, gradually dismantled all of the old cladding over the course of a week. Their route in and out of the ship was closed off from the remainder of the carrier by plywood bulkheads and fencing on the dockside and the material was placed in covered trucks and driven off to a special disposal unit. Once this task had been completed, a new team moved in to re-cover the boilers and pipes with a 'safe' material. It took almost a fortnight to clean up the resultant white deposit everywhere, and this caused me to have a serious argument with the Refit Project Manager.

It had always been drilled into me, from the time I had been a youngster, that if one made a mess anywhere one cleaned it up as soon as possible. This was not so in the dockyards, where 'cleaning squads' were employed. However, cleaning and tidying was not always carried out, especially on Friday afternoons: rubbish was frequently left lying around over the weekend, creating a potential fire hazard. Where carpenters had been working up forward in the ship, for example, heaps of wood shavings and chippings might be left in the flats. Sure enough, one weekend the ship experienced a fire, although, fortunately, it was quickly extinguished and very little damage resulted other than some scorched bulkheads and melted linoleum tiles. The Refit Manager agreed, after some persuasion, that in future all workmen would clean up before leaving a job.

Late in the autumn of 1980 *Hermes* was edged out of her refit dock and positioned once again alongside the Northwest Wall Jetty. Captain McKenzie was promoted Admiral and appointed Flag Officer Gibraltar. His relief was to be Captain Lynn Middleton, an old personal friend of mine. Lynn took up temporary quarters in a flat in Southsea, and while we were on the same Tactical Course at HMS *Dryad* he invited me to take up residence with him until we all moved back on board. Personally, I did not think it right that a Commander (Air) should be sharing the same accommodation as his Captain while his Executive Officer was living in the Naval Barracks. He understood when I explained my refusal. Lynn and I had always got along together very well, ever since he had been an cadet and I an Upperyardman aboard *Indefatigable*. In different circumstances I would, of course, have accepted the offer.

Work was proceeding well aboard the carrier. Her engine components were being re-installed and the furnace re-lined with new firebricks. One day, while discussing Sea Harrier operations with FOF3's Aviation Staff Officer, I glanced out of the office window and over towards the dockyard I saw black smoke issuing from the ship's funnel. It was far too thick to be the result of a normal furnace light-up, and when I returned dockyard fire engines and firemen were in attendance alongside. There had been a blaze in the boiler room; apparently the new firebricks in 'A' boiler had taken fire. Although the flames had been extinguished, considerable damage had been done to the furnace, which meant that it had to be overhauled once again. The dockyard personnel were extremely diligent and within a week had completed the re-work, and the boiler was ready for relighting. This time all went well.

The next big event was an exercise called 'Tempest', when all the new electronics that had been installed were tested both for operation and mutual interference. It soon came to light that the new aircraft radio system did not function very well. The Admiralty had in its wisdom awarded the contract for building the system and equipment to two different companies, Plessey supplying the transmitters and Racal the receivers, and the equipment did not match well. Each company blamed the other for the problems, of course, but in truth they lay squarely at the doors of the Admiralty. The difficulty was finally resolved and we had a system, which was, supposedly, 'state of the art' and gave us clear communications.

Once the dockyard refitting work had been completed the ship was painted from stem to stern. It was decided that, as the carrier had not been officially decommissioned or paid off, the only route open to the Captain was to organise a rededication ceremony, to which Admiral of the Fleet Lord Terence Lewin would be invited together with his wife, Lady Lewin, as guests of honour. Lord Lewin had been one of the Captains of *Hermes* when Lynn had served aboard as the CO of 809 (Buccaneer) Squadron. Aircraft from the carrier's air group were flown aboard while the ship was alongside, one of 800 Squadron's Sea Harriers being displayed on the after lift, the lift one-third raised and with the aircraft parked at an angle to show off its shape and colour scheme. Astern of the lift on the flight deck, but visible from the hangar, were parked three helicopters, two Sea Kings and a Wessex.

A full church service was held on board with numerous dignitaries, Admirals, members of the Board of Admiralty, officers and '*Hermes* people' and their families in attendance. Lord Lewin gave the rededication speech, the national anthem was sung, and then the partying began. It was a wonderful day, enjoyed by everybody who attended. On completion, those personnel not required for duty proceeded on weekend leave.

* * *

Christmas 1980 leave came and went. With the rededication ceremony over, the ship was readied for sea and her post-refit trials. Winter was more or less finished but there was still some bad weather about with strong winds. It was planned to leave before the end of March one mid-afternoon at the top of a spring tide. The wind had been gusting thirty knots or more all day, and it looked as though our departure would be postponed. I was in Flyco at the allotted time and Lynn came through and asked me for my opinion. I advised him to stand by, to await a time when the wind would decrease to about fifteen knots, which I could judge by the passage of lines of clouds. Eventually he was able to give the order to slip the mooring lines, steer port half rudder and proceed slow astern on the port propeller, two tugs pulling the ship off the jetty and helping to turn the stern to port. We turned into Fareham Creek, where we stopped and then went slow ahead on both propellers, and with a tug still attached to our bows and one following we headed for the harbour entrance and Spithead. Once we were clear of the harbour entrance the tugs left us and we were on our own, having completed our refit in little over a year: *Hermes* was once again a living, sea-going ship.

— 31 —

Caribbean Cruise

IT IS A WONDERFUL sensation to feel a ship moving once again under one's feet, knowing that she is alive after having spent over a year as an immobilised steel hulk. The wind had moderated considerably since leaving Northwest Wall Jetty. We proceeded slowly down-Channel checking all systems throughout the ship. In general we were very fortunate in having few post-refit failures and defects.

Before leaving Portsmouth, I had embarked the ASW Sea King and Commando helicopters and the day following our departure I embarked some of 800 Squadron's Sea Harriers, assigned as part of our air group. The 'ski-ramp' had not yet been not cleared for Harrier operations, but we were allowed to use the after part of the flight deck for vertical take-off and landing. Before leaving British waters, the 'ski-ramp' would be fully cleared for Harrier operations, by RAE Bedford and A&AEE Boscombe Down. In the meantime the flight-deck crews would gain valuable experience in handling both helicopters and fixed-wing aircraft. In addition, it would be good experience for our new Lieutenant Commander (Flying), Brian Clark, who had little or no familiarity with fixed-wing operations, especially of 'jump jets'. It gave me a great sense of pride knowing that *Hermes* was once again a 'fixed-wing' carrier, albeit with an entirely new type of fighter. The ship had to steam over the degaussing range at Portland to establish whether there had been any change to her magnetic profile. The new 'ski-ramp', with its extra steel, would make some difference, but otherwise everything remained much as it had been before.

While at Portland FOF3 had decided to embark for a short while. *Hermes* was anchored about a mile east of the harbour in Weymouth Bay, thick with fog at the time, but a landing craft under the control of the Ops Room, using radio and radar, was despatched inshore to collect the Admiral. The landing craft disappeared into the fog and a short while later the coxswain called in to say that he had the harbour entrance in sight. The Operations Room staff now began to relax until a radio call was received from the Admiral asking what had happened to his boat, whereupon the staff erupted into near-panic. After repeated radio calls, nothing was heard from the vessel, but after what seemed an inordinate period of time the coxswain called in to say that he had gone aground on some rocks.

'What rocks?' he was asked.

'Well, there is the Lulworth Cove Inn nearby. Does that mean anything?'

The Marine coxswain had driven his craft ashore at considerable speed half a mile north of us, tearing the bottom out of the boat. He had not used his compass, nor bothered to check its alignment or the chart he was carrying on board; what he had taken to be the walls of the harbour entrance were the tall white cliffs and rubble at Lulworth Cove. There were a number of red faces around the ship that day and both the Captain and the Admiral were hopping mad. It had been an utterly stupid accident involving a craft of which the Navy had very few. We had failed in the a simple task of collecting our 'boss' from ashore; the finger of scorn was pointing at us!

After the completion of the degaussing trial *Hermes* was re-anchored in Weymouth Bay for a couple of days. FOF3 wanted to return to his head-quarters at Fort Southwick and the engineers wanted to return an electrical cooking range top to the dockyard for repair. It was decided to carry out both tasks using the same Wessex helicopter, to be flown by a US Marine Corps exchange Major. The cooker top was loaded into the helicopter's main cabin, and the Admiral climbed into the right hand seat next to the pilot. A green light was given for the pilot to take-off and he lifted a few inches off the deck, only to flop back reporting that he was too heavy for take-off. I then suggested that he carry out a running take-off from the after part of the flight deck, but our Marine Major was not to be persuaded. The pilot shut the helicopter down and FOF3 climbed out. I knew that some 'flak' would be coming my way very soon.

The Captain called for me and demanded to know what on earth was going on, and I told him the facts as I knew them. The ship's AEO had asked the Engineering Department how much the cooker top weighed and had been told 350 pounds, and that was accepted. I then instructed the AEO to check the cooker top and its weight was found to be almost double that quoted by the Engineering Department. It was reloaded, the helicopter was defuelled to bring the it within take-off limits and the flight was rescheduled for the early afternoon. I am sure that the Major was suffering from nerves at having an Admiral setting alongside him: any other pilot would have made a running take-off. However, with everything adjusted, we would with luck have a successful take-off after lunch.

In the position that *Hermes* was anchored, our helicopter would have to transit the military firing range off Lulworth Cove. The procedure was to file a flight plan, which would be cleared by both Portland Air Traffic and Lulworth Range Control. As soon as the pilot lifted off he would switch through our Approach Control to the Portland Radar Control, which would then be respon-sible for controlling the aircraft through the area of the range. The Lulworth Range Control Officer gave his clearance, stating that he had only one test firing to make that afternoon, which would not interfere with the helicopter's flight. Off went our helicopter, and as it crossed the range a shell exploded about a mile and a half inshore of it. FOF3 saw the explosion. I was sitting in my after cabin going through some papers when the Operations Officer burst in to tell me the news. I told him to remain 'mum' about it for the time being but to gather as much information as possible before informing the Captain. At that precise moment I could see no reason for getting very excited: no harm had been caused to person or aircraft. I calmly awaited the inevitable.

It was a quiet sunny morning and I was in Flyco going through the signal log when the Captain called me from the bridge.

'Wings, can you come and see me straight away?'

I dropped everything and walked quickly to the bridge to find Lynn sitting in his bridge chair with the Staff Navigating Officer standing alongside him, glaring at me.

'What's all this I hear about the Admiral being almost shot down yesterday, Wings?' enquired the Captain.

'No he was not, sir!' I replied.

The Staff NO immediately laid into me.

'Oh yes he was!' he interjected.

'Were you there?' I asked.

'No I was not, but I take what my Admiral says as being correct.'

'Well, your Admiral is grossly exaggerating the event. The shell that was fired was a test shot of short range and it fell well inshore of the helicopter by a mile and a half. In addition, the ship had nothing whatsoever to do with the control of the helicopter, which was under the control of Portland Radar. A flight plan had been filed as required, and once the aircraft was airborne it was the responsibility of Portland to control its flight and to liaise with the Lulworth Range Officer. As far as I am concerned everything was conducted correctly and the helicopter was not in danger at all. And, by the way, do not question me about the flight and controlling of aircraft, which is my profession. I do not question you about your navigational ability.'

Lynn almost had to separate us: I had never been so angry in all my Naval service. The officer was overstepping his position and rank, was trying to call into question my competence and in my opinion was attempting to stir up trouble in the ship. Lynn thanked me and said that he would have a word with Portland, and the matter was laid to rest for the time being.

Lynn was going ashore later that morning and he would raise the subject with the Captain of Portland. Portland's Commander (Air) and his Operations Officer visited the wardroom that day and stayed for lunch. I tackled him about the incident and he promptly turned on me, saying that it was all *Hermes*' fault. I asked him how on earth could it be our fault when a proper flight plan had been issued and Portland Radar had taken control of the helicopter, and knew the status of the firing range at the time. It seemed to me that there was a great deal of backsliding going on here, with everybody trying to place the blame on us. I could not believe what I was hearing. I asked him why his radar had not controlled him around the range or to the north of it. There was silence, except that Portland's 'Wings' still insisted that the incident was our fault. It was very obvious to me that neither I nor anyone else in the ship was going to make much progress with officers who behaved in such an obstinate manner.

I was fairly sure of what had happened. The Lulworth Range Safety Officer had probably given permission for the Wessex helicopter to transit the range and then allowed the test firing of one shell, knowing that it was to be fired with a reduced charge. It was the only firing due to be carried out that day, and because of the low charge it was of short trajectory and would have caused no harm to the helicopter. However, an RSO would normally allow up to two or three times the trajectory range as a safety trace for the depth of the danger area, in case something went wrong and the projectile travelled further than intended. FOF3 saw the shell hit the water and knew that it was some distance off and no threat to him, his pilot or his aircraft, but he wanted to have some fun at *Hermes'* expense. It was certainly within his nature to do so. Personally, I found the incident trivial and exaggerated, but it caused a good deal of unnecessary aggravation among officers, a ship and an air station.

* * *

The main reason for visiting Portland was to gain some sea training, especially for the 'first- timers' but also for the ship's company as a whole. After spending ten days working up in the Portland Sea Training Areas, Flag Officer Sea Training's staff came aboard to examine and test us. The examination would last a day and was designed to see whether we were ready to join the Fleet as a fighting unit; it was rather like FONAC's inspection of an air station, although this visit was more to determine how we coped with various emergencies and kept the ship fighting. The tests were not confined to seaborne incidents but also to land-based emergencies such as an earthquake and the devastation that might be caused by a hurricane; the Royal Navy is renowned for providing assistance to countries that have been severely affected by natural disaster.

One sacred rule governing exercises that is always, or should always be, observed, whatever the circumstances, is that the safety of an aircraft and its crew must not be jeopardised. For some unknown reason FOST's Staff failed the anemometers. Brian Clark was trying to land-on a Sea King and was experiencing wind direction problems. I was busy dealing with another difficulty when Lynn Middleton dashed into Flyco exclaiming that the anemometer was inaccurate and wondering why 'Little F' was trying to land a helicopter facing the wrong way. Brian quickly waved the helicopter off and then instructed the pilot to land the other way, using the ship's ensign and funnel smoke for wind direction and strength.

I was absolutely fuming that FOST Staff had been so crass as to carry out such a stunt, and said so in no uncertain terms to both the Staff Aviation Officer and Staff Captain. Their immediate response was that the incident could happen 'for real' during a battle. I conceded that yes, it certainly could, and we would be aware of any battle damage, but they had tried to sneak in an incident that was in itself dangerous and likely to have caused an aircraft accident. Lynn Middleton calmed me down, but my point was received and understood by the Admiral's Staff and there the matter rested.

The ship passed FOST's inspection with flying colours, and he signalled the Admiralty and FOF3 that *Hermes* and her people were ready both for sea and for war. Lynn then steamed us to a Weymouth Bay anchorage, where we rested for the night, recovering from the ordeal of the inspection.

* * *

The day after FOST's inspection we steamed round to Lyme Bay for Sea Harrier 'ski-ramp' trials. Teams from MoD (Navy), RAE Farnborough, RAE Bedford and British Aerospace embarked for the trial. Danny Norman, ex FAA and a former CO of 800 Squadron, was included in the BAe team They brought one of their own Sea Harriers, fully instrumented for measuring all sorts of parameters during a take-off. In addition, an exit camera was installed together with an electrical wire spanning the width of the ski-ramp at the forward end, the purpose being to measure the aircraft's exit speed. The camera was triggered as the nose wheel passed over the cable but the system failed to function satisfactorily because the cable was dislodged by the wheel and eventually broke—exactly the experience during the trials at RAE Farnborough's 'ski-ramp'.

The trials went very well indeed until the last launch, when for a moment I truly thought that we were about to have the first Sea Harrier accident. It was almost dusk and the test pilot from BAe was taking off into a red and orange sky, the sun having just dipped below the horizon. The aircraft looked fine from Flyco and the FDO was given a 'Green' to launch the jet. The acceleration and run-up the ramp all seemed normal but then, as the aircraft left the ramp, it sank heavily towards the sea. I grabbed the console and was on the point of hitting the 'Crash' button, when the aircraft started to gain height. I quickly asked the pilot what had gone wrong but all he would say was 'I'll tell you when I land back on board.' When the pilot arrived in Flyco I asked him what had happened and he explained that there was nothing wrong with the aircraft: he had forgotten to select 60 degrees 'down' on the nozzles and had realised his mistake only as he was leaving the ramp. Following this incident we instituted a primary check by the FDO, in which he signalled the pilot to select nozzles 'down' before raising his 'Green Flag' for the launch, and a secondary check from Flyco. Within twenty-four hours we had a minimal clearance for the 'ski-ramp' and within a month a full day-and-night clearance. We were now fully operational, and over the next week, with 800 Squadron embarked, we gained experience in using the ramp for all rolling take-offs with both 'clean' and ordnance-loaded aircraft.

There were a couple of problems with the 'ski-ramp', both affecting navigation from the bridge. The top of the ramp was some 25 feet high, and this effectively blocked the view out on the port bow: any vessel or object approaching from that quadrant was lost from view at about one and a half or two miles. The other problem concerned the colour of the ramp on the starboard side. It had been painted the normal warship grey, but at a certain angle the sun's rays were reflected straight into the bridge area, producing a glare. This was overcome by painting the starboard side of the ramp dull black.

The first problem, however, was to remain with us, and of course was of particular concern when entering harbour. Consequently, during this man-oeuvre, we positioned an FDO at the top of the ramp using his flight-deck radio to relay the position of any other vessel to the bridge.

After the Sea Harrier trial we joined up with RFA *Olmeda* and refuelled before returning to Portsmouth. I was standing in Flyco when Lynn Middleton came in and asked me whether I had ever conned the ship during a Replenishment at Sea operation. I replied that I had not, and before I knew it I was standing out on the starboard bridge wing controlling the ship's engine revolutions while the XO steered the ship from the same position. Quite naturally, I suppose, I used the terms 'Up revs' or 'Down revs' when changing the number of engine revolutions. Lynn did not like that: I had to say 'Up ten revolutions both engines' or 'Down revolutions both engines', which was the recognised way of giving engine commands to the ship's conning crew—which seemed to me to be rather verbose. All the same, it was great fun keeping *Hermes* in the correct position alongside her tanker.

* * *

It was now midsummer and the carrier had returned to Portsmouth so that various minor defects could be rectified by the Dockyard—and of course so that the Petty Officers' celebrated cooker top could be replaced. Navy Days were upon us, and the ship was prepared for a multitude of visitors over the weekend, which happened to be the late August Bank Holiday. The ship was dressed overall and aircraft were ranged and placed on display on the flight deck. Enclosures were placed around the aircraft and squadron personnel conducted groups of half a dozen people around their charges. These Navy Days are very special to people of the various naval ports because it allows them to see the ships and people that their fathers, brothers and uncles work on or serve in. They are also very beneficial in terms of Navy recruitment.

As soon as the Navy Days had been completed the ship proceeded to sea once again, but this time our destination would be Mayport, Florida. However, before leaving British waters we had to conduct a trial over the 'measured mile' off Looe, Cornwall, to check and calibrate our log (the ship's 'speedometer'). Although it was a quiet day, the sky was heavily overcast and had all the portents of an equinoctial gale blowing in from the Atlantic. Apart from a few hiccoughs, however, the trial went well, and on completion we headed for Plymouth Sound, where the ship anchored for the last run ashore before heading out into the Atlantic. While we were at Plymouth a small Royal Marine detachment was embarked together with the four Wessex Mk 5 commando helicopters—the Flight being commanded by the same Flight Lieutenant RAF as before—and four Sea Kings. We were now prepared, if required, for any operations in the Caribbean.

The autumn weather was upon us as we steamed out into the South Western Approaches. As we passed the southern tip of Ireland the ship was turned north-west, heading for Rockall. There had been, and still was, a great deal of wrangling over this piece of barren and isolated rock sitting way out in the North Atlantic, about two hundred miles north-west of mainland Britain. Most Britons knew of the rock only as the name for one of the BBC Shipping Forecast sea areas, and the fact that storms seemed to be always present there. The Irish were trying to claim sovereignty over the rock for the purposes of mineral rights—oil, for example, probably exists in the area—because they believed the rock to be within their 200-mile sea limit. The United Kingdom was making similar claims. Lynn Middleton decided to replant the Union flag at the top of the rock, take photographs and have them published in the British newspapers. The task was given to the embarked Royal Marine detachment.

By the time *Hermes* arrived in the vicinity of Rockall the gale had blown itself out but there was still a heavy sea running. A plinth had been built atop the rock at some time in the past and there was a tabernacle for taking a flagstaff. Half a dozen marines embarked in a helicopter were flown over and within the hour they had the flagstaff erected and the Union flag flying stiffly in a Force 6 breeze. I expect the next storm that came through knocked staff and flag down, but in the meantime we obtained some excellent propaganda photographs, which were transmitted ashore and duly appeared in the press. Lynn was delighted!

* * *

We headed off now to a position about 400 miles south of Iceland. It had come to our attention that the USS *John F. Kennedy* was somewhere in the area, and Lynn thought it a good idea to carry out a search followed by a dummy attack against her with our small air group. We made a calculated guess that *Kennedy* was about 200 miles north of us, so we launched Sea Harriers in pairs against her, with the Sea Kings simulating missile attacks. It did not take our aircrew long to locate her by electronic means: the huge 'super carrier' was steaming along quite happily when, out of the blue, four Sea Harriers suddenly swooped across her flight deck, taking the Americans completely by surprise.

One of our Sea Kings came very close to being lost during this little exercise. It is standard procedure in a helicopter that the onboard compasses are aligned with the ship's heading by flying parallel alongside the flight deck. In this instance the Sea King crew failed to carry out this fundamental check and it was nearly their undoing. They should have returned back on board two hours later but we received a radio call to the effect that they could neither see nor find the ship at the centre of the grid system being used at the time, nor did they have the ship on their radar. In fact, based upon their radio transmissions, they were to the north-north-east and flying away from us. On my way to the Operation Rooms I obtained from the Navigation Officer the bearing of the sun. Not much progress had been made by the time I arrived in the Ops Room so I had the duty Ops Room Officer ask the pilot whether he could see the sun, and back came a reply in the affirmative. 'Tell him to point his helicopter at the sun, realign his compass to this bearing, and come home,' I instructed. Lynn turned the ship towards the helicopter, *Hermes* accelerated to full power and within twenty minutes the Sea King was in visual range. It landed back on board with about 200 pounds of fuel remaining—enough for half an hour's more flying before ditching. Lynn wanted to hang the crew but I suggested that perhaps they had learnt their lesson and urged him to leave the matter in the hands of the Squadron commander: we have all, or nearly all, 'been there' in similar circumstances and ended up with the inevitable red faces.

I was very interested in this compass error, so I obtained a boat's hand compass and carried out some headings checks on the flight deck, at each helicopter landing spot comparing the compass bearing with that of the ship's heading. The most accurate spots were those abaft the island and the greatest errors were found to be forward of the island, the most glaring being an error of 145 degrees at No 1 helicopter spot. Obviously the new 'ski-ramp' was causing a great deviation—and would have the same effect on an aircraft's compass either on the flight deck or when flying alongside. These errors also varied considerably according to whether the degaussing loop was switched on or not. After gathering all this information I had the Sea Harrier and helicopter pilots re-briefed on aligning their aircraft compasses before departing the ship and, thankfully, we had no further incidents of this sort.

The weather had deteriorated rapidly over the past few hours. The wind and sea had both risen and soon we were approaching severe storm conditions—Force 11 on the Beaufort scale. The two carriers were now in sight of one another and the American Admiral and the *Kennedy*'s Captain asked to come aboard and look over *Hermes*. They arrived in one of their Sea Kings, and after quick introductions on the bridge to the various heads of department they were taken by Lynn down into the Operations Room. While in the Ops Room, the Operations Officer passed me a message just received from the US carrier requesting that their Admiral and Captain remain on board *Hermes* until the seas had moderated; the American ship was pitching outside limits. The USN Admiral read the message and he exploded. 'Tell those knuckleheads if the Brits can fly so can we!' he roared, and a couple of hours later he and *Kennedy*'s Captain lifted off to land, quite safely, aboard their own ship. Looking across at our companion we could not see any reason why there was concern about the ship pitching: she appeared very stable— hardly any movement was visible—while the old *Hermes* was almost standing on end!

Conditions became steadily worse as the afternoon wore on, the wind finally reaching Force 11. *Hermes* and her support ships were 'taking it green' over the bows and their forefoots were often well clear of the water. Waves were breaking over the new 'ski-ramp' and across our bridge, and free water was washing across the flight deck. Owing to the sudden increase in sea heights and wind we were 'caught with our pants down' and the Sea Harriers were standing in a foot of salt water. As soon as conditions moderated, the aircraft were towed aft to the lift, where they were washed down with fresh water and sprayed heavily with WD40 to prevent any corrosion.

The weather conditions had not been forecast: they had blown up as if out of nowhere, which I understand is quite normal for that part of the North Atlantic during the autumn. In company with the *Kennedy* group we steamed slowly towards Florida, and after covering 400 miles we had reached calm seas and wind and an air temperature in the seventies. We joined up with the USS *Savannah* and refuelled from her, and then the ship's company had an afternoon of sports and barbecue on the flight deck with Brian Clark participating in a flight deck marathon, which he won. During the evening the flight deck was prepared and the aircraft ranged for our entry into Mayport.

During the refuelling from *Savannah* the CO of the US Navy Sea King squadron, together with some of his officers from *Kennedy*, came aboard for lunch as guests of our Sea King Squadron officers. It was a pleasant occasion, but a couple of days later the USN CO lost his life along with the rest of his crew in a crash of their helicopter. The cause was probably some sort of rotor failure, but as the wreckage sank quickly into very deep water no definite cause could be established. Lynn requested that *Kennedy* forward the condolences and sympathy of the *Hermes* people to the victims' families and loved ones, the Squadron and the ship. The accident seemed so unnecessary, especially when both ships were so close to their destination. All through my life and naval career I have found it extremely difficult to accept air accidents, especially when one knows the people involved and indeed may have been laughing and talking with them only hours beforehand. Some people I know try not to establish close friendships with anybody in the aviation world for fear of being hurt—although I could never be like that.

Our approach into Mayport was made in very hazy conditions and it was not until we were within a couple of miles of the harbour that we could start to make out the shoreline and buildings. *Kennedy* had gone in ahead of us and was tied up at the big carrier berth just inside the entrance. Our ship's company, dressed in full whites, lined the flight deck and island. The ship looked a picture as she steamed slowly into Mayport and took up the berth on the opposite side of the harbour. The whole purpose of going to Mayport was to carry out some additional refit work for which the Admiralty had allocated $210,000. After docking it was up to the Engineer Officer and the Shipwright to negotiate with the Americans to complete this additional work within the allocated budget—a tough task!

* * *

The next three weeks were a time of relaxation for the ship's company—except for the Engineering Department, which was toiling long and hard. The XO placed the ship in Tropical Routine. I received a letter from May telling me that our beloved cat Tinkerbell had died following a roadside accident. It was not really known what had happened to her, except that she was found dying near our front gate. With the vet just two doors away May rushed the poor animal to him but she had passed away before he could do anything. It looked as if she had been hit by someone on a bicycle or had been severely kicked. Her loss affected the whole household. As I was reading May's letter there was a knock on my cabin door, and when I opened it there was Lynn Middleton. He was feeling rather lonely and suggested that we take the Land Rover over to the Officers' Club for a beer or two. Having just heard about Tinkerbell, I needed a drink to calm me down.

When Lynn and I arrived at the Club the place was humming with officers from *Hermes*. A great cheer went up as we entered, he immediately ordered a couple of large jugs of ale and the party gathered more way. One of the officers asked Lynn what he thought our future might be. He said that he believed that we might end up in the South Atlantic. Whether he knew more than he was letting on I do not know, but if not it was indeed a prophetic reply.

As soon as the $210,000 had been spent we slipped our moorings and headed south for the Virgin Islands; FOF3 had embarked, intent on a cruise in the Caribbean. Sea Harrier and Sea King flying was carried out en route, involving bombing and strafing practice and anti-submarine sonar training. We anchored off St Thomas in the American Virgin Islands for a long weekend. It had been intended to stay there for ten days, but an American carrier entered the anchorage and FOF3 instructed Lynn to weigh anchor and go elsewhere; he was not having large numbers of British and American sailors mixing ashore to cause trouble. The anchor was weighed and we steamed to Virgin Gorda in the British Virgin Islands. It was while we were there that we lost an exchange Army REME sergeant from the Commando helicopter flight.

The Flight had been disembarked at Beef Island off Tortola conducting training with the embarked marines. Sergeant White had requested that he be allowed to visit a yacht show at another nearby island, returning in time for the re-embarkation the following Monday morning. The Flight Commander granted his request and off he went—never to be seen again by anyone in his Flight or aboard ship. We discovered that he had arrived at the show and was seen, and he had then boarded a sailing yacht crewed by girls to return to Beef Island, whereupon the yacht, the girls and Sergeant White vanished. A large-scale search was conducted by the ship, the US Coast Guard, police and customs officials but to no avail. To this day no evidence has emerged as to what might have happened; the hapless crew may have fallen foul of drug smugglers and been murdered and their yacht used for smuggling before being scuttled, but this is all speculation. The mystery remains.

En route to the British Virgin Islands we received a message from 'Mac' Melhuish, who had been at Lossiemouth with Lynn and me during the early days of the Buccaneer bomber. After returning home from having served with CBNS in Washington, DC, he had retired from the Royal Navy and become a professional charter yacht skipper in the Caribbean. Soon after we anchored he came aboard for lunch in the Captain's cabin with a bevy of girls he had crewing for him. They had been collected by our landing craft, but when it was time to depart the sea turned so rough and they had to re-board the craft by Jacob's ladder from the stern boat boom. Another problem presented itself. We had about five or six hundred officers and men ashore enjoying a banyan party on the beach at the time, and they were now stranded. The Sea Kings were therefore ranged, all the personnel made their way to a small airfield close by and after four hours of ferrying we managed to lift off everyone and all the ship's recreational equipment.

The following morning we weighed anchor and with all our helicopters re-embarked we proceeded to the waters north of Puerto Rico to conduct some flying exercises. We had just completed night flying when I spotted a red anti-collision light off our port quarter. Eventually, instead of crossing astern, it turned towards and approached us. There had been one or two garbled radio calls on our approach frequency which, we subsequently discovered, had come from the aircraft approaching us—which turned out to be a US Navy Sea King helicopter. He was waved on board by the FDO and the two pilots came up to Flyco. They had come from the USS *Dwight D. Eisenhower*, the latest American nuclear strike carrier, which was working up her air group to the north of us. We knew she was in the area but had been told that she was over 300 miles away and not fifty. The helicopter pilots delivered an invitation for us to visit their new carrier the following morning, which was gladly accepted.

The following day we hove-up on the *Eisenhower*'s port quarter and con-ducted cross-deck operations with our Sea Harriers, and then I flew across in one of our Sea Kings to pay a visit. We were conducted to the main briefing room for their air group, and to my amazement the Carrier Air Group Com-mander turned out to be none other than Captain Tom Treanor from VX-4 days. He was surprised to see me too, because the last time we had met he was at NAS Oceana as a Lieutenant Commander. He had not changed at all and was very much in control of events; he was well liked by his fellow officers and it was obvious that he was enjoying himself. After being shown around the ship we said farewell and flew back to *Hermes*, whereupon the ship set course for Bermuda.

* * *

While we had been with *Eisenhower* the weather had been far from perfect, with dull overcast skies and heavy seas running. The US carrier had been pitching quite badly, and several of her F-14s had bolted before being trapped. However, the following day broke bright and sunny with calm seas, and it was now obvious that we were going to have a happy visit. Bermuda would be our final port of call, and we would spend a long weekend there,

The ship was brought to anchor about a mile from Hamilton, the capital of the island, half a mile from the old RN Dockyard. We could not go alongside because the berths were reserved for cruise liners, which called frequently. Within hours of anchoring, officers and men were boating ashore to visit the island and make their last-minute purchases before returning home. Ber-muda is a fine place for a visiting yacht, or for staying at one of the expensive hotels which have their own entertainment, but I personally would soon become bored. It has become very much a tourist trap and an excellent place in which to shop for gifts for the family and friends back at home, but otherwise it holds nothing special for me. After our long weekend stay, the anchor was weighed and we were on our way home to Portsmouth and Christmas.

The passage back across the North Atlantic went very quickly, and we were soon steaming up-Channel. The Air Group was disembarked, the Sea Harriers and Wessex 5s to Yeovilton and the Sea Kings to Culdrose. Lynn took us into Portsmouth and berthed the ship alongside the South Railway Jetty. It was planned to stay in harbour until late January 1982, when the ship would go to sea once again for another work-up of the Air Group. In the meantime, everybody would proceed on Christmas leave and then attend training courses before going back to sea.

Over the past weeks, at Lynn's insistence, I had been revising and updating the Air Department War Orders. I am sure that Lynn knew more about what lay ahead concerning the ship's programme than he admitted. First, I had to find out just how many aircraft we could embark in the event of war. Working with the Aircraft Control Room Officer, I used silhouettes to establish the number of Sea Harriers and helicopters that could be accommodated and operated effectively. Outriggers were used to allow the Sea Kings to be parked with their tails overhanging the sides of the flight deck, an arrangement similar to that used in World War II for aircraft fitted with tail wheels. We finally managed to pack in nearly fifty aircraft. Then I went through those sections that dealt with Pilots' Notes, then the section that dealt with aircraft paint schemes. In most cases aircraft limits were waived, except where we knew it would be dangerous to go beyond those laid down by Boscombe Down. All aircraft would be painted blue-grey, top and bottom, and the white in the recognition roundels would be painted out. Numerals and lettering would be repainted in black. The orders were finally completed at about the time we arrived back in Portsmouth.

One day in early December 1981 Lynn called me into his cabin for a chat. He said that he intended to have me relieved earlier than planned; I had already served two years and David Dobson had promised me two and a half because of the refit programme. However, if I stayed until the end of the period promised, the incoming Commander (Air) would have barely two weeks in the chair before entering the next major NATO exercise, which in Lynn's opinion was far too short a period for anyone to learn the ropes. I reluctantly agreed with him. He showed me the names of those who had been put forward to be the next 'Wings' and one of these was Robin Shercliff. Lynn was for having Robin and I wholeheartedly agreed. He came aboard a week before Christmas 1981. I moved out of my cabin into a spare on the starboard side of the carrier, showed Robin around the ship and the departments and introduced him to all the important personnel, especially those within his own department. Then, with the Air Department, we had a run ashore to the Oyster Bar in old-town Portsmouth.

A day later I bade farewell to Lynn and the ship and was on my way home to Bexhill. David Dobson had given me my new appointment, which would be my last in the Navy before retiring: I would join the Directorate of Naval

Overseas Training, based in the Old Admiralty Buildings in London. My time aboard *Hermes* had been very happy and I was very saddened at having to leave her. However, I knew that Robin, whom I had known from the days at DNAW when we shared the same office, would be a very effective and capable Air Department 'boss'.

X

GOODBYE TO THE ANDREW

— 32 —

Back to the MoD

MY TIME in the Royal Navy was nearly over when I joined DNOT in the wing of the Old Admiralty Arch spanning The Mall leading up to Buckingham Palace. It was a cold and bleak morning when I presented myself to my new Director, Captain Brian Evans. Like me, he was also heading for retirement, having been passed over for 'Flag' rank. The Deputy Director was Commander Marx, who had also failed to make Captain's rank. All the remaining officers in the Directorate were more or less in the same position, having been ruled out for higher rank, due to retire or taking early retirement. I felt as though I were joining a department of 'has-beens'! However, they were all excellent, hard-working officers, still very much dedicated to the Navy and the job in hand.

The task of DNOT was mainly to arrange training both for foreign naval forces and for British personnel about to take up appointments as SNOs, such as the posting in the West Indies. An additional task for the Directorate was to sell surplus naval equipment to foreign navies, and it was in this area of concern that I would first 'wet my feet'. The Deputy Director was engaged in the sale of HMS *Lincoln* to the Bangladeshi Navy. The representatives were shown over the frigate, and it was bought 'as seen', a maritime term often used in the purchase of ships but not including gun breeches or ammunition. These items are never sold with a warship: they are bought separately, after the vessel has been delivered to the buyer's country, in order to forestall any untoward incidents involving third-party countries. The policy was to be of considerable concern to the Bangladeshis. As it happened, the Royal Navy had only very limited supplies of ammunition for the guns aboard this class of frigate, but after much argument it was agreed that the breeches and ammunition would be included in the sale but that they would be delivered separately. We certainly did not want any of our old weapons being turned against us or our friends before they reached their destination.

The frigate was steamed from Chatham to Portsmouth and then the new owners tried to start bargaining. They demanded in a most persuasive way that they be topped up with fuel and oil before leaving; they even demanded a library of 'blue' films for the wardroom. The Deputy Director almost exploded. What sort of service did they think the Royal Navy to be? We did not supply such films, and we had no intention of providing any! The frigate eventually departed. The crew appeared to have some problems navigating through the Mediterranean, and also had problems at the Suez Canal because of improper clearances, although when the Egyptians were told that there were neither gun breeches nor ammunition on board they were allowed to pass into the Red Sea—whereupon DNOT heaved a sigh of relief.

Once the sale of *Lincoln* had been completed and all the attendant disputes resolved, someone said to me, 'Welcome to DNOT. Now you have first-hand experience of some of the difficulties we have to contend with from time to time.' I obviously had a great deal to learn, but no doubt I would do so quickly and discover how to cope with the various tasks and 'wrinkles' in whatever form they presented themselves. Quite a few were lying in wait.

The next projects to land on my desk were the sale of two *Leander* class frigates, HMS *Dido* and HMS *Juno*, to the Royal New Zealand Navy and the sale of HMS *Invincible* to the Royal Australian Navy to replace the ageing HMAS *Sydney*, a light fleet carrier that had seen better days. The sale of the two frigates—both of which had been commanded by friends of mine, the former by Doug Borrowman and the latter by Ray Lygo and Ted Anson—presented no problems as far as the RN was concerned: they were two of the original ships of their class and over twenty-five years old. However, that of *Invincible* was a different matter. We were by then at war with Argentina, fighting over the Falkland Islands, and *Invincible* was in the thick of the action: here we were, trying to sell a warship while it was in battle. It simply did not make sense. What would the position be if the sale went through only for the carrier to be sunk? I do not believe that anybody even stopped to consider this possibility at any time during the negotiations. I began to feel that I was working and living with an unrealistic group of people who were failing to see the wood for the trees

The sale of *Dido* and *Juno* went ahead in a straightforward manner. There was a series meetings both at MoD and with the RNZN at New Zealand House, and the RN Project Team also flew out to RNZN headquarters in Wellington to complete the sale. The trip to Wellington had been arranged six weeks ahead of time, and on the appointed day I went straight from my lodgings in Putney to Heathrow Airport, the remainder of the team coming in from Bath, MoD and MoD (PE) by their own means. As it happened, I was the first to arrive and be checked in, and I ensured that we all had our assigned seats in the Club Class section of the airliner. There was one hiccough: one of the MoD (PE) representatives was an ex RNZN officer and was travelling on to Wellington from Auckland under his own steam. He would be in the capital ahead of us, visiting his daughter, while we were driving south in a hired car from Auckland. Once I had sorted everything out satisfactorily—or so I thought—I retired to the bar for a beer and to await the arrival of the others.

The flight was eventful, a strike amongst the airline's catering staff and a mix-up over our seating arrangements at Heathrow, a landing at a monsoon-drenched Karachi during which our 747 aquaplaned and an engine that refused to start at Perth all contributing to a memorable experience. Our troubles did not end there, for while driving the final leg from Auckland to Wellington Commander 'Rob' Robinson, our Engineer Officer from Bath, managed to attract a speeding fine from the New Zealand police and Neil McLoughlin, our MoD (PE) senior civil servant heading the sales team, suffered a bout of food poisoning.

When we arrived in Wellington the city was still experiencing the effects of a Force 10 storm that had been ravaging the area. It had been very violent, and when we left after our breakfast the following day there was plenty of evidence. A month earlier a ferry boat had been lost in the Cook Strait separating the North and South Islands, and in another storm a Russian cruise liner had gone on the rocks north of Nelson on South Island in the same general area. The Cook Strait is frequented by violent storms owing to its narrowness and the change in the water temperature from tropical to polar on either side of the islands. Our London RNZN liaison officer from New Zealand House, who had flown out ahead of us, met us on Monday morning and escorted us to the RNZN Headquarters. I was surprised at the size of the establishment, which was not much bigger than my squadron office block at Yeovilton. We were all introduced to the RNZN Chief of the Naval Staff and were then left to hammer out the final details and sign the various documents of sale.

Aspects that had not been too clearly defined back in Britain were the training arrangements for courses covering the ships' electronics and the Ikara anti-submarine missile system. It was learnt that the two ships would be renamed HMNZS *Wellington* (ex *Dido*) and HMNZS *Southland* (ex *Juno*). It had been intended originally to rename *Juno* HMNZS *Nelson*, but this could not be done because there was already in existence an HMS *Nelson*—the Royal Naval Barracks at Portsmouth. It is the tradition in the Royal Navy that when a new ship is named the silver and trophies held in storage are handed over to the ship, but in this instance it could not be done because the RNB had them all.

Once the signing ceremony had been completed I apparently put my foot in it with the RNZN Chief of the Naval Staff. I casually remarked that the RNZN was acquiring a couple of fine ships that at that time the Royal Navy could ill-afford to lose—the Falklands War having recently seen the loss of HMS *Sheffield*—although they were due to be replaced by two new Type 23 frigates. He got the impression that we did not want to sell them and was quickly on the telephone to Captain Evans, who would be awaiting my return. From what he said, I received the strong impression that the RNZN was not in a financial position to buy two replacement frigates at that time, although I am sure that reasonable terms were arranged to enable the sale to go ahead.

That evening a cocktail party was given at the Vice-Chief's home to celebrate the signing over of the two frigates. We had one day more before leaving, so we spent the time individually sightseeing and shopping in Wellington. There are some wonderful vistas overlooking Cook Strait and I thoroughly enjoyed myself wandering around, wishing only that May and the girls could have been with me. At the end of the day we threw a small cocktail party for our RNZN guests in the hotel, and after our farewells we boarded a turboprop airliner for a flight back to Auckland.

Our wait at Auckland Airport was quite short and we were soon aboard a BA 747 heading back to London, via Melbourne, Perth, and Karachi. Before we knew it, our wheels were touching down at Heathrow. After reporting to DNOT I took a long weekend off and drove south to Bexhill to see May and the girls again.

As soon as I had returned to DNOT the following Monday morning the Deputy Director informed me that the Director wanted to see me immediately. I was uneasy about the way he spoke, and when arrived at his office he asked me, after the usual pleasantries, what I had said to the RNZN Chief of the Naval Staff to upset him. I explained that all I had said was that they were acquiring two fine warships which we could ill afford to lose at the current time but that they would be replaced shortly by two new Type 23 frigates, then under construction. I saw nothing wrong with that statement: the information had been published in all the newspapers, and for the New Zealander to get upset over what I said was ridiculous; otherwise, why on earth would a team fly all the way to New Zealand to confirm a sales agreement? I explained also that I had found him to be a strange officer and a rather unhappy individual who, I felt, was having second thoughts about the deal. Brian Evans said that he had always thought the Admiral to be something of an 'oddball'.

Even though the frigate sale had gone through, the training for the New Zealanders had to be arranged in order for them to receive it before ownership of the vessels could be assumed. *Dido* was the first ship to be transferred, and she left Portsmouth with her new name, *Wellington*, painted on her port and starboard quarters. She was taken via the Panama Canal, Tahiti and the Samoan Islands and then on to New Zealand. They had to wait a little longer for *Juno*, which was still in commission, but she was finally handed over in the late summer in a short ceremony held at Portsmouth Dockyard, attended by Naval Home Command and his RM band. It was sad to see one of our old ships depart for another country, even though this country was a member of the British Commonwealth.

* * *

Before the sale of *Dido* and *Juno* had been completed, I had started preparations for the sale of HMS *Invincible*. It seemed to me odd that DNOT had been tasked to set up this sale, especially when we had only two of these vessels, plus the old light fleet carrier *Hermes*, although admittedly a third 'through deck cruiser', HMS *Ark Royal*, was expected in a couple of years. The Royal Navy was actually very lucky to have *Invincible* and the new *Illustrious* because, as related earlier, the then First Sea Lord, Admiral of the Fleet Sir Varyl Cargill Begg, was bent on preventing the Navy from commissioning any form of aircraft carrier.

When *Invincible* entered service it was the intention of the Navy to have two of the class in commission at any one time with the third laid up in reserve until one of the two went in for refit. The reason was the availability of manpower. The Armed Forces were being reduced in strength in order to save money and because the country's commitments overseas had been pared. In order to manoeuvre around the reduction in manpower the FAA commissioned several reserve helicopter squadrons that operated over the weekends or went to war when the necessity for their presence arose. There was, as a result, a rush to join the reserve squadrons by personnel completing their time and due to leave the naval service. It would therefore have been possible, if need be, fully to man the third ship of the class.

At the time of the negotiations with the Royal Australian Navy *Invincible* was in the South Atlantic in the thick of the Falklands War. Together with *Hermes* and many other warships, she had departed from Portsmouth fully laden with Royal Marines, their transportation and their weapons, plus Harriers and helicopters. My sales asset was on its way to a war zone, and I could not be sure whether it would return safely; moreover, I was uncertain whether I would be at DNOT for much longer.

One day Brian Evans called me into his office and asked me how long it would take to wrap my projects up and hand them over to somebody else. I had been earmarked by my Appointing Officer to go south to the Falkland Islands as the shore-based Officer-in-Command of air power. It seemed that I was about to have my war. I told Brian that it would take less than a day, and he told me to do it. I went back to Putney to pack my bags and await further orders from DNOA (X) as to where I should go, sat down and had tea with Ingrid, my old landlady, and watched the BBC News on the television. The programme was showing the recapture of Port Stanley by British forces and the Union flag being rehoisted. I knew then that I would not be going, and a short time later the telephone rang.

'Hi, Punchy,' the voice said. 'It's the Appointer again. Have you been watching the TV news?'

'Yes I have, and I suppose you don't need me now.'

'That's right!'

I was told to relax, unpack my bags and go off and have a beer.

It seemed odd that I had missed almost every conflict in which all my friends had been involved and that, yet again, my services were not required. Jonathan Todd, my closest friend, was in the Cabinet Office as a Captain giving advice to the Prime Minister; Robin Shercliff, my old DNAW friend, was now in my chair aboard *Hermes* as 'Wings'; and here was I trying to sell ships which we sorely needed. It made no sense at all.

— 33 —

Finale

MY WAR had come and gone, and so I went back to work as usual in DNOT. They were most surprised to see me. I gathered back all my old projects and set about the sale of *Invincible* with renewed vigour. With the end of the Falklands War, the project gathered pace. A team of RAN officers had been set up in Bath to finalise the purchase of both the ship and various equipment. With the impending arrival of the new *Ark Royal* into the Fleet, the requirement for the old *Hermes* was fast disappearing and she was now also up for sale. She had one more commission under the command of Captain Roger Dimmock before being paid off. She was a fine ship and in excellent condition structurally, electronically and mechanically. Moreover, she was fitted out to operate the Sea Harrier, and it was hoped that whoever bought her would also purchase the aircraft. Her one drawback was the fact that she still ran on 'black oil'; indeed, she and the Royal Yacht *Britannia* were the only two remaining ships in the Royal Navy to use this fuel, all the others being propelled by diesel oil, which could be used also by jet aircraft and helicopters.

A final meeting was held at Australia House in London to discuss the sales agreement, chaired by the RAN's equivalent of the RN's Comptroller of the Navy. I sensed at the time that he was holding back, and that he had no intention of signing on behalf of his Government or the RAN: he was too 'nit-picking', even though it had long been decided that *Invincible* was the right ship for the RAN. A few days later my suspicions were to be proved correct.

The Australians had a new Labour Government that was bent on cutting back the country's Armed Forces and saw no reason for spending a large proportion of the defence budget on a new carrier for which they felt they had little need. They were travelling the same route that the British Labour Party had taken back in the late 1960s and early 1970s. The Americans had persuaded them to buy F-111 aircraft to replace the RAAF's ageing Canberra bombers, plus a new fleet of US-designed anti-submarine frigates and Sea-hawk helicopters.

In many ways I was happy, as were many other British naval officers and civil servants. The RN could ill afford to sell *Invincible* or, for that matter, any of its frigates. *Hermes*, as the last traditionally powered big ship, had to go, and the personnel so released were required to man the new ships that were now starting to enter service. In the event, a buyer for the old carrier appeared from a most unsuspected quarter. The Indian Navy's elderly light fleet carrier *Vikrant* was fast falling apart at the seams and needed replacement. *Hermes* was just the ship, and they were prepared to buy not only the Sea Harrier to go with her but also the Westland Sea King anti-submarine helicopter. The Navy and the Government were very pleased with these sales, which went ahead together accompanied by a training package for the air and ground crews

* * *

Every day was filled with excitement in DNOT. In addition to the ship sales, we were trying to establish a Coast Guard and Frontier Force security course for the Saudi Arabians. When I first arrived at the Directorate, Commander Peter Gregory was the Project Officer for this task. However, shortly after my arrival, Peter's project came to an untimely end—or so we thought. It was not long after the Australian fiasco that the Director came up to me and dropped a file on my desk. It was Peter's old project, which was 'on' again. Fortunately the Deputy Director was dealing with the *Hermes* sale as the Lead Project Officer, so I plunged immediately into this new task. Peter was still with us and so I was able to glean a lot of valuable information from him, but there was still plenty of telephoning and legwork to be undertaken in order to bring the project back on line once again.

Although I had dealt with a foreign nation before while serving at CTTO, dealing with Arabs was something entirely different. Australians and Indians were in a sense 'family', and one knew more or less where one was going with them, but with the Arabs I had serious doubts. Peter and I had nothing but trouble with them, both as regards their general attitude and because of their tendency to 'shift the goal posts' at regular intervals. During Peter's tenure as the Project Officer, for example, having completed the arrangements the Saudis had suddenly cancelled them. DNOT and many other organisations were seriously embarrassed, particularly as other international training had been postponed in order to accommodate the Saudis' wishes. All the agencies involved in the course had insisted that the Saudis be taught technical English, which was essential in order fully to understand what they were taking on. However, they insisted that they could speak English, having been taught the language by the Pakistanis and Koreans (!). Although, at the time, this was the main reason that they pulled out of the planned courses, there were others—as I was about to find out in the not too distant future.

Going back over old ground and trying to convince the various British agencies to set up the same courses yet again was very difficult indeed. Quite naturally, most of them were very reluctant to do anything more. However, by 'sweet talking' and gentle persuasion I managed somehow to resurrect the old courses, but this time based upon various 'windows of opportunity' relating to when they, the Saudis, could attend; I was determined that this time they would not dictate to us when they could attend tuition. I made it quite clear to the Army Major at the Saudis' London Embassy that dates were non-negotiable once agreed, and that if he cancelled for any reason he would have to go elsewhere: we in Britain could not upset and offend other nations just to satisfy his country's whims.

I managed to arrange most of the courses, including the English language course, which would take place at the Army School of Language in Beaconsfield, Buckinghamshire. Visits were made to the Saudi Embassy but I began to have serious doubts about our clients' sincerity. On one occasion, during discussions with the Saudi Major, two eighteen-year-old Saudi Midshipmen burst into the room to talk to him, whereupon he disappeared with them for well over an hour. He neither excused himself nor said when he would be back. I then asked the other officer in the room what on earth was going on and he apologised, admitting that he was unsure when the Major would return. In fact he reappeared half an hour later but immediately announced that it was then 12.30 p.m., the Embassy closed for the day at 1.00 and the meeting was therefore over. He offered neither an apology nor an invitation to convene a further meeting for the next day. I left in disgust.

Two days later I received a telephone call from the Foreign Office. The civil servant introduced himself and asked me whether I could arrange security courses for the Saudi Arabian Coast Guard and Frontier Force. I enquired as to who might have requested this training, to be told that it was Major ———— from the Saudi Embassy. I explained that I had been in the process of setting up this training for many weeks with this gentleman, that my predecessor, Commander Gregory, had done the same and that the Saudis had cried off at the last moment. What was going on? After a short silence, back came the comment 'Oh, I see. You have not had any dealings with the Saudis before? Well, now you are experiencing how they operate!'

Still seething, I took the bull by the horns and telephoned the Saudi Major. I had made it quite clear, I said, that one of the conditions for the courses was that all attending them must also attend the Army's course at Beaconsfield, no matter what might be their command of English. The course was duly arranged through the British Council, and everything went well until a week or so before Christmas 1982, when a young lady at the Council telephoned me, requesting that I go across and see her immediately as she had a serious problem. When I arrived she showed me a letter stating that the Saudis had arrived, in company with their families—aunts, uncles and grandparents. It had been intended that one Saudi student would be accommodated within each bed and breakfast establishment so that they were compelled to speak English; now there was no way that English would ever be spoken outside the classroom. I returned to DNOT pulling my hair out.

I immediately telephoned the Saudi Major and laid down the rules for the English language course. I patiently explained that it was essential that there be only one Saudi per bed and breakfast establishment, otherwise the students would not learn the language properly. If they wished to have their families with them, then those people had to be accommodated elsewhere,

410

otherwise I would cancel the course and present his Government with a bill for failing to follow military training standards and requirements. There was a long silence, but eventually he said that he would sort it out and I heard no more.

Some time later I was sitting quietly at my desk reading through various papers and documents when the telephone rang. The Saudi Major was on the other end. 'Oh, Commander. Our Defence Minister, Prince ——, is due here any day. We have decided to postpone the security courses until we have discussed the matter with him. I will not have an answer as to when we will be able to reschedule them again until our meeting. This will not happen until after your Christmas celebrations.' There are times when one feels like leaping from Tower Bridge.

We had heard at this time that our Deputy Military Attaché in Riyadh was due to return home for retirement from the Army. He spoke some Arabic, my time at DNOT was coming to an end and it was felt that if this Lieutenant Colonel could be persuaded to join DNOT for a short time to finalise the Coast Guard and Frontier Force training course it would solve our problems. At the same time, DNOT was moving across Whitehall into renovated accommodation within the Old War Office building and I would move 'sideways' into the Directorate General of Naval Manpower and Training, which covered both men and women in the Naval Service. The Director was Rear Admiral Nicholas Hunt, who had been *Ark Royal*'s XO during one of my appointments to the ship. I would serve out my time in DGNMT until I retired in July 1983, seven months hence and just before my fiftieth birthday. I would have a month's leave prior to finally being mustered out of the Royal Navy and placed on the Retired List on 22 August 1983. I was disappointed that I had not brought the Saudi Arabian training scheme to a successful conclusion. At one point I really thought that I had won through, but it was not to be.

* * *

I was not idle for long. As soon as I arrived at DGNMT—many of the officers in whose air office were old friends from way back—I had an Air Traffic Control Officer, together with a Meteorological Branch manning problem, to sort out. These did not take long, but then I became involved in the sale of Lynx helicopters, plus an air and ground crew training package, to the Nigerian Navy. The Nigerians had arranged for basic helicopter flying training with a private company operating out of Weston-super-Mare, Somerset. I personally was not happy about this arrangement, but the Nigerians said that it cost them less than the Royal Navy training. What they did not appreciate was the fact that they were receiving inadequate flying hours before proceeding on to the Lynx helicopter, a fast and powerful machine. Nothing would budge them, however; and in any case they had already signed up and were therefore legally bound.

Then one of the Nigerians asked when flight-deck training would commence. All the RN representatives looked at each other: what flight-deck training?

411

'The flight-deck training that is included in the overall training package,' came the reply.

'There is no flight-deck training. You were told quite clearly—and it is recorded in the minutes, of which you have a copy—that flight-deck training was over and above all other training being given to your Navy.'

'No! It was our understanding that the training package included *all* training.'

This was a serious *impasse,* and we all took a break to mull the matter over. A check through the recorded minutes revealed that the Nigerians were trying to obtain something for nothing. When we returned to the meeting room, the RN Team Leader told the Nigerians what the position was; however, as a gesture of goodwill, he would include, gratis, some very limited flight-deck training. He then went through every section of the agreement line by line, ensuring that they understood everything, and then made them sign each individual page of the document so that there would be no future misunderstanding. They did not like it; but they signed.

* * *

While still serving in DNOT, I started making plans as to what I would do once I left the Navy. Many of my brother officers had gone into industry or the aviation world, but I thought that perhaps I might do something entirely different. After serving others for nearly thirty-three years I yearned for a pursuit that would be under my personal control. Although May and I still had our bed-and-breakfast business, I had the urge to do something else. All my life I had been extremely keen on sailing, and while glancing through a copy of *Yachting World* I saw an advertisement for a Moody 27 sailing yacht. Made of fibreglass, she was naturally of light construction, and she was fitted out with a Bermudan rig and sail plan. Consequently she was easy to handle though probably not capable of withstanding bad weather and heavy seas.

One evening I drove south to Burlesdon near Southampton, where Moody had their main sales office and display of yachts. I went aboard the 27 but quickly determined it to be far too small for my intended use of chartering; moreover, the freshwater pipes were badly arranged in the main saloon berth lockers, thereby restricting stowage space. I began to have serious doubts about the suitability of the yacht for chartering or even sail training: it was fine as a day sailing boat, but that was all. In the adjacent berth lay a Moody 31, a much larger and roomier yacht. I took the opportunity to look over the craft thoroughly, but once again I had doubts. It had one great disadvantage: when the dining table top was lowered from its stowage on the main bulkhead, it blocked the way to the forward cabin and heads. Thus, like the 27, it was struck off my list.

The following weekend I drove again to Burlesdon to view the two yachts but this time with May, Naomi, Dee Dee and Kim our lodger. Without any prompting on my part, they all came up with the same opinion as I had, and the two boats were crossed off my list permanently. We drove around to

Hamble to look at the Westerly yachts, and the moment we stepped aboard the Konsort we knew instinctively that we had found the right vessel; the Westerly Fulmar tied up alongside was even better, but the Konsort was within our pocket. We placed a marker on the boat, and agreed to a test sail the following day. This particular yacht was a 'bilge keeler'—that is, she had two iron bilge keels, enabling the craft to sit upright when dried out or if she had been unintentionally run aground during a falling tide. In theory, moreover, she would sail to windward better because the leeward keel would dig deeper into the water as the boat heeled, thus providing better lateral resistance. Westerly's sailing demonstrator, a retired merchant marine master with certificates in both steam and sail, took us out on to Southampton Water; after a couple of hours we were convinced and on our return agreed to buy the demonstration vessel. A week later, at the Southampton Boat Show, we handed over our deposit and the vessel was ours. Westerly gave us many extra sails but would not part with the 'cruising chute'. A marine mortgage was arranged and we now had a beautiful sailing yacht, christened *Naomidee* after our two daughters.

My main purpose for buying a Konsort was to start a yacht chartering business, earning enough money to pay for both the mortgage and marina berth. When not chartering, we would have a good yacht for our own pleasure, and for the girls to grow up with. Naomi was not a good sailor but Dee Dee took to the pastime like a duck to water; indeed, in short order she would become a Yachtmaster Instructor, in fact the youngest in the country. The Konsort was a fine, stable, safe sailing craft and one with plenty of space for four or five people. In gale force winds I never had any difficulty beating to windward with a storm jib and the mainsail with three reefs. To me the class was the safest of small sailing yachts and, above all, one of the best on which to learn sailing. I would purchase two more of the class a few years later.

* * *

It was about this time that my domestic troubles began. May and I had become quite estranged for various reasons. She had become anorexic, whether due to my behaviour or a desire on her part to lose weight, I do not really know. At the same time, my mother's health was deteriorating fast and, with my time in the naval service coming to an end, life seemed to be nothing more than an utter disaster.

A year before Mum died, we held a celebration at St Norbert's for my parents' golden wedding anniversary. All the family attended, including Aunt Alice (my father's sister and last remaining sibling), Uncle Wilf and family. Unfortunately, my siblings Brian, Anthea and Jacqueline were living on the other side of the world and could not make it, but Theresa, the youngest, was there. May cooked the dinner and everybody thoroughly enjoyed themselves, including Mum and Dad. Apart from giving May a business interest, it was for occasions like this that we had bought St Norbert's. It was a wonderful and friendly home and was ideal for family gatherings, although it had taken a great deal of hard work by both May and I to bring the house back to its former glory.

During the autumn of 1982 mother became very ill and spent much of her time in St Helen's Hospital at Ore on the eastern side of Hastings. She had been using a 'walker' in order to move around at home, and when she experienced her third fall her locum doctor, a young man straight out of medical school, determined that she should be in hospital. What none of us knew at the time was mother had suffered three heart attacks, resulting in the three falls. All this was a great strain on my father, who was himself not in the best of health, especially after he had suffered a heart attack while in California. I returned home and together with May visited Mum in hospital. She was finally placed in an Intensive Care ward run by an former Paratroop Medical Corps nurse. The evening before she died, Dad went home early as he was feeling extremely tired and I stayed with her until 11.30 and then returned to Bexhill. The following morning, at half past four, my bedside telephone rang and the Duty Sister informed me that my mother had passed away five minutes earlier. I immediately dressed and drove over to Camber to see Dad and tell him the sad news that we had all been expecting. He took it quite calmly although I was angry with myself for having left her when I did: she had passed away alone, with no family around her. It is something for which I will never really forgive myself. All my friends said that I should not berate myself, but I feel that I should have been there with her if only to hold her hand. Dying people, even when unconscious, do not feel alone when in their mind they sense the warmth of a family member touching them.

My mother's funeral was held a week later at Camber church, and a wake was held in the small home which she and Dad had shared for the past ten or fifteen years. All her old friends and family turned up, which cheered my father up considerably. He was feeling quite lonely now and although I tried to entice him to Bexhill he wanted to stay at Camber. Eventually my youngest sister Theresa drove over from Finchingfield in Essex and took him back with her. He stayed there until he passed away.

With the last load of my parents' effects driven away to Finchingfield, it really was the end of an era. Apart from Uncle Jim's daughter Joy, who lived in Rye under her married name Band, there were now no Dousts in the district at all. The family had been around Rye, Peasmarsh, Udimore, Winchelsea and Rye Harbour for over three centuries. The locals thought the world of Dad, and they would miss him very much: he was Rye Harbour and Rye Harbour was him!

* * *

My time at DGNMT was quite short—about six months. Although I had several projects, they really did not amount to much. I was still keen on there being just one officer corps instead of the three Officers' Naval Lists, i.e. the General, Special Duties and Supplementary, the last being that on which I served as a permanent officer. In the General and Special Duties

Lists, officers could serve up to the age of 53 years, extending this to 55 if there were an opening for them. However, some 70 per cent of the naval officers' corps were serving on the Supplementary List, yet these officers were restricted in the type of appointment they could hold (although I had been an exception) and they had to retire at the age of 50. To me it all seemed most unfair, especially when four out of five serving on the General List could be promoted to Commander's rank and three out of four Commanders could make Captain's rank. It was my opinion, and that of many others, that promotion to higher rank should be based upon ability and potential. There were far more officers on the Special Duties and Supplementary Lists who had potential for higher rank than on the General List. In some cases outstanding officers were recognised and transferred to the General List, but the fact that the opportunity existed did not mean that it was encouraged.

I hawked my paper around the corridors of the Naval Staff, but I was up against stiff opposition from the old and bald—senior officers who believed that the General List represented the *crème de la crème* of the officer corps and that the only thing that mattered was ship command. Commanders from DNPlans and DNOR would come into my office, having seen 'Commander, Royal Navy' below my doorplate, asking what ship had I commanded. I would retort that I had had naval air squadron command with the potential capability of delivering more explosive power than that dropped during the whole of World War II, to which the response would be, 'Oh that's not the same as having ship command!'

While at DGNMT I managed to persuade Admiral Hunt, my Director, that the way ahead was for a single officer corps. He saw the logic of what I was trying to put forward but said that I would meet stiff opposition. He was right. I remember floating the idea to Keith Somerville-Jones on the way to lunch one day, and he was absolutely against it. Many GL officers would recoil, suddenly see their future promotions in jeopardy if there were just one officers' list, the reason being of course that so many of them did not match up to those who were serving on the Supplementary or the Special Duties lists.

I left a copy of my paper with Admiral Hunt, but I was doubtful whether anything would come of it. With my imminent departure from the Navy, I am sure that he did not want to rock the boat, especially when he was in the running for further promotion and elevation to knighthood. Many changes have taken place since my departure from the RN, however, and I would think that it is just a question of time before the Service travels the route that I was advocating. The WRNS, which had been, since its formation, a separate branch of the Navy though not subject to military law, was brought within that law before I left; a few years later the WRNS became fully integrated into the Royal Navy and its officers became fully commissioned naval officers, wearing gold braid on their uniforms, holding sea-going appointments and becoming pilots and aircrew within the FAA. This later change would not have happened during the reign of Admiral of the Fleet Sir Edward Ashmore, the First Sea Lord who quite openly stated that no woman would ever go to sea or pilot an aircraft while he had anything to do with the RN. However, the change has taken place, and if I may say so it is a change for the good of the naval service: in my opinion there are many women officers who are just as capable as, if not more capable than, their male counterparts.

* * *

Towards the end of my time at DGNMT I set off to spend a weekend in a South Kensington Hotel for a two-day short course designed for all ranks leaving the Armed Forces for civilian life. It was a most interesting course because it brought home to all of us what we were about to face in the outside world, having lived a semi-cloistered life for so many years. The Armed Forces had always looked after their own. It was impressed upon us by our lecturers that life on the outside was entirely different, and it would require some adjustment for all. In the big wide world, 'number one'—i.e. oneself—was more important than anything else. A few weeks later I attended another leaving course at the Army Training Centre at Eltham in south-east London. There were officers of greater seniority attending this course, including Malcolm Carver, with whom I had served in 800 Squadron and DNAW. He was retiring as a Captain and had obtained a post as the Secretary to Lincoln's Inn.

At the end of June 1983 I left DGNMT for good, having been appointed to HMS *Nelson*, the RNB at Portsmouth, to attend a four-week cabinet maker's course: I had decided that if I was going to be my own boss in civilian life, running a yacht business, I might as well improve my carpentry skills. Our instructor was an excellent fellow and very patient with all of us. He went through the process of keeping one's tools clean and sharp, and how to select wood. I decided to make a magazine holder, and for the task I bought some mahogany sheeting from a wood yard in Portsmouth. At the end of the four weeks, we were all given our certificates, and the course took the instructor for a 'pub lunch' in Southsea. When I returned to the wardroom I loaded my ready-packed bags into my little old Renault, paid my mess bill, signed out of the mess and drove home to Bexhill to commence my separation leave. After almost thirty-three years, my time in the Royal Navy had finally come to an end. Looking back, I was not quite sure where all the time had gone, but it had been a wonderful career in which I had made many friends. Now a new way of life lay ahead of me, and as I drove east along the M27 motorway I wondered what was in store for me. In an hour and a half I would be with my family every day, for the rest of my life, and not half way around the world as a guardian of the Realm, the Commonwealth and Dominions, the seas and the oceans . . .

Epilogue

EW PEOPLE can honestly say that they have done what they wanted to do from the beginning of their lives. I can still remember, as if it were only yesterday, telling Dad and Uncle George in the small living room at Inkerman Cottages that I wanted to go to sea as a naval gunner. Uncle George had told me not to worry: one of these days I would. I did indeed go to sea, not as a surface but as an aerial 'gunner'. It is still difficult to believe that I more or less succeeded in achieving my objective.

Looking back over my life, there have been moments when I wish that I had done something else. I could have been a civil engineer, and if old Mr West, my boss after leaving school, had had his way I would have been one. However, the calling of the sea was much stronger and I decided to join 'the Andrew'. From the moment I made up my mind, moreover, I was determined to make commissioned rank, although, admittedly, in those early days I was in such a rush that I was not quite sure where I was going. There were many occasions when I might have acted and behaved in an entirely different manner. I hurt other people as well as myself, but somehow I managed, I think, always to rise above the occasion. I suppose that this was because of the discipline installed into me by the Navy, and how it taught me to be self-reliant. There is no doubt that sailors and naval officers are a breed apart from their Army and Air Force counterparts: a sailor, once at sea, has only himself and his crew to rely upon for help; he cannot dash round to his neighbour to ask for help. The sea levels everybody down to a single base, no matter from which family, section of society or nation one hails.

I enjoyed my time in the Royal Navy—a lifetime of almost thirty-three years, years during which I met all sorts of people and made many friends and acquaintances. My decision was the right one: no other life would have given me the same breadth of experience. A naval life is not necessarily for everybody, but it was for me. It still amazes me how everybody accepts a sailor to their bosom as a person of kindness and compassion. A sailor has, in my opinion, more understanding of the world than somebody who earns his living off the land. Life at sea can be an experience of sheer beauty and calm and at other times it can be utterly terrifying.

417

At sea, every man is the same as the next, no matter his position, colour or nationality, whether his country is at peace or at war. It is astonishing how sailors forget all feelings of animosity and anger when rescuing sailors of another nationality: no matter who those in trouble may be, they are casualties of the sea and deserve as much help and assistance as anyone else. I will always remember the young Russian seamen we rescued at night from the Mediterranean: they were treated with complete respect and kindness, even though this was the time of the 'Cold War' and they were, potentially, our enemies.

All sailors have a quick sense of humour and may make fun of a situation at someone else's expense, but without rancour. It is clean fun, and nothing is ever done in bad taste. Historically, on rare occasions a sailor's way of life has been seriously upset and he has withdrawn his labour; his actions are known as mutiny—a very serious offence. Usually when the case has been investigated, however, it is discovered that one or more officers have failed signally in their duties and responsibilities, causing severe hardship. In such instances the officers concerned have quickly been removed to other ships or duties, their careers ruined. However, an officer who gains the respect of 'his' people will be followed to the ends of the earth. One can always tell if a ship is properly run. The demeanour of her gangway staff is always pleasing, and one is welcomed aboard with friendliness and a smile. Captains and Executive Officers who praise their men in daily orders, even though the reason may be trivial, are loved by them.

I never regretted a single day of my naval career. It was my choice to join the naval service, and I was as proud as Punch when I donned His Majesty's uniform, even though, 'all skin and bones', I faintly resembled a string bean (a far cry from my present bodily shape!). However, the blue serge did itch like fury, and I could not wait to go ashore to Bakers, the naval tailors in Portsmouth, to be fitted out in a suit made of the finest material available. In those days Bakers was situated on Commercial Road just past the Guildhall, in a most imposing establishment with huge, glass-fronted, mahogany doors. Now that part of Portsmouth has been redeveloped and Bakers is located just past the RNB in a cheap retail shop, its glory days long gone.

When I gave my name at Bakers the assistant remarked, 'Oh, sir, we have another Doust on our books—Instructor Commander Doust. Is he related to you?'

'Well, no, he is not—not that I know of.'

'He has retired now and is an educational advisor to the Saudi Arabian monarch, King Faisal.'

Once I had established myself in the Navy I discovered that there were other Dousts serving in some capacity or other. There were Dousts in the FAA besides myself, and there was of course Victor Doust who worked out of Bath as a ship designer and was responsible for designing CVA-01.* There was also a Captain Doust RNR, the Navy's salvage expert throughout World War II, who finally retired to Hong Kong to manage and run his own huge

---

* See Chapter 23.

salvage business. Now, with my retirement from the naval service, the line of Dousts has been broken.

Many people have asked me why I joined the Royal Navy, seemingly under the impression that it had something to do with a good pay packet and flaunting oneself in a smart uniform. I joined because I was thereby offered a goal in life and an opportunity to serve both my country and my sovereign. It never occurred to me that I might have to make the supreme sacrifice of losing my life, either in battle or in an accident. I had always considered myself a 'policeman' of the seas and oceans, trained to keep open the lifelines of the nation, the Commonwealth and the Dominions. I was extremely fortunate in that I stayed around until the end; many of my friends were not so lucky and lost their lives in East Africa, Singapore, Borneo and, more recently, the Falkland Islands. They fought gallantly and gave of their best so that we all might see our tomorrows. I for one will never forget them; they will always be in my prayers.

There were times when I did my wife and family a great wrong and hurt; on occasion one has no idea of the repercussions that a decision may have. My difficulties happened at a time when I should have been looking forward to starting a new life with them; instead, I entered a new world with a very shaky domestic life wondering just how long my family would stay together—and at a time when we all needed each other so much. I was about to have the greatest challenge of my life, but it would be almost eight years before it would return to a relatively balanced level. There is little doubt that many of my friends and acquaintances did better than me, but we all started off on the same footing and with the same opportunities. I certainly do not envy them in any way. If I could live my life all over again I would certainly follow the same career, though on reflection I would have conducted my personal life in a much better way than I did. I would have thought more about others, especially my family. Fortunately for me, the domestic problems I hinted at earlier proved to be temporary.

No boy or girl, man or woman can go wrong by joining the Royal Navy. It offers a marvellous life, an experience that can never be forgotten. The Navy builds men and women of character, strength, intelligence and compassion and with an understanding for one's fellow human beings. It is also a wonderful preparation for whatever lies ahead: there is to my mind little doubt that men and women who leave the Navy for civilian jobs are far ahead of their counterparts in civilian life. Naval people are a breed apart from society, and society recognises this.

Since retiring I have lost both my parents and my youngest sister Theresa, to whom I was very close indeed. It is not until one's close relatives are no longer around that one realises just how much they mean. Other siblings live on the other side of the world in Australia and my other surviving sister lives in southern California. May has now lost all of her family except for her elder sister Margaret, who lives at Ambleside, Cumbria. Both of our daughters have grown up and have a family. Naomi, after sixteen years of marriage to an Air Force husband, is, much to our sorrow, now divorced. Dominique—Dee Dee—and her husband serve in the US Coast Guard as Chief Petty

Officers. Dee Dee, who was christened aboard *Ark Royal*, teaches navigation and seamanship to new cadets at the USCG College at Yorktown, Virginia. They both have a family, Naomi an eleven-year-old son Michael, and Dee Dee a five-year-old daughter Holly and another year-old daughter Willow.

On leaving the Navy I did start my chartering business and eventually had about seven 30- to 40-foot yachts in my fleet. I combined it with a sailing school, which I bought from a young man who had suffered a stroke. The school was a wonderful challenge, and I thoroughly enjoyed teaching people the rudiments of sailing and navigation. After moving to California, May and I gave up the charter business and sailing school and closed down our bed-and-breakfast establishment. We restarted a couple of businesses but because of the Gulf War trade fell away and so we closed these and took up working for other companies. We own our own house in Virginia, where we now live, thoroughly enjoying our surroundings, and the glorious weather, but still very much English at heart and in our thoughts.

Appendix

Aircraft Types and Models Flown by the Author

Single Piston Engine
Boulton Paul Sea Balliol T Mk 21
De Havilland Tiger Moth
Hunting Percival Provost T Mk 1

Twin Piston Engine
Avro Anson Mk 1
Beech UC-45J
Bristol Brigand B Mk 1
De Havilland Sea Devon C Mk 20
De Havilland Dominie
Grumman S-2F Tracker
Hunting Percival Sea Prince C Mk 1

Single Turboprop
Fairey Gannet T Mk 5
Westland Wyvern TF Mk 2
Westland Wyvern S Mk 4

Helicopters
Westland Lynx HAS Mk 2
Westland Sea King HAS Mk 1
Westland Wasp HAS Mk 1
Westland Wessex HAS Mk 1
Westland Wessex HAS Mk 3
Westland Wessex HU Mk 5
Westland Whirlwind HAR Mk 10
Westland/Aérospatiale Gazelle HT Mk 2

Single Jet Engine
De Havilland Vampire T Mk 11
De Havilland Vampire T Mk 22
De Havilland Vampire FB Mk 5
De Havilland Vampire FB Mk 9
De Havilland Sea Venom FAW Mk 21
De Havilland Sea Vampire F Mk 21
Hawker Hunter F Mk 4
Hawker Hunter GA Mk 11
Hawker Hunter T Mk 8
Hawker Hunter T Mk 8B
Hawker Sea Hawk F Mk 1
Hawker Sea Hawk FB Mk 3
Hawker Sea Hawk FGA Mk 4
LTV F-8E Crusader
LTV F-8H Crusader
LTV F-8K Crusader
McDonnell Douglas TA-4F Skyhawk

Twin Jet Engine
Blackburn Buccaneer S Mk 1
Blackburn Buccaneer S Mk 2
Gloster Meteor T Mk 7
McDonnell-Douglas F-4B Phantom
McDonnell-Douglas F-4G Phantom
McDonnell-Douglas F-4J Phantom
McDonnell-Douglas F-4K Phantom
Supermarine Scimitar F Mk 1

Abbreviations & Glossary

A1/2	Qualified Flying Instructors' categories, A1 representingthe pinnacle of knowledge, flying ability and instructional ability.
A25	RN Aircraft Accident Reporting Form.
A&AEE	Aircraft & Armament Experimental Establishment.
A of F	Admiral of the Fleet. The highest rank in the Royal Navy.
AA	Anti-aircraft
AAIU	Aircraft Accident Investigation Unit.
ACDS (OR)	Assistant Chief of the Defence Staff (Operational Requirements).
ACM	Air Chief Marshal (of the Royal Air Force).
ACNS (O)	Assistant Chief of the Naval Staff (Operations).
ACRO	Aircraft Control and Ranging Officer.
ADSL	Automatic Depressed Sight Line. A dive-bombing mode invented by Lieutenant Commander Chris Mather RN.
(AE) (P)	(Air Engineer) (Pilot). A Royal Navy officer qualified in both disciplines.
AED	Air Engineering Department.
AEN	Advanced Evaluation Note. (USN)
AEO	Air Engineering Officer.
AEW	Airborne Early Warning. Radar system carried by aircraft (or the aircraft itself) providing long-range warning to both sea and land forces of an impending enemy threat.
AFB	Air Force Base.
AFC	Air Force Cross. Awarded to both RN and RAF aircrew who have performed above the normal call of duty.
AFO	Admiralty Fleet Order. Now superseded by DCI (Defence Council Instructions) (Navy).
AIB	Admiralty (or Aircrew) Interview Board.
AIRTEVRON FOUR	Air Test and Evaluation Squadron 4 (VX-4). (USN)
AMCO	Air Maintenance Control Office(r).
Andrew, The	The affectionate name given to the Royal Navy, said to be based upon the name of one Lieutenant Andrew Miller RN, who impressed so many men into the Service during the 1700s that it became known as 'Andrew's Navy'.
AOM	All Officers Meeting. (USN)
ARP	Air Raid Patrol.
ASW	Anti-Submarine Warfare.
ATC	Air Traffic Control; Air Training Corps.
ATR	Army Training Room. A room set aside for the Forward Air Controlling team aboard a carrier.

ATTDU	Aerial Torpedo and Trials Development Unit. Manned by both RN and RAF personnel.
AV	Attack Vehicle. US term for a ground attack aircraft or fighter.
AVCAD	Aviation Cadet.
AVO	Amps, Volts and Ohms. Measuring meter.
AWG	Air Weapons Gear.
AWI	Air Warfare Instructor.
AWOL	Absent without leave.
B1/2	Qualified Flying Instructors' categories. Both of these categories are awarded on completion of the CFS course, B1 to those students who have obtained 80 per cent or more overall for the whole of their course grades. After taking up an instructional appointment a B2 QFI is re-categorised to B1 after three months in the job.
BA	British Airways.
BAC	British Aircraft Corporation.Formed in 1960 from the amalgamation of the Bristol, Vickers-Armstrong, English Electric and Hunting aircraft manufacturing companies.
BAe	British Aerospace. Formed in 1977 from the amalgamation of BAC, Hawker Siddeley Aviation and Scottish Aviation. Expanded and reorganised in 1999 as BAe Systems.
BBC	British Broadcasting Corporation.
BEA	British European Airways.
BEF	British Expeditionary Force.
BEM	British Empire Medal. Awarded to enlisted men and women for outstanding service to the community and the Armed Forces.
BOAC	British Overseas Airways Corporation. Forerunner of BA (q.v.).
BOQ	Bachelor Officers' Quarters. USN term, equivalent to the RN wardroom.
BQM	Aerial target powered by a small jet engine and launched either from a ground ramp or from an aircraft.
BSA	British Small Arms. British company that produced small arms, motor cycles and sports cars.
Bullpup	US-manufactured air-to-surface guided missile, offically designated AGM-12.
C-in-C	Commander-in-Chief.
CAG	Carrier Air Group.
CAP	Combat Air Patrol.
CAS	Chief of the Air Staff. (RAF)
CATWEP	Clearance, Aircraft Trials and Weapons.
CBNS	Chief of the British Naval Staff (in the United States).
CCA	Carrier Controlled Approach. Similar to the ground-based GCA system.
CDS	Chief of the Defence Staff.
CENTO	Central Treaty Organisation. A military alliance involving Great Britain, Turkey, Pakistan and Persia (Iran), formed in 1955 and disbanded in 1979.
CFI	Chief Flying Instructor.
CFS	Central Flying School. (RAF)
Chag	Chain arrestor gear. Equipment sited on a runway to stop aircraft with a tail hook. Generally deployed for a landing aircraft that has suffered a complete hydraulic failure.
Changi	The site of the notorious World War II Japanese camp for Allied prisoners of war. Used by the RAF as an air base after the war and now the site of Singapore International Airport.
'Charlie time'	The time at which the first deck landing is made by an aircraft from a group recovering to its carrier.

Clutch Radar	North-West European NATO Air Defence Radar.
CNO	Chief of Naval Operations. (USN)
CNS	Chief of the Naval Staff (RN)
COD	Carrier Onboard Delivery.
COMAIRMAT	Commander Air Material. Based at USNAS Miramar, San Diego, California. (USN)
Commander.	Naval officer rank immediately below that of Captain.
Commander (Air).	The head of an RN air department.
COMOPTEVFOR	Commander Operational Test and Evaluation Force. Based at Norfolk, Virginia. (USN)
CPO	Chief Petty Officer. A senior naval NCO.
Corpen	Executive order given to a fleet or squadron of ships to turn a prescribed number of degrees in unison.
CREA	Chief Radio Electrical Artificer.
CTTO	Central Trials and Tactics Organisation. Based at RAF High Wycombe, Buckinghamshire.
CVA	Carrier Vessel Attack.
CVH	Carrier Vessel Helicopter.
DAWG	Digital Air Weapons Gear. Digital version of the AWG. (US)
DC	Douglas Commercial (aircraft).
DDNOT	Deputy Director of Naval Overseas Training.
DEO	Deputy Engineer Officer.
Derry Turn	An aerobatic turn first demonstrated by John Derry, a test pilot who was killed in 1952 at RAE Farnborough while demonstrating the DH 110 twin boom fighter—the prototype for the Sea Vixen.
DGNA	Director General of Naval Aircraft.
DNAE	Directorate of Naval Aircraft and Equipment.
DGNMT	Director General of Naval Manpower and Training.
DGWE	Director of Guided Weapons and Electronics.
DH	De Havilland (Aircraft Company).
DLG	Guided missile destroyer.
DNAE	Directorate of Naval Aircraft and Equipment.
DNAP, DNPlans	Directorate of Naval Planning.
DNAW	Directorate of Naval Air Warfare.
DNOA (E)	Directorate of Naval Officers' Appointments (Engineers).
DNOA (X)	Directorate of Naval Officers' Appointments (Executive).
DNOR	Directorate of Naval Operational Requirements.
DNOT	Directorate of Naval Overseas Training.
DO	Divisional Officer.
DPR (RN)	Director of Public Relations (Royal Navy).
DSO	Deputy Supply Officer; Distinguished Service Cross.
ECG	Electro-cardiograph.
EM	Electrician's Mate. RN substantive rate.
EW	Electronic Warfare.
FAA	Fleet Air Arm. The RN's Air Branch, which was controlled by the RAF from 1918 to 1939. Also Federal Aviation Administration, the US equivalent to the CAA.
FAC	Forward Air Control(ler). The directing of ground attack aircraft over a field of battle or against enemy targets.
FAF	French Air Force.
FDEO	Flight Deck Engineer Officer.
FDO	Flight Deck Officer. The aviation officer responsible for controlling the movement of aircraft on the flight deck, especially during their launch and recovery.
FFO	Furnace Fuel Oil. A heavy-grade oil used originally in ship's boilers. It has now been superseded by diesel oil, which can be used in both marine and aircraft gas turbine engines.

425

Firing range	An area set aside for the release of practice weapons at sea or over the land.
Flag 'Foxtrot'	The alphabetical flag 'F' flown at a carrier's yardarm when she is conducting flying operations.
Flag rank	A naval officer of commodore rank or higher.
Flight Lieutenant	RAF officer's rank equivalent to a naval Lieutenant or army Captain.
FLIR	Forward-Looking Infra-Red. A system whereby an object can be detected in low light by means of its heat emissions.
Fly 4	The aircraft parking area alongside a carrier's island.
Flyco	The Flying Control position on the inboard port side of a carrier's island superstructure.
FM	Field Marshal. The highest rank in the British Army.
FOAC	Flag Officer Aircraft Carriers. Superseded by FOF3 (q.v.).
FOF3	Flag Officer Third Flotilla. Formerly FOAC.
FOFT	Flag Officer Flying Training. Superseded by FONAC (q.v.).
FONAC	Flag Officer Naval Air Command. Also acts as the Fifth Sea Lord when the Admiralty Board discusses aviation matters.
FOSNI	Flag Officer Scotland and Northern Ireland.
FOST	Flag Officer Sea Training.
Form A700	The RN's aircraft maintenance log.
FOST	Flag Officer Sea Training.
FW	Focke-Wulf. German World War II aircraft manufacturer.
FYC	Findhorn Yacht Club, Morayshire, Scotland. Now known as the Royal Findhorn Yacht Club.
(G) (P)	(Gunnery) (Pilot). A Royal Navy officer qualified in both disciplines.
GD	General Duties (officers' list). A list of officers who have risen from the enlisted ranks to commissioned rank.
GDP	Gun Direction Platform. Also Gross Domestic Product.
GHQ	General (Army) Headquarters.
GI	Gunnery Instructor.
GL	General Officers' List. Officers who have joined the Royal Navy through RN Britannia College, Dartmouth. They may have been transferred also from either the GD or the SL list. In addition, some enlisted ranks may have also gained elevation to this list through the Upperyardman scheme of promotion.
GMU	Guided Missile Unit. (USN)
'Green Berets'	Royal Marine Commandos.
'Green Endorsement	A citation placed in a pilot's or navigator's logbook indicating that he has performed a feat of above-average airmanship.
'Green Flag'	The flag used by the FDO (q.v.) indicating to a naval pilot that he is cleared to launch from a carrier's catapult or make a free or vertical take-off from the flight deck.
'Gully-gully' man	An Egyptian pavement or dockside seller offering goods by barter.
HMO	Health Maintenance Organisation (US)
HRH	His/Her Royal Highness.
'Ice Cream Trolley'	A trial electronic device used on a carrier's flight deck to set up a Sea Harrier's navigational and weapon system prior to take-off.
IFTU	Intensive Flying Trials Unit. An RN squadron charged with testing a new aircraft entering service and to develop procedures and tactics for its use.
ILS	Instrument Landing System. Used by pilots to make a safe approach to and landing on a runway in bad weather.
IRE	Instrument Rating Examiner. An experienced flying instructor who gives instrument flying training, monitors the standards of pilots' instrument flying ability and tests pilots annually.
Jack Tar	See Tar.

KRB	Kent River Board.
Krewe	Name given to a New Orleans family or group of friends.
LABS	Low Altitude Bombing System. A means of releasing nuclear weapons by 'tossing' them at low altitude during a half-loop.
LAX	Los Angeles International Airport.
Lieutenant	RN officer's rank equivalent to Captain's rank in the Army.
Lieutenant Commander	RN officer's rank equivalent to Major's rank in the Army.
'Little F'	Lieutenant Commander (Flying).
LLTV	Low-Light Television. An advanced television system capable of operating in conditions of extremely poor visibility.
LRTEM	Leading Radio Electrician's Mate.
LRMP	Long Range Maritime Patrol (aircraft). An aircraft endowed with a prolonged reach and endurance and reach, deployed to search out enemy threats on or beneath the oceans.
LSO	Landing Safety Officer, an aviator who is responsible for ensuring that a pilot makes a safe approach to and landing on a carrier's flight deck.
MAD	Magnetic Anomaly Detector. An electronic device capable of detecting changes in the earth's magnetic field caused by the presence of a large metallic object such as a submarine.
MADDLS	Mirror and Dummy Deck Landing System. Used ashore to train pilots in the art of deck landing.
Marshal of the Royal Air Force	The highest rank in the RAF, equivalent to Admiral of the Fleet or Field Marshal.
Master Green	An experience pilot's instrument rating which allows him to fly in all weather conditions.
'Mayday'	The international distress call, made when a vessel or aircraft is in dire emergency and the lives of its crew or passengers are at severe risk. Immediate assistance is required.
MF	Medium frequency (radio).
MoD	Ministry of Defence.
MoD (N)	Ministry of Defence (Navy). Responsible for RN and RM matters.
MoD (PE)	Ministry of Defence (Procurement Executive). Responsible for providing equipment and weapons for the three Armed Forces and the Royal Marines.
MNIB	Member of the National Institute of Business.
MTBF	Mean Time Between Failures.
MTP	Maintenance Test Pilot. An engineer pilot who tests an aircraft after major overhaul or maintenance.
NA	Naval Aircraft. The letters placed in front of a Naval Staff Requirement aircraft number.
NAAFI	Navy, Army and Air Force Institute. Organisation responsible for providing retail items and groceries (and also restaurant and bar facilities) for members of the British Armed Forces and their families at reduced cost.
NAC	Naval Air Command. (USN)
NAR	North American Rockwell.
NAS	Naval Air Station.
NASU	Naval Air Support Unit. Stores and provides replacement aircraft for naval squadrons and flights.
NATO	North Atlantic Treaty Organisation.
NAVAIR	Naval Air Systems Command. (USN)
NAWC	Naval Air Weapons Center. (USN)
NFC	Naval Flying Cross. (USN)
'No Foreign'	An American security classification. For American eyes only, i.e. not cleared for disclosure to foreign nationals.

427

OAL	Officers' Appointments List.
OEG	Operational Evaluation Group.
OFS	Operational Flying School.
'Old Man', The	An affectionate name given to a ship's Captain.
'Olde Blighty'	An affectionate name for Great Britain.
OOD	Officer of the day. The officer nominated on a daily basis to be responsible out of working hours for the maintenance of the discipline, security and general administration of an establishment or vessel.
ORI	Operation Readiness Inspection.
OTS	Over the Shoulder. A method of delivering a bomb whereby the weapon is released in a vertical loop after passing through 90–110 degrees. The bomb climbs to some 16,000 feet and then topples and falls earthwards. Used in the delivery of nuclear ordnance.
'Our man'	The British Government's representative (in a foreign country).
OV	Operational Evaluation.
PAF	Pakistani Air Force.
Patuxent River	The USN aircraft test facility based alongside the geographical feature of the same name in Maryland, some 60 miles south-east of Washington, DC.
PCH	Pacific Coast Highway. The road which runs the length of the US Pacific coast.
PLM	Pilot Launch Mode.
PTI	Physical Training Instructor.
Pusser's	Item obtained from an RN store as distinct from a similar item obtainable elsewhere. The word is a corruption of 'paymaster's'.
PX	Post Exchange. The US equivalent of the British NAAFI.
Qantas	Australian airline, originally the Queensland and Northern Territories Air Service.
QFI	Qualified Flying Instructor. Awarded after an instructor has passed through the RAF's Central Flying School.
RAAF	Royal Australian Air Force.
RAE	Royal Aircraft Establishment.
RAF	Royal Air Force.
RAFVR	Royal Air Force Volunteer Reserve
RAN	Royal Australian Navy.
RAS	Replenishment at Sea. Method of reprovisioning a warship with weapons, fuel, stores and other supplies while underway at sea. May be carried out by helicopter or by means of cables and pipes linking two ships.
RAT	Ram air turbine. A device which, when exposed to the airflow, provides emergency electrical and hydraulic power by means of the air pressure acting upon it.
RCAF	Royal Canadian Air Force.
RCN	Royal Canadian Navy.
RDAF	Royal Danish Air Force.
'Red Flag'	USAF weapons school for practising realistic flying tactics and missions, based at Nellis Air Force Base, Nevada. Attended by all NATO air forces.
REM	Radio Electrician's Mate. An RN substantive rate.
RFA	Royal Fleet Auxiliary.
RFC	Royal Flying Corps.
RHSC	Rye Harbour Sailing Club. Located by the River Rother.
RIO	Radar Intercept Officer. USN equivalent to the RN's Observer.
RM	Royal Marines.
RMS	Royal Mail Ship.
RN	Royal Navy.

RNAS	Royal Naval Air Service. Became the Fleet Air Arm in 1918 and was controlled by the newly formed Royal Air Force until 1939.
RNH	Royal Naval Hospital.
RNLI	Royal National Lifeboat Institution. A fleet of rescue boats located strategically around the British Isles for the purpose of rescuing people and seamen in distress at sea.
RNLO	Royal Naval Liaison Officer.
RNVR	Royal Navy Volunteer Reserve.
RNZN	Royal New Zealand Navy.
RPO	Regulating Petty Officer. RN 'policeman'.
RR	Rolls-Royce. An engineering company formed by Messrs Rolls and Royce engaged in the manufacture of engines and prestigious cars.
RRE	Royal Radar Establishment.
Run ashore	Liberty leave.
RYA	Royal Yachting Association. A British organisation formed in the 1960s to improve the standards of boating and yachting within the United Kingdom.
SAAF	South African Air Force.
SACLANT	Supreme Allied Commander Atlantic.
SAR	Search and Rescue.
SARBE	Search and Rescue (Radio) Beacon.
SASO	Senior Air Staff Officer. (RAF)
SATCO	Senior Air Traffic Control Officer.
SBA	Sick Berth Attendant.
SEATO	South-East Asia Treaty Organisation.
SL	Supplementary List (of officers in the RN).
SMAC	Special Maintenance Air Course.
SNLR	Services No Longer Required. A polite way of saying that one is no longer required in the Royal Navy as an enlisted man.
SNO	Senior Naval Officer. (RN)
SP	Senior Pilot
SSB	Single side band (radio)
'Strikeback'	An annual major NATO seaborne exercise in the North Atlantic and Norwegian Sea.
'Styx'	The NATO reporting name for the Soviet (Russian) SS-N-2 surface-to-surface missile.
TACAN	Tactical Air Navigation. An air navigational aid which gives a pilot range and bearing from a specific beacon.
Tailhook Convention	An annual get-together organised by the USN for all its aviators who have made an arrested landing aboard an aircraft carrier (i.e. by using a 'tailhook'). Used to be held in a Las Vegas hotel and was paid for in the main by the US aviation manufacturers who supplied equipment and aircraft to the Navy.
Tar	An affectionate name given to a Royal Navy seaman of yesteryear who tarred his pigtails. The blue jean collar was introduced to prevent his uniform from being spoilt by the tar. He was also known as 'Jack'—hence the name 'Jack Tar'.
'Tempest'	A test carried out aboard RN ships to check the compatibility of newly installed electronic equipment (i.e. to ensure that there is no mutual interference).
Their Lordships	The five Sea Lords of the Admiralty Board.
'Top Gun'	The Air Weapons Flying School at USNAS Miramar, San Diego, for pilots and RIOs (q.v.). Created by VX-4, it is very similar the Fleet Air Arm's Air Warfare Instructors' School that existed at Lossiemouth.
Trekker	A South African immigrant who travelled overland by ox-cart to the Transvaal.

UDI	Unilateral Declaration of Independence (with particular reference to Rhodesia in 1965).
Upperyardman	A seaman who was considered the best and most experienced and was trusted to work the topsails in a full-rigged sailing ship. By contemporary extension, the rank given to enlisted men who have been selected for officer training.
USAF	United States Air Force. Created out of the US Army Air Forces in 1947.
USCG	United States Coast Guard.
USMC	United States Marine Corps.
USN	United State Navy.
USNAS	United States Naval Air Station.
V-Bomber	One of the RAF's three strategic jet bombers—Vulcan, Victor and Valiant—in service in the 1950s, 1960s and 1970s and equipped to carry the 'nuclear deterrent'.
VF	USN fighter squadron.
VFX	USN Experimental Fighter.
VTAS	Fighter Tactical Air Sight. (US)
VX	USN Air Test and Evaluation Squadron.
Wren	The colloquial name given to a member of the WRNS (q.v.).
WRNS	Women's Royal Naval Service.
XO	Executive Officer. The second-in-command of a British warship or naval establishment. Also the second-in-command of a USN air squadron.
Zeppelin	A large German-built rigid airship named after Count von Zeppelin, who designed and built these craft.
Zulu	The Earth's time zone covering a longitudinal region 7½ degrees either side of the Greenwich Meridian, representing one hour of time.

Index

*Note: Ranks quoted in this Index are those held by individuals when first
acquainted with the author and therefore are not necessarily the final ranks attained.*

A

A-3 Skywarrior, *see* Skywarrior
Abbeville, 25
Aberdeen, 121, 152, 167, 210
Aberdonian, The, 266
Aberporth, 350
Abrahams, Lieutenant Commander Russell, 347, 348, 349–50
Active, HMS, 358
Aden Protectorate, 181, 192, 201, 204, 206, 209; *see also* Aden, RAF
Aden, RAF, 168, 175, 179, 192
Admiralty Interview Board (AIB), 35, 42, 43–4
Advanced Air Weapons Training Squadron, 108
Advanced Flying Training, 67, 68ff.
Aero Medical School, *see* Seafield Park
Afrika Korps, 40
Agusta, 313
Air Days, 86, 291; at St Merryn, 124; at Lossiemouth, 15, 214, 217–18, 292; at Aden, 179–80, at Point Mugu, 234; at Yeovilton, 291–2, 304, 306; at Culdrose, 304
Air Department War Orders, 398
Air Shows: Farnborough, 179; *see also* Air Days
Air Test and Evaluation Squadron Four (AIRTEVRON FOUR), *see* VX-4
Air Torpedo and Trials Development Unit (ATTDU), 57ff.
Air Traffic Control, French, 194
Air Training Corps (ATC), 27; *see also* cadets
Air Weapons Section (Whale Island), 187
Aircraft Accident Investigation Unit (AAIU), 96, 99, 139, 322–3, 352
Aircraft and Armament Experimental Establishment (A&AEE), *see* Boscombe Down
aircraft maintenance: in US Navy, 247–9; in Fleet Air Arm, 249
airships, 19–20

Airwork Services, 271, 308
Alaska, 257
'Alaskan highway', 376, 377, 380
Albacore, Fairey, 89
Albatross, Grumman, 107
Algeciras Bay, 282
Algeria, 193
All Officers Meeting (AOM), 250
Allen, 'Gubby', 28
Allison, Air Marshal, 291
Alvestoke Torpedo Range, 59
Anacapa, 256
Anamba Islands, 191
Anderton, Lieutenant Nigel, 67, 79, 80
Andover, RAF, 352
Andoya, 107
Andrew, HRH Prince, 364, 371–2, 375, 376; and British press, 372, 374–5
Anne, HRH Princess, 358
Anselmo, Ailene, 254, 255
Anselmo, Lieutenant Phil, 253, 254–5, 264
Anson, Avro, 27
Anson, Captain Ted, 217, 285, 404
Anstruther Cup, 28
Anthea (ex *La Toquette*, motor yacht), 20, 21, 28
Anti-Submarine OFS Course, 76
Arbroath, 143
Arcachon, 350—1
Archangel, 332
Ark Royal, HMS, (1938), 282
Ark Royal, HMS, (1955), 88, 93, 94, 97, 108, 359, 411, 420; author's service aboard, 99–105, 125, 150, 164, 168—9, 170ff., 264, 269, 271ff., 301, 324—5, 326ff., 365; embarks 831 NAS, 99; visits USA (1955), 101–2; and Fleet Review (1957), 103; and Wyvern landing problems, 104–5; refit to, 184; relieved by *Eagle* in far East, 206; retention in Royal Navy of, 262; and problems with arrester system aboard, 272–3, 276–7, 278; Harrier trials aboard,

275–6; in NATO exercises, 276–7; flight-deck lighting aboard, 278; collides with Soviet DLG, 283–4; aids HMS *Hampshire*, 284–5; visit to Barbados by, 330; visit to Fort Lauderdale by, 330–1, 339; visit by HM Queen Elizabeth the Queen Mother to, 331–2; making of BBC documentary aboard, 335–8; visit to Puerto Rico by, 337–9; and rescue of US submariner, 337–8; problems with catapults aboard, 339–40; repairs at Norfolk Navy Yard to, 339–40
Ark Royal, HMS, (1985), 262, 406, 408
Armada, Spanish, 225
armament practice: in Sea Hawk, 80, 122; in Wyvern, 100, 103; in Buccaneer, 191–2; *see also* bombing, Bullpup missile, gunnery, rockets, Sidewinder missile
Armed Forces Pay Review Board, 291
Armée de l'Air, l', *see* French Air Force
Army, British, 314
Army Training Centre, 416
Arran, Isle of, 48, 49
arrester hooks, problems with, 104
Arrow, Avro, 261
Aruba, 367
Asahan Range, 172, 191
Ashmore, Admiral of the Fleet Sir Edward, 415–16
Ashford (Kent), 23, 27, 29, 50, 265, 348
Assistant Chief of the Defence Staff (ACDS), 316–17
Assistant Chief of the Naval Staff (ACNS), 316–17
Athens, 41
Atkins, Upperyardman Pete, 69–70
Atkinson, Lieutenant Neville, 140
Auckland, 404
Australia House, 408
Australia Shield, 194
autogyro, 20
Automatic Depressed Sight Line (ADSL), 187–8, 192, 213, 216
AV-8A, *see* Harrier
AVCAD programme, 227, 245, 255
Avon, Rolls-Royce, (engine), 354
AWG-10 (radar), 241, 242, 248; *see also* AWG-14 (radar), 241OV-63
Azores, 337

B
'back-classing', 62, 64, 126
Backus, Cadet, 144
'Badger', *see* Tu-16
Bailey, Lieutenant Commander Peter, 143
Baja California, 256, 257
Baker, Joy, 125
Baker, Richard, 159
Bakers of Portsmouth, 75, 418
'Balbo formation', 214, 292, 327, 329
Ballangen (Norway), 105
Band (née Doust), Joy, 22, 414
Banff (Scotland), 141, 150

Banff National Park, 229
Bangladeshi Navy, 403–4
banyan parties, 181
Barbados, 330
Barnard, Commander 'Butch', 218
Barnden, Captain, 357
Barnden, Mr (author's headmaster), 25, 26, 357
Barracuda, Fairey, 89
Bastick, Lieutenant Tony, 89, 91, 94
Bath, 21, 278, 339, 379, 404, 405, 408, 418
Bathurst, Commander Ben, 319
Battle of Britain, 65, 66, 82, 179, 270
Bawtry, 145
Baylis, Admiral Luis Le, 239
BBC, *see* British Broadcasting Corporation
Beachy Head, 115
Beadsmore, Lieutenant Commander Ed, 288
'Bear', *see* Tu-95
Beaufighter, Bristol, 26
Beaufort scale, 394
Beaverbrook, Lord, 373
Bedford, author's wartime evacuation to, 22, 107, 159
Bedford, RAE, 104–5, 162–3, 272, 275, 278, 281, 307, 313, 328; and Sea Harrier 'ski-ramp', 387, 391
Beeching, Lord, 348
Beira Patrol, 208–9
Belknap, USS, 232
Benghazi, 209
Bennett, Commander Nick, 344–5
Bermuda, 375, 376, 397–8
Bexhill (-on-Sea), 302–3, 334, 342, 349, 356, 363, 378, 398, 406, 414, 416
Bickley, Lieutenant Mike, 329–30, 331
Billett, Lieutenant Bill, 154, 155, 156, 191
Billingham, Lieutenant Joe, 310, 311
'Billtong', Exercise, 175
Binbrook, RAF, 304
Binghy Creek, 328
bird strikes, 197–8
Birkenhead, 331
Biscarrosse, 350–1
Biscay, Bay of, 183, 218, 282
Bitter Lakes, 182
Black, Commander, 39
Black, Group Captain George, 305
Black (néePeacock), Margaret, (author's sister-in-law), 419
Blake, HMS, 312, 363, 382
Bland, Lieutenant Malcolm, 119, 120
Blattman, Mr, 19, 21
Bleakley, Sub Lieutenant, 140–1
Blitz, London, 23–4
Blue Angels, The, (US Navy aerobatic team), 245, 372
Blue Funnel Line, 27–8
Board of Inquiry, 298
boats, ship's, 365–6
Bodø, 333
'bogeys', 304

bomb sight, 187
Bomber Command, RAF, 270
bombing exercises, 80, 94, 100, 132, 153, 163, 186, 193, 214, 292—3, 396; see also *Torrey Canyon*
Booth, Lieutenant Gerry, 176
Bordeaux, 350, 351
Borrowman, Lieutenant Commander Doug, 285, 287, 294, 299, 307, 309, 311, 315, 323, 404
Boscombe Down, A&AEE, 97, 150, 273, 294, 398; and Canberra T Mk 22, 308–9; and Buccaneer, 318; and Sea Harrier 'ski-ramp', 387
Bosham, 114, 115
Bournemouth, 46–7
Bovingdon, RAF, 37, 42
BQM targets, 237, 238, 338–9
Brabazon, Bristol, 167
Bracklesham Bay Range, 94
Brawdy, RNAS, 87, 88, 100,101, 112, 137, 183, 217, 352, 353
Bridger, Lieutenant David, 125, 135, 136, 145
Brigand, Bristol, 59
Briggs, Commander, 324
Bristow, Lieutenant Michael, 67
Britannia, Bristol, 167—8, 209
Britannia, HMY, 103, 358, 408
Britannia Airways, 209, 213
British Aerospace (BAe), 285; and 'ski-ramp' trials, 391
British Aircraft Corporation (BAC), 307–9, 315
British Broadcasting Corporation (BBC), 334; and Rhodesia Crisis, 208; World Service of, 208; makes documentary aboard *Ark Royal*, 336–8
British Council, 410
British Expeditionary Force (BEF), 23
British Overseas Airways Corporation (BOAC), 265
British press, behaviour of, 372–3, 376
British Ropes, 272–3, 278
British West Indian Airlines, 173
Brize Norton, RAF, 265, 342
Brook, Alan, (author's cousin), 135
Brook, Brian, (author's cousin), 135
Brook, Malcolm, (author's cousin), 135
Brook, Roy, (author's cousin), 135
Brook, William, (author's uncle), 135, 303
Brooks, Reverend Oscar, 128, 129
Brough (Yorkshire), 186, 318
Brown, Lieutenant Commander Ivan, 132, 139
Brown, Lieutenant Commander Mike, 131, 135
Browning, Commander Bill, 228, 254–5
Bruggen, RAF, 304–5, 352
Bryant, Wing Commander, 290–1
Buccaneer, Blackburn, 53, 238, 242, 275, 276—7, 279, 308, 318, 327, 329, 331, 332, 352, 363, 396; in SAAF service, 212; as aerobatic aircraft, 217
S Mk 1, 186ff., 211ff., entry into service of, 184–5; development and description of, 186; weapon system for, 186–7, 194–5, 202; as photo-reconnaissance aircraft, 205; flying characteristics of, 206; and Rhodesia Crisis, 208
S Mk 2, 209, 211ff., 360, development and description of, 211; early problems with, 214–15; at RAF Honington, 270, 271; comparison with MRCA of, 317; and Martel programme, 351
Buccaneer Conversion Course, 156, 184
Buccaneer Weapon System Manual, 211, 212–13
Bullpup missile, 180, 191–2
Bulwark, HMS, 70
Burgess, Lieutenant Commander Peter, 311, 324
Burlesdon (Hampshire), 412
Burnham-on-Crouch (Essex), 321
Burns, Lieutenant Richard, 149—50, 273
Butterworth, RAAF, 206
Button, Lieutenant Commander Sandy, 234, 264

C
C-121, see Constellation
C-130 Hercules, see Hercules
C-131, Convair, 243
cadets, 155, 385; teaching of, 143
Cairngorm Mountains, 310
Cairo Airport, 97
California, 161, 220, 223ff.; sailing off, 256–7
Californian Current, 257
Callabasas, 263
Camarillo, 231, 259; Golf Club, 245
Camber, 24, 75, 83, 114, 129, 135, 220, 265, 302, 348, 414
Camber Sands, 23, 95
Cameron Highlanders, 164
Cammell Laird (shipbuilders), 331
Campanella, Joe, 254
Campbell, Captain, 48
Campbell, Commander Ian, 132
Camperdown, HMS, (battleship), 52
Canada, 229
Canada, Avro, 261
Canadian Army, 24
Canberra, English Electric, 146, 189, 317, 318, 408; and Suez Crisis, 97; in PAF service, 179; PR Mk 7, 308; T Mk 22, 307—9
Cannes, 245
'Capricorn', Exercise, 303–4
Cardew, Upperyardman Phil, 49, 64, 79, 81, 145
Cardington, RAF, 23
Cargill Begg, Admiral of the Fleet Sir Varyl, 262, 406

Caribbean Sea, 256, 329, 338, 364ff., 392

Carne, Lieutenant Commander Dickie, 145

Carr, Lieutenant Commander Paddy, 288, 295

Carrier Controlled Approach (CCA), 272, 334, 371

Carrier Onboard Delivery (COD), 209

Carver, Lieutenant Commander Malcolm, 190, 202, 307, 311, 312, 315, 319, 416

Caspard, Lieutenant Colin, 141, 142, 145

Cassidi, Admiral, 329

Catalina Island, 257

catapult training, 162

Cazaux, 350–1

Centaur, HMS, 190

Centaurus, Bristol, (engine), 37, 39, 40

Central Flying School (CFS), 129, 132, 146

Central Park (New York), 102

Central Tactics and Trials Organisation (CTTO): author's service with 347ff., 409

Central Treaty Organisation (CENTO), 179

Centurion, HMS, 303

'Chag' arrester system, 197, 198–9

Chamberlain, Neville, 22

Chambers, Lieutenant Nicholas, 100

Changi, RAF, 168, 190, 191, 192, 206

Channel Islands Harbour, 256

Charing Cross station, 265

Charles, HRH Prince, 217, 303, 306

Chase, Lieutenant Commander, 203–5

Châteauroux, 194

Chatham, 403

Chichester, 94, 108, 114–15

Chief of the British Naval Staff (CBNS), (in USA), 239, 243, 342, 345, 396

Chief of the Naval Staff (CNS), 159, 285, 314

Chilton, Commander Pat, 162

China Lake, see Naval Air Weapons Center

Chipmunk, de Havilland, 130

Chivenor, RAF, 158

Christchurch, RRE, 312–13

Clark, Lieutenant Commander Brian, 387, 390, 395

Clarke, Lieutenant Commander Nobby, 87

Clearance, Aircraft Trials and Weapons (CATWEP), 318

Clutch Radar, 295, 301

Clyde, River, 218, 324

Clymping, 83

Coast Guard and Frontier Force, Saudi Arabian, 409–11

cockpit design, US, 226, 247

Coggan, Donald, (Archbishop of Canterbury), 298

Cohu, Wing Commander Jerry, 288, 289–90, 294–5

'Cold War', the, 418

Colley, Surgeon Lieutenant Commander Ian, 92–3

Collingwood, HMS, (RN Electrical School), 29–30, 33–5, 36, 37, 42, 43, 44, 45, 46, 143

Combat Air Patrol (CAP), 179, 332

Comet, de Havilland, 354

Commander Operational Evaluation Force (COMOPTEVFOR), 230, 262–3

Commando Helicopter Project, 346–7

Concorde, BAC/Aérospatiale, 261

Congress, US, 263

Coningsby, RAF, 288, 351; Phantom Symposium at, 290–1

Constellation, Lockeed C-121, 244

Constellation, USS, 255

Cooke, Lieutenant David, 135

Coote, Mr, 17

Cope, Lieutenant Eddie, 131, 146, 147, 148, 152–3, 156, 245

Copeland, Lieutenant Andy, 146, 153

Copenhagen, 294

Cornishman, The, 335

Coronation (of HM Queen Elizabeth II), 46, 310; Fleet Review, 47, 52–3

Country Life (magazine), 266

courts-martial, 250, 322–4, 382–3

Covesea Lighthouse, 215

Cowling, Commander David, 324, 341

Cowling, Lieutenant Commander 'Smokey', 89

Crampton, Mr, 25

Cranwell, RAF College, 65, 145, 347, 358

Crater City (Aden), 209

Crawley, Leonard, 28

Credland, Lieutenant Bill, 276

cross-deck operations (with US Navy), 102

Crusader Ground Attack Project, 226, 230

Crusader, LTV F-8, 225, 226–7, 239, 245, 246–7, 248, 255, 264

Cubi Point, USNAS, 192

Culdrose, RNAS, 57, 70, 76, 99, 101, 112, 113, 120, 123–4, 152, 183, 217, 218, 293, 296, 303, 398; author's service at, 326–7

Cunningham, Admiral Sir Andrew, 201

Cunningham, Lady, 201

Cunningham, Lieutenant Randy, 237

Curaçao, 366–7

Customs & Immigration, British, 280

CVA-01 (aircraft carrier), 261–2, 270, 288n, 319, 418

Cyprus, 97, 282

D

Daily Express, 372–3, 374–5

Daily Mail, 94

Daily Mirror, 372

Daily Telegraph, 28, 310

Dakota, Douglas DC-3, 178

Dalachy airfield, 80

Dallas, USNAS, 256, 369

Darlington (town), 134

Darlington, Lieutenant Commander Mike, 307

Dartmouth, Royal Naval College, 26, 143, 364, 371

David, Lieutenant Commander John, 61

David, Group Captain Mervyn, 347–8
Davidson, Flight Lieutenant Neil, 158
Davis, Lieutenant Commander Brian, 301
Davis, Commander Carl, 349
DAWG-14 (radar), 248, 251
Day, Lieutenant Keith, 177
deck-landing practice, author's, 100, 189
decompression chamber, 67
Defence White Paper (1966), 269
degaussing, 387
Del Mar, 255
Delta Dagger, Convair F-102, 246
Demon, McDonnell, 161
'Derry Turn', 180
Deveron, River, 163
Devonport Dockyard, 88, 97, 101, 189, 190, 277, 278, 280, 331, 333, 334, 339–40
Devorak, Major 'Shad', 230
Diaper, Don, 28, 135
Diaper, Eunice, 263
Diaper, Esse, 129
Diaper, Guv, 129, 263
Diaper, Kimberlie, 263
Dido, HMS, 404–6
Dieppe, wartime raid on, 24
Dillingham, Flight Lieutenant 'Scrubber', 65–6
Dimmock, Lieutenant Roger, 112, 193, 408
Director General of Naval Aircraft (DGNA), 104, 194
Director of Guided Weapons and Electronics (DGWE), 313, 314
Directorate General of Naval Manpower and Training (DGNMT), author's appointment to, 411, 414–16
Directorate of Naval Air Warfare (DNAW), 104, 142, 147, 194, 269, 270, 272, 278, 285, 291, 295, 303, 328, 346, 373, 399, 416; and author's Buccaneer Weapon System Manual, 212, 213; author's appointment to, 209, 300, 302, 305, 307ff., 358–60
Directorate of Naval Aircraft and Equipment (DNAE), 272, 278, 295, 303, 307, 309
Directorate of Naval Officers' Appointments (DNOA), 142, 150, 269, 281, 302, 303, 310, 311, 324, 355, 373, 407
Directorate of Naval Operational Requirements (DNOR), 415
Directorate of Naval Overseas Training (DNOT), 398–9, 409, 410; author's appointment to, 403ff.
Directorate of Naval Planning (DNAP), 415
Directorate of Naval Plans, 324
Disbandment Movement Order, 303
Divisions: Captain's, 34, 212; Sunday, 47; in US Navy, 249–50, 251–2; Station, 291; Full Dress (Admiral's), 292
Do 17, Dornier, 23
Dobson, Lieutenant David, 269, 355–6, 358, 398
Dominie, de Havilland, 97, 132–3

'donkey's plonk', 198
Donnington, 289
Donnolly, Lieutenant Commander Dave, 318
Douglas (Isle of Man), 322
Doust (née Peacock), May, (author's wife), 130, 285, 356, 358, 406, 412; author meets at Culdrose, 125–6, 326; author's engagement to, 128–9; author's marriage to, 134–5; at Lossiemouth, 136, 137–8, 161, 164, 167, 183–4, 194, 210, 217, 327; at Point Mugu, 223ff., 250ff., 259ff.; at Bexhill, 302, 305, 307, 310, 334–5, 342, 378, 395–6, 413–14
Doust, Anthea, (author's sister), 17, 24, 413
Doust, Brian, (author's brother), 17, 20, 23, 24, 28, 29, 90, 413
Doust, Captain, 419
Doust, Dominique ('Dee Dee'), (author's daughter), 225, 263, 302, 305, 335, 378, 412–13, 420
Doust, George, (author's uncle), 417
Doust, Jacqueline, (author's sister), 17, 24, 413
Doust, James (author's uncle), 21, 22, 24, 228–9, 266, 414
Doust, John, (author's father), 19, 22, 26, 27, 29, 75, 114, 228–9, 265, 302, 320, 321–2, 413, 414, 417; as Rye Harbour Master, 17–18, 24–5, 95; and interest in boats, 20–1; retirement of, 265
Doust, Margaret, (author's mother), 17, 18, 20, 23, 25–6, 29, 75, 194, 302, 320, 413, 414
Doust, Naomi Elizabeth, (author's great grandmother), 17
Doust, Naomi, (author's daughter), 161, 184, 194, 210, 219, 224ff., 242, 263, 302, 305, 335, 378, 412–13, 419–20
Doust, Theresa, (author's sister), 93, 419
Doust, Victor, 261, 418
Doust, Wilfred, (author's uncle), 413
Doust, Instructor Commander, 418
Doust-Clark, Holly, (author's granddaughter), 420
Doust-Clark, Willow, (author's granddaughter), 420
Dover, 321
Dr Gray's Hospital (Elgin), 138, 195, 211
Draftees' Office, 36, 43
Drake, Sir Francis, 225
Drake's Island, 337
Driscoll, Lieutenant Willie, 237
Dryad, HMS, 356–7, 358, 367, 385
Dulles Airport, 341
Dunbar-Dempsey, Lieutenant David, 175, 302
Dundee Royal Infirmary, 160
Dunfermline, 354, 355
Dungeness, 116, 210, 321
Dunkirk, evacuation of, 23
Dunnolly, 115—16
Dwight D. Eisenhower, USS, 397

Dyce, RAF, 130

E

E-2C Hawkeye, see Hawkeye
Eagle, HMS, 84, 87, 88, 89, 92, 104, 159, 188, 189–90, 282, 324; and Suez Crisis, 97–8; hangar accident aboard, 98; author's service aboard, 105–7, 190ff., 198ff.; and encounters with Soviet Navy, 200–1; relieves Ark Royal in Far East, 206; is damaged at Plymouth, 277–8
Eagle, Rolls-Royce, (engine), 90
Eagle, Lieutenant John, 156
Eagles, Lieutenant Dave, 281
Easingwold, 134
Eastwood, Kenny, (author's cousin), 97
Eatwell, Lieutenant John, 190
Eberle, Rear Admiral Jim, 332
Edinburgh, 134, 167, 210, 290
Edinburgh, HRH the Duke of, (Prince Philip): visits Ark Royal, 101; and Fleet Review (1957), 103
Edward, Bob, Lieutenant, 102, 112–14, 281, 209, 311, 324, 328–9
Edwards, Lieutenant, 178
Eglinton, RNAS, 70
Egyptian Air Force, 182
Eilat, (Israeli destroyer), 238
Eilean Mhor, 219, 266, 281; sale of, 286
Eisenhower, General, 356
El Adem (Libya), 154, 168
El Centro, USNAS, 236
Electrical Officers' Training School, 36
'Eleven Plus' examination, 26
Elgin, 121, 138, 144, 161, 164, 195, 210, 220, 266
Elizabeth, HM Queen, (the Queen Mother), 331–2
Elizabeth II, HM Queen: Coronation of, 64, 310; and Fleet Review (1953), 47, 52–3; and Fleet Review (1957), 103
Ellen Louise (ketch), 28
Elliott, Lieutenant David, 373
Empire Test Pilots' School, 86, 97, 157
Empson, Captain Derek, 40, 188, 200
Enterprise, USS, 234
Escape and Evasion Exercise, 50–1, 163
Eureka (California), 229
Evans, Captain Brian, 403ff.
Evans, Rear Admiral 'Crash', 88
Evans, Air Chief Marshal Sir David, 348–9
Eve, Lieutenant Commander, 119
Excellent, HMS, 109, 119
exercises, NATO, 40, 274, 276, 279–80, 282, 332–3

F

F-4 Phantom, see Phantom
F-4J/AWG-10 Project, see OV-63
F-8 Crusader, see Crusader
F-14 Tomcat, see Tomcat
F-18 Hornet, see Hornet

F-86 Sabre, see Sabre
F-102 Delta Dagger, see Delta Dagger
F-104 Starfighter, see Starfighter
F-111, General Dynamics, 260–1, 318, 319, 408
Faisal, King, 418
Falklands War, 271, 364, 404, 407, 4008
Fareham, 29
Fareham Creek, 386
Farmer, Flight Lieutenant Mike, 158
Farnborough, RAE, 86, 97, 157, 261, 307, 310, 311, 312, 314, 391
Farquhar, Lieutenant Commander Stan, 83, 88, 89, 94, 96, 97, 112–13
Featherstone, Lieutenant Neville, 288, 292
Federal Aviation Administration (FAA), 256
Fell, Captain Michael, 40, 155
Fernbank Maternity Hospital, 17
Ferranti, 187, 194, 241
Ferranzano, Commander Fred, 246–7, 252
Fiat, Società per Azioni, 315
Fielding, Ray, 219, 269
Fighter Operational Flying Training, 76
fighter pilots, requirements of, 78–9
Fighter Tactical Air Sight (VTAS), 260
Filfla, 100, 193
Filton (Gloucestershire), 17
Finchingfield (Essex), 414
Findhorn (Morayshire), 355
firearms policy, in USA, 252–3
Firefly, Fairey, 44, 46, 83
Firestreak missile, 93, 154
Firth, Lieutenant, 105
'Fishbed', see MiG-21
Fisher, Captain, 48, 49
Flag Officer Aircraft Carriers (FOAC), 208, 329, 332, 333, 340
Flag Officer Flying Training (FOFT), 147, 189, 195, 217–18, 271, 287
Flag Officer Naval Air Command (FONAC), 212, 213, 287–8, 295, 302, 303, 306, 345, 349, 390; inspects RNAS Yeovilton, 292–4
Flag Officer Scotland and Northern Ireland (FOSNI), 277, 322
Flag Officer Sea Training (FOST), 390–1
Fleetlands (RN Aircraft Repair Yard), 98, 137, 157
Fleming, Sub Lieutenant Clive, 85–6
flight-deck lighting system, 198
Flight Safety Centre: FAA, 327–8; UK (Air), 353; Lossiemouth, 353
Flight Safety Trophy, 232, 233
'Flook', 94
Flowers, Lieutenant, 98
Flying Fortress, Boeing B-17, 23
Flying Training Command, 62
Ford, Lieutenant Commander John, 158–9, 161, 164, 280, 287
Ford, RNAS, 80, 100, 101, 104, 107ff., 170, 194, 195, 348, 350; author's service at, 82ff.
Forres (Morayshire), 219, 269

Fort Lauderdale, 330–1, 339; visit by *Hermes* to, 374–5
Fort Southwick (Sussex), 356, 388
Forward Air Control (FAC), 105, 160, 172–3, 201–2
Forward-Looking Infra-Red (FLIR) devices, 312, 313
Foster, Captain Jim, 224, 234, 241, 245, 246, 251ff., 262, 264, 369–70
Foster, Commander, 224
Fox, Upperyardman Peter, 49, 79
Franklin, Sub Lieutenant, 138–9, 185
Fremantle, 169
French Air Force, 350–1
French Navy, 93
Frenz, Sub Lieutenant Ian, 162
Friendship, Fokker, 233
Front Line Armament Practice (FLAP), 91
Frost, Lieutenant Commander Jack, 286
Future Policy Section, 309, 311, 319
FW 190, Focke-Wulf, 24, 25
Fyffe, Lieutenant Commander Al, 132, 133

G

Gadfly (yacht), 412
Galland, Adolf, 260
Gan, RAF, 168
Ganges, HMS, 58
Gannet, Fairey, 70, 81; AS.4, 83, 99, 101, 103, 104, 112, 114, 120, 137, 143, 171, 175, 192, 209, 269, 270, 277, 279, 299–300; AEW Mk 3, 217–18, 262, 271, 327; T Mk 5, 271, 327
Garrards, 96
Garvie Island, 155–6, 188
Gaulle, *Général* de, 350
Gault, Joan, 220, 266
Gault, Peter, 220
Gavin, Lieutenant John, 349
Geneva Convention, 50
George V, HM King, 18
George VI, HM King, 331
Georgetown (Grand Cayman), 367
Gerard-Pearse, Admiral, 320
Gibraltar, 44, 99, 101, 183, 218, 282, 285, 337, 364
Gick, Captain Percy, 89
Giddings, Air Marshal Peter, 317
Gieves (of Old Bond Street), 75, 335
Giles, Lieutenant Chuck, 202
Gleadow, Lieutenant Andrew, 198–9, 207–8
Goblin, de Havilland, (engine), 69, 85, 160
Goddard, Lieutenant Peter, 301, 319–20, 324, 359
Godden, Dick, 44
Gosport, RNAS, 57ff., 84, 98, 303; *see also Siskin*, HMS
Government, British, 340; and defence cuts, 261, 269–70
Graf Zeppelin (airship), 19
Graham, Captain Wilf, 331, 336, 339
Grand Canyon, 226

Grand Harbour, *see* Malta, Valletta
Grant (née Tillman), Rose, (author's great aunt), 320
Grantham (Lincolnshire), 61
Gray, Lieutenant Commander Alan ('Gus'), 89, 90, 95, 99, 108
Gray, CPO, 39
Green, Donald, (author's cousin), 320
Green (née Lee), Winnie, (author's aunt), 320
Greenwich Village (New York), 102
Greer-Rees, Lieutenant Nigel, 309–11
Gregory, Commander Peter, 409
Griggs, Lieutenant Alan, 105, 195–6
Ground Controlled Approach (GCA), 142, 197, 296
Ground School: at RAF Syerston, 62, 67; at RAF Valley, 68, 75; at RNAS Lossiemouth, 77; at HMS *Excellent*, 109, 114, 119; at RAF Little Rissington, 123; at NAS Miramar, 226; at RNAS Yeovilton, 271
Gulf War, 420
'gully-gully' men, 183
Gunn, Commander Max, 234
gunnery, fighter, 78—9
Gypsy Queen, de Havilland, (engine), 132
Gyron Junior, de Havilland, (engine), 184, 204

H

Haines, Upperyardman, 63, 67
Halfar, RNAS, 39, 98, 100, 101, 193
Hall, Lieutenant, 105
Hall, Sub Lieutenant, 98
Hall, Wally, 313, 315, 319, 210, 359
Hallam, Lieutenant, 138
Halliday, Lieutenant Commander Gus, 99, 105
Hamble (Hampshire), 413
Hamilton (Bermuda), 376, 397
Hampshire, HMS, 284–5
Harper, George, 23
Harrier, Hawker Siddeley, 275–6, 292, 351, 407; AV-8A, 373–4
Harstadtfjord, 105–7
Hartwell, Lieutenant Barry, 108
Harvard, North American, 62, 63, 65, 67
Harvey, Lieutenant Commander Mike, 199
Haslar, RN Hospital, 45, 84, 93, 148, 196, 272
Hastings (Sussex), 348, 414
Hawaii, 234
Hawarden (Flintshire), 354
Hawkeye, Grumman E-2C, 239
Hawley, Captain Bill, 301–2, 349
Hayr, Wing Commander Ken, 275
Healey, Dennis, 261
Hedgeler, Bert, 21
Hefford, Commander Freddie, 273–4
Heisner, Lieutenant Commander, 251
Helena (Montana), 229
'Helicopter Geriatric Course', 326–7
Helliwell, Lieutenant Commander Rob, 202

Hercules, Lockheed C-130, 295, 339
Hermes, HMS, 74, 140, 151, 152, 333, 406; author's service aboard, 355–6, 358, 360, 363ff, 385ff; in Caribbean, 364ff, 387ff, 395ff; refit to operate Sea Harriers, 379ff; rededication of, 385–6; and dummy attack on USS John F. Kennedy, 393; compass errors aboard, 394; refit at Mayport, 395; and rendezvous with USS Dwight D. Eisenhower, 397; in Falklands War, 407; sale of, 408–9
Hermione, HMS, 382–3
Heron, de Havilland, see Sea Heron
Higgins, Commander Jerry, 227, 234, 243, 251ff.
High Wycombe, RAF, 347ff.
Hillsdon, Lieutenant Reg, 48, 334
Hindenburg (airship), 19
Hitler, Adolf, 17, 22, 25
Hoddinott, Lieutenant Graham, 28, 3401
Hollis, Lieutenant Commander, 30
Holyhead, 72, 75, 363
Hong Kong, 173, 174, 191, 192, 419
Honington, RAF, 270, 271, 327, 352, 359
Honolulu, 234
Hopkins, Captain Frank, 93
'Hormone', see Ka-25 'Hormone'
Hornblower, Lieutenant Commander Mike, 187, 188, 190, 201–2
Hornchurch, RAF, 42, 43
Hornet, McDonnell Douglas F-18, 246, 256
House of Joy (New Orleans), 370
Howard, Upperyardman Dave, 75, 140, 311, 346, 359; in 726 NAS, 157, 161–2, 169, 211, 213, 216–17, 219–20; in 800 NAS, 172, 175, 201, 202, 207, 209
Howells, PO Sally, 131, 156
Hoy, 51
Hudson River, 102, 223
Humphreys, Lieutenant George, 84, 89, 99
Humphries, Marshal of the RAF Sir Michael, 285
Hunneyball, Lieutenant Chris, 301
Hunt, Lieutenant Jeff, 340–1, 342
Hunt, Lieutenant Reg, 64, 66, 84, 85, 89, 109–11, 148
Hunt, Rear Admiral Nicholas, 411, 415
Hunter, Captain, 173
Hunter, Hawker, 149, 151, 168; F Mk 4, 147, 156, 179, 352, 353; T Mk 7, 146, 311; T Mk 8, 108, 121, 141, 143, 145, 146, 152, 183, 190, 202, 216; GA Mk 11, 146–7, 183, 288
Hurricane, Hawker, 40
Hynett, Lieutenant Maurice, 154–5

I
'Ice Cream Trolley', 275
Idiens, Commander Simon, 287, 296–9, 349
Idiens, Debbie, 299
Il-38 'May', 279
Ilchester Hotel, 286

Illustrious, HMS, 262, 406
Implacable, HMS, 46—52
Indefatigable, HMS, 44–52, 57, 119, 299, 385
Indian Navy, 136—7, 409
Indonesia, 206
inertial navigation system (INS), of Harrier, 275
inflight refuelling, 193–4, 304
Ingham, Commander James, 359
Instructors' Flying Course, 65
Intensive Flying Trails Unit (IFTU), 107–8; see also Naval Air Squadrons: 700S
Invergordon, 103
Inverness (California), 259
Inverness (Scotland), 121, 140, 355
Inverness Flyer, The, 210
Invincible, HMS, 262, 324, 379; proposed sale to RAN of, 404, 406–7, 408; in Falklands War, 407
Iowa class (battleships), 280
Iraq, RAF operations in, 59
'Irongate', Exercise, 190–1
Ismalia, 182

J
Jaguar, SEPECAT, 311, 352, 353
Jahor Bahru, 172
Janvarin, Rear Admiral H. R., 195
Jarvis, Rear Admiral John, 327
Jet Provost, Hunting Percival, 302
John F. Kennedy, USS, 393–5; accident involving, 232, 253–4; and dummy attack on, 393
John, Augustus, 62
John, Admiral of the Fleet Sir Caspar, 62–3
Johnston, Commander Martin, 346
Johore Strait, 206
'Jolly Green Giant', 354
Jon's Bar (Pensacola), 372
Jones, Midshipman Brian, 143
Josselyn, Lieutenant Ian, 119
Jouitt, Lieutenant Jim, 84
Junk Island, 192
Juno, HMS, 285–6, 404–6
Jupiter, HMS, 175–6
Justice, James Robertson, 155

K
Ka-25 'Hormone', 333
Kai Tak, RAF, 154
Kai Tek Aviation, 192
Kalafrani Barracks, 42
Kanak, 97, 182
Karachi, 178, 179
Keast, Major Don, 226, 232, 233–4, 237–8, 242
Keighley-Peach, Lieutenant Commander, 77
Keith (Banffshire), 163
Kelly, Lieutenant Commander John, 86
Kemble, RAF, 146
Kemp, Lieutenant Commander Kenny, 131, 135

Kennedy, Robert, 252
Kennett, Lieutenant Commander John, 146; in 736 NAS, 157, 160, 211, 212, 213, 223; in 800 NAS, 175, 179, 181, 184; in 809 NAS, 186, 187, 188
Kent River Board, 28, 114
Kenyatta, Jomo, 178
Kerr, Lieutenant Nick, 173–4, 301
Khartoum, 168
Khormaksar, RAF, 203, 209
Kidd, Admiral, 340
Kilimanjaro, Mount, 178
Kinch, Lieutenant Gerry, 288, 289, 304
King, Dr Martin Luther, 227
King, Lieutenant Bob, 84, 85, 89, 99, 300, 340
King, Lieutenant Peter, 207
King's Cross station, 167, 266
Kinloss, RAF, 140, 349, 354–5
Kirby, Commander 'Rip', 298
Kirk, Captain David, 194, 217
Kirkwall (Orkney Islands), 89
Kluse, Commander Chuck, 256
Knapp, Lieutenant Commander Jeremy, 346
Koch fasteners, 298
Konsort (yacht), 413
Kor el Fakem, 180
Korean War, 50, 151
Krewe Ball, 368–9, 370
Kuala Lumpur, 172, 206

L

La Guardia airport, 224, 265
La Toquette (motor yacht), 20
Laing, Commander Duncan, 207
Lajes (Azores), 337–8
Lakehurst, USNAS, 19
Lakenheath, RAF, 354
Lancing College, 356
Land's End, 282, 289, 292, 337, 356
Landing Safety Officer (LSO): importance of, 88; duties of, 271
Las Vegas, 230, 243–5, 246
Lawrence, Midshipman Michael, 62, 72
Le Fanu, Captain Mike, 107, 158–60
Le Havre, 194
Leahy, Captain 'Spiv', 319
Leander, HMS, 292
Leander class, 404
Lee, Annie (author's grandmother), 23, 24, 320
Lee, Horace ('Horie'), (author's uncle), 23, 26, 320
Lee, William (author's grandfather), 23, 24, 93, 320
Lee-on-Solent, RNAS, 42, 44, 96, 99, 112, 147, 148, 201, 271, 294, 300; Sailing Club, 148
Leeuwarden, RNethAF, 295, 300–1
Leney, Harry, 27–8
Leonard, Commander Stan, 151–2
Leonides, Alvis, (engine), 62

Leuchars, RAF, 194, 304, 327, 332; as base for F-4Ks, 270, 288, 303, 305, 306, 349
Lewin, Admiral of the Fleet Lord, 285, 385
Lewis, Flight Lieutenant Gordon, 145, 150
Lewis, Flight Lieutenant Peter, 130
Lexington, USS, 371
Lightning, English Electric, 304, 317
lights, anti-collision, 351–4
Lincoln, Avro, 90
Lincoln, HMS, 403–4
Linton-on-Ouse, RAF, 99, 130, 131, 137, 302
Lists, Officers' Naval, 363, 414–15
Little Rissington, RAF, 65, 109, 122ff., 308
Littlehampton, 90, 114
loft-bombing, 275
London, HMS (cruiser), 26
Long Beach, 225, 257
Looe, 392
Los Angeles, 224, 253
Lossie Hotel, 91
Lossiemouth, RNAS, 75, 76, 84, 109, 119, 170, 183, 265, 281, 287, 292, 305, 306, 319, 331, 353, 363. 373; upgrading of, 51–2; author's service at, 77ff., 91–2, 131ff., 145ff., 186ff., 194ff., 211ff., 269, 270–1; routine at, 78; origins and suitability of, 78, 131, 270; and Fleet Review (1957), 103, snow-clearing at, 160; is transferred to RAF, 270; Freedom of the Town conferred on RN at, 327
Lossiemouth (town), 51, 327
Lossiemouth Fighter School, 301
Lossiemouth Sailing Club, 153
Love, Lieutenant John, 301–2
Low Altitude Bombing System (LABS), 184, 214
Low-Light Television (LLTV) sensors, 311–12, 313
Lucas, Captain Dennis, 355
Luftwaffe (World War II), 22–3, 25, 260
Lulworth Cove, 388
Lulworth Range, 388–90
Lundy Island, 47, 99, 296, 301
Luqa, RAF, 37, 291, 328
Luton, 23, 209, 213
Lutter, Sub Lieutenant Dave, 102, 103, 105, 106
Luxor, 182
Lydd Firing Range, 116
Lygo, Captain Raymond, 40, 273, 277–8, 279, 285–6, 404
Lyme Bay, 391
Lyneham, RAF, 137, 164, 289, 295, 328
Lynx, Westland, 326, 327; and Nigerian Navy, 411–12

M

MacCreadie, Alex, 220
MacCreadie, Jane, 220, 266
MacFarland, Alastair, 355
Macfie, Lieutenant Andy, 170

MacGregor, Mr, 20
Mackie, Surgeon Commander Ian, 58, 155, 207, 299
Maggs, Sub Lieutenant Maurice, 109–11
Magister, Fouga, 93
maintenance, see aircraft maintenance
Maintenance Test Pilots' Course, 97
Major Fields of Research, 313–14
mal de mer, 377
Malacca Strait, 175, 206, 207
Malaya, 191, 206; RAF operations in, 59
Maldive Islands 168
Malibu (California), 224
Malibu of Birdham (ketch), 321
Malindi (Kenya), 176
Mallerstang (Westmoreland), 134
Mallett, David, 321–2
Malta, 183, 282, 285, 324; deployment of Theseus to, 36ff.; deployment of Ark Royal to, 99–101; deployment of Eagle to, 190, 193, 201
Malta Times, 285
Maltby, Commander Jeff, 294
Malvern, RRE, 312–13
Manadon, RN Engineering College, 48, 97
Mancais, Lieutenant Commander 'Jock', 137, 142
Manchett, Lieutenant Sammy, 288, 289, 293, 306
Mann, Kathy, 266
Manning, Lieutenant Charles, 142, 146
Manston, RAF, 139
Mardi Gras, 368–70
Margaret (ex lifeboat), 20–1
Marham, RAF, 189
Marines, Royal, see Royal Marines
Marines, Royal Netherlands, 367
Markey, Major Ron, 251–2, 263, 264–5
Markley, Lieutenant Commander, 203–5
Marsh, Flight Lieutenant, 126–7
Marshall, Lieutenant Bruce, 232, 237, 262
Marshall, Caroline, 224
Marshall, Lieutenant Peter, 162, 169, 170, 174–5, 178, 179, 224–5, 228, 233, 234, 271, 287, 296
Martel missile, 350–1, 358
Martin, Commander Ian, 108
Martin-Baker Aircraft Co., 225
Marx, Commander, 403
Mather, Lieutenant Chris, 121, 122, 145, 147, 152–3, 154, 156, 186ff.
Matthews, Lieutenant Peter, 213, 310, 313, 315, 323
Maughan, Air Marshal Charles, 348–9, 352
'May', see Il-38
May, Castle of, 331, 332
Mayflower, 225
Mayport (Florida), 395
McCandless, Lieutenant Commander 'Jock', 131, 133, 137, 138
McCarthy, Upperyardman Dennis ('Mac'), 58, 84, 89, 98, 99

McClean, Lieutenant Ron, 131
McConnackie, Commander Ian, 107
McDonald, Mr, 223–4
McDonnell Douglas, 248
McFall, Gerry, 89, 104
McGee, Isabel, 75
McGee family, 72, 75
McIntosh, Commander Ian, 102, 317
McKenzie, Captain David, 363, 369, 371, 382, 385
McKeown, Lieutenant Commander 'Paddy', 113, 121, 122, 146, 151
McKeown, Lieutenant Ron, 233–4
McLoughlin, Neil, 405
Mears, Lieutenant David, 119, 121, 285
'measured mile', 392
Mediterranean Fleet, 36
Melhuish, Lieutenant Commander 'Mac', 239–40, 396
Merlin, Rolls-Royce, (engine), 124
Merlin, Westland, 313, 359
Messerschmitt-Bölkow-Blohm, 315
Meteor, Gloster, 77, 79, 100, 130, 137; T Mk 7, 131, 139
Meteorological Branch, RN, 411
Meteorological Office, 132, 315
Micklem, Gerald, 28
Middleton, Commander Lynn, 271, 292–3, 294, 340–1, 342, 385, 386, 389ff.
MiG fighters, 182, 183
MiG-21, 316
MiG-29, 261
Milham, John, 70
Miller, Lieutenant Commander, 119
Millett, Lieutenant Commander Paul, 133
Mills, Lieutenant Commander Don, 97, 157–8, 161–2, 169, 170, 171, 175, 179, 184, 186, 242, 296
Mills, Drucie, 161, 242
Milltown, (satellite airfield for Lossiemouth), 79, 144, 157, 160, 184
Milne, Lieutenant Commander Arthur, 147
Milner, Lieutenant Commander 'Dusty', 271, 309, 311
mines, 95, 103–4
Ministère de la Défense, 350, 351
Ministry of Defence (MoD), 108, 181, 189, 194–5, 212, 213, 278, 279, 285, 291, 298, 306, 307ff., 339, 346, 351, 391, 404; Procurement Executive (PE), 193, 298, 307–9, 311, 316, 318, 350, 352, 404, 405
mirages at sea, 175
Miramar, USNAS, 224ff., 242, 247, 255, 258, 259
Mirror and Dummy Deck Landing (MADDL), 160–1
missiles, see Firestreak, Martel, Phoenix, Sea Slug, Sidewinder, Sparrow, 'Styx'
Mississippi Delta, 368, 371
Mitchell, Percy, ('Our Percy'), 27
Mizpah, MV, 25
Mojave Desert, 237

Mombasa, 175, 176–7, 179, 190, 192, 202
Mombasa Club, 202
Monsell, Lieutenant Commander Derek, 137, 138, 141–2, 271, 281
Montana, 229
Monterey, US Navy College at, 227, 255
Moody (boatbuilders), 412
Moorcraft, Lieutenant Colin, 119, 120
Moore, Lieutenant Jimmy, 100–1, 131, 138, 142, 143, 275
Moray Firth, 155
Morgan, Upperyardman John, 72
Morrison, Lieutenant Commander Don, 77, 87
Morro Bay, 259
Morton, Lieutenant Commander Bobby, 234, 248
Morton, Lieutenant Tony, 329–30, 351, 358
Mosquito, de Havilland, 27
Mottram, Flight Sergeant, 63, 66–7
Mountbatten, Admiral of the Fleet Lord Louis, 53, 186
Mountbatten, RAF, 90
Mozambique, 178, 208
MRCA, see Multi Role Combat Aircraft
Mugabe, Robert, 208, 209
Mullender, Chief Petty Officer Roy, 172
Multi Role Combat Aircraft (MRCA), 315–17; comparison with Buccaneer of, 317
'murder boarding', 263
Murray, Lieutenant Commander, 142

N

NA.39, Blackburn, 53, 108, 186; see also Buccaneer, Blackburn
Nairobi, 175–8
Naples, 41–2, 294
Nash, Lieutenant Commander 'Lofty', 299–300
Nasser, Abdul, 181
National Parks Trust (US), 256
National Physical Laboratory (NPL), 275
National Service, 29, 73, 90
NAVAIR, see Naval Air Systems Command
Naval Air Squadrons and Units:
  700 NAS, 83
  700S NAS, 108
  707 NAS, 303, 306
  736 NAS, 77, 119, 131–2, 137, 141, 142, 145, 146, 151, 156, 171, 175, 194, 209, 242, 269, 281; author's service with, 157ff., 212ff.
  736B Flight, 212, 213
  738 NAS, 48, 76, 87, 151, 156, 183, 212; author's service with, 130, 131ff., 145, 218; trains Indian pilots, 136–7
  751 NAS, 114
  764 NAS, 80, 83ff., 97, 109, 110, 131, 132, 136, 151, 170, 183, 194, 281; relocates to Lossiemouth, 108; author's service with, 114, 119–21, 142–3, 145ff.; disbandment of, 306

  766 NAS, 132
  767 NAS, 87–8, 228, 233; author's command of, 285, 287ff.; disbandment of, 303, 305–6
  781 NAS, 151, 271, 294, 295, 322
  796 NAS, 70
  797 NAS, 124
  800 NAS, 155, 160, 161, 211, 213, 219, 275, 281, 391; author's service with, 164, 170ff., 186ff., 332, 416; aerobatic team formed by, 179–80; and Bullpup missile, 180; re-equips with Buccaneer, 184, 186; embarks aboard Eagle, 188, 190, 198; night exercises by, 197; embarks aboard Hermes, 387
  800X NAS, 193
  801 NAS, 156, 305; receives Buccaneer S.2s, 212
  803 NAS, 150, 154
  807 NAS, 108, 133
  809 NAS, 187, 194, 211, 276, 281, 285, 303, 329, 358
  813 NAS, 84, 87, 89, 99, author's service with, 105–7, 112, disbandment of, 114
  815 NAS, 199
  824 NAS, 284, 333, 341, 359, 367; and rescue of US submariner, 337–8
  827 NAS, 84, 87, 89
  830 NAS, 87, 89, 92, 97, 98, 99, 104, 112, 316
  831 NAS, 87, 88, 172, 242; at RNAS Ford, 89–98, 107, 109–14, 195; aboard Ark Royal, 99–105; disbandment of, 108, 114
  849 NAS, 99, 218, 281, 286, 299, 303, 346; author's service with, 123–5, 271; HQ Flight, 269, 327
  890 NAS, 175, 179
  892 NAS, 228, 279, 282, 288, 292–3, 301, 303, 305, 338–9, 340
  897 NAS, 87, 123
  898 NAS, 87, 100, 102
  899 NAS, 87
  1832 Channel Air Division, 83
Naval Air Support Unit (NASU), 157, 172, 173, 184, 190, 194, 207, 269
Naval Air Systems Command (NAVAIR), 235, 246, 251, 263
Naval Air Warfare Training School ('Top Gun' School), 236–7, 258
Naval Air Weapons Center, 237–8, 359
Naval Caravan Association, 131
Naval Instrument Flying School, 145, 147
Naval Intelligence Section, 359
Naval Legal Branch, 278, 322
Naval Missile Center (NMC), 235, 243, 254, 260; see also Pacific Missile Center
Navex, 304–5
Navigational and Operations School, 356; see also Dryad, HMS
Navigational School (RAF Swinderby), 64
Navy Days, 86, 392
Navy League, 227–8

Navy, Army and Air Force Institute (NAAFI), 30, 242; at Scapa Flow, 50; at Invergordon, 103; at RAF Gan, 168; at RAF Aden, 193; at RAF Khormaksar, 203
Neilson, Commander John, 278
Nellis AFB, 246, 258
Nelson, HMS, 382, 405, 416
New Orleans, 368
New Orleans, USNAS, 369
New York, 223–4, 264, 266
New Zealand House, 404, 405
Newark Hospital, 64
Newby, Lieutenant Commander Gil, 87–8, 97
Newcastle Airport, 333
Newman, Lieutenant Commander Peter, 157, 161–2
Newton airfield, 65–6
Nichols, Lieutenant Jeremy, 170, 179
Nicholson, P. S., 219, 269
Nigerian Navy, helicopter training for, 411–12
night exercises, 197
night vision devices, 311–13
Nimrod, Hawker Siddeley, 354–5, 359
Nixon, President, 228
'No Foreign', 237–8, 241, 250, 260
Norfolk (Virginia), 101, 230, 254, 256, 263
Norfolk, USNAS, 339
Norfolk Hotel (Nairobi), 178
Norfolk Navy Yard, 339–40
Norman, Lieutenant Commander Danny, 179, 391
North American Rockwell (NAR), 261
North Atlantic Treaty Organisastion (NATO), 40, 52, 53, 78, 105, 107, 238, 274, 276, 279, 282, 292, 301, 332, 340, 371
North Cape, 279, 332
North Foreland, 321–2, 356
North Front, RAF, 150, 282
North Island, USNAS, 239, 260
Northard, Lieutenant Bob, 119, 299, 334, 341
Northern Scotsman, 212
Norwegian Sea, 274, 279, 288, 332
Notley, Lieutenant Commander Tim, 261, 264
Noyes, Lieutenant Roy, 135, 136

O

O'Connor, Lieutenant Rod, 296–8
Oakington, RAF, 69, 72
Oakland (California), 228
Oceana, USNAS, 254, 258, 339
Oceanic Hotel (Mombasa), 176, 190
Oceanside (California), 225
Odiham, RAF, 346
Old Admiralty Buildings, 399
Old Faithful, 229
Olmeda, RFA, 341, 369, 392
Operational Evaluation Group (OEG), 262
Operational Flying School (OFS): at Lossiemouth, 77ff., 108, 130, 132, 136, 142, 143, 150, 170, 271; at Yeovilton, 132, 149, 298
Operational Readiness Inspection (ORI), 92, 188–9
Orion, HMS (cruiser), 18
Orion, Lockheed P-3, 23
Orkney Islands, 140
Orlando, 257
ornithopters, 293–4
Oslo, 280
Ossington airfield, 66
Otago, HMNZS, 169, 174
OV-63, Project, 228, 234ff., 243, 248–9, 251, 258, 259, 262—3, 264
'Overlord', Operation, 356
'Over-the-Shoulder' (OTS) attacks, 173–4, 214
Oxnard, 224, 233, 256
Oxley, Lieutenant Commander George, 292–3
Oxnard AFB, 246

P

P-3 Orion, *see* Orion
Pacific Coast Highway (PCH), 224, 225
Pacific Missile Center, 239–41; *see also* Naval Missile Center Point Mugu
Pacific Missile Range, 240; *see also* Point Mugu
Pack, Group Captain John, 349, 354, 358
Packhard, Lieutenant Martin, 126, 129, 130
Paddington station, 167, 335, 342
Pakistani Air Force, 178–9
Panavia, 315
Parachute Brigade, 97
Parfitt, Lieutenant John, 47
Paris, 350
Park, Air Commodore George, 347, 349
Park, Lieutenant Steve, 190, 191, 199–200, 202, 296
Parker, Captain Dougie, 94, 212
Patuxent River, 149, 373; *see also* Naval Air Weapons Center
Peacock, Thomas, 27
Pearce, Lieutenant Dick, 192, 193–4, 197, 201ff., 214, 217
Peasmarsh, 265, 414
Pensacola, USNAS, 84, 102, 119, 126, 136; visit by *Hermes* to, 371–5
Pentagon, The, 230
Pepe, Lieutenant Bill, 301
Pepper, Lieutenant, 77
Persian Gulf, 157, 175, 181
Pett (Sussex), 135
Phantom Symposium, 290–1
Phantom, McDonnell F-4, 226, 232–3, 246, 247, 255, 264; weapon system of, 235–6; F-4B, 235–6, 258
F-4G, 235–6
F-4J, 235–6, 238, 242, 287, 327–8; weapon system of, 240–1, 248–9, 251, 257–8, 259; *see also* OV-63

F-4K, 233, 241, 242, 262, 279, 318, 327, 331, 332, 338, 349; introduction to service of, 269; night flight-deck trials for, 273–4; in 767 NAS, 287ff.; Sidewinder firings by, 338–9; and Sparrow missile, 340

F-4M, 241, 290, 294, 318; and MRCA, 317

Philip, Prince, see Edinburgh, HRH the Duke of

Philippines, 192

Phoenix missile, 260

Photographic Reconnaissance School, FAA, 83

Photographic Unit (at Lossiemouth), 195, 196

photo-reconnaissance sorties, 205

Pierozzi, Captain Nello, 224, 234, 245, 372

Pierozzi, Marcia, 245

Pilot Launch Mode (PLM), 235, 241

Pinhey, Lieutenant Commander Roger, 188, 340

Piraeus, 40, 41

Pitchfork, Flight Lieutenant Graham, 213

planeguards, 169, 175

'Pluto' fuel system, 24

Plymouth, 29, 143, 183, 274, 280, 335, 392; entrance to, 277, 336–7; Naval Hospital at, 310

Point Mugu, USNAS, 223ff., 242ff.

Pollock, Captain Michael, 170, 173ff.

Ponter, Lieutenant Bob, 147–8

Port Hueneme (California), 242, 256

Port of Spain (Trinidad), 364–5

Port Said, 98, 182–3, 201

Port Stanley, 407

Port Suez, 181

Portland, RNAS, 44, 46, 53, 229, 312, 387–9

Portsmouth, 43, 57, 59, 324, 364, 376, 385, 395, 398, 403; RN Barracks at, 45, 382, 405, 416; Dockyard, 230, 406

Portsmouth Airport, 35

Post Exchange (PX), 242

Pre-Flight Training, 58ff.

Prentice, Percival, 67

Price, Commander Pridum, 209

Prince of Wales, HMS, (battleship), 191

Project OV-63, see OV-63

Provost, Percival, 62ff., 72, 126

Provost Branch, Royal Air Force, 347–8

Puerto Rico, 329, 337–40, 397

Pulau Tioman, 171

Pye, (née Doust) Gertrude, (author's cousin), 228–9

Pye, Archie, 228–9

Python, Armstrong Siddeley, (engine), 59–60, 89–90, 96

Q

Qantas, 163

Queen Elizabeth 2, (passenger liner), 218–19

Queen Mary, RMS, 233

Queen's Flight, the, 331

R

Rabat, 100

Rae, Flight Lieutenant Ray, 131, 138–9

Raffles Lighthouse, 207

railway system, 'rationalisation' of, 348

ram air turbine (RAT), 297, 301–2

Ramsgate, 115

Rapide, de Havilland, 132

Ratcliffe, Michael, (author's grandson), 420

Ravensden, 23

Rawbone, Lieutenant Commander Ray, 87, 123, 146, 170, 179, 290

Rawlings (née Diaper), Eunice, 224

Rayleigh, HMS, 126

'Red Flag' Range, 258

Red Sea, 168, 181, 193, 201

refits, ships', 379ff.

refuelling, inflight, 141

Replenishment at Sea, 392

Repulse, HMS, (battlecruiser), 191

Rhodesia, 208–9

Richardson, Lieutenant Don, 157, 171, 175, 179, 184, 207, 213, 216

Richardson, Upperyardman Dave, 70, 72

Richens, Lieutenant Rod, 184–5

Rift Valley, East Afican, 178

Riyadh, 411

Robb, LREM, 37, 38–9

Robertson, Lieutenant Robbie, 100–1

Robinson, Commander 'Rob', 405

Rockall, 392–3

rockets, 2-inch, 163, 202, 203–4, 208, 292

Rolls-Royce, 316

Rommel, Erwin, 40

Roosevelt Roads, USNAS, 329, 330, 337, 339, 340

Rosen, Al, 237, 262

Ross, Commander Don, 312

Rother, River, 321

Rowan Thompson, Lieutenant, 77

Rowbotham, Commander John, 176–7

Roxburgh, Captain, 205

Royal Air Force (RAF), 29, 62, 217, 249, 265; and Tiger Moth trainer, 20; and Suez Crisis, 97; catering by, 168; and Buccaneer, 213, 318; and F-111, 261;transfer of RN personnel to, 262; relationship with Fleet Air Arm of, 270; and Major Fields of Research, 314; and MRCA project, 317, and anti-collision lights, 351–3

Royal Air Force Germany, 285, 290, 294, 295, 360

Royal Air Force Regiment, 347

Royal Air Force squadrons:
No 1, 275–6
No 8, 286, 327
No XV, 360
No 43, 228, 288
No 120, 354

Royal Australian Air Force (RAAF), 90

Royal Australian Navy (RAN), 119, 138

Royal Canadian Air Force (RCAF), 52
Royal Canadian Navy, 77
Royal Danish Air Force (RDAF), 294
Royal Fleet Auxiliaries, 262
Royal Flying Corps (RFC), 62, 270
Royal Manhattan Hotel, 265, 266
Royal Marines, 120, 346, 379, 392, 407
Royal National Lifeboat Institution (RNLI), 322
Royal Naval Air Service (RNAS), 57, 62, 270
Royal Navy, author's views on importance of, 417—19
Royal Navy Branches and establishments:
  Electrical Branch, 28, 29
  Marine Branch, 29
  Recruiting Station, Charing Cross, 29
  Seaman Branch, 29, 33
  See also under individual locations
Royal Netherlands Air Force, 295, 300–1
Royal New Zealand Navy, 404–6
Royal Sovereign Lightvessel, 95
Ryce, Lieutenant Bill, 184
Rye (Sussex), 24, 71, 75, 76, 107, 114, 128, 134, 265, 348, 357, 414; see also Rye Harbour
Rye Grammar School, see schools
Rye Harbour (Sussex), 18, 24, 115, 228, 229, 265, 348, 414; author's father as Harbour Master at, 17, wartime memories of, 23ff.; Sailing Club, 28; see also Rye, St Mary's Church, schools

S

S2F Tracker, see Tracker
S-70 Seahawk, see Seahawk
Sabre: Canadair, 52; North American F-86, 179
safety, flight, 345–6; see also Flight Safety Centre, Flight Safety Trophy
Sailor (BBC television programme), 337–8
St David's (Pembrokeshire), 296
St Elmo's fire, 197
St Helen's Hospital, 414
St Leonards, 266
St Leonards-on-Sea, 266, 334
St Louis, 248
St Martin-in-the-Fields, 201
St Mary's Church (Rye), 22, 128, 134
St Mawgan, RAF, 354
St Merryn, 124
St Moritz, 298
St Norbert's, 303, 307, 335, 413–14
Salinas airport, 246
Salt Lake City, 230
San Clemente, 225
San Diego, 224, 239, 245, 255, 260
San Francisco, 227, 229, 257, 259
San Miguel, 256
Sanderson, Lieutenant Commander 'Sandy', 191
Sandison, Bobby, 84, 89, 95–6, 109, 212
Sandison, Colonel, 96, 212

Sandison Trophy, 96–7, 195, 212
Santa Barbara Channel, 256, 264
Santa Cruz, 256
Santa Monica, 224
Santa Rosa, 256
Saratoga, USS, 102, 245
SARBE, 140, 296
Saudi Arabia, security course for, 409–11
Sausman, Sub Lieutenant Peter, 81
Savannah, USS, 395
Saville, Jimmy, 333-4
Scadding, Lieutenant Commander Malcolm, 180
Scapa Flow, 50
schools: Church School, Rye Harbour, 22; Gordonstoun, 28; Rye Grammar, 21, 40, 44, 70–1, 131, 159, 347; Rye Junior, 24, 357; Rye Modern, 27; Bedford Grammar, 159; Gordonstoun Boys', 217
Scimitar, Supermarine, 108, 132, 141, 142, 143, 145, 149, 150, 154, 155, 157ff., 170ff., 205, 310; height restrictions for pilots of, 137; weapons trials with, 162–3; aerobatics in, 179–80; and Bullpup missile, 180; withdrawal from service of, 184
Sea Balliol, Boulton Paul, 123–5
Sea Devon, de Havilland, 124, 151
Sea Fury, Hawker, 37, 40, 77
Sea Harrier, BAe, 261–2, 278, 327, 359, 408; Staff Target for, 309, 311, 324, 363ff.; aboard Hermes, 379ff., 387ff; and 'ski-ramp' trials, 391–2; make dummy attack on USS John F. Kennedy, 393; colour scheme of, 398; sale to India of, 409
Sea Hawk, Hawker, 77, 83ff., 101, 104, 108, 112–13, 123, 131, 132, 136–7, 140, 147, 183, 218, 305; armament of, 79; ejection from, 79; and Suez Crisis, 97; F Mk 1, 76, 80; F Mk 4, 121–2; formation flying in, 141–2
Sea Heron, de Havilland, 151, 271, 294, 305, 322–4
Sea King, Westland, 262, 274, 277, 279ff., 296, 330ff., 364, 367, 392; replacement project for, 313; and rescue of US submariner, 337–8; embarked aboard Hermes, 387, 390, 395ff.; make dummy attack on USS John F. Kennedy, 393–4; sale to India of, 409
Sea Knight, Boeing-Vertol, 371
Sea Prince, Hunting Percival, 125, 215, 302
Sea Slug (missile), 284
Sea Vampire, de Havilland, 109
Sea Venom, de Havilland, 80, 98, 99, 101, 104, 119, 122, 124, 130, 132ff.
Sea Vixen, de Havilland, 108, 131, 132, 135, 143, 145, 149, 154, 156, 162, 171, 173, 175, 179, 186, 191, 199, 204, 207, 234, 238, 241, 279, 281, 288, 299, 308, 327; landing accidents by, 269
Seafield Park, 147–8, 150, 163, 264
Seahawk, Sikorsky S-70, 408

Search and Rescue (SAR), 140, 142, 151, 171, 271, 274, 283, 296, 300ff., 328, 334, 341, 363
Seattle, 229
Seleta, RAF, 172
Selsey Bill, 110–11, 115
Senior Officers' War Course, 299
Seven Stones Reef, 216
Shackleton, Avro, 140, 286, 327, 354
Sheffield, HMS, 405
sheikhs, 181
Shell Mex House, 311, 314
Sheppard, Lieutenant Peter, 131, 135, 136, 143, 145, 153
Shercliff, Lieutenant Robin, 398–9, 407
Sherman, Lieutenant 'Tank', 108
Shetland Islands, 276, 354
Shoreham (Sussex), 115
Sidewinder missile, 162–3, 237, 260, 303; in Vietnam War, 235; firing practice with, 338–9
sight: mirror landing, 269; helmet-mounted, 259–60
Sigonela, USNAS, 198
Singapore, 164, 168, 171–2, 175, 190–1, 192, 206, 208
Sirrett, Commander Vic, 327
Siskin, HMS, 57, 58, 67, 73
'ski-ramp' (on Hermes), 380—1, 387; trials with, 391–2; at RAE Bedford, 387, 391
Skyhawk, Douglas A-4/TA-4, 225, 226, 247
Skyhawk Instrument Training School, 225
Skyraider, Douglas A-3, 99, 101, 104, 125
Skywarrior, Douglas A-3, 153
Slater, Captain Jock, 324
Smart, Flight Lieutenant Graham, 198, 213
Smeeton, Admiral, 195
Smith, Dr, 259, 263
Smith, Ian, (Prime Minister of Rhodesia), 208–9
Smith, Lieutenant Jack, 154–5, 156, 168, 191
Smith, Sub Lieutenant Jerry, 108, 112–14
Smith, Lieutenant Mike, 108
Socotra, 205
Somerville, Leading Airman, 335
Somerville-Jones, Lieutenant Keith, 184–5, 358–60, 415
Souter, Captain, 134
South African Air Force (SAAF), 212
South Petherton (Somerset), 296
South Stack lighthouse, 69
Southampton Boat Show, 413
South-East Asia Treaty Organisation (SEATO), 171, 191
Southern California State Hospital, 231
Southland, HMNZS, 405; see also Juno, HMS
Southsea, 385, 416
South-Western Approaches, 392
Souza, Lieutenant Peter de, 157
Soviet Navy, interference with RN operations by, 53, 200–1, 280, 282—4, 333

Spafford, Treavor ('Sam'), 84, 89, 92, 94, 96, 102, 108, 110, 172, 207; is awarded Sandison Trophy, 97
Sparrow missile, 237, 238, 260, 303–4, 340; in Vietnam War, 235
'special weapons', 154
Spey, Rolls-Royce, (engine), 209, 295, 304, 354
Spitfire, Supermarine, 65, 77
Spithead, 52, 271, 272
Spokane (Washington), 229
Springfield, Chief Petty Officer (GI), 30, 34–5
Squadron Command Examination, 215, 216
squadrons, see Naval Air Squadrons, Royal Air Force squadrons, United States Marine Corps squadrons, United States Navy squadrons
SR.177, Saunders-Roe, 93–4
Staff Officer, duties of, 92
Staff Targets, 309, 311, 314, 315–17
Stanley, Captain Dave, 310, 311, 319–20, 325
Starfighter, Lockheed F-104, 300–1
Stewart, Lieutenant Commander, 119
Stewart, Lieutenant Arthur, 142, 145, 146
Stonehouse (Barracks), 334, 346
Stotfield Hotel (Lossiemouth), 216
Strike Command, RAF, 347, 353; Flight Safety, 349
'Strikeback', Exercise, 105
'Styx' missile, 206, 238
Subic Bay, 149, 192
Suez Canal, 181–2, 183, 190, 193, 198, 201, 404; see also Suez Crisis
Suez Crisis, 58, 123, 181, 182; background to, 97; 831 NAS in, 98; FAA casualties in, 98
Sullivan, Upperyardman Pat, 73–4
Sun, 372
Sunset Ceremony, 285
Supreme Allied Commander Atlantic (SACLANT), 340
Sverdlov (Soviet cruiser), 53, 186, 283
Sweetie Pie (author's cat), 219–20, 286, 335
Swept Wing Conversion Course, 145, 146, 183
Swinderby, RAF, 64, 213
Swindon, 167, 265, 342
Swithinbank, Lieutenant Commander Phil, 107
Sydenham, 98, 108, 156, 305, 306, 322
Sydney, 163
Sydney, HMAS, 404
Syerston, RAF, 60, 61ff., 68, 125, 355

T
T-33, Lockheed, 227, 233, 237
T-54 tank, 97
tactics, fighter, 78
Tahoe (California), 259
Tailhook Convention, 243–5
Tain Range, 80, 153, 155, 187, 202, 214

'taking it green', 394
Tallman, Commander Jack, 234, 238
Tangmere, RAF, 27, 86, 111
Tanner, Clive, 229, 230
Taranto raid, 63
Tarbat Ness, 155
target-towing, 79
Tartar, HMS, 299
Tarver, Commander Alan, 303
Taylor, Flight Lieutenant, 64, 66
Teague, Commander 'Tooter', 227, 235, 247
Teddington, 320
Teledyne Ryan, 245
'Tempest', Exercise, 385
Tenby Lightvessel, 48
Tengah, RAF, 171ff., 190, 206
tensions, racial, (in USA), 227, 250–1, 370
Terror, HMS, 168
TFX programme, 260; see also F-111
Thanksgiving Day, 231, 263
Theseus, HMS (aircraft carrier), 36, 46;
    author's service aboard, 37ff.; flight-deck
    operations aboard, 39–40
Thompson, Lieutenant Commander Rowan,
    161
Thompson, Lieutenant Tommy, 27, 68
Thorney Island, RAF, 154
'through-deck cruiser', 261–2, 324; see also
    Invincible class
Thurleigh (Bedfordshire), 23
Tibbets, Captain Sir Michael, 376
Tiger Moth, de Havilland, 20, 27, 35, 44, 66,
    143
Timber (author's dog), 144, 184, 219, 220,
    335
Tinkerbell (author's cat), 335, 395–6
Tobermory (Isle of Mull), 134
Todd, Lieutenant Jonathan, 219, 310, 407
Tofts, Lieutenant Commander Jock, 89, 92,
    95, 97, 100, 107, 110, 111, 119, 317, 323;
    and Wyvern colour scheme, 94; commands
    Scimitar IFTU, 108; commands 807 NAS,
    108
Tomcat, Grumman F-14, 247, 261, 397; see
    also VFX programme
Tonbridge, Mrs, 21
'Top Gun' School, see Naval Air Warfare
    Training School
Tornado, Panavia, see Multi Role Combat
    Aircraft
Torness (Inverness-shire), 304
Torpoint–Plymouth ferry, 336
Torrey Canyon, 216–17
Tracker, Grumman: S2F, 149, 228, 246—7;
    US-2F, 234
Trafalgar Club, 27
Traffic Separation Scheme, 280
Training Flight, F-4K, 303
Transvaal, 218
Treacher, Admiral Sir John, 192
Treanor, Joy, 253–4
Treanor, Lieutenant Tom, 234, 253–4

Trenchard, Major Hugh, 62
Trent (Dorset), 298–9
Trinidad, 364–5
Tristram, Lieutenant Commander Michael,
    273
Troon (Ayrshire), 49
Tropicana Hotel (Las Vegas), 244
Trucial Oman, 180; Scouts, 175
TSR.2, BAC, 270
Tu-16 'Badger', 279, 332
Tu-95 'Bear', 279
Turkish Air Force, 179
Turner, Matilda, 159
Type 23 frigates, 405, 406

U
UC-45, Beechcraft, 227, 228
Udimore (Sussex), 414
Unilateral Declaration of Independence
    (UDI), see Rhodesia
unions, dockyard, 364
United Services Club, 154
United States, SS, 223
United States Air Force (USAF), 258; rescues
    author, 107; parade customs in, 251
United States Marine Corps (USMC), 192,
    288; conducts AV-8 trials aboard Hermes,
    373–4
United States Marine Corps squadrons:
    VMF-92, 234
    VMF-96, 234
United States Navy (USN), 40, 136, 192, 213,
    223ff,. 242ff., 259ff., 288; author's
    appointment to, 219, instrument flight
    practice in, 225; aircrew losses over
    Christmas period, 231–2, 263–4;
    establishes Safety Center, 233; standards
    of flying in, 247; training procedure in,
    247, 258; aircraft maintenance in, 247–8;
    combating narcotics in, 250; courts-martial
    in, 250; Airborne Early Warning Division
    in, 255; Fleets in, 258; and Koch fasteners,
    298
United States Navy squadrons:
    VCR-35, 234
    VF-101, 258
    VF-121, 225, 235–6, 242, 258
    VFT-125, 225
    VX-3, 243
    VX-4, 161, 328, 359, 369, 370, 372;
        author's service with, 223ff., 242ff., 259ff.
US-2F, see Tracker

V
V-1 missile, 25–6
'V-Bomber' force, 317
Vaerlose, RDAF, 294
Valletta, 37, 42, 100
Valley, RAF, 57, 67, 68ff., 288, 289, 354
Vampire, de Havilland, 62, 68, 72–3, 83, 85,
    86–7, 108, 125–6, 130, 134, 137, 151;
    aerobatics in, 73; stall turns forbidden in,

72–3; FB Mk 5, 68, 69; FB Mk 9, 68; T Mk 11, 68, 69, 77, 99, 126, 136; T Mk 22, 77, 85, 90, 91, 121, 131, 133, 136, 139, 147
Vancouver, 229
Vanguard, HMS, (battleship), 43–4
Varsity, Vickers, 64, 265
Vaughan, Barbara, 242
Vaughan, Lieutenant Commander Dai, 157, 242
VC-10, Vickers, 265, 342
Venables, Lieutenant Dave, 169, 213
Ventura, 256; County Police, 250
VFX programme, 260–1; *see also* Tomcat
Victor, Handley Page, 304
Victoria station, 342
Victoria, HMS, (battleship), 52
Victorious, HMS, 149, 156, 191
Victory, HMS, 230
Vietnam War, 226, 234–6, 241, 258, 259, 263
'viffing', 275
Viking, Vickers, 36–7, 42
Vikrant, INS, 136n, 409
Vincent, HMS, 58
Vincent, Lieutenant Commander, 89
Virgin Islands, 396
Viscount, Vickers, 355
vortex generators, value of, 205, 211, 318
Vulcan, Avro, 213

W
Wagon Wheel (motel), 225
Wallasey, 322–3
Walling (née Peacock), Nancy, (author's sister-in-law), 134
Wallis, Barnes, 261
Walsh, Lieutenant Tony, 356, 363
Walwyn, Lieutenant Commander Peter, 186–8, 192, 194–5, 209, 211, 212, 242, 243
Walwyn, Maureen, 242
Wandsworth, 359
Wangchi, 174
Warsaw Pact, 291
Warton (Lancashire), 307–8
Washington (DC), 243, 246, 341–2
Waterloo station, 310
Watson, Lieutenant Willie, 146, 184, 211
weapons trials, 162–3, 186–8, 191–2; with Buccaneer S.2, 212, 214
Webster, Flight Sergeant John, 126
Webster, Lieutenant John, (i), 119, 124
Webster, Lieutenant John, (ii), 124
Wellington (New Zealand), 404–5
Wellington, HMNZS, 405–6; *see also Dido*, HMS
Wessex, Westland, 389; Mk, 2, 331; Mk 5, 326, 327, 333, 364, 392, 398
West Freugh, RAE, 132–3, 163, 188
West Indies Station, 299, 375, 376
West Malling, RAF, 27
West, Mr, 417
Westerly (boatbuilders), 413

Westinghouse, 240–1
Westland Aircraft Company, 90, 101
Westoby, Flight Lieutenant 'Toby', 145
Wetherby, 266
Weymouth, 356, 357
Weymouth Bay, 387, 388, 391
Whale Island, 109, 120, 151, 154, 187, 195, 378; *see also Excellent*, HMS
Wheatley, Lieutenant Peter,89, 91, 92, 94, 100, 108, 110,111
Whirlwind, Westland, (helicopter), 326
White, Admiral, 239
White, Sergeant, 396
Whitworth, Air Commodore, 129
Wigg, Lieutenant Alfie, 40, 131
Wight, Isle of, 364
Wilcox, Lieutenant Commander George, 242–3
Wilkinson, Lieutenant Les, 215–16
Wilkinson, Lieutenant Richard, 146
Willemstad (Curaçao), 366–7
Williams, Sub Lieutenant John, 108
Willis, Admiral Sir Algernon, 24
Wilson, Upperyardman 'Tug', 46
Wilson, Sub Lieutenant Chris, 163
Wilton (Wiltshire), 346
Winchelsea (Sussex), 17, 24, 26, 348, 414
Wings Parades: at RAF Syerston, 65; at RAF Valley, 75, 76
Winton, Lieutenant John de, 124, 146, 281
Wirdnam, Flight Lieutenant Dickie, 78, 79
Wittering, RAF, 276
Women's Royal Army Corps (WRAC), 25
Women's Royal Naval Service (WRNS), ('Wrens'), 125, 326, 358, 364, 415
Wood, Lieutenant Curly, 157, 163–4
Woodard, Lieutenant Bob, 190, 191, 202, 356, 357, 358
Woolgar, Lieutenant Commander, 328
Workentin, Chief Petty Officer, 248–9
World War II, author's memories of, 22–6
Worth, Lieutenant Commander Jack, 223, 328, 329, 330–1, 334
Wrath, Cape, 156
Wright, Lieutenant, 234–5
Wyvern, Westland, 58, 59, 80, 84ff., 89ff, 111, 112–13, 125, 348; performance of, 84; squadrons equipped with, 84; colour scheme of, 94; armament of, 95; problems with arrester hooks of, 104; author's ejection from, 106–7, 159; disbandment of squadrons equipped with, 108; aerobatics in, 109; S Mk 4, 89

Y
Yachting World (magazine), 412
Yarmouth, HMS, 283
Yellowstone National Park, 229–30
Yeovil, 302—3, 306, 356
Yeovil General Hospital, 300
Yeovilton, RNAS, 112, 113, 137 147, 170, 183, 190, 194, 197, 239, 242, 271, 286,

363; Sea Venoms at, 80, 101; author's interviews and examinations at, 123, 145, 215–16; Sea Vixens at, 131, 132, 234, 238, 308; F-4Ks at, 242, 270, 273, 281, 285, 322–3, 382, 405; F-4K Ground School at, 271; author's service at, 285, 287ff., 345–7; and Canberra T Mk 22, 309
York, 167

York, Duke of, see Andrew, HRH Prince
Yorktown, US Coast Guard College at, 420
Yosemite National Park, 229

Z
Zebbie (author's cat), 219, 335
Zimbabwe, see Rhodesia